The Pro

Eleventh West Coast Conference on Formal Linguistics

The Proceedings of the

Eleventh West Coast Conference on Formal Linguistics

edited by Jonathan Mead

Published for the
Stanford Linguistics Association
by the
Center for the Study of Language and Information

Printed in the United States

ISBN 1–881526–12–7
ISSN 1042–1068

∞The recycled, acid-free paper used in this book meets the minimum requirements of the American National Standard for Information Sciences—Permanence of Paper for Printed Library Materials, ANSI Z39.48-1984.

Contents

Prosodic Target and Vocalic Specification in the Ibibio Verb

AKINBIYI AKINLABI & ENO URUA
Rutgers University and University of Uyo, Nigeria

In recent literature (for example, Yip 1992) it has been shown that a language may not necessarily foot its lexical roots, but may impose a particular foot structure on root plus affix combinations. In this paper, we propose that Ibibio[1] verb roots in combination with a variety of suffixes target a disyllabic trochee with two templates, though the verb roots themselves are not independently footed. Our argument is that without such an assumption, phonological generalizations regarding root - suffix structures cannot be captured. The immediate consequence of this is that the minimal word may not be equivalent to the minimal foot, contrary to the proposals of McCarthy and Prince (1986, 1990), and others. Secondly, we show that while CV suffixes form a heavy - light disyllabic trochee with the root, V suffixes attract a light - light template. These targets are met regardless of the underlying weight of the verb root. These weight requirements involve both vowel lengthening and shortening which we show are better captured by a prosodic approach rather than a segmental rule approach. Finally, we show that given the assumption of a disyllabic trochee vocalic specification in the Ibibio verb is completely predictable. Only the first vowel of the verb root need be underlyingly specified. The second vowel of the disyllabic foot (usually a suffix) is always derived from the first one by spreading. Any subsequent suffix vowel is determined by default specification.

1. Assumptions

1.1. Prosodic Morphology

A few theoretical assumptions provide the ingredients of our analysis. First,

---

[1] Ibibio is spoken by about five million people in Akwa Ibom State in the Niger-Delta region of Nigeria (Connell 1987). Greenberg (1963) classifies it under the Benue Congo branch of the Niger-Congo family. It is subclassified as a Lower-Cross language of the Cross-River subfamily. Williamson's (1989) classification groups it as part of the Lower Cross branch of Delta Cross, along with the closely related languages Efik and Anaaŋ.

Ibibio has a fair amount of dialect variation. The dialect we will be discussing in this paper is that spoken in Uyo, the location of the state headquarters, and in the Etinan local government area. This is close to what Essien (ms.) refers to as General Ibibio.

the analysis is worked out within the prosodic theory (Hyman 1985; McCarthy and Prince 1986, 1990; Hayes 1989; Archangeli 1991; and others). Following McCarthy and Prince (1990), we shall assume two of the fundamental theses of prosodic theory as follows (see McCarthy and Prince 1990,209):

(i) Prosodic Morphology Hypothesis: Templates are defined in terms of authentic units of prosody: mora (μ), syllable (σ), Foot (F), prosodic word (W), and so on.

(ii) Template Satisfaction Condition: Satisfaction of template constraints is obligatory and is determined by the principles of prosody, both universal and language-specific.

McCarthy and Prince (1986) also propose the following distinct Foot types (see also Hayes 1987):

(1) [σ σ] syllabic trochee
[μ μ] moraic trochee / bimoraic foot
[σ_{μ} $\sigma_{\mu\mu}$] iambic foot

It is crucial to note that verb roots in Ibibio are not footed. Ibibio verb roots, we propose, are usually monosyllabic: they may be CVVC[2] wààk "tear", CVC wàt "paddle", or just CV wà "sacrifice". Each of these may be used in isolation, that is, without any suffix. We can therefore assume that the minimal word in Ibibio is a monomoraic CV. Given the prosodic theory, the foot structures in (1) also serve as minimal template requirements that footed items must satisfy. If there were a minimal foot requirement on Ibibio verb roots, for example, a moraic trochee or a bimoraic foot, we expect CV verbs to be lengthened to CVV *wàà "sacrifice" in isolation, making them minimally bimoraic (with each vowel dominated by a mora μ). This does not happen.[3] Secondly, if CVVC verb roots were to constitute a moraic trochee on their own, they could not form part of another (moraic) trochee. The fact however is that they do, through V suffixation: wààk "tear", wàɣá "be torn to pieces". We therefore conclude that verb roots are not footed in isolation.

1.2. Syllabification and Weight By Position

We assume a theory of syllabification in which moraification of coda consonants is independent of general syllabification (Hayes 1989; Archangeli 1991; and others). Syllabification maps vowels to one or two moras and maps single consonants to syllables as onsets and codas. Codas, like onsets, are thus nonmoraic at this stage of the derivation. Coda consonants are assigned moraic weight at a later stage of the derivation by a rule of "weight by position", making

[2] A number of verbs in Ibibio have the form Ci/u V (C). We analyze the initial Ci/u in these forms as CG. Such forms are therefore CGV(C), and not CVVC sequences. See also footnote (4)

[3] Ibibio does not have an underlying contrast between CV and CVV, but such contrast may be derived: dá "stand/wait", ń dáá "I waited and waited [i.e. I waited for a long time]". Therefore any attempt to derive CV from CVV by rule is doomed to fail.

CVC syllables bimoraic, and thus heavy in languages where they behave as such. We would assume that the stage at which coda consonants become moraic is language dependent. The version of the rule adopted here is that suggested by Archangeli:

(2) Weight -By-Position

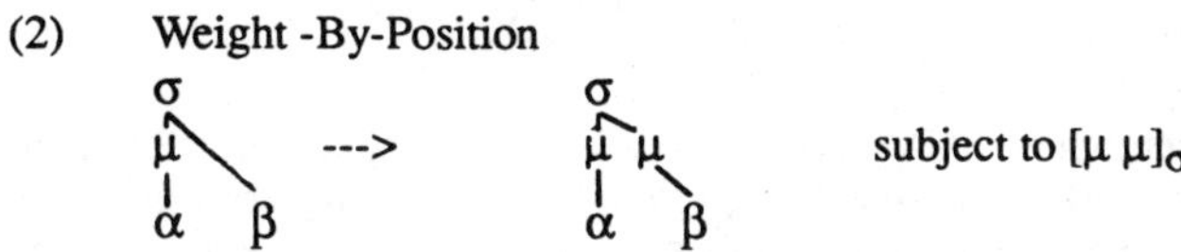

Given the above theory, there is a universal bimoraic limit on syllable size (but see Hayes (1989) for evidence of some languages with trimoraic syllables). For example the application of "weight by position" (2) to a CVVC structure results in vowel shortening, giving CVC.

The universal two mora per syllable limitation and hence Weight -By - Position is motivated in Ibibio by one important fact: Ibibio contrasts only two vowel lengths, as seen in wààt "sprinkle [e.g., powder in stew]" wàt "paddle", and not three (as for example in certain dialects of German, Hayes 1989). There is not enough evidence to motivate trimoraic syllables in Ibibio, as the CVVC roots might superficially suggest. In isolation or in peripheral position, we assume that final consonants are extraprosodic, thereby maintaining vowel length contrasts.

1.3. Underspecification

Finally, Ibibio operates a six vowel system / i e a ɔ o u / (Kaufman 1968). Adopting radical underspecification we assume the following underlying structure for Ibibio vowels, in which the vowel /e/ is completely underlyingly unspecified for any of the features [high], [low], and [round] with which we specify Ibibio vowels (See Archangeli 1984, 1988, Pulleyblank 1986, 1988, Clements 1987, Steriade 1987, etc., for various versions of underspecification theory.)

(3) Underlying Vocalic Specification in Ibibio

	i	e	a	ɔ	o	u
high	+					+
low			+	+		
round				+	+	+

We propose that suffix vowels are underlyingly unspecified. In an Ibibio verb root + suffix combination (within the foot), the suffix vowel is derived either by spreading from the verb root, or by default specification. In cases where the suffix falls outside the foot, no spreading takes place; the vocalic quality of the suffix is then completely determined by the application of default rules which predictably result in vowel [e]. The motivation for underspecification in Ibibio lies not just in its ability to account for the vowel [e], but also in its ability to account for vocalic spreading which we discuss shortly.

2. Foot Structure in Ibibio

In spite of the fact that verb roots are not footed, there is evidence that the morphology of the Ibibio verb contains a disyllabic foot; which forms the domain of several phonological processes. Ibibio verb roots may take a variety of suffixes which are either CV or V.

2.1. The CV Suffix

Ibibio has a number of CV suffixes which are homophonous. They are generally considered verbal extensions (Essien 1990) marking verb negation, reversion of action, and relative clauses. In each of these cases, the melodic form of the CV suffix depends on the verb root, but it generally takes the same form in all its functions. We will discuss only the negative suffix here, which we assume to be / kv́/ (a /k/ followed by an unspecified vowel). We present its forms after CVC, CV, CVVC verb roots in that order.

(i) CVC Roots

After CVC verbs, the suffix is completely assimilated to the verb root but the verb remains unchanged as shown in (4).

(4)	kòp	"hear"	...kòp-pó	"... not hearing"
	yét	"wash"	...yét-té	"... not washing"
	dát	"take/pick up"	...dát-tá	"... not taking"
	kɔ̀k	"vomit"	...kɔ̀k-kɔ́	"... not vomiting"
	dóm	"bite"	...dóm-mó	"... not biting"
	bòn	"father a child"	...bòn-nó	"... not fathering a child"
	sàŋ	"go"	...sàŋ-ŋá	"... not going"
	kɔ̀ŋ	"knock"	...kɔ̀ŋ-ŋɔ́	"... not knocking"

(ii) CV Roots

After CV verb roots the suffix takes the form of a gamma [ɣ] and a vowel identical to the preceding vowel,[4] but the CV root now becomes CVV.

(5)	kǎ	"go"	...kàà-ɣá	"... not going"
	sé	"look"	...séé-ɣé	"... not looking"
	nɔ̀	"give"	...nɔ̀ɔ̀-ɣɔ́	"... not giving"
	dá	"stand"	...dáá-ɣá	"... not standing"

(iii) CVVC Roots

Finally, after CVVC roots, the suffix is also completely assimilated to the root, but the root becomes CVC.

(6)	fáák	"wedge between two objects"	fák-ká	"remove wedged object"
	kɔ́ɔ́ŋ	"hang on hook"	kɔ́ŋ-ŋɔ́	"remove from hook"

[4] In these and the preceding examples, we have excluded high vowel roots. We will discuss these later, because they involve additional complications.

A clear generalization is obvious from the shape of the derived negated verbs: whatever the underlying form of of the verb root, the root-suffix outcome has to take the form of a heavy (bimoraic) syllable followed by a light (monomoraic) syllable. All of the data can be accounted for if we assume that the prosodic target is a disyllabic trochaic foot. We propose the following foot template for Ibibio:

(7) Ibibio Foot Template 1:
$[\sigma_{\mu\,\mu}\ \ \sigma_{\mu}]$ heavy - light trochee

We propose that assimilation takes place to accommodate the suffix within this disyllabic foot structure. The foot is constructed left to right, and is consonant initial. Note that Ibibio does not have stress prominence, so evidence for the prosodic foot can only be sought from other parts of the phonology. Aside from phonological weight (observed above), three processes, all of which are restricted to this prosodic structure, indicate that the first syllable is more prominent than the second, as expected of a trochee. (i) /k/ completely assimilates to the last consonant of closed syllable roots, (ii) Stop weakening converts /k/ to a continuant [ɣ] after roots ending in vowels, and (iii) the suffix vowel is completely assimilated to the verb root vowel. Outside of this disyllabic trochee, none of these processes takes place. For example, the negative suffix takes the invariant form [ké] after disyllabic verbs, no matter the segmental melody of the of the disyllabic verb.

(8)	dáppá	"dream [vb.]"	...dáppá-ké	"...not dreaming"
	dámmá	"be mad"	...dámmá-ké	"...not being mad"
	dɔ́kkɔ́	"tell"	...dɔ́kkɔ́-ké	"...not telling"

(9)	sàŋá	"walk"	...sàŋá-ké	"...not walking"
	kɔ́ŋɔ́	"choke"	...kɔ́ŋɔ́-ké	"...not choking"

The suffix melody in the the examples in (4) - (6) can be accounted for by three foot based rules: i) Consonant Gemination, ii) Vocalic Spreading, and iii) (Oral) Stop Weakening. We propose that these rules take the foot as their domain since they operate to completely assimilate the suffix within the foot structure. Prosodic versions of these rules may be formulated as follows (symbols such as [k], [o], etc., represent the root nodes of the relevant segments in these and subsequent rules):

(10) Consonant Gemination

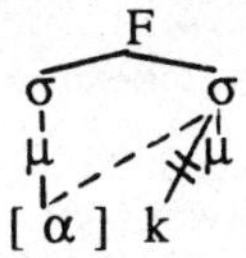

F
σ σ
μ μ
[α] k

[α is a coda consonant]

(11) Vocalic Spreading

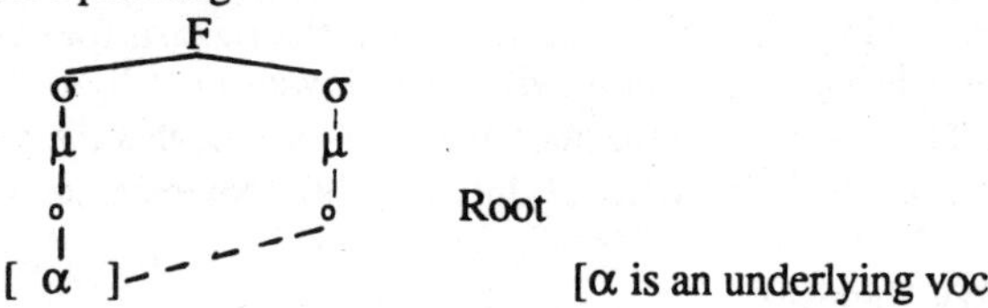

[α is an underlying vocalic feature]

(12) (Oral) Stop Weakening

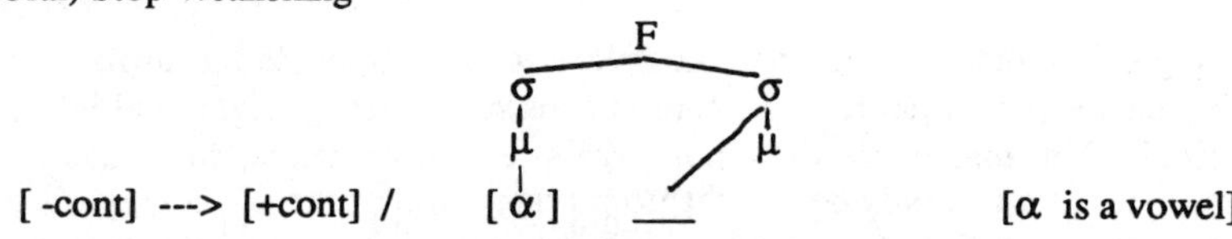

Consonant Gemination (10) spreads the root node of a preceding coda consonant to delink the /k/ onset of the following suffix within the same foot thereby completely assimilating /k/. The coda requirement ensures that it applies only to final consonants of CVC roots, and not vowels in CV verbs. The formulation in (10) also indicates that coda consonants are mora bearing at the time the rule applies, making closed syllables heavy. This is justified by two reasons. First, CVC roots function as heavy syllables in terms of template satisfaction in Ibibio, they are therefore bimoraic (after the application of weight-by-position). Secondly, Hayes (1989) shows that geminate consonants of the type we have in (4) and (6) are dominated by at least one mora. Since onsets are not weight bearing (Hyman 1985, Hayes 1989, and others), and since one half of the geminate serves as the coda of the preceding syllable while the other serves as the onset of the following syllable, the first half of the geminate has to bear the mora.

We find justification for Consonant Gemination (10) from the fact that Ibibio completely forbids clusters of two diverse obstruents within and across morphemes.[5] Therefore, it lacks such forms as dép-kɛ́ 'not buying', found in closely related Efik (see Welmers 1973). When such forms arise across morphemes which cannot be accommodated in a foot, a vowel (an unspecified mora) is inserted and is footed with the preceding stem as shown by the following reduplicated example in (13).

(13)	kèèt	--->	kèèt kèèt	--->	kèr<u>ẹ</u>kèèt
	"one"		(reduplication)		"one by one / one each"[6]

The second rule, Vocalic Spreading (11), ensures that the suffix vowel is

[5] Two types of phonetic clusters exist in Ibibio, both of which occur in the onset position. The first are CG clusters as in /diɔ́k/ --->[djɔ́k] "be bad", /tuàk/--->[twàk] "push", etc. The second arise from vowel deletion in fluent speech: /ťidé/ --->ťiré-->[trě] "stop", /fùdó/---->fùró--->[frǒ] "jump". Even such phonetic clusters are barred from syllable/morpheme final positions, and across morphemes.

[6] A form like [kèèt kèèt] cannot be footed because the second syllable of the Ibibio foot has to be light. Ibibio forbids a heavy-heavy foot template.

completely identical to the root vowel, as long as the vowel is within the disyllabic foot. It thus completely assimilates a suffix vowel. Since this spreading has to apply across consonants, we assume that it refers to terminal vowel features in the feature geometry (Clements 1985, 1990; Sagey 1986; McCarthy 1988; and others). In the case of /e/, which has no underlying feature specifications, default rules specify both the root and suffix vowels.

Finally, (Oral) Stop Weakening (12) converts the underlying /k/ of the suffix to a gamma. Stop Weakening is actually a more pervasive process in the language, and /k/ weakening above is only part of its realization. The stops [p, t, k] are productively weakened to [β, ɾ, ɣ] respectively in intervocalic position, comprising either the second consonant of a disyllabic (CVCV) verb (14) or the final consonant of a closed syllable followed by any vowel initial morpheme (15) (see Cook 1968 and Welmers 1973 for a description of an identical process in Efik). Each of these two contexts is equivalent to a light-light trochee, which we will motivate later. (Material enclosed in parenthesis fall outside the foot.)

(14)	tòβó	"make an order"
	tǐré	"stop"
	fèɣé	"run"

(15)	dwòp	"ten"	dwòβ è (bà)	"twelve" [ten plus two]
	èfɨt	"fifteen"	(è)fɨɾ è (nààŋ)	"nineteen" [fifteen plus four]
	úfɔ̀k	"house"	(ú)fɔ̀ɣ ì (bà)	"two houses"

Note that intervocalic occurrence is not enough for (Oral) Stop Weakening. For example, the vowel prefixes of nouns do not trigger (Oral) Stop Weakening, as the examples in (16) show. Vowel prefixes are thus extraprosodic. (Recall that the foot is formed from left to right and it is consonant initial.) Therefore (Oral) Stop Weakening (12) is a foot based process.

(16)	étáp	"saliva"	íkɔ́t	"bush"
	étó	"stick"	ɔ̀kɔ́	"fence"
			àkàm	"prayer"

Though the rules in (10) - (12) will correctly derive the suffix melody, they do not account for changes in the verb root. Applying these rules alone will not account for the vowel lengthening in (5) and vowel shortening in (6). This problem straightforwardly handled within a prosodic approach. Given the assumption that Ibibio operates a disyllabic trochee- type of foot structure, CV suffixes target a heavy - light trochee in combination with the verb root. If we assume that the relevant foot template requirement must be satisfied by the output of the foot structure irrespective of the underlying form of the verb root, then the vowel lengthening in (5) and vowel shortening in (6) are accounted for. Vowel lengthening and vowel shortening take place only to satisfy the (target) template.

An alternative non-prosodic approach fails to capture the same generalization. For example, a possible non-prosodic account is to assume that a vowel is lengthened by rule before the CV suffix if it occurs after a CV (open syllable) root . This solution accounts for the data in (5), but it raises an unanswered (and possibly unanswerable) question: why should lengthening occur in a CV root, and not in any other root? The fact that this lengthening has nothing to do with an open syllable, or with the CV suffix, is confirmed by the absence of lengthening in CVCV verbs before /kv́/ as in (9): sàŋá "walk", sàŋá-ké "...not walking" cf *[sàŋáá-ké] / *[sààŋá-ké]. If lengthening had anything to do with either an open syllable or with a CV suffix, then a form like *[sàŋáá-ké] or *[sààŋá-ké] will be wellformed.

A non-prosodic account may once again postulate a vowel reduction rule, shortening long vowels before geminate consonants, as in (6). The problem however is that no such rule can adequately capture vowel shortening in Ibibio, since vowels may become short even when they are not followed by geminate consonants: wààk "tear", wàɣá "be torn to pieces". (See section (2.2) for a discussion of examples like these.)

Therefore, in both cases a rule based approach is inadequate, since it is unable to predict all the facts.

As pointed out earlier, a prosodic approach does not have these problems. Sample derivations of [kàà-ɣá] "...not going", [fák-ká] "remove wedged object" which employ the above prosodic proposals are given below in (17) and (18) respectively.

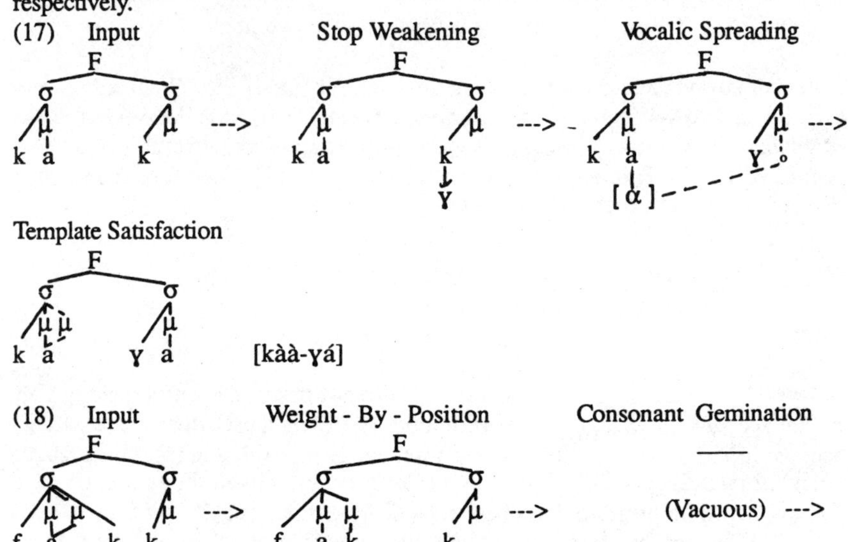

Vocalic Spreading

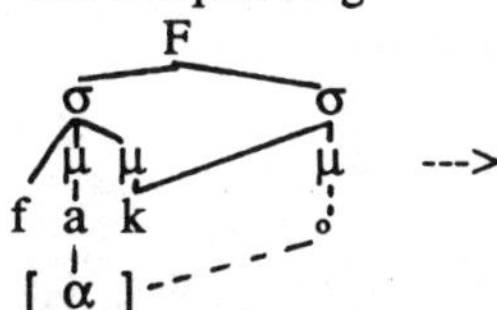

Template Satisfaction

——

The above account makes certain predictions. The first is that if the input structure contains a heavy root, then no lengthening takes place. All the examples in (4) confirm this. Therefore, CVC roots count as heavy, making final consonants of such roots moraic by Weight - By - Position as proposed above. Secondly if the root contains a light syllable (CV), then it will become heavy by lengthening[7] through Template Satisfaction. The examples in (5) as well as <u>all</u> cases of CV roots to our knowledge undergo this lengthening without exception. The surface presence of long vowels with underlying CV roots is thus accounted for. In the case of CVC roots, there is no lengthening because the template is already satisfied with the presence of the final consonants which, as we proposed above, are moraic.

Finally, as seen in the derivation (18), vowel shortening in (6) is achieved through syllabification and weight-by-position. Weight-By-Position assigns the second mora of a CVVC root to the final consonant, resulting in vowel shortening. This happens at the input to the foot in Ibibio irrespective of whether the final consonant is followed by another consonant or by a vowel, thus achieving a generalization missed by a segmental rule approach.

2.2. The V Suffix.

The foregoing section was devoted to the assimilation of the CV suffix /-kv́/ to the verb root, which as we showed takes place within a targeted (disyllabic) heavy-light trochee. Aside from the CV suffix, Ibibio also has a vowel suffix (i.e., an onsetless monomoraic syllable). We assume that it is underlyingly unspecified for any vocalic features. It creates the reflexive or the agentless passive form of a verb. In all of the data available to us, the suffix appears only after CVC and CVVC roots.

(19) With CVC Roots

yàt	"wear a hat"	yàrá	"wear a hat on oneself"
dòt	"place on top of"	dòró	"place on top of oneself"
wèt	"write"	wèré	"be written"
kɔ̀p	"lock"	kɔ̀βɔ́	"be locked"

[7] The correct spreading result is guaranteed because spreading takes place from left to right in Ibibio suffixes (and from right to left in prefixes), deriving the correct [kàa-ɣá] instead of *[kàk-ká] which will result from a right to left spreading.

(20) With CVVC Roots

béék	'remove corn" [with finger from cob]	béɣé	"be removed [of corn]"
wààk	"tear"	wàɣá	"be torn to pieces"

It is important to separate these examples from those in (4) - (6) where the suffix (i.e., /kv́/) has an onset. In the above cases, since the suffix is an unspecified vowel (mora) without an onset, Consonant Gemination (10) is not triggered. Rather, there is a weakening of the final oral stop of the verb root through (Oral) Stop Weakening (12). Verb roots which occur with both the negative suffix and the agentless passive suffix as in (21) clearly reveal the distinction between them.

(21)

wèt	"write"		wèré	"be written"
	cf	...wèt-té	"not writing"	
bɔ́t	"create/mold"		bɔ́rɔ́	"be shaped"
	cf	...bɔ́t-tɔ́	'notcreating/molding'	
kɔ̀p	"lock"		kɔ̀βɔ́	"be locked"
	cf	...kɔ̀p-pɔ́	"unlock"	

Again there is a clear generalization from the reflexive/passive forms in (19) and (20). Whatever the input weight, the root+suffix combination ends up as two light (monomoraic) syllables. The data in (19) and (20) can be accounted for if we assume that the (prosodic) target template is a light - light disyllabic trochee. We give this second template as follows:

(22) Ibibio Foot Template 2

$[\ \sigma_{\mu}\quad \sigma_{\mu}\ ]$ light - light trochee

The assimilation of this suffix is therefore also foot based. The crucial difference in this suffix however is that it forms a light - light disyllabic trochee with the preceding root. Again, this target template is always satisfied regardless of the underlying moraic structure of the verb root.

The derivation of the examples in (19) and (20) follows a similar pattern to the ones already given. The examples employ Vocalic Spreading (11) and (Oral) Stop Weakening (12) (where applicable), both foot based processes which are already motivated above. A point worthy of note is that the roots start out being heavy, but end up as light. CVVC roots (in (20)) end up being monomoraic. This is achieved through template satisfaction. Weight - By - Position converts the long vowel to a short one by making the coda moraic (in 20), and template satisfaction explains the rest. In this case, the target template is light - light, and so there is further mora loss. A CVC and a CVVC root become equivalent after Weight-By-Position (stage (23b) below), and the rest of the derivation follows the same pattern. Weight-By-Position applies before resyllabification in Ibibio, even when we have a vowel suffix. The early application of Weight-By-Position is justified by the behavior of high vowels which we cannot discuss here for reasons of space. We provide a sample derivation of wàɣá 'be torn to pieces' (from 20) below:

(23a) Input

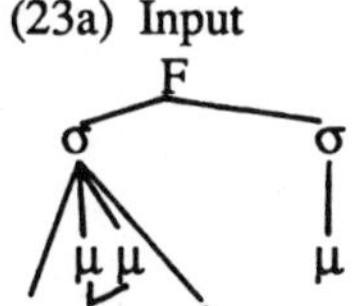

(b) Weight - By - Position

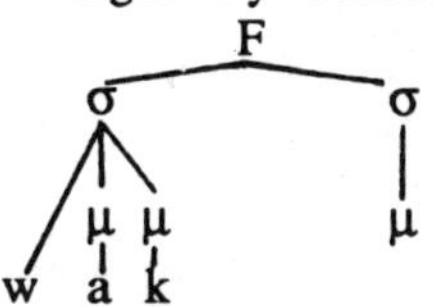

(c) Resyllabification

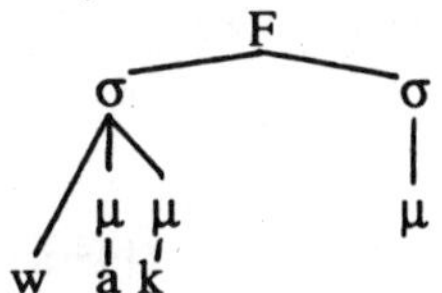

d) Stop Weakening [8]

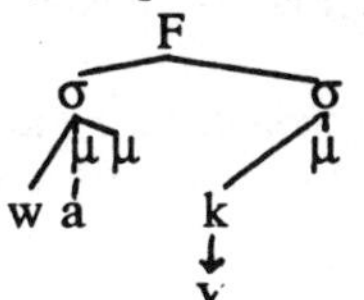

(e) Vocalic Spreading

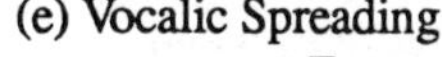

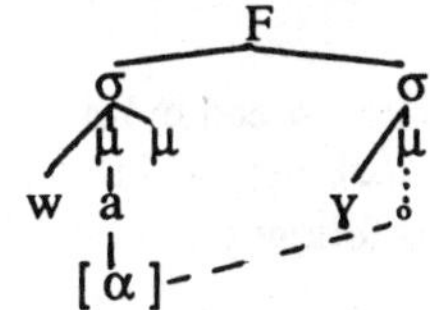

(f) Template Satisfaction

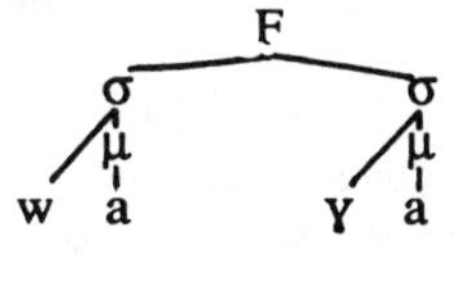

In the foregoing sections we have shown that the minimal word in Ibibio is a monomoraic CV. We have have also shown that the foot in Ibibio is a disyllabic trochee. If the above account is correct, then the Ibibio minimal word is **not** equivalent to the minimal foot, contrary to the proposals of the prosodic theory (for example, McCarthy and Prince 1986, 1990). However instead of abandoning this proposal altogether, we link its failure in Ibibio to the fact that lexical roots are not footed in isolation, as we showed earlier. We propose the following condition limiting the applicability of the minimality principle:

(24) <u>Condition on Minimality</u>
Minimal word is minimal foot only if lexical roots are footed.

3. Vocalic Specification

Given the above idea of the disyllabic trochee, a number of important generalizations about vocalic specification in the Ibibio verb are achieved. First, the vocalic specification of the (trochaic) foot is completely predictable. As seen above only the verb root vowel is underlyingly specified, the suffix vowel is derived by spreading from the root.

Our assumption, as proposed above, is that Ibibio Vocalic Spreading involves the propagation of the terminal vowel features. Each feature may be spread independently of other features, and only the plus values of these features may spread, since only these are underlyingly specified. However, of the three vowel features [high], [low] and [round], only the last two, [low] and [round], may spread. The feature [high] does not spread in Ibibio. Therefore of the six

[8] We adopt this order to uniformly make (oral) Stop Weakening apply between two syllables within the same foot, as is the case when [kv] is suffixed to CV roots, illustrated in (36) above. Stop Weakening may well take place earlier, that is, immediately after Vowel Centralization, since it is foot based.

vowels / i e a ɔ o u /, only four [e a ɔ o] may occur in suffixes. Suffixes never have high vowels:

(25)	kpǐ	"cut [with matchete]"	...kpǐi-ɣé	"...not cutting"
	dí	"come"	...díí-ɣé	"...not coming"
	dù	"be alive"	...dùù-ɣó	"...not living"
	kpù	"be in vain"	...kpùù-ɣó	"...not being in vain"

The fact that the feature [high] does not spread in Ibibio may be accounted for with a language particular constraint blocking the propagation of [+high] between syllables.[9] We state this constraint as follows:

(26) [+high] spreading constraint

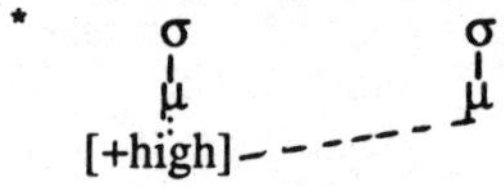

```
*      σ            σ
       |            |
       μ            μ
       :            |
  [+high]- - - - - -
```

In combination with underspecification, our proposal works as follows. Given the underlying vocalic specification in (3), the spreading of [+low] alone results in vowel [a]. The spreading of [+round] alone results in vowel [o]. Spreading both features results in [ɔ], and spreading no features at all results in vowel [e] (through default specification). If the feature [high] does not spread as proposed here, then there is no spreading in case the root vowel is /i/, since its only underlying specification is [+high]. The result then is vowel [e], again by default specification. And finally, if the root vowel is [u], only the feature [round] may spread, resulting again in vowel [o]. This completely accounts for the four vowels which occur in suffixes.

If only the first vowel of the verb is specified, and if disyllabic verbs constitute trochaic feet on their own, the prediction is that disyllabic verbs will have identical vowels. This prediction turns out to be correct. (Note that in the case where the first vowel of the root is high, the second vowel will be nonhigh given the constraint that high vowels do not spread between syllables.)

(27)	dáppá	"dream [vb.]"	sàŋá	"walk"
	dámmá	"be mad"	kɔ́ŋɔ́	"choke"
	dɔ́kkɔ́	"tell"	fèɣé	"run"
	tèmmé	"explain"	bɔ́ɣɔ́	"overtake"
	díkké	"be frightened"		
	díppé	"lift up"		

Finally, vocalic specification beyond the foot is also accounted for. If Vocalic Spreading (11) is foot bound, then vocalic specification in suffixes beyond the foot

[9] This constraint is independently motivated by the fact that the result of vocalic spreading is never a high vowel in Ibibio; either in prefixes or in suffixes.

will not be derived by spreading since spreading stops with the foot. This generalization is also borne out by fact. In all of such cases the suffix vowel is specified by default, and is invariably [é] as the negative forms of the above verbs, given in (28) below show.

(28)	...dáppá-ké	"not dreaming"	...sàŋá-ké	"not walking"
	...dámmá-ké	"not being mad"	...kɔ́ŋɔ́-ké	"not choking"
	...dɔ́kkɔ́-ké	"not telling"	...fèɣé-ké	"not running"
	...tèmmé-ké	"not explaining"	...bɔ́ɣɔ́-ké	"not overtaken"
	...díkké-ké	"not being frightened"		
	...díppé-ké	"not lifting up"		

4. Conclusion

In the foregoing sections we have argued for a number of positions. Languages with unfooted lexical roots may target prosodic categories in the morphology. The Ibibio verb system operates a targeted disyllabic trochee with two templates: heavy - light and light - light. These templates are determined by whether the suffix is a CV or a V respectively, and they must be satisfied regardless of the underlying moraic structure of the verb root, with the result that mora count may be increased or decreased (usually by vowel lengthening or shortening). It is interesting that these suffixes should require different foot templates, since they are both monomoraic. This fact clearly requires further research. Several phonological processes that take place between verb root and suffix in Ibibio are foot bound, and any suffixes outside the foot fall beyond the scope of such processes. Given the foot structure, the vocalic specification of the Ibibio verb is predictable. Verb roots may be underlyingly specified for vocalic features (or they may be unspecified). The second vowel of a verb, usually a suffix which forms a disyllabic foot with root, is derived by spreading from the the root, resulting in most cases in an identical vowel. If this proposal about the foot structure of Ibibio is correct, then the proposal that the minimal word is always equivalent to the minimal foot (McCarthy and Prince 1986,1990) has to be restricted to languages in which lexical roots are footed, otherwise it is invalid.

Notes

*Earlier versions of this paper benefited from comments by Yetunde Folarin Schleicher and Francis Oyebade. Our great indebtedness to Brian McHugh, Douglas Pulleyblank and Donca Steriade is obvious throughout this version. All remaining errors are, of course, our responsibility.

References

Archangeli, D. 1984. *Underspecification in Yawelmani Phonology and Morphology* Doctoral Dissertation, MIT, Cambridge, MA.

Archangeli, D. 1988. Aspects of Underspecification Theory. *Phonology* 5: 183 - 207.

Archangeli, D. 1991. Syllabification and Prosodic Templates in Yawelmani. *Natural Language and Linguistic Theory* 9: 231 - 284.

Clements, G. N. 1985. The Geometry of Phonological Features. *Phonology Yearbook* 2: 225 - 252.

Clements, G. N. 1987. Towards a Substantive Theory of Feature Specification. *NELS* 17: 79-93.

Clements, G. N. 1990. Place of Articulation in Consonants and Vowels: A Unified Theory. To appear in *L'Architecture et la Geométrie des Représentations Phonologiques*, eds. B. Laks and A Rialland, Paris: Editions du C.N.R.S.

Connell, B. 1987. Temporal Aspects of Labiovelar stops. *Work in Progress* 20, Department of Linguistics, University of Edinburgh.

Cook, T.L. 1968. The Efik Consonant System. Ms, University of Ibadan.

Essien, O.E. 1990. *A Grammar of the Ibibio Language*. Ibadan: University Press Limited.

Greenberg, J. 1963. *The Languages of Africa*. (IJAL 29,1. Publication 25 of the Indiana University Research Center in Anthropology, Folklore and Linguistics.) The Hague: Mouton and Co.

Hayes, B. 1987. A Revised Parametric Metrical Theory. *NELS* 17: 274 - 289.

Hayes, B. 1989. Compensatory Lengthening in Moraic Phonology. *Linguistic Inquiry* 20: 253-306.

Hyman, L.M. 1985. *A Theory of Phonological Weight*. Dordrecht: Foris Publications.

Kaufman, E.M. 1968. *Ibibio Grammar*. Doctoral dissertation, University of California, Los Angeles.

McCarthy, J. 1988. Feature Geometry and Dependency: A Review. *Phonetica* 43: 84 -108.

McCarthy, J. and A. Prince. 1986. Prosodic Morphology. Ms, University of Massachusetts, Amherst and Brandeis University.

McCarthy, J. and A. Prince. 1990. Foot and Word in Prosodic Morphology the Arabic Broken Plural. *Natural Language and Linguistic Theory* 8: 209-284.

Pulleyblank, D. 1986. *Tone in Lexical Phonology*. Dordrecht: Reidel.

Pulleyblank, D. 1988. Vocalic Underspecification in Yoruba. *Linguistic Inquiry* 19: 233-270.

Sagey, E. 1986. *The Representation of Features and Relations in Nonlinear Phonology*. Doctoral dissertation, M.I.T.

Steriade, D. 1987. Redundant Values. *CLS 23: Parasession on Autosegmental and Metrical Phonology*, 339 - 362.

Welmers, William. 1973. *African Language Structures*. Berkeley: University of California Press.

Williamson, Kay. 1989. Benue Congo Overview. in *The Niger Congo Languages*, eds. J. Bendor-Samuel and R.L. Hartell, 3 - 45. Lanham: University Press of America.

Yip, M. 1992. Prosodic Morphology in four Chinese Dialects. *Journal of East Asian Linguistics* 1: 1 - 35.

Agreement Asymmetries in Arabic

MAHER BAHLOUL & WAYNE HARBERT
Cornell University

In this paper we consider an asymmetry between two sets of nominal features in Arabic, which differ according to the contexts in which phrasal heads are inflected in agreement with them. The basic contrasts in Arabic agreement are well known, and have been analyzed in an extensive literature which we cannot review here (cf., e.g., Fassi-Fehri (1984), Abd El Moneim (1989) Mohammad (1990), Benmamoun (1990, 1992a)). As the contrast between (1a) and (1b), (2a) and (2b) shows, Arabic verbs agree in number with preverbal but not postverbal subjects.

(1) a. qadim-a (/*qadim-uu) al-ʔawlaadu
came-3MS came-3MP the-boys-3MP
'The boys came'
b. al-ʔawlaadu qadim-uu (/*qadim-a) [t]
the-boys-3MP came-3MP came-3MS
'The boys came'

(2) a. qadim-at (/*qadim-ataa) al-bint-aani
came-3SF came-3DF the-girl(F)-3D
'The two girls came'
b. al-bint-aani qadim-ataa (/*qadim-at) [t]
the-girl(F)-3D came-3DF came-3SF
'The two girls came'

These same examples show that postverbal subjects, as well as preverbal subjects, control agreement on the verb with respect to the features of gender and apparently person. The basic question we wish to address here is why there should be such an asymmetry between these two types of features. In the course of developing an answer, we will point out that a widely assumed descriptive generalization about the distribution of number agreement is not quite accurate.

One solution that suggests itself for this split in agreement features is that person/gender features and number features are associated with different functional head positions. We might envision, for example, an inner and an outer AGR position, and claim that different phi features are inherently associated with each of these positions--number with the outer AGR^0 and person/gender with the inner one. Such an account would accord well with the radically extended X-bar proposal of Schlonsky (1989), under which every Phi-feature heads its own projection, and under which clausal structure includes distinct number phrases, gender phrases, and person phrases. Along with Benmamoun (1990), however, we argue against such an approach. Our first argument is based on the behavior of agreement in the compound tense examples in (3)-(5), which show clearly that number agreement is not associated with a single head position.

(3) kaan-at ta-ktub-u al-bint-aani darsa-humaa
was-**3FS** **3F**-write-**S** the-girl-**3D** lesson-FD
'The two girls were writing their lesson'

(4) a. kaan-at al-bint-aani ta-ktub-aani [t] darsa-humaa
was-**3FS** the- girl-**3D** **3F**-write-**D** lesson-DF
'The two girls were writing their lesson'
b.* kaan-at al-bint-aani ta-ktub-u [t] darsa-humaa
was-**3FS** the-girl(**F**)-**3D** **3F**-write-**S** lesson-FD

(5) a. al-bint-aani kaan-ataa [t] ta-ktub-aani [t] darsa-humaa
the-girls(**F**)-**3D** was-**3FD** **3F**-write-**D** lesson-FD
'The two girls were writing their lesson'
b.* al-bint-aani kaan-at [t] ta-ktub-aani [t] darsa-humaa
the-girl-**3D** was-**3FS** **3F**-write-**D** lesson-FD

In these examples, T^0 is occupied by the auxiliary *kaana*. The lexical verb occupies a lower position in the structure--according to Bahloul (in prep), it has been raised to the functional head position of an Aspectual projection (Asp). The proposed tree is illustrated in (6):

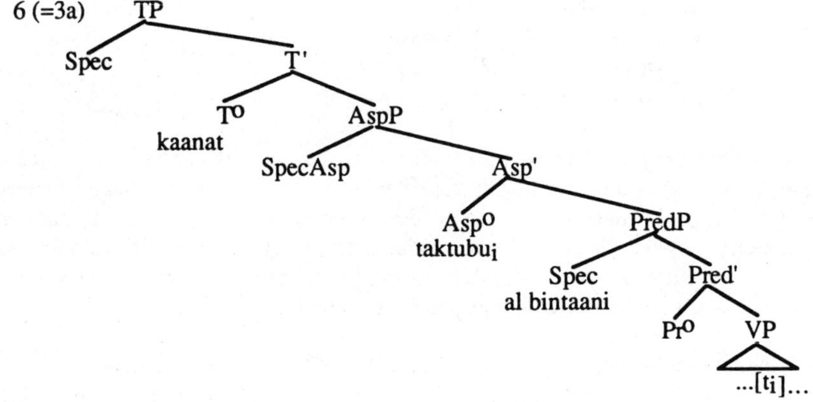

When the subject follows the raised verb (i.e., occurs in an internal subject position, which we take, following Bowers (1990), to be Spec Pred), subject and verb agree only in person and gender, as in (3). Notice, moreover, that in (3) *kaanat,* the auxiliary, also agrees with the in situ subject in gender but not number. When the subject is preposed to a Spec position between *kaanat* and the verb as in (4a)--the Specifier position of the Aspect projection, under our analysis--, the verb agrees with the subject in number as well as gender. *Kaanat,* however, remains singular in (4a), but continues to exhibit feminine agreement. When the subject is preposed all the way to SpecTP, as in (5a), both *kaanataa* and the lexical verb agree with it in number as well as person and gender. Similarly, in (7), the negative auxiliary *laysa* is seen to agree with a subject in number only if that subject is preposed to the Spec position of its projection:

(7) a. lays-a ya-dri-i al-walad-aani mataa [pro] yu-saafir-aani
Neg-**3MS** **3M**-know-**S** the-boy-**3D** when **3M**-travel-**D**
'The two boys do not know when they are traveling'
b. lays-a al-walad-aanii ya-dri-yaani [t] mataa [pro] yu-saafir-aani
Neg-**3MS** the-boy-**3D** **3M**-know-**D** when **3M**-travel-**D**
c. al-walad-aanii lays-aa ya-dri-yaani [t] mataa [pro] yu-saafir-aani
the-boy-**3D** Neg-**3MD** **3M**-know-**D** when **3M**-travel-**D**
d. *al-walad-aanii lays-a ya-dri-yaani [t] mataa [pro] yu-saafir-aani
the-boy-**3D** Neg-**3MS** **3M**-know-**D** when **3M**-travel-**D**

This shows that there can be multiple occurrences of number agreement within a clause. We must accordingly reject at least the hypothesis that the number feature is associated with a unique functional projection in the clause. It is, of course, possible, though unlikely, that a hypothesized Number Phrase recurs within clausal structure. We find it much more plausible to interpret the paradigm in (3)-(5) as suggesting that, in fact, number agreement is not localized in only certain functional projections, but that it may be licensed on a verb occurring in any functional head position, just in case directly licensed by a subject nominal (or the trace of one) occurring in a Spec-Head relation with that functional head. This view is borne out by consideration of the fact that the same patterning is evidenced in other projection systems. This point is illustrated in (8)-(10). Quantifiers agree with their DP complements in number when the latter are preposed but not otherwise.

(8) a. nafsu al-mašaakili tuqliqu-hu
same the-problems-**PF** disturb-him
'The same problems disturb him'
b. al-mašaakilu nafsu-haa (/*nafsu) tuqliqu-hu
the-problems-**PF** same-**PF** same-S disturb-him

(9) a. xaraja jamiiʕu an-naasi
left-3S all-**S** the-people-**PM**
'All the people left'

b. xaraja an-naasu ajamaʕuun (/*jamiiʕu)
left-3S the-people-**PM** all-**P** all-**S**

(10)a. xaraja kilaa ar-raʔiisayni
left-SM both the-presidents-**DM**
'Both presidents left'

b. xaraja ar-raʔiis-aani kilaa-humaa (/*kilaa)
left-SM the-presidents-**DM** both-**DM** both-**S**

(11) shows a possible similar alternation, involving definiteness agreement.

(11)a. darras-tu xamsata ṭullaab-in
teach-Perf-1S five students-Gen
'I taught five students'

b. darras-tu **aṭ**-ṭullaab-a **al**-xamsata (/*xamsata) [t]
teach-Perf-1S **the**-students-Acc **the**-five five
'I taught the 5 students'

The generalization which emerges is that number agreement (and, apparently, definiteness agreement) may be licensed on the heads of functional projections of a variety of sorts, just in case the licensing DP (or its trace) occurs in a direct Spec-Head relation with that functional head position at S-structure. Those heads do not agree with arguments left in lower positions in the structure.

However, what about agreement with respect to other features--e.g., gender? As (3) shows, agreement with respect to gender features obtains even when the DP controlling gender agreement has not been raised to the Specifier position of the functional projection containing the verb at S-structure. Moreover, in (3) gender agreement obtains between *kaanat* and the postverbal subject even though they have not been in a Spec-Head relation at any point in the derivation. Following Benmamoun (1992a) we will adopt the view that agreement here is licensed under a second type of relationship--that of government (cf. also McCloskey 1986). The verb in (3) agrees with the postverbal subject in Spec Pred because the verb is in Asp^0, and from that position it minimality-governs Spec Pred, as seen in tree (6). To account for the feminine singular agreement on *kaanat* in (3), we assume that the agreement feature assigned to the verb through its government relationship with the postverbal subject is in turn passed upward, again through agreement under government, to T^0--which governs the projection of the verb.

The question that arises, however, is why number features may not be similarly licensed through agreement under government, but rather require a direct Spec-Head relationship, as appears to be the case. In other words, if agreement is licensable under government at all, why can number agreement not be so licensed in Arabic? The account of Benmamoun (1992a) is as follows: In principle, agreement under government and agreement under a Spec-Head relation are both possible, regardless of the features involved. However, if the verb in INFL acquires both number features and person features from a postverbal subject through government by agreement, this will result in an INFL fully specified for all phi-features. This INFL is in turn coindexed with an expletive pro in Spec IP through Spec-Head agreement, and, by hypothesis, the full agreement of INFL identifies that <u>pro</u> as a thematic <u>pro</u>. This <u>pro</u> subject therefore competes with the postverbal subject for the single external theta-role, and a violation of the Theta Criterion results. Such a violation can be avoided only if INFL is not fully specified for all agreement features. Thus, full agreement with the postverbal subject is disallowed.

There are, in our estimation, certain possible problems with such an account. We note, for example, that (12) is well-formed. Here, the imperfect verb is fully marked for person/gender, in the prefix, and number, in the suffix *-u*. The source for this singular number agreement marker is not the postverbal dual subject, of course; rather, we assume that it is either licensed by an expletive <u>pro</u> in Spec I (that is, Spec T in our analysis) or assigned by default. Whatever its source, however, it remains the case that the verb in INFL here is specified for all phi-features. If the presence of full agreement were sufficient to force <u>pro</u> to be interpreted as thematic, then a theta-theoretical violation should arise in (12) as well, contrary to fact. Thus, it appears not to be the case that the verb in VS order must remain unspecified for number. Rather, its number morphology simply cannot be controlled by a postverbal subject.

(12) [pro] ta-ktub-u al-bint-aani darsa-humaa
3F-write-**S** the-girl-**3D** lesson-FD
'The two girls wrote their lesson'

Second, if the requirement is simply that INFL must not be fully specified for agreement, in order to avoid identifying pro as thematic, it remains unclear, as Benmamoun notes, why that requirement could not alternatively be satisfied by the suppression of person/gender agreement, rather than number agreement.

It is also not clear that the account extends readily to other languages. In Welsh, as in Arabic, number agreement with postverbal, nonpronominal subjects is similarly suppressed, yet there is no evidence in Welsh for a position for expletive subjects distinct from that of postverbal subjects in general. When overt expletives occur, as in (13), their distribution is the same as that of other postverbal subjects.

(13) Mae hi wedi synnu pawb y bydd angen mwy o arian
Is 'she' Perf surprise everyone that will-be need more of money
'It surprised everyone that more money will be needed'
(Awbery 1976:105)

There is also arguably no room for a preverbal expletive in Welsh. The order of the postverbal subject relative to the sentential negator *dim* in Welsh in such sentences as (14a) suggests that that subject is not in the internal subject position (which we identify as Spec Pred), but that it has been raised out of that position, across NegP, to the outer subject position, Spec IP. Accordingly, we claim that in Welsh, VSO order results from the raising of the subject to Spec I and the inflected verb to Co. This leaves no room for an expletive subject. Note that in Welsh, unlike Arabic, there is no possibility for the subject to move to a preverbal nonoperator position--that is, no evidence from subject raising for a preverbal subject position.[1] Nonetheless, Welsh shares with Arabic the prohibition against number agreement with postverbal subjects--suggesting that this prohibition is not in fact linked to properties of expletives in Spec IP.

Finally, it appears that the claimed prohibition of number agreement between verbs and postverbal subjects in Arabic, from which earlier accounts have proceeded, is not absolute. Here, a comparison with Welsh is again instructive. In Welsh, as in Arabic, full NP subjects do not trigger number agreement in the verbs preceding them, This is seen in (14a). As (14b) shows, however, postverbal pronominal subjects do control number agreement.

(14)a. Dydy'r doliau 'na ddim yn rhy ddrud
Not-is (Sg)-the dolls those NEG Pr too expensive
'Those dolls are not too expensive.'
b. Dydy-n nhw ddim yn rhy ddrud
Not-are-Pl they Neg Pr too expensive
'They are not too expensive.'

This appears to be the case in Arabic as well. Pronoun subjects in Arabic typically cannot appear postverbally, since they are subject to obligatory fronting to Spec IP They can be enabled to remain postverbal, however, by conjoining them with NP's. As (14c) shows, the verb then does agree in number with the pronoun, as in Welsh.[2]

[1] As Awbery (1990) notes, in colloquial Welsh the subject can follow the negative element dim, as well as precede it under some circumstances, as in (i):

(i) Ond nese dim Data tro (Awbery 1990)
But not-would-do Neg Dad turn
'But Dad would not do the trick.'

This supports the view that that subjects occurring to the left of dim are not in the inner subject position, but have been raised to Spec I.

[2] Fassi-Fehri (1984: 109) also gives an example of a stressed contrastive, nonconjoined plural pronoun remaining in postverbal position. Here too, there is plural agreement.

(14)c. xaraj-uu /*xaraj-a [hum wa Sami]
left-**3MP** left-**3MS** they and Sami
'They and Sami left'

That is, there is number agreement with postverbal subjects in both languages, just in case the subject is pronominal. Why should this be so? We might suppose that the difference between pronominal and nonpronominal subjects is the result of a movement of postverbal pronominal subjects, e.g. to a position which is more local to INFL than the position of full NP subjects--by cliticization, for example. This, however, cannot be the correct answer. Number agreement obtains in (14c) even though the pronoun, as a conjunct within a coordinate structure, is inaccessible to movement. Compare also example (20f) below, from Welsh. Even if we set aside the Coordinate Structure Constraint, the pronoun in (14c) cannot have been moved out of the conjoined subject to some higher but still postverbal position reserved for pronominal subjects. If it had been moved out of the conjoined NP, then we should expect it to be further fronted obligatorily to Spec IP, just as other unconjoined noncontrastive pronominal subjects are.

The account we wish to propose for the observed distribution of agreement features is the following. We adopt Benmamoun's insight that there are two types of relationships which can license agreement--the Spec-Head relation and the government relation. However, we propose that the choice is not free, but depends on the source of the features in question. We claim that **gender** features are inherent features of lexical nouns. In languages with gender distinctions, nouns are typically associated with an invariant gender. On the other hand, definiteness, for example, is not an inherent feature of lexical head nouns, but a feature of the functional category Determiner, and therefore of DP's. Recent analyses (including Valois (1990) and Ritter (1990)) have also claimed the same status for number. We refer you especially to Ritter (1990), who argues at length for Hebrew that gender inflection is assigned to nouns through lexical affixation, while number inflection is associated with the head of a functional projection Num, and acquired by nouns through syntactic head raising.

Our account makes crucial use of this difference in the source of these two types of features. It also exploits the notion of PROJECTION SYSTEM being developed by Isabella Barbier at Cornell, based on insights in Abney (1987). The idea is defined formally in (15a), but an ostensive definition might suffice here. Consider the tree in (15c). The claim is that a lexical head and its projection plus all of the functional projections uniterruptedly dominating it form a single Projection System. The unique lexical head in such a system is the Base of the Projection System. (15a) also allows functional heads to count as Bases of Projection Systems, in cases where there is no other candidate--i.e., in cases where those functional heads do not select a Lexical Phrase as their complement. This provision is made to accommodate pronouns, which we take to be intransitive DP's or NumP's, following Ritter (1990) and others. In other words, a path traced downward through a stack of functional projections eventually terminates, either with a lexical projection or with a functional projection--e.g., a pro-DP or pro-NumP-- with no complement. This stack of functional projections plus its terminus together define a Projection System, with the bottommost phrase counting as its Base.

(15)a. A Projection System is a maximal set of phrases $Z_1^{Max}...Z_n^{Max}$ such that:

i. Z_j^0, the head of Z_j^{Max}, governs Z_{j-1}^{Max}

ii. For every Z_k^{Max}, k>1, the head Z_k^0 of Z_k^{Max} is a functional head

iii. Z_1^0 is either a lexical head or a functional head with no complement.

b. Z_1^0 is the Base of its Projection System.

c.

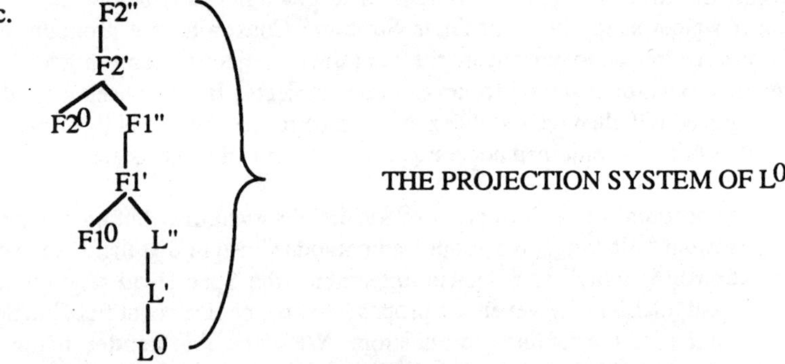

The higher functional layers in such a Projection System are transparent to the projection of features from the Base. Thus, for example, in (16), the plural feature of the lexical noun <u>grapes</u> is accessible for the purpose of subject agreement, just in case <u>bunch</u> is interpreted as a quantifier--i.e., as a functional head.

(16) A bunch of grapes are on the table

We claim that for certain grammatical processes defined in terms of government, only features originating on the Base of a Projection System are evaluated. In particular, we propose the restriction in (17) on agreement under government in Standard Arabic, and in Welsh.

(17) Only those features which originate on the Base of a Projection System are evaluated for agreement under government.

This yields straightforwardly the observed asymmetry between gender and number agreement in Arabic. Gender features originate on lexical N's, hence on the Bases of Projection Systems. They are thus visible for agreement under government. Number features are features of the functional head Num, as schematized in (18a).

They are accordingly not features of the Base node in Projection Systems terminating in lexical N's, and are invisible to such agreement.[3]

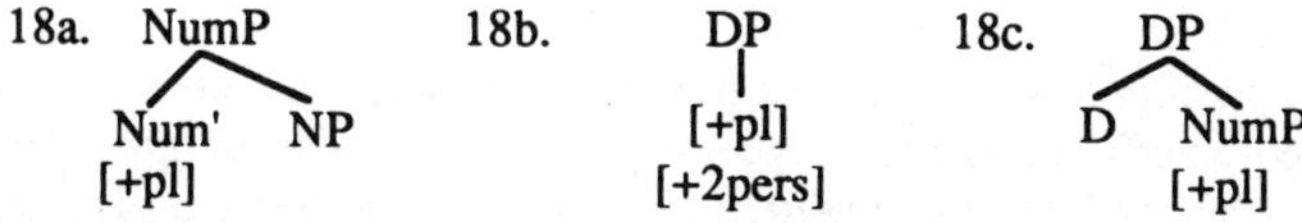

The crucial difference between plural full NPs and plural pronouns is that pronouns, following Ritter (1990) and others, are taken to be DP's or NumP's without internal structure, which are directly associated with Person, Gender and Number features. This is schematized in (18b) and (18c). Since they do not select NP complements, these DP's or NumP's terminate Projections Systems, and therefore count as Bases of those Projection Systems. Their person/number features are therefore Base features. Following Ritter, we hold that person features have only the values [±1 pers] and [±2 pers], third person being a default. These features are, moreover, only associated with pronouns, where they count as Base features, as we have defined them.(Cf. also Lapointe (1984:72).) It is accordingly predicted, given Principle (17) that number features on pronouns, but not number features in full NP's, will be visible for agreement under government, and that person features on pronouns will also be visible for this kind of agreement.

This proposal also provides an account for such examples as (19), in which gender agreement is shown to be controlled by the lexical head of the projection system, bypassing the quantifier. (The reader is referred to Benmamoun (in preparation) for a quite different characterization of these constructions.)

---

[3] A word is perhaps in order here about nonhuman plural subjects in Arabic. With these, there is no number agreement even when the subject is in preverbal position. Moreover, the plurals of such nouns trigger uniform feminine gender agreement on the verb, as in (ii):

(i) al-qiṭṭu naama
the-cat(Sg)Masc-Nom sleep-Perf-3MS
'The cat (masc) slept'

(i) al-qiṭaṭ-u xaraj-at
the-cat(Pl)-Nom left-3FS
'The cats slept'

These examples show that the presence of plural number is not sufficient to trigger number agreeement. DP's can control plural agreement only if they have both a [±Pl] feature, projected from Num^0, and [+human], projected from N^0. We propose further that feminine agreement in (ii) results from the fact that Num^0 [+plural] selects for an abstract Feminine gender feature on its N^0 complement when the latter is nonhuman. A similar account can be devised for the Broken Plurals of Classical Arabic.

(19) xaraj-at baʔḍ-u al-fatayaat-i
came-**F** some-Nom the-girls-**F**-Gen
'Some girls left'

We will now attempt to show that this proposal also has some other positive empirical consequences for Arabic agreement. In particular, it provides a straightforward account of the striking alternations in gender agreement illustrated in (20), which have been pointed out by Mohammad (1990) and Benmamoun (1992b).

(20)a. [al-waladu wa al-bintu] xaraj-aa
the-boy(**M**) and the-girl(**F**) left-**DM**
'The boy and the girl left'
b. [al-bintu wa al-waladu] xaraj-aa
the-girl(**F**) and the-boy(**M**) left-**DM**
c. xaraj-at [al-bintu wa al-waladu]
left-**3SF** the-girl(**F**) and the-boy(**M**)
d. xaraj-a [al-waladu wa al-bintu]
left-**3SM** the-boy(**M**) and the-girl(**F**)

In (20a), we see that a conjoined subject consisting of a masculine conjunct and a feminine conjunct triggers dual masculine agreement on a verb in SV order. We will not concern ourselves for the moment with the precise mechanism of feature addition which yields this result, but simply note that a masculine NP conjoined with a feminine NP yields a coordinate structure with the gender feature Masculine, and that this feature controls agreement on the verb. The contrast between (20a) and (20b) shows that this is independent of the relative order of the conjuncts. In both, the verb in SV order agrees with the composite gender feature of the topmost node. Strikingly, however, in VS order a very different pattern emerges. The verb is singular, as expected, but its gender inflection is determined by which of the two conjuncts is the closer to it. In (20c) it is feminine, since the feminine conjunct is initial. In (20d) it is masculine, since the masculine conjunct is initial. This pattern of agreement is also found in other languages with conjoined subjects in VS order. See Corbett (1984) for Russian and McCloskey (1986) for extensive discussion of Irish. (20f) shows the same effect for person. Person agreement in Standard Arabic is with the initial pronoun in a postverbal conjoined subject.

(20)e. xaraj-ta [ʔanta wa Sami]
left-**2MS** you and Sami
'You and Sami left.'

(21a-c) show that the same holds true of Welsh.

(21)a. Fe fyddi [di a fi]'n mynd i'r parti (Alun Hughes, p.c.)
Comp will-2S you and I Pr go to-the party
'You and I will go to the party'

b. Wyt [ti a dy dad] yn cyrraedd yfory? (Alun Hughes, p.c.)
Are-2S you and your Dad Pr arriving tomorrow?
'Are you and your father arriving tomorrow?'

c. Ydy [dy dad i ti] 'n cyrraedd yfory? (Alun Hughes, p.c.)
is-3S your Dad and you Pr arriving tomorrow
'Are your father and you arriving tomorrow?'

Our account of these facts starts from the structure assumed by Benmamoun (1992b) for coordinate XP's, under which they conform to the template imposed by X-bar theory. As seen in (22), the conjunction is held to be the head of a phrase, and the first conjunct is its Specifier.

22.

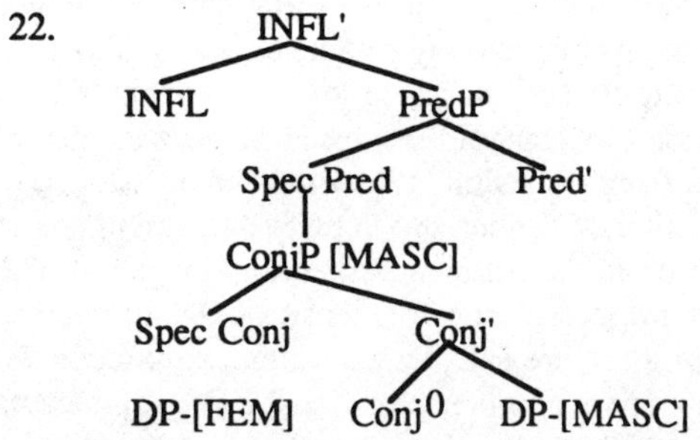

This proposal appears to be very similar to the Boolean Phrase hypothesis argued for by Munn (1989, 1992). Now, as Benmamoun notes, under the assumption of an appropriate definition of minimality government, INFL in configuration (22) governs the Specifier of the Conjunction Phrase, since that Spec is not more locally c-commanded by any other head. Accordingly, INFL may agree in gender with the DP in Spec Conj position, through agreement under government. It may not agree with the second conjunct--the complement of $Conj^0$-- since the complement is in the domain of a more local head. This accounts for the impossibility of feminine agreement in (20d). In fact, in order to make this work under the assumptions we have adopted, some additional provisions are needed. If conjunctions are heads at all, it appears that they must be functional, rather than lexical heads. This is suggested at least by the fact that they are closed class elements, not belonging to a major word class. If this is so, then the complement NP in (22) constitutes the Base of a Projection System extending upward to Conjunction Phrase. Given that features of Bases of Projection Systems are projected freely upward through those systems, why is it that in (20d), for example, the feminine feature of the noun in the complement phrase is not available for purposes of agreement? We propose that it is because the normal projection of these features is disrupted in such cases by the fact that the head of the Conjunction Phrase is simultaneously assigned a second abstract gender feature through Spec-Head agreement with the DP in its Specifier position. Because of these competing phi features--one from the Base of the Projections System and one from the Specifier of the phrase, the Conjunction Phrase receives a composite gender feature, counting for purposes of agreement as Masculine. This feature is what determines agreement in the Spec-Head agreement cases in (20a,b).

Given, however, that INFL also governs the whole Conjunction Phrase in (22), in addition to minimality-governing the DP in its Spec position, we must ask why in a case like (20c) INFL can only agree with the feminine feature of the DP in the Specifier of ConjP, and not with the composite masculine feature belonging to the ConjP as a whole. In Standard Arabic, at least, Masculine agreement is not possible in (20c), unlike the Spec-Head agreement case of (20a). McCloskey (1986) addresses this question for Irish by defining government in such a way that (in that language) in conjoined structures the leftmost conjunct (Spec Conj, in our account) while the mother node (ConjP in our analysis) is not. Government by a head, so defined, in effect skips over the topmost node of conjoined structures and relates the head uniquely with the leftmost conjunct (a possibly parameterized option). We propose, however, that no such stipulative modification of government is necessary. Rather, the behavior of postverbal conjoined subjects in these languages follows without further specification from provision (17), which we introduced to account for the difference in distribution of gender and number agreement. The Conjunction Phrase and its daughter nodes form a Projection System. The masculine feature on ConjP is not projected from the Base of the Projection System. Rather, it is the product of a feature calculation which compounds the gender feature of the Specifer and that of the complement, yielding [Masc] in cases where the two are distinct, regardless of the order of the conjuncts. Accordingly, we predict that this feature cannot be consulted for the purpose of agreement under government, because it does not originate on the Base of the Projection system as required by (17). Feminine agreement thus emerges as the sole possibility in (20c). A similar account is available for person agreement; in the Welsh (21a), person agreement cannot be with the composite first-person plural feature of the whole Conjunction Phrase, since that feature does not originate on the Base of the ConjP but is rather the result of the computation of the features of both conjuncts. It is thus invisible, given (17), and, [+2 pers] agreement with the Specifier of ConjP is again the only choice here.

Agreement in Arabic with conjoined objects appears to exhibit a similar patterning, though there are interesting differences. (23a,b) show that when the first member of the conjoined object is a pronoun, the verb (obligatorily) occurs with a clitic encoding the phi-features of that pronoun. We take this clitic to be an object agreement marker.

(23)a. šaahad-tu-hum$_i$ [hum$_i$ wa al-bin-ta]
see.PRF-1S-**3MP** them.MP and the-girl-ACC
'I saw them (M) and the girl'

b. šaahad-tu-hunna$_i$ [hunna$_i$ wa al-walad-a]
see.PRF-1S-**3FP** them.FP and the-boy-ACC
'I saw them (Fem) and the girl'

Unlike the subject case, however, when both of the conjuncts of a conjoined object are full NP's, there is no encoding of agreement at all, even with respect to gender. This is shown in (23c,d):

(23)c. šaahad-tu [al-walad-a wa al-bin-ta]
see.PRF-1Sg the-boy-ACC and the-girl-ACC
'I saw the boy and the girl'

d.* šaahad-tu-hum$_i$ [al-ʔawlaad-a$_i$ wa al-bin-ta]
see.PRF-1S-**3MP** the-boys-ACC and the-girl-ACC

We take this to be a result of the way in which the morphology bundles phi-features. In the case of subject agreement, e.g., in the perfect *qadim-at-aa* 'came-Fem-Dual' or the imperfect *ta-ktub-aani* 'Fem-write-Dual', the morphemes for gender and number are isolable, and it is possible to coindex an argument with one without coindexing it with the other. It appears that the object agreement morphemes, on the other hand, are portmanteau morphemes, in which gender and number features are bundled together. Suppose that an argument can be coindexed with such a morpheme only if (a) it matches the morpheme in all features, and (b) it is in a position from which it can legitimately license all of them. Since (17) rules out the licensing of number agreement under government, except in the case where the controlling argument is a pronoun, number agreement with the object in (23d) is blocked. The object therefore cannot be coindexed with the agreement morpheme. However, this also prevents the encoding of gender agreement, and there can therefore be no agreement at all.

Principle (17) thus accounts for three apparent anomalies in agreement in Arabic, some of which have counterparts in other languages. First, it accounts for the difference between gender and number agreement with full NP subjects in postverbal positions. Only gender, not number, is visible to agreement under government. Second, it accounts for the difference between pronoun subjects and full NP postverbal subjects with respect to number agreement. Number is a Base feature only on pronouns--not on full NP's. Finally, it accounts for the fact that agreement with postverbal conjoined subjects is controlled by the first conjunct, rather than by the whole conjoined phrase.

We conclude by noting that other varieties of Arabic exhibit a pattern of agreement different from the one described here for Standard Arabic. As Benmamoun notes, in some dialects--in particular, Morroccan and Tunisian Arabic-

-number agreement is possible, and in fact, required, between verbs and postverbal, as well as preverbal subjects. We have illustrated this for Tunisian Arabic in (24).

(24)a. [e] xarj-u l-wlaad (V S)
left-**3MP** the-boys
'The boys left'
b. l-wlaad xarj-u (S V)
the-boys left-**3MP**
c. * xraj l-wlaad
left-**3MS** the-boys

Space does not permit a full discussion of the differences between these dialects and Standard Arabic which result in these differences in agreement possibilities. We believe that in these dialects agreement is achieved not through government of the postverbal subject by INFL but through chain formation between that postverbal subject and the expletive in Spec I, along the lines proposed in Harbert and Toribio (1991). This is therefore an instance of agreement under a Spec-Head relationship, mediated through Spec I, and number agreement is possible. Under the typology of chain formation developed in Harbert and Toribio, that sort of chain can be formed only if the expletive in Spec I is phonologically empty. Benmamoun has noticed that the Spec I expletive behaves differently in Standard Arabic than in Morroccan (and Tunisian) Arabic. In particular, in contexts of nonnominative case assignment, it can be overtly realized in SA but not TA. The possibility of spell-out for the expletive in Standard Arabic reflects that it has at least potential phonological content. We propose, therefore, that the difference between Tunisian Arabic and Standard Arabic might be that Standard Arabic doesn't allow chain formation between expletives in Spec IP and postverbal subjects because Spec IP is not radically empty in that language.

Postverbal conjoined subjects also control number agreement in Tunisian Arabic; according to the seven informants we consulted, agreement in most cases must be with the whole conjoined phrase, as in (25), and not with the first conjunct. There are some puzzling exceptions to this, which we do not understand at this point: when there is a referential dependency between the two conjuncts, as in (26), or if one of the conjuncts is a pronoun, as in (27), our informants strongly prefer agreement with the first conjunct over agreement with the whole conjoined NP, even though they disallow this otherwise. We believe that considerations of salience are involved here.

(25) xarj-u / ?? xraj [maher w nabil]
left-**3P** left-**3SM** maher and nabil
'Maher and Nabil left'

(26). xraj /?*xarj-u [haaka ir-raajil w wild-u]
left-3MS left-3P that the-man and son-his
'That man and his son left'

(27) xraj /* xarj-u [huwa w sami]
left-3S left-3P he and sami
'He and Sami left'

In any case, these examples show, at least, that agreement under government is still possible in Tunisian Arabic, as well as agreement through coindexation with Spec IP, though the former is disfavored except under special circumstances.

Interestingly, however, in Tunisian Arabic object agreement works the same as in Standard Arabic: full NP objects (conjoined or unconjoined) fail to trigger object agreement of any sort, as seen in (28), while pronominal objects (conjoined and unconjoined) obligatorily control full agreement, as in (29).

(28)a. šrii-t ktaab
buy.PRF-1S book
'I bought a book'

b. *šrii-t-u ktaab
buy.PRF-1S-3MS book.MS

c. šrii-t [l-ktub w kurraṣa]
buy.PRF-1S the-books(M) and notebook
'I bought the books and a notebook'

d. *šrii-t-him [l-ktub w kurraṣa]
buy.PRF-1S-3P the-books(M) and notebook

(29)a. *šrii-t-u (huwa)
buy.PRF-1S-3MS it
'I bought it'

b.* šrii-t (huwa)
buy.PRF-1S it

c. šrii-t-him [huma w kurraṣa]
buy.PRF-1S-3P them (3P) and notebook
'I bought them and a notebook'

d. *šrii-t [huma w kurraṣa]]
buy-PRF.1S them(3P) and notebook

These facts would appear to support further the analysis of subject agreement we have proposed for Tunisian Arabic. Under that account, the reason there can be full agreement (including number agreement) with postverbal, nonpronominal subjects in TA is that subject agreement need not involve agreement under government in such cases. Rather, it may involve Spec Head agreement, mediated by the empty expletive in Spec I whose presence is insured by the Extended Projection Principle. Tunisian Arabic differs from Standard Arabic only in that such chain formation is unavailable in SA, and therefore agreement between a verb and a postverbal subject in SA must be agreement under government. This leads to the prediction that number agreement should fail in TA, too, in cases where there is no expletive in Spec position with which the postverbal NP could form a chain. In such cases, agreement can only obtain under government, and it is then regulated by (17). This appears to be borne out in cases of object agreement such as (28d).

* We would like to thank Elabbas Benmamoun for his generosity in sharing work in progress with us, from which the present paper has benefited substantially. Additional thanks are due to audiences at Cornell University and WCCFL for their insightful questions.

REFERENCES

Abd El-Moneim, A.A. 1989. *The Role of INFL.* Ph.D dissertation, The University of Connecticut.

Abney, S. 1987. *The English Noun Phrase in its Sentential Aspect.* Ph.D dissertation, MIT.

Awbery, G. M. 1976. The Syntax of Welsh. Cambridge: Cambridge University Press.

_____. 1990 Dialect Syntax: A Neglected Source for Welsh. *Syntax and Semantics 23*, ed. R. Hendrick, 1-25. New York: Academic Press.

Bahloul, M. (in preparation). *The Syntax and Semantics of Aspect, Tense, and Modality.* Ph.D dissertation, Cornell University,

Benmamoun, E. 1990. "Infectional Morphology: Problems of Derivation and Projection". ms., USC.

_____. 1992a. "Structural Conditions on Agreement". Proceedings of NELS 22.

_____. 1992b (in preparation). *Functional Categories: Problems of Projection, Representation and Derivation.* PhD. Dissertation, USC.

Bowers, J. 1990. "The Syntax and Semantics of Predication". ms. Cornell University, Ithaca.

Corbett. G. G. 1984. Agreement: A Partial Specification Based on Slavonic Data. *Agreement in Natural Language* ed. M. Barlow and C. A. Ferguson, 23-53, Stanford: CSLI.

Eid, Mushira. 1991. "Verbless Sentences in Arabic and Hebrew". *Current Issues In Linguistic Theory* 80, Perspectives On Arabic Linguistics III, ed. Bernard Comrie & Mushira Eid, 31-61. Amsterdam: John Benjamins.

Fassi-Fehri, A. 1984. Agreement in Arabic, Binding and Coherence. *Agreement in Natural Language* ed. M. Barlow and C. A Ferguson, 107-158. Stanford: CSLI.

Harbert, W. & A.J. Toribio.1991. "Nominative Objects". *Cornell Working Papers in Linguistics* 9: 127-192.

Lapointe, S. 1984. Toward a Unified Theory of Agreement. *Agreement in Natural Language* ed. M. Barlow and C. A. Ferguson, 67-87, Stanford: CSLI.

McCloskey, J. 1984. Inflection and Conjunction in Modern Irish. *NLLT* 4: 245-281.

Mohammad, M.A. 1990. "The Problem of Subject-Verb Agreement in Arabic: Towards a Solution". *Current Issues In Linguistic Theory 63, Perspectives On Arabic Linguistics I*, ed. Mushira Eid, 95-125 Amsterdam: John Benjamins.

Ritter, E. 1990. "Cross-linguistic Evidence for Number Phrase." *Functional Categories*, ed. C. Lefebvre et. al.

Schlonsky, U. 1989. "The Hierarchical Representation of Subject Verb Agreement". ESCOL 6.

Valois, D.1990. "The Internal Syntax of DP and Adjective Placement in French and English". Proceedings of*NELS* 21.

Null Pronominals in the Context of NP and QP

ELABBAS BENMAMOUN
University of Southern California

1. Introduction

In this paper, I show that the quantifier *kull* patterns with N in that both head a lexical projection complement of D, the head of DP. This parallelism stems from the observation that both assign genitive Case and carry the Case assigned to the DP projection. However, while both Q and N allow an empty thematic pronominal in their Spec position, they impose different structural conditions on its identification and licensing. I shall propose that this difference between NP and QP may be explained by the theory that N, as opposed to Q, is a thematic role assigner and, correlatively, an inherent Case-assigner. I adopt and generalize Belletti's (1988) proposal that morphology does not absorb inherent Case. This allows N (head of NP) to license its pro locally while forcing the Spec of Q to raise to a Case position.

2. The Structural Parallelism Between NPs and QPs

Consider the following sentences from Standard Arabic:[1]

(1) zaa?a kull-u l-?awlaad-i
came all-Nom the-children-Gen
'All the children came'

(2) kull-u l-?awlaad-i zaa?uu
all-Nom the-children-Gen came
'All the children came'

(3) ra?aytu kull-a l-?awlaad-i
I saw all-Acc the-children-Gen
'I saw all the children'

---

*I wish to thank Joseph Aoun, Audrey Li, Barry Schein and Maria-Luisa Zubizarreta for their help and suggestions.

[1]We follow Fassi Fehri (1989) and Mohammad (1987, 1990) that the VSO order is derived by verb movement to I leaving the subject in the Spec of VP.

In (1)-(3) the quantifier *kull* constitutes with the NP *?awlaad* a complex constituent. This constituent has all the characteristics of the Construct State (CS) in Arabic (Aoun 1978, Mohammad 1987 and Fassi Fehri 1982,1989) for Arabic, and Borer 1984, Ritter 1987, and Siloni 1990 for Hebrew). In CS structures in Standard Arabic, the head noun carries the Case assigned to the whole projection and assigns genitive Case to the NP following it as shown in (4), (5) and (6):

(4) zaa?a 9amm-u l-?awlaad-i
came uncle-Nom the-children-Gen
'The children's uncle came'

(5) ?amm-u l-?awlaad-i zaa?a
uncle-Nom the-children-Gen came
'The children' uncle came'

(6) ra?aytu 9amm-a l-?awlaad-i
I saw uncle-Acc the-children-Gen
'I saw the children's uncle'

In (4) the noun *9amm* carries nominative Case and assigns genitive to the NP *l-?awlaad*. I assume with Fassi Fehri (1989), and Mohammad (1987) that the CS in Arabic is basically a DP having the structure given in (7).[2] The head noun is generated as head of the complement of D, namely NP. It raises to D and assigns genitive Case under government to the DP in Spec of NP (but see below). Moreover, once in D the head noun gets the Case assigned to the whole DP.[3,4]

(7)

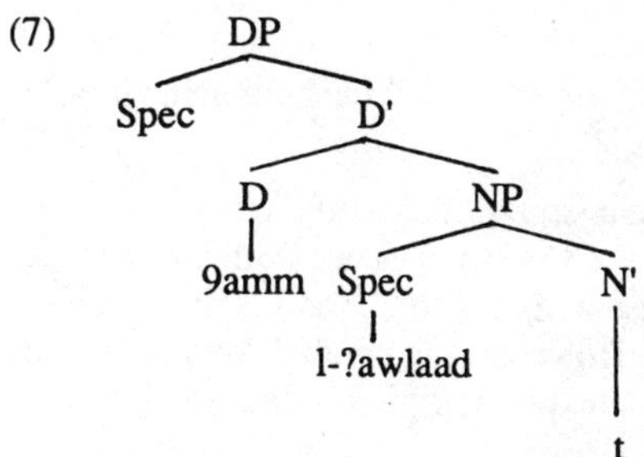

Since the exact structure of the construct state in Arabic is not the main focus of this paper, we will put any further discussion of it aside merely noting the syntactic parallelism between phrases containing regular nouns and their

[2]However, we do not assume the details of the DP structure defended in the above-mentioned works especially the location of the demonstrative and the definite article. But since the details are not relevant here, we will put the discussion of that problem aside.

[3]Fassi Fehri (1989) proposes that Case by I, V and D in Arabic is assigned uniformly to the right.

[4]The earliest consideration, as far as I know, of a derivation of the Construct State in Arabic by raising of N was considered, but not adopted, in Aoun (1978: p28).

counterparts containing the quantifier *kull*.

Going back to (1), (2) and (3), notice in particular that the quantifier in (1), (2) and (3) behaves exactly as the noun *9amm* in (4), (5) and (6). It gets the structural Case assigned to the whole projection and assigns genitive Case to the NP to its right. This suggests that the constituents in (1), (2) and (3) containing the quantifier *kull* are DPs on a par with the structures of the DP subject in (4) and (5) and object in (6). Therefore, we can safely conclude that the projection containing the quantifier *kull* is as in (8), namely a DP.[5] I will refer to the lexical projection headed by Q as QP following essentially Fassi Fehri (1982: 217) and Shlonsky (1991a,b).

(8)

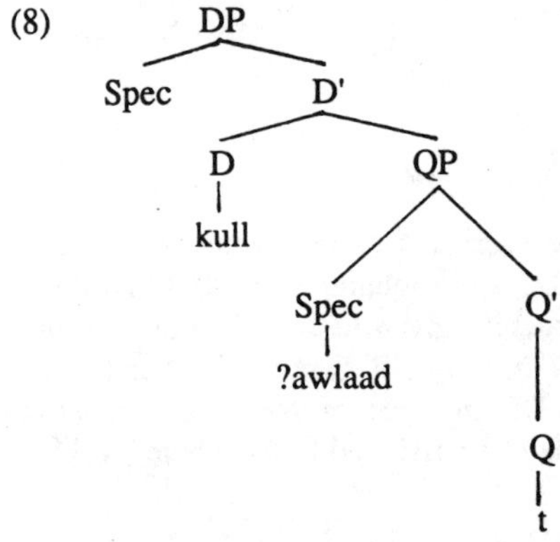

Notice that the only difference between (7) and (8) is that the complement of D is an NP in the former and a QP in the latter.

Assuming the structure in (8), we account straightforwardly for the structural parallelism between Q and the N head of the Construct State. Both are located in D at SS, a position where they get the Case assigned to DP and from which they assign genitive Case to their DS specifier. However, the parallelism shown above between NP and QP breaks down in the context of null pronominals.[6]

3. Pro-drop in the context of QPs and NPs

Both the Spec of N and the Spec of Q can be empty in which case an agreement

---

[5]This supports Sportiche's (1988) argument that Q is not a VP adverb but part of the projection containing the NP. However, while Sportiche considers Q, in French at least, as NP adjunct or NP determiner, in Arabic it is clear that Q is a head since it displays all properties of heads. It assigns Case and get the Case assigned to the DP projection. We will also show below that it displays another property of heads, namely identification of empty pronominals. In Schlonsky (1990 and 1991a,b) it is proposed that the NP is generated as complement of Q and extracted via the Spec position.

[6]Another difference between NP and QP is that the latter exhibits the process of Q-float. For a detailed analysis of Q-float in Hebrew see (Shlonsky 1991a,b).

clitic on Q and N is obligatory as shown by the following sentences from Moroccan Arabic.[7]

(9) zaa 9amm-hum
came uncle-their
'Their uncle came'

(10) 9amm-hum zaa
uncle-their came
'Their uncle came'

(11) 9amm-hum fi-d-daar
uncle-their in-the-house
'Their uncle is in the house'

(12) zaaw kull-hum
came all-them
'They all came'

(13) kull-hum zaaw
all-them came
'They all came'

(14) kull-hum fii d-daar
all-them in the-house
'They are all in the house'

We will assume that the clitic is generated on N and Q and that the Spec of QP/NP is an empty position. Thus, all the specifiers of QP and NP in (9)-(10) have the DS DP representation in (15):

---

[7]The same facts obtain with the possessive preposition *dyaal*:

(i) hada le-ktaab dyaal le-wlaad kull-hum
this the-book of the-children all-them
'This is the book of all the children'

(ii) * hada le-ktaab dyaal kull-hum
this the-book of all-them

(iii) hada le-ktaab dyaal-hum kull-hum
this the-book of-them all-them
'This is the book of all the children'

(15)

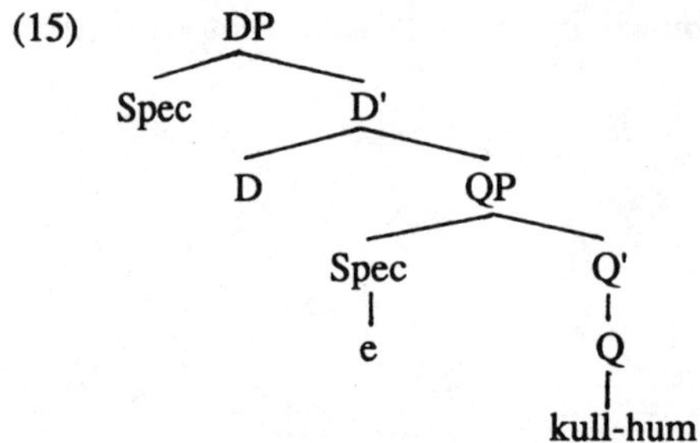

Given the inventory of empty elements there are four candidates for the Spec QP position. PRO is ruled out since Spec QP is governed by Q (which moves into D) and presumably PRO cannot occur in governed context. Moreover, movement to Spec DP may not save PRO since that position is also governed externally.[8] It cannot be a variable either since there is no overt operator that may bind it. Moreover, the following sentence shows that positing an empty operator is not possible since the Spec of CP is already filled by a *wh*-operator:

(16) skun tlaqa-hum kull-hum
who met-them all-them
'Who met them all'

The remaining possibilities are pro and NP trace. These two options are not incompatible since a moved pro can leave an NP trace. Moreover, if Spec QP is occupied by a trace, it entails that its local antecedent is in DP (for minimality reasons). Thus the viable candidate for the empty Spec QP is pro. Accordingly, the D-Structure representation of the above quantified DPs is as in (17):

(17)

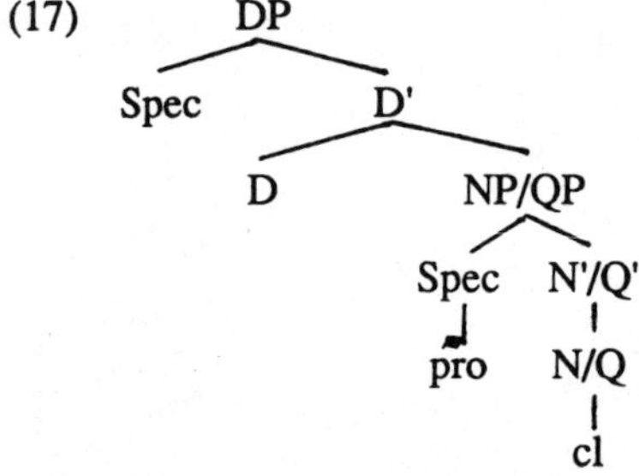

Positing a pro in Spec NP/QP raises the issue of licensing and identification. Rizzi (1986) argues that (thematic) pro needs both licensing and recoverability

---

[8]Moreover, non-controlled PRO is usually non- specific:

(i) To go there is fun

However, in all the sentences above the reference is to a specific NP.

(identification).[9] As far as recoverability is concerned no problem arises. In the configuration in (15) pro is identified by the clitic on N/Q under Spec-head agreement. However, things are not as straightforward with licensing. Rizzi (op.cit.) proposes that licensing is done under Case assignment. If this is correct, then it follows that pro in (9)-(14) is Case-marked. Moreover, that, in turn, entails that N and Q are in D at SS which means that Case realization for Spec N and Case assignment and realization for Spec Q apply under government.

Therefore, as far as (9)-(12) are concerned it seems that Q patterns with N in being able to license and identify its null pronominal specifier. However, this conclusion is not correct since while both allow for the null pronominal, when the DP containing QP occurs in the context of a verb, noun or preposition, we get some surprising effects. In addition to the agreement clitic on Q the head governing the DP also carries an agreement clitic identical to the one carried by Q.

(18) tlaqiit-hum kuul-hum
I met-them all-them
'I met them all'

(19) hada 9amm-hum kull-hum
this uncle-them all-them
'This is the uncle'

(20) msiit m9a-hum kull-hum
I went with-them all-them
'I went with all of them'

Notice both Q and the verb, noun and preposition carry an agreement clitic in (18)-(20) respectively. This striking fact does not exist with DPs containing NPs:

(21) *tlaqiit-hum 9amm-hum
I met-them uncle-them

(22) * hada ktaab-hum 9amm-hum
this book-them uncle-them

(23) *msiit m9a-hum 9amm-hum
I went with-them uncle-them

Moreover, absence of this "doubling" phenomenon in the context of Q results in ungrammaticality:

---

[9]Licensing is separated from identification/recoverability (Rizzi 1986) both for theoretical and empirical reasons. Empirically, it accounts for the fact that expletive pro requires formal licensing whereas thematic pro requires both licensing and identification (see Mohammad (1987, 1990)) for discussion of the properties of the expletive pronominal in Standard Arabic). Theoretically, the separation of licensing and identification as conditions on null pronominals seems to be equivalent to the separation of head government and antecedent government/binding as conditions on traces (Aoun et al. 1987, Rizzi 1990 among others).

(24) * tlaqiit kull-hum
I met all-them

(25) * hada 9amm kull-hum
this uncle all-them

(26) * msiit m9a kull-hum
I went with all-them

The main questions that arise are the following:

(i) What is the nature of this doubling?

Put differently, what is the clitic on the head governing the DP in (18)-(20)? Moreover, why is this doubling absent in subject position and the sentence is still grammatical? This is especially the case with (14) which, unlike (12) and (13), does not contain a verb inflected for agreement with the QP subject.

(ii) Why is this doubling absent in the context of DPs containing NP?

Starting with the first question, the data in (18)-(20) seem to be just another instance of an independent phenomenon in Arabic, namely that a pronominal governed by a non-nominative Case assigner is always lexicalized. For example, in Standard Arabic the complementizer *?anna* 'that' assigns accusative Case to Spec IP:

(27) qaala Omar ?anna T-Taalib-a xaraja
said Omar that the-student-Acc left
'Omar said that the students left'

Obviously, when the subject is not governed by *?anna* it surfaces with nominative Case:

(28) xaraja T-Taalib-u
left the-student-Nom
'The student left'

What is relevant for the present concern is that the pronominal subject, which in other contexts would be null, is here lexicalized when governed and assigned Case by *?anna*. The following sentence shows the contrast between subject pro marked with nominative Case as in (28) and the same pro in accusative context. The latter is lexicalized.

(29) qaala Omar ?ann-hu xaraja
said Omar that-him left
'Omar that he left

To account for presence of the clitic we will make the natural assumption that Arabic has the filter in (30) that in effect requires the lexicalization of a non-Nominative Case-marked pro (Mohammad 1987, Aoun 1982 and Travis 1984:

p245):[10]

(30) Lexicalization Condition
* pro if non-Nominative
[+Case]

Turning back to (18)-(20) it is natural to conclude that the clitic on the verb, noun and preposition is the pro that has been lexicalized under government by a non-nominative Case assigner as required by the Lexicalization Condition. As to why there is no doubling in (12)-(14) this follows from the fact that pro is in a nominative context. Notice that the conclusion that the clitic on the head governing DP is a lexicalized pro follows from the assumption that the head governing DP, governs and Case-marks the head and the specifier of DP. The cliticization facts strengthen the assumption that Spec DP can be externally head governed.

If this analysis is on the right track, (24)-(26) are all ruled out by the filter in (30). For example, in (24) pro in Spec QP is governed and Case-marked by the verb.

However, notice that for the pro-lexicalization analysis to work, pro has to be in Spec DP at SS. The obvious question is what forces pro to move to Spec DP rather than stay in Spec QP as is the case with lexical QP specifiers in (1)-(3)? Unlike lexical specifiers which have the option of not moving out of Spec QP, pro must move as required by our analysis.

So the question is why must pro move out of Spec QP? Since this obligatory movement is specific to pro, it is natural to suspect that it may have to do either with identification or licensing in the sense of Rizzi (1986).

Suppose that it is identification, then movement of pro could be required by a Spec-head agreement requirement on identification. That requirement would have to be at SS given the assumption that pro is in Spec Q at DS. Movement to Spec DP puts pro in a Spec- head agreement relation with Q in D and it also puts it within the government domain of all heads that govern the DP. Therefore, under

---

[10]We formulated the filter as a condition on pro rather than on empty categories in non-Nominative contexts to exclude wh-traces from lexicalization:

(i) snu kliti e
what (you)ate
`What did you eat'

There are different reasons that may be invoked to explain why variables are not subject to (30). Notice that the the variable is part of a chain that contains a lexical element (Wh-phrase). We might capitalize on this and assume that association with a lexical element exempts the variable from lexicalization. Another way to implement the same basic idea is to allow the variable to transfer Case to the lexical Wh- phrase. This would entail a slight modification of the definition of variable from being Case-marked to being in a Case position. One suggestive piece of evidence that the latter may be correct comes from formal English where an accusative marked Wh-phrase may occur in Spec CP:

(i) Whom did you meet e

such an analysis the doubling effect is a consequence of the structural condition on identification which puts pro in a context where it would be subject to the lexicalization condition in (30).

At this point it is relevant to bring into the discussion the second question, namely the reason for the absence of the doubling effect in the context of NPs. If the pro Spec of Q is moved to Spec DP for identification which results in lexicalization, then given the fact that doubling is a consequence of movement to Spec DP, the reasonable conclusion is that the pro Spec of NP does not move to Spec DP at SS. That amounts to saying that N identifies pro under government as opposed to Q which identifies it under Spec-head agreement. Thus, (21-23) would be ruled out by failure of pro to be identified since it is not governed by N at SS.

However, while the stipulation that nouns identify pro under government and Q does so under Spec-head agreement derives the right empirical facts, it would be desirable if that difference could be reduced to independent properties.

Since Case is a requirement on the licensing of pro the main hypothesis to consider is that pro is moved to Spec DP to be Case-marked and consequently licensed. That would entail that Q cannot assign Case to pro in Spec QP while N can. However, it is clear from (1)-(3) that Q can Case-mark its lexical specifier when the latter remains in Spec QP at SS.

Suppose that Q cannot assign Case to pro and thus the latter is forced to a Case position, then the question is why cannot Q assign Case?

This question can be answered if we adopt the theory of Aoun (1981) and assume that clitics absorb Case.[11] If this assumption is correct it follows that when Q carries the clitic, it cannot Case-mark pro. Consequently, if pro stays in situ the structure would be filtered out since pro would not be licensed by a Case-assigner. Therefore, the only way out is for pro to move to a Case-marked position.

With respect to NPs the situation is more complex. The logic of our analysis leads us to the conclusion that N Case-marks pro. However, this needs to be qualified since N carries the agreement clitic which in principle should absorb Case. Suppose following (Chomsky (1985) that N assigns inherent Case which may be related to its being a thematic role assignment. Now suppose that the clitic absorbs only structural Case leaving inherent Case intact, following Belletti (1988) where it is claimed that passive morphology does not deprive the verb of its "ability to assign inherent partitive Case". It is necessary if in the following sentence (reproduced from Belletti (op.cit.)) nominative Case assigned to the expletive is not transferred to the postverbal subject:

(31) Il a été tué un homme.
there has been killed a man

---

[11]On the issue of absorption see also Borer (1984), Chomsky (1981), Jaeggli (1982) and references cited there.

Apparently, the inherent partitive Case assigned by the passive verb is enough to satisfy the Case filter (and/or visibility).

Therefore, if inherent Case cannot be absorbed by the morphology (passive or agreement) then it is not surprising that pro Spec of NP does not move to Spec DP at SS since it is licensed by the inherent Case it gets from N under Spec-head agreement at DS. On the other hand, Q, which is not a thematic role assigner, assigns only structural Case which does get absorbed by the morphology (passive and agreement) and is consequently unable to license its null pronominal specifier.[12,13]

Before closing this section, we will briefly discuss one alternative analysis for the pro-drop facts. One might argue that the agreement clitic on Q is a pronominal base-generated in Spec QP and subsequently cliticized on Q in D:

[12]Notice that though N does not assign structural Case it still needs to raise to D to support the Case assigned to the DP projection (as suggested by Jospeh Aoun).

[13]It was brought to my attention that this analysis does not carry over to numerals especially those that presumably have a Construct State representation:

(i) xamasat-u kutub-in
five-Nom books-Gen
`Five books'

However, it is clear that numerals are different from Q in other respects. For example, in Moroccan Arabic, the numeral may assign the so called partitive Case:

(ii) xamsa dyal-le-ktub
five of-the-books
`Five books'

And it does not allow null pronominals:

(iii) a. *xamsat-hum
five-cl
b. *xamsa dyal-hum
five of-cl

This suggests that ultimately any account for the idiosynchratic behavior of *kull* will have to factor in other properties such as the type of Case assigned.

(32) DS:

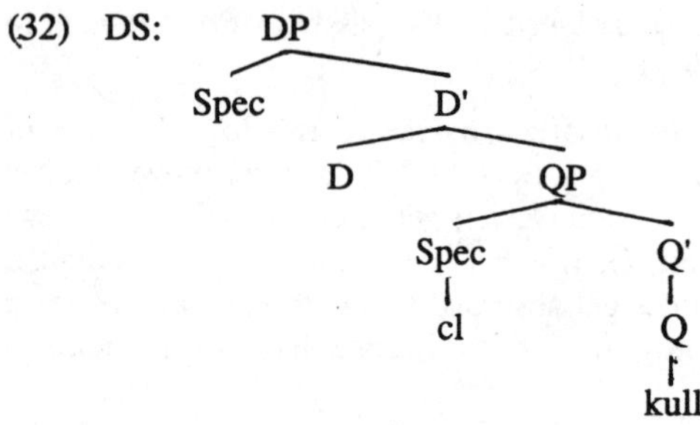

SS:

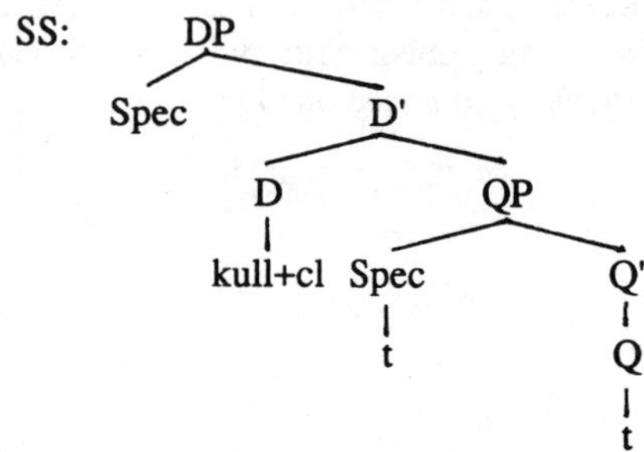

However, such an analysis is not empirically adequate. First, it does not explain the ungrammaticality of (24-26) which under this alternative analysis would be equivalent to (1-3). The only difference is that in (1-3) Spec QP is lexical. Second, it does not explain the doubling effect and why it occurs only in non-nominative contexts. In other words, it does not explain the contrast between (18-20) and (14) for example. This nominative/nonnominative asymmetry is not predicted under the alternative analysis.

However, the main advantage of the pronominal analysis is that it derives the complementary distribution between the lexical specifier of Q and the clitic.

(33) * kullu-hum ?al-?awlaad
all-them the-children

Under our analysis (33) is ruled out by the fact that the clitic absorbs Case leaving the lexical NP Caseless at SS in violation of the Case filter.[14]

[14]Another alternative is to assume that the clitic is a realization of features related to pro base- generated in Spec DP. However, instead of generating the features directly on Q one could argue that they are generated directly on the verb, noun or preposition. Due to identification, pro triggers Spec- head agreement with Q which explains the agreement morphology on Q. This is empirically inadequate since it does not carry over to (14) where there is no local head that would identify a base-generated pro in Spec DP. In other words, it does not predict the Nominative/Non-Nominative asymmetry noted above and accounted for by the filter in (30).

References

Aoun, J. 1978. Structure Interne du Syntagme Nominal en Arabe: l'?idafa. ms.

Aoun, J. 1981. *The Formal Nature of Anaphoric Relations*. Ph.D. dissertation, M.I.T.

Aoun, J. 1982. Expletive PROs in *M.I.T. Working Papers in Linguistics* A. Marantz & T. Stowell (eds.).

Aoun, J., N. Hornstein, D. Lightfoot and A. Weinberg 1987. Two Types of Locality. *Linguistic Inquiry*, 18.

Belletti, A. 1988. The Case of Unaccusatives. *Linguistic Inquiry* 19, 1-34.

Borer, H. 1984. *Parametric Syntax*. Dordrecht: Foris.

Chomsky, N. 1981. *Lectures on Government and Binding*. Dordrecht: Foris.

Chomsky, N. 1985. *Knowledge of Language: Its Nature, Origin, and Use*. Praeger.

Fassi Fehri, A. 1982. *Linguistique Arabe*. Rabat, Morocco.

Fassi Fehri, A. 1989. Generalized IP structure, Case, Inflection and VS Word order *M.I.T. Working Papers in Linguistics*, Laka et.al eds.

Jaeggli, O. 1982. *Topics in Romance Syntax*. Dordrecht: Foris.

Mohammad, M. 1987. On the Parallelism between IP and DP Proceedings of WCCFL.

Mohammad, M. 1990. *The Sentential Structure of Arabic*. Ph.D. dissertation, U.S.C.

Ritter, E. 1987. NSO Noun Phrase in Modern Hebrew. in J. McDonough and B. Plunkett (eds.), *Proceedings of NELS*, 17, pp. 521-537.

Rizzi, L. 1986. Null Objects in Italian and the Theory of pro. *Linguistic Inquiry* 17, 501-558.

Rizzi, L. 1990. *Relativized Minimality*. Cambridge: MIT Press.

Shlonsky, U. 1990. Floating Quantifiers in Hebrew paper presented at NELS 21, Montreal, Quebec.

Shlonsky, U. 1991a. Quantifier Phrases and Quantifier Float Proceedings of NELS 21.

Shlonsky, U. 1991b. Quantifiers as functional heads: A Study of Quantifier Float in Hebrew *Lingua* 84, 159-180.

Siloni, T. 1990. Hebrew Noun Phrases. ms University of Geneva.

Sportiche, D. 1988. A Theory of Floating Quantifiers. *Linguistic Inquiry* 19, 425-449.

Travis, L. 1984. *Parameters and Effects of Word Order Variation*. Ph.D. dissertation, M.I.T.

Nominally Absolutive is not Absolutely Nominative

JONATHAN DAVID BOBALJIK
Massachusetts Institute of Technology

0. Introduction*

The literature on Ergativity abounds with analyses attempting to reconcile the well known Case and Agreement patterns of Ergative/Absolutive (E/A) languages with a constrained theory of Universal Grammar. With the notable exception of Levin & Massam's analysis of Niuean (Levin & Massam 1985, Massam 1985), the majority of contemporary analyses within the "GB" framework equate the ABSOLUTIVE (ABS) Case of the E/A languages to the NOMINATIVE (NOM) of Nominative/Accusative (N/A) languages (cf. Bittner 1988, in prep, Bok-Bennema 1991, Murasugi in prep).

In the present paper, I will present an analysis taking the opposite tack. That is, in a sense to be made explicit presently, I am claiming that the phenomena associated with E/A languages can be better understood if we look at the ABS as the structural parallel of the N/A ACCUSATIVE (ACC) Case. In particular, I will show (section 2) that such an approach straightforwardly captures the Binding facts discussed in most analyses without recourse to obligatory A′-movement and reconstruction of subjects, a mechanism which is

* The present work represents a section of a larger work in progress. Thanks are due to many people for comments and criticisms of the entire work, too numerous to mention here. For specific comments on this paper, I would like to thank Maria Bittner, Tony Bures, Noam Chomsky, Jody di Piseto, Ken Hale, Alec Marantz, Kumiko Murasugi, David Pesetsky, Suzanne Urbanczyk, an audience at MIT, the WCCFL XI audience, and the very patient WCCFL XI editors. It should go without saying that all errors in this paper are my own...

to be dispreferred due to evidence from Weak Crossover and related phenomena. Further (section 3), I will introduce data from non-finite constructions in Inuit languages which support an approach along the lines of the one which I am defending here, but are at best hard to reconcile with an approach equating the ABS and NOM Cases.

1 Ergativity - The Phenomenon and Analyses

In discussing Ergativity in a comparative light, terminology always presents an initial problem. It is the notions "subject" and "object" themselves which are at stake and thus these terms are to be avoided, yet strictly semantic or thematic labels are often misleading. In this paper, I will use a slightly modified version of the terminologies introduced in Dixon (1979) and Bittner & Hale (1992): The argument corresponding to the *Agent* of a transitive Agent-Patient verb will be called the *A-argument*, and the argument corresponding to the *Patient* will be called the *P-argument*. This will be extended beyond strictly Agent-Patient verbs to all transitive verbs which mark their arguments after this pattern (1a). The sole argument of intransitive verbs will be called the *S-argument* (1b).

(1) a **Pat** touched / saw / met **Sam**.
A-argument **P-argument**

b **Dale** ran / arrived / etc....
S-argument

In these terms, then, the phenomenon of Ergativity can be characterised by systems which show Case and/or Agreement patterns as exemplified by the table in (2):

(2) Case and Agreement Systems

	N/A system	E/A system
A-argument	NOM	ERG
S-argument	NOM	ABS
P-argumet	ACC	ABS

In N/A systems, the S-argument pattens with the A-argument, in opposition to the P-argument. In E/A systems on the other hand, it is the P-argument with which the S-argument patterns, in opposition to the A-argument.

There are two characteristics which the ABS Case shares with the NOM Case cross-linguistically. Firstly, as evident from the table in (2), these are the Cases which are realised (at least abstractly) on some argument regardless of the transitivity of the clause. And secondly, both have a tendency (though this is by no means universal) to be morphologically the least marked case in a given system (see Bittner in prep, chapter 1). As noted in the introduction, this has led to many analyses in which the two are taken to be equivalent Cases (at least abstractly). Under such analyses, intransitive clauses in the two language types are (in all relevant respects) isomorphic. The differences, then, are differences in the realisations of arguments of transitive clauses between the language types. The ERGATIVE (ERG) Case is seen in different analyses to be a by-phrase (Hale 1970), a PP or KP (Bittner 1988, in prep), a genitive NP (Bok-Bennema 1991, Johns 1992), or an abstract equivalent of the ACC (Murasugi 1991).

In the spirit of Levin & Massam (1985) and Massam (1985), I am claiming that the opposite view can and should be maintained: that the ABS can be equated with the ACC and that the ERG and NOM correspond. This approach implies that the arguments of transitive clauses across the language types pattern similarly, and that the differences lie solely in Case and Agreement in intransitive clauses. In particular, looking first at transitive clauses I argue that the ERG NP stands in exactly the same relationship to the ABS NP as the NOM does to the ACC. Under this view, to whatever extent "subject" and "object" are coherent notions, then these labels apply in both language types to the A-argument and P-argument, respectively, of transitive clauses and that the Case and Agreement paradigms reflect this.

The second part of this claim is that intransitive clauses pattern differently between the two language types. If the ABS Case is the same (abstract) CASE as the ACC then this claim amounts to a claim that the sole NP of intransitive clauses in E/A languages is marked with the ACC Case and that the NOM is not realised. But what does this mean more formally?

More formally, this hypothesis has two parts. Firstly, it is a necessary part of most theories within the GB framework that they admit of a statement along the lines of (3):

(3) Case X is obligatorily assigned / checked.

where "Case X" refers to some abstract structural Case. Generally, Case X is taken without discussion to be the NOM Case, and analyses of Ergativity which claim that ABS=NOM retain this. However, in a framework which posits a distinction between two *structural* Cases (NOM & ACC) on the one hand, versus *inherent* or *semantic* Cases, on the other (e.g. Chomsky 1986, 193), there is no *a priori* reason to assume that "Case X" is necessarily NOM. Hence, I propose this is a logical place for the introduction of a parameter into UG. Essentially, (3) requires that *a* structural Case be realised in all representations, whereas what I will call the *Obligatory Case Parameter* (4) allows for the parameterisation of which structural Case is assigned.

(4) *Obligatory Case Parameter (OCP)*[1]

a In N/A languages, CASE X is NOMINATIVE (=ERG)
b In E/A languages, CASE X is ABSOLUTIVE (=ACC)

Such a parameter has a very natural working out in the "Articulated IP" framework in which both structural Cases are reflexes of the SPEC,Head relationship in Functional AGR Phrases, at some level of representation (see, e.g. Pollock 1989, Chomsky 1991 and subsequent work). For reference, I present the tree in (5) modelled on Chomsky's conception, though I have called his AGR-S and AGR-O "AGR-1" and "AGR-2" respectively to avoid confusion with the "subject" and "object" mnemonics. I assume without discussion that all arguments are generated VP-internally.

(5) The Articulated IP Tree

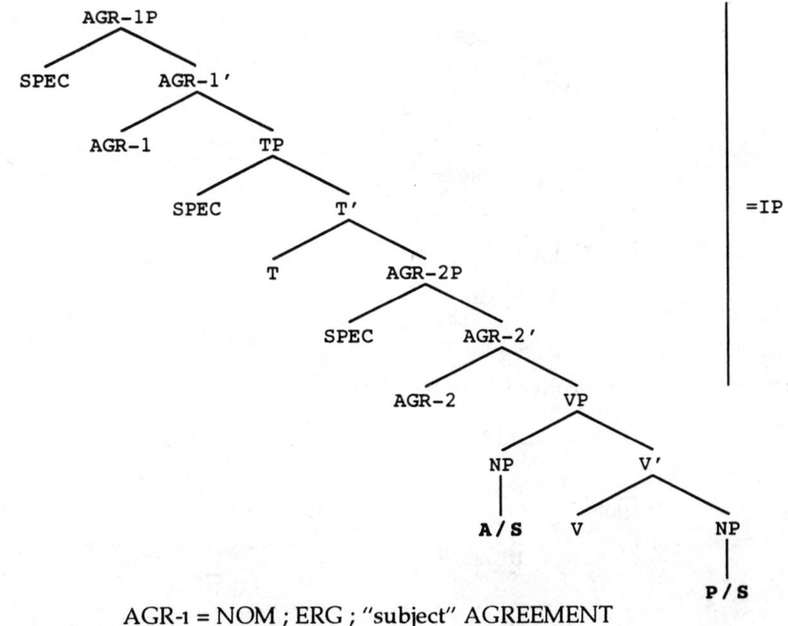

AGR-1 = NOM ; ERG ; "subject" AGREEMENT
AGR-2 = ACC ; ABS ; "object" AGREEMENT

[1]The formalisms in (3) and (4) are intentionally very similar to (one of) the "Conditions on Case Assignment" and the "Case Parameter" in Levin & Massam (1985) and Massam (1985). As noted in the text, (3) is a basic element of most theories, and there are crucial differences in the implementation and realisation of (4) between this work and the works cited. For reasons of space, a discussion of these differences is well beyond the scope of this paper.

Recast, the OCP in this framework would be a parameterisation of which AGR (or AGR-Phrase) is "active" in intransitive constructions. In N/A languages it is AGR-1 which is active, thus NOM is realised on the S-argument, whereas in E/A languages it is AGR-2 which is active, thus the ACC (though called ABS) is realised. The ABS and NOM Cases are thus similar only in that they are the obligatory Cases of the different language types. Presumably, the observed morphological tendency towards a null morpheme for these Cases is a reflection of this obligatory status.

Combining the representation in (5) with the central hypothesis of the paper, i.e. the parameter in (4), the derivation in (6) is the only possible derivation for transitive clauses in both N/A and E/A language types, whereas the representations of intransitive clauses will be either as in (7a) or (7b) depending upon the setting of the OCP. In both (6) and (7) I have omitted details irrelevant to this paper, such as the role of TP and the locus (i.e level) of movement of the V and NPs to the IP complex.

(6) Transitive Clause

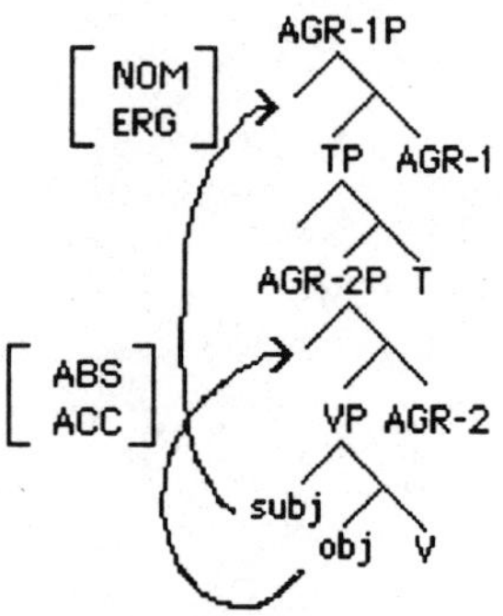

(7) Intransitive Clause

a NOM/ACC

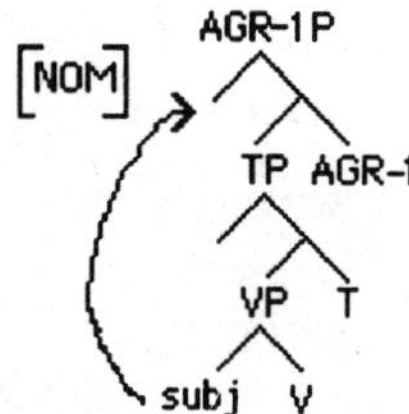

b ERG/ABS

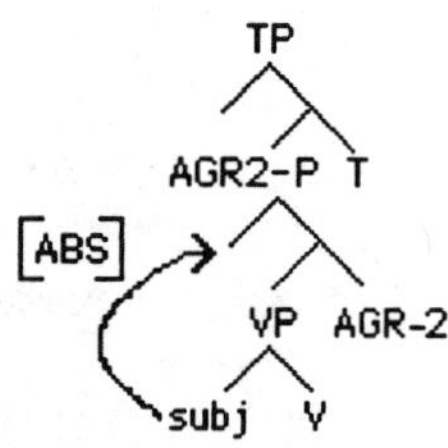

It is worth noting at this point that there is nothing in the present discussion which hinges on the adoption of the AGR-Phrase framework as the mechanism for the representation of structural Case. The crucial point is that the parameterisation is of structural Cases, and what follows can be straightforwardly translated into a framework without AGR-Phrases which has two structural Cases.

2 A-argument/P-argument Asymmetries: N/A and E/A languages

The asymmetrical distribution of anaphoric and pronominal elements is considered one of the canonical diagnostics for the relative structural positions of arguments within a language. This is exemplified in part by the distribution of *-self* anaphors in English in (8):

(8) a Mary$_i$ saw herself$_{i/*j}$(... in the mirror).
b * Herself$_{i/j}$ saw Mary$_i$ ...

Such asymmetries are generally presumed to be derived from Principles A and B of the Binding Theory (9):

(9) *The Binding Theory* (Chomsky 1981, 188)

A An anaphor must be A-bound in its governing category.
B A pronoun must be A-free in its governing category.

where α ***binds*** β iff α and β are co-indexed and α c-commands β.

Such an account provides a ready explanation for the asymmetry in (8). In (8a), the anaphor *herself* must be bound (i.e. coreferent with) a c-commanding element in its governing category. The grammaticality on the coindexing where *herself* = *Mary* indicates that the position of the NOM in English c-commands that of the ACC. Example (8b) indicates by similar logic that this relationship is asymmetrical – the ACC NP does not c-command the NOM. Similar data are familiar from a wide spectrum of N/A languages.

Anderson (1976) discusses the behaviour of a number of E/A languages with respect to the distribution of anaphors and pronouns. I will discuss briefly a few canonical examples from three unrelated E/A languages and then turn to a slightly more elaborate discussion of the Inuit languages. In all the languages under discussion, as in many other E/A languages, the patterns consistently and unambiguously show that the asymmetry between the A-argument and P-argument of N/A languages carries over straightforwardly to the E/A languages. The conclusion we will be forced to is that the ERG NP asymmetrically c-commands the ABS, just as the NOM c-commands the ACC, at whatever level the Binding Conditions A and B hold.

2.1 Basque Reciprocals

The examples in (10) - (11) show that the reciprocal *elkar* "each other" in Basque (language isolate, The Basque Country) may occur as an ABS argument of a transitive clause, where it is bound (i.e. c-commanded) by the ERG A-argument (10a), but that it may not occur as the ERG argument (10b). This is exactly the pattern exemplified by the English anaphor *herself* in (8) above.

(10) a mutil-ek elkar ikusi dute
boys-ERG ea.oth.ABS see AUX.3sA/3pE
"The boys saw each other."

b * elkar-rek mutil-ak ikusi ditu(zte)
ea.oth-ERG boys-ABS see AUX.3pA/3sE(3pE)

As with N/A anaphors, the Basque reciprocal is illicit as the ABS S-argument of an intransitive clause (11a), though it is permitted as an oblique anteceded by the S-argument (11b).

(11) a * elkar etorri dira
ea.oth.ABS come AUX.3pA
* "Each other came"

b elkar-rekin etorri dira
(pro) ea.oth-COM come AUX.3pA
"They came with each other."

(all examples from Hualde (1988:317))

2.2 Niuean Reflexive Particle

The reflexive particle in Niuean (Polynesian: Niue, New Zealand), *nī*, for the relevant purposes shows the same distribution pattern as the Basque reciprocals just discussed. The ABS pronoun in a transitive clause may host the reflexive particle, in which case the antecedent is the local ERG NP (12), but the ERG NP may not itself be marked reflexive (13).

(12) a Kitia he tama fifine a ia nī he fakaata.
see ERG child female ABS her REFL in mirror
"The girl sees herself in the mirror."

b Ko e tele nī kia e koe a koe nī ?
PRES kick EMPH Q ERG you ABS you REFL
"Are you kicking yourself ?"

(13) * Ko e tele kia e koe nī a koe?
PRES kick Q ERG you REFL ABS you
"Are you kicking yourself ?"

Further, as in Basque, an oblique NP in a transitive clause may be reflexive and bound by the local ABS S-argument (14a), though such an ABS NP in an intransitive clause may not be reflexive (14b).

(14) a Matakutaku a ia i a ia nī.
frightened ABS he AGT PERS he REFL
"He's frightened of himself."

b *Matakutaku a ia n̄ī i a ia.
frightened ABS he REFL AGT PERS he
(Niuean examples all from Seiter 1979:78-79)

2.3 Abkhaz Reflexive Agreement

Abkhaz (NE Caucasian: former Georgian Soviet Socialist Republic, Turkey) does not typically show Case marking on nouns and pronouns, but has a relatively rich agreement system. Transitive verbs agree with both an A-argument and a P-argument for number and in the third person singular, gender. The agreement morphology displays an E/A pattern in that the P-argument and S-argument trigger the same set of agreement markers. Reflexives are formed with the noun *-xe* "head" preceeded by a possessive marker. The examples in (15) demonstrate this with 1s and 3sf. In both examples, the (non-overt) pronouns trigger ERG (A-argument) agreement, while in both examples, the "reflexive" X's head triggers 3sn ABS (P-argument) agreement. For contrast I have given examples with different ABS agreement markers in (16).

(15) a l-xe y-l-ba-yt'
3sf-head(n) 3snA-3sfE-see-PRES
"She sees herself."

b s-xe y-z-ba-yt'
1s-head 3snA-1sE-see-PRES
"I see myself."
(examples from Anderson 1976, 16, attributed to G Dumézil)

(16) a ala lara d-a-ba-yt'
dog(n) 3sfpron 3shumanA-3snE-see-PST
"A dog saw her."

b sara iara də-z-ba-yt'
1spron 3smpron 3shumanA-1sE-see-PST
"I saw him."

c wara sara sə-w-ba-yt'
2spron 1spron 1sA-2sE-see-PST
"You see me."
(informant)

As Section 3 will deal principally with the Inuit languages, in the next subsection, I will discuss in a little more depth the position of Inuit with respect to the phenomena just seen, and I will show that even though it lacks overt anaphoric elements in argument positions, it can still be shown to conform to the well known paradigms of the Binding Theory in the same way as all the other E/A languages mentioned above.

2.4 Inuit and the Binding Theory

Unlike Basque, Niuean, and Abkhaz, there are no overt reflexive arguments in Inuit, though there is a reflexive pronoun *iŋmi / immi* which occurs in oblique positions (cf. Bittner 1992). Simple reflexives in the language (e.g. Mary saw herself) are indicated by the use of intransitive morphology on a transitive verb (17c).

(17) a Jaani-up natsiq kapi-jaŋa.
J-ERG seal.ABS stab-[**+trans**].3s/3s
"Jaani stabbed a seal."

b Jaani pisuk-**tu**q.
J.ABS walk-[-**trans**].3s
"Jaani is walking."

c Jaani kapi-**ju**q.
J.ABS stab-[-**trans**] 3s
"Jaani stabbed himself."

Inuit does, however, have possessive markers which, in the third person, alternate between a reflexive and a non-reflexive form. Thus:

(18) a Piita-up anaana-**ni** nagligi-jaŋa.
Piita-ERG mother-**POSS.3s/refl/**ABS love-3s/3s
"Piita loves his mother." (his = Piita)

b Piita-up anaana-**ŋa** nagligi-jaŋa.
Piita-ERG mother-**POSS.3s**/ABS love-3s/3s
"Piita loves his mother." (*his = Piita)

Such elements are familiar, of course, from the Scandinavian (*sin* vs. *hans*) and Slavic (*svoj* vs. *ego*) languages, for example, Russian:

(19) a Ol'ga ljubit **svoju** mamu.
O.NOM loves **her.REFL**.ACC mother.ACC
"Olga loves her mother." (her = Olga).

b Ol'ga ljubit **eë** mamu.
O.NOM loves **her**.ACC mother.ACC
"Olga loves her mother." (*her = Olga)

In N/A languages, the distribution of these possessives in simple clauses is predictable from the Binding Theory, on the plausible assumption that the reflexive possessives are anaphors and that the non-reflexive forms are pronominals. The most straightforward prediction from the Binding Theory is that an anaphoric possessive should not be licit when (a part of) the matrix A-argument, as it would not have a c-commanding antecedent. This is, of course, well known for the N/A languages (e.g. for Russian as seen in (20a)).

Following the discussion of Basque, Niuean, and Abkhaz, we would predict that the same would hold for Inuit – that the reflexive possessive should be illicit construed with the matrix ERG argument. Example (20b) shows that this is clearly borne out:

(20) a * **Svoja** mama ljubit Ol'gu.
her.REFL.NOM mother.NOM loves O.ACC
*"Her$_i$ mother loves Olga$_i$."

b * Anaana-**mi** Piita nagligijaŋa.
mother.**3s/REFL/**ERG Piita-ABS loves
* "His$_i$ mother loves Piita$_i$."

More interestingly, a non-reflexive (i.e. pronominal) possessive construed with the A-argument should result in an ambiguity. That is, as the position of the possessor of the A-argument (SPEC,NP or SPEC,DP or whatever) neither c-commands nor is c-commanded by the position of the P-argument, the two should be free to corefer or not without violating condition B (or C) of the Binding Theory. This is well known from e.g. Russian (21a) and holds just as well for Inuit (21b):

(21) a **Eë** mama ljubit Ol'gu.
[**her**.NOM mother.NOM] loves O.ACC
"Her$_{i/j}$ mother loves Olga$_i$." (her = or ≠ Olga)

b Anaana-**ŋata** Piita nagligijaŋa.
[mother.**3s**/ERG] Piita-ABS loves
"His$_{i/j}$ mother loves Piita$_i$. (his = or ≠ Piita)

To sum up, the paradigms just presented from a number of genetically unrelated E/A languages show clearly that the Binding Theoretic asymmetries between A- and P- arguments familiar from N/A languages carry over directly to the E/A languages. With respect at least to this range of phenomena, the ABS NP stands in the same relation to the ERG as the ACC does to the NOM in the N/A languages, and not the other way round. We can thus only conclude, as others have noted (cf. esp. Anderson 1976), that the ERG NP asymmetrically c-commands the ABS NP at whatever level the Binding Conditions hold.[2]

[2]Chomsky (1992 and fall lectures 1991) has suggested that as the Binding Conditions are conditions on interpretation, they can hold only at the interpretive interface (LF). If this is so, this would immediately preclude accounts of Ergativity in which the Binding Conditions may be satisfied at one level (e.g. S-structure) and then the relationships between the arguments "undone" by subsequent (e.g. LF) movement. For this paper, I leave this as an undecided issue, though I believe it is a point in favour of the present analysis that it is consistent with a more restrictive framework which precludes parameterisation of the locus of the Binding Conditions and which allows the Binding Conditions to be sensitive to a revised notion of A/A' positions which would classify movement for Case-theoretic reasons (and possibly only for these reasons) as A-movement. A fuller discussion of this is beyond the scope of the present work.

Further, it is important to note that this asymmetrical c-command relationship cannot be a relationship derived by A′-movement. That is, if one were to make the assumption that ABS = NOM (i.e., the opposite assumption from that proposed here) and that the ABS NP receives Case in SPEC,IP, then in order to account for both the descriptive fact that the unmarked word order of e.g. Inuit or Abkhaz is ERG – ABS – V, and the structural asymmetries implicated by the Binding Theoretic evidence presented above, one would have to posit movement of the ERG A-argument across SPEC,IP to some higher position such as SPEC,CP (Bittner in prep) or an adjoined position (Bok-Bennema 1991). Such movement, when coreferent elements are involved, is the canonical configuration for Weak Crossover effects, as exemplified in (22):

(22) Weak Crossover I - Movement to SPEC,CP across SPEC,IP.

a Who$_i$ t_i loves his$_i$ mother ?
b * Who$_i$ does his$_i$ mother love t_i
(with the meaning – For which x : x's mother loves x)

(23) Weak Crossover II - Topicalisation (Adjunction to IP)

a His$_i$ teacher, John$_i$ really admires t_i.
b * John$_i$, his$_i$ teacher really admires t_i .

If unmarked transitive clauses in E/A languages were derived by A′-movement of the ERG A-argument across the ABS P-argument in SPEC,IP, then we would expect either that all instances of coreference in the language are ungrammatical, which is clearly not the case, or that they are all instances of the Weak Crossover configuration, but that Weak Crossover effects are not seen in E/A languages (as has been claimed even for some N/A languages). The data in (24)-(25) shows that Weak Crossover is indeed well attested in E/A languages. Thus the grammatical sentences and the asymmetrical c-command of the ABS by the ERG can not be derived by A′-movement of the ERG across the ABS.

(24) Basque

a Bere ama nork maite du ?
his mother-ABS who-ERG love AUX 3sA/3sE

b Nork maite du bere ama ?
who-ERG love AUX.3sA/3sE his mother-ABS

(both) "Who$_i$ loves his$_i$ mother ?"

c ?* Bere amak nor maite du ?
his mother-ERG who-ABS love AUX.3sA/3sE

d ?* Nor maite du bere amak ?
who-ABS love AUX.3sA/3sE his mother-ERG

(both) ?* "Who$_i$ does his$_i$ mother love ?"

(J. Ormazabal, pc)

(25) Nisgha (Tsimshian: Western Canada)

a næ-t ʔæn-sipˡən-s nɔxʷ-t
who-3E REL-love-DM mother-3s
"Who$_i$ loves his$_{i/j}$ mother ?"

b næ-gat ɬ ti-sipˡən-s nɔxʷ-t
who-one ND FOC-love-DM mother-3s
* "Who$_i$ does his$_i$ mother love ?"
"Who$_i$ does his$_j$ mother love?"

(Belvin 1985, Urbanczyk 1992)

Most other analyses of Ergativity acknowledge the Binding Theoretic asymmetries and propose various mechanisms for dealing with them and with the related Word Order and Weak Crossover facts. The point of the discussion here is that under my analysis the Binding relations in the E/A languages look the same as their N/A equivalents because they are the same. These facts require nothing further than what is independently motivated for more familiar N/A systems. In the next section, I discuss a perhaps surprising prediction of the analysis at hand along these lines.

3 On the Behaviour of Non-Finite Clauses

In N/A languages in general, the A- or S- argument of a Tenseless ([-T]) clause (e.g.. gerund or infinitive) cannot be marked NOM, nor can it trigger agreement with the verb. Unless it receives Case from elsewhere (Exceptional Case Marking, complementisers like *for,* etc.), then it is restricted to what is generally called PRO. It is in some abstract sense present in the construction as can be seen by coreference phenomena and the like, but it cannot surface as a lexical NP, due presumably to its lack of Case. The P-argument, on the other hand, is subject to no such restrictions conditioned by the valence of [T]. Briefly: the arguments which would in tensed clauses receive NOM Case are in tenseless clauses barred from receiving Case or triggering Agreement in the tenseless clause, while ACC arguments may receive Case and trigger agreement in both tensed and tenseless environments. This is summarised in (26), and relevant examples are given in (27) from English, and in (28) and (29) from Miskitu (Misumalpan: Nicaragua, Honduras) and Swahili (Bantu: E. Africa), respectively, N/A languages which show subject and object agreement on the verb.

(26) Case & Agreement in non-finite clauses: N/A languages

(a) NOMINATIVE argument: *Case, *Agreement [A-, S-argument]
(b) ACCUSATIVE argument Case Agreement [P-argument]

(27) a John tried {PRO / *John / *him} to leave.

b John tried {PRO / *John / *him} to congratulate himself/Mary/...

(28) a Utilya luki-sa [yang mai kaik-ri].
U(name) think-3s [I 2sACC see-1.PAST]
"Utilya thinks that I saw you."

b Utilya luki-sa [yang wa-ri]
U think-3s [I go-1PAST]
"Utilya thinks that I went."

c Utilya [mai kaik-aia] want-sa.
U [2sACC see-INF] want-3s
"Utilya wants to see you."

d Utilya [w-aia] want-sa.
U [go-INF] want-3s.
"Utilya wants to leave."
(Miskitu examples provided by Tom Green, pc)

(29) Ni-na-taka ku-ki-soma (kitabu hiki).
I-pres-want KU-7Obj-read (7book 7this)
"I want to read it/ this book"
(Vicki Carstens, pc)

Within the AGR framework adopted here, the common hypothesis is that AGR-1 is in some non-trivial sense defective in the environment of [-T]. Thus, as NOM Case and Agreement are seen as reflexes of the SPEC,Head relationship with this head, when it is defective, this relationship cannot license Case or Agreement.

Recalling the central thesis of this paper, that ABS Case is the relationship in AGR-2, I proposed the transitive and intransitive derivations in (6) and (7b), repeated here, for E/A languages.

(30) a Transitive Clause b Intransitive Clause

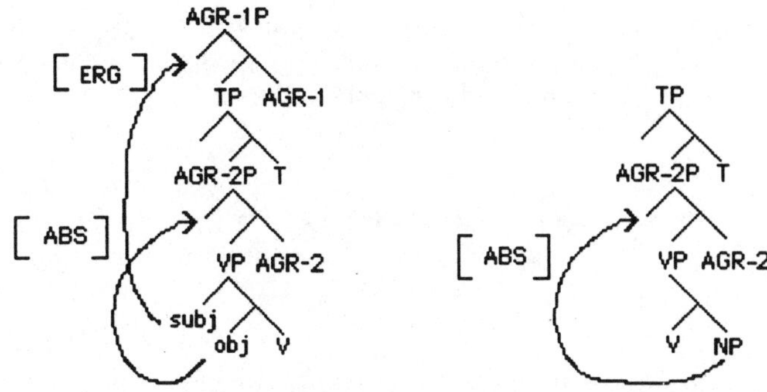

If we extend the hypothesis that AGR-1 is in some sense "defective" in the environment of [-T] to these structures, we would predict that transitive infinitives in E/A languages should behave like their N/A counterparts. That is, as the derivation in (30a) is supposed to be that for N/A languages as well as E/A languages, the A-argument, which in a tensed clause would be marked for ERG [=SPEC,Head in AGR-1] should not be allowed to receive Case or trigger Agreement in the [-T] clause, just as in N/A languages. Also parallel to N/A languages, the P-argument which is marked ABS via its association with AGR-2 should not have any special restrictions peculiar to [-T] environment. It should show Case and trigger Agreement.

The intransitive derivation for E/A languages in (30b) is different from the N/A intransitive derivation in that the S-argument receives (ABS) Case in AGR-2. If it is AGR-1 which is defective in a non-finite environment then the prediction is that in intransitive clauses the ABS S-argument should be free to realise Case and Agreement. Thus corresponding to (26) for N/A languages, my analysis would predict (31) for E/A languages. The key point to note is the difference in the (predicted) behaviour of the S-argument (the sole argument of intransitive clauses) in the two language types.

(31) Case and Agreement in Non-Finite Clauses: E/A languages

(a)	ERGATIVE argument:	*Case	*Agreement	[A-argument]
(b)	ABSOLUTIVE argument:	Case	Agreement	[P-,S-argument]

Unfortunately, most of the E/A languages under consideration do not have constructions which readily correspond to "infinitives". Many languages use subjunctive clauses and/or nominalised forms to express what in the Indo-European languages and others is expressed by means of a non-finite form of the verb. The Inuit languages do, however, have a non-finite form, indicated by the "mood"-morpheme *-llu-*, which is used in more or less the constructions we would expect non-finite forms, that is, as a complement to verbs like "promise" (with subject control) and with gerundive (e.g. "while") clauses. Clearly, we have here a testing ground for the prediction noted above.

The examples in (32 a and b) show that, in Inuit, the transitive part of this prediction is clearly borne out.

(32) a [Miiqqat ikiu-ssa-llu-**git**] niriursui-vutit.
[children.ABS help-FUT-LLU-**3pABS**] promise-IND.2sABS
'You promised to help the children.'
(Bittner, in prep, 52)

b aŋuti-rujug-šuaq aavir-šuaq uniar-lu-**gu** tiki-lir-suq
man-very.big-ABS [whale-big-ABS trail-LLU.3s] come-begin-PRT
'... the big man who began to come [trailing the big whale] ... '

(simplified, from Bergsland 1955)

In these examples, the embedded clauses are non-finite, as indicated by the morpheme *-llu-*, underlined in the glosses, and furthermore the verbs bearing this marker agree only with the ABS P-argument of their clause. In both examples, the A-argument (which must be construed as coreferent with the matrix subject) is illicit in the lower clause, i.e., it corresponds to PRO. For instance, by examining the Case and Agreement morphology, we see unambiguously that in (32b) the NP *aŋutirujugšuaq* "the big man" is in the matrix clause. It is marked ABS and so syntactically cannot be the A-argument of the embedded, transitive clause . Further the embedded verb *uniarlugu* 'trail-LLU-3s' shows agreement only with the ABS P-argument *aaviršuaq* 'whale'. Contrast (32b') which shows agreement for 3rd person A- and P-arguments:

(32) b' ... uniam-**ma-gu** 'because he was trailing it'
(e.g. 3sERG/3sABS agreement)

The argument corresponding to the ERG argument in a [+T] clause is disallowed in a [-T] clause in Inuit, as expected. Turning to the intransitives, the prediction in (31) is again borne out.

(33) a Aggi-ssa-llu-**tit** niriusui-vutit
come-FUT-LLU-**2s** promise-IND.2s
'You promised to come'
(Bittner, in prep, 51)

b agi-ssa-vlu-**tik** uqar-put
come-FUT-LLU-**3p-REFL** say-IND.3p
'they said (of themselves) that they would like to come'
lit: 'they said (of themselves) to come'
(Woodbury 1975, 84 attributed to Kleinschmidt 1851)

(34) a qaammaššuaq uqalualaar-tuaŋŋuar-lu-ni niri-lir-put
[moon.man.ABS tell.stories-continue-LLU-4s] eat-start-3p
"The moon man continuing to tell stories, they started to eat."

b niviarsiaq sikkir-luni kiina-ŋŋu-a nui-rataŋŋuar-puq
[girl.ABS giggle-LLU-4s] face-little-3s appear-at.last-3s
"The girl giggling, her little face appeared at last."
(Bergsland 1955)

In (33) - (34) the embedded non-finite intransitive verbs show agreement for an ABS (e.g. S-) argument in contrast to both ERG (A-arguments) and the S-arguments in N/A languages (cf. (27a) and (28d) above). Further, in (34) the embedded S-arguments are lexically present and are marked for ABS as well as triggering agreement. In both (34a&b) the Case and Agreement morphology shows unambiguously that the embedded S-arguments are for all syntactic tests, inside the lower clause. For example, in (34a), the embedded agreement is singular, agreeing with the NP *qaammaššuaq* "moon man", whereas the matrix agreement is plural agreeing with the non-overt A-argument "they" of the verb *nirilirput* "they started to eat".

4. Conclusion

In conclusion, it is the aim of this paper to support the more general claim that the grammars of individual languages are straightforwardly derivable from a highly constrained Universal Grammar via a very few parameters. That is, the range of syntactic variation among languages is presumed to be due to the interaction of these parameters with each other and with a restricted set of universal principles.

The analysis I have proposed in this paper is that the sole systematic difference between N/A languages and E/A languages is the setting of a low-level parameter, what I have introduced as the Obligatory Case Parameter, which dictates which of the two structural Cases must be realised in clauses which have only one non-oblique argument. Under such an analysis, the well-known behaviour of arguments in E/A languages with respect to the Binding Theory does not require the introduction of new mechanisms into Universal Grammar. The patterns of the distribution of anaphoric and pronominal elements in E/A languages looks exactly like the pattern in the N/A languages because it is, under this analysis, the same pattern. Further, and more strikingly, the predictions for E/A languages regarding the distribution of Case and Agreement in non-finite clauses are entirely straightforward only on the type of analysis argued for here. In particular, any analysis which equates the ABS Case of the E/A languages with the NOM of N/A languages will predict, if anything, entirely the opposite paradigms as those clearly exemplified by the data from the Inuit languages.

References

Anderson, Stephen. 1976. On The Notion Of Subject in Ergative Languages. *Subject and Topic*, ed C. Li, 1-23. New York: Academic Press.

Belvin, R. 1985. Nisgha Syntax And The Ergativity Hypothesis: An Analysis Using the Government and Binding Model. *Proceedings of the 20th International Conference On Salish And Neighbouring Languages, University of British Columbia, August 1985.*

Bergsland, Knut. 1955. *A Grammatical Outline of the Eskimo Language of West Greenland.* Oslo: Skrivemaskinstua.
Bittner, Maria. 1988. *Canonical and Non-Canonical Argument Positions.* Doctoral dissertation, U Texas Austin.
Bittner, Maria. in prep. *On Case And Scope.* ms. Rutgers
Bittner, Maria & Ken Hale. 1992. Ergativity ms. Rutgers & MIT.
Bok-Bennema, Reineke. 1991. *Case and Agreement in Inuit.* Doctoral dissertation, Tilburg University.
Chomsky, Noam. 1981. *Lectures on Government and Binding.* Dordrecht: Foris.
Chomsky, Noam. 1986. *Knowledge of Language.* New York: Praeger.
Chomsky, Noam. 1991. Some Notes on Economy of Derivation and Representation. *Principles and Parameters in Comparative Grammar,* ed. R. Friedin, 417-454. Cambridge: MIT Press.
Chomsky, Noam. 1992. A Minimalist Program for Linguistic Theory. ms. MIT.
Dixon, R. M. W. 1979. Ergativity. *Language* 55:59-138.
Hale, K. L. 1970. The Passive and Ergative in Language Change. *Pacific Linguistics Studies in Honour of Arthur Capell,* ed. S. A. Wurm and D. C. Laycock. (Pacific Linguistics) Sydney: Australia National University.
Hualde, Jose I. 1988. Case Assignment in Basque. *Anuario del seminaro de filologia Vasca "Julio De Urquijo",* XXII:313-330.
Johns, Alana. 1992. Deriving Ergativity. *Linguistic Inquiry* 23.1:57-87
Kleinschmidt, Samuel. 1851. *Grammatik der grönländischen sprache.* [cited in Woodbury (1975)]
Levin, Juliette & Diane Massam. 1985. Surface Ergativity: Case/Theta Relations Reexamined. *Proceedings of North Eastern Linguistics Society XV,* ed. S. Berman, 286-301. Amherst: GLSA.
Massam, Diane. 1985. *Case Theory and The Projection Principle.* Doctoral Dissertation, MIT. [Distributed by MIT Working Papers in Linguistics].
Murasugi, Kumiko. 1991. The Role of Transitivity in Ergative and Accusative Languages: The Cases of Inuktitut and Japanese. paper presented at the Association of Canadian Universities for Northern Studies' Third National Student Conference on Northern Studies, Ottawa, October 1991. [to appear in proceedings in *The Musk Ox*]
Murasugi, Kumiko. in prep. *NP-Movement and the Ergative Parameter.* Doctoral dissertation, MIT.
Pollock, Jean-Yves. 1989. Verb Movement, Universal Grammar, and the Structure of IP. *Linguistic Inquiry* 20:365-424.
Seiter, William. 1979. *Studies in Niuean Syntax.* Doctoral dissertaion, UC San Diego.
Urbanczyk, Suzanne. 1992. Ergativity and AGR-O in Nisgha. ms. U Mass, Amherst.
Woodbury, Anthony C. 1975. *Ergativity of Grammatical Processes: A Study of Greenlandic Eskimo.* Master's Thesis, U Chicago.

Jonathan David Bobaljik
Department of Linguistics and Philosophy
20D-219, MIT, Cambridge, MA, 02139
BOBALJIK@MIT.EDU

Marshallese Suffixal Reduplication

DANI BYRD
University of California, Los Angeles

This paper will discuss suffixal reduplication in Marshallese, a Micronesian language of the Pacific. An understanding of Marshallese syllable structure will be important in understanding its reduplication process and the interaction of reduplication and epenthesis. Marshallese reduplication appears to have two distinct patterns. The reduplicative suffix added to words ending in CVC is of the form CVC while the reduplicative suffix added to words ending in CVVC is of the form VVC, apparently lacking an onset consonant. I will propose an analysis of Marshallese reduplication within the framework described by Steriade (1988) which explains both types of Marshallese reduplication as the result of a single process. I will show that Marshallese demonstrates a very unusual type of reduplication within the typology of reduplication outlined by McCarthy and Prince (1986) filling an otherwise unexplained but nonprincipled gap in this typology. The proposed analysis of Marshallese reduplication will be compared to a new analysis of Tzeltal verbal reduplication. Finally, I will describe Marshallese epenthesis which produces the surface forms of the reduplicated words.

1. Marshallese Syllable Structure

Marshallese is a Micronesian language spoken on the Marshall Islands of the Pacific. There are two main dialects of Marshallese, Ratak (eastern) and Ralik (western), which occasionally differ in pronunciation. The data in this paper will be from a native speaker of the Ratak dialect.[1]

The consonant inventory of Marshallese is shown in (1):

[1]All data included in this paper are taken from transcriptions made by Ian Maddieson and the author while working with a native Marshallese speaker, Dinah Young. Many thanks are due to Professor Maddieson and Mrs. Young for their time and effort. Additionally, I thank Donca Steriade for much advice, discussion, and insight regarding the analysis of the Marshallese data. Of course all errors are my own responsibility.

(1)

	light plain or palatalized	heavy velarized	rounded
oral stops			
velar	--	k	q
labial	p	b	--
dental	j	t	--
nasal stops			
velar	--	ŋ	ŋʷ
labial	m	m̦	mʷ
dental	n	n̦	nʷ
laterals	l	l̦	lʷ
trills	d	r	rʷ
(This orthography is taken largely from Bender, 1969)			

The Marshallese language has 12 surface vowel qualities: four front and four central unrounded vowels and four back round vowels. The transcription used in this paper is shown in (2) below.

(2)

	front	central	back
high	i	ɯ	u
higher mid	e	ɤ	o̝
lower mid	ɛ	ə	o̞
low	æ	a	ɒ

The front vowel occur in the neighborhood of light consonants; the central in the neighborhood of heavy consonants, and the back in the neighborhood of round consonants. The exact distribution of these surface qualities and their underlying phonological analysis is not clear, and the reader is encouraged to see Bender (1969) and Choi (in preparation).

Marshallese contrastive vowel and consonant length. Minimal pairs of these alternations are given in (3) and (4).[2]

(3)	dam	forehead	daam	your blood
	bat	hill	baat	smoky
	mat	cooked	maat	finished
	mæŋ	fall	mææŋ	pandamus leaf
	tok	to land, settle	took	ashamed
	je̝n	lets	je̝e̝n	chain
	jæn	from	jææn	cents

[2]Lists (3) and (4) are partially due to Bender (1969).

(4)	eta	my name	etta	to be in the early months of pregnancy
	ebat	he is slow	ebbat	he is late
	elan	squall	ellan	to spread something apart
	ele	possessed by a demon	elle	to bear fruit or flower; serves you right
	ine	seed	inne	yesterday
	ebo	I caught you	ebbo	it's ripe

Marshallese syllables are of the following types: CV, CVV, CVC, and CVVC. Stress falls equally on long and closed syllables in a word and no secondary stresses are used in the language.[3] Light syllables are unstressed and syllables created by epenthetic vowels (to be discussed later) have the lowest level of prominence. No tautosyllabic consonant clusters occur in the language.

Under a moraic theory of syllable weight (Hyman, 1985 and McCarthy and Prince, 1986), the structure of stem CV_iV_i and CVC syllables will be bimoraic, as shown in (5). This is supported by the stress facts in the language. All closed and long syllables of a word receive stress while monomoraic syllables, CV and V, do not.

(5)

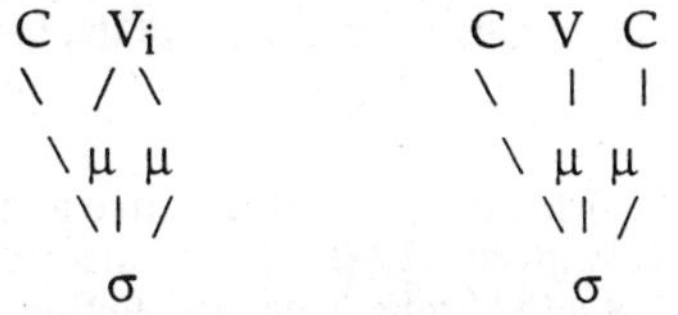

```
C  Vi          C  V  C
\  / \         \  |  |
 \ μ  μ         \ μ  μ
  \ | /          \ | /
    σ              σ
```

Sequences of unlike vowels do occur in the language but appear to be bisyllabic[4], ie, a sequence of the a CV and V syllable.

We are then left with the question of how CV_iV_iC syllables should be represented. These syllables occur only word finally and in structures where the coda consonant is geminate, ie. the structure $C_1VVC_2C_2V$...[5], although these sequences are not common. This pattern can be seen in the words given in (7).

(7)	jɛraaṃṃan	fortunate
	weeppæn	improved

The moraic representation of the geminate consonants after long vowels is an open question, as geminate consonants are generally considered to be moraic. Here, however, the preceding vowel is long thereby making the syllable already bimoraic. The question of the appropriate syllable structure for the words like those in (7) will not be further addressed here as these are the only examples of such words I have

---

[3]Ian Maddieson, personal communication.

[4]Ian Maddieson, personal communication

[5]Such words may derive historically from compounding and place assimilation.

collected, and they are not relevant to the reduplication data or analysis described below.

I suggest that the word final extra heavy syllables be represented as bimoraic, having the coda consonant share the final mora of the syllable template. This structure is shown in (8).

(8)
```
 C  V  C
  \ / \ /
  \ μ  μ
   \ | /
     σ
```

Cross-linguistic evidence suggests that a syllable may be maximally bimoraic (see Hyman, 1985), in the unmarked case. As will be shown, a trimoraic structure for this syllable would prevent the possibility of a unified analysis of reduplication patterns in the language. We will see that a proposal suggesting that the final consonant is extrametrical is also untenable.

While all other syllables in the language have a one-to-one or many-to-one to one (in the case of long vowels assuming a single root node) mapping of moras to segments, the CVVC syllable type has a one-to-many mapping. Consonant clusters in coda would also produce a one-to-many mapping; however, Marshallese does not allow tautosyllabic consonant clusters. I will suggest that this one-to-many mapping is a non-optimal syllable type whose limited distribution in Marshallese is relevant to our understanding of reduplication in the language.[6]

2.0 Reduplication

Reduplication in Marshallese is used to form the causative and the intensive. The process is fairly but not entirely productive. There are two patterns of reduplication. In the first, a suffix is added which has the melody and syllable structure of the final stem syllable. Examples of this type are shown in (9). (A [+] indicates the addition of a grammatical marker prefixally.)

(9) Pattern 1

jæj	slippery	jæj-jæj	bragging, very slippery
ŋar	bite	ŋar-ŋar	bite hard
laq	most recent	laq-laq	far away, long ago
lɤŋo̞ŋ	fear	lɤŋo̞ŋ-ŋo̞ŋ	very afraid
mok	tired	e+mok-mok	very tired
ebbok	to make full	ebbok-bok	puffy
bok	sand	e+bok-bok	sandy
bo̞k	carry	eb+bo̞k-bo̞k	she is a gossip
ro̞ŋ	ear	ja+ro̞ŋ-ro̞ŋ	deaf
ennon	aroused	ennon-non	(sexually) aroused
enno	delicious	enno-no	very delicious

[6] I thank Donca Steriade for her discussion of such structures with the author.

tǫ	rope	ka+tǫ-tǫ	hang up
yu	coconut soft meat	kay+yu-yu	collect coconut soft meat
awa	hour	ka+awa-wa	kill time

(these data do not represent surface phonetic realizations as the discussion of epenthesis later will indicate more explicitly.)

The second phonological pattern of suffixal reduplication is found in words having long vowels and a coda consonant in their final syllables. This pattern appears to differ from Pattern 1 in that the reduplicated syllable seems to lack an onset. Examples of this pattern are given in (10).

(10) Pattern 2

baat	smoke	e+baat-aat	smokey
jook	ashamed	e+jook-ook	shy, bashful
naan	talk, word	kɤ+kɤn+naan-aan	talkative
kǫǫn	piglet	ka+kǫǫn-ǫǫn	to own a piglet
kɤjeek	fire	ka+kɤjeek-eek	firey, blazing
tææŋ	popular	tææŋ-ææŋ	(very) popular
jitɯɯl	steel	jitɯɯl-ɯɯl	very magnetic
mææṇ	burn, warm	e+mææṇ-ææṇ	burning
mææṛ	lie, fib	e+mææṛ-ææṛ	he is a fibber

Long vowels do not surface in word final position due to a process of word final vowel shortening. The reduplicated form of a CVV final stem surfaces with a short vowel in word-final position. For example, the reduplicated form of */baataa/* 'father' is realized as [baata] and will surface in its reduplicated form as *baataa-ta* 'priestly'.

3. Reduplication Analysis

Adopting the above syllable structure and Steriade's (1988) theory of reduplication, a unified account of Marshallese reduplication becomes possible. Recall that Steriade proposes that "templates are not strings of concrete, fillable slots, but rather abstract conditions on the prosodic weight and syllabic organisation of strings" (Steriade, 1988, p. 146). If the weight parameter of the reduplicative suffix is specified as a bimoraic syllable both patterns of reduplication can be explained as the result of a single process. The analysis of the CVC pattern of reduplication, Pattern 1, is straightforward. The entire word with its accompanying syllable structure is copied, suffixed, and trimmed to a bimoraic syllable. The derivation is shown in (11).

(11)

input:	ebbok	to make full
copy:	ebbok-ebbok	
prosodic weight:	ebbok-bok	
output:	ebbokbok	puffy

Furthermore, the reduplication of words ending in CVVC syllables which seems to affix an onsetless suffix can now be given a straightforward explanation. This structure is represented in (12).

```
(12)  C V C     +   C V C
       \ /\|         \ /\|
        \μ μ          \μ μ
         \|/           \|/
          σ             σ
```

Recall that we suggested that the one-to-many mode of association of moras to segments, ie. the extra heavy syllable, is less preferable than a one-to-one or many-to-one mapping. Such syllables are in fact only allowed in Marshallese finally or as parts of geminate structures internally. In the case of a reduplicated stem with a final CVVC syllable, the sequence must resyllabified after affixation in such a way as to make a regular heavy syllable out of the now word internal extra heavy stem syllable. The final stem consonant reassociates as an onset to the suffixal reduplicated syllable. Here, it becomes relevant that Marshallese does not permit complex onsets (or any tautosyllabic consonant clusters). This forces the original suffixal onset to delete to yield a simplex onset. The original coda consonant is now the onset of the reduplicated syllable. The derivation is shown in (13).

```
(13a)   j i t ɯ ɯ l + j i t ɯ ɯ l      ------>      j i t ɯ ɯ l ɯ ɯ l

              C  V  C - C  V  C    (d. below)
              \  /  \ \   / \/
               \μ  μ   \  μ  μ
                \|/     \  |/
                 σ         σ
```

(13b)

a. input:	jitɯɯl
b. copy:	jitɯɯl-jitɯɯl
c. prosodic weight:	jitɯɯl-tɯɯl
d. get rid of extra heavy syllables:	jitɯɯ.ltɯɯl
e. no complex onsets:	jitɯɯ.lɯɯl
f. output:	jitɯɯlɯɯl

Resyllabification, creating an illicit onset, occurs to remedy the illicit word internal occurrence of an extra heavy syllable rather than deletion of the offending stem final coda consonant. It seems likely that a rule deleting the second consonant in complex onsets is a less marked rule than one deleting (word internal) coda consonants. Steriade (1988) states that complex onsets appear to simplify systematically by eliminating non-initial consonants. Marshallese corrects the illicit syllable structure created by the reduplication of CVVC forms by resyllabification. Then a common rule of onset simplification occurs.

Steriade's (1988) framework for reduplication is adopted here over a copy-and-associate framework as introduced by Marantz (1982) and developed in the work of Yip (1982), Broselow and McCarthy (1983), Levin (1983), Kiparsky (1986), and others] which considers the shape of reduplicated affixes to be independent of their base as are normal affixes (Steriade, 1988). In Steriade's reduplication framework, the template has no independent existence and arises as a result of weight and syllable markedness parameter settings which are satisfied independently of one another using a full copy of the base *and* its syllable structure. This framework is preferred here, a copy-and-associate framework, for reduplication whereby a template is affixed and the melody copy then associated or mapped to it does not have a mechanism to account for the transfer of vowel length from the stem to the reduplicated affix. (Note that the proposal of McCarthy and Prince (1987), however, does account for length transfer by adopting the insertion of the lexical specification of the base in lieu of copying and assuming that "all and only the lexically specified properties of the input are available for association.") Steriade comments that Clements (1985), Davis (1985) and Kiparsky (1986) have "noted that many instances of reduplication cannot be derived [by a copy-and-associate model] unless the first step is to link a syllabic segment to the V slot of the template." (1988, p. 86) Steriade suggests that these instances actually demonstrate "not the need to give priority in association to Vs but rather the fact that partial reduplication copies not just segments but also syllable structure." (1988, p. 87) This is the position adopted in the analysis presented below.

To continue the description of Marshallese reduplication, recall the cases of the vowel-final words and the process of final vowel shortening. The relevant derivation is given in (14).

(14)

input:	baataa
copying:	baataa-baataa
prosodic weight:	baataa-taa
final-vowel shortening:	baataa-ta
output:	baataata

The reduplicated forms of true CV-final words like /awa/ look like syllable copying resulting in /ka+awawa/ (shown in (15)) but in fact are due to a combination of the requirement of template satisfaction and the rule of word final vowel shortening. The final vowel in *kaawawa* is lengthened in order to maximally satisfy the template but then undergoes word final vowel shortening.

(15)

input:	awa
copying:	(ka+) awa-awa
prosodic weight:	kaawa-wa
template satisfaction:	kaawa-waa
final vowel shortening:	kaawa-wa
output:	kaawawa

Although there is no empirical evidence to show that this vowel lengthening occurs to fill the template, arguments by McCarthy and Prince and others suggest that a reduplicative template must be satisfied if possible in the language. As Marshallese does have long vowels, we infer that the template is satisfied but that this final long vowel doesn't surface due to the independently motivated rule of word-final vowel shortening.

Although sequences of unlike vowels are uncommon in Marshallese, there are a few examples of reduplication in such words. These forms are shown in (16).

(16) pi.o cold pi.yo.yo very cold
de.o̧ pretty de.o̧.yo̧ very pretty
ki.o̧ orange ki.yo̧.yo̧ orangey
(where [y] is a palatal glide)

An explanation for the presence of glides in the reduplicated forms is available if the final syllabic stem vowel is analyzed as having a glide in onset position. This follows the line of Bender's (1969) analysis in which he posits a light glide, [y], and a round glide,[w], in the language noting that the glides are "often heard mainly in [their] effect on the neighboring vowels" (p. xviii). Clearly, a glide must exist as an onset in the second syllable of the stem because it appears in the reduplicated affix and is an unrounded glide rather than the rounded glide which would be predicted by a rule of glide insertion between two round vowels. The choice of a iV or iyV transription was rather arbitrary in most cases because of its contextually predictability after the first vowel of the stem. No phonological contrast between VV and VGV exists. The glide in the suffix is copied from phonological material in the base; however transcription of the glide in the stem final syllable was somewhat arbitrary due to the natural acoustic transitions after a front vowel. The stem internal glide appears to be transcribed more reliably when followed by an affix in which the glide is clearly present.

4. Marshallese Fills an Unexplained Gap

Marshallese is very unusual with respect to its weight parameter for reduplication. McCarthy and Prince (1986) state that they have found no cases of bimoraic syllable suffixation (p. 41). They do cite examples of suffixal minimal word/foot reduplication in Manam, bisyllabic reduplication in Siriono, and monosyllabic reduplication in Kamaiura (with an onset) and in Tzeltal (purportedly without an onset). They comment regarding the lack of any bimoraic syllable suffixation that "[t]his gap does not appear to be a principled one; the relative rarity of suffixing reduplication, joined with the relative rarity of bimoraic reduplicative affixes, is sufficient to account for it."(McCarthy and Prince, 1986, p. 41) Under the proposed analysis, Marshallese appears to fill an otherwise unexplained gap in reduplication typology. A bimoraic syllable weight parameter for the reduplicative suffix in Marshallese then appears theoretically economical in that two apparently different patterns of reduplication are given a unified analysis, as well as being of interest as an example of a rare type of suffixal reduplication.

5. A Note on Tzeltal Reduplication

Tzeltal, a Mayan language of Mexico has a reduplication process which is similar in certain ways to that of Marshallese. McCarthy and Prince (1986) offer an example of reduplication in Tzeltal in which the reduplicated suffix has the form VC. They say, "Tzeltal appears to add only a rhyme, deriving its onset from phonological material already present in the base " (McCarthy and Prince, p. 41, 1986) Several examples are given in (17).

(17) Pattern A (Berlin, 1963)

nit	nititan	push
net'	net'et'an	press
haš	hašašan	feel with palm
čol	čololan	make rows
p'uy	p'uyuyan	grind in fingers

McCarthy and Prince (1986) claim that this reduplication pattern arises because of a transparent morphological juncture between stem and affix with respect to the Onset Rule. Because the morphological juncture is transparent, the association process whereby segments are mapped to the morphological template will reach into the stem to obtain an onset consonant for the suffixal template. The stem final consonant is disassociated from its coda position and reassociates as an onset in the suffix. The suffix initial consonant is then prevented from association because the onset position of the template has already been filled. McCarthy and Prince (1986) state that their analysis explains the restriction of VC affixes to suffixal position. They state that the Tzeltal case parallels cases of prefixal reduplication which they describe in Mokilese, Orokaiva, and Ponapean. They claim that these language likewise have a transparent morphological junctures between prefix and stem. However, it is not clear that the cases are in fact parallel. In the Tzeltal case the suffix initial consonant does meet the template requirements for an onset, is closer than the stem final consonant, and, according to their analysis, is available for association. The delinking and reassociation of the stem final consonant as the suffixal onset requires right to left association in suffixes which is a counterexample to Marantz' (1982) observed correlation between the type of affixation (i.e., prefixal or suffixal) and the direction of association of the reduplicative melody--R to L in suffixes. The prefixal cases of Mokilese, Orokaiva, and Ponapean differ from the Tzeltal case in that the prefix final consonant is the only available consonant and associates to an empty stem onset position. In comments on these cases, McCarthy and Prince (1986) state that "the ultimate shape of a reduplicated sequence is sensitive in subtle ways to the character of syllabification in a language. When syllabification across the prefix-stem boundary is permitted...an extra consonant will be taken to fill an empty onset position (p. 16)." It is unclear if any independent evidence exists, in these languages or in the reportedly opaque boundary languages of Kaingang, Sudanese and Ilokano, to support the status of transparency or opaqueness of affixal morphological boundaries as a language specific variable. I would suggest that McCarthy and Prince are correct that the ultimate prosodic shape of the reduplicative affix is sensitive to the prosodic character of the language, but that the Tzeltal case can be explained more straightforwardly without stipulations as to the special status of the morphological boundary.

When one examines Tzeltal verbal reduplication more closely, one finds that there are two patterns of reduplication for the transitive and intransitive verbs of Tzeltal. Most verbs appear to reduplicate the entire final syllable: CVC -> CVC-CVC. This pattern of reduplication sometimes prespecifies a vowel and/or consonant in the rhyme. This is the type of Tzeltal reduplication described in Steriade (1988). Examples are given in (18) below.

(18)	Pattern B	(Berlin, 1963)	
p'ik	to touch lightly	p'ikp'ik	to touch it lightly, repeatedly
c'al	to make ready for carrying	c'alc'an	to continue carrying cargo
		(final n prespecified)	

The only two desinences which have a reduplicative suffix lacking the stem onset are the classes of verbs which require an additional -VC suffix *after* the reduplicative suffix (Berlin, 1963). This is the type shown in (17). The grammatical[7] VC suffix is *-an* for the transitive verbs (shown above) and *-et* for intransitive verbs. Whenever this grammatical suffix is not present, the final syllable reduplicates retaining the same onset consonant which is seen in the stem. Under the McCarthy and Prince (1986) account, the verbs which take a -VC grammatical suffix after the reduplicative suffix (Pattern A) would have a transparent morphological boundary between stem and the reduplicated affix over which syllabification may operate, but the verbs which do not have this grammatical suffix (Pattern B) would have to have an opaque boundary between stem and reduplicative affix so that the association process would be prevented from reaching into the stem to map the stem final consonant to the onset position of the suffix. The suggestion that the transparency of this boundary may vary within a language's verbal reduplication process is unattractive, and a better explanation should be sought.

I suggest that, as in Marshallese, prosodic requirements of the language can be called upon to explain the lack of an onset in the Pattern A Tzeltal case. Under Steriade's (1988) framework adopted in this paper, reduplication proceeds normally producing an affix by copying the melodic and prosodic structure of the stem. The addition of the final -VC grammatical suffix, however, alters the prosodic structure of the word. Resyllabification makes the coda of the reduplicative suffix the onset for the grammatical suffix. Tzeltal mainly has CV and CVC syllables. VC and V syllables occur word medially in words like ha.e.tik and las.le.iʃ (Berlin, 1962). After creation of an onset for the grammatical -VC suffix, a reduplicated CVC form will have the form CVC.CV.Can. The derivation to this point appears in (19):

(19)

a. input:	nit
b. copy and grammatical suffix:	nit-nit+an
c. onset rule:	nit.ni.tan

A consideration of prosodic structure in Tzeltal is relevant here. While neither Berlin (1962) nor Kaufman (1971) offer an systematic description of stress in Tzeltal. Berlin states that two main patterns of primary stress or accent exist: sometimes stress is on the final syllable and sometimes on the penult. An examination of Berlin (1962) and Kaufman (1971) shows that stress falls on the penult in words ending in vowels.[8] These words are mostly borrowed from Spanish:

(20)	kirsánu	Christian	
	kawáyu	horse	
	báka	cow	
	kálto	sou	(*sic* Kaufman 1971, p.13)
	kostúmpre	custom	

Stress falls on the final syllable in the native forms, which generally end in a closed syllable, and in those borrowed forms that end in a closed syllable:

---

[7]I use the term grammatical here only to differentiate between this final suffix and the reduplicative suffix which both appear as VC sequences.

[8]There is some "morphophonemic" variation between final and penultimate stress in the words which Berlin describes as penultimately stressed (Berlin, 1962).

(21)	winík	man
	yaʔtík	today
	ganár	earning
	migél	Michael

Kaufman and Berlin use the orthographic <h> to denote a voiceless non-syllabic vowel with the same articulation as the adjacent tautosyllabic vowel (Kaufman, 1971, p. 8). These syllables also appear to count as heavy with respect to stress:

(22)	kahpéh	coffee
	lasmahmáh	they fight
	huhukáh	each

When primary stress is on the final syllable, secondary stress falls on the antepenultimate and on alternating syllables before that in longer words, apparently without regard to weight. If only one syllable precedes the primary stress (whether it is on the penult or final) the secondary stress falls on that syllable (Berlin, 1962). Berlin's examples include: *yàʔtík, t'ùʃahík, and h-poʃtàwanéh.* In words ending in a light syllable (generally borrowed), primary stress falls on the penult and secondary stress two syllables before it on the pre-antepenult. Berlin's examples include: *tà-pínka, hùn-wárti, and ta-tènehápa.*

The data has clear gaps but the account that seems compatible with all available examples would be that Tzeltal creates bimoraic left-headed feet from right to left. This would explain the pattern of primary stress being final in words ending in a heavy syllable, and penultimate in words ending in a light syllable. This being the case, the form resulting from step c in (19), [nit.ni.tan], will yield a final bimoraic foot of the form CVC and a preceding unfootable monomoraic syllable trapped word internally between two acceptable bimoraic feet.[9]

(23)

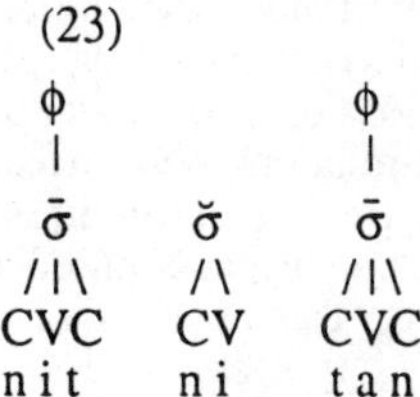

If the first two syllables here were incorporated into a single foot, the foot would be trimoraic rather than bimoraic. In order to make an acceptable bimoraic foot out of the sequence, the final moraic stem coda consonant is resyllabified.[10] As in Marshallese, this consonant is prosodically incorporated into a following onset which is then simplified. The complete derivation appears in (24):

[9]I thank Donca Steriade for her discussion of this possibility with me.

[10]Note that when a grammatical suffix of the form -CV is added to a reduplicated form, Pattern B results, and the original onset consonant is not lost. So, *pas* 'to make it' reduplicates with the grammatical suffix *-ta* to yield *paspasta* 'to continue to make it' (Berlin, 1962). Final light syllables occur in the language and are allowed presumably by extrametrically when preceded by heavy syllables; ie., unfootable, or extrametrical, syllables are allowed peripherally.

(24)

a. input:	nit	to push it
b. copy and grammatical suffix:	nit-nit+an	to push it rapidly in a crooked or curvy path
c. onset rule:	nit.ni.tan	
d. make bimoraic feet (R to L): (in order to do this the first syllable must be monomoraic, so resyllabify)	[ni.tni][tan]	
d. no complex onsets:	ni.ti.tan	
e. output:	nititan	

In support of the requirement of cluster simplification in step (d), we note that no more than one coda consonant is allowed before a morphological boundary, and native morphemes have no onset clusters (Kaufman, 1971). (s and š may create clusters when prefixed to a root.) Kaufman (1971) lists three possible forms for native roots: CV, CVC, and CVhC. (Geminate consonants do not occur.) While loans from Spanish retain all or most consonant clusters, Berlin notes that onset clusters in these words are broken up by the insertion of an epenthetic vowel (Berlin, 1962). This limited distribution of consonant clusters motivates the delinking of the original onset consonant of the reduplicative suffix after resyllabification creates a new onset from the stem final consonant. Since Tzeltal does not generally allow C1C2 onsets, the output of (20d) must be fixed. This is accomplished by deleting C2.

Under this analysis, the two patterns of reduplication, whole syllable suffix and onsetless syllable suffix, in Tzeltal can be understood as a single process. An appeal to the Pattern A type of reduplication to support the rhyme as the reduplicative template accompanied by the postulation of a "transparent" morphological juncture does not appear to be a fully explicit account of the Tzeltal verbal reduplication. Both patterns of Tzeltal reduplication must be examined, and both can be considered to form a suffix of the entire final syllable of the stem. Foot structure requirements of the language account for the loss of the original onset in the reduplicative affix in the verbs which require a grammatical -VC suffix in this form. We see that apparent differences in the surface prosodic structures of the base and the copy in both Marshallese and Tzeltal can be accounted for by considering the prosodic requirements of each language. The stem coda becomes an onset in Marshallese because a trimoraic syllable is impossible and in Tzeltal because a trimoraic foot is impossible.[11] In both cases the onset clusters then simplifies losing the second consonant. Seemingly different patterns of reduplication within each of the languages whereby an onsetless reduplicative suffix appears in some cases and a complete syllable in others can be unified under a single analysis when requirements of prosodic structure are considered. These facts support the general conclusion that no VC or VVC templates are necessary.

5. Marshallese Vocalic Epenthesis

In order to derive the final surface forms of the Marshallese reduplicated words, a description of epenthesis in Marshallese is required. An epenthetic vowel is inserted, both within and across words, between two stops which differ in their primary place of articulation, ie. between heterorganic consonants. The

[11] A comparable phenomenon is encountered in Ibibio where a long vowel shortens in a CVVC verbal stem before a CV suffix in order to satisfy footing requirements in the language (Akinabi & Urua, 1992).

reduplicated forms given in (9) where adjacent closures are created by reduplication are realized after epenthesis as shown in the following examples:

(25)	lɤŋo̟ŋ	->	lɤŋo̟ŋŋo̟ŋ		--------------------
	mok	->	e+mokmok	->	e+mokəmok
	ebbok	->	ebbokbok	->	ebbokəbok

Stop clusters having the same primary place of articulation but differing in their secondary place of articulation do not give rise to a mediating epenthetic vowel. While such clusters are unusual in Marshallese, epenthesis is impossible for the native speaker.

(26)	*epenthesis prohibited in:*		
	l̩æntɤn	lantern	palatalized alveolar+velarized alveolar
	bujentɤm̩a	balloon	palatalized alveolar+velarized alveolar
	ellal̩lal̩e	a down-to-earth person	velarized lateral+palatalized lateral

Recall that the Marshallese consonant inventory includes only stop consonants with the exception of the lateral and glides.[12] Laterals appear to behave irregularly with respect to the epenthesis process. This fact is not surprising in light of the somewhat ambiguous status of constriction degree, ie. stop vs. continuant, which lateral liquids often have. In light of the fact that the consonant inventory includes only stops, Marshallese epenthesis can be described in the following way: two adjacent closure gestures are disallowed.[13] Phrase-final consonants are allowed without a following epenthetic vowel as no closure gesture follows them, and stop sequences differing only in secondary place also surface without epenthesis as the secondary constriction is not a closure.

Recalling that the CVC syllables will always receive stress, one might wonder whether a rule of epenthesis is a stress conspiracy preventing two clashing stresses. This does not appear to be the case, however, as all heavy syllables are stressed, including CVV syllables which *can* immediately precede or follow other heavy syllables thereby yielding adjacent stresses. Given that the language systematically releases even phrase final consonants and that there is no prohibition on adjacent stresses, a more accurate explanation of the data is offered by an analysis prohibiting two adjacent closure gestures. Such underlying sequences surface with an intervening epenthetic vowel.

Itô (1989) has suggested that cases of epenthesis similar to that of Marshallese can be explained by the existence of a Coda Filter which prevents a Place node from being singly linked to a coda consonant (Itô, 1989; Itô, 1986), shown here in (27).

---

[12] The trills behave like the full stops with respect to epenthesis and are sometimes phonetically prestopped.

[13] I thank Donca Steriade for her discussion of this analysis with the author.

(27) Coda Filter (from Itô, 1989)

```
*        C]σ
          |
       [PLACE]
```

When the Coda Filter is violated because the coda consonant has an independent place component epenthesis occurs to resolve the violation by turning the consonant into an onset for an epenthetic vowel. While the Coda Filter might appear to explain epenthesis in Marshallese word-internal closed syllables, there are several problems with postulating a Coda Filter for Marshallese. First, closed syllables are allowed word finally; no final epenthetic vowel is inserted. A Coda Filter with no special conditions would predict that word final consonants should be prohibited. Secondly, there are no cases of epenthesis between extra heavy CVVC syllables and a following consonant. When such syllables are derived word internally due to the reduplication process, resyllabification, not epenthesis, occurs.

In order to explain the reduplication and epenthesis facts, one might postulate that the final consonant in extra heavy syllables is extraprosodic and that such consonants are licensed only word finally.[14] This approach combined with a Coda Filter leads to incorrect predictions. Recall that these extra heavy syllables *are* separated from a following consonant across word boundaries by an epenthetic vowel such as that formed in the reduplicated form of [ebbok] which surfaces as [ebbokəbok]. A Coda Filter wouldn't predict this as the extraprosodic final consonant should not be seen by a Coda Filter. Additionally, Steriade (1982) shows that languages having a Coda Filter and final extrametricality will allow two consonants at word edges (Itô, 1989 and Itô, 1986). Marshallese does not allow such sequences.

Although these above objections to postulating a final stray consonant in the extra heavy syllables rely on an interaction with a Coda Filter, there are problems with an analysis postulating final extrametricality of the coda consonants of extra heavy syllables, even without the assumption of a Coda Filter. Such an analysis would assert that coda consonants in the language are extrasyllabic just in case they are in a syllable with a bimoraic vowel. Syllables with a short vowel and a coda consonant would be bimoraic, not having extrasyllabic coda consonants. The final consonant in an XCVC# sequence cannot be extraprosodic since it carries weight as indicated in the stress pattern; i.e. closed syllables receive primary stress, regardless of their position, just as do syllables containing a long vowel.

Because of the inadequacies encountered in postulating a Coda Filter or final extrametricality or both to describe the Marshallese epenthesis and reduplication data, I have proposed an analysis of these facts which describes both patterns of reduplication and the surface forms created by epenthesis as a result of prosodic requirements of the language which limit the distribution of extra heavy syllables and prohibit two consecutive closure gestures. Phrase final consonants, geminate consonants, and consonants differing only in secondary place may surface without epenthesis occurring.

---

[14]This leaves aside the word internal CVVC syllables where the final C is part of a geminate consonant.

6. Satisfying Prosodic Requirements in Marshallese

The proposed analysis of reduplication in Marshallese suggests that the language appears to conform to prosodic requirements using resyllabification, deletion, and epenthesis mechanisms. Illegitimate stop sequences are created in the derivation of both Pattern 1 and Pattern 2 of Marshallese reduplication. In deriving surface forms of the reduplicated words, Pattern 1 (repeated here in (28)) yields two abutting CVC syllables.

(28)	Pattern 1			
	lɤŋo̞ŋ	fear	lɤŋo̞ŋ-ŋo̞ŋ	very afraid
	mok	tired	e+mok-mok	very tired
	ebbok	to make full	ebbok-bok	puffy
	ro̞ŋ	ear	ja+ro̞ŋ-ro̞ŋ	deaf
	ennon	aroused	ennon-non	(sexually) aroused
	enno	delicious	enno-no	very delicious
	to̞	rope	ka+to̞-to̞	hang up
	yu	coconut soft meat	kay+yu-yu	collect coconut soft meat
	awa	hour	ka+awa-wa	killtime

This pattern cannot surface when two heterorganic stops occur adjacently. In these cases, epenthesis must occur yielding the surface forms. This produces the surface forms shown in (29).

(29)	Pattern 1--surface forms			
	lɤŋo̞ŋ	fear	lɤŋo̞ŋŋo̞ŋ	very afraid
	mok	tired	e+mokəmok	very tired
	ebbok	to make full	ebbokəbok	puffy
	ro̞ŋ	ear	ja+ro̞ŋəro̞ŋ	deaf
	ennon	aroused	ennonnon	(sexually) aroused
	enno	delicious	ennono	very delicious
	to̞	rope	ka+to̞to̞	hang up
	yu	coconut soft meat	kay+yuyu	collect coconut soft meat
	awa	hour	ka+awawa	killtime

Pattern 2 (repeated here in 30) arises when two extra heavy syllables abut after reduplication.

(30)	Pattern 2			
	baat	smoke	e+baat-baat	smokey
	jook	ashamed	e+jȯok-jook	shy
	naan	talk, word	kɤ+kɤn+naan-naan	talkative
	ko̞o̞n	piglet	ka+ko̞o̞n-ko̞o̞n	to own a piglet
	kɤjeek	fire	ka+kɤjeek-jeek	blazing
	tææŋ	popular	tææŋ-tææŋ	very popular
	jitɯɯl	steel	jitɯɯl-tɯɯl	very magnetic
	mææn̩	burn, warm	e+mææn̩-mææn̩	burning
	mæær	lie, fib	e+mæær-mæær	he is a fibber

The Pattern 2 structure, at this point in the derivation, cannot meet the syllable structure requirements of the language because extra heavy syllables are disallowed word internally (excepting in the case where the final consonant is geminate) and because complex onsets are prohibited. Marshallese fulfills prosodic requirements by resyllabification of the coda consonant making it an onset and deletion of the second consonant in the resulting complex onset. Epenthesis does not occur. Thus, the surface forms shown in (31) are produced.

(31) Pattern 2--surface forms

baat	smoke	e+baataat	smokey
jook	ashamed	e+jookook	shy
naan	talk, word	kɤ+kɤn+naanaan	talkative
ko̦o̦n	piglet	ka+ko̦o̦no̦o̦n	to own a piglet
kɤjeek	fire	ka+kɤjeekeek	blazing
tææŋ	popular	tææŋææŋ	very popular
jitɯɯl	steel	jitɯɯlɯɯl	very magnetic
mææn̩	burn, warm	e+mææn̩ææn̩	burning
mæær̩	lie, fib	e+mæær̩æær̩	he is a fibber

Thus we see the following distribution of epenthesis and deletion in creating acceptable syllables in reduplicated forms.

(32)

	CC ->		Epenthesis CəC	Resyllab. & Deletion CØ
Pattern 1	ron-ron	->	ronəron	*ronon
Pattern 2	jook-jook	->	*jookəjook	jookook
			coda+onset	onset cluster

The prohibition of two adjacent closure gestures appears to be satisfied through epenthesis in the case of a heterosyllabic cluster, ie. an adjacent coda and onset, and by deletion in a derived tautosyllabic cluster, ie. a complex onset. These processes and the distributional restrictions placed on extra heavy syllables serve to determine the prosodic realization of words in this Marshallese morphological process.

6. Conclusion

In conclusion, I have described how both patterns of Marshallese suffixal reduplication are the result of a single process of affixation with a bimoraic syllable weight parameter. This analysis unifies the two apparently different patterns of reduplication in the language: the apparently onsetless reduplicative suffix in one pattern and the more common suffixation which retains an onset in the other. I have compared the proposed analysis of Marshallese reduplication with a new analysis of the facts of Tzeltal verbal reduplication. I have explained the process of epenthesis which creates the surface realization of the Marshallese reduplicated forms as a prohibition against two adjacent closure gestures. Finally, I have noted that Marshallese bimoraic syllable suffixation demonstrates a very unusual type of reduplication within the typology of reduplication outlined by McCarthy and Prince (1986) filling an otherwise unexplained but nonprincipled gap in this typology.

Appendix

Unusual Phonemes of Marshallese and Corresponding Transcriptions

j	laminal palatalized palato-alveolar stop or fricative
t	velarized apico-alveolar stop
r	apical dento-alveolar stop
q	labialized velar stop
b	velarized bilabial stop
ḷ	velarized lateral
l̓	palatalizedlateral
ṇ	velarized alveolar nasal
n	palatalized alveolar nasal
ṃ	velarized bilabial nasal
ɯ	high central vowel
a	low central vowel
ọ	higher mid back vowel
ǫ	lower mid back vowel
y	palatal glide
ɤ	higher mid central vowel

References

Akinlabi, A. and E. Urua. 1992. Prosodic targets and vocalic specification. presentation at WCCFL XI, 1992 to appear in the *Proceedings of WCCFL XI*, 1992..

Bender, Byron. 1969. *Spoken Marshallese.* University of Hawaii Press.

Berlin, B. 1962. Esbozo de la Fonología del Tzeltal de Tenejapa, Chiapas, *Estudios de Cultura Maya*, 2.17-36.

Berlin, B. 1963. Some semantic features of reduplication in Tzeltal. *International Journal of American Linguistics*, 29,3, pp. 211-218.

Broselow, E. and J. McCarthy. 1983. A theory of internal reduplication. *The Linguistic Review*, 3, 25-38.

Choi, J. dissertation in preparation at UCLA.

Clements, G.N. 1985. The problem of transfer in nonlinear morphology. *Cornell Working Papers in Linguistics*, 7., 68-73.

Davis, S. 1985. On the nature of internal reduplication. Ms, Indiana University.

Itô, J. 1986. *Syllable Theory in Prosodic Phonology.* Ph.D. dissertation, University of Massachusetts, Amherst. Published by Garland Publishers, 1988.

Itô, J. 1989. A prosodic theory of epenthesis. *Natural Language and Linguistic Theory* 7:217-259.

Kaufman, T. 1971. *Txeltal Phonology and Morphology.* UCPiL, 61, UCPress, Berkeley.

Kiparsky, P. 1986. *The phonology of reduplication.* Ms, Stanford University.

Levin, J. 1983. Reduplication and prosodic structure. Ms, MIT.

Marantz, A. 1982. Re reduplication. *Linguistic Inquiry*, 13. 435-482.

McCarthy, J. 1979. *Formal Problems in Semitic Phonology and Morphology.* Ph.D. dissertation, MIT, Cambridge, Massachusetts. Published 1985, by Garland Publishers, NY.

McCarthy, J. 1981. A prosodic theory of nonconcatenative morphology. *Linguistic Inquiry*, 12, 373-413.

McCarthy, J. and A. Prince. 1986. Prosodic Morphology. manuscript, University of Massachusetts, Amherst, and Brandeis University, Waltham.

McCarthy, J. and A. Prince. 1987. Quantitative transfer in reduplication and templatic morphology. in Linguistic Society of Korea (ed.), *Linguistics in the Morning Calm* 2, Hanshin Publishing Co., Seoul, pp. 3-35.

Steriade, D. 1982. *Greek prosodies and the nature of syllabification.* Ph.D. dissertation, MIT.

Steriade, D. 1988. Reduplication and syllable transfer in Sanskrit and elsewhere. *Phonology* 5:73-155.

Yip, M. 1982. Reduplication and C-V skeleta in Chinese secret languages. *LI* 13, 637-661.

The Role of Agreement and Modality in Palauan

LYNN CHERNY
Stanford University

Palauan is a Western Austronesian language with VOS order (Georgopoulos 1984) exhibiting the WH-AGREEMENT effect described by Georgopoulos (1985a,b, 1991). A similar phenomenon in Chamorro, a related Austronesian language, has been discussed extensively in Chung (1982, 1991). WH-Agreement is the morphological alternation in the verb that results when arguments are preposed. In Palauan, this is realized as an alternation in mood.

In this paper, I reanalyze the WH-Agreement data presented by Georgopoulos, using verb raising to a functional category I call MoodP (or MP), motivated by a licensing requirement for A′ binders, which is similar in spirit to Rizzi's (1989) WH-Criterion. I state this licensing requirement in terms of proper government, and suggest that agreement is crucial to this government, at least within the A′ functional projections (cf. Chung 1991). I examine two agreement configurations: Spec-Head relationships, and agreement along an EXTENDED PROJECTION, in the sense of Grimshaw (1991). Some of the morphological alternations that accompany WH-Agreement appear to be sensitive to the different configurations for agreement.

1. Structure of Palauan

I will assume the base form of a Palauan sentence is a head-initial structure, with specifiers on the right, as in (1):

(1)

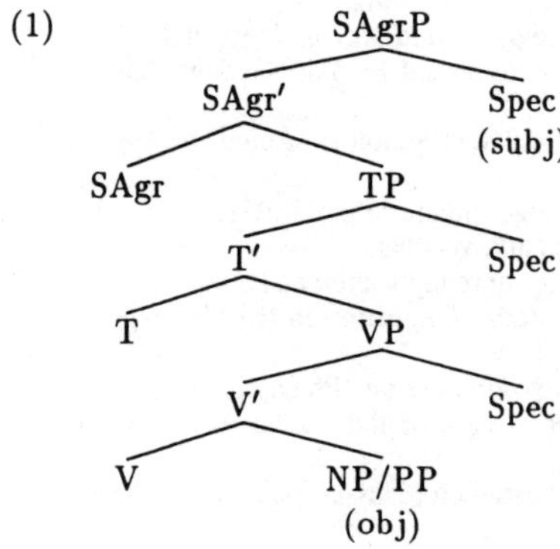

Sentences in (2) illustrate basic word order.[1] Object agreement suffixes only appear on perfective verbs, and direct objects are encoded in PPs if there is no object agreement.[2]

(2) a. Imperfective, realis:
ng-ulemengch er a choch-il a bilis.
R/3s(subj)-IMP-bite P CM foot-3s(poss) CM dog
The dog was biting its own foot.

b. Perfective, realis:
ng-kiltmeklii a uloal a Peter.
R/3s(subj)-PERF-clean-3s(obj) CM floor CM Peter
Peter cleaned the floor.

2. Morphology

Before discussing the WH-Agreement facts in more detail, I will introduce some basic morphology.

In Palauan, pro-drop occurs obligatorily in the presence of a governing agreement affix, for subjects, objects, and possessor NPs (see (3)). Where agreement is not a proper governor, overt pronouns appear. Resumptive pronouns alternate with gaps according to the presence of governing agreement in extraction constructions as well. I will assume, following Georgopoulos (1985a,b), that *pros* and overt pronouns can both be A′-bound variables; the pronouns and A′ binders are base-generated, the latter being subject to the licensing condition that I will present. I'll use the movement metaphor to make things clearer, however.

The only agreement marker I will discuss is the subject agreement prefix, in bold in (2a,b). Subject agreement is marked with sets of prefixes that also encode a modality distinction: there is one set that encodes realis, glossed with an '**R**' in this paper, and another that encodes irrealis, glossed with '**IR**'. Irrealis mood is signalled solely by the irrealis set of subject agreement prefixes, but I assume like Georgopoulos (1985a,b) that realis is the mood the verb expresses with or without the overt realis agreement marker.

Irrealis mood shows up on the verb in modal constructions such as conditionals, in negative sentences, in imperatives, and in some adverbial phrases (see (3a,b), with '**R**' and '**IR**' prefixes).

(3) a. Negative, irrealis:
Ng-diak k-secher.
not-PRES **IR/1s(subj)**-sick.
I'm not sick.

[1] Abbreviations used in the glosses:

R: realis	IR: irrealis
IMP: imperfective	PERF: perfective
CM: constituent marker	P: preposition
COMP: complementizer	FUT: future
DEM: demonstrative	

[2] All of my data are taken from Georgopoulos (1985a,b) unless otherwise indicated.

b. Conditional, irrealis:
A l-engar er ngii a ududek,
CM **IR/3(subj)**-be P it CM money,
e **ak**-mo er a Guam.
then **R/1s(subj)**-go-PRES P CM Guam.
If I had money, I'd go to Guam.

3. The WH-Agreement Facts

Movement phenomena in Palauan display an interesting interaction between agreement and modality marking. The subject AGR morpheme is overt and realis in a normal VOS sentence as in (2), but when the subject is preposed, the subject agreement marker disappears, as in (4a). (As stated above, the mood is still assumed to be realis when no agreement prefix appears.) When a nonsubject (either possessor, object, or oblique) is preposed, the subject marking is irrealis (and hence overt), as in (4b).

(4) a. Subject topicalization (no overt agreement):
A rengalek a rirellii a present el mo er a sensei.
children **R**-PERF-do-3s(obj) present COMP go P teacher.
The children made a present for the teacher.

b. Object topicalization:
A present a l-lirellii a rengalek el
IR/3s(subj)-PERF-do-3s(obj)
mo er a sensei.
go P teacher
The children made a present for the teacher.

This pattern of agreement and irrealis marking occurs with WH-movement as well as topicalization (hence the name 'WH-Agreement'). WH-phrases may be either in situ (as in (a) in (5) through (7)) or in a position to the left of the main clause, prefixed with a cleft marker (as in (b) in (5) through (7)), with no difference in meaning. WH-in-situ sentences do not show irrealis agreement, but show realis overt agreement marking, unless there is a semantic trigger for irrealis (e.g., a conditional or negative); Georgopoulos (1985a,b) concludes therefore that the irrealis alternation in WH-Agreement is syntactically triggered at S-Structure.[3]

(5) a. Subject in situ:
ng-osiik er ngak a techang?
R/3s(subj)-IMP-look.for P me who
Who is looking for me?

[3]Possessives behave like other nonsubjects in WH-movement as well as in topicalization, although I do not give those examples here (Georgopoulos 1985a).

b. Preposed subject (no overt agreement):
ng-techa a kileldii a sub?
CL-who **R**-heat-PAST-3s(obj) soup.
Who heated up the soup?

(6) a. Oblique in situ:
ke-milerar tiang el mo er teang?
R/2s(subj)-PERF-buy-3s(obj) DEM COMP go P who?
Who did you buy this for?

b. Preposed oblique:
ng-ker **le**-bilsk-au a buk er ngii a Ruth?
CL-where **IR/3(subj)**-PERF-gave-2s(obj) book P it Ruth
Where did Ruth give you the book?

(7) a. Object in situ:
ng-omelacha a ngera er a mlai a Sabeth?
R/3s(subj)-put what P car Sabeth
What is Sabeth putting in the car?

b. Preposed object:
ng-ngera a **le**-silseb-ii a seelil?
CL-what **IR/3(subj)**-PERF-burn-3s(obj) friend-poss
What did his friend burn?

The WH-Agreement effect can therefore be summarized:

Preposed Subjects: no subject agreement, mood assumed to be realis.
Preposed Nonsubjects: irrealis subject agreement mood marking appears.

4. Previous Analyses

Previous analyses of this alternation in mood associated with argument preposing have focused on the link between irrealis and A′ binding but failed to explain the relationship between irrealis, subject agreement marking, and modal environments in general (Georgopoulos 1985a,b, 1991; Haik 1990). For Georgopoulos (1991), WH-Agreement (or A′-Agreement) is a phenomenon distinct from local Spec-Head agreement (or A-Agreement); the former she asserts to be agreement of Case features between the verb and the A′-bound variable or clause containing the variable. This Case agreement principle is stated as a disjunction that simply distinguishes subject variables (with nominative Case) from nonsubject variables (with non-nominative case). Since Case is not overtly marked in this language, and there is therefore no evidence that Case is what triggers WH-Agreement, the generalization is at best a descriptive one stating that subject variables trigger unmarked realis mood and nonsubject variables trigger irrealis agreement in A′-binding constructions. Georgopoulos's generalization in terms of Case does not explain the lack of overt subject agreement in subject-preposed sentences; and it does not explain why an alternation in **mood** is the result of the supposed Case agreement.

I maintain as an alternative that the phenomenon of WH-Agreement is a local agreement relationship between the verb and the preposed argument, triggered by the licensing of the A′-binder, rather than a long-distance agreement between the verb and the the abstract Case of the variable. In the usual case this local agreement takes the form of Spec-Head coindexing.[4] This analysis has the beneficial consequence of reducing the WH-Agreement phenomenon to a familiar operation in grammatical theory. My approach also illuminates the role of mood in licensing A′ binders; and I suggest conditions under which overt morphological agreement appears or fails to appear.

5. Analysis

I propose extending the phrase structure given in (1) to the A′ categories CP and MP.[5]

I adapt some ideas from Whitman (1989) and Bhatt and Yoon (1991) regarding the structure and function of CP and MP. Whitman (1989) proposes for Korean that topic position is [Spec, MP] and MP dominates TP. He notes that modal morphemes cooccur with Topics, and certain complementizers select modal clauses. Clearly in Palauan, mood is partly determined by presence of a topic (as shown in (4)). Furthermore, Georgopoulos (1985a,b) notes that one of the complementizers, *el kmo*, selects a realis clause when there is no overt operator following it. Josephs (1975, 436) describes this complementizer in some circumstances as 'implying that the speaker is fairly sure about the factuality of what he has heard', which is consistent with the semantically realis mood it selects (as in (8)).[6]

---

[4]Georgopoulos (1991) also tries to invoke Spec-Head coindexing, but still requires long-distance percolation of Case features along the A′ chain; this approach is problematic if one respects the notion of agreement locality in Grimshaw (1991).

[5]I am in fact agnostic about the existence of an actual functional projection for Mood; I use this as a label to indicate the functionality I associate with some projection under CP and above TP. This projection could also be considered to be another CP with slightly different properties from the CP dominating it, as in Bhatt and Yoon (1991). I use the label MoodP to stress that the properties are more closely related to verbal inflection than to complementation. Another alternative, of course, would be to consider the MP as another SAgrP, Spec-initial and with different functions from the canonical head-initial SAgrP below it. The higher SAgrP would then function as an A′ position for preposed arguments and also play the role my MP plays as far as generating modality is concerned. It is not clear to me, however, that these notational differences would make substantially different claims as long as the functionality of the heads is still being spelled out the same way.

[6]Example from Josephs (1975, 436). The evidence that *el kmo* selects realis when there is no overt operator beside it comes from long distance extraction cases, in which the complementizer's selection properties override the 'trace of WH-movement' effect, which occurs in Palauan as in Chamorro (Chung 1982). Long distance extraction of nonsubjects ordinarily

(8) **Ak**-rirenges [el kmo a sensei a mlad er a elii].
R/1s(subj)-hear-PAST COMP teacher **R**-die-PAST P yesterday
I heard (about the fact) that the teacher died yesterday.

Along with hosting topics and other preposed items, MP is where modal morphemes are generated for constructions like imperatives and conditionals, which are irrealis even without a preposed phrase. As I showed earlier in (1), the basic clausal structure is head-initial, governing canonically to the right. I will just assume without further extensive comment that in their base positions, arguments are licensed by heads which canonically govern them, generally P, V, N, SAgr. In the A′ categories above SAgrP, however, Specs precede heads (see tree (9); this is true for Chamorro as well, where the only Spec-initial category is CP (Chung 1991)).

(9)

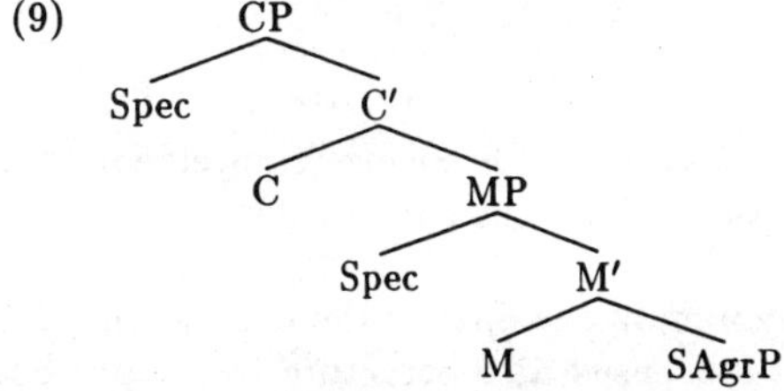

I assume that overt subject agreement is due to verb raising at least to SAgr, and potentially to M; these nodes are associated with an agreement functionality. (SAgr is intrinsically associated with a morphological agreement role as an agreement head; but M is also associated with an agreement function in Palauan, since mood is determined by a separate set of subject

---

results in irrealis verbs between the head and foot of the chain, as in (a) below. When the operator *ng-ngera* is moved higher in the sentence to another preclausal position (which does not affect the meaning of the sentence), the verb following *el kmo* becomes realis, as seen in (b). The other verbs between the operator and variable *ngii* are irrealis as expected (examples from Georgopoulos 1985b):

(i.) a. a Moses **ng**-dilu [el kmo ng-ngera$_i$ a **l**-ulengiil
Moses **R/3s(subj)**-said COMP CL-what **IR**/3(subj)-IMP-wait
er ngak [el **bo** **k**-uruul er ngii$_i$]]?
P me COMP **IR-FUT** **IR/1s(subj)**-do P it
What did Moses say that he was waiting for me to do (it)?

b. ng-ngera$_i$ a **le**-dilu a Moses [el kmo **ng**-milngiil
CL-what **IR**/3s(subj)-said Moses COMP **R**/3s(subj)-IMP-wait
er ngak [el **bo** **k**-uruul er ngii$_i$]]?
P me COMP **IR-FUT** **IR/1s(subj)**-do P it
What did Moses say that he was waiting for me to do (it)?

I do not discuss long extraction in this paper. One clear ramification of my analysis is that there must be traces in intermediate Comps that also require proper government in order to explain the 'trace of WH-movement' effect, contra Georgopoulos (1991).

agreement affixes.) Irrealis agreement obligatorily requires verb raising to M. Realis agreement, as the default, may or may not be accompanied by verb raising to MP.

To illustrate the simple derivation of a VOS sentence (e.g., (2a,b)): in the tree in (10), the V moves up to SAgr and since the subject is in situ, the overt agreement form results from Spec-Head coindexing (and the canonical government configuration).

(10)

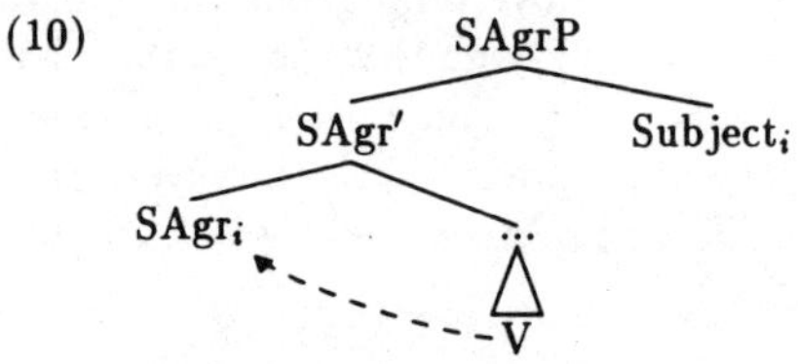

6. Preposed Arguments

My analysis of WH-Agreement rests on the licensing requirement that I assume for phrases in the A′ projections. I set this out in (11):

(11) **Licensing Hypothesis**: Any item in the Spec of the non-canonical, A′ functional projections must be licensed at S-Structure by proper head government. Proper head government for these functional categories requires an agreement relationship (as in Chung 1991). This relationship may either occur through:

(1) an explicit Spec-Head coindexing configuration, or

(2) via an inherited coindexation over an extended projection (Grimshaw 1991) with no intervening functional head that is phonologically overt.[7]

6.1 Preposed Nonsubjects

To illustrate, let us first look at the WH-Agreement effect caused by preposed nonsubjects. I assume that [Spec, MP] is where preposed arguments land (I discuss CP later). The reflex of the 'agreement' relationship in the case of nonsubjects in MP is the surfacing of the irrealis morpheme, via V raising to M. In (12), V raises to M in order to produce a Spec-Head coindexed configuration satisfying the proper head government requirement for A′ operators (from (11)'s clause (1)). The subject in situ is still governed by the SAgr via the Government Transparency Corollary (Baker 1988).

[7]Chung (1991) relativizes her definition of proper head government for traces according to the lexical versus functional status of a head; my analysis focuses on the licensing of base-generated A′ operators instead. For both of us, agreement is necessary for functional heads to govern properly. I adopt Chung's proposal that an overt functional head blocks this agreement relationship if it is not the agreeing governor itself.

(12)

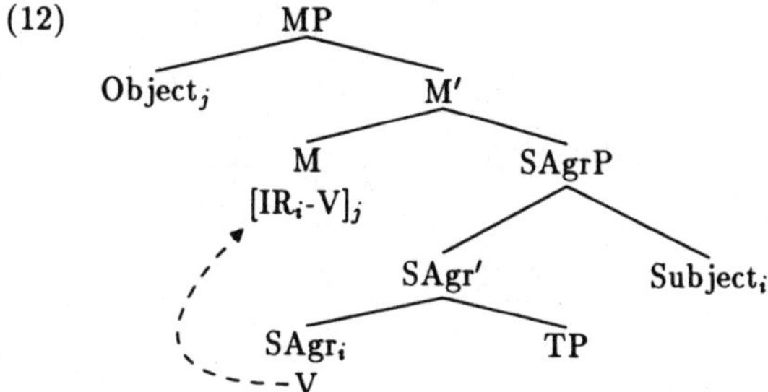

6.2 Preposed Subjects

Preposed subjects, as seen above, result in no overt agreement marking on the verb and therefore have realis mood. If there is in the general case a government-via-agreement relationship, we must wonder what is special about preposed subjects with respect to this agreement. I propose it is their 'nearness' to their base position where agreement ordinarily licenses them canonically. If we invoke the notion of EXTENDED PROJECTION in Grimshaw (1991), which captures just such a locality between elements in different maximal projections, we can formalize the appropriate agreement relationship between SAgr and MP.

Grimshaw (1991) suggests that the functional categories C and I are projections of the lexical category V. In her terminology, V (and I and C) are EXTENDED HEADS of the extended projections IP and CP; the projection nodes all share categorial features, but there is an ordering relation on them (which she achieves by assigning ordered F VALUES to each head). Selection and agreement are relationships that appear to be nonlocal and require percolation of information up extended projections from heads to higher functional nodes. Only members of an extended projection allow this transmission of information. Grimshaw (1991) gives examples of C and [Spec, IP] agreeing in West Flemish, and main clause verbs selecting subordinate clause verb mood past overt complementizers in English and Romance; she analyses these as cases of percolation along projections.

In my analysis, the verbal extended projection includes maximal projections for SAgrP and MP. As a head in the extended projection, the SAgr node may transmit information to projections above it; or, put more declaratively, the SAgr node's properties are visible to the nodes above it. We capture this observation with clause (2) of the licensing requirement in (11). Agreement information may be inherited from the complement of M if M is not specified for it, as in Grimshaw (1991) (a nonovert M is not specified for any relevant features, I assume). Thus SAgr itself is capable of abstractly governing the [Spec, MP] via this agreement, since MP forms an extended projection with SAgrP. This might be viewed as percolation of the index SAgr inherently has (as an agreement head) up the tree to [Spec, MP], as in (13):

(13)

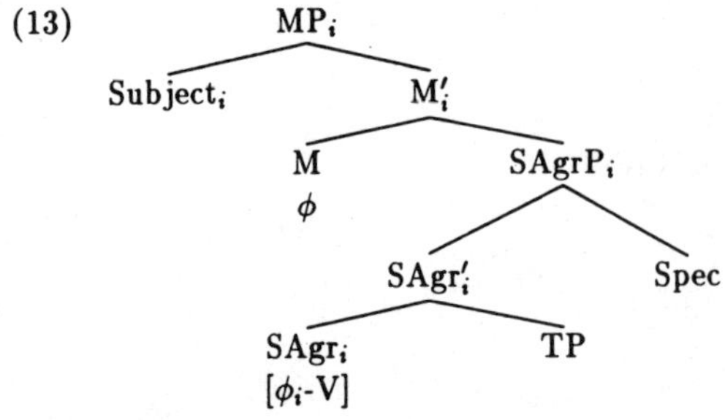

The verb therefore does not have to raise to support M, since raising is not required to govern the preposed subject; subject preposing is therefore 'easier' in an economical sense. In fact subject preposing is highly productive (productive enough for Josephs (1975) to claim that the basic word order is SVO; but see Georgopoulos (1984) for arguments based on word order in subordinate clauses, focus effects on clause-initial arguments, and structural parallelism between topicalization, question formation, and relativization that suggest the order is most plausibly VOS underlyingly).

It should be clear that I am making a formal distinction between the mechanism of abstract agreement in the grammar and agreement as it surfaces morphologically (see also Georgopoulos (1991) for such a distinction). Via the mechanisms of index percolation up a projection and Spec-Head coindexing (which may be viewed as a type of index percolation within a projection (Grimshaw 1991)), grammatical agreement is represented, but only under certain conditions can this grammatical agreement surface as overt morphological agreement.

The surfacing of overt agreement morphology is sensitive to the presence of a Spec-Head relationship: overt agreement surfaces if the subject is in situ in [Spec, SAgrP]. Recall that I assume A$'$ binders are actually generated in MP and bind resumptive pronouns (overt or *pro*); the 'preposed' subject in [Spec, MP] has therefore never been in a Spec-Head relationship with SAgr, and hence there is no overt agreement (as would be expected if it had been base-generated in SAgrP and moved from there). The lack of overt morphological agreement when the subject is preposed is an indication that there is no Spec-Head relationship within MP for preposed subjects, and that instead, the agreement and government result via the extended projection. I show in section 8 that in fact, Spec-Head relationships within MP are possible even for subjects, and result in the expected overt agreement.

Note that in (13), if a nonsubject were in [Spec, MP] and the verb did not raise to M, the nonsubject would not be properly governed since the nonsubject requires the Spec-Head agreement relationship for its government; this is because there is no head nearby which is inherently coindexed with it (to percolate an index from).

7. The 'WH-Criterion'

Rizzi's (1989) WH-Criterion seems to provide some plausible support for why a preposed argument might require a local head governor. Informally, the WH-Criterion states that there is a Spec-Head relationship required between preposed WH elements and a [+WH] INFL.

WH-Criterion:

a. Each [+WH] X^0 must be in a Spec-Head relation with a WH-phrase.

b. Each WH-phrase must be in a Spec-Head relation with a [+WH] X^0.

This generally requires I raising to C in the Romance languages, and thus partly explains Subject-Aux inversion with nonsubject extractions. The [+WH] INFL is abstract in these languages, however. The situation in Palauan MP instantiates this relationship overtly, with irrealis morphology as the [+WH] reflex. Note that the [+WH] Spec-Head requirement in Palauan only goes one direction: irrealis mood, although being the result of a (nonsubject) argument in [Spec, MP], is not necessarily a reflection of [Spec, MP] being filled, since the verb raises in modal constructions as well, with empty [Spec, MP]. (In other words, only clause (b) holds at S-Structure in Palauan; or else M is not inherently specified for [+WH] but gets the feature via coindexing with a preposed argument.)

Preposed subjects in MP do not require verb raising, however. It must be noted that even in the English and French cases Rizzi presents, preposed subjects behave differently with respect to requiring a [+WH] Comp. Example (14d) illustrates that the INFL does not raise to C.

(14) a. [What did [John t burn?]]

b. [*What [John burned?]]

c. [Who [burnt the chips?]]

d. [*Who did [t burn the chips?]]

Rizzi (1989) analyses subject extraction by chain, with [+WH] remaining in INFL, not moving to Comp because the subject trace at the tail of the chain in [Spec, IP] satisfies the criterion of Spec-Head association with the [+WH] in I (and by transitivity of agreement, the head satisfies the criterion). Rather than invoke the mechanism of a chain, I suggest that the government relationship between SAgr and a preposed subject is satisfied via the extended projection and so the verb does not need to, and therefore does not, raise to M.

8. Independent Mood Requirements

Since mood is a bound morpheme, verb raising to M is required for semantically irrealis sentences like imperatives, conditionals, negatives, and some adverbial clauses. If, as I have claimed, the licensing of preposed arguments merely requires a local (agreeing) head governor, then the actual mood on the verb should be irrelevant, since only the structural configuration and resulting coindexation should matter. Hence it should be possible for an irrealis mood to appear on a subject preposed sentence, if the semantic mood requires it.

This is verified by Georgopoulos (1985b), and the example in (15) supports the prediction:[8]

(15) A Droteo a dimlak **lo**-lim a biang.
  Droteo Neg-PAST **IR/3s(subj)**-drink beer.
  Droteo didn't drink any beer.

In (15) the negation triggers irrealis, but when the subject is preposed, the mood is still marked irrealis; hence, there is overt agreement.

We might further speculate that if realis is a possible mood generable in MP[9] (as well as being the default unmarked mood), then we should be able to find overt realis subject AGR cooccurring with preposed phrases, whether subject or nonsubject, since in either case a Spec-Head relationship will occur if the verb raises to M. It appears that this is possible for yes/no questions, as shown in (16b,c); they may optionally bear subject agreement in realis even when the subject is preposed. When they do not show overt realis agreement, intonation alone signals their yes/no question status. (These options resemble the options in English, where intonation alone can indicate that a question is being asked, or Subject-Aux inversion occurs. The verb raising to M is the Palauan equivalent of Aux raising to C.)

(16) a. Preposed nonsubject declarative (irrealis):
  a bangk a **l**-ulleng a bebil er a udoud er
  bank **IR/3(subj)**-borrow some P money P
  ngii a demak.
  it father-1s(poss)
  My father borrowed some money from the bank.

[8]There are unfortunately no examples of the irrealis verb and subject immediately adjacent in either Georgopoulos (1985a) or Josephs (1975). A native speaker would be required to confirm the claim with precisely the right data.

[9]Perhaps as a remnant of a formerly more complex modality system, in which realis obligatorily required verb raising as well.

b. Preposed nonsubject yes/no question (realis with agreement):
a bangk **ng**-lileng a bebil er a udoud er ngii
bank **R/3s(subj)**-borrow
a demam?
father-2s(poss)
Did your father borrow some money from the bank?

c. Preposed subject yes/no question (realis with agreement):
a demam **ng**-lileng a bebil er a udoud er a bangk __?
father-2s(poss) **R/3s(subj)**-borrow
Did your father borrow some money from the bank?

(17)

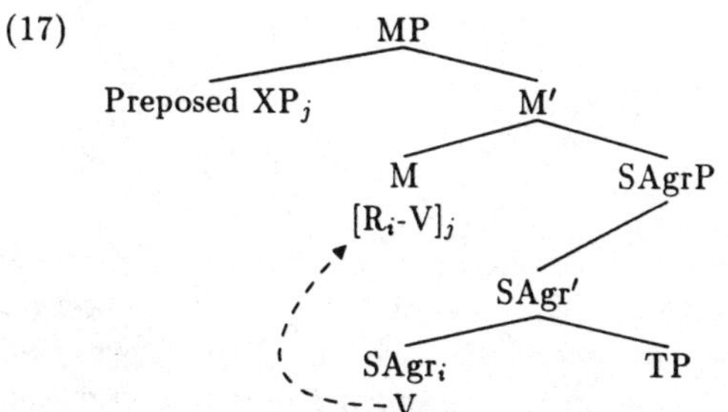

In the tree in (17), the index j results from the Spec-Head relationship, and i from the subject agreement marking incorporated in the realis prefix. If a subject is preposed, the index i will be equal to j. If a nonsubject is preposed, as in (16b), i will not be equal to j; if it were, a Principle C violation would occur as a result of the coindexed nonsubject and in situ subject. The Spec-Head coindexing is the relevant agreement relationship for the satisfaction of (11), so the i is irrelevant in the nonsubject-preposed case.

If verb raising is possible in either realis or irrealis moods, we might wonder why preposed nonsubjects result in irrealis rather than realis agreement marking when the semantic mood of the clause is assumed to be realis (Georgopoulos 1985a,b). Irrealis may be the syntactic reflex of most WH-agreement for the semantic reason that WH-questions indicate a degree of ignorance or doubt on the part of the speaker, which correlates with irrealis mood in some languages (Palmer 1986). However, this partial semantic explanation clearly does not generalize to all preposed arguments in Palauan, since topics also trigger the same mood as WH-operators. The extension of the effect to topics may be a result of the syntacticization of a partly semantically motivated phenomenon. An explanation in terms of markedness may be an alternative: if the mood that resulted from verb raising for licensing preposed arguments were always realis, this raising would be string-vacuous and so invisible, hence unlearnable (since realis is the mood when all arguments are in situ). Irrealis, as the mood that unambiguously arises from verb raising to M, renders the government requirement more transparent.

10. Doubly-Filled Comp

Palauan in fact appears to allow doubly-filled Comps, as Georgopoulos (1985a,b) has documented. The proposal earlier for CP dominating MP becomes useful when we consider the behavior of two A′ operators, which presumably under this account, fill the Specs of CP and MP, as in (18a,b):

(18) a. Subj Obj IR-V:
[$_{cp}$ ng-techa [$_{mp}$ a ngera [a l-oruul]]]?
CL-who what **IR/3(subj)**-do
Who does what?

b. Obj Subj R-V:
*[$_{cp}$ ng-ngera [$_{mp}$ a techa [a meruul]]]?
CL-what who **R**-do?
Who does what?

The grammaticality of example (18a) is predicted by our definition of proper head government in the A′ categories. The non-overt C is not a potential head governor, so the incorporated subject agreement under M can govern the subject by the same index percolation up the extended projection, as in tree (19):

(19)

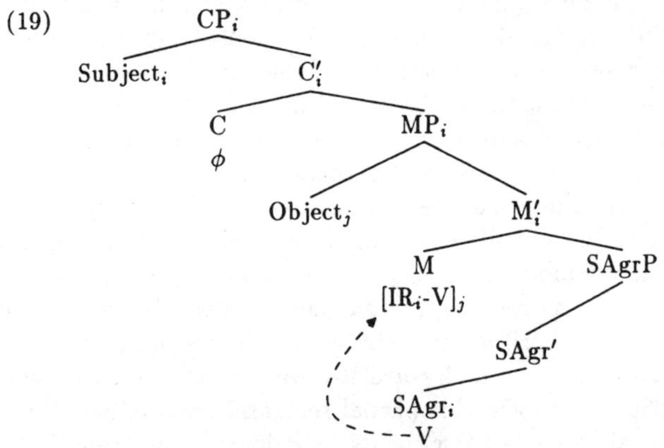

The object in (19) is in the required Spec-Head configuration and therefore governed as well. (Notice that, critically, it is the incorporated SAgr that governs the subject in [Spec, CP]; the node SAgr cannot govern it past the raised verb that is phonetically overt in M, under my definition of government.)

However, the reverse order of arguments in CP and MP, as in (18b), is not a proper government configuration, as shown in (20):

(20)

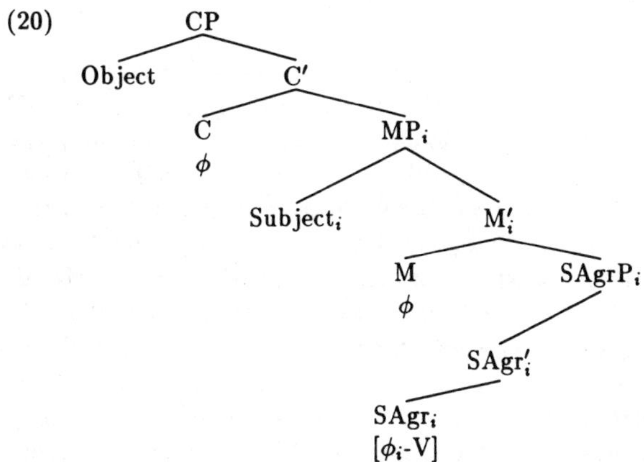

Here the object is not in a proper government configuration: there is no Spec-Head relationship with a raised verb, since the verb has not raised. SAgr, not being coindexed with the object, cannot govern it along the extended projection via MP, as it does for the subject.

We might ask whether inserting a complementizer into C would create the proper government configuration for the object. Complementizers in Palauan do not inflect, and so are not capable of bearing agreement features; I hypothesize that they are not proper governors. There is, in fact, evidence supporting this hypothesis from embedded clauses with the complementizer *el kmo* (Josephs 1975, 435):

(21) a. Embedded clause's subject in MP:
A Toki a omuachel [$_{cp}$ el kmo [$_{mp}$ a Droteo a sechel-il.]]
Toki **R**-IMP-tell COMP Droteo **R**-boyfriend-3s(poss)
Toki is telling us some story about Droteo being her boyfriend.

b. Embedded clause's subject in CP:
A Toki a omuachel er [$_{cp}$ a Droteo el kmo
Toki **R**-IMP-tell P Droteo COMP
[$_{mp}$ **ng**-sechel-il.]]
R/3s(subj)-boyfriend-3s(poss)
Toki is telling us some story about Droteo being her boyfriend.

The option of preposing the subject of the embedded clause to the position *before* the complementizer is available, as in (21b), but when this occurs, the argument raises and becomes an 'object' of the main verb, according to Josephs (1975). Note, in (21b), the insertion of the preposition before *Droteo*. This might be explained if we assume that the C is not a proper governor, and the main clause is able to provide one in exceptional cases.

11. Conclusion

I have proposed that for Palauan, there are certain licensing conditions that must be obeyed when A′ binders appear in the Comp categories CP and MP, conditions which are strictly configurational and result in the apparent WH-Agreement facts we have observed. The head movement account I propose explains the morphological alternations between overt irrealis and non-overt realis triggered by nonsubjects and subjects respectively; the crucial difference between the alternation is the proximity of SAgr to the A′ categories MP and CP, and the possibility of government via an extended projection. I further suggest that the surfacing of overt agreement forms may be sensitive to whether a Spec-Head configuration obtains within an appropriate functional phrase. Finally, a proposal for verb raising to a Comp category as an explanation for Palauan WH-Agreement unifies the Palauan account with proposed accounts for WH-Agreement effects in other languages, like Irish (Chung and McCloskey 1987) and Kikuyu (Clements 1985).

References

Baker, M.C. 1988. *Incorporation.* University of Chicago Press.

Bhatt, R., and J. Yoon. 1991. On the Composition of COMP and Parameters of V2. In *Proceedings of the West Coast Conference on Formal Linguistics* 10, ed. Dawn Bates, 41–52. Stanford Linguistics Association.

Chung, S. 1982. Unbounded Dependencies in Chamorro Grammar. *Linguistic Inquiry* 13:39–77.

Chung, S. 1991. On Proper Head Government in Chamorro. In *CLS 27-I: Papers from the Twenty-Seventh Regional Meeting,* ed. L. Dobrin et al.

Chung, S. and J. McCloskey. 1987. Government, Barriers, and Small Clauses in Modern Irish. *Linguistic Inquiry* 18, 173–237.

Clements, G.N. 1985. Binding Domains in Kikuyu. *Studies in the Linguistic Sciences* 14.

Georgopoulos, C. 1984. Palauan as a VOS Language. *Papers from the Fourth International Conference on Austronesian Linguistics.*

Georgopoulos, C. 1985a. *The Syntax of Variable Binding in Palauan.* Doctoral dissertation, University of California at San Diego.

Georgopoulos, C. 1985b. Variables in Palauan Syntax. *Natural Language and Linguistic Theory* 3: 59–94.

Georgopoulos, C. 1991. On A- and A′-Agreement. *Lingua* 85: 135–169.

Grimshaw, J. 1991. Extended Projection. Manuscript, Brandeis University.

Haik, I. 1990. Anaphoric, Pronominal, and Referential INFL. *Natural Language and Linguistic Theory* 8: 347–374.

Palmer, F. 1986. *Mood and Modality.* Cambridge University Press.

Rizzi, L. 1989. Speculations About Verb Second. To appear in *Grammar in Progress,* ed. J. Mascaro and M. Nespor. Dordrecht: Foris.

Whitman, J. 1989. Topic, Modality, and IP Structure. In *Harvard Studies in Korean Linguistics* 3, ed. S. Kuno et al., 341–356.

Weakly and Strongly Novel Noun Phrases

CLEO CONDORAVDI

Center for the Study of Language and Information, Stanford University

1 Introduction

Standard theories of indefinite NPs, including both those that analyze them as inherently existentially quantified and those that analyze them as non-quantificational, variable contributing elements, predict that indefinites always have existential force if outside the scope of any operator, that they assert rather than presuppose existence, and that they are never anaphoric.[1] Those theories, moreover, in which indefinites can inherit the force of the operator whose scope they are under (Kamp 1981, Heim 1982, Chierchia 1992) predict that an indefinite will have non-existential force only if in the restriction of an operator.

In this paper, I show that there are indefinites which, in one of their readings, although not in the scope of any operator do not have existential force and presuppose rather than assert existence. I argue that this kind of reading arises when an indefinite is evaluated with respect to a context entailing its descriptive content, in a sense to be made precise. I cast my analysis within the novelty theory of indefiniteness (Heim 1982), revising it in order to allow for indefinites which are felicitous with respect to contexts entailing their descriptive content. I distinguish between two types of indefinite NPs according to the types of felicity conditions they are associated with. STRONGLY NOVEL NPs are indefinite NPs which are associated with a novelty condition both with respect to their index and their descriptive content. WEAKLY NOVEL NPs are indefinite NPs which are associated with a novelty condition only with respect to their index.

2 The Functional Reading of Bare Plurals

Two influential analyses of the bare plural have sought a unified treatment for its existential and generic readings. One treats bare plurals as kind-denoting terms (Carlson 1977). The other treats bare plurals as indefinite NPs (Gerstner & Krifka 1987, Krifka 1987, 1990, Wilkinson 1988), relying on the analysis of indefinites developed by Kamp (1981) and Heim (1982) as inherently non-quantificational NPs contributing a free variable and conditions on that variable. It distinguishes between two types of genericity and analyzes one type as involving a sentential dyadic modal

[1]Thanks to T. Davis, D. Farkas, M. Gawron, C. Piñón and S. Zucchi for very useful discussions.

operator binding free variables in its restriction.

Both analyses are designed to account for the following two generalizations: (*i*) if the bare plural has a universal reading, then the reading for the whole sentence is generic; (*ii*) if the reading for the whole sentence is episodic, then the bare plural has an existential reading.[2] In this section I show that English bare plurals exhibit a universal reading which arises both with individual-level predicates in non-generic sentences, violating (*i*), and with stage-level predicates in episodic sentences, violating (*ii*). I call this reading the FUNCTIONAL READING since, as will be shown in section 5, a contextually salient function is implicated in its analysis.

2.1 Functional Reading with Individual-Level Predicates

A prediction of the standard indefiniteness analysis of bare plurals is that the universal reading of a bare plural, as of any indefinite, will arise only in quantificational contexts. Such contexts require the presence of an overt adverb of quantification, a modal, or implicit genericity.

A universal reading, however, arises in a wider range of contexts which cannot be assumed to be quantificational. Consider (1a) and three possible continuations, (1b)–(1d).

(1) a. In 1985 there was a ghost haunting the campus.
  b. Students were aware of the danger.
  c. The students were aware of the danger.
  d. There were students who were aware of the danger.

Intuitively, (1b) appears synonymous with (1c). Unlike (1d), (1b) does not make an existential assertion but, like (1c), it is an assertion about the totality of the contextually relevant students, whose existence in the actual world seems to be presupposed by both (1c) and (1b). Although the bare plural receives a universal reading, (1b) is not generic in any obvious way; it does not express a non-accidental generalization about students in general, nor a regularity about the occurrence of awareness in other situations in which a ghost was haunting the campus. Rather, (1b) expresses a generalization restricted to the actual students on campus on a particular occasion.

2.2 Functional Reading with Stage-Level Predicates

The universal reading of bare plurals also shows up with stage-level predicates in purely episodic contexts. (2b) can be understood either as an existential statement about some opponents of the proposal, or as a statement involving the totality of the opponents of the proposal.

(2) a. The proposal will be voted on tomorrow.
  b. Opponents demanded that the vote be shifted to next week.

The former reading is the expected one for a bare plural in an episodic context, but the latter is inconsistent with the generalization, which all existing theories of the bare plural take for granted, that there is no universal reading for the bare plural construed with a stage-level predicate in an episodic sentence.

[2]For Carlson (1977) these two implications are equivalences.

2.3 Genericity and the Functional Reading

In order to establish that the bare plural in (1b) is not within the scope of an operator, I show that (1b) is not generic—an interpretation which in any case does not square with our intuitions about the meaning of (1b). I present three arguments that further distinguish between the generic and the functional interpretation.[3]

The first argument is based on the contextually restricted nature of the generalization expressed by the functional reading. Implicit contextual restrictions, supplied by the context of utterance, are present with the functional reading of the bare plural. For example, (1b) is no more general than (3b), where the restrictions are part of the descriptive content of the NP. In order for (1b) to be true, the actual students on campus in 1985 have to have been aware of the danger. Moreover, if no students other than the ones on campus at that time were aware of the ghost's appearance, (1b) would still be true.

(3) a. In 1985 there was a ghost haunting the campus.

b. Students on the campus at that time were aware of this fact.

While the context of utterance affects the descriptive content of a bare plural NP with the functional reading, it cannot do so for generic indefinite NPs. Krifka (1987), among others, observed that generic statements do not accept implicit contextual restrictions, provided by the context of utterance on the basis either of previous linguistic discourse or of some salient facts established by the extralinguistic context, and assumed that adverbial quantifiers and the implicit generic operator, in contrast to nominal quantifiers, do no quantify over a contextually restricted domain of individuals. If the perceived functional reading were an entailment of a generic reading, the bare plural would not be contextually restricted. If contextual restrictions are not part of the generic interpretation, then they cannot come for free in the functional reading.

The second argument is based on the implication of existence in the actual world associated with the functional reading. Unlike generic statements, (1b) implies the existence of students on campus in 1985 in the actual world. That this is a nontrivial implication can be perhaps better appreciated if we consider a bare plural with additional descriptive content, as in (4b).

(4) a. In 1985 there was a ghost haunting the campus.

b. Students with police connections were aware of the danger.

c. But there were no students with police connections on campus in 1985.

Although the existence of individuals satisfying the descriptive content of the bare plural cannot in general be taken for granted, (4b) certainly implies that there were actually students with police connections on campus in 1985. Continuing the discourse comprised of (4a) and (4b) with (4c) leads to a contradiction. If the generic interpretation were the only interpretation for (4b), no implication of existence would be guaranteed since (4b) could be true, and even entail the equivalent actual generalization, even if no students with police connections actually existed on campus in 1985.

[3]The same arguments apply to a bare plural construed with a stage-level predicate, as in (2b).

Intersentential anaphora provides an additional piece of evidence for this implication. The bare plural of (1b) and (4b) can be the antecedent of a pronoun in intersentential anaphora: each of these sentences can be felicitously continued by (5). Note that the contextual restrictions are present in the interpretation of the pronoun as well: *they* picks out the students (with police connections) on campus at the time of the ghost's appearance, not just the students (with police connections) in the actual world at large.

(5) They had been informed by the police.

Intersentential anaphora in (5) is possible only if the indefinite antecedent asserts existence in the actual world (Karttunen 1976). For most theories this generalization amounts to there being no modal/generic operator present or to the indefinite taking wide scope relative to such an operator.[4] If (1b) and (4b) must entail existence in the actual world in order for anaphora to be possible, the bare plural is not in the scope of a generic operator.

The third argument is based on the scopal interaction between the bare plural and overt quantificational adverbs and modals. The universal force of the bare plural persists even when an overt adverb of quantification with non-universal force is present, which shows that the bare plural is not bound by the adverb of quantification. (6b) is about the totality of the contextually relevant students while the adverb of quantification has a temporal reading.[5]

(6) a. In 1985 there was a ghost haunting the campus.
b. Students were usually aware of this fact.
c. Most students were aware of this fact.

Since its interpretation does not depend on the adverb of quantification, the bare plural of (6b) must outscope it. If the bare plural were within the scope of the adverb of quantification, it would be bound by it and (6b) would appear synonymous with (6c), contrary to fact.

Adverbs like *normally* or *typically* are generic operators and can be used as diagnostics for a true generic reading because they cannot be stripped of their modal force. When they are added to examples like (1), they can lead to infelicity, as in (7).

(7) a. In 1985 there was a ghost haunting the campus.
b. (#)Normally/Typically students were aware of the danger.

On the infelicitous reading of (7b), the bare plural picks out the totality of the contextually relevant students in the actual world. (7b) is infelicitous to the extent that the quantification induced by the generic operator is vacuous; quantification is vacuous because the bare plural is not within the operator's scope.[6] (7b) may also have an interpretation in which the bare plural is within the scope of the generic operator, but in that case the bare plural is not contextually restricted, and no claim is made about the actual students associated with the campus during the time of

[4]Except if modal subordination is involved (Karttunen 1976, Roberts 1989).

[5]In fact, because the adverb of quantification has a temporal reading the sense of *be aware* shifts to *be consciously aware* in (6b) so that the predicate can be interpreted as temporally relativizable.

[6]Unlike modals, generic operators cannot quantify only over possible worlds.

the ghost's appearance. The generic operator can also be interpreted as quantifying over temporally individuated situations. In that case, the bare plural outscopes the operator and exhibits the functional reading, a situation parallel to that of (6b).

The functional reading surfaces with modals as well, when the bare plural takes wide scope with respect to the modal. (8b) has a reading in which the students are taken to be the actual students on campus.

(8) a. A ghost is haunting the campus.
b. Students should be aware of the danger.
c. Unfortunately, they are not.

The anaphora in (8c) is possible precisely because (8b) entails the existence of students in the actual world.

To sum up, the evidence presented argues that the functional reading cannot be explained away as an entailment or an implicature of a generic generalization. Rather, it must be recognized as the actual interpretation of the bare plural.

2.4 Contextual Restrictions

On its functional reading a bare plural can be contextually restricted, in contrast to a bare plural within the scope of adverbial operators. In this section I show that bare plurals not only can but must be contextually restricted on their functional reading. I call this effect the POSITIVE CONTEXTUAL SENSITIVITY of the functional reading. However, the functional reading systematically excludes certain types of contextual restrictions. I call this effect the NEGATIVE CONTEXTUAL SENSITIVITY of the functional reading.

NPs are often dependent on the context of utterance to supply information that determines their interpretation either by restricting their domain of quantification or by providing an additional condition for their descriptive content. The role that the context plays in restricting the interpretation of NPs may be viewed either as a purely pragmatic phenomenon, or as the result of an interplay between semantics and pragmatics: the semantics makes available a certain parameter whose value is determined by pragmatic factors, such as saliency, discourse coherence, etc. Under either view, whether an NP in a given context of utterance is interpreted as contextually restricted or not, or which contextual restrictions are chosen, depends solely on pragmatic considerations.

Bare plurals with the functional reading are different in this respect: the implicit contextual restrictions on the bare plural are part of its meaning as they not cancellable. The discourse in (9) is contradictory.

(9) a. In 1985 a ghost was haunting the campus.
b. Students were aware of the danger.
c. However, none of the students associated with the campus was aware of the danger.

If the bare plural is construed as having a generic reading, no contradiction arises, as in (10).

(10) a. A ghost is haunting the campus.

b. In general, students are aware of this kind of danger.

c. However, none of the students associated with the campus is aware of this kind of danger.

For indefinites, in general, there might be a preference for a contextually restricted reading, which, however, can always be overridden if, for instance, it leads to contradiction. The discourse in (11), for example, is perfectly coherent.

(11) a. In 1985 a ghost was haunting the campus.

b. Some students were aware of the danger.

c. None of the students associated with the campus was aware of the danger.

Although the indefinite in (11b) can, in principle, be interpreted as contextually restricted with the contextual restrictions contributed by (11a), the presence of (11c) rules out this kind of interpretation. The crucial point is that the meaning of the indefinite in (11b) is such that it is compatible with any number of contextual restrictions, or none at all, while that of the bare plural in (9b) requires a specific kind of contextual restriction.

Not only should the bare plural be contextually restricted but the contextual restrictions must be provided by the discourse prior to the utterance of the bare plural. Consider the difference between the discourses in (12) and (13).[7]

(12) a. A burglar was roaming Santa Clara county.

b. Deputy sheriffs were aware of the danger.

c. #They had been sent from LA county to investigate.

(13) a. A burglar was roaming Santa Clara county.

b. Several deputy sheriffs were aware of the danger.

c. They had been sent from LA county to investigate.

The same point is also made by cases in which the sentence containing a bare plural is first in a discourse with the NP that can provide the contextual restrictions in the following sentence, as in (14).

(14) a. Students were roaming the streets.

b. A school nearby had ended classes early.

In that case, the bare plural has only an existential reading although the next sentence can, and in fact does, provide additional restrictions for it.

Necessary as the contextual restrictions may be for the functional reading to arise, not any contextual restriction is possible. (15c) still expresses the same generalization as (1b) in the context of (15a) and (15b), not the more contextually restricted one corresponding to *every student in this dormitory*, although the context provides the information for the extra restriction.[8] This reading is easily available for the definite in (15d) and the quantificational NP in (15e).

---

[7]I owe these examples to Tony Davis.

[8]Admittedly, a discourse comprised of (15a), (15b) and (15c) sounds incohesive. Rather than being at odds with the point being made here, this can be taken as further support for it, since the more contextually restricted reading is absent even when discourse cohesiveness would require it. Such a discourse would in any case improve if it were followed by something that would justify the shift from one group of students to the other, e.g., *The students of the dormitory have, moreover, taken strict precautions*.

(15) a. There is a ghost haunting the campus.
b. There are 500 students in this dormitory.
c. Students are aware of the danger.
d. The students are aware of the danger.
e. Every student is aware of the danger.

Similarly, in a deictic context, like that of (16), the bare plural receives the same reading as (1b), not the more contextually restricted one picking out the perceptually salient students.

(16) Context: We know that there is a ghost haunting the campus. We are standing in front of the library and we can both see several students.
Students are afraid to enter the library.

While the perceptually salient students can be taken as providing the evidence for the generalization, the generalization is not restricted to them as far as the meaning of (16) is concerned. (16) can also be taken as evidence that referential use of the bare plural is not sufficient for the functional reading to arise.[9] That it is not necessary is shown by all the examples considered so far.

2.5 The Presupposition of Existence

A bare plural on its functional reading implies existence in the actual world, without, however, asserting existence. If it did, it would have an existential reading. Rather, a bare plural with the functional reading presupposes existence, which means that it can be taken for granted that entities satisfying the descriptive content of the NP plus the additional contextual restrictions exist in the actual world.

That students with police connections exist is a precondition for a felicitous utterance of (17b) and of the negated (17c) and must be taken for granted by the discourse participants.

(17) a. In 1985 there was a ghost haunting the campus.
b. Students with police connections were aware of the danger.
c. Students with police connections were not aware of the danger.

Moreover, the contextual restrictions are part of what is presupposed. What must be taken for granted for a felicitous utterance of (17b) or (17c) is not simply the existence of students with police connections at large, nor the existence of such students on some campus or other, but the existence of students on the campus that makes (17a) true.

The fact that the implicit contextual restrictions are part of the presuppositional content of the bare plural explains why the information contributed by them is not cancellable, as shown by (9) and (12), and why they are only provided by prior discourse, as shown by (12) and (14).

An interesting contrast arises when the bare plural is construed with a stage-level predicate, which allows for either the existential reading or the functional reading.

[9]See Ludlow & Neale (1991), who develop a taxonomy of the distinct uses of indefinites and characterize the corresponding utterance contexts.

If the bare plural in (2) is interpreted existentially, the existence of opponents of the proposal need not be taken for granted for a felicitous utterance of (2). If, on the other hand, the bare plural receives the functional reading, the existence of opponents of the proposal must be taken for granted for a felicitous utterance of (2).

A central characteristic of presuppositions, and one that distinguishes them from assertions, is that they are inherited, possibly in a modified form, by complex constructions containing the presupposition-triggering element. I will concentrate here on one-case conditionals since I am focusing on the functional reading in non-quantificational contexts.

Indeed, the existential presupposition associated with the bare plural on its functional reading is projected in the usual fashion in conditional sentences, as in (18a) and (18b).

(18) a. If students with connections in the police department are aware of the danger, they will inform the rest.

b. If a ghost is present on the campus, students with police connections are aware of the danger.

c. If a ghost is present on the campus, there are students with police connections

In (18a), where the bare plural is in the antecedent, the presupposition that there are students with connections in the police department is inherited by the whole conditional, as expected. (18b), where the bare plural is in the consequent, also seems to presuppose that there are students with connections in the police department. Although the predicted presupposition for (18b) is a weaker one, namely the proposition expressed by (18c) (Karttunen & Peters 1979, Heim 1983), the stronger presupposition is associated with the conditional under the assumption that the presence of a ghost makes no difference one way or another with respect to the existence of students with police connections on the campus.

2.6 Bare Plurals in Greek

Can the functional reading of bare plurals be derived from some other distinguishing property that they have, like having no overt determiner or their homogeneity of reference? While these roperties may be necessary, they are not sufficient, on empirical grounds. Bare plural indefinite NPs in Greek have no overt determiner and are homogeneous in reference but they nevertheless lack the functional reading.

The familiar contrast between the aspectual effects of bare plurals and other types of NPs (Carlson 1977, Dowty 1979) shows up in Greek as well:

(19) a. #I Maria skotone merika kounelia epi dio ores.
the Mary killed-IMP some rabbits for two hours
'Mary killed some rabbits for two hours.'

b. I Maria skotone kounelia epi dio ores.
the Mary killed-IMP rabbits for two hours
'Mary killed rabbits for two hours.'

(20) a. I Maria skotose merika kounelia mesa se pende lepta.
the Mary killed-PERF some rabbits in five miniutes
'Mary killed some rabbits in five minutes.'

b. #I Maria skotose kounelia mesa se pende lepta.
the Mary killed-PERF rabbits in five miniutes
'Mary killed rabbits in five minutes.'

Bare plural indefinite NPs, however, do not have universal force except when in the scope of an operator and do not exhibit the functional reading. The bare plural gets an existential reading with the individual-level predicate in (21b)[10] and this is its only possible interpretation in this context.

(21) a. Ena fandasma trigirizi sto panepistimio.
a ghost wanders in-the university
'A ghost is haunting the campus.'

b. Fitites ehoun ip opsin tous ton kindino.
students have under view their the danger
'There are students who are aware of the danger.'

Bare plurals do not exhibit the functional reading with stage-level predicates either. The bare plural in (22) has only an existential reading.

(22) Andipali tou ipopsifiou ipostiriksan pos ...
Opponents the-GEN candidate-GEN claimed that
'There were opponents of the candidate who claimed that ...'

This provides one more argument that the functional reading cannot be the result of some pragmatic factors since those would come into play in Greek as much as in English. Thus, an analysis of the functional reading should be such that this cross-linguistic variation can be easily stated.

2.7 Summary

A successful analysis of the functional reading must account for the universal force of the bare plural in the absence of an operator, the occurrence of the reading with both individual-level and stage-level predicates, the apparent synonymy of the bare plural with the definite in certain contexts, the positive and negative contextual sensitivity, and the presence of the existential presupposition.

An obvious possibility is to say that the bare plural is ambiguous between an indefinite and a definite interpretation. After all, it appears to be in free variation with the corresponding definite in certain contexts, and it has an existential presupposition, the hallmark of definiteness. However, one important observation is that the bare plural never has an anaphoric reading, that is a definite reading where an explicit antecedent is available. Putting together the evidence from the presupposition facts and the negative contextual sensitivity facts, we arrive at the following generalization: a bare plural on its functional reading is associated with an existential presupposition but it is never anaphoric. In fact, it is in free variation with the corresponding definite only when the definite is neither anaphoric nor deictic.[11]

The real challenge, therefore, is to account for the properties of the functional reading while maintaining that the bare plural is an indefinite NP. The question then

[10]This is in general possible in Greek.

[11]I use 'anaphoric' and 'deictic' as descriptive terms. The analysis of definites by Kamp (1981) and Heim (1982) makes all definites anaphoric semantically, even those that one would not characterize this way on descriptive grounds.

is in what way the theory of indefiniteness should be revised in order to accommodate the functional reading. I will take the novelty theory of indefiniteness proposed by Heim (1982) as the starting point, but along the way I will have to modify it in certain crucial respects. Bare plurals in English are indefinite descriptions which always require a novel index, but which can be felicitous in a wider range of contexts than standard indefinites.

3 The Novelty Theory of Indefiniteness

Heim's (1982) novelty/familiarity analysis of (in)definiteness is couched within a theory of meaning in which the meaning of a linguistic element is specified in terms of the effect it has on a given body of information. Extending proposals by Stalnaker (1979), Heim construes this body of information as a file and specifies the interpretation of definite and indefinite NPs in terms of their file change potential. One of the advantages of this conception of meaning is that both the assertive and the presuppositional content of a given element can be formulated in terms of the same theoretical construct, i.e., the file. Assertions update files, whereas presuppositions are checks on files.

Specifically, files are construed as pairs consisting of a set of natural numbers, called the domain of the file (Dom(F)), and a set of assignment function–possible world pairs, called the satisfaction set of the file (Sat(F)). Every file determines a proposition, construed as a set of worlds, called the world set of the file (W(F)); W(F) is the set of worlds in which the file is true. The file change potential of a formula ϕ is a possibly partial function from files to files (symbolized as $+\phi$), such that $\text{Dom(F)} \subseteq \text{Dom}(\text{F}+\phi)$ and $\text{Sat}(\text{F}+\phi) \subseteq \text{Sat(F)}$. The presuppositions ϕ may be associated with are construed as felicity conditions of ϕ with respect to a file specifying the conditions under which the function $+\phi$ is defined.

The felicity conditions associated with definite and indefinite NPs are covered by the Extended-Novelty-Familiarity-Condition, given in (23) (Heim 1982, 369–70).

(23) EXTENDED-NOVELTY-FAMILIARITY-CONDITION:
For ϕ to be felicitous with respect to a file F, for every NP_i in ϕ it must be the case that:

a. if NP_i is [–def], then $i \notin \text{Dom(F)}$

b. if NP_i is [+def], then $i \in \text{Dom(F)}$ and if NP_i is a formula,[12] F entails NP_i.

The Extended-Novelty-Familiarity-Condition contains an index condition for both definites and indefinites but a descriptive content condition only for definites. The descriptive content condition in (23b) captures the intuition that definites presuppose their descriptive content.[13] Although (23a) does not contain a statement that directly captures the intuition that indefinites assert their descriptive content,[14] this is a consequence of the novelty of their index, given a general condition that Heim imposes on files, Condition B, which is stated in (24) (Heim 1982, 304).

[12]This is to distinguish between pronouns, which correspond to variables, and descriptions, which correspond to open formulas.

[13]F entails NP_i iff $\text{Sat(F)} \subseteq \text{Sat}(\text{F}+\text{NP}_i)$ iff for every $\langle f, w\rangle \in \text{Sat(F)}$, $f(x_i) \in [\![\text{CN}]\!]_w$, where CN is the common noun predicate of the NP.

[14]This amounts to the following: in order for an indefinite NP_i to be felicitous with respect to a file F there must be some $w \in \text{W(F)}$ such that for every f and every $j \notin \text{Dom(F)}$ $f(x_j) \notin [\![\text{CN}]\!]_w$.

(24) For every file F, any world w and every $n \notin \text{Dom}(F)$: if f and g are two assignment functions that are alike except insofar as $f(x_n) \neq g(x_n)$, then $f \in \text{Sat}_w(F)$ iff $g \in \text{Sat}_w(F)$.

Condition B ensures that a file does not cross-reference to discourse referents not already introduced, or, in somewhat more technical terms, that a file does not impose conditions on a variable whose index is not in the domain. Coupled with the definition of truth for files it predicts that an indefinite not in the scope of an operator will always have existential force.

More generally, Heim's theory has the consequence that the entailment relation between a file and a formula is a strong one: for example, in order for a file F to entail some atomic formula ϕ it has to entail the propositional information carried by ϕ and it must have a fixed assignment for all indices in ϕ, in other words, ϕ must contain no novel indices. As a result, it makes the following predictions about non-quantificational NPs: (a) an NP asserts existence iff it introduces a new discourse referent, (b) an NP presupposes existence iff it is anaphoric on an already existing discourse referent.[15]

The evidence from the functional reading argues that we must allow for NPs which do not assert existence but introduce a new discourse referent. In order to allow for such NPs, we have to make room for a somewhat weaker entailment relation. This is the relation of a file entailing another file, discussed in the next section.

4 Strong and Weak Novelty

As we saw in section 2, a central fact about the functional reading is that the bare plural seems to presuppose existence without being anaphoric. Within the file change framework, this means that the file prior to the update with the bare plural must entail the descriptive content of the NP, without, however, having a fixed assignment for the index of the NP. Therefore, we should first make precise how exactly that entailment is to be formulated and then we should specify how the analysis of indefiniteness should be revised so as to allow for indefinites that are felicitous with respect to files entailing their descriptive content.

The new conception of a file F entailing the descriptive content of an NP that we need is roughly this: the file should entail that some individual has the property given by the common noun predicate of the NP without requiring that that individual correspond to any discourse referent. In more technical terms, all the worlds in the world set of F should be such that they contain some such individual (i.e., for every $w \in \text{W}(F)$ there is some f such that for some k $f(x_k) \in [\![\text{CN}]\!]_w$) but that individual is not the value for a variable with an index in Dom(F) (i.e., $k \notin \text{Dom}(F)$). For a file F to have this property it should satisfy the condition in (25).

(25) For every $\langle f, w \rangle \in \text{Sat}(F)$ there is some g agreeing with f on Dom(F) such that for some $k \notin \text{Dom}(F)$ $g(x_k) \in [\![\text{CN}]\!]_w$.

Updating F with NP_i will then result in no addition of propositional information (no elimination of worlds); the effect of the update with the indefinite will simply be to fix the assignment for its index (introduce a new discourse referent), which will

[15] If the NP is within the scope of an operator, then asserting and presupposing existence in the technical sense will not coincide with the intuitive sense.

result in the elimination of a class of assignment functions. The entailment relation then is such that $W(F)=W(F+NP_i)$ but $Sat(F)\not\subseteq Sat(F+NP_i)$.

More generally, if two files F and F_1 are such that they determine the same proposition, i.e., $W(F)=W(F_1)$, but may differ with respect to the variables they have a fixed assignment for, i.e., $Dom(F)\subseteq Dom(F_1)$ and $Sat(F)\not\subseteq Sat(F_1)$, then F entails F_1. The definition of this entailment relation is given in (26). See also Heim (1987, fn. 4).

(26) F entails F_1 iff for every $\langle f, w\rangle \in Sat(F)$ there is some g agreeing with f on Dom(F) such that $\langle g, w\rangle \in Sat(F_1)$.

Indefinites may then be distinguished according to whether they are felicitous with respect to files entailing their descriptive content in the sense specified above or not.[16] I call those indefinites that are felicitous with respect to such files WEAKLY NOVEL, and those indefinites that are not, STRONGLY NOVEL. A weakly novel indefinite is associated only with a felicity condition requiring the novelty of its index, as in (27). A strongly novel indefinite is associated with two felicity conditions, one requiring the novelty of its index and the other the novelty of its descriptive content, as in (28).

(27) For NP_i, where NP_i is weakly novel, to be felicitous with respect to a file F it must be the case that $i\notin Dom(F)$.

(28) For NP_i, where NP_i is strongly novel, to be felicitous with respect to a file F it must be the case that both (a) and (b) hold:

a. $i\notin Dom(F)$,

b. F does not entail $F+NP_i$.

Strongly novel indefinites are the standard indefinites covered by Heim's analysis. However, because we are now allowing for weakly novel indefinites, the felicity conditions of strongly novel indefinites have to be augmented by a condition requiring the novelty of their descriptive content.[17] Weakly novel indefinites, by contrast, are the indefinites whose existence is established in this paper and which motivate the revisions in the theory of indefiniteness.

The set of admissible files and the range of interpretations of a weakly novel indefinite will properly include those of a strongly novel indefinite. Any indefinite, whether weakly or strongly novel, updating a file not entailing its descriptive content will have an existential reading if not in the scope of an operator. This is guaranteed by (29b) below. A weakly novel indefinite updating a true file F that entails its descriptive content will not get an existential reading: if F entails the existence of individuals satisfying the descriptive content of the NP, then the file resulting from the update with the NP cannot fail to be true as long as the assignment to the variable with the index of the NP is to those individuals whose existence is entailed by F. The revised version of (24) given in (29).

(29) For every file F, any world w and any two assignment functions f and g that agree on Dom(F):

[16]For definites we can preserve Heim's analysis. Definites presuppose their descriptive content in the stronger sense of (23b): an admissible file F for a definite NP_i must entail NP_i and not just $F+NP_i$.

[17]Note that (28b) achieves exactly what the statement in fn. 14 requires.

a. if F entails some F_1, then if for every novel index $j \in Dom(F_1)$ there is some f' agreeing with f on every index except possibly on some $k \notin Dom(F)$ and there is some g' agreeing with g on every index except possibly on some $l \notin Dom(F)$ such that $f'(k)=g'(l)=h(j)$, where h is such that $h \in Sat_w(F_1)$, then $f \in Sat_w(F)$ iff $g \in Sat_w(F)$;

b. otherwise, $f \in Sat_w(F)$ iff $g \in Sat_w(F)$.

Note that we have preserved some of the intuition behind Condition B: a file cannot impose conditions on any particular index not in its domain but we have now allowed for a general (existential) statement over indices not in the domain.

5 The Functional Reading

Bare plurals in English are weakly novel NPs and differ therefore from standard indefinites, like the other indefinites in English or bare plurals in Greek, in that they impose a weaker requirement on files for felicity, namely all they require is that their index be novel with respect to the domain of the file. The standardly recognized interpretations of a bare plural, which are also those of a strongly novel indefinite, arise when it updates a file not entailing its descriptive content. The functional reading arises when it updates a file which entails its descriptive content.

What gives rise to files entailing the descriptive content of some indefinite NP? More concretely, let us see how the functional reading arises for the bare plural in (1b). Let (30a) and (30b) be the logical form representations of (1a) and (1b), respectively, and F the file obtained after the update with (30a).[18]

(30) a. $ghost(x_m)$ & $campus(x_j)$ & $haunt(x_m,x_j,x_l)$ & $in\text{-}1985(x_l)$

b. $students(x_i)$ & $be\text{-}aware(x_i,\phi)$

Given that it is part of general background knowledge that campuses have students, we can assume the existence of a function $s^{student}$ which assigns to each campus in the universe of discourse a set of individuals who are students on that campus.[19] Given the existence of such a function, the file F may be updated as in (31), whereby its domain remains unchanged and its satisfaction set is changed to include only pairs whose worlds are such that some set of individuals is the value of the function $s^{student}$ applied to the campus verifying (30a).

(31) $Dom(F_1) = Dom(F)$
$Sat(F_1) = \{\langle f, w\rangle \in Sat(F)$: there is some g agreeing with f on Dom(F) and some $k \notin Dom(F)$ such that $g(x_k) = s^{student}(f(x_j))$ in $w\}$

If $Sat(F_1)$ is non-empty, F_1 contains the information, not contained in F, that the campus verifying (30a) has students. Since for all worlds in the world set of

[18]I have given the predicate *be aware of* a formula as its second argument, assuming that it is a propositional attitude predicate even when its syntactic argument is an NP. The variables x_m, x_j and x_l are individual-denoting while the variable x_i is set-denoting. For the sake of simplicity I do not make a notational distinction in (30) between individual and set-denoting variables or between predicates having individuals and those having sets in their extension.

[19]Contextually salient functions of this type have been invoked for the analysis of E-type pronouns (Cooper 1979, Heim 1990, Chierchia 1992), interrogatives (Engdahl 1986, Ginzburg 1992), and indefinite NPs with the modifier *certain* (Hintikka 1986). We can assume that the existence of such a function is also responsible for satisfying the familiarity condition of the definite in (1c).

F_1 it holds that there is some set of individuals who are students on that campus, F_1 entails the descriptive content of the bare plural *students* (i.e., F_1 entails $F_1 + \mathit{students}(x_i)$) but it does not entail $\mathit{students}(x_i)$ since the assignment to x_i could be anything whatsoever.[20] In fact, F_1 entails the decsriptive content of the bare plural plus its implicit contextual restrictions, hence the positive contextual sensitivity of the functional reading.[21] F_1 can then be updated with (30b):

(32) $\mathrm{Dom}(F_2) = \mathrm{Dom}(F_1) \cup \{i\}$
$\mathrm{Sat}(F_2) = \{\langle f, w\rangle \in \mathrm{Sat}(F_1)$: $f(x_i) = s^{student}(f(x_j))$ and $f(x_i)$ is aware of the danger in $w\}$

How do we ensure that the function $s^{student}$ assigns to $f(x_j)$ the set containing all the students on $f(x_j)$? For this we can adopt a strategy used in effect by Gawron, Nerbonne & Peters (1991) and Chierchia (1992):[22] instead of assuming that there is a single $s^{student}$, let us assume that there is a family of such functions, each mapping a given campus to a different set of students on that campus. One of them will be such that it has as its value the set of all students on that campus. Under the additional assumption that the truth or falsity of what is said should be constant across different values of the functions $s^{student}$ for a given campus, the appropriate choice for $s^{student}$ should be that whose value is the set of all students on that campus.

The functional reading will only arise in contexts that provide enough information so as to make available a salient function relating one kind of individual to another kind of individual and to trigger the addition of information about the existence of certain individuals. Intuitively, therefore, a bare plural on its functional reading presupposes existence although it is not associated with a felicity condition requiring the entailment of its descriptive content.

The update from F to F_1 is the result of accommodation; it is the kind of informational accommodation[23] advocated by Heim (1982, 1983), except that the accommodation does not occur in order to satisfy the felicity conditions of some element. Rather, F is updated so that the resulting file can entail a certain piece of information because as discourse participants we are willing to take certain facts for granted , namely that if a world contains an entity of a certain kind (e.g., a campus) it will also contain an entity of another kind (e.g., students on that campus). This is of course a contingent fact—it is a property of some worlds but not of others—and that is why the update from F to F_1 is non-trivial.

References

Carlson, Gregory N. 1977. *Reference to Kinds in English.* Doctoral dissertation, University of Massachusetts, Amherst.

Chierchia, Gennaro. 1992. Anaphora and Dynamic Binding. *Linguistics and Philosophy* 15:111-183.

[20]If $\mathit{students}(x_i)$ is to be felicitous relative to F_1, then $i \notin \mathrm{Dom}(F_1)$.

[21]The negative contextual sensitivity is due to the non-anaphoricity of the bare plural, a consequence of the novelty of its index.

[22]Gawron, Nerbonne & Peters (1991) use it to get uniqueness for singular E-type pronouns, Chierchia (1992) for the universal reading of donkey-pronouns.

[23]This term is meant to distinguish this kind of accommodation from representational accommodation proposed by several recent works, which involves the addition of a certain piece of structure into a given representation.

Cooper, Robin. 1979. The Interpretation of Pronouns. *Syntax and Semantics 10: Selections from the Third Groningen Round Table*, eds. Frank Heny and Helmut S. Schnelle, 61–92. New York: Academic Press.

Dowty, David. 1979. *Word Meaning and Montague Grammar*. Dordrecht: Reidel.

Engdahl, Elizabet. 1986. *Constituent Questions*. Dordrecht: Reidel.

Gawron, Mark, John Nerbonne, and Stanley Peters. 1991. The Absorption Principle and E-Type Anaphora. CSLI Report No. CSLI–91–153 RR–91-12.

Gerstner, Claudia and Manfred Krifka. 1987. Genericity. To appear in Joachim Jacobs, Arnim von Stechow, Wolfgang Sternefeld and Theo Vennemann *Handbuch der Syntax*. Berlin: W. de Gruyter.

Ginzburg, Jonathan. 1992. *Questions, Queries and Facts: A Semantics and Pragmatics for Interrogatives*. Doctoral dissertation, Stanford University.

Heim, Irene R. 1982. *The Semantics of Definite and Indefinite Noun Phrases*. Doctoral dissertation, University of Massachusetts, Amherst.

Heim, Irene R. 1983. On the Projection Problem for Presuppositions. *Proceedings of the West Coast Conference in Formal Linguistics*, vol. 2, eds. Michael Barlow, Daniel. P. Flickinger, and Michael T. Westcoat, 114–125. Stanford Linguistics Association.

Heim, Irene R. 1987. Where Does the Definiteness Restriction Apply? Evidence from the Definiteness of Variables. *The Representation of (In)definiteness*, eds. Eric J. Reuland and Alice G. B. ter Meulen, 21–42. Cambridge: MIT Press.

Heim, Irene R. 1990. E-Type Pronouns and Donkey Anaphora. *Linguistics and Philosophy* 13:137–177.

Hintikka, Jaakko. 1986. The Semantics of *A Certain*. *Linguistic Inquiry* 17:331–336.

Kamp, Hans. 1981. A Theory of Truth and Semantic Representation. *Formal Methods in the Study of Language*, eds. Jeroen Groenendijk, Theo Janssen, and Martin Stokhof, 277–321. Amsterdam: Mathematisch Centrum.

Karttunen, Lauri. 1976. Discourse Referents. *Syntax and Semantics, vol. 7*, ed. James McCawley, 363–385. New York: Academic Press.

Karttunen, Lauri & Stanley Peters. 1979. Conventional Implicature. *Syntax and Semantics: Presupposition, vol. 11*, eds. Choon-Kyu Oh and David A. Dinnen, 1–56. New York: Academic Press.

Krifka, Manfred. 1987. Syntax and Semantics of Definite and Indefinite Generics. Partly in collaboration with Claudia Gerstner. Manuscript, Universität Tübingen.

Krifka, Manfred. 1990. Genericity: An Introduction. Manuscript, University of Texas at Austin.

Ludlow, Peter & Stephen, Neale. 1991. Indefinite Descriptions: In Defense of Russell. *Linguistics and Philosophy* 14:171–202.

Roberts, Craige. 1989. Modal Subordination and Pronominal Anaphora in Discourse. *Linguistics and Philosophy* 12:683–721.

Stalnaker, Robert C. 1979. Assertion. *Syntax and Semantics, Vol. 9: Pragmatics*, ed. Peter Cole, 315–332. New York: Academic Press.

Wilkinson, Karina. 1988. Genericity and Indefinite NPs. Manuscript, University of Massachusetts, Amherst.

Pharyngealization in Palestinian Arabic: The Implications for Feature Theory

STUART DAVIS
Indiana University

0. Introduction

Researchers in feature geometry such as Trigo (1991) and Goad (1991) have recently put forward the view that the feature retracted tongue root (henceforth, [RTR]) is dependent on the Pharynx Node. In this paper I argue based on data from the spread of pharyngealization in a dialect of Palestinian Arabic that the feature [RTR] can be a feature located under the Tongue Height Node (which is sometimes called the Tongue Position Node or Aperture Node). Such a node has been posited in a variety of very recent works in feature theory including Odden (1991), Wiswall (1991), Lahiri and Evers (1991), and Clements (1991). I will argue that the pharyngealized coronal phonemes of the Southern Palestinian dialect under consideration, which are shown in (1), have an underlying representation reflected in (2).

(1) /Ṭ/, /Ṣ/, /ð̣/[1]

(2) Proposed UR of a Pharyngealized Coronal (or Emphatic)

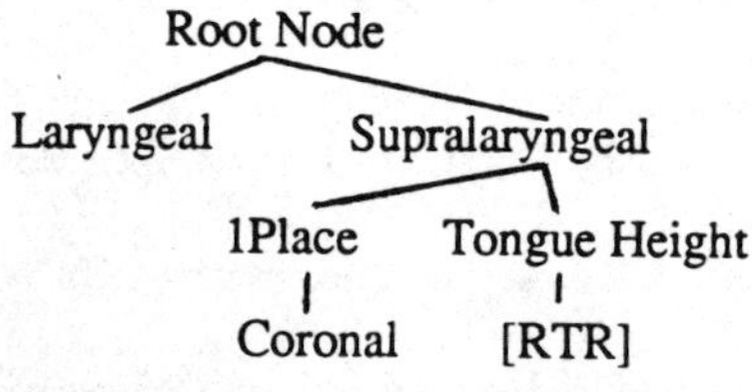

---

*I wish to thank Salman Al-Ani, Yasir Al-Mallah, Ellen Broselow, Daniel Dinnsen, Morris Halle, Elizabeth Hume, Jonni Kanerva, Yongsung Lee, Paul Newman, Mary Niepokuj, David Odden, and Elisabeth Selkirk for useful discussion and comments concerning various aspects of this paper. Any errors in this paper are my responsibility.

[1]Our discussion on pharyngealization will ignore the emphatic /Ṛ/. Younes (1991) has shown that /Ṛ/ is subject to several rules of depharyngealization that do not apply to the other emphatic consonants. Consequently, the patterns of pharyngealization spread from /Ṛ/ is different than the spreading patterns of the other emphatics.

I will support the representation in (2) for the pharyngealized coronals of Palestinian Arabic based on evidence from the spread of pharyngealization, from the nature of phonotactic constraints among root consonants, and from cinefluorographic film of Arabic emphatic consonants reported in the phonetics literature. All three types of evidence converge to support a representation like that in (2). However, I will also argue that at some stage in the derivation the emphatic consonants do acquire the Pharynx Node by redundancy rule so that a later representation of an emphatic consonant would be as in (3).

(3) Representation of a Pharyngealized Coronal

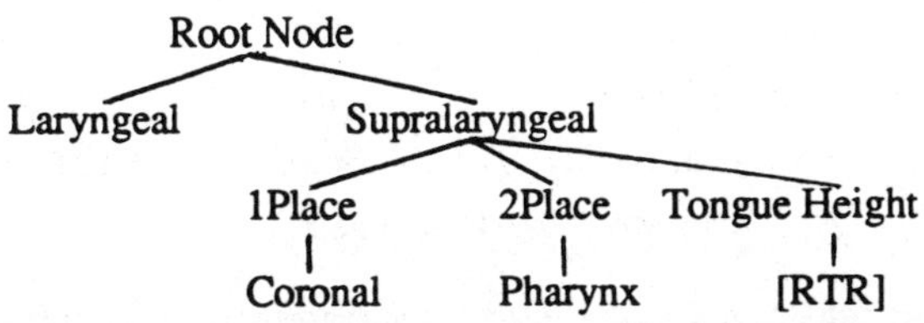

In the first section of this paper I present the data showing the patterns of pharyngealization spread in the Palestinian dialect under consideration. In the second section I present my analysis of the pharyngealization data and offer arguments supporting the view that the emphatic consonants underlyingly have the representation in (2) and later acquire the Pharynx Node as in (3). Finally, in the third section, I briefly discuss some implications that the proposed analysis has for feature theory.

1. Data

It is well known that in the Arabic dialects, pharyngealization spreads from an underlying emphatic consonant. The precise extent or domain of pharyngealization varies greatly among the dialects. On one extreme is a dialect such as Cairene Arabic as discussed in Schulte (1985) and Younes (1991), where (normally) if a word has an underlying emphatic consonant then the whole word is pronounced as pharyngealized. On the other extreme is a dialect such as Abha Arabic spoken in Saudi Arabia and discussed by Younes (1991) where pharyngealization only spreads to an immediately preceding or following low vowel. Many other dialects fall between these two extremes. Moreover, in some of these other dialects pharyngealization may be blocked by the presence of certain phonemes. What is very interesting is that in several Arabic dialects, phonemes that block the spread of pharyngealization only do so in one direction but not in the other. One such dialect where this phenomenon occurs is Palestinian Arabic. Consider the data in (4) and (5) which reflects the speech of my consultant who is a speaker of a Southern Palestinian dialect. The data are similar to the Palestinian dialects examined by Card (1983) and Schulte (1985), but are different from the Northern Palestinian dialect of Herzallah (1990) and Younes (1991), though the right-to-left pharyngealization spread illustrated by the data in (4) seems to be characteristic of Palestinian Arabic in general. (The following conventions for transcription are used throughout this paper: The underlying pharyngealized phonemes are indicated with a dot underneath. The surface pharyngealized sounds are indicated in capital letters, and the surface nonpharyngealized sounds are shown in small letters. The symbol /j/ represents a voiced palatoalveolar affricate.)

(4) Words displaying the leftward spread of pharyngealization

a. BALLAAṢ	"thief"	e. MANAAFIḌ̣	"ashtrays"
b. ħAḌḌ	"luck"	f. XAYYAAṬ	"tailor"
c. ?ABSAṬ	"simpler"	g. TAMŠII ṬA	"hair styling"
d. BAAṢ	"bus"	h. ʕAṬšaan	"thirsty"

(5) Words displaying the rightward spread of pharyngealization

a. ṢABAAħ	"morning"	e. Ṭiin-ak	"your mud"
b. ?AṬFAAL	"children"	f. ṢAyyaad	"hunter"
c. ṬUUB-AK	"your blocks"	g. ʕA Ṭ šaan	"thirsty"
d. ṬWAAL	"long (pl.)"	h. ḌAjjaat	"yell (pl.)"

The data in (4) illustrate that the leftward spreading of pharyngealization starts from the emphatic coronal consonant and extends to the beginning of the word. No phonemes block the leftward spread of pharyngealization. The data in (5) illustrate the rightward spread of pharyngealization. The words in (5a)-(5d) show that pharyngealization normally spreads rightward from the emphatic coronal consonant to the end of the word. However, the words in (5e)-(5h) show that the phonemes /i/, /y/, /š/ and /j/ block the rightward spread of pharyngealization.[2] These phonemes, though, fail to block the leftward spread of pharyngealization as shown by the words in (4e)-(4g).[3] It is incumbent upon any analysis of the data in (4) and (5) to account for the asymetry of the opaque segments. That is, an analysis must account for why phonemes like /i/, /y/, /š/, and /j/ block rightward spreading but fail to block leftward spreading.

---

[2]In Card's (1983) data it is only long /i/ and word-final /i/ that block the spreading. In her data, word internal instances of short /i/ are not opaque. In the speech of my consultant both long /i/ and short /i/ block rightward spreading. Examples of words in which short /i/ blocking rightward spreading include [Ṣinaaʕa] 'industry' and [Ṣiħħa] 'health'. Also, it is worth noting that Card did not investigate the blocking behavior of /j/. In the dialect of my consultant it patterns with /i/, /y/ and /š/ in that it blocks rightward spreading as in (5h) but fails to block leftward spreading as in [MAjAṢṢAṢiš] 'it did not solidify'.

[3]Card (1983) claims that the phonemes /i/, /y/, and /š/ do block the leftward spread of pharyngealiztion. However, the only relevant data that Card considered is the comparison of /š/ in the word /šaṬṬ/ 'shore' and /šatt/ 'become distracted'. Judging from her spectrograms, in these words the initial /š/ sounds are somewhat similar acoustically. One would need, though, a prefix on a word like /šAṬṬ/ to see if pharyngealization truly spreads leftward beyond the /š/. In this regard, Schulte (1985) notes that in her brief discussion of Palestinian Arabic (Jerusalem dialect) that /š/ does not seem to block rightward spreading as reflected by (4g), [TAMŠIIṬA]. Moreover, Younes (1991) notes that the phonemes /i/, /y/ and /š/ do not block the leftward spreading of pharyngealization, and, as noted, these phonemes do not block leftward spreading in the speech of my consultant. Consequently, Card's statement that certain phonemes block both leftward and rightward spread of pharyngealization may not be right.

2. Analysis and Evidence

2.1 The Rightward Spread of Pharyngealization

Let us first consider the data in (5) in which /i/, /y/, /š/, and /j/ act as a natural class in that they are opaque to the rightward spreading of pharyngealization. These sounds are all coronals and they can all be considered as [+high]. Such sounds could have the feature geometric representation in (6).

(6) Representation of /i/, /y/, /š/, and /j/[4] (Differences between these are not indicated.)

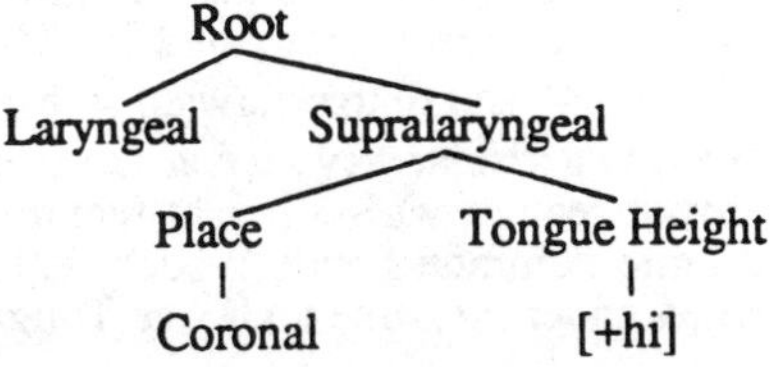

Now, it is well known from articulatory studies on the Arabic emphatic consonants by researchers such as Ali and Daniloff (1972) and Ghazeli (1977) that pharyngealized coronals involve to a great extent the retraction of the tongue root. This suggests that the pharyngealized coronals have the feature geometric representation in (7) with the feature [+RTR]. (The feature [RTR] was also used to characterize the emphatic consonants by Broselow (1979) in her study of Cairene Arabic.)

(7) Representation of a Pharyngealized Coronal

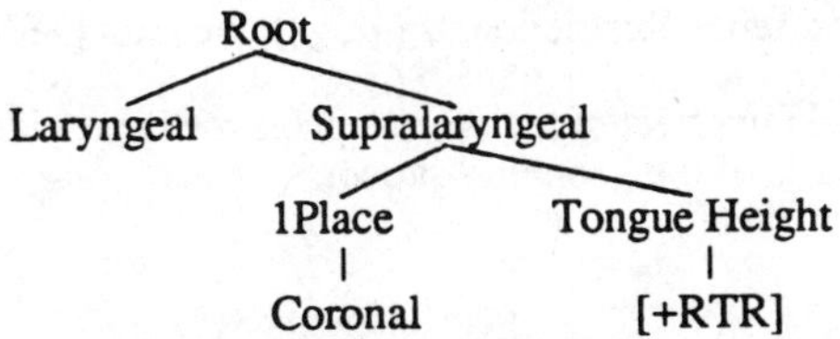

In (7), I represent [+RTR] as being under the Tongue Height Node rather than under the Pharynx Node as proposed by Trigo (1991) and Goad (1991). I will specifically argue for this representation in Section 2.1.2.

Given the representations in (6) and (7), there is a very clear reason why /i/, /y/, /š/, and /j/ function as opaque phonemes. They are subject to the feature cooccurrence restriction given in (8).

4The consonants /š/ and /j/ are not normally represented as [+hi] in feature geometric representations; rather, they are often represented with the feature [-anterior] under the coronal node. However, as Lahiri and Evers (1991) note, many languages have rules that convert dental or alveolar type sounds into palatoalveolars when before a high vowel. This suggests, then, that palatoalveolars like /š/ or /j/ may be represented with the feature [+high].

(8) Feature Cooccurrence Restriction on [+high] and [+RTR]:
If [+high], then not [+RTR]

Feature cooccurrence restrictions involving [+high] and [+RTR] (or [-ATR]) are discussed at length by Archangeli and Pulleyblank (1991). They show that a feature cooccurrence restriction like that in (8) is phonetically grounded in that the raising of the tongue for the feature [+high] is antagonistic to the backing of the tongue required for the feature [+RTR] (or [-ATR]). Numerous examples can be cited from a wide variety of languages in which such restrictions play an important role. One example would be Yoruba vowel harmony as analyzed by Archangeli and Pulleyblank (1989) where the [-ATR] (or [+RTR]) feature of a vowel can only spread to a vowel that is [-high]. Another example would be Salentino Italian metaphony as discussed by Calabrese (1988) in which a filter is posited that prevents the cooccurrence of the features [+high] and [-ATR] on the same phoneme. The opaqueness of /i/, /y/, /š/, and /j/ to rightward spreading as reflected in the data in (5) can be understood in a similar way. It constitutes another example of the interaction of a tongue root feature with a height feature. The fact that cooccurrence restrictions are quite common between such features constitutes evidence that they are represented under the same node, the Tongue Height Node shown in (6) and (7).

Given the feature cooccurrence restriction in (8), the rule of Rightward Spread can be formulated as in (9).

(9) Rightward Spread
- a. Trigger: Pharyngealized coronals /Ṭ/, /Ṣ/, /ð̣/
- b. Target: Any Phoneme
- c. Operation: Spread the feature [+RTR]
- d. Direction: Left-to-Right (i.e., rightward)
- e. Domain: word
- f. Mode: Unbounded
- g. Feature Cooccurrence Restriction: if [+high], then not [+RTR]

A derivation showing the blocking effect of the opaque phoneme is provided in (10), with only the relevant parts of the geometry shown.

(10)
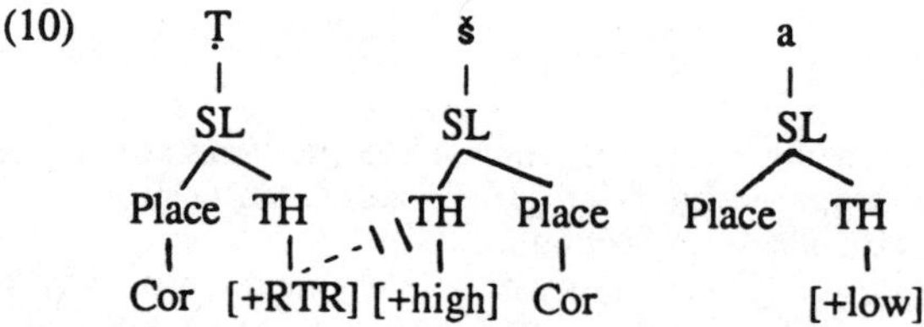

Given the cooccurrence restriction in (8), the [+RTR] feature of the /Ṭ/ is prevented from spreading to the /š/, and thus due to locality, cannot spread beyond it to the following low vowel. On the other hand, with words like those in (5a-d) where there are no underlying [+high] phonemes, the rule of Rightward Spread extends to the end of the word.[5]

---

[5]This crucially assumes that /w/ and /u/ are specified for [+back] and not for [+high]. Alternatively, though, one can view the feature cooccurrence restriction in (8) as pertaining to [+high] sounds that are coronals.

2.1.2 Evidence for the location of [RTR]

Now, in the analysis of the rightward spreading of pharyngealization that I have offered in the previous section, the feature [RTR] is represented as being located under the Tongue Height Node, as seen in (7). This is contrary to the recent proposals of Trigo (1991) and Goad (1991) in which [RTR] is a feature dependent on the Pharynx Node. Instead of (7), one can posit that the pharyngealized coronals have the representation in (11) with a secondary place or V-Place Pharynx Node. (I am not concerned here with the specific relationship holding between primary and secondary place.)

(11) Representation of a Pharyngealized Coronal

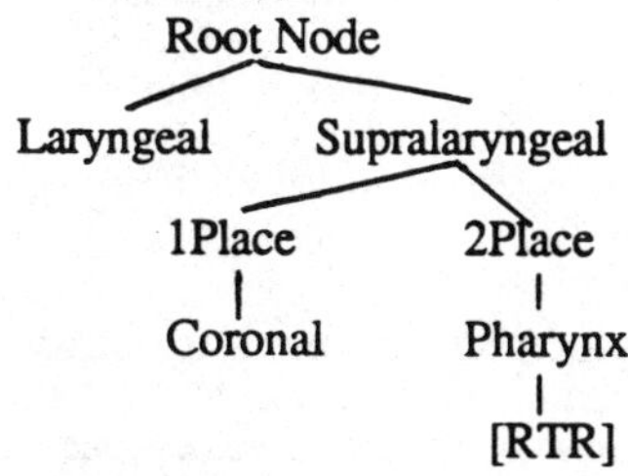

While seemingly the representation in (11) and (7) are equally as adequate in capturing the rightward pharyngealization patterns as shown in data like in (5), I offer three arguments that (7), where [RTR] is under the Tongue Height Node, is the more accurate underlying representation of the emphatics.

The first argument centers on the nature of the feature cooccurrence restriction in (8) that disallows [+RTR] from spreading onto a phoneme that is [+high]. A cooccurrence constraint between two features, such as [+RTR] and [+hi] is suggestive of, but not proof of, those two features being dominated by the same node. In fact, Goad (to appear) contends that a negative constraint between two features like that in (8) means that those two features are in a complementary relation dominated by the same node. Consequently, the nature of the restriction in (8) is at least quite suggestive that [+high] and [+RTR] are under the same node. Now, given that [high] is not a feature dependent on the Pharynx Node, then, if [high] and [RTR] are under the same node, they would be located under the Tongue Height Node.

A more compelling argument for pharyngealized coronals having the underlying representation in (7) comes from the nature of the cooccurrence restrictions on root consonants. As Greenberg (1950) and McCarthy (1991) have observed, Arabic has a number of morpheme structure conditions that disfavor roots containing consonants that are articulated with the identical place articulator. So, for example, Arabic roots tend not to contain more than one labial consonant or more than one velar consonsant. McCarthy notes that this constraint also holds for sounds made with the Pharynx Node. Thus, for example, one tends not to find a true pharyngeal consonant cooccurring in the same root with another true pharyngeal; also one tends not to find true pharyngeal consonants in the same roots with laryngeal consonants or with (most) uvular consonants. However, pharyngealized coronals do cooccur with the true pharyngeals and laryngeals. McCarthy, who views the pharyngealized coronals as having a secondary place Pharynx Node, is thus forced to restrict the constraint to sounds having the primary place Pharynx Node. Given the representation in (7), though, it follows automatically that the emphatic sounds would not participate in root cooccurrence constraints with true pharyngeals since emphatics lack the Pharynx Node.

Now, while pharyngealized coronals do not normally participate in root cooccurrence constraints with true pharyngeal sounds, Herzallah (1990) notes a restriction that prevents the coocurrence of a [+continuant] emphatic to the left of a back velar in the same root. This restriction, illustrated by the data in (12), also pertains to the Southern Palestinian dialect of my consultant. The initial consonant in (12a) and the interdental in (12b) are arguably underlyingly pharyngealized coronals. They are represented as such in the orthography, but more importantly they are pronounced as emphatic in speech of high style as well as in other dialects. This means that the word-initial underlying emphatic in (12a) and the interdental in (12b) depharyngealize as a result of the presence of the back velar later in the word. The back velar sounds which trigger depharyngealization are given in (13).

(12) a. /Ṣadaga/ -----> [sadaga] "charity"
b. /ʔað̣yag/ -----> [ʔaðyag] "narrowest"

(13) /x/, /ɣ/, /g/

However, this depharyngealization only occurs if the pharyngealized coronal is to the left of the back velar. When the emphatic is to the right of the back velar, the expected leftward spread of pharyngealization takes place. This is shown by the data in (14).

(14) a. /maxxaṬ/ -----> [MAXXAṬ] "he blew his nose"
b. /xabaṢ/ -----> [XABAṢ] "mix randomly"

The question that arises then is if pharyngealized coronals have the representation in (7) without a Pharynx Node why do they seem to participate in an OCP (Obligatory Contour Principle) type delinking just with the back velars. Insight into a possible answer to this question comes from Goad's (1989) analysis of flattening or pharyngealization in the Athapascan language Chilcotin. According to Goad (1989), Chilcotin has two types of dorsal sounds; one triggers flattening of an adjacent vowel and the other does not. The dorsal sound that triggers flattening are uvulars. Goad characterizes these as having the feature [+RTR]. The [+RTR] feature of the uvular then spreads to an adjacent vowel. Similarly, I would posit that the back velars in (13), which are historically uvulars, have the feature [+RTR] underlyingly. Given this view, then, an OCP-type constraint disallowing two [+RTR] consonants within the same root becomes relevant. In each of the underlying representations shown in (12) and (14) there is a back velar and a pharyngealized coronal both of which would have the [+RTR] feature. Whenever two [+RTR] consonants cooccur in the same root the leftmost of the two [+RTR] features delinks. This is seen clearly in (12a) where, given the representation in (7) for pharyngealized coronals, the delinking of the [+RTR] feature on the /Ṣ/ results in it becoming [s]. The rule of rightward spread would not subsequently apply in (12a) since /Ṣ/ loses its [+RTR] feature. Moreover, there is no subsequent pharyngealization of any type since the [+RTR] back velar in (12a) is not a trigger for pharyngealization. Furthermore, the data in (14) are handled in an identical manner. In (14b), for example, the back velar /x/ and the /Ṣ/ are both underlyingly [+RTR] in the same root. The OCP applies delinking the [+RTR] feature of the initial /x/. However, since the word-final /Ṣ/ does not lose its [+RTR] feature, leftward spreading will apply so that the initial /x/ will surface as pharyngealized. Derivations for (12a) and (14b) are summarized in (15) and (16).

(15) Proposed derivation of (14a)

a. Underlying Representation (note: /Ṣ/ and post velar /g/ are both [+RTR])	/Ṣadaga/
b. OCP: Delink the leftmost of two adjacent [+RTR] features	sadaga
c. Rightward Spread (9)	DNA
d. Leftward Spread	DNA
e. Phonetic Representation	/sadaga/

(16) Proposed derivation of (15b)

a. Underlying Representation	/xabaṢ/	
b. OCP: Delink the leftmost of two adjacent [+RTR] feature	xabaṢ	(/x/ loses its RTR feature)
c. Rightward Spreading (9)	DNA	
d. Leftward Spreading	XABAṢ	
e. Phonetic Representation	[XABAṢ]	

There are several advantages to this analysis. Firstly, there is no need for ordering the OCP effect between the rules of Leftward Spread and Rightward Spread as in Herzallah's (1990) analysis (which I do not detail here because of space limitations). The OCP constraint prohibiting the appearance of two [+RTR] consonants in the same root comes into play at the beginning of the derivation. Secondly, this analysis captures what is special about the back velars in Palestinian; they are [+RTR]. Notice that in dialects where the corresponding sounds of (13) are not back velars (in many dialects they are uvulars or glottals), there are no restrictions involving these and the emphatics. That is, the underlying /Ṣ/ in (12a) surfaces as such in other dialects. Finally, we neatly account for why cooccurrence restrictions only occur between the emphatics and post velars and not between emphatics and pharyngeals or laryngeals. Emphatics do not have a Pharyngeal Node, as proposed in (7), and the restriction holding between pharyngealized coronals and post velars involve the feature [+RTR].

There is one further argument that supports the representation in (7) for the pharyngealized coronals. The argument comes from various phonetic studies that examined the actual articulation of the emphatic sounds of Arabic. Several of these studies have concluded that the pharyngealization of the emphatic sounds in Arabic is completely implemented by the retraction of the tongue root.

Ghazeli (1977:68-76) did a cinefluorographic study of Southern Tunisian Arabic. This dialect is similar (though not identical) to the Palestinian dialect under consideration in its patterns of rightward spreading and leftward spreading. Ghazeli observed that the articulatory gesture involved in the articulation of a pharyngealized coronal included a secondary articulation that consisted of '...a rearward movement of the back of the tongue towards the back wall of the pharynx...' He also noted for the emphatics that, "...there is no contraction of the laryngopharynx such as that observed during the pharyngeal consonants [ħ] and [ʕ]... [n]either is there an upward displacement of the larynx that can be attributed to pharyngealization..."

Ali and Daniloff (1972) even went as far as rejecting the terms pharyngealization or velarization for Arabic emphatic consonants because, in their cinefluorographic study of Iraqi Arabic, the pharyngeal constriction was implemented almost completely by the rearward movement of the tongue root, with the back wall of the pharynx and the velum not playing and significant role.

I would take the results of such studies as constituting articulatory evidence for the proposal in (7). Arabic pharyngealization seems to be implemented primarily by the retraction of the tongue root and not by movements of the larynx and/or pharyngeal wall. This is captured by the representation in (7) which, as I have tried to argue in this section, is supported by both phonetic and phonological evidence.

2.2 The Leftward Spread of Pharyngealization

The remaining question for the analysis posited so far is the following: if the feature co-occurrence restriction in (8) accounts for why the opaque phonemes /i/, /y/, /š/ and /j/ block the rightward spread of pharyngealization in Palestinian Arabic, how come these same phonemes fail to block the leftward spread of pharyngealization, as shown by the data in (4e)-(4g)? Our suggestion here is simple, the rule of Leftward Spread does not involve the spreading of the feature [+RTR], rather it involves the spreading of the secondary place Pharynx Node. The Pharynx Node would be specified by redundancy rule for any consonant that is [+RTR]. The redundancy rule would have to be ordered before the rule of Leftward Spread perhaps by something like Archangeli's (1984) Redundancy Rule Ordering Constraint. Thus, when the rule of Leftward Spread applies the pharyngealized coronal would have the representation in (17).

(17) Representation of a Pharyngealized Coronal

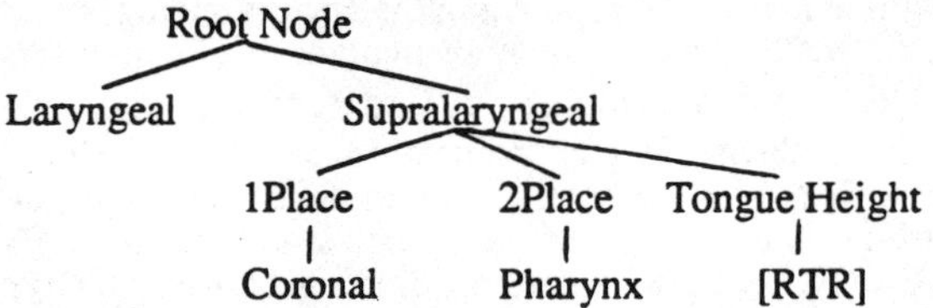

If Leftward Spread involves the spread of the secondary place Pharynx Node then no phonemes would block leftward spread. The feature cooccurrence restriction in (8) involves the feature [+RTR]. The Pharynx Node is not subject to a similar feature cooccurrence constraint. The rule of Leftward Spread can be formalized as in (18).

(18) Leftward Spread
- a. Trigger: Pharyngealized coronals /Ṭ/, /Ṣ/, /ð̣/
- b. Target: Any Phoneme
- c. Operation: Spread the secondary Place Node Pharynx
- d. Direction: Right-to-Left (i.e., leftward)
- e. Domain: word
- f. Mode: Unbounded
- g. Feature Cooccurrence Restriction: None

Some sample derivations are given in (19) and (20).

(19) Derivation of [ṬUUBAK] "your blocks"

Underlying Representation	/Ṭuubak/
Rightward Spread (9)	ṬUUBAK
Leftward Spread (18)	DNA
Phonetic Representation	[ṬUUBAK]

(20) Derivation of [ʕAṬšaan] "thirsty"

Underlying Representation	/ʕa Ṭ ša a n/
Rightward Spread (9)	blocked due to 9g
Leftward Spread (18)	ʕA Ṭ ša a n
Phonetic Representation	[ʕA Ṭ ša a n]

While admittedly, the arguments for leftward spreading involving the secondary Pharynx Node are not as strong as the arguments for rightward spreading involving the feature [+RTR], the analysis offered here does capture that the two spreading processes are different and are subject to different conditions. Moreover, while in my analysis the rule of Leftward Spread involves the redundant Pharynx Node, it is worth mentioning that it is not uncommon for a redundant feature to spread in assimilation processes. One can point to cases where nasal consonants trigger voicing assimilation or to weakening rules where perhaps some redundant feature of a vowel spreads to a following consonant.

Crucially, though, the above analysis provides a straightforward account for why phonemes like /i/, /y/, /š/, and /j/ are opaque to pharyngealization spread in one direction but not in the other. Rightward Spread involves the spreading of the feature [+RTR] while Leftward Spread involves the spreading of the Pharynx Node. Since the spreading processes are different, they are subject to different conditions. Thus, it is only the spread of [+RTR] which is subject to the cooccurrence restriction with the feature [+high] given in (8). The leftward spreading of the Pharynx Node is not subject to any condition.

3. Implications

There are several implications that the above analysis of Palestinian Arabic pharyngealization has for recent proposals in feature theory. One implication concerns the representation of opaque phonemes. Archangeli and Pulleyblank in various works show that the opacity of certain phonemes to spreading processes may be accounted for by a feature cooccurrence restriction rather than positing that the opaque phonemes have the opposite value of the spreading feature. Archangeli and Pulleyblank (1991) point out that feature cooccurrence restrictions involving [+RTR] (or [-ATR]) and [+high] are very common. Such restrictions are understandable because retracting the tongue root is antagonistic to a high tongue position. The Palestinian Arabic case then constitutes another example where the opacity of certain phonemes are accounted for by a feature cooccurrence restriction.

A second implication is that in Palestinian Arabic the feature [+RTR] can be under the Tongue Height Node rather than dominated by the Pharynx Node as posited in Trigo (1991) and Goad (1991). If [+RTR] were under the Pharynx Node for pharyngealized coronals then the leftward spread of the Pharynx Node for data like that in (4) would entail the spreading of the feature [+RTR]; and so the phonemes /i/, /y/, /š/ and /j/ would be predicted wrongly to block the leftward spread of pharyngealization. This problem does not arise in the present analysis in which [RTR] is under the Tongue Height Node. The leftward spread of the Pharynx Node does not entail the spread of the feature [+RTR].

Nonetheless, I do not want to propose that [RTR] is always located under the Tongue Height Node. Instead, I would posit that the location of [RTR] is parameterized; for some languages or dialects it is located under the Tongue Height Node while for other languages or dialects it is located under the Pharynx Node. For example, in Cairene Arabic discussed by Younes (1991) or in Moroccan dialectal Arabic discussed by Goad (1991), there are no opaque phonemes and spreading occurs both leftward and rightward throughout the word. Additionally, the root cooccurrence constraints are different than in Palestinian Arabic. This means that for Cairene Arabic and Moroccan Arabic there is no independent evidence for positing that [RTR] should be located under the Tongue Height Node. And, in these dialects, [RTR] is probably best analyzed as being under the Pharynx Node as in Goad (1991).

A third implication, somewhat indirect, relates to the work of Clements (1991) in which he posits an Aperture Node for tongue height. Clements's Aperture Node only dominates one feature, [open], but the feature [open] may appear simultaneously on several autosegmental tiers. Clements's model is shown in (21).

(21)

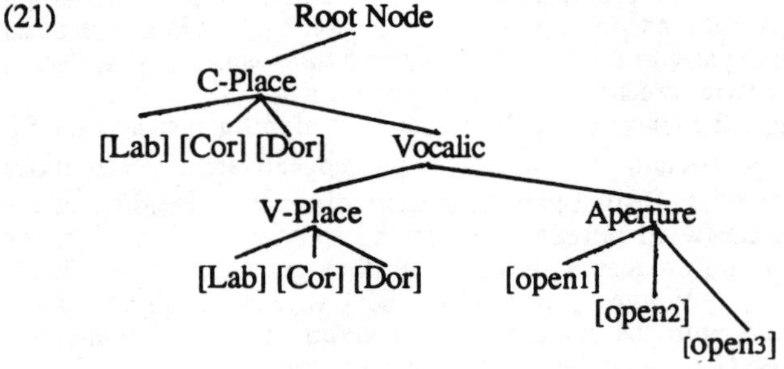

Crucially, on this view features like [high], [low], and [ATR] have no role. One possible problem with Clements's model, then, is that it becomes more difficult to express feature cooccurrence restrictions like that posited for Palestinian Arabic in (8) which, as Archangeli and Pulleyblank (1991) have shown, are quite common cross-linguistically. While it may be possible to express a restriction like that in (8) in Clements's model, the precise statement of a restriction like that in (8) would be dependent on the specific vowel inventory of the language because the nature of the vowel inventory determines how many instances of the feature [open] need to be present. To the extent that feature cooccurrence restrictions like that in (8) involving features like [high], [low], and [ATR] are common cross-linguistically, their expression presents a problem for Clements's model in which such features normally play no role.

In summary, I have argued for a representation of the pharyngealized coronals of Palestinian Arabic as in (7) in which the [+RTR] feature is located under the Tongue Height Node and where there is no separate Pharynx Node. Evidence supporting this representation comes from the nature of the phonemes that are opaque to pharyngealization spread, the types of root cooccurrence restrictions that are found in Palestinian Arabic, and the actual articulation of pharyngealized coronals which, according to work in the phonetics literature, largely involves the retraction of the tongue root without a contraction of the laryngopharynx as found in true pharyngeals. The main implications of the analysis is that it supports a view that phonemes can be opaque as a result of feature cooccurrence restrictions and it offers a case where the feature [RTR] is located under the Tongue Height Node rather than the Pharynx Node. In discussing this, I have proposed that the location of [RTR] in feature geometry is parameterized; in some languages or dialects it is a feature under the Tongue Height Node while in other languages or dialects it is located under the Pharynx Node.

References

Ali, L. and R. Daniloff. 1972. A Contrastive Cinefluorographic Investigation of the Articulation of Emphatic-Nonemphatic Cognate Consonants. *Studia Linguistica* 26:81-105.

Archangeli, D. 1984. *Underspecifcation in Yawelmani Phonology and Morphology*. Doctoral dissertation, MIT.

Archangeli, D. and D. Pulleyblank. 1989. Yoruba Vowel Harmony. *Linguistic Inquiry* 20:173-217.

Archangeli, D. and D. Pulleyblank. 1991. *Combinatorial Specification*. Unpublished ms., University of Arizona and University of British Columbia.

Broselow, E. 1979. Cairene Arabic Syllable Structure. *Linguistic Analysis* 5:345-382.

Calabrese, A. 1988. *Towards a Theory of Phonological Alphabets*. Doctoral dissertation, MIT.

Card, E. 1983. *A Phonetic and Phonological Study of Arabic Emphasis*. Doctoral dissertation, Cornell University.

Clements, G. 1991. Place of Articulation in Consonants and Vowels: A Unified Theory. *L'Architecture et la Géométrie des Représentations Phonologiques*, ed. B. Laks and A. Railland. Paris: CNRS.

Ghazeli, S. 1977. *Back Consonants and Backing Coarticulation in Arabic*. Doctoral dissertation, The University of Texas.

Goad, H. 1989. On the Feature [rtr] in Chilcotin: A Problem for the Feature Hierarchy. *Arizona Phonology Conference* 2:20-31.

Goad, H. 1991. [ATR] and [RTR] are Different Features. *West Coast Conference on Formal Linguistics* 10:163-173.

Goad, H. To appear. Dependency and Complementarity in Vowel Geometry. *The Linguistic Review* 8.

Greenberg, J. 1950. The Patterning of Root Morphemes in Semitic. *Word* 6:162-181.

Herzallah, R. 1990. *Aspects of Palestinian Arabic Phonology: A Non-linear Approach*. Doctoral dissertation, Cornell University.

Hoberman, R. 1989. Parameters of Emphasis: Autosegmental Analyses of Pharyngealization in Four Languages. *Journal of Afroasiatic Languages* 2:73-97.

Lahiri, A. and V. Evers. 1991. Palatalization and Coronality. *Phonetics and Phonology* 2:79-100.

McCarthy, J. 1991. *The Phonology of Semitic Pharyngeals*. Unpublished ms., University of Massachusetts.

Odden, D. 1991. Vowel Geometry. *Phonology* 8:261-289.

Schulte, M. 1985. *The Word and the Syllable in the Spread of Emphasis in Cairene Arabic*. Unpublished Masters paper, University of Arizona.

Trigo, L. 1991. On Pharynx-larynx Interactions. *Phonology* 8:113-136.

Wiswall, W. 1991. *Tunica Partial Vowel Harmony*. Paper presented at the Arizona Phonology Conference, University of Arizona.

Younes, M. 1991. *Emphasis Spread in Three Arabic Dialects*. Unpublished ms., Cornell University.

The Principle of Contrastiveness

HELEN DE HOOP
University of Groningen

0. Introduction

Whether an object in Dutch can scramble into the position before a sentential adverb or not seems to be dependent on several factors. One involves the characterization of NPs in terms of weakness and strength, as languages in which scrambling occurs exhibit a weak-strong effect. Another factor that restricts the possibilities of scrambling involves the contrastiveness of the predicate. These two generalizations can be combined into a universal semantic principle, the principle of contrastiveness, that also satisfactorily accounts for some other environments in which a distinction between weak and strong readings on NPs can be observed.

1. Scrambling and strong readings

In Dutch, definite or strong NPs may scramble freely, as is illustrated in (2), where the object has scrambled into the position before the adverb:

(1) dat Els gisteren de/alle/de meeste eenhoorns geaaid heeft
that Els yesterday the/all/most unicorns caressed has

(2) dat Els de/alle/de meeste eenhoorns gisteren geaaid heeft
that Els the/all/most unicorns yesterday caressed has
"that Els caressed the/all/most unicorns yesterday"

Furthermore, a weak NP can only scramble if it can get a strong reading. I use the term *strong reading* as a comprehensive term for referential/ specific, partitive, generic, and generic collective readings. I will briefly review those readings.

Fodor and Sag (1982) present evidence for a lexical ambiguity in indefinite NPs, contra the idea that indefinites always denote existential quantifiers. Consider (3):

(3) A horse of mine is pregnant

The indefinite NP in (3) can have either a referential or an existential reading. The existential reading just states that the set of pregnant horses of mine is not empty, whereas the referential reading refers to a specific individual, for instance, Shannon. In the latter case, the interpretation of the indefinite is comparable to the interpretation of a proper name or a demonstrative. I will not repeat the arguments of Fodor and Sag, but I think they convincingly show that indefinites can have a referential reading, although I do not agree with them that we are dealing with a lexical ambiguity. Instead, I assume that the ambiguity is a matter of different readings, probably triggered by syntactic factors.

A second type of a strong reading on a weak NP is the partitive reading of cardinals. It has been observed in the literature that determiners such as *some*, *many*, and the numerals, can have two readings, one of which is called weak or existential, the other one strong or partitive. Consider Milsark's (1977) example in (4):

(4) Some unicorns appeared on the horizon

On its existential reading, *some* is unstressed; on its partitive reading, the meaning of *some* can be paraphrased as *some of the*. Milsark observes that individual level predicates always trigger strong readings; in (5) *some unicorns* can only get a partitive reading, due to the individual level predicate:

(5) Some unicorns are white

More arguments can be provided which show that cardinal determiners are ambiguous between these two readings. Partee (1988) shows that in adjectival positions, only the existential reading arises:

(6) a. the many horses
b. the three horses

In Dutch, the adjectival character of *veel* 'many' is sometimes reflected in adjectival inflection; an example is given in (7):

(7) Els heeft vele eenhoorns geaaid
Els has many$_{+\text{infl}}$ unicorns caressed
"Els caressed many unicorns"

In (7) *vele* 'many' bears adjectival inflection and it strongly favours an existential reading. In general, adjectival inflection seems only appropriate in case of an existential reading.

Partee (1988) sketches a possible analysis of the two readings of *many* within the framework of D(iscourse) R(epresentation) T(heory). The existential reading follows if *many* is taken to be indefinite, consisting of a zero determiner and an adjective. The strong, quantificational reading is captured if *many* is treated as operator, just like strong determiners such as *every* and *most*. Such an analysis can be given for the two readings of all cardinals (not only *many*, but also *some* and the numerals).

Another instantiation of a strong reading is the so-called generic reading. English bare plurals, for instance, can receive either an existential or a generic reading, as observed by Carlson (1977). He notes that not all predicates allow both a generic and an existential reading for indefinites. Consider (8) and (9):

(8) Unicorns were eating grass
(9) Unicorns are white

In (8) the stage level predicate favours an existential reading on the bare plural subject, whereas the individual level predicate in (9) only allows a generic reading. If we take a generic reading to be a strong reading, then this is perfectly coherent with Milsark's principle that says that individual level predicates trigger strong readings on their subjects. For more arguments, I refer to De Swart (this volume).

A special case of a generic reading is constituted by generic cardinals (cf. Hoeksema 1983, Partee 1988). Some examples are given in (10):

(10) a. Ten boys can't form a soccer team
b. One swallow does not make a summer

Obviously, the cardinals in these constructions receive a weak, collective reading. Hoeksema analyzes them as adjectives interpreted as cardinality predicates of groups. This is in accordance with the observation that in Dutch, *veel* 'many' can bear adjectival inflection in this type of construction:

(11) Vele haartjes maken een borstel
many$_{+\text{infl}}$ hairs make a brush

If we conclude that the cardinals function as adjectives here, then the genericity of these constructions must be due to the zero determiner, just as in the case of bare plurals. So, the numeral gets a weak, cardinal reading, but the NP as a whole gets a strong, generic reading.

In environments where syntactic factors trigger strong readings on weak NPs, we find support for the use of *strong reading* as a comprehensive term. For instance, as was already noted, individual level predicates trigger strong readings on their subjects. In (12)-(15) all possible strong readings are triggered by individual level predicates. Note that the strong readings put between brackets are not the only possible strong readings. For example, the subject in (13) can also get a referential reading. But none of the subjects can get a weak, existential reading; this is due to the individual level predicate:

(12) A friend of mine is paleontologist *[referential]*
(13) Two fishes are black *[partitive]*
(14) Fishes are vertebrates *[generic]*
(15) Three fossils are more expensive than two *[generic collective]*

One other such context is constituted by object scrambling in Dutch. Scrambling an object into the position before the adverb triggers all possible strong readings:

(16) dat Els een (zekere) eenhoorn gisteren geaaid heeft *[referential]*
that Els a (certain) unicorn yesterday caressed has
(17) dat Els twee eenhoorns gisteren geaaid heeft *[partitive]*
that Els two unicorns yesterday caressed has
(18) dat Chris eenhoorns altijd tekent *[generic]*
that Chris unicorns always draws
(19) dat Chris tien eenhoorns altijd tekent *[generic collective]*
that Chris ten unicorns always draws

In conclusion, object scrambling triggers strong readings on weak NPs, where strong can be referential, partitive, generic, or generic collective, dependent on the nature of the determiner, the type of predicate and other syntactic factors, such as adverb choice. The reason these readings are called *strong* is because they pattern with strong NPs in their syntactic behaviour. Recall that strong objects in Dutch may always scramble, as was illustrated in (2).

If a weak NP cannot get a strong reading, then scrambling is not possible. This can be witnessed in (21):

(20) dat Els gisteren eenhoorns geaaid heeft
that Els yesterday unicorns caressed has
(21) * dat Els eenhoorns gisteren geaaid heeft
that Els unicorns yesterday caressed has

The reason why (21) is ill-formed is that the only possible strong reading for a bare plural is a generic reading, but such a reading is blocked in (21), due to the stage level predicate in combination with the adverb *gisteren* 'yesterday'.

2. Contrastiveness of the predicate

A second factor that plays a role in whether an object can scramble or not in Dutch is the contrastiveness of the predicate (cf. De Hoop 1990).[1] Object-scrambling results in ungrammatical sentences in (22)-(24), intuitively because the predicate is not contrastive, i.e. cannot bear contrastive stress:

(22) * omdat ik een kat altijd heb
because I a cat always have
"because I always HAVE a cat"

(23) * omdat een krant enkele artikelen altijd bevat
because a newspaper some articles always contains
"because a newspaper always CONTAINS some articles"

(24) ?? omdat ik tulpebollen altijd plant
because I tulip-bulbs always plant
"because I always PLANT tulip-bulbs"

A verb can bear contrastive stress when alternatives are available. Verbs like *have* and *contain* are typically non-contrastive; for a verb like *plant* in (24) it is easier to find a context that makes the sentence interpretable, as can be seen in (25):

(25) omdat ik tulpebollen altijd plant en niet opeet
because I tulip-bulbs always plant and not up-eat
"because I always plant tulip-bulbs and don't eat them"

Modification of a predicate such as *planten* 'plant' will also lead to well-formed sentences, witness (26) and (27):

(26) omdat ik tulpebollen altijd in de tuin plant (en niet in het bos)
because I tulip-bulbs always in the garden plant (and not in the forest)
"because I always plant tulip-bulbs in the garden (and not in the forest"

(27) omdat ik tulpebollen altijd onmiddellijk plant (en ze niet laat wegrotten)
because I tulip-bulbs always immediately plant (and them not let rot)
"because I always plant tulip-bulbs immediately (and don't let them rot)"

---

[1] This term was initially introduced in De Hoop and De Swart (1989).

Apparently, contrastive stress is possible in (25) to (27), which means that the predicates are members of a set of similar predicates that function as alternative predicates with respect to the object *tulpebollen* 'tulip-bulbs'. The only way in which the oddness of sentences such as (22) to (24) can be imitated in English, is by stressing the predicate, as indicated in the translations.

Rooth (1991) argues that intonational focus in English has a uniform semantic import, which can be related to the intuitive notion of contrast within a set of alternative elements. Obviously, in Dutch, scrambling of the object yields the same effect. Thus, the verbs in (22) to (24) cannot bear contrastive stress, because there are no alternatives available. In order to account for these observations, I use Rooth's notion of a contrast set *C*, a pragmatically determined set of alternative predicates.

Rooth (1985) analyzes focus in terms of *alternative semantics*, a semantics based on the idea of sets of alternatives, called *P-sets*. P-sets are defined semantically. For instance, the P-set of sentence (28) contains all properties of the form *R-ing Fossil Fishes from Solnhofen*:

(28) Jackie only READ Fossil Fishes from Solnhofen

Obviously, the set of all properties of this form includes properties based on all sorts of choices for *R*, such as the relation *being born in the same millenium as the author of Fossil Fishes from Solnhofen*. Rooth (1991) points out that this yields the wrong semantics for a sentence such as (28). That is, in Rooth (1985) the semantics of (28) would be of the form given in (28'):

(28') for any property P, if P is of the form *R-ing Fossil Fishes from Solnhofen* and Jackie has P, then P is *reading Fossil Fishes from Solnhofen*

As the example sketched above shows, the condition in (28') will not be satisfied, but it would be if one takes into consideration only a set of relevant properties as substitutes for *reading Fossil Fishes from Solnhofen*. This set, *C*, should be a subset of the whole P-set and might be rather small in particular uses. Semantics just constrains C, while it has to be pragmatically determined what C actually is.

We can use Rooth's notion of a contrast set C to account for the intuitions set forth in the above concerning the requirement on contrastiveness of the predicate in case of object-scrambling. For example, the C-set for (24) could contain two predicates *plant* and *eat* (note, however, that the context has to determine what C actually is). Evidently, more relations are imaginable between me and tulip-bulbs, but the domain of quantification is not this whole set of alternative predicates, but a contextually limited subset of it. In order to make sure that the contrast in

(24) is not trivial, the C-set must at least contain one predicate other than *plant*.

To put it differently, the intonational focus in (24) expresses contrast, and this contrast must be appropriate. In Dutch, scrambling the object yields the same semantic effect. This means that the C-set of the predicate should at least contain one alternative predicate. In other words, in order to make scrambling of the object possible, the cardinality of the C-set of the predicate should be at least two. Typically non-contrastive predicates such as *have*, *contain*, etc. will not meet this condition.

3. The principle of contrastiveness

So far, we have seen that whether an object can scramble or not is dependent on at least two factors. Firstly, an object can only scramble if it can get a strong reading. Secondly, an object can only scramble if the predicate is contrastive. I would like to combine these two generalizations in the following way: an object can only get a strong reading if the predicate is contrastive. I assume that strong readings must be attributed to the type of NP, namely the type of a generalized quantifier. In other words, an object is interpreted as a generalized quantifier if and only if it gets a strong reading. I will not go into the question of what the type of NPs on a weak reading is, but informally I claim that weak NPs are interpreted as part of the predicate rather than as real arguments (cf. De Hoop, in prep.).

I furthermore claim that the principle just formulated does not only hold for object NPs, but more generally for all NPs of type $<<e,t>,t>$, the type of a generalized quantifier. Hence, it can be stated as under (29):

(29) PRINCIPLE OF CONTRASTIVENESS (POC)
For all NPs Q of type $<<e,t>,t>$ and predicates P: Q(P) is only appropriate if $\|P\| \in C$ & $|C| \geq 2$

4. The power of POC

The principle as put in (29) nicely account for some other environments where a distinction between weak and strong readings can be observed. Take for instance the well-known facts in (30):

(30) Jackie has some/*some of her/*all sisters

Lack of a contrastive predicate blocks a generalized quantifier type of the object. Hence, only a weak reading is allowed. Note that sentence (30) differs from, for instance, (31):

(31) Jackie has some/some of her/all books

In (31), an alternative predicate for some of the/all books could be that

JANE has them, in which case the C-set contains two members. The sisters in (30) cannot vary in that way, they are tied up to Jackie.[2] This means that the only contrast that can be achieved is through the plain verb *have*, but this verb is usually non-contrastive in that its C-set only contains one member. If it is replaced by for instance *hit*, then the requirement of contrastiveness is satisfied again:

(32) Jackie hits some/some of her/all sisters

The principle of contrastiveness also explains the paradigm in (33)-(34). In Dutch the subject of an existential sentence can have a strong, partitive reading (cf. De Hoop 1990).

(33) * Er zijn twee van de katten
there are two of the cats
(34) Er zijn twee van de katten ziek
there are two of the cats ill

Comorovski (1988) and Hoeksema (1989) independently argue that a difference should be made between existential sentences with and without an XP-coda, for "bare" existential sentences do not allow an implicit or explicit partitive as their subject, whereas existential sentences with a coda do.[3]

Instead of making a principled distinction between two kinds of existential sentences, I claim that the difference in grammaticality between (33) and (34) is due to the principle of contrastiveness. The subject in (34) has a strong (explicitly partitive) reading, which means that the type of the NP is $<<e,t>,t>$. The use of such a type of NP argument is only appropriate in case of a contrastive predicate. The predicate *zijn* 'be' in (33) is typically non-contrastive (the C-set of this predicate only contains *to be*), which accounts for the ill-formedness of this sentence. In (34), on the other hand, the predicate is *ziek zijn* 'be ill' and its C-set might contain, for instance, *be healthy*. Therefore, the strong, partitive reading on the subject is allowed.

That it is the principle of contrastiveness that explains the difference between (33) and (34), rather than the absence or presence of a

---

[2]This is because *sister* is a relational noun, unlike for instance *book*. Landman and Partee (p.c.) have proposed a semantic analysis according to which a sentence such as *Jane has every sister* comes out as ill-formed because it expresses a tautology, papaphrasable as "for all y, if y is a sister of Jane, then y exists". Tautologies do not generally lead to ill-formedness, however, and Landman and Partee's approach highly depends on the semantic analysis of *have*. I think the principle of contrastiveness is more generally capable of accounting for the facts.

[3] Both Comorovski and Hoeksema discuss English examples. Since partitives in English existential sentences are at best marginal or exceptional, I use Dutch examples.

lexical coda, can easily be shown in Dutch, as in Dutch other verbs than the typical non-contrastive ones are allowed in existential sentences. Consider (35):

(35) Er slapen twee van de katten
there sleep two of the cats

Sentence (35) is as good as the one in (34), despite the fact that there is no coda present. Yet, the partitive is permitted here, as it does not violate the principle of contrastiveness; the C-set of *slapen* 'sleep' obviously contains more elements, e.g. *be awake*.

Some related facts are observed by Zwart (1991). In Dutch PPs can usually be extraposed, as shown in (36) and (37):

(36) Ik geloof dat de katten in de tuin spelen
I believe that the cats in the garden play
(37) Ik geloof dat de katten spelen in de tuin
I believe that the cats play in the garden

The interpretation of (36) is not the same as the interpretation of (37), however. (36) can be uttered as an answer to the question *What are the cats doing?*, whereas (37) must be an answer to the question *What are the cats doing in the garden?* In other words, in (36) the predicate is *play in the garden*, whereas in (37) the predicate is *play*. Extraposing the PP is only possible if this PP can function independently as the realization of an argument. If it is necessarily interpreted as part of the predicate, then it has to remain in its preverbal position.

Now, compare (37) to (39):

(38) Ik geloof dat de katten in de tuin zijn
I believe that the cats in the garden are
(39) * Ik geloof dat de katten zijn in de tuin
I believe that the cats are in the garden

The ill-formedness of (39) can again be analyzed as a violation of the principle of contrastiveness. The subject of the subordinate clause has a strong, referential reading and hence, the predicate should be contrastive, which is not possible for the plain verb *be*. In (38) the predicate is *be in the garden*.

This phenomenon can also be observed in existential sentences, as pointed out by Zwart (1991):

(40) dat er veel katten in de tuin waren
that there many cats in the garden were
"that many (of the) cats were in the garden"

(41) dat er veel katten waren in de tuin
that there many cats were in the garden
"that there were many cats in the garden"

In Dutch existential sentences, weak subjects can get either a weak or a strong reading. If the subject in (40)-(41) gets a strong reading, then the predicate must be contrastive. In (40), this is no problem, as *be in the garden* is contrastive. In (41), however, the predicate *be* cannot be contrastive, which leaves the weak subject reading as the only reading possible in (41). This is exactly what happens. So, in (40) the subject gets a weak, existential or a strong, partitive reading, but in (41) only the weak, existential reading is available.

Zwart (1991) analyzes these observations differently. He claims that two types of existential sentences must be distinguished, one in which the expletive is analyzed as a raised predicate (following Moro 1991), and one in which the expletive is analyzed as a meaningless element that is freely inserted at S-structure and replaced at LF by the associated NP (cf. Chomsky 1986). The latter type of existential sentence allows both weak and strong readings, whereas the former type only allows an existential reading on the subject. If a PP is extraposed as in (41), it cannot function as a small clause predicate anymore and therefore *er* 'there' must be the raised small clause predicate. Hence, only an existential reading is possible. Although Zwart's analysis thus differs from mine, the idea that an extraposed PP cannot function as small clause predicate anymore, is compatible with my view that it cannot function as part of the predicate anymore. I do not need to make a principled distinction between two types of existential sentences, however.

One more illustration of how my analysis works is found in the following paradigm. The verb *zitten* 'sit' in Dutch has two readings, a non-literal, non-contrastive reading that can be translated as *be* and an ordinary contrastive reading *sit*.

(42) dat veel taalkundigen in de kroeg zitten
that many linguists in the pub sit
"that many (of the) linguists are in the pub"

(43) dat veel taalkundigen zitten in de kroeg
that many linguists sit in the pub
"that many (of the) linguists SIT in the pub"

(44) dat er veel taalkundigen in de kroeg zitten
that there many linguists in the pub sit
"that many linguists are in the pub"

(45) dat er veel taalkundigen zitten in de kroeg
that there many linguists sit in the pub
"that many linguists are/sit in the pub"

In (42) the subject is in standard position, which means in Dutch that it gets a strong, partitive reading.[4] The predicate is *in de kroeg zitten*, (literally 'sit in the pub', but meaning 'be in the pub'), which is contrastive. In (43) the PP is extraposed, so that it does not belong to the predicate anymore. The contrastiveness of the predicate must now reside in the verb *zitten* 'sit', which means that only the literal meaning of the verb is obtained. Sentence (31) can only mean that it holds for many linguists that they SIT in the pub and do not stand or walk around.

In (44) and (45) the subject is VP-internal, which in Dutch means it can have both a weak and a strong reading. In (44) both possibilities are open; either the subject gets a weak, existential reading (there are many linguists in the pub), or it gets a strong, partitive reading (many of the linguists are in the pub). In (45) the PP is extraposed; if the subject gets a strong reading, then the predicate must be contrastive, and we get a reading that is similar to (43), but it is also possible that the subject gets a weak, existential reading (like in (44)); then the interpretation of (45) is that it is a statement about the pub: there are many linguists there.

5. A semantic explanation

The question arises what deeper layer of explanation there might be for the relation between quantification and contrastiveness reflected in POC. It has become a common view in the literature that quantification involves tripartite structures, consisting of a quantifier and two arguments; the first argument can be called the restrictor, and the second argument the nuclear scope. This way of dividing quantificational structures can be generalized to various kinds of quantificational stuctures, as pointed out by Partee (1990). Partee (1991) shows that there is a correlation between topic and restrictor and similarly, between focus and nuclear scope. This might explain the fact that the restrictor is often associated with presupposition accomodation.

The principle of contrastiveness is essentially a principle concerning the relation between quantificational NPs (the quantifier and the restrictor in a tripartite structure) and their predicate (the nuclear scope). The predicate must be contrastive in that alternative predicates must be available in the C-set of the predicate. In other words, the predicate that functions as the second argument of the quantifier must be significant. A predicate that is non-contrastive has no alternatives, hence has no new information to add to the restrictor part. In fact, non-contrastive predicates are in a way already presupposed as part of the restrictor. In (46) and (47) the object has scrambled, which means that it gets a strong reading. Following the principle of contrastiveness, the predicate must be contrastive in these examples:

[4]Unlike English, subjects in standard subject position in Dutch necessarily get a strong reading (cf. Reuland 1988, Rullmann 1989).

(46) * omdat ik nachtmerries altijd droom
because I nightmares always dream
"because I always DREAM nightmares

(48) omdat ik nachtmerries altijd 's nachts droom
because I nightmares always at night dream
"because I always dream nightmares AT NIGHT"

Obviously, nightmares only exist by virtue of being dreamt, *dream* is therefore a presupposition of *nightmares*, hence it belongs to the restrictor if *nightmares* gets a quantificational (generic) interpretation. We can argue that the nuclear scope is either empty or filled with a dummy, already presupposed element. In fact, this is how Szabolcsi (1986) characterizes certain predicates in Hungarian that do not allow for a strong reading. She calls these predicates *bleached* or *empty* predicates and suggests that these predicates do not assign a Θ-role to their object.

In (48) the nuclear scope contains the predicate *dream at night*, which is contrastive: a possible alternative is *dream during the day*. In other words, POC states that constructing a quantificational, tripartite structure is only appropriate if the nuclear scope contains a predicate that is not presupposed already, not a dummy or empty predicate. This is not surprising (it is not a coincidence that the second argument of a quantifier has been called the *nuclear scope*, this argument is in fact what the statement should be all about): a real argument (a quantificational NP) must not hang in the air, but needs a significant (i.e., contrastive) predicate.

POC should not be confused with a prohibition on expressing tautologies in natural language. The following tautology is not prohibited by POC and accordingly, it is perfectly grammatical:[5]

(49) Every linguist is a linguist

The quantificational NP requires a contrastive predicate, and *be a linguist* is indeed a contrastive predicate as its C-set contains more than one member. So, despite the fact that the predicate that goes into the nuclear scope is a repetition of the predicate that occupies the restrictor (and as a consequence turns the whole expression into a tautology), it is not a dummy or empty predicate. The well-formedness of (49) is therefore in accordance with POC.

6. Conclusion

In Dutch only NPs on a strong reading can be scrambled, a condition that seems to be observed in all languages. A second factor that plays a role in whether an object can scramble or not is the contrastiveness of the

---

[5]Thanks to Cleo Condoravdi for drawing my attention to this.

predicate: an object can only scramble if the predicate is contrastive. The two restrictions on object scrambling are combined and generalized to all NPs in the semantic Principle of Contrastiveness (POC). It states that a predicate whose C-set does not contain two or more members blocks a generalized quantifier (strong) reading of an NP. The principle can account for several other environments in which a distinction between weak and strong readings is observed. A semantic explanation of POC must be sought in the way in which quantificational structures are built up (in three parts). The second argument of a quantifier, the nuclear scope, should not be occupied by an empty, dummy, or already presupposed predicate.

Acknowledgements

I thank Barbara Partee as well as the audience in Los Angeles for helpful discussion, and Ale de Boer for checking the English. This research was supported by the Foundation for Linguistic Research, which is funded by the Dutch organization for research, NWO (grant 300-171-005).

References

Carlson, Gregory. 1977. *Reference to Kinds in English*. Doctoral dissertation University of Massachusetts, Amherst.

Chomsky, Noam. 1986. *Knowledge and Language*. New York: Praeger.

Comorovski, Ileana. 1988. *Discourse and the Syntax of Multiple Constituent Questions*. Doctoral dissertation Cornell University.

Fodor, Janet and Ivan Sag. 1982. Referential and Quantificational Indefinites. *Linguistics and Philosophy* 5:355-398.

Hoeksema, Jack. 1983. Plurality and Conjunction. *Studies in Modeltheoretic Semantics*, ed. Alice ter Meulen, 63-83. Dordrecht: Foris.

Hoeksema, Jack. 1989. *Review of The Representation of (In)definiteness*, eds. Eric Reuland and Alice ter Meulen. *Language* 65:115-125.

Hoop, Helen de. 1990. Restrictions on Existential Sentences and Object-Scrambling: Some Facts from Dutch. *The Proceedings of the Ninth West Coast Conference on Formal Linguistics*, ed. Aaron Halpern, 277-288. Stanford University.

Hoop, Helen de. in preparation. *Case Configuration and Noun Phrase Interpretation*. Doctoral dissertation University of Groningen.

Hoop, Helen de and Henriëtte de Swart. 1989. Over indefiniete objecten en de relatie tussen syntaxis en semantiek. *GLOT* 12:19-35.

Milsark, Gary. 1977. Toward an Explanation of Certain Peculiarities of the Existential Construction in English. *Linguistic Analysis* 3:1-29.

Moro, Andrea. 1991. The Raising of Predicates: Copula, Expletives and Existence. *MIT Working Papers in Linguistics* 15:119-181.

Partee, Barbara. 1988. Many Quantifiers. *Proceedings of the Fifth Eastern States Conference on Linguistics*, ed. Joyce Powers and Kenneth de Jong, 383-402. The Ohio State University.

Partee, Barbara. 1990. Domains of Quantification and Semantic Typology. To appear in *Proceedings of the 1990 Mid-America Linguistics Conference*, ed. Frances Ingemann. University of Kansas.

Partee, Barbara. 1991. Topic, Focus, and Quantification. To appear in *Proceedings of SALT I.*

Reuland, Eric. 1988. Indefinite Subjects. *Proceedings of NELS 18*, 375-394.

Rooth, Mats. 1985. *Association with Focus*. Doctoral dissertation University of Massachusetts, Amherst.

Rooth, Mats. 1991. A Theory of Focus Interpretation or What is the Source of Association with Focus Ambiguities. Manuscript University of Stuttgart.

Rullmann, Hotze. 1989. Indefinite Subjects in Dutch. Manuscript University of Massachusetts, Amherst.

Swart, Henriëtte de. this volume. Genericity, Conditionals and the Weak/Strong Distinction.

Szabolcsi, Anna. 1986. Indefinites in Complex Predicates. *Theoretical Linguistic Research* 2:47-83.

Zwart, Jan-Wouter. 1991. Expletive Raising and Expletive Replacement in Dutch. To appear in *Proceedings of ESCOL 8*.

Genericity, Conditionals and the Weak/Strong Distinction

HENRIËTTE DE SWART
University of Groningen

0. Introduction[1]

The interpretation of indefinite NPs in sentences and discourse is an important topic in modern linguistic research. For quite some time, the Discourse Representation Theory (DRT) advanced by Kamp (1981) and Heim (1982) has been the leading paradigm. It has been pointed out, though, that this account does not respect the principle of compositionality of meaning. In many respects, compositional reinterpretations of DRT have the same descriptive power as DRT, because they focus on the same data. Until now, there has not been much discussion of linguistic arguments favoring one or the other approach. In this paper, I will show that the semantics of indefinite plurals in French may be used as evidence in favor of an interpretation of indefinites as existential quantifiers, rather than as variables. The crucial issues here are the treatment of genericity and symmetric/asymmetric readings of conditionals.

1. The unselective binding approach

Kamp (1981) and Heim (1982) propose a quantifier free treatment of definite and indefinite NPs in terms of variables: indefinite NPs introduce "new" variables, definite NPs identify "old" variables in the discourse representation. A variable introduced by an indefinite NP is either bound by an unselective quantifier or captured by a discourse operator of existential closure. This approach accounts for discourse anaphora as in (1) and for so-called "donkey anaphora" as in (2):

(1) A dog came in. It lay down under the table.

(2) (a) Every farmer who owns a donkey beats it.
(b) If a farmer owns a donkey he always beats it.

---

[1]I wish to thank Ale de Boer, Peter Blok, Jack Hoeksema, Helen de Hoop, Brigitte Kampers-Manhe, Hillig van 't Land, Rita Landewerd, Sjaak de Meij and Co Vet for helpful comments on an earlier version of this paper. A grant from the Dutch Organization for Scientific Research is hereby gratefully acknowledged.

The pronoun *it* in the second sentence of (1) picks up the discourse referent introduced by *a dog* in the first sentence. The quantified conditional under (2b) is represented by the formula under (3b), which is equivalent to the standard first order predicate logical formula in (3c):

(3) (a) If a farmer owns a donkey he always beats it.
(b) $\text{Always}_{x,y}$ [[farmer(x) & donkey(y) & own(x,y)] → beat(x,y)]
(c) ∀x∀y [[farmer(x) & donkey(y) & own(x,y)] → beat(x,y)]

The unselective quantifier *always* binds the two variables *x* and *y*; they are added as indices on the quantifier. A similar analysis is provided for (2a). This account of discourse and donkey anaphora is extended to account for generic NPs and bound variable readings. Carlson (1978) already observed that the interpretation of bare plurals depends on the predicate:

(4) (a) Cats were playing in the garden.
(b) Cats are intelligent.

The bare plural has an existential reading in the subject position of the stage-level predicate in (4a). With individual-level predicates, the bare plural always gets a generic interpretation as in (4b) (cf. Kratzer (1989) and Diesing (1990) for more discussion). Heim treats generic readings by means of a phonologically unrealized operator, which functions as an unselective binder. A sentence like (5a) or (5b) then gets the representation in (5c):

(5) (a) A cat (usually) has green eyes.
(b) Cats (usually) have green eyes.
(c) GEN_x [cat(x)] [have-green-eyes(x)]

GEN is interpreted as default quantification over "normal" cases. The general idea is that an indefinite NP gets a generic reading if the variable it introduces is interpreted in the restrictive clause (the first argument) of the quantifier and an existential reading if it ends up in the nuclear scope (the second argument). Whatever is responsible for the generic character of (5a) and (5b), it cannot be the fact that a variable is bound by a quantifier. The mechanism of an operator binding a variable cannot be responsible for the generic character of the NP all by itself, as variable binding does not necessarily induce genericity, as the behavior of determiners shows:

(6) (a) Most cats have green eyes.

(b) Most_x [cat(x)] [have green eyes(x)]

Also, the indefinite NP *a donkey*, which gives rise to the donkey pronoun *it* in (2a) and (2b), is not in general characterized as a generic NP. So genericity is not just taking over the quantificational force of the binder. If the variable binding mechanism itself is not responsible for the meaning effects of genericity, the phenomenon should be attributed to the binder at hand. Accordingly, it is claimed that quantifying adverbs (short: Q-adverbs) like *usually* are to be regarded as generic quantifiers, similar to the operator GEN. This means that the generic character of (5a) and (5b) is located in the Q-adverb *usually*. But Q-adverbs do not always function as generic quantifiers, as the non-generic (7) shows:

(7) Last month, Paul always walked to school.

A view of Q-adverbs as generic quantifiers is thus overgeneralizing. Just like determiners, they may, but need not express generic quantification.

2. The French paradigm

A problem for the unselective binding approach to genericity is that the analysis is hard to extend to definite NPs:

(8) The Alsatians are (usually) fat.

Given that definite NPs are supposed to identify "old" variables which have been introduced earlier in the discourse representation, it is unclear whether the unselective binding mechanism can be applied to these cases. Now, sentences like (8) are not very frequent in English, but they turn out to be the typical expression of genericity in French:

(9) (a) Un Alsacien est (généralement) obèse.
An Alsatian is (usually) fat.
(b) *Des Alsaciens sont (généralement) obèses.
INDEF-PL Alsatians are (usually) fat.
(c) Les Alsaciens sont (généralement) obèses.
DEF-PL Alsatians are (usually) fat.

(9a) is the immediate counterpart of (5a), but (9b) is unacceptable. Instead of (9b), we use (9c) to express generalizations. Indefinite plurals in contexts which give rise to an existential reading allow discourse anaphora, just like their English counterpart (10). They also give rise to donkey pronouns, as in (11):

(10) Hier soir, *des terroristes basques* ont essayé d'enlever le Premier Ministre.
Ils n'ont pas eu de chance: *ils* ont été arrêtés ce matin.
Yesterday evening, *Basque terrorists* tried to kidnap the Prime Minister.
They were not very lucky: *they* have been arrested this morning.

(11) (a) Tous les paysans qui ont *des ânes têtus les* battent.
All farmers who have *stubborn donkeys* beat *them*.
(b) Généralement, si un paysan a *des ânes têtus* il *les* bat.
Generally, if a farmer has *stubborn donkeys*, he beats *them*.

If we take the occurrence of discourse anaphora and donkey pronouns as the main criterion for variable like behavior, *des* N behaves just like singular indefinites and bare plurals in English. Note, however, that the sentences in (10) and (11) concern non-generic readings of indefinite NPs. If an English bare plural takes up a generic interpretation or combines with a Q-adverb, we cannot use *des* N in the French translation of the sentence, but we have to use the definite plural *les* N:

(12) (a) *Des chats ont les yeux verts.
INDEF-PL cats have green eyes.
(b) Les chats ont les yeux verts.
DEF-PL cats have green eyes.

(13) (a) *Des chats ont toujours les yeux verts.
INDEF-PL cats always have green eyes.
(b) Les chats ont toujours les yeux verts.
DEF-PL cats always have green eyes.

Something similar may be observed in the object position of verbs of affection like *admire, like, detest.* Carlson (1978) observes that these predicates select the generic interpretation of the bare plural object:

(14) Marie always detests Swedish tennis stars.

These facts have a parallel in German and Dutch. Scrambled positions of the object correspond with a universal reading of the indefinite (15b), while unscrambled positions preferably yield existential readings (15a) (cf. Kratzer 1989, De Hoop and De Swart 1990):[2]

(15) (a) Anne heeft daarvoor geen tijd, omdat ze altijd werkstukken zit te corrigeren. [existential reading]
Anne does not have time to do that, because she is always correcting papers.
(b) Anne's begeleiding wordt erg gewaardeerd, omdat zij werkstukken altijd corrigeert. [universal reading]
Anne's supervision is very much appreciated, because she always corrects papers.

If an existential reading for the indefinite object is absent for verbs of affection, we expect the scrambled position to be preferred. This prediction is borne out by the sentences under (16):

(16) (a) ... omdat Marie Zweedse tennissterren altijd haat
... because Marie Swedish tennis stars always detests
(b) ...??omdat Marie altijd Zweedse tennissterren haat
... because Marie always Swedish tennis stars detests

In (16a), the object is scrambled out of the VP and the sentence has the same interpretation as (14). The contrast in (16) can be explained if we assume with Kratzer (1989) that a position inside the VP (as in 16b) favors an existential interpretation, whereas an indefinite NP outside the VP (16a) corresponds with a variable which ends up in the restrictive clause of the quantifier. The latter results in a universal/bound variable interpretation. Unlike German and Dutch, French does not allow scrambling of the direct object. The contrast in (15) corresponds with an alternation between an indefinite plural (17a) and a definite plural (17b):

(17) (a) Anne n'a pas le temps de faire cela, parce qu'elle est toujours en train de corriger des dissertations. [existential reading]
Anne does not have time to do that, because she is always correcting INDEF-PL papers.
(b) Tout le monde aime travailler sous la direction d'Anne, car elle corrige toujours les dissertations. [universal reading]
Everyone likes to work under Anne's supervision, for she always corrects DEF-PL papers.

The class of verbs of affection in French contains predicates like *admirer* ('admire'), *détester* ('detest'), etc. Indefinite plurals are not allowed in the object position of these verbs, one has to use a definite plural:

---

[2]Sometimes, a "specific" or "referential" reading of *a* N or *een* N is possible instead of a generic one, but I will not discuss such interpretations (cf. Fodor and Sag 1982).

(18) (a) Marie déteste toujours les joueurs de tennis suédois.
Marie always detests DEF-PLUR Swedish tennis stars.
(b) *Marie déteste toujours des joueurs de tennis suédois.
Marie always detests INDEF-PLUR Swedish tennis stars.

(18a) is the immediate counterpart of (14) and (16a). (18b) is unacceptable on the individual-level interpretation of the predicate, because *des* N cannot have a generic interpretation and the sentence disallows an existential interpretation of the indefinite object. The ungrammaticality of (18b) is thus related to the unfelicity of (16b).

At first sight, this presents a very fuzzy picture. On the one hand, the observations concerning discourse and donkey anaphora suggest that *des* N does instantiate variable behavior. But then we would also expect to find examples in which this NP is bound by a generic or quantificational operator. However, the examples under (12), (13), (17) and (18) show that *des* N refuses to be interpreted as a bound variable in the restrictive clause. Intuitively, this is related to the fact that French *des* N is a typically existential and predicative expression, which always provides new information. Therefore, it tends to end up in focused positions, where it is existentially closed off. Note that its focused position leaves open the possibility of the indefinite being interpreted as part of the restrictive clause. This then allows for iteration of binding as in donkey sentences.

The behavior of *des* N is problematic for the unselective binding approach. Of course, we could add a special condition to the grammar of French, which would require *des* N to be always captured by existential closure. But this immediately raises the question why there is such a special rule needed for French. In the case of scrambling in German and Dutch, we have syntactic clues to help us get the interpretation right. The position of a VP-internal object is structurally different from the one of a scrambled object and the rules Kratzer (1989) formulates are meant to capture the influence of structural positions on interpretation. The interpretation of *des* N, however, is not related to its syntactic position. It seems to be an inherent semantic property of the indefinite plural that it never provides the variable to be quantified over. And this, of course, runs counter to the whole spirit of the variable analysis. These observations suggest that the behavior of French *des* N favors an approach under which indefinite NPs are interpreted as existential quantifiers. An independent argument in favor of such an analysis is provided by (a)symmetric readings of conditionals.

3. Symmetric and asymmetric readings of conditionals

Symmetric and asymmetric readings of conditionals have been studied in relation to the proportion problem (Kadmon 1987, Chierchia 1990). The problem arises when a non-universal quantifier is regarded as an unselective quantifier binding more than one variable:

(19) Most women who own a dog are happy.

Suppose there are ten women in our domain of discourse. One of them owns 50 dogs and she is happy, the other nine women own exactly one dog each and they are miserable. Intuitively (19) is false in this situation. However, the unselective binding analysis of *most* predicts its truth, because the unselective quantifier binds pairs of women and dogs. This approach fails to capture the intuition that in a sentence like

(19) we want to quantify asymmetrically (and count dog-owning women), instead of quantifying symmetrically (and count woman-dog pairs). Kadmon points out that relative clauses usually give rise to asymmetric quantification, whereas their conditional counterparts may express either symmetric or asymmetric quantification. Consider (20a) and (20b), which express quantification over an indefinite subject and an indefinite object respectively. As Bäuerle and Egli (1985) point out, a donkey pronoun related to the antecedent subject or object favors the corresponding asymmetric reading:

(20) (a) In general, when a famous actress promotes a Dior perfume, she earns a lot of money. [symmetric or subject asymmetric]
(b) In general, when a famous actress promotes a Dior perfume, it sells well enough. [symmetric or object asymmetric]

Imagine a situation in which a certain actress promotes 10 Dior perfumes, and does not earn a lot of money (say because her advisors did not bother to negotiate a good contract). Suppose 5 other actresses promote one Dior perfume each and they were smart enough to negotiate well, so they earn a lot of money. Then (20a) is false under a symmetric reading (10 of the 15 pairs do not meet the consequent), but it is true under the subject asymmetric reading, in which we claim that actresses who promote Dior perfumes earn a lot of money. On the other hand, imagine a situation in which a certain Dior perfume is promoted by 10 famous actresses and it is a great success. Moreover, 5 other Dior perfumes are promoted by one actress each, but they are too expensive, so nobody buys them. In this situation (20b) would be true under a symmetric reading (10 of the 15 pairs meet the consequent). However, it is false under the object asymmetric reading in which we claim that perfumes promoted by a famous actress sell well, because only 1 perfume out of 5 sells well.

Donkey pronouns are not the only clue to obtaining asymmetric readings. Focus also helps to bring out a particular reading: focus on the object works in favor of the subject asymmetric reading, whereas deaccenting the object more easily yields the object asymmetric interpretation (cf. Kratzer 1989, Chierchia 1990, Partee 1991 and De Swart 1991). Wasow (1972, 77-8) already drew attention to the close relationship between stress and anaphora. He points out that anaphora lead to a reduction in stress, except when the stress is contrastive. He relates this to a more general phenomenon, viz. that stress is reduced on items which do not introduce new information. If we adopt this perspective, it is not surprising that anaphora and focus work together to establish asymmetric readings. In French, we get the same sets of readings; (21) is the translation of (20):

(21) (a) En général, quand une actrice connue fait de la publicité pour un parfum Dior, elle gagne beaucoup d'argent. [symmetric or subject asymmetric]
(b) En général, quand une actrice connue fait de la publicité pour un parfum Dior, celui-ci se vend bien. [symmetric or object asymmetric]

If we replace one of the singular indefinites by a plural indefinite, we observe that only one of the two configurations can have an asymmetric reading:

(22) (a) En général, quand une actrice connue fait de la publicité pour des parfums Dior, elle gagne beaucoup d'argent. [symmetric or subject asymmetric]
In general, when a famous actress promotes INDEF-PL Dior perfumes, she earns a lot of money.
(b) En général, quand une actrice connue fait de la publicité pour des parfums Dior, ceux-ci se vendent bien. [symmetric only]
In general, when a famous actress promotes INDEF-PL Dior perfumes, they sell well enough.

(23) (a) En général, quand des actrices connues font de la publicité pour un parfum Dior, elles gagnent beaucoup d'argent. [symmetric only]
In general, when INDEF-PL famous actresses promote a Dior perfume, they earn a lot of money.
(b) En général, quand des actrices connues font de la publicité pour un parfum Dior, celui-ci se vend bien. [symmetric or object asymmetric]
In general, when INDEF-PL famous actresses promote a Dior perfume, it sells well enough.

This distribution of interpretations can be explained on the assumption that asymmetric readings are similar to generic/universal/bound variable readings. As observed in section 2, *des* N is a typically existential and predicative expression, which naturally ends up in focused positions. Therefore, an NP of the form *des* N in subject position favors an object asymmetric reading and the other way around. This is in accordance with the distribution of donkey pronouns in (22a), so it is only natural to interpret the sentence in terms of asymmetric quantification over actresses who promote Dior perfumes. The distribution of donkey pronouns in (22b) however, suggests an object asymmetric reading just as in (20b)/(21b). In French, this reading would be paraphrased using the definite plural *les*: "En général, les parfums Dior promus par une actrice connue se vendent bien".[3] The paraphrase shows that the object is supposed to provide the variable for the Q-adverb to quantify over. This is something which *des* N does not do, so the sentence only has a symmetric interpretation. If we want to use plurals which can have a universal/bound variable reading, we have to use definite NPs. There is a sharp contrast between the indefinite plural in (22b), which blocks a subject asymmetric reading and the definite plural in (24a), which allows such a reading:

---

[3]Cf.:

(i) Des parfums Dior tels que Miss Dior, Dune et Poison se vendent bien.
INDEF-PL Dior perfumes, such as Miss Dior, Dune and Poison sell well.

(i) is not ungrammatical, but it does not have the desired universal interpretation of the object. *Des* parfums has an existential reading, meaning 'some' or 'certain'.

(24) (a) En général, quand une actrice connue fait de la publicité pour les parfums Dior, ceux-ci se vendent bien. [symmetric or object asymmetric]
In general, when a famous actress promotes DEF-PL Dior perfume, they sell well enough.
(b) En général, quand les actrices connues font de la publicité pour un parfum Dior, elles gagnent beaucoup d'argent. [symmetric or subject asymmetric]
In general, when DEF-PL famous actresses promote a Dior perfume, they earn a lot of money.

A similar reasoning accounts for the distribution of readings in (23). (23b) has the same set of readings as (20b)/(21b), but (23a) lacks the subject asymmetric reading of (20a)/(21a). Note that this reading is present in (24b), which contains a definite instead of an indefinite plural in subject position. These observations are hard to account for in the unselective binding approach, which claims that in symmetric readings both indefinites yield bound variables, whereas in asymmetric interpretations one of the indefinites is existentially closed off. In section 2, I argued that the only way to explain the behavior of *des* N would be to assume that it is always captured by existential closure. This would predict that the symmetric interpretation is blocked, which it obviously is not. On the other hand, if the symmetric reading would lead us to assume that bound variable interpretations exist after all, it is unclear why an asymmetric reading in which *des* provides the variable for the quantifier to bind is unavailable.

Summing up, we can say that the behavior of French *des* N does not readily fit into the model of DRT. The unselective binding mechanism provides an account of discourse anaphora and donkey sentences, but it fails to see that genericity and bound variable readings are basically a different issue. In order to grasp the semantics of indefinites in general and of *des* N in particular, we should realize that generic indefinite NPs are strong. Genericity may then be regarded as the typical way for a certain class of weak NPs (such as indefinite singulars and English bare plurals) to take up a strong reading. I claim then, that the weak/strong distinction is the clue to a better understanding of the phenomenon of genericity in general and of the behavior of French indefinites in particular.

4. The weak/strong distinction

Usually, the discussion concerning strong readings of weak NPs focuses on expressions such as cardinals and *many/few* N:

(25) (a) One white bird is just as expensive as two black birds.
(b) Two cats were playing in the garden.
(c) Two cats have green eyes.
(d) Many cats have green eyes.

These NPs sometimes take up a collective generic reading as in (25a). Collective generic readings are not very frequent for *many/few* N, though. In most contexts which involve a weak/strong alternation, such as the subject position of stage-level and individual-level predicates, we observe a contrast between weak existential readings (25b) and strong partitive (25c) or proportional readings (25d). Milsark (1977) was the first to formulate this as a restriction which individual-level predicates such as *have green eyes* impose on the interpretation of the subject NP, in contradistinction to stage-level predicates such as *to play in the garden.* Recall that the stage/individual contrast also plays a role in the interpretation of singular indefinites and bare plurals (cf. (4) in section 1). Although strong (partitive or proportional) readings are quite natural for numerals and *many/few*, they are not easy to obtain for a N and bare plurals (but see footnote 2). Singular indefinites or bare plurals usually take up a generic reading if they occur in positions which are restricted to strong NPs, as Carlson (1978) already observed. These observations suggest that it is only natural to account for genericity as one way for weak NPs to take up a strong reading (cf. De Hoop, to appear). Genericity can be regarded as the typical way for indefinite singulars and English bare plurals to become strong.

Returning to the French case, we may relate the ungrammaticality of (26) to a reluctance of the French NP *des* N to take up a strong reading, be it partitive-proportional or generic:

(26) *Des chats ont les yeux verts.
INDEF-PL cats have the eyes green.

Clearly, French indefinite plurals do not like either of these ways to become strong. However, Galmiche (1986) points out that, if *des* N is forced to take up a strong reading, it is interpreted as a partitive:

(27) Des fauteuils sont bancals.
INDEF-PL armchairs are shaky.

According to Galmiche the indefinite plural selects a contextually determined subset of the armchairs as the referent of the NP. The best paraphrase for this sentence is then "Some armchairs (of a set which is somehow salient in the discourse situation) are shaky". This reading of *des* N is strictly restricted to situations in which such a subset is relevant and can be properly selected from a discourse given or presupposed set.

The observations made by Galmiche (1986) suggest that *des* N is closer in behaviour to cardinals and *many/few* N than to *un* N/ *a* N/ bare plurals and like these is not well suited for the expression of genericity. We may conclude that from a linguistic point of view, an interpretation of *des* N as an existential quantifier is preferable to an analysis in terms of variables. So let us now turn to compositional reinterpretations of DRT.

5. Dynamic existential quantifiers

Kamp (1981) and Heim (1982) introduce a treatment of indefinite NPs as variables because a classical predicate logical analysis cannot account for the discourse anaphor in (1) and the donkey pronoun in (2), as the relevant variable is not in the scope of the existential quantifier:

(28) (a) $\exists x\,[\text{dog}(x)\ \&\ \text{came-in}(x)]\ \&\ \text{lay-down}(x)$
(b) $\forall x[[\text{farmer}(x)\ \&\ \exists y[\text{donkey}(y)\ \&\ \text{own}(x,y)]] \rightarrow \text{beat}(x,y)]$

If we want to return to a treatment of indefinite NPs in terms of existential quantifiers, we should develop representations very similar to those under (28), but without the binding problems classical first order logic gives rise to. In the literature we find solutions to this problem which appeal to the notion of dynamic existential quantifiers. Groenendijk and Stokhof (1990, 1991) introduce dynamic existential quantifiers which differ from their static counterparts of classical predicate logic in that they provide an "anchor" for variable assignments in subsequent sentences to attach to. This allows for binding relations beyond sentence boundaries. Leaving the technical details aside, we can say that dynamic existential quantifiers pass on the variable binding to the next sentence which is dynamically conjoined with it. Interpreting the indefinite NP in terms of a dynamic existential quantifier gives (29a) the representation under (29b). It is translated as in (29c), which can be rewritten as (29d):

(29) (a) A dog came in. It lay down under the table.
(b) **Ed** [dog(d) ; come-in(d)] ; lay-down(d)
(c) $\lambda p \exists x[\text{dog}(x) \wedge \text{come-in}(x) \wedge \{x/d\}{}^{\vee\wedge}[\text{lay-down}(d) \wedge {}^{\vee}p]$
(d) $\lambda p \exists x[\text{dog}(x) \wedge \text{come-in}(x) \wedge \text{lay-down}(x) \wedge \{x/d\}{}^{\vee}p]$

(29c) shows that in the first sentence the variable assignment anchors the discourse marker *d* to the individual *x*. This variable assignment is carried on to the next sentence: $\{x/d\}$ tells us that subsequent occurrences of *d* will also be attached to *x*. The pronoun *it* can then be interpreted as referring to the same individual *x*. This approach accounts for discourse anaphora, but also for donkey sentences. Chierchia (1990) uses this idea to develop an interpretation of Q-adverbs in terms of dynamic conservative generalized quantifiers over cases. A sentence like (30a) is translated as in (30b):

(30) (a) When a man is in the bathtub, he always sings.
(b) **Always** $(\lambda c \exists x[\text{man}(x) \wedge \text{in-the-bathtub}(x) \wedge {}^{\vee}c])$
$(\lambda c[\exists x[\text{man}(x) \wedge \text{in-the-bathtub}(x) \wedge \text{sing}(x) \wedge {}^{\vee}c])$
(c) $\forall c(\exists x[\text{man}(x) \wedge \text{in-the-bathtub}(x) \wedge {}^{\vee}c]) \rightarrow$
$(\exists x[\text{man}(x) \wedge \text{in-the-bathtub}(x) \wedge \text{sing}(x) \wedge {}^{\vee}c])$
(d) $\forall x[[\text{man}(x) \wedge \text{in-the-bathtub}(x)] \wedge [\text{sing}(x)]]$

This interpretation of the classical donkey sentences involves a scopal relation between adverbial quantifiers over cases and dynamic existential quantifiers over individuals. (30c) says that every case in which a man is in the bathtub, is a case in which that man sings. This is equivalent to (34c), because cases are singleton sets of assignments to discourse markers. There is no need to go into the technical details of this analysis right here. The interested reader is referred to the literature to see how the idea of a dynamic existential quantifier is implemented in a dynamic and compositional, Montague-like grammar. What Groenendijk and Stokhof, Chierchia and others convincingly show is that discourse and donkey anaphora can be treated equally well in a framework in which indefinites are treated as Generalized Quantifiers, provided one gives them the right, dynamic interpretation.

The Dynamic Montague grammar account for the interpretation of indefinites has certain advantages over the unselective binding approach, because it yields a compositional interpretation of discourse and donkey anaphora. Moreover, it provides an interesting view on the French paradigm. Given that all indefinites are interpreted as existential quantifiers, this approach is less counterintuitive than the unselective binding approach. But as far as generic/bound variable readings are concerned, this approach inherits the problems pointed out with respect to the unselective binding mechanism. Iteration of binding does not provide a real insight into the phenomenon of genericity, just like plain variable binding did not. For the

French case, this implies for instance, that it remains a mystery why *des* N allows for iteration of binding in the case of donkey sentences, but why it refuses to take up a generic/bound variable reading. Notwithstanding the attractiveness of the dynamic existential quantifier approach, then, it seems that there is something missing yet. Let us therefore take a look at the treatment of symmetric and asymmetric readings of conditionals Chierchia develops in the framework of DMG.

5. Symmetric and asymmetric readings of conditionals

Chierchia's (1990) treatment of asymmetric readings is based on his analysis of determiners in relative clause constructions. In constructions such as (19), the head noun provides the set of individuals (i.e. a set of women) the determiner quantifies over. The relative clause specifies a dependent property (cf. Barwise 1987). The translation of the *when*-clause in (31) under the symmetric reading is given as the set of cases in which there is an actress and a Dior perfume standing in a promoting relation:

(31) When a famous actress promotes a Dior perfume
$(\lambda c \exists x \exists y[\text{famous-actress}(x) \wedge \text{Dior-perfume}(y) \wedge \text{promote}(x,y) \wedge {}^{\vee}c])$

In asymmetric readings of conditionals, one of the indefinites is singled out as the element that characterizes the set of cases the Q-adverbs quantifies over. The configuration of donkey pronouns, but also focus and pragmatic information may help to circumscribe the type of situation we are talking about. This means that one quantifies over the background of the antecedent (cf. also Partee 1991). The part of the antecedent which is in focus has a role similar to that of a relative clause.

Technically, this is realized in Chierchia's system by an operation of existential disclosure, which turns the existentially quantified NP into a dynamic property, and adds it as an index onto the Q-adverb. For the subject asymmetric reading, this is done by dynamically conjoining the proposition in (32a) with a proposition which identifies x with u. Via (32c), this leads to the set of famous actresses u which have the property of promoting a Dior perfume. Instead of quantifying over cases, the Q-adverb now takes a set of individuals as its arguments:

(32) (a) When a famous actress promotes a Dior perfume
(b) $(\lambda u[\lambda p \exists x \exists y[\text{actress}(x) \wedge \text{perfume}(y) \wedge \text{promote}(x,y) \wedge {}^{\vee}p]\ ;\ \uparrow x = u])$
(c) $(\lambda u[\lambda p \exists x \exists y[\text{actress}(x) \wedge \text{perfume}(y) \wedge \text{promote}(x,y) \wedge x{=}u \wedge {}^{\vee}p]])$
(d) $(\lambda u[\lambda p \exists y[\text{actress}(u) \wedge \text{perfume}(y) \wedge \text{promote}(u,y) \wedge {}^{\vee}p]])$

The object asymmetric reading is obtained in a similar way and gives us the set of Dior perfumes promoted by a famous actress:

(33) $(\lambda w[\lambda p \exists x[\text{perfume}(w) \wedge \text{actress}(x) \wedge \text{promote}(x,w) \wedge {}^{\vee}p]])$

Existential disclosure opens the way for variable binding and the type shift of the Q-adverb guarantees the appropriate truth conditions. This is a very interesting solution to the problem under consideration. Discourse anaphora, donkey anaphora and symmetric readings are accounted for in terms of dynamic existential quantifiers. Existential disclosure is only necessary in the case of asymmetric readings of conditionals, where it allows for variable binding. Furthermore, we may impose certain conditions on the operation of existential disclosure. For example, we require that it is only allowed for indefinite singulars and bare plurals which provide background information and exclude application to indefinite NPs in focus.[4]

6. Towards an analysis

We can give an interesting application of Chierchia's analysis by extending the operation of existential disclosure to generic and other bound variable readings. Generic NPs crucially depend on a presupposed set of relevant individuals. It is the presupposition bearing character of generic NPs which relates them to other strong NPs (cf. Diesing 1990). Unlike Diesing, however, I do not think that this is related to indefinites lacking quantificational force. Recall for instance that cardinals, which at least carry a numerical value can end up here and create collective generic readings. On the other hand, the French indefinite *des* N, which does not carry any more quantificational information than the English bare plural, never gets a generic interpretation. Therefore, I wish to claim that it is not an issue of quantificational force, but a matter of background/foreground structure, which is closely related to the way in which a weak NP takes up a strong reading. It is well known that genericity is closely tied up with focus and a classical pair of sentences illustrating this is given in (39):

(34) (a) Beavers build dams.
(b) Dams are built by beavers.

This leads to the conclusion that an indefinite NP can only be generic if it is used to characterize the set of elements for the generic operator or the adverb of quantification to quantify over. In a DMG-like framework, this appeals to an operation of existential disclosure. This characterization of genericity also explains the restrictions on the interpretation of the French indefinite plural *des* N. *Des* N does not occur in generic sentences, because it is a typically predicative expression. Therefore it always ends up in focused positions, where it cannot provide a set for the quantifier to operate on, and so cannot take up a generic reading. In French the contrast between (34a) and (34b) is grammaticized as expected:

(35) (a) Les castors construisent des barrages.
DEF-PL beavers build INDEF-PL dams.
(b) Les barrages sont construits par des castors.
DEF-PL dams are built by INDEF-PL beavers.

The focused position of *des* N leaves open the possibility of it ending up in the antecedent of a conditional, which implies iteration of binding as in donkey sentences. However, it does not create asymmetric readings.

---

[4]There are also some disadvantages to Chierchia's solution. For instance, it is crucial to adopt a type shift and interpret the Q-adverb as an expression which quantifies over sets of individuals. It would be more attractive to let Q-adverbs range over situations or eventualities, as I argue in de Swart (1991, 1992). An implementation of Chierchia's approach in an event-based semantics is possible if we use a more fine-grained identification of situations for symmetric than for asymmetric readings. Asymmetric readings would then require meaning postulates such as (i) which allow for two events to be regarded as "the same" although the assignment to one of the discourse markers is different:

(i) $\forall e \forall e'$ [[$\exists x \exists y$ actress(x) & Dior-perfume(y) & promote(x,y,e)] &
[$\exists x \exists z$ $z \neq y$ & actress(x) & Dior-perfume(y) & promote(x,y,e')]] $\rightarrow$ e=e'

It is not quite clear why exactly *des* N is sensitive to background/ foreground structure in this way, but the phenomenon is consistent. Similar observations can be made with respect to indefinite mass nouns of the form *du/de la* N. Moreover, this seems to be a more general property which recurs in other Romance languages, like Spanish and Italian. For instance, Belletti (1988) points out that bare plural nouns in Italian can only take up an existential reading, and never become generic. Similarly, Laca (1990) discusses examples which demonstrate the restriction of Spanish bare plurals and bare mass nouns in object position to existential interpretations. Although a detailed discussion of other Romance languages is beyond the scope of this paper, the evidence from the literature shows that indefinites in Romance languages display a behavior which is essentially different from the English paradigm. An extension of the discussion to examples from French and related languages then opens up interesting new perspectives on the interpretation of indefinite NPs.

References

Barwise, J. 1987. Noun phrases, generalized quantifiers and anaphora, in: P. Gärdenfors (ed.) *Generalized quantifiers*, Dordrecht: Reidel, 1-30.

Bäuerle, R. and U. Egli 1985. Anapher, Nominalphrase und Eselsätze, *Arbeitspapier des Sonderforschungsbereichs* 99, Konstanz.

Belletti, A. 1988. The case of unaccusatives, *Linguistic Inquiry* 19, 1-34.

Carlson, G. 1978. *Reference to kinds in English*, New York: Garland.

Chierchia, G. 1990. Anaphora and dynamic logic in: *Quantification and anaphora I*, Dyana report R2.2.A, 37-78.

Diesing, M. 1990. *The syntactic roots of semantic partition*, Ph.D. dissertation UMass, Amherst.

Fodor, J. and I. Sag 1982. Referential and quantificational indefinites, *Ling and Phil* 5,355-398.

Galmiche, M. 1986. Référence indéfinie, événements, propriétés et pertinence in: J. David and G. Kleiber (eds.). *Déterminants: syntaxe et sémantique*, Paris: Klincksieck,41-71.

Groenendijk, J. and M. Stokhof 1990. Dynamic Montague Grammar, in: L. Kálmán e.a. (eds.). *Proceedings of the second symposium on logic and language*, Budapest.

Groenendijk, J. and M. Stokhof 1991. Dynamic predicate logic, *Ling and Phil* 14, 39-100.

Heim, I. 1982. *The semantics of definite and indefinite NPs*, Ph.D. dissertation UMass, Amherst.

de Hoop, H. (to appear). *Case configuration and noun phrase interpretation* Ph.D. dissertation University of Groningen.

de Hoop, H. and H. de Swart 1990. Indefinite objects, in: *Linguistics in the Netherlands 1990*, Dordrecht: Foris, 91-100.

Kadmon, N. 1987. *On unique and non-unique reference and asymmetric quantification*, Ph.D. dissertation. UMass, Amherst.

Kamp, H. 1981. A theory of truth and semantic representation, reprinted in: J. Groenendijk, T. Janssen and M. Stokhof (eds.) 1984. *Truth, interpretation and information*, Dordrecht: Foris, 1-41.

Kratzer, A. 1989. Stage-level and individual-level predicates, ms. UMass, Amherst.

Laca, B. 1990. Generic objects: some more pieces of the puzzle, *Lingua* 81, 25-46.

Milsark, G. 1977. Toward an explanation of certain peculiarities of the existential construction of English, *Linguistic Analysis* 3, 1-29.

Partee, B. 1991. Topic, focus and quantification, *Proceedings of SALT 1*

de Swart, H. 1991. *Adverbs of quantification: a generalized quantifier approach*, Ph.D. dissertation, University of Groningen.

de Swart, H. 1992. Quantification over time in: J. van der Does, J. van Eijck (eds.). *Generalized Quantifier theory and its applications*, Amsterdam: ITLI, 377-401.

Wasow, T. 1972. *Anaphoric relations in English*, Ph.D. dissertation, MIT.

On the Role of Agreement for Government

VIVIANE DEPREZ
Rutgers University

Introduction

The purpose of this paper is to compare two distinct approaches to the role of agreement in the grammar, that of Rizzi (1990), in which agreement is viewed as affecting the governing capacity of heads, and that of Deprez (1989 & following) which construes agreement as a condition on barrier transparency. The comparison is here limited to two empirical domains, subject extractions and VP deletion, both standardly assumed to invoke a government relation between a functional head and an ec, C° and the subject trace on the one hand, I° and the deleted VP, on the other. While much attention has been paid to the role of agreement in subject extractions (Rizzi 1990, Frampton 1990), little has been said about its relevance to other governing relations. Although I will discuss subject extractions, it is my goal here to present little known facts about VP deletion in French and Romance which, I will argue, are relevant to an adequate definition of the role of agreement as a licensing condition in the grammar.

I. Agreement and Head government

Rizzi (1990) proposes that the role of agreement is to affect the governing power of a head. This proposal is central to his account of subject extractions which focuses on the government capacity of C°. In Rizzi's view, C° is a head universally inert for government. Thus, given a conjunctively defined ECP (antecedent & head government), subject extractions such as (1a) are ruled out, because the subject trace fails to be properly head governed. In (1b), however, the ECP can be satisfied because agreement with *t'* in Spec CP (manifested here by *qui*) transforms C° into a proper head governor for the subject trace *t*.

(1) a. *Qui$_i$ crois-tu que [t$_i$ a vu Jean]
    b. Qui$_i$ crois-tu [t'$_i$ qui [t$_i$ a vu Jean]]
       Who do you think saw John

The assumption that agreement plays a central role in subject extractions is empirically well supported. In various languages, such as those in (2), C° manifests a special form, elegantly analyzed as resulting from Spec-head agreement (SHA) with an intermediate trace.

(2) a. Den vent die hier geweest heet (West Flemish)
the man that has been here
b. Vi vet hvem *(som) snakker med Marit (Norwegian)
c. Vi ved hvem *(der) taler med Marit (Danish)
We know who is talking with Mary
d. Kimoun ou kwe *(ki) we Jan (Haitian Creole)
Who do you think saw John

But as I will show, Rizzi's specific proposal about the non-governing status of C° and the role of agreement is problematic in several respects, and, particularly, for languages such as English in which agreement is not manifest. To account for the standard *that-t* effect, Rizzi proposes that C° agreement in English is limited to empty Cs. Thus, somewhat paradoxically, only empty Cs can become head governors. Although plausible for (3a), the proposal is more difficult for structures such as (3b) where AUX in C° carries overt agreement features.

(3) a. *Who do you think [t that [t saw John]]
b. *[Who$_i$ did$_j$ [t$_i$ t$_j$ see John]]

For (3b), furthermore, the assumption that C° is inert for government prevents head government not only of the subject trace but also of the AUX trace. Since I° to C° is otherwise permitted, it cannot be assumed to generally fail the ECP. Thus, Rizzi suggests, the head government requirement of the ECP must be relaxed for traces of X°, although, crucially, not for traces of XPs. This results in a non-homogeneous definition of the ECP for heads and maximal projections.

The restriction of agreement to empty C° is itself problematic, with respect to the *anti-that-t* effect manifested in subject relative clauses (RC) and cleft sentences as in (4). The facts, here, seem rather to demand that it be the overt C° which agreement turns into a head governor for the subject trace, not the empty one.

(4) a. a man [t that [t saw John]]
b.*a man [C° [t saw John]]
c. It's John [t that [t saw Mary]]
d.*It's John [t C° [t saw Mary]]

To counter this difficulty, Rizzi proposes to abstractly distinguish four types of Cs, distributed as in (5), and two types of C-agreement, Spec-head agreement (SHA) and predicative agreement (PA), the latter obtaining directly between the RC head noun and the head of the adjoined CP.

(5)

+wh -pred	I wonder what C° you saw
+wh +pred	the thing which C° you saw
-wh +pred	the thing that you saw
-wh -pred	I know that you saw it

In English, SHA is then restricted to empty [-pred] Cs, and PA to overt [+pred] Cs. Crucially, both agreements are assumed to have the same effect on the governing capacity of C°. As the reader can compute, this proposal accounts for the paradigm in (4). But further problems arise. Consider for instance (6a), whose structure is given in (6b):

(6) a.*the woman I know the book that wrote
   b. the woman$_i$ I know [the book$_j$ [$_{CP}$that$_j$ [$_{IP}$t$_i$ wrote]]]

In (6b), the C° of the lower relative clause, is overt. It can thus undergo PA with the adjacent RC head noun *book* and become a proper head governor. This, however, has the unwanted consequence that, in such cases, subject extractions should violate only subjacency, not the ECP, since head government of the subject trace by C° obtains.[1] To prevent this problem, a further restriction is needed. Rizzi proposes that an X° can turn into a proper governor only if it agrees both with its specifier and with its direct complement, here IP. The necessity of this restriction is further illustrated by the phenomenon in (7). (7) shows that C° agreement is not possible with non-subject extractions. We observe here, an anti-agreement effect which is as robust as the agreement effect in (2).

(7) a.*Qui crois-tu [$_{CP}$ t qui [$_{IP}$ Jean a vu t]]
   Who do you believe John saw ?
   b.*Den vent [$_{CP}$ t die [$_{IP}$ Jan gezien heet t]]
   the man that John has seen
   c.*Vi vet [$_{CP}$ hvem som [$_{IP}$ Marit snakker med t]]
   We know who that Mary talks to
   d.*Vi ved [$_{CP}$ hvem der [$_{IP}$ Marit taler med t]]
   We know who that Mary talks to
   e.*Kimoun ou kwe [$_{CP}$ t ki [$_{IP}$ Jan te we t]]
   Who do you believe John saw

To sum up, in the domain of subject extractions, Rizzi's proposal that the role of agreement is to affect the governing power of a head is problematic on two counts. First, a number of stipulations are needed to specify which inert heads may or may not be sensitive to agreement. Second, the context of government activation must be distinguished from that of SHA agreement and must be constrained so as to avoid over-application both with subject extractions out of wh and RC islands and with overt C° agreement. In Rizzi's approach, this constraint is stipulated and remains unexplained.

These are essentially conceptual problems. But Rizzi's approach to agreement faces some empirical problems when we try to extend its scope to other functional heads such as, for instance, I°. There is a well known difference between English on the one hand, and French and other Romance languages on the other hand, with respect to VP deletion. As illustrated in (8) and (9), English licenses VP deletion while Romance does

---

[1]Although in (6), antecedent government of the subject trace may arguably fail to obtain, this remain insufficient to lead an ECP violation. Subjects like objects bear thematic indexes. Thus binding, which requires no local antecedent government, should obtain. As noted by Rizzi himself, the same problem arises with subject extractions out of wh-islands.

not. As Zagona (1982), (1988) and Lobeck (1986) have argued, VP deletion is possible only when the deleted VP is governed by I°. In view of this requirement, this known contrast can be understood to follow from a parametric difference in the governing status of the respective I°s. But if, as Rizzi proposes, agreement can affect the governing power of a head, we do not expect any difference to arise. It is clear, indeed, that in each of these languages, I° agrees with its subject. As a result, we expect I° to always be able to govern a null VP, contrary to fact.

(8) a. Paul left and Mary did [e] too
  b. Paul has succeeded and Mary has [e] too
  c. Paul was arrested and Mary was [e] too

(9) a.*Jean a dormi et Paul a [e] aussi
  b *Juan a dormido y Pedro ha [e] tambien
  c.*Gianni ha dormido y Pedro ha [e] anche
  John has slept and Peter has [e] too}

Note furthermore that Rizzi's view, leads somewhat puzzling crosslinguistic differences with respect to the governing capacities of functional heads. In French, C° must be assumed to become a head governor under SHA but I° must not and in English, overt C° cannot become a head governor under SHA but overt I° can. The conceptual problems reviewed above and the rather unexpected extended consequences just mentioned concur to suggest that a different conception of the role of agreement in government is needed. We turn to such a proposal in the next section.

II. Agreement as a condition on barrier transparency

The approach to be summarized here construes agreement as affecting not the government status of heads but rather the barrierhood of functional projections. The intuitive content of the idea is as follows. In the present Principle and Parameter framework, heads of functional projections are taken to be bundles of syntactic features. It is thus rather natural to assume that if two functional heads share some features, and here, I will only be concerned with phi-features, their respective projections become, non-distinct and can be taken to form, in some sense, "extended projections" of one another. That is, through feature percolations of the standard type between heads and projections, the projections of heads sharing features also share features and are thus non-distinct. We can therefore expect them to be transparent to certain grammatical relations and, in particular, to movement and government. The proposal then, is that agreement can establish a relevant feature sharing relation between two projections and thereby ensure their transparency. As a possible formal characterization of this idea, I propose to extend the definition of L-marking of Chomsky (1986), which concern conditions on barrier transparency, as in (10):

(10) X° L-marks YP iff X° governs YP and
  i. X° = lexical i.e. [+/- N,V] or
  ii. X° agrees with the head of YP (Phi(X) Phi(Y) = 0)

Let us first observe the functioning of this definition in cases such as (1) repeated here in (12). Assuming that IP like other maximal projections is a barrier, (12a) will be ruled out, because SHA between C° and the extracted subject has not occurred. C° and I° share no phi-features so that IP is not L-marked. It remains a barrier which prevents head and antecedent government of the subject trace.

(12) a. Qui crois-tu [t_i que_j [$_{IP:i}$ t_i est parti]]
b. Qui crois-tu [t_i qui_i [$_{IP:i}$ t_i est parti]]

In (12b), however, since SHA has occurred, C° shares phi-features with IP, now L-marked (i.e. non-distinct) and thus transparent to government. Note that the transitivity of agreement between a specifier ZP, a head X° and its YP complement is here a basic condition for barrier transparency and follows naturally from the current assumptions about functional projections. As a consequence, we expect SHA to have an effect on government relations only if it establishes this transitivity of agreement. Otherwise, although it may freely occur, it will have no effect. A first result of this view is that it provides an immediate account for the anti-agreement effect of (7)=(13) and for the island effect of (6)=(14) with no added stipulation:

(13) Qui crois-tu [t_i qui_i [$_{IPj}$ Jean a vu t]]

(14) the $woman_j$ I know a book [Op_i $that_i$[$_{IPj}$$t_j$ wrote t_i]]

In (13) and (14), indeed, the required transitivity of agreement does not obtain. I° in (13) bears the phi-feature of its own specifier, the NP *Jean*, while C° bears the phi-feature of the extracted object. As a result CP and IP remain distinct and no government relation obtains across the non-L-marked IP barrier. Similarly for (14).[2] A second important consequence of the present approach is that it requires no stipulation about the governing capacity of C°. Indeed, the failure of head government in (12a) follows here from the general prohibition of government across a barrier, not from the stipulation, now superfluous, that C° is not a head governor. This is no doubt a desirable consequence, but one which requires a different account for (3). The central key to an account of (3) developed in Deprez (1991) and only briefly summarized here, is the conjecture that the status of (3) is not a direct effect of the ECP but results rather from broader principles of Economy (Chomsky (1989)). Consider first (3b) for which I will assume the structure given in (15a), where wh-movement of the subject has occurred but I° to C° has not:[3]

(15) a. [Who_i C_i[$_{IPi}$ t_i INFL leave]]
b.*[Who_i did_i [$_{IPi}$ t_i t'_i leave]]

In (15a), the conditions for barrier transparency are met. After SHA with *who*, the [+wh] empty C° bears the features of the extracted subject which are identical to those of IP. Thus IP is L-marked and government obtains. Although these conditions are also met in (15b) where I° to C° has occurred, (15b) is clearly a more complex derivation, since it involves one more movement. Given that this additional movement is not required for the satisfaction of any UG principles, (15b) will be ruled out under general considerations of

---

[2]A more detailed account of the anti-agreement effect is developed in Deprez (1991) where phi-feature agreement is related to the A/A' status of a position.

[3]Cf M-A Friedeman (1989) for empirical arguments supporting this structure.

Economy favoring the shortest possible derivation compatible with UG constraints.[4] In case of non-subject extractions as in (16), IP transparency cannot obtain through SHA since the transitivity of agreement between I° and C° will fail.

(16) a.*What John bought ?
b. [What$_i$ C$_i$ [$_{IPj}$ John bought t$_i$]]

Here then, I° to C° is required, and is not a superfluous movement. Note that, in contrast to Rizzi's, the present account requires no stipulated distinction between X° and XPs with respect to the head government requirement of the ECP. As long as I° does not agree with a non-subject, I° to C° movement will always ensure the C/IP agreement. Thus, IP will not be a barrier and head government of the trace of I° can be satisfied. Turning now to (3a), namely the classic *that-t* effect, note that here too Rizzi's stipulation about the non-governing status of the complementizer *that* is superfluous. It is in fact sufficient to assume that *that* is immune to agreement to exclude (3a). This latter assumption, however, remains stipulative. Furthermore, as we have discussed, it fails to provide an interesting account of the *anti-that-t* effect in (4) above. It should thus be eliminated. Due to space limitation, I can only briefly sketch an approach based on the theory of agreement presented here (See Deprez (1991)). This approach derives the *that-t* effect and the *anti-that-t* effects from the interaction of the English particular phenomenon of *that*-deletion and general principles of Economy. Suppose, that, in English, *that*-deletion expresses an option to realize sentences either as CPs or as IPs. That is, assume that when C° is lexically realized, sentences are CPs, and when it is empty and devoid of features (i.e. -wh), sentences are IPs. If so, sentences where *that* deletes, and among them RCs, have two possible representations, one with CP as in (17b) and one with IP as in (17a), assuming, with Chomsky (86), that [-wh] empty operators, need not occur in a CP specifier.

(17) a.*the man [Op [$_{IP}$ t left]]
b. the man [$_{CP}$ Op that [$_{IP}$ t left]]

(17a) is excluded by a conjunctive ECP since there is no appropriate head governor for the subject trace. The N head which does not c-command it cannot head-govern it. In (17b), however, the head government requirement can be satisfied by the overt C°. The C° *that* is here assumed to agree with the operator in its specifier so that the transitivity of agreement required for barrier transparency obtains.[5] This proposal, (which extends naturally to clefts) provides a simple account for the *anti-that-t* effect.

The next problem to consider is the *that-t* effect. Given our assumptions, sentential complements also have two possible representations, (18a) and (18b):

---

[4]More specifically, we may assume that this movement is permitted only when associated with a distinct interpretation, namely something like insistence. Note, incidentally, that in Rizzi's theory, this possibility is excluded.

[5]The movement of the empty operator in Spec CP is here required by the ECP, since agreement must obtain to satisfy head government, not by the nature of the operator.

(18) a. Who do you think [$_{IP}$ t left]
b. Who do you think [$_{CP}$ t that [t left]]

Here, in contrast, the ECP can be satisfied in both structures. In (18a), IP is L-marked by the matrix verb which also head-governs the subject trace. In (18b), after SHA in CP, IP is transparent and the subject trace can be head governed by *that*. Why then is (18b) excluded? As proposed by Chomsky, it is only when general principles of grammar are satisfied that Economy can play a discriminating role. In (18), this condition is met and we can assume that the derivation (18a) will be chosen since it is clearly simpler than (18b). Under the view proposed here, the *that-t* effect is excluded not by the ECP but by Economy considerations. Note, furthermore, that no stipulations about the status of C° with respect to government or agreement are needed. There is no need to stipulate that C° is not a head governor, nor to posit an abstract distinction between two *that* [+/-pred], nor to distinguish two types of abstract agreement. The peculiarities of English subject extractions are here subsumed under more general principles and C° in English need not differ from C° in French, except with regards to deletion, a distinction which is, in any event, independently required. Clearly, however, a condition of success for this account is that it should not enforce obligatory complementizer deletion in all cases. There are essentially two possible approaches to this question. Either agreement itself could be assumed to be the costly operation in (18b) or the derivation for non-subject extractions should be cost equivalent independently of the presence of an overt complementizer. Both solutions are discussed in Deprez (1991).

To sum up, I have shown that construing agreement as a condition on barriers transparency permits an account of subject extractions which requires no stipulations on the governing status of C° and which naturally restricts the effects of agreement on government to configurations in which agreement transitively obtains between an X°, its specifier and its complement. The next section will extend the proposed theory to I° in cases of VP deletion.

III. Romance clitic-VP-deletion

Although, as discussed above, VP deletion is generally not licensed in French and other Romance languages, there are, however, some cases, illustrated in (19), in which a construction akin to VP deletion is possible. In this section, I will concentrate on this construction, which I call Clitic-VP-Deletion (CLVD), and argue that the conditions of its licensing involves the same transitivity of agreement which we have seen at play in subject extractions. In the last part of this section, I return to the English/Romance distinction with respect to VP deletion and propose a solution compatible with and dependent on the present theory of agreement.

(19) a. Jean sera photographié et Paul le sera aussi
b. Gianni fu fotografato e lo fu anche Paolo
c. John fue retratado y Pedro lo fue tambien
John was photographed and Paul was too

As can be seen in (19), CLVD involves a deleted participle which appears to be resumed by a clitic. In similarity with VP deletion, CLVD is licensed in conjunctions or by a participle mentioned in a previous sentence, as in (20).

(20) a. Jean sera photographié Lundi. Marie le sera aussi
John will be photographed Monday. Mary will be too

That CLVD does not simply involve the deletion of a head is shown in (21) where both a V and its complement are deleted.

(21) a. Ce dossier a été confié a Marie et, selon toute probabilité, celui-ci le sera aussi.
This work was entrusted to Mary. That one will be too
b. Son premier tableau a été mis au musée, celui-ci le sera surement aussi.
Her first painting was put in a museum, that one will be too

There is, however, a clear difference between VP deletion and CLVD: the latter is essentially limited to passive contexts.[6] As shown in (22), the presence of the clitic cannot by itself ensure the grammaticality of CLVD in active intransitive constructions:

(22) a.*Jean a dormi et Paul l'a aussi
b.*Gianni ha dormido e Paolo lo ha anche
c.*Juan ha dormido y Pedro tambien lo ha
John has slept and Peter has it too

If as (20) & (21) suggest, CLVD bears similarity to VP deletion, this restriction is puzzling. Assuming following Zagona (1988) that null VPs must be licensed under government by I°, how can it be accounted for? It would seem, at first view, that the contrast between (19) and (22) should be attributed to the properties of their respective auxiliaries. Note, however, that as shown by (23), the auxiliary *être* cannot by itself license a null VP:

(23) a.*Jean sera photographié et Marie sera aussi
b.*Gianni fu fotografato e fu anche Paolo
c.*John fue retratado y Pedro fue tambien
John was photographed and Paul was too

Thus, to simply posit a distinction in government capacities between *être* and *avoir* is insufficient. Indeed, if we were to assume that *avoir* cannot be a governor for a null VP but that *être* can, the ungrammaticality of (23) would remain unexplained. Clearly, the licensing of CLVD must involve a relation between the auxiliary in I° and the resumptive clitic. It has been proposed by Kayne (1989) that the contrast between (19) and (22) may

---

[6]Other contexts in which CLVD occurs are copular sentences and some unaccusative constructions:

(i) Jean est furieux et Pierre l'est aussi
John is mad and Peter is too.

(ii) Les fleurs sont tombees mais les feuilles ne le sont pas
The flowers have fallen but the leaves have not

This shows that like VP deletion, CLVD can occur with various types of predicates.

be due to a difference in the Case assigning properties of the auxiliaries. Since the pro-predicate clitic *le* in (19) is identical in form to a regular object clitic, Kayne suggests that it may need Case. Assuming that *avoir* is not a Case assigner, (21) can then be simply excluded as a violation of the Case filter. That the auxiliary *avoir* is not a Case assigner is most probably correct. But it is quite doubtful that *être* should be assumed to differ from it in this regard. When we consider their respective non-auxiliary forms, it seems rather that it is *avoir*, not *être*, which manifests some Case assigning property. As shown in (24a), *avoir* can take a NP complement. As shown in (24b), it appears, furthermore, to be able to assign Case to the subject of a small clause in an ECM fashion.

(24) a. Jean a un ami
John has a friend
b. Jean a un ami (de) malade
John has a friend sick (i.e., who is sick)

Être, on the other hand, licenses only predicative NPs, which arguably do not require Case, if, as proposed by Chomsky (1981), Case is a condition on theta-assignment. Furthermore, it cannot assign Case to the subject of a small clause.

(25) a. Jean est un ami
John is a friend
b.*Il est un ami (de) malade
There/it is a friend sick (who is sick)

Given that the Case-assigning property of the non-auxiliary *être* is at best controversial, it seems rather doubtful that the passive auxiliary could be taken to be a Case assigner. More generally, it appears, in any event, that a distinction in the lexical property of the auxiliary is insufficient to account for the restriction on CLDV licensing. Indeed, as shown in (26), impersonal passives which are constructions requiring *être* do not license CLVD:[7]

(26) a.*Il sera tiré sur le bateau et il le sera sur le train
There will be shooting on the boat and there will be it on the train
b.*Il sera procedé a la revision de ce procès et il le sera a la revision de cet autre
There was proceeded to the review of this trial and there was it to the review of this other
c.*Il a été arreté beaucoup de gens aujourd'hui et il le sera aussi demain
There will be arrested may people today and there will be it tomorrow too

Besides auxiliary selection, another well known difference between the passive constructions in (19) and the active constructions in (22) is the behavior of their participles with respect to agreement. Passive participles always agree with their subjects, active participles never do, although, in appropriate contexts, they may agree with an object. It has been proposed by Kayne (1989) that past participle agreement involves Spec-head

---

[7]Other constructions which require *etre* but do not license CLVD are reflexive constructions such as (i):

(i) *Jean s'est lave et Pierre se l'est aussi
John washed himself and Peter did too.

agreement with a functional projection, latter termed AGR-0 in Chomsky (1989), located above the participle projection. Under this view, the structure of Romance compound tenses is as in (27):[8]

(27) ...$[_{IP}$...I°...$[_{AGRP}$...AGR-O...$[_{VP}$ participle]]]

Passive participle agreement with a derived subject can then be understood as resulting from the successive movement of the NP through the specifier of AGR-O as in (28):

(28) $Jean_i$ sera $[_{AGRP}$ t'_i AGR $[_{VP}$ arreté t_i]]

I will assume that the clitic which appears in the CLVD construction is in fact the head of AGR-O. That is, under normal conditions when the VP is present, AGR-O is a bound morpheme which fuses with the participle under head-movement. When the VP is deleted, however, the AGR-head is stranded and surfaces as a clitic. Under this view, the structure of the examples with a null VP in (19) is as in (29):

(29) $[_{IPi}$ $Jean_i$ sera $[_{AGRPi}$ le $[_{VP}$e]]

Note that in (29), it is no longer the I° head which directly dominates the null VP but rather the head of the functional projection. We may then assume that it is this head which head-governs the null VP. The licensing of CLVD will then depend on the relation between the clitic and the I°. As discussed above, in passive constructions, AGR-O bears the features of the sentential subject, due to Spec-head agreement. As a result, AGRP-O and I°, itself agreeing with the subject, bear the same phi-features. Within the present theory of agreement, this has the consequence that AGRP-O can now be L-marked by the functional head which dominates it, namely I°. Thus government across this projection will obtain. Assuming that in the CLVD passive constructions, this agreement relation is encoded, possibly because of layered traces or some equivalent mechanism independently needed for a movement derivation of passives in VP-deletion, the AGRP-O projection will be L-marked by I° so that the movement of the clitic to I° will be licensed since its trace can be head and antecedent governed. In active constructions, on the other hand, AGR-O never agrees with the sentential subject. This means that in such cases, I° bears different phi-features from AGR-O. As a result, the projection of AGR-O is not L-marked by I° and remains a barrier. The consequence for active CLDV is that the movement of the clitic heading AGR-O will be excluded by the ECP, since its trace can neither be head nor antecedent governed across the AGRP-O barrier. As a result, (22) whose structure is given in (30) will be excluded.

(30) *$[_{IPj}$ $Jean_j$ l' a $[_{AGRPi}$ t $[_{VP}$ ec]]

The proposed analysis has several interesting consequences. First, as required under Zagona's theory of null VP constructions, the null VP in CLVD is appropriately head governed by an inflectional head. Second, the contrast between (19) and (22) is accounted for independently of the lexical property of the auxiliary and with no stipulation regarding the governing status of I°. We can assume that all X° are head governors. Their actual governing effects follow from their L-marking capacity subsumed under the present

[8]Further possible expansions of IP are here omitted for ease of exposition.

theory of agreement. In similarity with C°, I° will head govern the trace of the clitic only if it L-marks its projection, that is, only if the transitivity of agreement required for L-marking is met. The proposed analysis further makes an important prediction. In constructions where agreement between the subject and the AGR-O does not obtain, CLDV will be excluded. This prediction is in fact confirmed by the ungrammaticality of (26). As shown by Kayne (1989), participle agreement in impersonal passive constructions in never possible, even when a post-verbal NP has been fronted under wh-movement:

(31) *Combien de filles crois tu qu'il sera invitées a cette soirée ?
How many girls do you think that there will be invited$_{+AGR}$ at this party ?

In other words, for reasons we will not get into (see Kayne 1989), the AGR-O projection is inert for agreement in these constructions. This, in the present view, is what explains the ungrammaticality of CLVD in (26). In absence of the transitivity of agreement required for L-marking, the AGR-O projection remains a barrier which prevents the government of the clitic trace by I°.

To sum up, I have argued, here that CLDV is licensed only when the conditions for the transitivity of agreement which is a condition for barrier transparency are met. These conditions are met through Spec-head agreement and head-head agreement between I° and AGR-O in passive constructions. They are not met in active or impersonal passive constructions since I° and AGR-O never agree.[9]

One question which remains is that of the distinction between English and Romance with respect to VP-deletion. An a priory plausible answer would be to assume that the distinction resides in the nature of I°. It has been proposed by Zagona (1982) that English I° has a "verbal" nature. Translated in the terms of the present approach, this would mean that English I° has properties comparable to V° and, as such, can L-mark its complement independently of agreement. In contrast, Romance I° could then be assumed to be more functional in nature, thus, requiring agreement to L-mark. As argued by Zagona (1988), however, this proposal is unsatisfactory in part because it predicts that V° should license null VPs, a prediction which as shown by (32) (= Zagona(88) # (10)) is not verified.

(32) *John was watching the movies and Paul started too.

Within the approach developed here, an alternative solution suggests itself. As is well known, English participles never agree, neither with a derived subject nor with an object. Furthermore, as shown by Pollock (1989), in English, contrary to French, adverbs can never intervene between a participle and its object NP. Within the framework adopted here, this suggests that AGR-O may in fact never be projected in English. Assuming this to be the case, we then have a simple solution for the distinction between English and Romance with respect to the licensing of null VPs. In English, since AGR-O is not present

---

[9]Although, as I argue, the transitivity of agreement between the subject I° and AGR-O is a necessary condition for the licensing of CLDV, it does not appear to always be a sufficient condition. Thus for instance, in the reflexive constructions mentioned in footnote 7 above, although past participle agreement with the subject obtains, CLDV is not licensed. The investigation of further conditions on CLDV is beyond the scope of the present paper.

in the structure, I° is directly adjacent to the null VP. That is, the structure of a null VP construction is schematically as in (33).

(33) $[_{IP}...I^{o}\ [_{VP}\ ec]]$

In this structure, L-marking is not required for the government of the null VPs. This predicts correctly that agreement will have no effect on VP-deletion. In Romance on the other hand, AGR-O is projected and thus intervenes between I° and the null VP. As a consequence, direct licensing of the null VP by I° is not possible. The licensing of null VP constructions in these languages must necessarily be mediated by the relation between I°, AGR-0 and the null VP. Under this view, the parameter accounting for the distinction between English and Romance with respect to VP-deletion resides simply in the fact that the functional projection of AGRPO is absent in the former and present in the latter. As a final remark, note that this proposal presents an interesting parallelism with the proposal made above for the licensing of subject extractions. Recall that to account for the French/English difference in this respect, I have suggested that CP, which is always projected in French, may be missing in English. Although the precise conditions under which functional heads are required to project in the syntax remains to be worked out, this parallelism is sufficiently striking to invite further investigation.

Conclusion

In this paper I have presented an account of the relation between C°, IP and the subject trace in extractions and between I°, AGR-O and the null VP in VP-deletion. Unifying these two apparently unrelated empirical domains is a theory of agreement, here construed as affecting barrier transparency.

References

Chomsky, Noam. 1981. *Lectures on Government and Binding*. Dordrecht: Foris

Chomsky, Noam. 1986. *Knowledge of Language*, New York: Praeger

Chomsky, Noam. 1989. Some notes on Economy of Derivation. *MIT Working papers in Linguistics* 10.

Deprez, Viviane. 1989. *On the Typology of Syntactic Positions and the Nature of Chains*. Ph.D dissertation, MIT

Deprez, Viviane. 1991. Economy and the That-t Effect. to appear Proceedings of WECOL 10.

Frampton, John. 1990. Parasitic Gaps and the Theory of Wh-chains. *Linguistic Inquiry* 21. Cambridge: MIT Press

Friedeman, Marc-Ariel. 1989. Le *Que* interrogatif. ms University of Geneva

Kayne, Richard. 1989. Facets of Romance past participle agreement. in Paola Beninca Ed *Dialect Variation and the Theory of Grammar*. Dordrecht: Foris

Lobeck, Anne. 1986.*Syntactic constraints on VP Elipsis*, Ph.D dissertation U. of Washington

Pollock, Jean-Yves. 1989. Verb Movement, Universal Grammar and the Structure of IP. *Linguistic Inquiry* 20:365-424 Cambridge: MIT Press

Rizzi, Luigi. 1990. *Relativized Minimality*. Cambridge: MIT Press.

Zagona, Karen. 1982. *Government and Proper Government of Verbal Projections*, Phd dissertation, U. of Washington.

Zagona, Karen. 1988. Proper government and Antecedentless VP in English and Spanish. *Natural Language and Linguistic Theory* 1: 95-128. Dordrecht: Kluwer

'Variable-Free' Syntax, Variable-Binding Syntax, the Natural Deduction Lambek Calculus, and the Crossover Constraint

DAVID DOWTY
Ohio State University

In recent work, Szabolcsi (1987, 1989) and Jacobson (1991a, 1991b) have endorsed 'variable-free syntax', a combinatory categorial grammar (CCG) in which combinators serve to 'bind' anaphoric arguments to NP antecedents or WH-words, without literally invoking variables in the syntax or even in the semantics of gaps and bound pronouns, along lines suggested in the work of V.W. Quine and in combinatory logic.

But how different is variable-free syntax, ultimately, from familiar syntactic analyses that use variables? In this paper[1] I will argue that the significance of eschewing variables is not what it probably first appears. Furthermore, the 'Natural Deduction' formulation of the Lambek Calculus (henceforth NDLC) proposed by Morrill (1989) and others and developed in Hepple (1990, 1991) perspicuously enables us to see how this is so, inasmuch as analyses in NDLC can be transparently converted to variable-free CCG analyses on the one hand, and to traditional index-and-binding analyses on the other. This framework is thus an interesting medium for theory comparison, in addition to its merits in its own right.

What we can see from this comparison is that important differences among the three approaches do exist, though they do not lie simply in the presence or absence of variables, but elsewhere: most importantly for the present paper, in the degree to which the familiar 'C-command constraint' on anaphoric binding is stated (or follows automatically), and, very strikingly, in the way that the (Strong and Weak) Crossover Constraint (Postal 1971, Jacobson 1977) is predicted to exist (to perhaps varying extents) in the CCG account of crossover (and related phenomena with functional questions and paycheck pronouns) that Jacobson (1991b) describes and in parallel analyses I will construct for NDLC. I will also discuss briefly the possibility of 'translating' such analyses into more traditional variable-and-binder theories and suggest points at which further investigation of such cross-theoretical relationships might be productive.

The Lambek Calculus (here specifically, the product-free, bidirectional Lambek calculus) differs from other versions of categorial grammar in its use of a SLASH INTRODUCTION rule, or **/-I**, in addition to the more familiar SLASH ELIMINATION

[1] I would like to thank Chris Barker, Mark Hepple and, Pauline Jacobson for very helpful discussion of this material. This is not of course to imply they will necessarily share my conclusions, and I alone am responsible for any remaining errors.

rule, or **/-E** (often called FUNCTIONAL APPLICATION). In the NDLC formulation these rules are (roughly) (1)-(2):

(1) **/-E**:

$$\frac{\begin{matrix}\vdots & \vdots \\ A/B:\ \alpha & B:\ \beta\end{matrix}}{A:\ \alpha(\beta)}\ /\text{-E}$$

(2) **/-I**:

$$\frac{\begin{matrix}[B]:\ v \\ \vdots \\ A:\ \alpha\end{matrix}}{A/B:\ \lambda v[\alpha]}\ /\text{-I}$$

(I omit here the mirror image versions of these rules, **\-E** and **\-I**, and I ignore also conditions on relative order of undischarged arguments necessary to preserve proper word order: see Hepple (1990:10-14) for details.) **/-I** can be seen as the analog of the rule of Conditionalization in propositional logic, in that it allows us to temporarily 'assume' an additional, hypothetical category B (indicated by square brackets) that is not actually present in the string in question and derive an analysis of that string plus the hypothesis as belonging to category A, but only if one later DISCHARGES this temporary hypothesis by **/-I**, i.e. further deriving from A the final category A/B. The semantic interpretations for **/-E** and **/-I** are added in (1) and (2) following the colons: **/-E** is interpreted as functional application, and **I-/** is equivalent to abstraction over a variable corresponding to the hypothesized category. A simple example of a derivation from A/B + B/C to A/C illustrates **/-I** in (3); an NDLC analysis of an English relative clause with gap is in (4):

(3)

$$\cfrac{\cfrac{A/B:\ \alpha \qquad \cfrac{B/C:\ \beta \qquad [C]:\ v}{B:\ \beta(v)}\ /\text{-E}}{A:\ \alpha(\beta(v))}\ /\text{-E}}{A/C:\ \lambda v[\alpha(\beta((v))]}\ /\text{-I}$$

(4)

who	John	says	Bill	loves	
rel/(s/np)	np	s\np/s	np	s\np/np	[np]

- s\np/np + [np] ⇒ s\np (/-E)
- np + s\np ⇒ s\np (\-E)
- s\np/s + s ⇒ s\np (/-E)
- np + s\np ⇒ s (\-E)
- s ⇒ s/np (/-I)
- rel/(s/np) + s/np ⇒ rel (/-E)

(5) [Rel who [S λx_i [S [N′ John] [V′ [V says] [S [N′ Bill] [V′ [V loves] [N′ x_i]]]]]]]

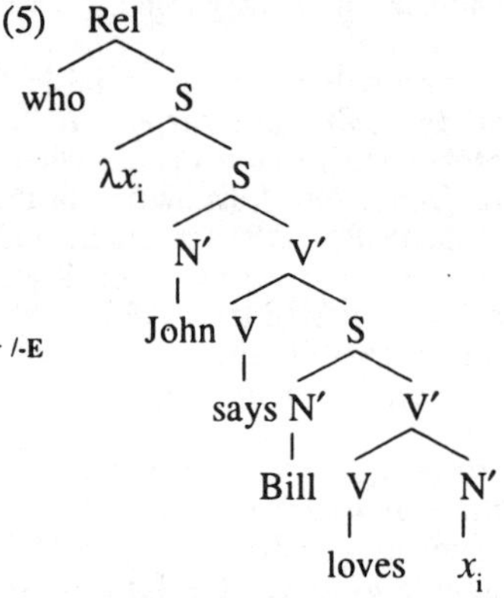

That is, in (4) we 'hypothesize' the additional np designated '[np]', prove that by including it the string *John says Bill loves* would be of category s, then use **/-I** to discharge this assumption and thereby show that the string without np is actually of category s/np: following Steedman (1987) I have assumed that a relative pronoun *who* is of category rel/(s/np) and thus can take this s/np as an argument.

A derivation such as (4) bears an obvious resemblance to a familiar LF for a relative clause in which the '[np]' corresponds to an empty category or trace and the operation of **/-I** corresponds to a (silent) operator binding this trace--in other words something like (5). This suggests an informal algorithm for converting a NDLC analysis to a more familiar trace-and-binding analysis:

(6) *Algorithm for NDLC-analysis to variable-and-binder analysis conversion:*

(a) convert NDLC derivation to nearest equivalent phrase-marker
(b) replace subsequently discharged assumptions with empty categories
(c) at points where **/-I** is used in NDLC derivation, insert a variable-binding operator coindexed with that empty category.

There is not much point in trying to make this algorithm more than informal, however, since the details of the phrase markers and categories in them in currently-accepted transformational analyses of binding will not match up too precisely with the those employed in Hepple's (1990) NDLC or current CCG analyses. But the relationship defined loosely in (6) will be clear enough for us to make useful comparisons below and suggest others.

However, Hepple (1990:13) correctly cautions us against taking this resemblance between discharged assumptions and empty categories too literally: the hypothesized category in a NDLC is 'not really there' but is simply part of the means to demonstrate formally that the string WITHOUT the hypothesized category is a well-formed expression of the indicated final functor category.

Probably the best way to appreciate this fact is to realize that, e.g., (3) above amounts to a proof of a theorem of NDLC that for any categories A/B, B/C and A/C: A/B and B/C can be combined directly to form A/C (in symbols, A/B + B/C ⇒ B/C) -- in other words, the familiar rule of functional composition in CCG. Since the syntax of NDLC has the structure of a formal deductive system, in which appeal to any valid theorem in a derivation is fully as appropriate as appeal to a primitive inference rule of the system, we would for example be perfectly entitled to derive the relative clause in (4) in the NDLC with the simpler 'Steedman-style' derivation (7) by appealing to this functional composition theorem (designated FC in the derivation):

```
(7) who            John    says     Bill       loves
    rel/(s/np)     np  T   s\np/s   np    T    s\np/np
                 s/(s\np)          s/(s\np)
                                   ------------------- FC
                                          s/np
                           ---------------------- FC
                                   s\np/np
                 ----------------------------- FC
                              s/np
    ------------------------------------------ /-E
                    rel
```

This in turn leads to the observation that ALL the combinators advocated by linguists for CCGs for natural languages (functional composition, type raising, and as will be illustrated below, combinators proposed by Jacobson) can be derived as theorems of the NDLC (or indeed in any version of the Lambek calculus).

Therefore, one way of viewing the relationship between the NDLC and CCG would be to see the NDLC as a system of 'meta-rules' which can be used to generate as theorems a variety of combinators which would then in turn constitute a combinatory categorial grammar, much as the meta-rules of GPSG generate a large set of phrase-structure rules that actually generate sentences:[2]

(8) *Algorithm for converting a NDLC analysis to a CCG analysis*

(i) Using NDLC derivations involving /-I, \-I (and other assumption-discharging rules to be discussed below), generate an appropriate stock of theorems which do not involve any hypothesized categories (e.g., theorems such as Functional Composition, Type-Raising, etc.).

(ii) Using these theorems as additional modes of combination (= 'combinators'), generate categorial derivations of all English sentences without using any hypothesized categories.

With this background, I turn to Jacobson's analysis of pronoun binding, functional questions, and paycheck sentences. Jacobson (1991b), like Hepple (1990, 1991), treats 'ordinary' bound pronouns as denoting the identity function. Thus the phrase *thinks that Mary said that he lost* in (9), assuming it is semantically built up by functional composition, would be semantically analyzed as (9'):

(9) Every man_i thinks that Mary said that he_i lost.

(9') $\mathit{think} \circ \lambda p[\mathit{say}(p)(m)] \circ \mathit{lost} \circ \lambda x x$
$= \lambda x[\mathit{think}(\mathit{say}(m, [\mathit{lost}(x)]))]$.

Note that this is a function from individuals x to a property (thinking that Mary says something about x), so the quantifier *every man* must be combined so as to bind TWO argument positions here. It might seem we should simply postulate a combinator (like Curry and Fey's 'duplicator' **W**) which converts a relation to a property and apply this to the meaning in (9), then just add the quantifier, but instead Jacobson motivates a slightly more complex combinatorial operation to use at this point, via functional questions and paycheck pronouns.

The so-called FUNCTIONAL QUESTION reading (Groenendijk and Stokhof 1981, Engdahl 1986) of a question (10) is one for which the answer does not denote a single individual, as does (11a), but in effect denotes a function, (11b). That is, on their analysis we can paraphrase the functional reading of (10) as (10') and its answer as (11b'):

---

[2] I should mention an objection to this (hypothetical) view of CCG. It is well-known that by taking certain sets of combinators as primitives (e.g., the four Curry and Feys (1958) combinators **B**, **S**, **C** and **I**), a system results which is equivalent to the Lambek Calculus, insofar as iterations and combinations of primitive combinators achieve the expressive capacity of variable binding as in the lambda calculus. However, smaller subsets of combinators result in more restricted systems, and both Steedman (1987) and Szabolcsi (1989) have explicitly argued that such 'sub-Lambek' systems make empirically desirable predictions about natural language syntax, in that they systematically rule out certain kinds of structures which do not in fact occur in human languages but which the full Lambek calculus would allow. This is not the place to debate this issue in general (cf. the previous citations for some discussion), except perhaps to note that the NDLC of Hepple is not really equivalent to a normal Lambek Calculus but rather has built into it a rich system of island and locality constraints and a c-command condition on binding that follows from the nature of the binding rule: if we translate from Hepple-type NDLC analyses into CCG, such constraints which would be stated unitarily in Hepple's NDLC might have to be stated as constraints on several independent primitive combinators in a CCG, so in this sense Hepple's approach might capture certain kinds of linguistic generalizations that a CCG would not.

(10) Who does every Englishman love?

(11) a. The Queen
b. His mother

(10') What is the function f such that *every-Englishman*(λx[*love*(f(x))(x)])

(11b') f is the *mother-of* function.

On this view the gap in (10) has complex meaning, which might be described as consisting of both an individual variable x bound by *every Englishman* and a variable f (over functions from individuals to individuals) bound by the WH-phrase. Jacobson proposes to capture this analysis in a CCG by postulating a new combinator **z**:

(12) Let F be a function of type <χ, <e, ψ>> (for χ and ψ variables over types). Then **z**(F) is a function of type <<e, χ>, <e, ψ>>, where **z**(F) = λg[λx[F(g(x))(x)]] (for g a variable of type <e, χ>).

(Jacobson, unlike Hepple, assumes a so-called 'polymorphic' correlation of semantic types with natural language categories: in particular, that when **z** combines with a predicate, that predicate changes the semantic type of its denotation but not its syntactic category.) Then the phrase *every Englishman loves* (in the embedded question in *John knows who every Englishman loves*) will have its meaning constructed via **z** and functional composition (indicated '°') as in (13). That is, this denotes the set of functions f that will map any individual x into the individual $f(x)$ that x loves, where x is a variable bound by *every Englishman.*

(13) *every-Englishman* ° **z**(*love*) =
every-Englishman ° λf[λx[*love*(f(x))(x)]] =
λf[*every-Englishman*(λx[*love*(f(x))(x)])]

As Jacobson notes, this analysis generalizes nicely to paycheck pronouns, such as the italicized pronouns in (14):

(14) a. The woman who put her paycheck in the bank was wiser that the one who put *it* in the Brown Credit Union.
b. Every graduate student deposited her paycheck, but every professor lost *it*.

The parallel with functional questions lies in the fact that the pronoun *it* in, e.g., (14b) depends anaphorically on both *her paycheck* and *Every professor*: the former because *it* refers to the paycheck of someone, but the latter because it is each professor's paycheck that is referred to, not each graduate student's: that is, *paycheck* provides the value of the function variable f, while *every professor* binds the individual variable x, to give $f(x)$, the denotation of the pronoun. As is actually anticipated in Cooper (1979), Jacobson notes that if we simply let the function in pronoun denotations range over ALL possible functions from individuals to individuals (with its denotation possibly supplied by context), 'ordinary' pronouns can be viewed as special instances of paycheck pronouns, since the identity function (which can be regarded as the f in an ordinary bound pronoun's denotation) is merely one such function. Jacobson's analysis of the second clause of (14b) proceeds by applying **z** to *lost*: (Thus the f function here is treated as a kind of definite discourse anaphora, as in Cooper's and Evans' E-PRONOUN analysis.)

(15) *every-professor*(**z**(*lost*))(f) = *every-professor*(λg[λx[*lost*(g(x))(x)]](f))
= *every-professor*(λx[*lost*(f(x))(x)])

At this point, let us turn to Hepple's analysis of anaphora and binding. As mentioned, WH-gaps are analyzed as hypothesized assumptions (of category np) that are later discharged by **/-I**. Pronouns are treated as (approximately) of category np/np and denote the identify function on individuals: they will always combine with a hypothesized np argument to their right to form a np (see (17) below). The reason for this combination of np/np and [np] is that a hypothesized argument must be involved in deriving bound pronouns, because hypothesized arguments are the ONLY means to achieve the semantic effect of 'binding' in NDLC, yet note that the pronoun itself cannot be the subsequently-discharged argument (i.e., the [np]), for this would predict it cannot have any syntactic realization. This NP binding rule, for reflexive and non-reflexive pronouns, called the BINDING INTERPRETATION RULE, or **BIR**, in Hepple (1991) is (16):

```
(16)    BIR:  [⊕B]^i: x
                 :                 where C is A\B or A/B
               C: f
             ─────────── BIR^i
             C: λx[f(x)]
```

Here A and B as well as C are of course variables over categories: for NP anaphora, the category B will be np and category C will be s\np (i.e., where the antecedent that does the np-binding is a subject) or s\np/np (where the antecedent is a direct object), etc. (The superscripting of the BIR application to match an index on the hypothesized category in (16) and in derivations below are for expository clarity and for more easily checking that a side condition on **/-I** is met (cf. footnote 1): they are not in any sense an essential 'coindexing' feature of the system.) Note that the rule does not change the category of the output but it affects the semantics: after BIR applies, the next np to combine with the A\np or A/np functor will both be interpreted as the argument of that functor and also 'bind' the argument position represented by the hypothesized np which is somewhere inside the interpretation of this functor.[3] An example is in (17), its semantics (17'):[4]

```
(17)  Every      man      loves        himself
      np/n        n /-E   s\np/np      np/⊕np        [⊕np]^i /-E
           np                          ──────────────────np /-E
                                     s\np   BIR^i
                                     s\np   \-E
                          s
```

[3] This semantic rule may be stated in such a way as to appear to make use of the notion of 'variable' in an essential way, but this is because the lambda-calculus has been used as the semantic meta-language in which to give the semantics for the language: alternative methods could have been used instead. Also, the use of a variable *f* in Jacobson's analysis in (15) is not essential, though for a different reason: See Jacobson (1991) for explanation.

[4] For simplicity of exposition, I have equivocated as to whether the category np denotes individuals or generalized quantifiers, using whichever is convenient in translations. This of course can easily be made consistent either by replacing np denotations by their 'sublimations' (the '$\lambda P[P\{x_0\}]$' of Montague Grammar) and treating verbs as higher-order predicates, or else by using higher-type categories for quantificational NPs, e.g., s/(s\np) for subjects, etc.

(17')	$[\oplus\text{np}]^i$	$\Rightarrow v_i$	*himself*	$\Rightarrow \lambda x[x](v_i) = v_i$
	loves himself	$\Rightarrow$	$love(v_i)$	
	BIR^i(*loves himself*)	$\Rightarrow$	$\lambda v_i[love(v_i)(v_i)]$	
	Every man loves himself	$\Rightarrow$	$every\text{-}man(\lambda v_i[love(v_i)(v_i)])$	

There is also independent motivation for the pronominal category np/np in Hepple's system: I have ignored up to now his theory of island and locality constraints, which is implemented via a system of (multiple) modal operators. Different kinds of bound arguments are actually represented by the variants of np and np/np categories in (18):

(18)	WH-gaps:	Δnp
	reflexive pronouns:	np/$\oplus$np
	non-reflexive pronouns:	□np/$\oplus$np

Although I cannot go into the details of this system of constraints here (see Hepple 1990, 1991 for this), I note (i) the absence of any operator in front of the left np for the reflexive category ensures that it must be bound within its clause or VP, (ii) the □operator in the non-reflexive category ensures that its binding is not subject to either clause-internal or WH-island binding conditions, and (iii) the Δ operator in the WH-gap category determines that WH-binding is subject to WH-islands but not a single-clause domain (in English) and is in addition motivated by Hepple's treatment of non-peripheral extraction, which is arguably superior to that in Steedman (1987). The operator I have symbolized '$\oplus$' here also appears in the Binding Interpretation Rule below but not anywhere else in the grammar, thus guaranteeing that the pronominal category np/$\oplus$np cannot combine with a real NP to give e.g.,**him John*, yet allowing all kinds of NP binding to be done by a single rule: this allows Hepple to effectively describe such complex conditions as those found with Icelandic reflexives, which must be bound within their clause in many contexts but can be bound outside them in certain others (Hepple 1990:166-174, 1991). Use of (variants of) np/np makes all this possible.

Consider now how an analysis of functional questions like Jacobson's can be cast in terms of Hepple's theory: it turns out that essentially no modification is needed. In Jacobson's analysis of the functional question *Who every Englishman loves*, the word *who* must take an argument of (semantic) type <<e,e>,t>, whereas *who* in ordinary non-functional questions take arguments of type <e,t>. As mentioned, Jacobson assumes a 'polymorphic' theory (in which the same syntactic category, indeed the same expression, can have multiple semantic types), and we could if desired possibly take this same approach in a NDLC, but in this paper I will assume semantic type is determined uniquely by syntactic category, as is usually done in Lambek-calculus analyses. This means that while *who* in ordinary questions will take an argument of category s/np, in functional questions its argument must be of category s/(np/$\oplus$np): *who* itself thus belongs to both Q/(s/np) and Q/(s/(np/$\oplus$np)), where Q is the category of questions.[5] Alternatively, we could assign *who* to the schematic category Q/(s/np\$), using \$ as in Steedman (1987). This is all we need to derive functional questions: the category np/$\oplus$np is of course the pronoun category in Hepple's theory, and a functional question will

[5] To make the 'extraction' subject to the proper island-constraints, the categories for *who* should include a 'Δ' operator, as do all WH-extraction triggers for Hepple, i.e., they should be Q/(s/Δnp) and Q/(s/Δ(np/$\oplus$np)). But I omit 'Δ' below to simplify the derivations. The rightmost category in (19) should then actually be $[\Delta\oplus\text{np}]^j$.

have TWO hypothesized categories in its derivation:

(19) who every Englishman loves

Q/(s/(np/⊕np)) np/n n s\np/np $[\text{np}/\oplus\text{np}]^i$ $[\oplus\text{np}]^j$ /-E

np np /-E

s\np BIR^j

s\np \-E

s /-I^i

s/(np/⊕np) /-E

Q

(19') $[\oplus\text{np}]^i$ $\Rightarrow v_i$

$[\text{np}/\oplus\text{np}]^j$ $\Rightarrow f_j$ (*N.B.* f *is of type* <*e,e*>)

$[\text{np}/\oplus\text{np}]^j\ [\oplus\text{np}]^i$ $\Rightarrow f_j(v_i)$

loves $\Rightarrow love(f_j(v_i)$

BIV^i(*loves*) $\Rightarrow \lambda v_i[love(f_j(v_i))(v_i)]$

every Englishman loves $\Rightarrow$ *every-Englishman*$(\lambda v_i[love(f_j(v_i))(v_i)])$

/-I^j(*Every Englishman loves*) $\Rightarrow \lambda f_j[$*every-Engl.*$(\lambda v_i[love(f_j(v_i))(v_i)])]$

Who every Englishman loves $\Rightarrow$ *who*$(\lambda f_j[$*every-Engl.*$(\lambda v_i[love(f_j(v_i))(v_i)])])$

The resulting functional interpretation is exactly the same as Jacobson's. Note that we did not need to stipulate an operator **z** in order to derive it: this is because **z** is in effect a mode of combination which is a theorem of Hepple's NDLC, a theorem whose proof is implicit in the above. To show it more compactly:

(20) A\B/C: α $[\text{C/B}]^j: f$ $[\text{B}]^i: x$ /-E

C: $f(x)$ /-E

A\B: $\alpha(f(x))$ BIR^j

A\B: $\lambda x[\alpha(f(x))(x)]$ /-I^j

A\B/(C/B): $\lambda f\lambda x[\alpha(f(x))(x)]$

Thus the theorem A\B/C: $\alpha \rightarrow$ A\B/(C\B): $\lambda f\lambda x[\alpha(f(x))(x)]$ is in effect a legitimate (unary) 'combinator' to use in NDLC derivations: Jacobson's **z** combinator is the specific instance of this where B = np (i.e., type e). (Category C is also equal to np in all cases discussed here.) We could if we wished appeal to this to give a shorter derivation of (19), namely (21), which would result in the same interpretation (which I omit). Here, I appeal to type-raising (**T** below) [6]
as well as **z**:

(21) who every Englishman loves

Q/(s/(np/⊕np)) np/n n /-E s\np/np Z

np T (s\np)/(np/⊕np)

s/(s\np) FC

s/(np/⊕np) /-E

Q

---

[6] I include this for (hopefully) greater clarity, though if as mentioned in note 4 the category 'np' is to be consistently replaced with s/(s\np), (s\np)\(s\np/np), etc., this step is unnecessary.

We can likewise extend this approach to Jacobson's **z**-analysis of paycheck pronouns: Like Cooper and Jacobson, we simply generalize the denotation of Hepple's pronouns of category np/⊕np from just the identity function (as Hepple specified) to ANY function of this type, in particular, one whose value can be supplied by the surrounding linguistic context. The second clause in (14b) (= *Every graduate student deposited her paycheck in the bank, but every professor lost it*) would be derived as in (22):

(22) Every professor lost it

Every: np/n, professor: n ⟹ (/-E) np
lost: s\np/np, it: np/⊕np, $[\oplus np]^i$ ⟹ (/-E) np^i
lost + np^i ⟹ (/-E) s\np ⟹ (BIR^i) s\np
np + s\np ⟹ (\-E) s

(22') $[\oplus np]^i \Rightarrow v_i$ $\quad$ *it* $\Rightarrow f$
it $[\oplus np]^i \Rightarrow f(v_i)$ $\quad$ *lost it* $\Rightarrow lost(f(v_i))$
BIV^i(*lost it*) $\Rightarrow \lambda v_i[lost(f(v_i))]$
every professor lost it $\Rightarrow$ *every-professor*$(\lambda v_i[lost(f(v_i))])$

In the last line of (21'), f is free and is contextually interpreted, thus the interpretation is that for each professor x, x lost $f(x)$, where f is the *paycheck-of* function. Once again, a single combinator like **z** could be derived in NDLC which would apply directly to the verb and pronoun without invoking the hypothesized [⊕np] or **BIR**, but I forego more details here.

As Jacobson notes, further configurations of arguments that can appear in functional questions require her to schematize her definition of **z** across categories in yet other ways besides the type variables in (12) (see Jacobson 1991b, definition (37)). But these 'other **z**'s' will also be provable as theorems in NDLC with Hepple's binding theory without any further generalization. Also, she notes empirical reasons why **z** cannot be a lexical operation but must apply to syntactic phrases (cf. her example (38)), and this too is predicted if we use the NDLC analysis (or derive the **z** combinator(s) via it).

I turn now to the familiar CROSS-OVER CONSTRAINT(S) (Postal 1971, Jacobson 1977), of which the so-called WEAK version is illustrated by the impossibility of the indicated coreferential interpretation in (23b) (vis-a-vis (23a)), and the STRONG version by (24a) vs. (24b):

(23) a. the man_i who loves his_i mother.
b. *the man_i who his_i mother loves.

(24) a. the $woman_i$ who John told $\_\_\__i$ that Bill loves her_i.
b. *the $woman_i$ who John told her_i that Bill loves $\_\_\__i$.

It is an interesting property of a system in which combinators do the work of variable binding, as well as of the Lambek Calculus, that each binding 'operation' binds exactly one variable 'position': there is no vacuous binding, and likewise no binding of multiple variable positions by the same binder (or quantifier).[7] In the lambda-calculus or in ordinary predicate logic, by contrast, a quantifier or lambda-operator may bind one, many, or no variables. Why this is so is perhaps easiest to see from what has been presented so far of the NDLC: in both the rule of **/-I** and Hepple's **BIR**, note that the rule is required to 'discharge' an assumption -- if one cannot be discharged, the rule cannot be applied. Also, once an assumption has been discharged, it cannot be discharged again by a later rule application. Thus there is a necessary one-to-one correspondence in each derivation between discharged assumptions (interpreted like variables) and binding operations.

This fact, however, does not imply that CCG and the Lambek calculus are powerless to deal with grammatical examples like (23a) and (24a) (in which a WH-gap and a pronoun are bound to the same head) or sentences like (25) or (26), with a NP binding two pronouns:

(25) Every man_i said that he_i admires himself_i.

(26) Every man_i said that the woman who knows him_i doesn't love him_i.

One way to generate many such examples in these theories is for one pronoun to bind another pronoun, then for the antecedent NP to bind the first pronoun (and therefore since coindexing is a transitive relation, the effect is the same as if the NP bound both pronouns). Careful reflection on Hepple's **BIR** or Jacobson's **z** will reveal that there is in fact nothing that would prohibit one pronoun from binding another, and this possibility is also motivated empirically for the 'sloppy' readings of VP-ellipsis cases like (27) and (28) (Jacobson 1991):

(27) He hates his mother, and so do I.
(28) They don't really respect themselves, but we do.

Another way of getting such multiple coindexing would be to apply **BIR** (or Jacobson's **z**) twice in succession to the same phrase just before it combines with the NP antecedent argument, e.g., $\mathbf{BIR}_i(\mathbf{BIR}_j($*said that ... him* $[\oplus \text{np}]^i$ *doesn't love him* $[\oplus \text{np}]^j))$. This possibility is in fact necessary for examples like (26) above (Jacobson 1991b), since neither pronoun is in a structural position where it can bind the other (more on that shortly).

In the case of one pronoun and one WH-gap both coindexed to the head of the WH-construction, i.e., the potential Crossover violations in (23) and (24), the situation is slightly different. The last method (the same binding operation applies iteratively) is not possible in this case in NDLC: whereas NP binding uses one NP argument to determine the semantic value of another and can be iterated if the binding np is itself a hypothesized category, the nature of the WH-binding precludes iteration, since its result is a relative clause or question, not a category that can be input to another binding rule. And we would not want to alter BIR to permit it to bind WH-gaps as well as pronouns, since it 'discharges' its hypothesized np-arguments and would thus not leave behind the 'unsaturated' category (i.e., a s/np after **/-I** applies) that a WH-word demands as argument.

---

[7] Jacobson (1991b) and Szabolcsi (1989) are of course also aware of this.

Rather, for examples (23) or (24) to be generated, either the gap must bind the pronoun, or the pronoun must bind the gap. In fact, in Hepple's binding analysis in the NDLC it turns out that nothing at all would prohibit a gap from binding a pronoun via **BIR**. In order to illustrate how this works in a sentence like (23a), it will be necessary to invoke some kind of 'Wrap' analysis, since in the CG literature it is well-known that the object NP arguments of verbs like *tell* and *persuade* must be less oblique than their infinitival or sentential complements, i.e., the object NP arguments must combine with the verb later than the other complement. But for simplicity of exposition, I will not adopt Hepple's way of reconstructing Wrap in the Lambek Calculus but adopt the expedient of 'inserting' a wrapped-in argument in the middle of a string and enclosing it in parentheses to show its status. A functor marked for wrapping-in its argument is indicated by '//', and '...' connects parts of a derivation contiguous prior to wrapping. Cf. (29):

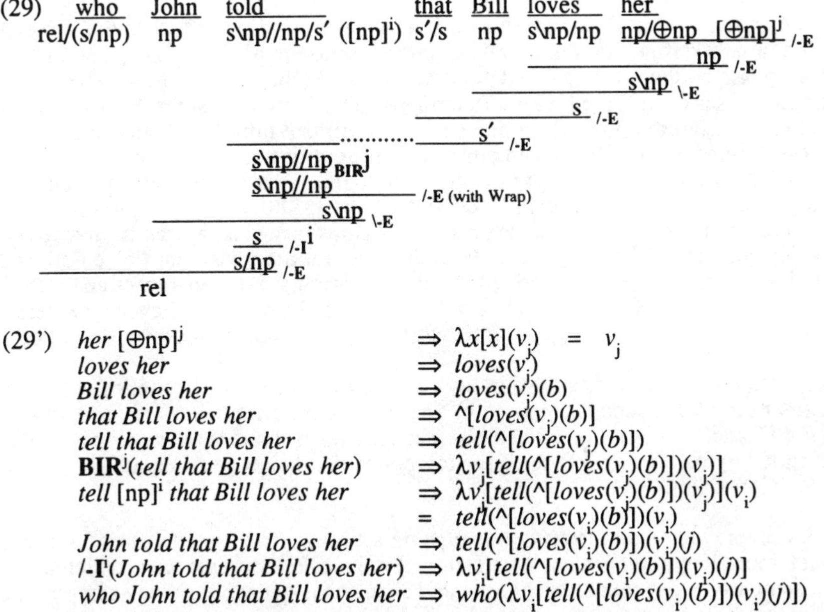

Could a pronoun also bind a WH-gap in this binding theory? (By *pronoun* here I mean a pronoun in np/⊕np plus hypothesized ⊕np). No it could not, first of all, because the hypothetical categories that are bound are actually distinct in Hepple's system (because of the need to make them subject to different island conditions): i.e. **BIR** discharges only the category ⊕np, while WH-words actually demand a clause containing a Δnp gap. But for the sake of argument, let us ignore this difference: even without it, a pronoun cannot bind a WH-gap for essentially the same reason that we cannot iterate a binding rule to get this case: the **BIR** discharges a hypothesized argument, while for a WH-construction we must have a remaining undischarged np at the point at which the final clause is produced, in order to use **/-I** to convert this s into the s/Δnp that the WH-word needs as its argument.

The final piece we need to complete the explanation of Crossover is the observation that the **BIR** (16) (cf. above), by its nature, enforces a kind of 'c-command' constraint between antecedent np and bound anaphor. This is because **BIR** discharges a category which has already been used earlier in the derivation of the functor C (= A\B or A/B) to which **BIR** applies: since expressions are derived 'bottom-up' (less confusingly with the present form of derivation diagram, 'from the inside out'), and since it is the argument of this (whole) functor C which is interpreted as the NP binding the discharged category, the argument of the functor C will necessarily be introduced later in the derivation (= 'higher' in the nearest corresponding phrase-marker) than the bound pronoun. The reason that **BIR** (or the parallel binding rule of Bach and Partee (1980)) not only does but must work this way is essentially a constraint of compositional semantics: given the standard Tarski-style semantics for variables binding, binders/quantifiers must be added to the expression containing a variable (or an otherwise unsaturated predicate, as in CCG), not vice-versa. Predicate logic also necessarily imposes a 'c-command' constraint between binders and variables for the same reason.

As has often been observed, this notion of 'command' is not quite the same as c-command defined on the usually-assumed phrase markers but is rather an 'obliqueness' notion, often dubbed F-COMMAND, based on the order in which various arguments are combined with a functor (which mirrors the steps by which their semantic interpretations are composed): an argument introduced later in the derivation F-commands any argument or constituent of that argument. In terms of obliqueness, a less oblique argument F-commands a more-oblique argument. (In fact, the NP-binding rules in Bach and Partee (1980) and the similar ones in Chierchia (1988) have this same property.)[8] But since (i) a gap can be antecedent for a pronoun but not vice-versa (and they cannot otherwise both be coindexed with the gap's controller), and (ii) an antecedent must F-command its anaphor, it follows that a WH-gap must always F-command the pronoun, never vice-versa, and this is exactly the configuration that (Strong and Weak) Crossover describes.

Essentially the same relationship on 'co-indexing' of bound pronouns and WH-gaps hold in Jacobson's (1991a,b) analysis of binding (via **z**) is in Hepple's NDLC, and her definition of **z** entails that a bound pronoun is always F-com.cp 2 manded by its binding NP, so as she too points out, her analysis entails the Crossover Constraint.

Moreover, Jacobson discusses in some detail how correct predictions from this fact about her anaphora analysis follow for Bach-Peters sentences (which arguably involve 'paycheck' pronouns) and functional questions. For example, the fact that (30a,b) are grammatical while (31a,b) are not:

(30) a. Every man_i who loves her_j kissed his_i $wife_j$.
b. Every man_i who loves her_j kissed the $woman_j$ who wrote to him_i.

---

[8] As noticed by Bach and Partee (1980) and commented on subsequently by several writers, there may be linguistic arguments for F-command over c-command from sentences like *The guru showed every woman herself* (vs. **The guru showed herself every woman.*) and *Mary talked to every man about himself* (vs. **Mary talked about every man to himself*), where a difference in c-command that would account for the assymmetry in anaphoric possibilities is hard or impossible to justify empirically. The F-command theory of obliqueness, on the other hand, entails that of any two subcategorized arguments, one is necessarily more oblique than the other, and evidence of of a phrase-structural difference is not required to motivate this.

(31) a. *Every man$_i$ who she$_j$ loves ___ kissed his$_i$ wife$_j$.
b. *Every man$_i$ who she$_j$ loves ___ kissed the woman$_j$ who wrote to him$_i$.

is attributable to the fact that *her* (and *she*) must be paycheck pronouns: though their apparent antecedent (as indicated by the subscripting) follows them, this provides only their 'function variable's' value: they must also have an individual variable 'bound' by *every man*, which in Jacobson's analysis or the above extension of Hepple's can happen only via being bound by a WH-gap: this is fine in (30), but in (31) it would violate Crossover. Similarly, the fact (observed by Robert May and discussed by Gennaro Chierchia) that (32) has a functional question reading but (33) lacks it can also be attributed to Crossover and is predicted by her analysis (as it is by the extension of Hepple's given above).

(32) Who does every Englishman love?

(33) *Who loves every Englishman?

However, there is one interesting difference: Jacobson (1991b) says that in a sense the way she has captured Crossover "is something of a stipulation; it follows from nothing deep about this system that there is no backward binding, for one could as well formulate a 'backwards' version of **z** -- call it **s** as given in [(34) here, her (64)]: (note that this is essentially the **S** combinator of Curry and Feys (1958) ...)" If **s** were also allowed in the grammar, Crossover violations would no longer be ruled out.

(34) for any function F of type $<s, <\chi, \psi>>$, $\mathbf{s}(F)$ is of type $<e,<<e,\chi>,\psi>$, where $\mathbf{s}(F) = \lambda x[\lambda g[F(x)(g(x))]]$ (for g a variable of type $<e,\chi>$)

Hepple's theory, it turns out, does not in fact permit an operator like **s** to be derived, though an additional condition which Hepple has imposed turns out to be crucial for this result: the regular Lambek calculus actually permits great flexibility in the hierarchy in which arguments combine with their functor, for example X/Y\Z ⇒ X\Z/Y (the so-called ASSOCIATIVITY rule) is a valid derivation in most versions of the Lambek calculus, yet this changes the relative obliqueness of the arguments X and Y, even though it leaves the word order they occur in unaffected. If unrestricted, this power would wreak havoc, as e.g. (35) illustrates. (This is simplified and not completely representative of Hepple's system in various ways, but it will serve to make the point for now: see Hepple (1990, ch. 4,5) for more complete discussion.) Its key feature is that the pronominal subject combines with the verb without the object (via **\-I**) and then **BIR** binds object and subject augments together, so that when the object is added it becomes the pronoun's 'antecedent':

(35)
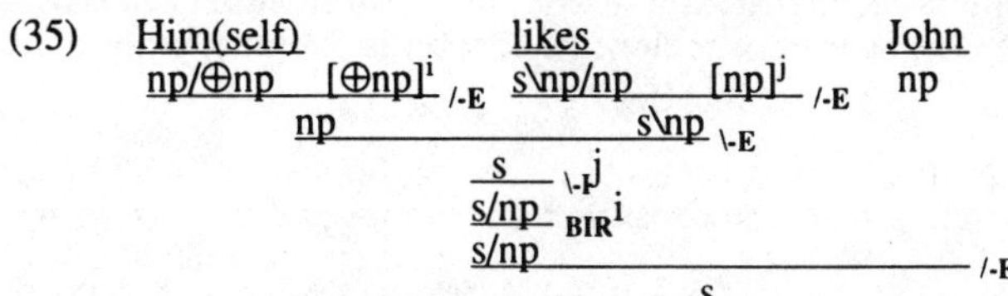

The relevant condition Hepple imposes involves distinguishing LEXICAL TYPES from other syntactic categories that arise from manipulation of categories in the course of a Lambek derivation: 'lexical type' is perhaps an unfortunate choice of a term for linguists, since it does not exactly refer to the contrast between 'lexical' vs 'non-lexical' categories in phrase-structure grammars but rather to the difference between 'normal' categories (as found in an applicative categorial grammar, i.e. without FC, type-raising) vs. 'abnormal' ones that arise from these special combinators (or /-**I**). For example, English lexical types include s\np (containing phrasal VPs as well as intransitive verbs) and s\np/np (phrasal TVPs or transitive verb), but, s/np is not a lexical type (normal English VPs never seek their single argument on the right side), nor is s/np\np. The lexical types, though not necessarily the other categories that a predicate can be shifted into in the Lambek calculus, indicate its true obliqueness hierarchy. Hepple then restricts the **BIR** (16) to apply only when the functor categories A/B or A\B are lexical types. E.g., since s/np is not a lexical type, the application of **BIR** to s/np in the next-to-last step in (35) is not legitimate. This distinction between lexical and non-lexical types is not without independent motivation in Hepple's overall theory, however, since it is also a key feature of his method of reconstructing 'wrap'. With this restriction to lexical types in place, the F-command constraint follows for the reasons already described above in connection with (16). Should it become necessary to treat other combinatory configurations besides those where **z** applies, the F-command constraint would extend to them automatically in the NDLC approach (insofar as they were all constructed using /-**I** and/or **BIR**), but it would in effect have to be observed again for each new combinator in a CCG. (The NDLC counterpart of Jacobson's **s** combinator would be a rule such as A/C/B: α $\rightarrow$ A/(C/B)/B: $\lambda x \lambda f[\alpha(f(x))(x)]$, the derivation of which would require applying **BIR** to A/(C/B)/B, but that input category would not, as far as I can see, be a lexical type in Jacobson's or anyone else's analyses of English.)

Thus the NDLC binding theory seems at this point to be more general and natural in the way it captures the F-command constraint than the primitive-combinator theory, insofar as the F-command constraint on anaphora ultimately arises from compositional semantics in lexical types, and the non-lexical types are after all found only the 'non-traditional' categories and 'funny constituents' of NDLC and CCG that do not appear in other theories.

I say 'seems to be', because the motivation for distinguishing between lexical and non-lexical types clearly demands further scrutiny. Hepple suggests that other syntactic processes might require essential reference to obliqueness, and since in both Lambek-calculus and CCG flexible category and constituent assignments arise that virtually obliterate normal obliqueness relationships, both theories would need to appeal to 'lexical type' to identify normal obliqueness if Hepple is right. But it remains to be seen exactly what these other processes are (besides anaphora binding and extraction) that require us to invoke obliqueness and exactly how they are to be analyzed. As mentioned, invocation of 'lexical types' is also necessary in Hepple's reconstruction of wrapping and treatment of word order, but it also remains to be seen whether this version is the most preferable one.

To summarize at this point, I have argued that the key features of CCG and NDLC which cause them to predict the Crossover Constraints and the significantly parallel 'crossover'-like behavior of paycheck pronouns and functional questions are not the superficial absence of variables in CCG (since after all NDLC has things that superficially look like variables) but rather those in (36):

(36) *Key features of NDLC and CCG (Jacobson) which predict Crossover:*

a. Each binding operation binds exactly one pronoun or WH-gap.
b. NP-binding is accomplished by an operation (**z** or **BIR**) applying to a np-functor (a s\np, s\np/np, etc.), with the interpretation that the argument of that functor 'binds' an anaphoric form within the functor.
c. WH-binding is accomplished by giving WH-words a category Rel/(s/np) (or Q/(s/np), etc.) taking a gapped-category as argument.
d. [A consequence of (b) and (c):] A WH-gap can bind a pronoun, but a pronoun cannot bind a WH-gap.
e. To prevent NP-binding from escaping its basic 'F-command' character, it must be restricted to apply to lexical types only, or else it must be stipulated that a 'downward-binding' operator like **z** is possible but an 'upward-binding' operator like **s** is not (and it is in the choice between these last two methods that CCG and NDLC seem to differ most significantly).

What would the corresponding conditions be in a variable-binding theory that would allow such a theory to make parallel Crossover predictions? Would such changes be compatible with other tenets of such theories? Would there be significant differences in the generality, economy, naturalness or other properties of the resulting analyses vis-a-vis CCG or NDLC? This is clearly not the place to try to answer these questions in full but I will close with a few preliminary observations.

I take it that the above (in conjunction with Jacobson 1991b) has suggested strongly that the most explanatory account of Crossover (and its parallels in paycheck pronouns and functional questions) is one that ultimately derives it from the compositional semantics of (the equivalent of) bound-variable interpretation, so the interesting challenge is to reproduce this in a GB-like or other bound variable theory. I see two potential sources of difficulty here: (i) just as non-lexical types or operators like **s** (which are needed in CCG for, among other things, getting wide-scope readings of more oblique NPs) are problematic, so the possibility of movement at LF as in Quantifier-Raising (needed for similar purposes) will potentially complicate the business of cashing in on the c-command constraint; (ii) particularly novel in many variable-binding theories (other than Montague Grammar) is the notion of one bound pronoun or empty category serving as binder for another bound pronoun, yet as emphasized above, this seems to be the key to capturing Crossover naturally. I stress that simply 'coindexing' a trace or bound pronoun with another bound pronoun is NOT adequate for this task, since coindexing is inherently a symmetric relation between two variables, whereas what is called for here is the asymmetrical relation between a binder and a 'bindee': the successful theory must allow a bound pronoun or gap to function simultaneously as both.

References

Bach, Emmon and Barbara H. Partee. 1980. Anaphora and Semantic Structure. *Papers from the Parasession on Pronouns and Anaphora,* 1-28. Chicago: Chicago Linguistic Society.

Cooper, Robin. 1979. The Interpretation of Pronouns. *Syntax and Semantics vol. 10: Papers from the Third Groningen Roundtable*, ed. by F. Guenthner and S. J. Schmidt, 61-92. New York: Academic Press.

Curry, Haskell B. and Robert Feys. 1958. *Combinatory Logic: vol. I.* Amsterdam: North Holland.

Chierchia, Gennaro. 1988. Aspects of a Categorial Theory of Binding. *Categorial Grammars and Natural Language Structures*, ed. by Oehrle, Richard T., Emmon Bach, and Deidre Wheeler, 125-152. Dordrecht: D. Reidel.

Engdahl, Elizabeth. 1986. *Constituent Questions*. Dordrecht: D. Reidel.

Groenendijk, Jeroen and Martin Stokhof. 1981. Semantics of WH-Complements. *Formal Methods in the Study of Language*, ed. by J. Groenendijk, M. Stokhof, and T. Jannsen, 153-182. Amsterdam: Mathematical Centre.

Hepple, Mark. 1990. *The Grammar and Processing of Order and Dependency: a Categorial Approach*, University of Edinburgh PhD dissertation.

Hepple, Mark. 1991. Command and Domain Constraints in a Categorial Theory of Binding. To appear the proceedings of the 8th Amsterdam Colloquium.

Jacobson, Pauline. 1977. *On the Syntax and Semantics of Crossing Co-Reference Sentences*. 1975 U. California Berkeley PhD diss. Bloomington: Indiana University Linguistics Club, 1979; also pub. by Garland, 1981.

Jacobson, Pauline. 1991a. Functional Questions, Paycheck Pronouns, and Variable Binding. Presented at the ASL/LSA Conference, LSA Summer Institute 1991.

Jacobson, Pauline. 1991b. Bach-Peters Sentences in a Variable-Free Semantics. To appear in the proceedings of the 8th Amsterdam Colloquium.

Morrill, Glyn. 1989. Intensionality and Boundedness. *Linguistics and Philosophy* 13.6:699-726.

Postal, Paul. 1971. Cross-Over Phenomena. New York: Holt, Rinehart and Winston.

Steedman, Mark. 1987. Combinatory Grammar and Parasitic Gaps. *Natural Language and Linguistics Theory* 5, 403-440.

Szabolcsi, Anna. 1989. Bound Variables in Syntax: Are There Any? *Semantics and Contextual Expression*, ed. by R. Bartsch et al., 295-381. Dordrecht: Foris.

Szabolcsi, Anna. 1987 [1992]. Combinatory Categorial Grammar and Projection from the Lexicon. Presented at the Symposium on Lexical Semantics, Stanford University, Ausust 1987. Revised version to appear in *Lexical Matters*, ed. by I. Sag and A. Szabolcsi, 241-386. Stanford: CSLI.

On the Status of Chamorro Wh-Agreement

MICHAEL DUKES
University of California, Los Angeles

Introduction

The Western Austronesian language, Chamorro, displays a grammatical process in which the wh-extraction of some category triggers the appearance of exceptional morphology on verbs which lie on the path between the extractee and the extraction site. Sandy Chung (1982, 1991) has analyzed this exceptional morphology as the realization of WH AGREEMENT (henceforth 'WhAgr'), a process in which the grammatical relation (or, as more recently proposed, the abstract Case (Chung 1991)) borne by a wh-trace is formally registered on a verb bearing some structural relation to that trace (Chung 1982, Chung & Georgopoulos 1988 (henceforth C&G)).

If Chung is essentially correct in claiming that the grammars of natural languages may allow 'special' agreement between verbs and wh-traces (in argument positions and, crucially, in 'intermediate COMPs'), then surfacy lexicalist theories of syntax such as Phrase Structure Grammar (Gazdar et al 1985, Pollard & Sag to appear) and Categorial Grammar must allow subcategorization for gaps and for elements containing gaps (as proposed for example in Goldberg's 1985 HPSG account of Chamorro WhAgr). This is a rather undesirable weakening of constraints on subcategorization because it essentially means that verbs must be able to vary in form depending on the internal structure of their arguments. In the case at hand, verbs must be allowed to subcategorize for the contents of the SLASH lists carried by their arguments. While the problem must ultimately be resolved according to empirical considerations, it is suspicious that Chamorro and the related language, Palauan, are the only languages for which such a requirement has (so far)

*I would like to thank Sandy Chung, Ed Keenan, Emily Sityar and Anna Szabolcsi for comments on various versions of this paper. None of them necessarily agrees with anything herein nor are they responsible for the remaining errors. I would also like to thank the participants at WCCFL XI for their questions and comments on this material. Please note that all examples in this paper come from Chung 1982 unless otherwise noted.

appeared necessary. It would thus be rather desirable if WhAgr could be analysed away in terms of more familiar grammatical processes[1].

Although WhAgr requires a rather unpleasant extension of agreement possibilities within PSG, it is apparently tractable. Things do not look so rosy however, for theories which do not recognize the existence of bound variable gaps, such as Combinatory Categorial Grammar (Steedman 1987, Szabolcsi 1992). As far as I can see, such a theory would be totally at a loss to account for a WhAgr phenomenon of the type proposed for Chamorro. There is simply no way to encode on a predicate the Case or grammatical relation of an argument containing a gap independently of the Case or grammatical relation borne by the higher filler (here I use 'gap' and 'filler' in a metaphorical sense). From the viewpoint of a gap-free theory then, it is rather important to show that Chamorro WhAgr is not agreement with gaps.

In this paper I hope to demonstrate that Chamorro WhAgr cannot be an 'agreement with gaps' phenomenon of the type proposed by Chung. If this conclusion is correct, and if it can be extended to the case of Palauan (a question I do not consider here), it suggests that a theory which does not even allow for an 'agreement with gaps' analysis is to be preferred over one that does. This conclusion can thus be seen as support for a theory like Combinatory Categorial Grammar or for a version of G/HPSG in which SLASH features are not available for agreement purposes.

In section 1, I start with a brief review of the form of WhAgr morphology and its distribution. In section 2, I outline some additional facts that undermine the claim that WhAgr morphology is 'agreement with gaps'. In particular, it will be shown that extraction and WhAgr morphology do not always cooccur in any given sentence and that the WhAgr morphology itself is best analysed as morphosyntactic information indicating nominalization or nonfiniteness. In section 3, I show how Chamorro WhAgr can be partially understood in terms of constraints on Wh extraction observed throughout the Western Austronesian family. Section 4 discusses some questions that remain unsolved under this account. Unfortunately, these unsolved questions are some of the most interesting ones.

1. An Outline of the WhAgr Phenomenon

The basic characteristics of the WhAgr phenomenon (at least those characteristics that initially motivated an 'agreement with gaps' analysis) are briefly summarized below[2]. Note that basic word order is VSO and that Wh movement involves movement of the question word to the left of the verb.

1.1 Subject WhAgr in Main Clause Questions

If the subject of a realis transitive clause (which usually triggers a type of subject agreement known as Ergative Agreement) is extracted, then *-um-* is infixed into the verb instead of the usual ergative agreement. This morpheme **um** is 'Subject WhAgr' (SWhAgr):[3]

---

[1]Thus Jacobson's (1987) objection to the inclusion of SLASH in the class of head features in Gazdar et al 1985 would remain valid, contra Hukari and Levine 1990.

[2]The summary presented in section 1 is distilled entirely from Chung 1982.

[3]Some abbreviations: 'Unm' stands for 'unmarked case' (which appears on subjects and objects), 'Loc' stands for 'locative case', 'Obl' stands for 'oblique case'.

(1a) Ha-fa'gasi si Juan i kareta
E3s-wash Unm the car
'Juan washed the car' (Normal Ergative (E) Agreement)

(1b) Hayi f-*um*-a'gasi i kareta
Who **um**-wash the car
'Who washed the car?' (SWhAgr)

In any other kind of clause (i.e., an intransitive or an irrealis clause), the usual agreement morphology shows up in questions that have undergone subject extraction. There is thus no overt SWhAgr morphology in such cases, although it is claimed that these verbs are covertly marked with a 'zero' SWhAgr morpheme (Chung 1991).

1.2 Object WhAgr in Main Clause Questions

If an NP which is a (non-derived) direct object (or a 'former' direct object that has not been promoted to subject (Chung 1982,50)) is extracted, then the verb may optionally be nominalized with the infix-*in*-. This morpheme **in** is 'Object WhAgr' (OWhAgr):

(2a) Ha-fahan si Maria i sanhilo'-ña gi tenda
E3s-buy Unm the blouse-her Loc store
'Maria bought her blouse at the store'

(2b) Hafa f-*in*-ahan-ña si Maria gi tenda ?
What **in**-buy-her Unm Loc store
'What did Maria buy at the store ?' (verb is nominalized with OWhAgr)

If a direct object is otherwise extracted and the verb is not nominalized then there is no unexpected morphology:

(2c) Hafa ha-fahan si Maria gi tenda ?
What E3s-buy Unm Loc store
'What did Maria buy at the store ?'

As was the case with 'covert' SWhAgr, unnominalized verbs with extracted objects are claimed to be marked with a null OWhAgr morpheme (Chung 1991).

1.3 Oblique WhAgr in Main Clause Questions

If an oblique NP (including certain kinds of instruments, extent phrases, comitatives and complements of stative verbs[4]) is extracted, then the verb is obligatorily nominalized:

(3a) Hu-punu' i lälu' ni niús
E1s-kill the fly Obl newspaper
'I killed the fly with the newspaper'

[4]All such obliques are marked with one of the two prepositional case markers **ni** or **yan**.

(3b) Hafa puno'-mu ni lälu' ?
What kill-your Obl fly
'What did you kill the fly with ?' (nominalization indicates OblWhAgr)

Although there is no overt Oblique WhAgreement morpheme, this obligatory nominalization is claimed to be the realization of OblWhAgr (Chung 1991).

1.4 WhAgr in Long Distance Questions

The agreement phenomena outlined above are also observed in long distance questions. If a Wh word is extracted out of a clause which is an argument of some verb, then that verb shows WhAgr morphology determined by the grammatical relation (or abstract Case) borne by the argument clause. We therefore observe chains of local WhAgr dependencies between verbs and arguments of verbs that have been extracted out of:[5]

(4a) Ha-istotba häm na malägu' i lahi-nmami ni kareta
E3s-disturb us Comp want the son-our Obl car
'It disturbs us that our son wants the car'

(4b) Hafa$_i$ *um*-istotba hao ni malago'-ña i lahi-mu e$_i$?
What **um**-disturb you Comp want-his the son-your
'What does it disturb you that your son wants?'

(5a) Si Juan ha-sangan-i yu' na un-bisita si Rita
Unm E3s-say-Dat me Comp E2s-visit Unm
'Juan told me that you visited Rita'

(5b) Hayi$_i$ si Juan ha-sangan-i hao b-*um*-isita e$_i$ si Rita ?
Who Unm E3s-say-Dat you **um**-visit Unm
'Who did Juan tell you visited Rita?'

In (4b), extraction of an oblique argument triggers nominalization of the embedded verb *malägu'* , and since the embedded clause is the subject of the main verb, we observe SWhAgr on *istotba*. In (5b), the subject of the embedded verb *bisita* is extracted, triggering SWhAgr in the embedded clause, while on the main verb *sangan*, there is no (overt) marking because its object argument was extracted out of and objects only optionally trigger (overt) OWhAgr.

1.5 WhAgr in Relative Clauses

WhAgr shows up in relative clauses (RCs) in exactly the same form as in questions. However there is one important contrast in the distribution of WhAgr in long distance RCs as compared to long distance questions. While WhAgr appears as usual on the most deeply embedded verb of a RC it preferably does not appear on higher verbs within a RC. Thus while chains of WhAgr markings are possible in long distance RCs (as in long distance questions) they are dispreferred.

[5]Note that the 'Dat' suffix *-i* indicates that the verb has undergone Dative Shift.

2. Some Empirical Problems for an Agreement Analysis

The phenomena described in section 1 have been accounted for along two basic lines:

(i) **GF WhAgr:** *A verb agrees in grammatical function with a constituent that is dependent on it and contains a gap* (Chung & Georgopoulos 1988,260)

(ii) **Abstract Case WhAgr:** *V agrees in Case with a clausemate that is a WHtrace (A and B are clausemates if and only if they are dominated by all the same S nodes)* (Chung 1991)

The actual formalization of these ideas within some grammatical theory or other is an interesting problem in itself, but here, I wish to concentrate solely on the empirical plausibility of the basic ideas underlying these proposals. The crucial notion involved in both these accounts is the claim that a (Wh) gap triggers agreement, either directly (as in (ii)) or indirectly (i.e., by virtue of its being contained in some constituent, as in (i)). It is this notion which I take issue with here. I hope to demonstrate that there is serious reason to doubt that the marking of WhAgr morphology necessarily involves the presence of Wh gaps, let alone agreement with those gaps. The agreement analysis of WhAgr morphology crucially relies on the use of a good deal of 'zero morphology' by which WhAgreement information is always marked on certain verbal categories even though it may never surface overtly. While the use of zero marking can often be perfectly well justified (in particular, if the zero marked forms otherwise behave just like the overtly marked forms), I will argue below that in this case, it only serves to obscure the true nature of the phenomenon under investigation because there are a number of crucial properties of WhAgr that depend solely on whether or not WhAgr is overt.

To support the contentions made so far in this section, I now turn to a more detailed examination of the three kinds of (overt) WhAgr described earlier.

2.1 Subject WhAgr is Infinitival

Overt SWhAgr (the morpheme **um**) is restricted to sentences involving transitive realis verbs (as exemplified in (1b)). However, a homophonous morpheme also appears in infinitival transitive realis complements of Equi and Raising verbs (Chung 1982,49; Topping 1973,185):

(6) Malägu' gui' b-*um*-isita si Rita
want he **um**-visit Unm
'He wants to visit Rita'

(7) Huchagi h-*um*-atsa i lamasa
I tried **um**-lift the table
'I tried to lift the table' (from Topping 1973,185)

Under the view that **um** is overt marking of agreement between a Wh trace and a verb, the examples in (6) and (7) must be accounted for by some process other than WhAgr because there is clearly no Wh trace in either sentence (nor is there any extracted element to bind such a trace). In other words, the infinitival **um** in (6) and (7) cannot be the same **um** as the one in (1). However, the fact that both elements are restricted exclusively to transitive realis verbs suggests that this conclusion is incorrect. Furthermore, there is a clear syntactic and semantic parallel between the extraction contexts and nonextraction contexts where **um** shows up; both contexts involve a 'missing' subject.

There is some rather direct evidence demonstrating that infinitival **um** is the same morpheme as SWhAgr **um**. Chung and Georgopoulos (1988,261) note a peculiar contrast in the properties of SWhAgr that depends purely on the overtness of the **um** morpheme:

(8a) Hayi$_i$ s-*in*-angane-nña si Juan as Maria [(*na) *um*-istótotba e$_i$ gui']
Who **in**-tell-his Unm Obl that **um**-disturb him
'Who did Juan tell Maria (*that) was disturbing him ?'

(8b) Hayi$_i$ s-*in*-angane-nña si Juan as Maria [na trinik e$_i$ as Miguel]
Who **in**-tell-his Unm Obl that trick(Pass) Obl
(covert SWhAgr)
'Who did Juan tell Maria that was tricked by Miguel ?'
(adapted from C&G's (20a,b))

The finite complementizer **na** may not introduce a clause whose main verb is overtly marked with SWhAgr, as in (8a), whereas **na** is allowed if it introduces a clause in which SWhAgr is supposedly covert, as in (8b). Under the agreement analysis of WhAgr, there is no principled explanation for the contrast observed between (8a) and (8b) because the overtness of the morpheme should be morphosyntactically irrelevant. The agreement analysis would require an ad hoc surface filter to block the cooccurrence of **na** and **um** within the same minimal clause.

A straightforward account of these occurrences of **um** can be provided if we adopt an analysis in which **um** is simply treated as a morpheme that derives the infinitival form of transitive realis verbs. Under this view, the Equi and Raising facts in (6) and (7) follow for free (by whatever mechanism it is that forces complements of these verbs to be nonfinite), as does the contrast observed between (8a) and (8b): since the embedded verb is nonfinite in (8a), it clearly cannot cooccur with the finite complementizer **na**. Example (8b), on the other hand, is fine since *trinik* is an ordinary finite verb with a gapped subject.

This analysis leads us to the following conclusions. Firstly, **um** clearly does not mark agreement with a Wh gap; it is an infinitival marker. Secondly, given this first conclusion, there is no remaining motivation for assuming the existence of any kind of covert SWhAgr. The mystery that the Chamorro SWhAgr data can now be seen as presenting is one of explaining why transitive realis verbs must be infinitival when their subject position is extracted from. I return to this question in section 3, but it must said at this point that I can find no theoretically interesting answer to it. One might appeal to the fact that nonfinite clauses are typically more easily extracted from than finite ones, but this leaves us with no obvious account of the contrast between transitive realis clauses and the other clause types. Nevertheless, there is some clear diachronic motivation for Chamorro SWhAgr, as we will see in section 3.

2.2 Object WhAgr is Passive Nominalization

Problems analogous to those observed in 2.1 for an agreement analysis of SWhAgr morphology can be shown to exist for an agreement analysis of OWhAgr. I note firstly that the gross characteristics of SWhAgr and OWhAgr are rather different, something one would not expect on the view that they involve the same grammatical process. While SWhAgr appears obligatorily on a restricted subclass of verb forms, the OWhAgr morpheme **in** is entirely optional and derives a nominalized form of any transitive verb. An agreement analysis cannot account for these differences in morphosyntactic properties without invoking a good deal of ad hoc feature instantiation on verb forms, since information such as 'nonfinite' or 'nominalized' is clearly not the kind of information that is shared as agreement between two syntactic elements[6].

Another problem for an agreement analysis is the fact that the OWhAgr morpheme **in**, like **um**, shows up in contexts that do not involve extraction but which are clearly related syntactically and semantically to the extraction cases. In Topping (1973) and Gibson (1980), **in** is referred to as a 'nominalizing infix' which, when attached to transitive verbs, yields a nominalized version of the verb:

(9) Hu li'e' i h-*in*-atsa
I see the **in**-lift
'I saw the thing that was lifted' (Topping 1973,102)

(10) Este i *in*-eppe-ku para guiya
This the **in**-answer-my for him
'This is my answer to him' (Cooreman 1984,398)

(11) I f-*in*-ahan-ña si Maria ni chetda ha na'-mänman yu'
the **in**-buy-her Unm Obl bananas 3s Caus-surprise me
'Maria's buying of the bananas surprised me'
(adapted from Gibson 1980,23)

The morpheme **in** in these examples seems to share the same morphosyntactic properties as OWhAgr. The **in**-marked verb in (9) denotes some entity which undergoes the action described by the verb. In other words, it appears to denote something which has the same properties as an object of that verb. The nominalized subject clause in (11) closely resembles the nominalized clause in (2b). However, the former sentence lacks an object gap, the object NP (*ni chetda*) being realized as an oblique[7].

These occurrences of **in**-nominals are closely related to verbal passive forms which also contain a morpheme **in**:

(12) Pära u-ku-**in**-entusi si Jose ni haga-ññiha
Fut. S3s-**Pass**-speak-to Unm Obl daughter-their
'Jose is going to be spoken to by their daughter'
(Chung 1981,316)

Again, there is an obvious 'object focus' that verbal passives share with the **in**-nominalizations discussed above. Under an agreement analysis, these three usages of **in** (i.e., as OWhAgr, as a verbal passive marker and as a nominal passive marker) are unrelated, a rather undesirable proliferation of homophonous morphemes in the language.

---

[6]Indeed it is difficult to see how, for example, the presence of a Wh trace in an intermediate Comp can alter the lexical category features of a predicate during the course of a derivation. Yet this is what the agreement analysis requires in order to produce a nominalized verb in a clause that is on an extraction path. Note too that this process must be entirely optional, since cases of overt and covert OWhAgr are assumed to be structurally isomorphic under the agreement analysis (but not under the analysis presented in section 3.)

[7]I assume that this contrast is due to the fact that the **in**-nominal in (11) is functioning as an argument (therefore, potentially 'saturated'), while the nominal in (2b) is a predicate (and therefore, necessarily requires an 'external argument').

A unified treatment of **in** can be provided straightforwardly if we simply abandon the idea that verbs agree with object traces. Bearing in mind that **in**-nominalization is entirely optional in extraction contexts, there is absolutely nothing that the grammar needs to say specifically about clauses containing object Wh gaps. **In**-nominals and ordinary (verbal) passives may freely occur in such contexts or not. In the analysis proposed in section **3** below, infixation of **in** into active verbal forms will be carried out as a lexical rule of verbal passive formation. The distinction between nominal passives and verbal passives will be captured by a simple category-changing lexical rule. The agreement analysis of **in**-nominalization can thus be seen as entirely redundant. There is no need to assume that (unnominalized) verbs are covertly marked with OWhAgr, since these forms will be treated as ordinary run-of-the-mill active transitive verbs whose objects have been extracted. The morphosyntactic differences between overt and covert OWhAgr, which were mysterious under the agreement analysis, are immediately accounted for.

2.3 Oblique WhAgreement is Nominalization

By now there is little point in maintaining an agreement analysis of WhAgr morphology just for the treatment of oblique extraction. While OblWhAgr is the only fully general variety of WhAgr, it is, like OWhAgr, a variety of nominalization, and thus susceptible to some of the same objections raised against OWhAgr in 2.2. There is no overt sharing of features between a predicate and argument, thus no 'agreement' in the usual sense of the word. As in the case of SWhAgr, I suggest that the puzzle raised by OblWhAgr be reinterpreted. The question we must ask is why it is that a verb must undergo bare nominalization if an oblique argument is extracted (or extracted from).

3. Accounting for WhAgr Morphology

I have suggested that the phenomenon of WhAgreement be reinterpreted as the triggering of certain morphosyntactic processes in extraction contexts that are independently available in nonextraction contexts. The fact that these processes can occur in nonextraction contexts (amongst other things) shows that it is not the presence of Wh gaps per se that triggers them. However, we must now provide some rationale for the appearance of this morphology in questions and relative clauses.

From the perspective of more widely known European languages, the Chamorro WhAgr facts may seem to lack any obvious grammatical motivation. However, from the viewpoint of the Western Austronesian (WA) languages, of which Chamorro is one, the appearance of WhAgr morphology is somewhat less remarkable. It can in fact be seen as a vestigial remnant of a family wide condition on extraction. I do not wish to suggest that the genetic relationship of Chamorro to other WA languages constitutes an explanation of why the Chamorro-particular facts are the way they are. This relationship does however provide some rationale for understanding how Chamorro ended up the way it is.

3.1 Extraction in Western Austronesian

Wh movement in WA languages (among them Malagasy, Tagalog and Indonesian) is typically governed by some version of a constraint (first formulated in Keenan 1972) that can be crudely stated as follows:

Austronesian Extraction Constraint[8]: **Extract Subjects Only**

In some languages, for example Malagasy and Tagalog, this constraint still holds quite firmly, while in others, such as Indonesian (and, as I will claim, Chamorro) there is a considerable loss of generality.

In Malagasy, relative clauses may only be formed on heads corresponding to the subject NP of the relative clause:

(13a)	ny	zazavavy	(izay) manasa	ny lamba
	the	girl	(that) wash	the clothes
		'the girl that's washing the clothes'		

(13b)	*ny	lamba	(izay) manasa	ny zazavavy
	the	clothes	(that) wash	the girl
		'the clothes that the girl is washing'		

(13c)	ny	lamba (izay) sasan	'ny	zazavavy
	the	clothes (that) wash(pass)	the	girl
		'the clothes that the girl is washing'		

(from Keenan 1976,265)

As can be seen in (13), an object NP can only be relativized if the verb is first passivized so as to 'promote' the object to subject. The obligatory appearance of passive morphology in questions and relative clauses can thus be seen as the Malagasy equivalent of Chamorro WhAgr; the morphology on the Malagasy verb 'agrees with' the grammatical relation of the extracted NP.

Restrictions similar to those found in Malagasy are observed in Indonesian, except that here the restrictions are typically preserved only in the formal register of the language (Chung 1978,370-5). Rules involving wh movement (relative clause formation, question formation and clefting) are restricted to subjects in the formal language. But in colloquial Indonesian, direct objects may be directly extracted in questions and they may also be clefted, although relative clause formation on objects is not allowed for all speakers (Chung ibid.).

Perhaps the closest approximation to the Chamorro phenomena can be observed in Philippine languages such as Tagalog. These languages typically have well developed systems of verbal voice morphology which mark some argument in each clause as 'most prominent'. In Tagalog, this most prominent argument is case marked with one of the nominative particles (**ang** or **si**), and is referred to as the subject NP in Kroeger (1991)[9]. Kroeger (1991,256) observes that elements extracted by Wh movement must be subjects:

(14a)	Ano	ang	ninakaw	ng-katulong	mo ?
	what	Nom	Perf.Objective voice-steal	Gen-maid	your

'What did your maid steal ?' (lit: 'what was stolen by your maid?')

---

[8]Keenan's (1972,173) formulation of this constraint was called the 'Basic Constraint'.

[9]The status of 'subjects' in the Philippine languages is actually the subject of a long standing controversy (Schachter 1976, Bell 1983). For our purposes the details of this controversy are not entirely relevant, although it is obviously the case that the picture of constraints on extraction presented here favours the view that **ang/si** marked NPs are indeed subjects. Nevertheless, the role of 'subjects' could be reconstructed (and perhaps should be) in terms of 'focus'.

(14b) *Ano ang nagkakaw ang-katulong mo ?
what Nom Perf.Active voice-steal Nom-maid your
'What did your maid steal ?' (Kroeger 1991,258)

Furthermore, constituents containing gaps must also be subjects (Kroeger ibid.). Thus Tagalog (like Malagasy) obligatorily violates the Sentential Subject Constraint in long distance Wh dependencies:

(15) Alin-ng kotse ang sinabi mo kay-Pedro
Which car Nom. Perf.ObjV-say you(Gen.) Dat.-Pedro

na binili ni-Linda ?
Comp Perf.ObjV-buy Gen-Linda
'Which car did you tell Pedro that Linda bought ?' (Kroeger 1991,264)
(lit: 'Which car was it told by you to Pedro that was bought by Linda?')

As was the case with the Malagasy data, the Tagalog voice 'agreement' is strikingly similar to Chamorro WhAgr.[10]

3.2 A Voice Analysis of WhAgr

It seems quite clear that contemporary Chamorro, like colloquial Indonesian, only partially obeys the Austronesian Extraction Constraint. The fact that objects may always be directly extracted with no unexpected morphology marked on the verb (as in (2c)) shows this quite clearly. However, in accounting for those cases where WhAgr does appear on verbs, it seems reasonable to suppose that we are dealing with a somewhat less general version of the same voice phenomenon observed in other WA languages. I will be assuming that overt WhAgr morphology in Chamorro indicates lexical modification of the argument structure of a predicate so as to 'promote' a gapped item to subject position. Notice that under this view, we need not state any direct dependency between a Wh gap and the voice morphology on the nearest verb. Voice morphology indicates dependencies between a verb and its arguments irrespective of the syntactic category of the arguments (i.e., whether they are traces or full NPs).

I will assume for convenience that voice morphology is assigned to verbs lexically and that it dictates the way in which syntactic grammatical relations must be linked to the semantic arguments of a predicate. Following the format for lexical category specification employed in Pollard & Sag (to appear), I employ subcategorization (SUBCAT) lists for lexical categories which are ordered in terms of the obliqueness of grammatical relations. 'Subject' corresponds to the least oblique argument (i.e., first element on the SUBCAT list), 'object' to the second least oblique element, etc. Voice morphemes can thus be viewed as elements that require a particular correspondence between SUBCAT lists and semantic arguments.

Verbs marked with OWhAgr (i.e., **in**-nominalizations) can now be treated in the following way. Firstly, we independently require a rule of (verbal) passive formation as given in (16):

---

[10]As Kroeger notes (1991,256). Indeed it seems more than likely that Chamorro **um** and **in** are cognate with the homophonous morphemes in Tagalog that mark 'active voice' and 'objective voice' respectively.

(16) **Passive Formation:**

[+V, -N, SUBCAT ⟨XP_1, XP_2,...⟩]

→ **in**+[+V, -N, SUBCAT⟨XP_2, ...,(XP_1[Case:Obl.])⟩]

OWhAgr forms are simply nominalized forms of these passives, as given by the category-changing rule in (17):

(17) **Passive Nominalization:**

in+[+V, -N, SUBCAT⟨XP_2, ...,(XP_1[Case:Obl.])⟩]

→ **in**+[-V, +N, SUBCAT⟨XP_2, ...,(XP_1[Case:Gen.])⟩]

As already noted, we need state no extraction-specific restrictions on the application of these lexical rules. Thus nothing else needs to be said about these forms.

Subject WhAgr can be treated as morphology that derives an infinitival active verb form from a finite one according to the lexical rule specified in (18):

(18) **Infinitive Formation:**

[+V,-N, +finite, +realis, SUBCAT ⟨XP_1, XP_2...⟩]

→ **um**+[+V,-N, -finite, +realis, SUBCAT ⟨XP_1, XP_2...⟩]

SWhAgr presumably had its origins as true 'active focus' morphology, as found in Tagalog and in the Chamorro actor focus construction (Topping 1973,243). Indeed, it is plausible that a more comprehensive grammar of Chamorro might directly derive infinitival verb forms from actor focus forms. I do not attempt this here.

Oblique WhAgr can be derived via a lexical rule similar to (17), such as the one given in (19):

(19) **Oblique Nominalization:**

[+V, -N, SUBCAT ⟨XP_1, (XP_2), XP_3[Case:**ni/yan**]⟩]

→ [-V, +N, SUBCAT ⟨XP_3, (XP_1[Case:Gen]), (XP_2[Case:Obl])⟩]

This rule, like (17), provides a straightforward account of the change in case marking properties induced by nominalization. These properties were rather mysterious under the agreement analysis since that account provided no obvious reason why wh-movement of one argument of a verb should induce changes in the case marking assigned to the remaining arguments.

3.3 Long Distance Questions and Relative Clauses

The analysis proposed here straightforwardly accounts for the fact that chains of local Wh agreement may show up in long distance questions and relative clauses. This agreement is simply a consequence of the lexical operations performed on the argument structure of predicates in order to ensure compliance with the Chamorro-particular version of the Austronesian Extraction Constraint. Under this view, it is no coincidence that Chamorro WhAgr resembles Tagalog or Malagasy voice morphology since fundamentally the same process is involved in all three languages.

What then of the contrast observed in 1.4 and 1.5 between long distance questions and relative clauses? Recall that while WhAgr shows up in long distance questions as usual, it need not (and preferably does not) show up in long distance relative clauses, except on the lowest verb. Thus taking OblWhAgr as an example, we require its obligatory presence in long distance questions (as in (20a)), but its optional presence in relative clauses (20b):

(20a) Fanu'i yu' [hafa na lepblu$_i$ malago'-mu [un-taitai e_i]]
show me what? Lkr book want-your(Nmnlzd) 2sg-read
'Show me what book you want to read'
(indirect question with obligatory OblWhAgr on *malägu'*)

(20b) Fanu'i yu' ni lepblu$_i$ [ni malägu' hao [un-taitai e_i]]
show me Obl book Comp want you 2sg-read
'Show me the book that you want to read'
(relative clause with no OblWhAgr marked on *malägu'*)
(adapted from Chung 1982,(77)a,b)

Chung (1982) proposes that relative clauses may either be the product of successive-cyclic movement of the relative NP, or they may be created via 'Controlled Pro Deletion' (i.e., deletion of a pronoun under coindexation with the head of the relative clause). Under the first strategy, chains of Wh Agreement result; under the second, they do not. This analysis suffices to derive a descriptively adequate account of the contrast (under the assumption that deleted Pro's become traces), however it relies on an unbounded process (Controlled Pro Deletion) which is rather unconstrained.

Within the framework presented here, there is an alternative account available which assumes that all relative clause formation is 'successive-cyclic' (in transformational terms). It was observed in section 3.1 that some speakers of colloquial Indonesian allow direct (i.e., without passivization) extraction of objects in questions but not in relative clauses. In other words, whatever version of the Austronesian Extraction Constraint it is that holds in their grammar is weaker with respect to questions than relative clauses. If we assume that a similar (but reversed) language-particular discrepancy holds in Chamorro, the contrast between the appearance of WhAgr in questions and relative clauses will follow without requiring appeal to two distinct varieties of relative clause formation[11]. What we will require is a Chamorro-particular version of the Austronesian Extraction Constraint that is somehow sensitive to the distinction between relative clauses and questions. But since we will need something similar anyway for Indonesian, this option seems distinctly preferable. The result is that verbs in relative clauses may, but need not, undergo the lexical processes outlined in (16)-(19), thereby deriving the optionality of WhAgr in such structures.

4. Some Remaining Questions

The analysis of Chamorro WhAgr presented in this paper has been shown to have a number of advantages over Chung's agreement proposal. However, there

---

[11]Within a PSG framework, the obligatoriness of WhAgr on the lowest verb should presumably be made to follow from the fact that this is the only verb that actually has a trace as an argument.

are a number of residual problems which I would briefly like to consider in conclusion.

Sandy Chung (p.c.) has pointed out to me that the use of WhAgr marked predicates is apparently rather unnatural in answers to Wh questions and may even be ungrammatical in some cases. It is clear therefore that the analysis presented here must (at the very least) be supplemented by some set of discourse-based preference orderings that determine appropriate usage of WhAgr forms. Such principles are also needed to account for the fact that Chamorro speakers apparently prefer not to use WhAgr forms in relative clauses even though the option is grammatically available to them[12].

Perhaps the most important question that remains to be addressed is the grammatical status of the Austronesian Extraction Constraint. I have appealed to this notion throughout as an independently required device, without saying much about how it should be instantiated in the grammars of Austronesian languages. It seems to be an unfortunate fact that most current theories of generative syntax have little or nothing to offer in the way of explanation for why it is that Wh movement must typically proceed from subject position in these languages[13]. It is of course possible to stipulate that Wh gaps must always bear a particular grammatical function (as in Kroeger's (1991,274) LFG account of Tagalog Wh extraction) or that Wh dependency paths must always proceed through a particular set of nodes in a tree. But such accounts are simply restatements of the problem. Theories that employ some kind of list-valued analysis of subcategorization (such as Categorial Grammar or HPSG) appear to offer at least the right kind of structural generalizations for capturing such constraints; but again, there is nothing inherent in the structure of either theory that forces wh movement to apply out of subject position. In the absence of any concrete proposals as to how this constraint should be grammatically implemented, I will speculate no further.

Finally, I must point out that both analyses discussed in this paper suffer from an important defect. Neither offers any explanation for the fact that the operation of WhAgr creates nonfinite constituents rather than finite ones. The correlation between nonfiniteness and greater freedom of extraction is well known, but, as in the case of the extraction constraint discussed above, current syntactic theory appears to offer no easy explanations for this correlation or its Chamorro-particular realization.

References

Bell, Sarah J. 1983. Advancements and Ascensions in Cebuano.*Studies in Relational Grammar 1*, ed. by D. Perlmutter. Chicago: University of Chicago Press.

Chung, Sandra. 1978. *Case Marking and Grammatical Relations in Polynesian.* Austin: University of Texas Press.

Chung, Sandra. 1981. Transitivity and Surface Filters in Chamorro. *Studies in Pacific Languages and Cultures in Honour of Bruce Biggs*. ed. by Hollyman, J. & A. Pawley. Auckland: Linguistic Society of New Zealand.

[12]It would be interesting to know to what extent such variations in the use of WhAgr forms are correlated with social or dialectal factors. Such information might bear on the hypothesis that non-subjects in Chamorro (like Indonesian) are becoming more accessible to extraction.

[13]Indeed, movement from within subjects has been explicitly banned in almost all versions of transformational grammar since Ross 1967.

Chung, Sandra. 1982. Unbounded Dependencies in Chamorro Grammar. *Linguistic Inquiry* . 13.39-77.

Chung, Sandra. 1989. On the Notion 'Null Anaphor' in Chamorro.*The Null Subject Parameter,* ed. by O. Jaeggli & K. Safir. Dordrecht: Kluwer.

Chung, Sandra. 1991. Sentential Subjects and Proper Government in Chamorro. *Interdisciplinary Approaches to Language: Essays in Honour of S.-Y. Kuroda,* ed. by C. Georgopoulos & R. Ishihara. Dordrecht: Kluwer.

Chung, Sandra & Carol Georgopoulos. 1988. Agreement with Gaps in Chamorro and Palauan. *Agreement in Natural Language,* ed. by M. Barlow & C. Ferguson.Stanford: CSLI.

Cooreman, Anne. 1984. A Functional Analysis of Passives in Chamorro narrative discourse. *Papers in Linguistics* .17(4).

Gazdar, Gerald, Ewan Klein, Geoffrey Pullum & Ivan Sag. 1985. *Generalized Phrase Structure Grammar*. Cambridge: Harvard University Press.

Gibson, Jeanne. 1980. *Clause Union in Chamorro and in Universal Grammar.* Ph.D thesis, UCSD.

Goldberg, Jeffrey. 1985. Lexical Operations and Unbounded Dependencies. *Proceedings of Regional Meeting of Chicago Linguistics Society* 21. ed. by W.H. Eilfort et al. Chicago: Chicago Linguistics Society.

Hukari, Thomas & Robert Levine. 1990. Jacobson on GKPS: A Rejoinder. *Linguistics and Philosophy 13,* 363-381.

Jacobson, Pauline. 1987. Review: Generalized Phrase Structure Grammar. *Linguistics and Philosophy 10,* 389-426.

Keenan, Edward. 1972. Relative Clause Formation in Malagasy (and Some Related and Not So Related Languages). *The Chicago Which Hunt* , ed. by P. Peranteau, et al. Chicago: Chicago Linguistics Society.

Keenan, Edward. 1976. Remarkable Subjects in Malagasy.*Subject and Topic,* ed. by C. Li. New York: Academic Press.

Kroeger, Paul. 1991. *Phrase Structure and Grammatical Relations in Tagalog.* Ph.D thesis, Stanford University.

Pollard, Carl. & Ivan Sag. to appear. *Agreement, Binding and Control (Information-Based Syntax and Semantics, volume 2).* Stanford: CSLI.

Schachter, Paul. 1976. The Subject in Philippine Languages: Topic, Actor, Actor-Topic or None of the Above. *Subject and Topic,* ed. by C. Li. New York: Academic Press.

Steedman, Mark. 1987. Combinatory Grammars and Parasitic Gaps. *Natural Language and Linguistic Theory 5.*

Szabolcsi, Anna. 1992. Combinatory Grammar and Projection from the Lexicon. *Lexical Matters,* ed. by I. Sag & A. Szabolcsi. Stanford: CSLI.

Topping, Donald. 1973. *Chamorro Reference Grammar*. Honolulu: University of Hawaii Press.

A Last Look at the 1AEX

PATRICK FARRELL
University of California, Davis

1. Framing the Problem

The 1-ADVANCEMENT EXCLUSIVENESS LAW (1AEX) of Relational Grammar (RG), paraphrased informally in (1), is proposed by Perlmutter and Postal (1984) (henceforth P&P) as — among other things — an explanation for the ungrammaticality of passives in English such as the (b)-examples in (2)-(3).

(1) There can be at most one advancement to subject per clause. (1AEX)

(2) a. The toothpaste oozed into the sink.
b. * The sink was oozed into by the toothpaste.

(3) a. Five dollars bought a lot of heroin in 1905.
b. * A lot of heroin was bought by five dollars in 1905.

The idea is that sentences like (2a) contain an UNACCUSATIVE verb: the final 1 is an initial 2 that advances to 1.[1] Similarly, sentences like (3a) contain an initial oblique that advances to 1. Passive fails in both cases because it would involve a second advancement to 1. The kind of RELATIONAL NETWORK (RN) schematized by the stratal diagram in (4) is prohibited by the 1AEX.[2]

---

[1] The following grammatical relations are employed in this paper: subject (= 1), direct object (= 2), indirect object (= 3), oblique (= Obl), predicate (= P), and chomeur (= Cho). In standard RG, various oblique relations (benefactive, locative, instrumental, etc.) are distinguished. I collapse these into one relation here, for the sake of simplicity.

[2] A relational network is a graph-theoretic object consisting of nodes, representing such linguistic elements as NPs, predicates, and clauses, and arcs that connect these nodes in such a way as to show constituency relations. The arcs are labeled for the grammatical relations that constituents bear and have coordinates that indicate the level(s), or strata, at which the relations hold. A stratal diagram displays the arcs in a format which, for the sake of perspicuity, suppresses coordinates in favor of horizontal lines indicating strata. The initial stratum is indicated by the uppermost line. Thus, constituent *A* in the diagram in (4) heads an initial *y* arc and a final 1 arc in clause *d* (i.e., bears the grammatical relation *y* in the initial stratum of clause *d* and the grammatical relation 1 in the final stratum).

(4)

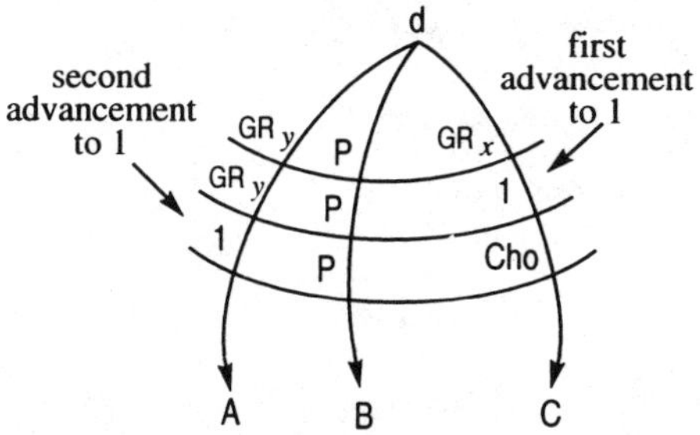

d
second advancement to 1
first advancement to 1
GR_y P GR_x
GR_y P 1
1 P Cho
A B C

There have been various empirical challenges to the 1AEX, most of which take the form of showing that unaccusative verbs can be passivized in one way or another.[3] There are three reasonable ways of responding to these challenges. The first would be to attempt to maintain the 1AEX as a principle of universal grammar by providing analyses of the apparently problematic cases that are compatible with its claims. Although Postal (1986, Ch. 5) pursues this kind of response at some length, not all of the problematic cases are dealt with and some do not seem to yield to satisfactory alternative analyses. For example, the interaction of locative inversion, passive, and unaccusative advancement in Bantu languages such as Kichaga and Chishona (Bresnan and Moshi 1990) poses a serious problem for the 1AEX that is amenable to neither the kind of solution considered by Postal nor any other, as far as I can tell. A second response would be to (effectively) parametrize the 1AEX, i.e., to maintain that it holds for some languages and not others. This is essentially what Baker (1988, Ch. 6) does with respect to the Government-Binding theory counterpart of the 1AEX — the claim that passive is an operation that suppresses the EXTERNAL ARGUMENT of a verb (see, for example, Jaeggli 1986 and Grimshaw 1990).[4] The third response would be to abandon the 1AEX entirely. If it could be shown that there are alternative accounts of phenomena attributed to the 1AEX that are, at least, no less illuminating, this latter alternative is clearly to be preferred in that it obviates the need for otherwise unmotivated analyses of counterexamples and makes it possible to eliminate a constraint on RNs that effectively bans what emerges from other fundamental assumptions of RG as a natural possibility. The goal of this paper is to show that the third response is worthy of consideration, since it is doubtful that there is any need for the 1AEX.

---

[3] Languages claimed to allow impersonal passives of unaccusatives include Turkish (Özkaragöz 1980), Sanskrit (Ostler 1979), Lithuanian (Timberlake 1982, Keenan and Timberlake 1985, Nerbonne 1982), and Irish and Estonian (Nerbonne 1982). A more serious challenge to the 1AEX comes from languages that apparently allow personal passives of clauses with unaccusative advancement, among which are Halkomelem Salish (Gerdts 1984, 1988b, Ch. 5) and certain Bantu languages (Bresnan and Moshi 1990).

[4] More specifically, although the passive morpheme (an 'incorporating' N for Baker) is generated in INFL in languages such as English, and thus necessarily receives the external θ-role of the verb, it can also be generated within the VP, allowing it to receive an internal θ-role. One result of these assumptions is that unaccusatives can be 'passivized' in the latter type of language.

2. Pseudopassives and Unaccusativity in English

Let us consider, to begin with, the contrast between grammatical English PSEUDOPASSIVES (also known as prepositional passives) such as those in (5) and ungrammatical ones such as those in (2b) and (6).[5]

(5) a. The students were spoken to by their parents.
 b. The house was paid for by the woman.
 c. The changes were asked for by the president.
 d. That solution was thought of by no one.

(6) a. * The package was accumulated on by dust.
 b. * The dome was collapsed under by the model.
 c. * The oven was melted in by the ice cube.
 d. * The hill was grown on by grass.

The assumptions under which the 1AEX can be appealed to in an account of this contrast are (i) that the clauses in (5) are initially UNERGATIVE (i.e., have an initial stratum in which there is no 2 arc and the clausal dependent expressed in the *by*-phrase heads a 1 arc) and (ii) that those in (6) are initially UNACCUSATIVE (i.e., have an initial stratum in which there is no 1 arc and the clausal dependent expressed in the *by*-phrase heads a 2 arc) and involve unaccusative advancement to 1, whereby the initial 2 advances to 1 prior to being placed en chomage by the passive advancement to 1. Only in the unaccusative passive clauses are there two advancements to 1 in violation of the 1AEX: the initial 2 first advances to 1 in the unaccusative advancement construction; the initial oblique (or 3) then advances to 1 (via an advancement to 2) in the passive construction. The stratal diagrams for (5b) and (6b) would be as shown in (7).[6]

(7)

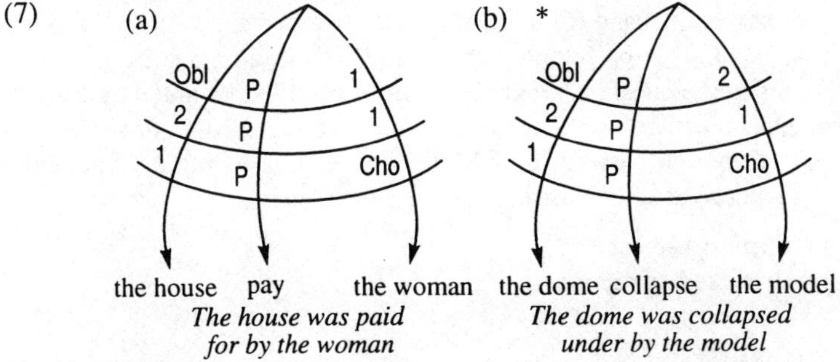

The house was paid for by the woman *The dome was collapsed under by the model*

The question that needs to be asked is whether there is an equally attractive alternative explanation for the contrast in (5) and (6) in which the 1AEX plays no role. I maintain that there is. There are two keys to understanding this alternative. The first is the assumption that the verbs in (5) are unergatives and those in (6) are

---

[5] The examples in (6) are from P&P.

[6] I follow Postal (1986) in the assumption that all passive clauses in English involve an advancement from 2 to 1 resulting in detransitivization. See below for some evidence that the advancee to 1 in a pseudopassive indeed heads a 2 arc.

indeed unaccusatives. The second is the claim that the pseudopassive construction does not involve an advancement to 2 as shown in (7); rather, the passive advancee to 1 is the initial 2 of a complex verb with a lexically incorporated preposition.[7] It is, thus, necessarily an initial 2 that advances to 1 in the pseudopassive construction. Since the verbs in (6) have the theme argument (the nominal expressed in the *by*-phrase) as their initial 2 and since there can be only one initial 2 per clause — as guaranteed by the STRATAL UNIQUENESS LAW (SUL) (Perlmutter and Postal 1983) — it follows that a passive advancement to 1 is not a possibility. That is to say, if the analysis of pseudopassives is as shown in (8a), an example such as (6b) would have to have the structure shown in (8b); however, this structure violates the SUL, since it has two 2 arcs in the initial stratum.

(8)

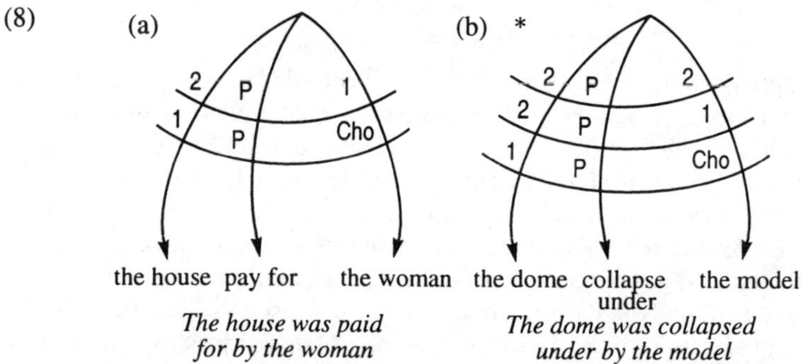

The house was paid for by the woman

The dome was collapsed under by the model

The unaccusative/unergative distinction is crucial to both my SUL-based account and a 1AEX-based account. The claim concerning the correct analysis of pseudopassives is what distinguishes the two. In order to motivate the 1AEX based on the contrast between (5) and (6), it would be necessary to show that the analysis of pseudopassives in (7) is preferable to that in (8). As it turns out, the empirical evidence bearing on the question weighs in favor of (8). First, as noted by Bresnan (1982), participial adjectives can be formed from the verb/preposition complex of a pseudopassive, in which case the modified noun expresses the argument that would be the advancee to 1, as illustrated by the examples in (9).

(9) a. an **unpaid for** car
    b. rarely **asked for** items

---

[7] This is essentially an RG-compatible version of Bresnan's (1982) analysis of pseudopassives. The chief difference is that although I too consider preposition incorporation to be a lexical phenomenon, I view passivization itself as a syntactic phenomenon (2–1 advancement), as in standard RG. The preposition incorporation idea (often called reanalysis) has been widely adopted in some form (e.g., Chomsky 1981, Hornstein and Weinberg 1981, van Riemsdijk 1978). Postal (1986, Ch. 6) argues convincingly against the claim that there is preposition incorporation in the active counterparts of pseudopassives. However, I have pointed out elsewhere (Farrell 1991, Ch. 3) that Postal's arguments do not bear on the issue of whether preposition incorporation underlies the pseudopassive construction itself and there is some evidence to support the claim that it in fact does.

Based on the systematic ungrammaticality of participial adjectives formed on the argument that advances to 2 in the 3–2 advancement construction, as shown in (10), in Farrell 1991, Ch. 3 I argue that there is a constraint on participial adjective formation in English that can be formulated as in (11).[8]

(10) a. The lady offered the children some candy. 3–2 ADVANCEMENT
b. The children were offered some candy. 3–2 ADVANCEMENT PLUS PASSIVE
c. * **unoffered** children *PARTICIPIAL ADJECTIVE

(11) A participial adjective is well-formed only if the noun it modifies expresses the initial 2 of the base verb.

If (11) is correct, the final 1 of the pseudopassive construction must be the initial 2 of a verb/preposition complex.

A second kind of motivation for the proposed analysis is that it makes possible an explanation for the impossibility of pseudopassives based on verbs that clearly take an initial 2 that is distinct from the nominal associated with the preposition. Consider, for example, the ill-formedness of pseudopassives of the following sentences — representative examples of what I take to be the systematic exclusion of pseudopassive structures containing more than one 2.

(12) a. They shot an arrow at the target.
b. * The target was shot at an arrow.

(13) a. We can't perform that symphony in this hall.
b. * This hall can't be performed in that symphony.

(14) a. Someone stole a lot of money from that store.
b. * That store was stolen from a lot of money.

If pseudopassives are made possible by the syntactic expression of what would otherwise be a 3 or oblique as an initial 2, it follows (from the SUL) that it can only occur in a clause in which there is no distinct initial 2.[9] An advancement to 2 analysis of pseudopassives, on the other hand, would not automatically explain the ungrammaticality of the (b)-examples in (12)-(14). Under such an analysis, the SUL could not be appealed to, since the final 1 in the (b)-examples would be an initial oblique rather than an initial 2. Given that an advancement to 2 (as well as a passive

---

[8] I also show that (11) is preferable to the constraint proposed in Levin and Rappaport 1986 and Rappaport and Levin 1988, according to which all the obligatorily expressed internal arguments of a verb must be expressed in a participial adjective construction. It should be pointed out that (11) is a necessary condition, but not a sufficient one (e.g., *Front vowels follow palatal consonants* is fine, but **(un)followed palatal consonants* is not).

[9] The tacit assumption here is that a 2 put en chomage by an advancement would be a bare NP, as in what I analyze as 3–2 advancement clauses ((10a) for example) as well as in the presentational *there* construction (*There was a bug in my soup*), in which I assume — following Perlmutter (1983a) — that the initial 2 is put en chomage by the dummy *there* which advances to 1. Themes, when expressed syntactically, are initial 2s as a general rule. When expressed as initial obliques they are marked by a preposition (usually *with*). As expected, a theme can be an initial oblique in some cases involving incorporated prepositions (for example, *The target was shot at with an arrow*; *The wallpaper was painted over with blue paint*). The key point is that 2 chomeurs, which are not marked with prepositions in English, do not occur in pseudopassives.

advancement to 1) would have to be sanctioned because of cases such as *The target was shot at*, it would have to be stipulated that an advancement to 2 of the kind associated with preposition incorporation could not take place in a clause with an initial 2, in order to rule out cases like (12b).[10] No such stipulation is required on the proposed analysis.

In sum, the best analysis of pseudopassives is one according to which the argument otherwise expressed in a prepositional phrase is the initial 2 of a verb/preposition complex. Given this analysis, the impossibility of pseudopassives of unaccusatives follows from the fact that the theme argument of unaccusatives is their unique initial 2.[11] There is no need to appeal to the 1AEX to explain the ungrammaticality of examples such as those in (6).

3. Funny Subject Constructions in English

P&P claim that clauses such as those illustrated by the (a)-examples in (15)-(18) involve oblique–1 advancement. That is, the highlighted nominals are initial obliques and final 1s.

(15) a. **Five dollars** bought a lot of heroin in 1827.
b. Melvin bought a lot of heroin for five dollars.
(16) a. **This cabin** sleeps twenty people.
b. Twenty people can sleep in this cabin.
(17) a. **1939** found the United States on the brink of disaster.
b. The United States was found on the brink of disaster in 1939.
(18) a. **Labor Day** saw the government's policy in shreds.
b. We saw the government's policy in shreds on Labor Day.

The idea is that the final 1s of the (a)-sentences apparently bear the same thematic relation as the corresponding obliques in the (b)-sentences. It is natural, then, to relate these sentences by oblique–1 advancement.[12] This analysis, together with the 1AEX, yields an account of the ungrammaticality of passives of the (a)-sentences:

---

[10] Some kind of stipulation with the same effect would be needed even if pseudopassives were analyzed as involving a direct oblique–1 advancement rather than oblique–2–1 advancement.

[11] This explanation extends to the case of so-called INVERSION predicates such as *matter* (as in *That doesn't matter to me*), which P&P claim have the experiencer as initial 1 and demotee to 3 and the theme as initial 2. Thus, the fact that pseudopassives such as **I am not mattered to by that* are not possible follows from the analysis of pseudopassives proposed here, in conjunction with the assumption that the theme is the initial 2. Whether or not the experiencer is an initial 1 that demotes to 3 or an initial 3 (or oblique) is an interesting but orthogonal question. The same explanation also extends to the impossibility of compound passives involving both regular passive and pseudopassive. Thus, the passive *Letters have been written to the president* cannot be pseudopassivized to yield **The president has been (been) written to by letters*. In this case, *the president* and *letters* cannot both be initial 2s of *written to*, which they would have to be in order for such a double passive to be grammatical.

[12] Under the assumption that they are thematic paraphrases in some relevant sense, it would be necessary to relate these sentences by oblique–1 advancement in a version of RG incorporating the Universal Alignment Hypothesis, according to which the corresponding nominals in thematic paraphrases necessarily bear the same initial grammatical relations. However, the Universal

(19) a. * A lot of heroin was bought by five dollars (in 1827).
b. * Twenty people are slept by this cabin.
c. * The United States was found on the brink of disaster by 1939.
d. * The government's policy was seen in shreds by Labor Day.

If the nominals expressed in *by*-phrases in the examples in (19) are initial obliques that advance to 1 prior to being put en chomage, the resulting structures are ill-formed because the passive advancement that puts them en chomage constitutes an illicit second advancement to 1.

The ungrammaticality of passive clauses such as those in (19) provides support for the 1AEX only if an equally viable alternative solution to this problem is not available. I will consider two possibilities, without taking a stand on which is correct. The logic of the argument is as follows. Since either of these two possibilities would account for the ungrammaticality of (19) at least as straightforwardly as the oblique–1 advancement analysis with the 1AEX, such examples motivate neither an oblique–1 advancement analysis of (15a)-(18a) nor the 1AEX.

Consider, to begin with, the question of whether there are two different predicate-argument structures in paraphrases like (15a-b). It is clear that the predicate of (15b) is one that has an agent argument. The predicate of (15a), on the other hand, apparently does not. When *buy* is used as it is in (15a) no agent argument can be expressed:

(20) * Five dollars bought a lot of heroin in 1827 by Melvin.

There are essentially two possible accounts of this: (i) *buy* is associated with a single argument structure and the advancement of *five dollars* puts en chomage an initial 1/agent that is necessarily unspecified and implicit, or (ii) the *buy* of (15a) is associated with an agentless argument structure derived from that of the *buy* of (15b). Since there is at least no obvious reason for preferring (i) over (ii), let us assume that (ii) is correct.[13] The argument structure of the *buy* of (15a) is, thus, either (21a) or (21b) (*amt* = amount — for lack of a better label for the thematic relation of *five dollars*).[14]

Alignment Hypothesis is itself highly problematic for reasons noted in Rosen 1984 and Farrell 1991, Ch. 4.

[13] Of course, if (i) can be shown to be correct, the argument being developed here does not go through. There are, I believe, verbs in English that are clearly associated with two distinct argument structures in precisely the way that I am claiming *buy* is. Consider, for example, *split* in the following two uses: *The man split the log with the wedge* and *The wedge split the log*. It can be argued that *the man* (the agent) is the initial 1 in the first sentence and the wedge (the instrument) is the initial 1 in the second. Evidence comes from the fact that the nominalizing suffix *-er* suppresses the initial 1 of a predicate (Farrell 1991, Ch. 3) and a phrase like *the log splitter* could be used to refer either to the man or the wedge. Further, if the 1AEX were assumed to be valid, the same conclusion would follow from the fact that both sentences can be passivized (at least for many speakers).

[14] What I have in mind with the term *argument structure* is a lexical specification of the number and semantic type (or thematic relation) of the arguments of a predicate and their

(21) a. *buy*: <amt/obl, theme/2>
b. *buy*: <amt/1, theme/2>

Suppose that (21a) is correct. If so, this *buy* appears in an RN with an unaccusative initial stratum. In order to satisfy the FINAL 1 LAW (Perlmutter and Postal 1983), there must either be an advancement to 1 or a dummy final 1 must be inserted. However, there is only one possible structure. The theme cannot advance to 1 and a dummy cannot be inserted:

(22) a. * A lot of heroin bought for five dollars in 1827.
b. * There bought a lot of heroin for five dollars in 1827.

It would therefore have to be stipulated that in such structures the oblique must advance to 1. We might encode this restriction in the argument structure, as follows:

(23) *buy*: <amt/obl⇒1, theme/2>

The key point here is that something special needs to be stipulated about clauses like (15a) if their final 1 is assumed to be an initial oblique, as it must be in order to engage the 1AEX to account for the ungrammaticality of (19a).

Suppose, now, that (21b) is chosen as the argument structure for the *buy* in question. It does not, of course, need to be stipulated that one of the arguments must advance to 1. However, the 1AEX cannot be engaged to account for the ungrammaticality of (19a). Still, it could simply be stipulated that the initial 1 cannot be put en chomage in this structure, which is equivalent to saying that passivization is impossible.[15] This stipulation would be essentially the opposite of that needed for the advancement to 1 analysis. The argument structure of the *buy* of (15a) would be (24).

(24) *buy*: <amt/1⇏cho, theme/2>

Unless it can be shown that (23) is preferable to (24), the ungrammaticality of (19a) provides no evidence for an oblique–1 advancement analysis of (15a) and the 1AEX. A similar line of reasoning holds concerning the analysis of the other (a)-examples in (15)-(18).[16] It is true, of course, that why, ultimately, passiviza-

---

[15] Another way of formulating the relevant constraint would be to say that the initial 1 must be the final 1.

[16] (16) is somewhat different than the other pairs, in that the number of nominals does not differ. Still, the *sleep* of (16a) is arguably a different predicate than the *sleep* of (16b), as can be seen by the fact that the former places different semantic restrictions on its arguments. *My mother sleeps in this cabin* and *Twenty people will not sleep in this cabin voluntarily* are fine; but **This cabin sleeps my mother* and **This cabin will not sleep twenty people voluntarily* are not. If these are not analyzed as two predicates with partially distinct semantics and distinct argument

tion is impossible remains an unanswered question under such an analysis. However, the 1AEX-based analysis provides a kind of answer to this question only by replacing it with another unanswered question, i.e., why the initial oblique argument of certain predicates must advance to 1. The number and kind of arbitrary stipulations is the same.

A second possible approach to the problem posed by the ungrammaticality of passive clauses corresponding to (15a)-(18a) is based on the idea that passivization in English is semantically constrained. Although it is clear that no simple thematic constraint could work, it is also clear that clauses with an agent and patient can virtually always be passivized and when the subject of an active clause cannot plausibly be construed as acting in some way on the direct object, passivization is generally not possible (Pinker 1989, Ch. 4), hence the contrast in (25).

(25) a. The man was murdered by his brother.
b. * A great voice was had by my mother.

The ungrammatical examples in (19) are intuitively closer to (25b) than (25a) in terms of their distance from the prototypical passive clause. I think it would be safe to say that if there is a viable, general semantic explanation for why some clauses passivize in English and others do not, this explanation is sure to cover the ungrammaticality of the sentences in (19).[17] As a concrete example, consider the case of (16). (16b) has, at least on one reading, essentially the same meaning as (16a). As is well known, the verb *sleep* can be (pseudo)passivized, under the right conditions, as shown by (26a). (16b), however, cannot:

(26) a. This bed has been slept in by someone.
b. * This cabin can be slept in by twenty people.

Whatever the precise condition that accounts for this contrast turns out to be, the explanation for it is undeniably semantic at some level. The passive subject of (26a) is understood as being affected by the sleeping, that of (26b) is not. If (16b) does not have the right semantics to be passivized, then (16a) surely does not either, whatever its syntactic structure happens to be. Crucially, some kind of (apparently semantic) constraint on passivization, which is likely to extend to cases like (19), is required for cases like (25b) and (26b) in any case.

In short, the fact that sentences like those in (15a)-(18a) do not passivize can be said to provide support for an oblique–1 advancement analysis and the 1AEX only in the unlikely event that a satisfactory formulation of what appears to be an independently motivated semantic constraint turns out to be impossible and (23) can be shown to be superior to (24).

---

structures, then the conditions on the advancement that relates (16b) to (16a) are quite unusual. It is, I believe, only the semantic contribution of *can* that gives (16b) essentially the same meaning as (16a).

[17] It might also, of course, cover the ungrammatical passive examples discussed in §2 — a result that would make it possible to liberate the explanation from the Unaccusative Hypothesis.

4. Cebuano Advancements

Drawing on the analysis presented in Bell 1983, P&P claim that the 1AEX explains the impossibility of multiple advancements to 1 in Cebuano. According to Bell, the final 1 of the Cebuano clause is the NP marked with what she calls the nominative case, which in any given clause can be one of various arguments depending on what voice marking appears on the verb. As shown by the following examples, when the initial 1 is the nominative-marked nominal (what I hereinafter call the pivot),[18] the verb is in the so-called active voice.[19]

(27) a. Magluto' **ang babaye** ug bugas sa kulon.
ACT-cook NOM woman OBL rice OBL ricepot
'*The woman* will cook rice in the ricepot.' (Bell's ex. 1)

b. Mosulat **si Linda** ug sulat gigamit ang lapis.
write-ACT NOM Linda OBL letter being used NOM pencil
'*Linda* will write a letter with the pencil.' (Bell's ex. 8a)

When the theme is pivot, the verb is generally in the objective voice, as shown in (28a). Although locative and instrumental voices have various uses, in most cases their use is predictable from the thematic relation of the pivot.[20] Locative voice is used, for example, with locative pivots (see (28b)); instrumental voice is used with instrumental pivots (see (28c)).

(28) a. Luto'on sa babaye **ang bugas** sa kulon.
cook-OBJ GEN woman NOM rice OBL ricepot
'The woman will cook *the rice* in the ricepot.' (ex. 4)

b. Luto'an sa babaye **ang kulon** ug bugas.
cook-LOC GEN woman NOM ricepot OBL rice
'The woman will cook rice *in the ricepot*.' (ex. 5)

c. Isulat ni Linda **ang lapis** ug sulat.
INS-write GEN Linda NOM pencil OBL letter
'Linda will write a letter *with the pencil*.' (ex. 8b)

The analysis proposed by Bell is that the sentences in (27) are monostratal active clauses. Among clausal dependents of finite verbs, so-called nominative case is used for final 1s. Oblique case is used for (certain) final obliques and for final 2s. Genitive case is used for 1 chomeurs. The active voice is used when there is no advancement to 1. The sentences in (28) all involve advancements to 1. In (28a) the initial 2 advances to 1 in the passive construction; in (28b-c) initial obliques advance to 1. The analysis of (28b), for example, is assumed to be as shown in the following stratal diagram.

---

[18] I use the term *pivot* with the understanding that it means the clausal dependent marked with the case that Bell calls nominative, and nothing more.

[19] I take the following liberty with Bell's examples: the English translation is always in the active voice with the pivot in italics. Bell gives examples in the objective voice in Cebuano English translations in the passive voice. It will become clear why she does this and why I do not.

[20] The situation is actually quite complex. See Bell 1983 for details.

(29)

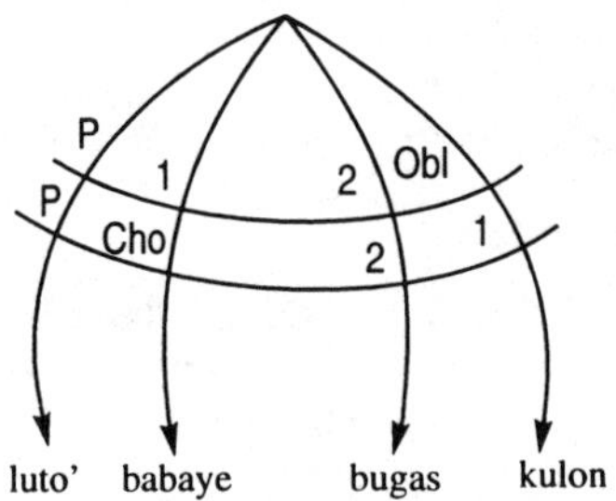

P&P observe that the various putative advancements to 1 in Cebuano are mutually exclusive and that the 1AEX provides an explanation for this. The problem is that Bell's analysis is probably wrong, as Cebuano is arguably better analyzed as a syntactically ergative language (Dryer 1978, Blake 1990, Ch. 7, Farrell 1991, Ch. 4), i.e., one in which the prominent relations are ERGATIVE (the 1 of a transitive stratum) and ABSOLUTIVE (the lowest-ranking nuclear term of a stratum).[21] An ergative analysis has been argued for in RG terms for related languages such as Ilokano (Gerdts 1988a) and Tagalog (De Guzman 1988) and is widely accepted for Philippine languages in general (Cooreman, Fox, and Givón 1988, Blake 1990, Ch. 7). Under such an analysis, the pivot is characterized as the final absolutive rather than the final 1. (28a) is not a passive clause but a monostratal transitive clause in which the theme is both initial and final 2 (and hence final absolutive as well). The so-called genitive case is more appropriately labeled 'ergative' case. The sentences in (27) involve ANTIPASSIVE: the initial 2 demotes to chomeur leaving the clause finally intransitive with the initial 1 as final absolutive. Clauses with locative or instrumental voice are applicatives of the usual sort. That is, they involve advancements to 2. The analysis of (28b), for example, would be as in (30).

(30)

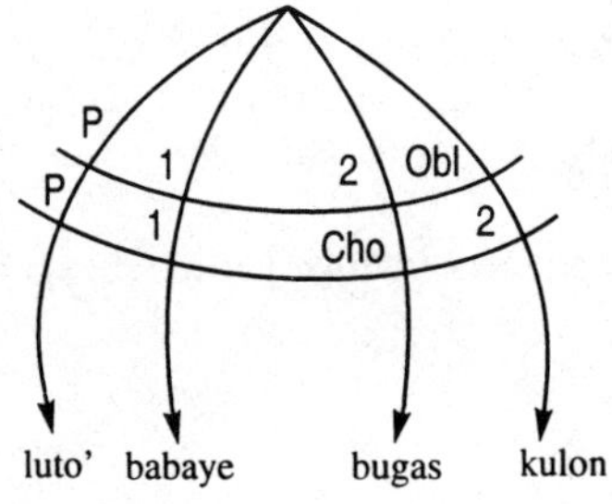

[21] 1 > 2 and the nuclear terms are 1 and 2. An ergative analysis can be shown to account straightforwardly for the various phenomena discussed by Bell. It is preferable inter alia in that it eliminates various typological anomalies that stand out under Bell's analysis. For example, there is a subject-only condition on reflexive antecedence that does not have to be formulated in such a way as to allow 1 chomeurs and disallow advancees to 1 as antecedents. See the cited references for further details.

The important point is that under the ergative analysis there are no advancements to 1 whatsoever in Cebuano. If there are no advancements to 1, it is logically impossible for the 1AEX to find support from this language.[22]

5. Impersonal Passives in Dutch

Citing data from Perlmutter 1978, P&P note that although impersonal passives of agentive intransitives are possible in Dutch, impersonal passives of unaccusatives are not, as illustrated by the following contrast:

(31) a. In de zomer wordt er hier vaak gezwommen.
'In the summer it is swum here frequently.'
b. * In de zomer wordt er hier vaak verdronken.
'In the summer it is drowned here frequently.' (P&P's exx. 106a-b)

The 1AEX provides a means of explaining this contrast, if it is assumed that impersonal passives are clauses in which a dummy is inserted as a 2 and advances to 1 putting a 1 en chomage. Since (31b) is initially unaccusative, it would have to involve an unaccusative advancement with a subsequent advancement to 1 by the dummy. The 1AEX, however, precludes the possibility of two advancements to 1. (31a) does not pose a problem because there is no unaccusative advancement.

The problem in this case is that there is apparently no independent motivation for the kind of unaccusative/unergative distinction needed in order to engage the 1AEX in an account of the distribution of impersonal passives. In fact, if the unaccusative/unergative distinction correlates with the lexical intransitive verb classes that can be established on the basis of auxiliary selection and prenominal *ge*-participle formation (Hoekstra 1984, Zaenen 1989), impersonal passive formation is not a reliable criterion of unaccusativity, since it picks out a partially distinct class, as noted by Perlmutter (1978) and Levin (1988). In particular, translating her LFG mapping theory analysis into RG terms, Zaenen shows that the conditions on auxiliary selection and prenominal *ge*-participle formation can be formulated as in (32), given the analysis of a certain class of intransitive verbs as unaccusatives.[23]

(32) a. When the final 1 heads a 2 arc, the auxiliary is *zijn* 'be'; otherwise it is *hebben* 'have'.
b. The noun modified by a prenominal *ge*-participle expresses its initial 2.

---

[22] The question of why apparent advancements to 2 are mutually exclusive is interesting but irrelevant for present concerns. See Farrell 1991, Ch. 4 for an answer to this question.

[23] It should be noted that (32b) is the same as (11). Like participial adjective formation in English, this phenomenon picks out the initial 2 of lexically transitive verbs and the principal argument of a subclass of lexically intransitive verbs. Only by treating the latter class as unaccusatives is it possible to express the condition as a generalization. Zaenen characterizes unaccusative verbs as nonpassive intransitives with an argument that is intrinsically marked [–r], like prototypical direct objects of transitive verbs (see also Bresnan and Zaenen 1990).

Unaccusatives such as 'fall', 'die', 'drown', and 'arrive' take *zijn* as their auxiliary in the compound past tense and allow for prenominal *ge*-participle formation, for example:[24]

(33) a. Hij **is** gevallen/gestorven/aangekomen. *zijn* AUXILIARY
'He fell/died/arrived.'
b. De gevallen/(pas) gearriveerde jongen. *ge*-PARTICIPLE FORMATION
'The fallen/(just) arrived boy.'

On the other hand, unergatives such as 'swim', 'sneeze', 'work', and 'sleep' take *hebben* and do not allow for prenominal *ge*-participle formation, as illustrated by the examples in (34).

(34) a. Hij **heeft** gezwommen/gwerkt/geslapen. *hebben* AUXILIARY
'He swam/worked/slept.'
b. * De geslapen/gewerkte jongen. **ge*-PARTICIPLE FORMATION
'The slept/worked boy.'

The idea that impersonal passives are possible with unergatives but not unaccusatives and that the 1AEX is responsible for this is problematic in two ways. First, there are verbs that are unergatives by the auxiliary and prenominal *ge*-participle criteria and do not form impersonal passives. The verb 'bleed', for example, takes *hebben* but does not form an impersonal passive:

(47) a. De man **heeft** gebloed. *hebben* AUXILIARY
'The man bled.'
b. * Er werd (door de man) gebloed. *IMPERSONAL PASSIVE
'There was bled (by the man).'

Zaenen shows that impersonal passives are possible only with verbs corresponding to 'controllable' eventualities (a class of verbs for which there are independent tests, such as ability to be combined with the adverb 'on purpose'). Thus, there is a semantic constraint whose effects subsume and go beyond those of the 1AEX, rendering it superfluous as an explanation for the distribution of impersonal passives.

Second, given a sentence whose aspect, as a whole, is atelic (a second semantic condition on impersonal passives), controllable unaccusatives can form impersonal passives:

(35) In dat hotel heb ik geen oog dicht gedaan, want er werd the hele nacht aangekomen en vertrokken.
'In that hotel I didn't sleep a wink, for there was the whole night arrived and left.'

As noted by Zaenen, it would not work to claim that 'arrive' and 'leave' are unergatives when they are used in atelic constructions, since the auxiliary is still *zijn* in such cases, as shown by (36).

---

[24] These and all subsequent Dutch examples are from Zaenen 1989 or are based on examples presented there.

(36) Er **zijn** hier urenlang reizigers aangekomen.
'There have here for hours travelers arrived.'

It is thoroughly reasonable to conclude, as Zaenen does, that the restricted distribution of impersonal passives in Dutch is due to conditions based on semantic factors that are similar to but distinct from the semantic correlates of the unaccusative/unergative distinction. The important implication from the perspective of this paper is that this phenomenon fails to motivate the 1AEX. Indeed, on the face of it, the 1AEX wrongly predicts (35) to be ungrammatical. P&P briefly discuss other languages that seem to have the same kind of restrictions on impersonal passives as Dutch. It is possible that closer inspection of these languages will reveal the need for the 1AEX. On the other hand, it is equally possible that similar language-specific semantic constraints recur in various languages. The fact that there are languages in which such constraints are not found (see footnote 3) suggests that it is initially preferable to view them as language-specific constraints rather than as manifestations of a law of universal grammar.

6. Conclusion

The status of the 1AEX has long been controversial. Problematic data from various languages has been presented by a number of researchers. A certain range of this data has been argued to be amenable to analyses that render it unproblematic (Postal 1986). Moreover, it is likely that some kind of salvaging analysis could be made available for virtually any empirical challenge. Against this background, it is unclear whether the 1AEX should be maintained, abandoned entirely, or parametrized. I have attempted to show that abandoning it is the best option, because it has no clear motivation to begin with. Although the issue is addressed here from an RG-internal perspective, the results have potentially broader implications. In particular, they call into question the desirability of such cross-theoretical counterparts of the 1AEX as the characterization of passive as suppression of the so-called external argument.

References

Baker, Mark C. 1988. *Incorporation: A Theory of Grammatical Function Changing*. Chicago: University of Chicago Press.

Bell, Sarah J. 1983. Advancements and Ascensions in Cebuano. In Perlmutter 1983b.

Blake, Barry J. 1990. *Relational Grammar*. Croom Helm Linguistic Theory Guides. London: Routledge.

Bresnan, Joan. 1982. The Passive in Lexical Theory. *The Mental Representation of Grammatical Relations*, ed. by Joan Bresnan. Cambridge, Mass: MIT Press.

Bresnan, Joan, and Lioba Moshi. 1990. Object Asymmetries in Comparative Bantu Syntax. *Linguistic Inquiry* 21.147–185.

Bresnan, Joan, and Annie Zaenen. 1990. Deep Unaccusativity in LFG. *Grammatical Relations: A Cross-Theoretical Perspective*, ed. by Katarzyna Dziwirek, Patrick Farrell, and Errapel Mejías-Bikandi. Stanford: CSLI and The Stanford Linguistics Association.

Chomsky, Noam. 1981. *Lectures on Government and Binding*. Dordrecht: Foris.

Cooreman, Ann, Barbara Fox, and Talmy Givón. 1988. The Discourse Definition of Ergativity: A Study in Chamorro and Tagalog Texts. In McGinn 1988.

De Guzman, Videa P. 1988. Ergative Analysis for Philippine Languages: An Analysis. In McGinn 1988.

Dryer, Matthew. 1978. Some Theoretical Implications of Grammatical Relations in Cebuano. University of Michigan Papers in Linguistics 2. Ann Arbor, Michigan.

Farrell, Patrick. 1991. *Thematic Relations, Relational Networks, and Multistratal Representations*. University of California San Diego dissertation.

Gerdts, Donna B. 1984. A Relational Analysis of Halkomelem Causals. *Syntax and Semantics 16: The Syntax of Native American Languages*, ed. by E.-D. Cook and Donna B. Gerdts, New York: Academic Press.

Gerdts, Donna B. 1988a Antipassives and Causatives in Ilokano: Evidence for an Ergative Analysis. In McGinn 1988.

Gerdts, Donna B. 1988b. *Object and Absolutive in Halkomelem Salish*. New York: Garland. Doctoral dissertation, University of California, San Diego, 1981.

Grimshaw, Jane. 1990. *Argument Structure*. Cambridge, Mass: MIT Press.

Hoekstra, Teun. 1984. *Transitivity: Grammatical Relations in Government-Binding Theory*. Dordrecht: Foris.

Hornstein, Norbert, and Amy Weinberg. 1981. Case Theory and Preposition Stranding. *Linguistic Inquiry* 12.55–91.

Jaeggli, Osvaldo A. 1986. Passive. *Linguistic Inquiry* 17.587–622.

Keenan, Edward L., and Alan Timberlake. 1985. Predicate Formation Rules in Universal Grammar. *Proceedings of the West Coast Conference on Formal Linguistics* 4. Stanford University, Stanford, Calif.

Levin, Beth, and Malka Rappaport. 1986. The Formation of Adjectival Passives. *Linguistic Inquiry* 17.623–662.

Levin, Lori. 1988. *Operations on Lexical Forms: Unaccusative Rules in Germanic Languages*. New York: Garland. Doctoral dissertation, MIT, 1986.

McGinn, Richard (ed.) 1988. *Studies in Austronesian Linguistics*. Monographs in International Studies, Southeast Asia Series, Number 76. Athens, Ohio: Ohio University Press.

Nerbonne, John A. 1982. Some Passives Not Characterized by Universal Rules: Subjectless Impersonals. *Grammatical Relations and Relational Grammar*, ed. by Brian D. Joseph, Columbus, Ohio: The Ohio State University.

Ostler, N. D. M. 1979. *Case-Linking: A Theory of Case and Verb Diathesis Applied to Classical Sanskrit*. MIT dissertation.

Özkaragöz, Inci. 1980. Evidence from Turkish for the Unaccusative Hypothesis. *Proceedings of the Sixth Annual Meeting of the Berkeley Linguistics Society*. University of California, Berkeley.

Perlmutter, David M. 1978. Impersonal Passives and the Unaccusative Hypothesis. *Proceedings of the Fourth Annual Meeting of the Berkeley Linguistic Society*. University of California, Berkeley.

Perlmutter, David M. 1983a. Personal vs. Impersonal Constructions. *Natural Language and Linguistic Theory* 1.141–200.

Perlmutter, David M. (ed.) 1983b. *Studies in Relational Grammar 1*. Chicago: University of Chicago Press.

Perlmutter, David M., and Paul M. Postal. 1983. Some Proposed Laws of Basic Clause Structure. In Perlmutter 1983b.

Perlmutter, David M., and Paul M. Postal. 1984. The 1-Advancement Exclusiveness Law. In Perlmutter and Rosen 1984.

Perlmutter, David M., and Carol Rosen (eds.) 1984. *Studies in Relational Grammar 2*. Chicago: University of Chicago Press.

Pinker, Stephen. 1989. *Learnability and Cognition*. Cambridge, Mass: MIT Press.

Postal, Paul M. 1986. *Studies of Passive Clauses*. Albany: State University of New York Press.

Rappaport, Malka, and Beth Levin. 1988. What to Do with θ-Roles. *Syntax and Semantics 21: Thematic Relations*, ed. by Wendy Wilkins. San Diego: Academic Press.

Rosen, Carol. 1984. The Interface between Semantic Roles and Initial Grammatical Relations. In Perlmutter and Rosen 1984.

Rosen, Carol. 1988. *The Relational Structure of Reflexive Clauses: Evidence from Italian*. New York: Garland. Doctoral dissertation, Harvard University, 1981.

Stowell, Timothy. 1981. *Origins of Phrase Structure*. MIT dissertation.

Timberlake, Alan. 1982. The Impersonal Passive in Lithuanian. *Proceedings of the Eighth Annual Meeting of the Berkeley Linguistics Society*. University of California, Berkeley.

van Riemsdijk, Henk. 1978. *A Case Study in Syntactic Markedness*. Dordrecht: Foris.

Zaenen, Annie. 1989. Unaccusativity in Dutch: An Integrated Approach. Xerox-PARC and CSLI, Stanford, MS.

Sikuani Stress and the Accentual Zone

HENRY GERFEN
University of Arizona

0. Introduction

In this paper I consider the puzzle of primary stress placement in Sikuani, a Guahibo language of Colombia. The most salient feature of the Sikuani stress system is that primary stress must fall within a word-final trisyllabic window or accentual zone (AZ).[2] I argue that the correct characterization of this zone requires a theory of stress which permits non-iterative footing (c.f. Hayes 1981, 1987, 1991, Hammond 1986, etc.). Furthermore, I claim that stress shift into the AZ provides empirical support for a model in which foot construction and head assignment are formally separate processes (Halle and Vergnaud 1987a,b).

The organization of this paper is as follows. In section 1, I claim that lexical accent is a property of Sikuani morphemes. In section 2, I provide the basic stress facts, showing that word stress contours are generally derived directly from morpheme concatenation. In section 3, I present an array of data involving main stress location, focussing on stress shift both into and within the AZ. Finally, in section 4 I propose an analysis of stress placement, making crucial use of non-iterative footing, as well as the formal separability of footing and head assignment.

1. Lexical Accent

Following Queixalós (1985), I assume that stress in Sikuani originates at the morpheme level. Morphemes are divided into two groups: i) those with lexical accent, and ii) those without. This division corresponds roughly to the functional versus content category of a morpheme. Examples of both are provided in (1).

---

[1]I would like to thank Dick Demers, Chris Golston, Mike Hammond, Pilar Piñar, and Iris Kao for comments and suggestions on earlier versions of this paper. All errors are my own.

[2]See also Everett and Everett (1984) on Pirahã and Steriade (1988) on Ancient Greek for discussions of similar word-final trisyllabic zones.

(1)

Accented Morphemes		Unaccented Morphemes	
nò	'tuber'	to	'negative'
wài	'summer'	tʰa	'instrumental'
à.ke	'scorpion'	be.he	'both'
ma.li.kài	'type of bird'	ha.wa	'small'
xài	'have, possess'	pe	'det.'
		xae	'because of'
		wi	'animate pl.'
		nae	'virtual mood'
		apo	'neg.'
		wa	'fem.'

Accented morphemes in isolation exhibit fairly regular patterns. Lexical accent generally falls on the penult or on a bimoraic syllable (there are no closed syllables in Sikuani: *VC]$_\sigma$). Given these two preferences, bimoraic penults are the most systematically accented syllables, yet the range is relatively wide, as seen in (2-8), where lexical accent is marked with a grave accent.

(2) Penultimate accent

xà.nü	'I'
yà.la	'porcupine'
mè.ne	'river'
wì.si	'good shooter'
wa.nà.li	'talisman'
da.hù.bi	'pets'
da.xì.ta	'all'

(3) Heavy syllable accent

kìu.li	'ant'
na.kùa	'world'
ko.tìa	'llama'
ma.rài	'type of bird'
ma.li.kài	'type of bird'

(4) Accent on heavy penult

u.mài.pia	'toponym'
kai.wìa.li	'type of ant'
pìa.lua	'piaroa'
kùa.lia	'type of insect'

(5) Penult accent before a heavy ultima

tʰì.kue	'type of bird'
kò.pʰia	'oso palmero'
ì.nae	'silex'

(6) Antepenult accent before a heavy ultima

mà.li.bai	'type of fish'

(7) Accent on an ultima after a heavy penult

pʰu.lia.wài	'a morning star'

(8) Non-penult accent in morphemes with no heavy syllables

a.kè	'cold'
tsì.ki.ri	'small'
ì.ku.li	'type of turtle'
ka.mà.la.pi	'type of insect'
tu.lì.ki.si	'necklace'

As shown below, word stress contours are determined in large measure by the distribution of lexically accented syllables. This is reminiscent of the stress domain phenomenon in Diyari (Poser 1986, Halle and Vergnaud 1987b), insofar as the stress contours of individual morphemes appear to be respected in the concatenated string. It is important to note, however, that lexical accent is not subject to the rigid constraints on stress placement found for concatenated strings.

2. Word Stress

Word stress contours are generated via the concatenation of both accented and unaccented morphemes. Though the system becomes quite complex as a result of the stress shift facts discussed below, the general pattern is straightforward. After morpheme concatenation, the rightmost accented syllable surfaces with main stress, while all other lexically accented syllables surface with secondary stress. Importantly, only lexically accented syllables surface with secondary stress, as seen in (9), where morphemes to the left of the arrow constitute the input to the string.[3]

(9) a. kabè + sà + pà + ta + me → kabèsàpátame
hand naked come asp. you 'you came with nothing'

b. owèbi + màta + è + to + t^ha → owèbimàtaétot^{h}a
deer head horn sg. instr. 'with the horns of the deer'

Given this pattern, a preliminary analysis of Sikuani word stress is formulated in terms of the constituentized grid of Halle and Vergnaud (1987a,b). Note in (10) that no feet are built on line 0, an option exploited by Halle and Vergnaud (1987a) for Vedic, though later rejected in Halle and Vergnaud (1987b). For Sikuani, this ensures the proper placement of secondary stresses in concatenated forms, as only lexical accents are placed on line 1.

(10) Word stress rules: a first pass

i. Stressable elements are syllables.
ii. Assign line 0 asterisks to all stressable elements.
iii. Assign line 1 asterisks to all lexically accented syllables.
iv. Construct a constituent on line 1, where line 1 parameter settings are [+Head Terminal; -Bounded; +Right]
v. Locate the head of the line 1 constituent on line 2.

The rules in (10) account for all secondary stresses in Sikuani by limiting line 1 asterisks to syllables already accented at the morpheme level (10iii). A right-headed word tree is then built on line 1, accounting for rightmost primary stress (10v). Stress shift facts motivating line 0 constituency, such as those adduced by Halle and Vergnaud (1987b) for Sanskrit and Russian, are unavailable,

[3]A note on diacritics: I use acute accents to represent primary stress in surface forms. Grave accents represent the location of lexical accent in morphemes prior to concatenation, as well as secondary stress in surface forms.

since stressed vowels are not subject to elision in Sikuani (Queixalós 1985). The absence of line 0 footing with be further exploited in 4.1 below. For now, a relevant derivation is provided in (11).

(11) Input: /kabè + sà + pà + ta + me/

```
                                                       *
(ii-       *   *   *            (iv         (*    *    *)
iii)   *   *   *   *   *   *    -v)      *    *    *    *    *    *
→      ka.be.sa.pa.ta.me        →       ka.be.sa.pa.ta.me
```

Output: [ka.bè.sà.pá.ta.me] 'you came with nothing'

3. Stress shift and primary stress

While the rules in (10) account for secondary stress placement in the language, the location of primary stress is more problematic. Two issues must be addressed: i) the systematic location of primary stress in the AZ of concatenated forms, and ii) the shifting of some rightmost lexical accents within the AZ to a following bimoriac syllable (c.f. Prince's 1990 WEIGHT TO STRESS PRINCIPLE).

3.1 The array of facts

As noted above, primary word stress must fall in the trisyllabic AZ. In the forms in (12), a heavy, lexically accented syllable surfaces in the AZ after concatenation.

(12) a. pa + wài	→	pa.wái	'this summer'
b. pa + wài+ yo	→	pa.wái.yo	'this summer (diminutive)'
c. pa + wài+ behe	→	pa.wái.be.he	'both summers'

The data in (13) provide cases of apparent stress shift from a lexically accented light syllable to a following heavy syllable within the AZ. Note in (13a) that there is no stress shift, as the rightmost lexically accented syllable of the word surfaces in the AZ and is not followed by a heavy syllable. In (13b-c), however, the accented syllable *pò* surfaces in the AZ, yet main stress is realized on the following heavy syllable, with concomitant loss of stress on *po*. In (13d) *pò* falls outside of the AZ, and stress again surfaces on the following heavy syllable.

(13) a. pò+na	→	pó.na	'goes'
b. apo+pò+nae	→	a.po.po.náe	'not go (3rd sg)'
c. apo+pò+nae+mu	→	a.po.po.náe.mu	'not go (2nd sg)'
d. pe+pò+nae+wa+yo	→	pe.po.náe.wa.yo	'the little walker'

The forms in (14) are significant in that stress shifts from a lexically accented light syllable to the rightmost heavy syllable in the AZ. This is clearest in (14b), where primary stress surfaces on the ultima *xáe*, rather than on the heavy penult *nae*.

(14) a. pò+nae+hitsia+nu →po.nae.hi.tsía.nu 'I'm going to go'
b. pe+pò+nae+xae →pe.po.nae.xáe 'because of his/her going'

Interestingly, the necessity of the trisyllabic AZ is not yet clear, since the data in (12-14) could be accounted for via a rule shifting main stress to the rightmost heavy syllable of a word. The forms in (15) show that this cannot be the case. In (15a) an accented heavy syllable surfaces with primary stress if it falls in the AZ, even if it is not the rightmost heavy syllable. Crucially, (15b) indicates that stress shift into the AZ itself is obligatory. Note that stress shifts from a lexically accented heavy syllable, just in case that syllable does not surface in the AZ.

(15) a. pìalua+wa → pía.lua.wa 'piaroa woman'
b. pìalua+nexa → pia.lúa.ne.xa 'for the piaroa'

If the AZ lacks a heavy syllable, the following array of facts emerges. As shown in (16)--and in (8) above--rightmost lexical accent is realized as primary stress if the rightmost lexically accented syllable surfaces in the AZ.

(16) a. tsìkiri+nò → tsì.ki.ri.nó 'small tuber'
b. tsìkiri+nò+yo → tsì.ki.ri.nó.yo 'small tuber(diminutive)'
c. tsìkiri+nò+yo+t^ha → tsì.ki.ri.nó.yo.t^ha 'with the small tuber (dim)'

The data in (17) show that if the syllable with rightmost lexical accent falls outside of the AZ, main stress surfaces on the first syllable of the AZ. As with the data in (13), stress shift into the AZ is characterized by a lack of expected secondary stress on the rightmost lexically accented syllable of the concatenated string. (17) reinforces the claim that stress cannot simply be shifted to a rightmost heavy syllable. In (17c) the final heavy syllable *nae* is outside of the AZ and thus cannot seat main stress.

(17) a. tsìkiri+hawa+yo → tsi.ki.ri.há.wa.yo 'tiny little thing'
b. tsìkiri+hawa+behe → tsi.ki.ri.ha.wá.be.he 'both little things'
c. pe+xài+nae+wi+behe → pe.xai.nae.wí.be.he 'both owners'

As the facts are somewhat confusing, a flow chart summarizing main stress placement is provided in (18).[4]

[4]One further complication for stress shift is found in the following:

i) pe+kóp^{h}ena+wa+xi → pe.ko.p^{h}e.na.wá.xi 'his/her little mothers in-law'
ii) tsíkiri+hawa → tsi.ki.ri.há.wa 'small thing'
iii) tsíkiri+wa → tsi.ki.ri.wá 'small female'

Here, the AZ lacks both a heavy syllable and a lexically accented syllable, and stress fails to shift to the first syllable of the AZ. Note that stress seems to fail to shift onto a syllable within the same

(18) Does the rightmost line 1 asterisk fall in the accentual zone?

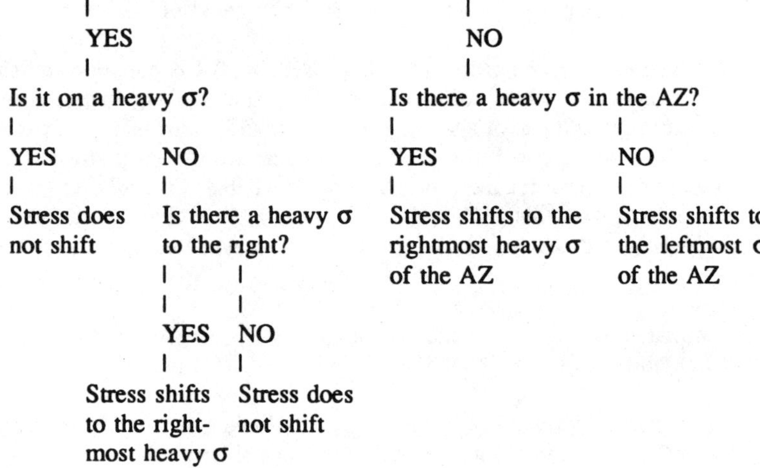

4. A solution

The chart in (18) reveals that Sikuani primary stress is characterized by two fundamental conditioning environments. First, primary stress must fall in the AZ. Secondly, primary stress falls on the rightmost heavy syllable in the AZ, except in cases such as (15a) *pía.lua.wa* 'piaroa woman'. I argue that these two observations provide a key to the puzzle of stress placement in that they suggest the interplay of two distinct processes in the derivation of the array of stress contours in (12-17). Specifically, one process locates stress in the accentual zone, while a later process shifts stress onto a heavy syllable in predictable contexts. Such an analysis, I claim, provides a maximally simple account of the data above.

4.1 Characterizing the AZ

The data in (17) are relevant to the first step in the analysis, as i) rightmost lexical accent falls outside of the AZ, and ii) the accentual zones of these forms lack heavy syllables. I take this to be the "default" case. Here, the attraction of stress into the AZ is manifested, without interference from the quantity-sensitive stress shift that is apparently triggered by the presence of bimoraic syllables in the zone. Significantly, in all three forms in (17), primary stress falls on the leftmost syllable of the AZ, that is, on the antepenult. Keeping this in mind, the solution to the problem of characterizing the zone is quite straightforward. First, in line

morpheme. That is, in these forms, main stress shifts past the antepenult, landing on the penult in (i-ii) and on the final syllable in (iii). In all three cases, the syllable located in antepenultimate position is also part of the lexically accented morpheme in the string. It thus appears that stress resists shifting to a location within the same morpheme in these forms. This contrasts with (15b), where stress shift of this type seems possible, if the syllable seating primary stress is heavy. I leave this problem for further investigation.

with the standard view of extrametricality (cf. Hayes 1982, Harris 1983, Archangeli 1984, Halle and Vergnaud 1987b[5]), a non-lexically accented word-final syllable is made extrametrical. Secondly, exploiting the absence of line 0 footing, a non-iterative syllabic trochee is constructed from right to left. Given the EXHAUSTIVITY CONDITION of Halle and Vergnaud (1987b), by which the rules of constituent construction apply exhaustively to a string, such footing is prohibited. However, Hayes (1987, 1991) includes an iterative/non-iterative parameter for foot construction (see also Hammond 1986). If the analysis here is on the right track, Sikuani would appear to constitute evidence in favor of a non-iterative parameter, as such footing permits the systematic parsing of the accentual zone in Sikuani words, without affecting the distribution of the lexical accents which surface as the only secondary stresses to the left in the string.

Consider, for example, the implications of exhaustive, left-headed binary foot construction for forms such as (16c), repeated here.

(16) c. /tsìkiri+nò+yo+t^{h}a/

```
   *   *     *
  (*) (*   *) (*   *)  <*>
 tsi.ki.ri.no.yo.t^ha
```
'with the small tuber'

In (16c), the footing algorithm parses the entire string, building three feet, each of which is supplied with a head. This parse correctly locates primary stress over the antepenultimate syllable via the construction of a right-headed word tree. Recall, however, that secondary stress in Sikuani is limited to non-rightmost, lexically accented syllables. Yet, here, a line 1 asterisk heads the foot (ki.ri), incorrectly predicting that secondary stress will surface on $[\text{ki}]_\sigma$.

Part of a formal solution to this problem might be found in Hammond (1989b), who argues on the basis of English secondary stress that lexical accent must be formally distinguished at line 0 (by a diacritic such as an *o*) from asterisks assigned by stress rules. Under such an assumption, one might build a right-headed word tree and invoke conflation. Since lexical accent is formally distinguishable at line 0, subsequent rules could then place line 1 asterisks only over lexically accented syllables, in effect replacing the secondary stresses lost through conflation. Such an approach, however, is needlessly complicated. First, we must introduce a new diacritic. And secondly, we are forced invoke conflation only because we have been forced to exhaustively parse the word. Non-iterative footing straightforwardly circumscribes the AZ, without affecting the location of secondary stress.

4.2 Headship

As Hammond (1989a) points out, the Halle and Vergnaud grid permits the separate manipulation of foot construction and head placement. This raises the

[5] See also Hammond (1991) for a less restricted approach to extrametricality.

possibility of exhaustively parsing Sikuani words into feet while not including a rule placing line 1 asterisks as the heads of the parsed constituents. Given Halle and Vergnaud's FAITHFULNESS CONDITION, line 1 lexical accents will be respected as heads during foot construction, while the boundaries of all headless constituents will be erased.

(19) Faithfulness Condition (Halle and Vernaud 1987b, pp.15-16)

The output of metrical structure respects the distribution of heads (accented elements), in the sense that each head is associated with constituent boundaries in the output structure and that these are located at the appropriate positions in the sequence. Constituent boundaries are erased in the output when none of the elements enclosed by the boundaries is marked as head.

Returning to the form in (16c) above, if no rule places line 1 asterisks as the heads of parsed constituents, the output of footing will be as in (20), where only lexical accents will surface as heads.

(20) Input: /tsìkiri+nò+yo+tʰa/

```
                                                   *
  *          *                    *                *
 (*) (*   *) (*   *)  <*>        (*)  *    *  (*    *)  <*>
tsi.ki.ri.no.yo.tʰa      →     tsi.ki.ri.no.yo.tʰa
```

Output: [tsì.ki.ri.nó.yo.tʰa] 'with the small tuber'

This would seem to correctly locate both primary and secondary stress, without invoking extra mechanisms such as conflation. It is unclear, however, that such an analysis would account for the data in (17), in which no lexical accent falls in the AZ. Without a rule placing line 1 heads above parsed feet, the boundary erasure clause of the Faithfulness Condition incorrectly predicts the absence of stress in the AZ in these forms.

I argue that with respect to Sikuani stress, the separability of footing and headship can be shown to be an advantage of the Halle and Vergnaud model, when viewed in conjunction with non-iterative foot construction. In fact, the separability of these two operations allows for a straightforward analysis of stress shift into the AZ. Let us first consider forms such as those in (17), which are accounted for as follows. After final syllable extrametricality, a single syllabic trochee is parsed from right to left. No line 1 lexical accent heads the foot, since the AZ in each of these forms lacks lexical accent. Furthermore, no line 1 lexical accent to the left of the parsed foot is the head of another foot, since constituent construction is non-iterative. Keeping the definition of Faithfulness in mind, we might characterize such elements as "free" heads, that is, heads without constituents. I claim that for the data in (17), the parsed foot is supplied with a head simply via the shifting of the closest, free line 1 accent.[6] This follows from a more general interpretation of Faithfulness, given in (21).

(21) Generalized Faithfulness

Lexical accents prefer to be the heads of constituents

This analysis provides a maximally simple account of stress shift in cases where no lexical accent surfaces in the AZ. If head assignment and foot construction were conceived of as a single operation, the grammar would require the addition of a highly specific rule deleting a rightmost lexical accent in concatenated strings, just in case this accent does not fall on a syllable within the AZ. Consider, for example, the contrast between (13d) and (16b), repeated here.

(13)	d. pe+pò+nae+wa+yo	→ pe.po.náe.wa.yo	'the little walker'
(16)	c. tsìkiri+nò+yo+tʰa	→ tsì.ki.ri.nó.yo.tʰa	'with the small tuber (dim)'

In (13d), no lexically accented syllable surfaces in the AZ, while in (16b), lexical accent falls on the antepenult. Under my analysis, the lack of secondary stress in (13d) is predicted. Simply, the lexical accent shifts in order to satisfy Generalized Faithfulness. In (16c), no shift is necessary, as lexical accent is already present in the AZ. Under an analysis in which heads are supplied automatically in foot construction (e.g., Hayes 1991), there is no clear account for why secondary stress fails to surface in (13d), yet surfaces predictably in (16c).

Formally, I posit the following three rules to be added to those in (10): 1) a rule of extrametricality; 2) a rule building a non-iterative line 0 constituent; and 3) a rule locating a head in the absence of lexical accent in the AZ.

(22) Revised stress rules

i. Stressable elements are syllables.
ii. Assign line 0 asterisks to all stressable elements.
iii. Assign line 1 asterisks to all lexically accented syllables.
iv. Make the last syllable of the word extrametrical if it has no line 1 asterisk.
v. Build a binary constituent on line 0 from right to left, where line 0 parameter settings are [+Head Terminal; +Bounded; +Left; -Iterative]
vi. If no line 1 asterisk heads the line 0 constituent, shift the nearest line 1 asterisk to head position. (Generalized Faithfulness)
vii. Construct a constituent on line 1, where line 1 parameter settings

---

[6]Note that this approach seems to endow lexical accent with autosegmental properties. I leave open, however, the question of whether lexical accents in Sikuani can be said to "float" or "associate" in the autosegmental sense. Hence, I have chosen to describe the process as one of "shifting" to head position. See Hagberg (1991) for arguments in favor of attributing autosegmental status to heads. See Hayes (1991) for an alternative, tonal approach to pitch accent in Winnebago.

are [+Head Terminal; -Bounded; +Right]

viii. Locate the head of the line 1 constituent on line 2.

A representative derivation for the forms in (17) is provided in (23).

(23) Input: /tsìkiri + hawa + yo/

```
(ii-iii)  1  *
          0  *  *  *  *  *  *     (iv-v)
→            tsi.ki.ri.ha.wa.yo      →
```

```
1  *                                           *
0  *  *  *  (*   *)<*>   (vi)   *  *  *  (*   *)<*>
 tsi.ki.ri.ha.wa.yo       →  tsi.ki.ri.ha.wa.yo
```

```
          2                *
(vii-     1  (             *   )
viii)     0  *   *   *  (*   *)<*>
 →            tsi.ki.ri.ha.wa.yo
```

Output: [tsi.ki.ri.há.wa.yo] 'tiny little thing'

Given Faithfulness, a lexical accent present on line 1 in the AZ is respected as the head of the non-iterative constituent, and (22vi) is inapplicable. This is true of the forms in (12) and (16). Sample derivations are provided in (24). Note also that extrametricality is inapplicable in (24a), as the final syllable bears lexical accent.

(24) a. Input: /tsìkiri + nò/

```
       2                          *
(ii-   1   *        *   (v-    (*          *)
(iii)  0   *   *  *  *  vii)     *   *   * (*)
→         tsi.ki.ri.no   →     tsi.ki.ri.no
```

```
       2              *
       1  (*          *)
(viii) 0   *   *   * (*)
→         tsi.ki.ri.no
```

Output: [tsìkirinó] 'small tuber'

b. Input: /tsìkiri +nò + yo/

```
(ii-    1    *         *       (iv-     *        *
(iii)   0    *   *   *   *   *    v)     *   *   *  (*)<*>
→          tsi.ki.ri.no.yo      →     tsi.ki.ri.no.yo

        2              *
(vii-   1   (*         *)
viii)   0    *   *   *   *  <*>
→          tsi.ki.ri.no.yo
```

Output: [tsìkirinóyo] 'small tuber (dim)'

4.3 Post stress shift

Importantly, the rules in (22) account for main stress placement in (12), (15), (16), and (17)--that is, in all the cases where main stress does not shift to a rightmost heavy syllable. The data in (13) and (14), however, exhibit stress shift to a rightmost heavy syllable both from within and from outside of the AZ. These cases, I argue, are best understood in terms of the regular stress rules of the language (those provided in 22), together with a later Post Stress Shift rule (c.f. Davis 1988) that shifts main stress from a light syllable to a following heavy syllable. This rule is formalized in (25).[7]

```
(25) Post Stress Shift:   *                    *
                          *                    *
                          *      *    →    *   *

                          μ (σ) μμ         μ (σ) μμ
```

While (25) seems to take a bit of a brute force approach to guaranteeing empirical coverage of the data in (13-14), the formal separation of regular stress placement and later weight-influenced stress shift accounts nicely for the asymmetry between the data in (14) and (15). Consider the contrast between (14b) and (15a).

14) b. pe+pò+nae+xae----->pe.po.nae.xáe 'because of his/her going'
15) a. pìalua+wa-------> pía.lua.wa 'piaroa woman'

In both forms, lexical accent falls on the antepenult. In (14b) the antepenult is monomoraic and main stress surfaces on the rightmost heavy syllable $[xae]_\sigma$.

---

[7]Note that as it is formalized, Post Stress Shift violates the CONTINUOUS COLUMN CONSTRAINT (CCC) (Prince 1983). I have no clear alternative to this formulation at present, although the possibility of applying the shift rule within the AZ but prior to main stress placement has been suggested to me by Michael Shalev (p.c.). Under such an approach, a line 1 asterisk would shift to a following heavy syllable, thus avoiding a CCC violation. Main stress would then be assigned over the rightmost line 1 asterisk in the word.

In (15a) the lexically accented syllable is heavy, and there is no stress shift to the following bimoraic syllable. It would thus seem that the need for a stress shift rule is motivated independently by this data.

In short, both heavy and light syllables are subject to stress shift into the AZ as part of the global stressing process of the language. Only light syllables undergo further shift at a later stage in the derivation. The application of (25) following main stress placement is shown in (26).

(26) Input: /pò + nae + hitsia + nu/

```
                           (iii     *
 *  *   *   *   *          -v)      *  *   (*    *) <*>   (vi)
po.nae.hi.tsia.nu           →      po.nae.hi.tsia.nu        →


                                                *
        *                  (vii-               (*    )
 *  *   (*    *) <*>       -viii)   *  *   (*    *) <*>
po.nae.hi.tsia.nu           →      po.nae.hi.tsia.nu


                                    *
POST                 (              *)
STRESS SHIFT          *   *   *     *   *
→                    po.nae.hi.tsia.nu
```

Output: [ponaehitsíanu] 'I'm going to go'

5. Conclusions

Interestingly, I find no words in which the AZ has the following two properties: 1) there is no lexically accented syllable present and 2) there are at least two heavy syllables, one of which is the antepenult. Given the approach to the problem of stress placement taken in this paper, the above analysis makes a clear prediction: main stress will not surface on the rightmost heavy syllable. This is because the rules in (22) will locate main stress on the heavy antepenult. As a consequence, the rule of Post Stress Shift will be inapplicable. Such a form, then, would provide a useful empirical test for the hypotheses advanced here.

With respect to the theoretical concerns of this paper, I have argued that Sikuani stress is best accounted for within a theory that permits non-iterative footing. Such footing is crucial in that it allows for the formal circumscription of the accentual zone without interfering with the completely predictable pattern of secondary stress in the language. In contrast, exhaustive metrification as defended most recently in Halle (1990), would require a far more complicated analysis of the stress contours found in these data. I have further argued that the phenomenon of stress shift into the AZ receives a maximally simple explanation if foot construction and head assignment are conceived of as formally distinct operations. In this way, much of the stress shift data can be derived from a more generalized interpretation of the Faithfulness Condition.

References

Archangeli, Diana. 1984. Extrametricality in Yawelmani, *The Linguistic Review* 4: 101-120.

Davis, Stuart. 1988. Syllable Onsets as a Factor in Stress Rules, *Phonology Yearbook* 5: 1-19.

Everett, Dan and Keren Everett. 1984. Syllable Onsets and Stress in Pirahã. *Proceedings of the West Coast Conference on Formal Linguistics* 3: 105-116.

Hagberg, Larry. 1991. *An Autosegmental Theory of Stress*, Ph.D.dissertation, U. of Arizona.

Halle, Morris. 1990. Respecting Metrical Structure, *Natural Language and Linguistic Theory* 8: 149-176.

Halle, Morris and J.R. Vergnaud. 1987a. Stress and the Cycle, *Linguistic Inquiry* 18: 45-84.

Halle, Morris and J. R. Vergnaud. 1987b. *An Essay on Stress*, Cambridge: MIT Press.

Hammond, Michael. 1986. The Obligatory Branching Parameter in Metrical Theory, *Natural Language and Linguistic Theory* 4: 185-228.

Hammond, Micheal. 1989a. Lexical Stress in Polish and Macedonian, *Phonology Yearbook* 6: 19-38.

Hammond, Michael. 1989b. Cyclic Secondary Stress and Accent in English, *Proceedings of the West Coast Conference on Formal Linguistics* 8: 139-153.

Hammond, Michael. 1991. Deriving Ternarity, U. of Arizona ms.

Harris, James. 1983. *Syllable Structure and Stress in Spanish: A Non-Linear Analysis*, Cambridge: MIT Press.

Hayes, Bruce. 1981. *A Metrical Theory of Stress Rules*, 1980 Ph.D. dissertation, MIT, revised version distributed by Indiana University Linguistics Club.

Hayes, Bruce. 1982. Extrametricality and English Stress, *Linguistic Inquiry* 15: 33-74.

Hayes, Bruce. 1987. A Revised Parametric Theory of Stress, *Proceedings of the Northeastern Lingustics Society* 17: 274-269.

Hayes, Bruce. 1991. *Metrical Stress Theory: Principles and Case Studies*, UCLA ms.

Poser, William. 1986. The Metrical Foot in Diyari, *Phonology Yearbook* 6: 117-148.

Prince, Allen. 1983. Relating to the Grid, *Linguistic Inquiry* 14: 19-100.

Prince, Allen. 1990. Quantitative Consequences of Rhythmic Organization Brandeis University ms.

Queixalós, Francisco. 1985. *Fonología Sikuani*. Bogotá: Instituto Caro y Cuervo.

Steriade, Donca. 1988. Greek Accent: A Case for Preserving Structure, *Linguistic Inquiry* 19: 271-314.

cgerfen@ccit.arizona.edu

On Raising and Lowering Shifts

HEATHER GOAD
University of Southern California

1. Introduction*

Raising and lowering shifts commonly occur in vowel systems. And yet, under the traditional analysis of height as a complex of binary features, it is impossible to express shifts in a unified way. This problem has led some scholars to consider alternative approaches to height. In several works in the late 60s and 70s, it was proposed that height be treated as a single multivalued feature; see, for example, Ladefoged (1966, 1973), Contreras (1969), McCawley (1973), Saltarelli (1973), and Lindau (1978). More recently, Schane (1984a,b), Clements (1989), and Hayes (1990) have advanced the view that height should be represented as multiple occurrences of an aperture component.

As we shall see shortly, these alternatives do allow for a unified account of raising and lowering shifts. However, a typology of shifts reveals fewer observed patterns than they actually predit should occur. In response to this, I provide yet another proposal for vowel height, one which is within the spirit of these alternative approaches, but one which I believe to be more restrictive.

2. Binary and n-ary approaches to height

In contrast to the binary approach of SPE (Chomsky & Halle 1968), the alternatives outlined above are collapsed under the label 'n-ary approaches'. Binary and n-ary alternatives are compared in (1) for front vowels in a three height system.

(1) *Some approaches to vowel height:*[1]
 a. *SPE:*
  i [+high]
  e [-high, -low]
  æ [+low]

[1] By limiting the discussion to the approaches in (1), I do not mean to imply that these are the only ones that have been proposed. On the contrary, several positions have been advanced which have grown out of a greater or lesser degree of dissatisfaction with SPE. I have chosen to focus on the proposals in (1), as they explicitly address the question of raising and lowering shifts.

b. *Multivalued Height:*
i [3high]
e [2high]
æ [1high]

c. *Particle Phonology:*
i
e |a|
æ |aa|

d. *Clements:*
i [-open1, -open2]
e [-open1, +open2]
æ [+open1]

The SPE proposal is given in (1a). Three heights are expressed with '+' and '-' values of two features, [high] and [low]. In (1b) is the multivalued feature approach, where numerical values are assigned to a single feature [high]. 1 is assigned to the lowest vowel in the system.[2] Numbers greater than 1 are assigned to vowels of higher height, determined by the total number of heights in the system. In (1c), height as represented in Schane's Particle Phonology is given. The approach has also recently been adopted by Hayes (1990).[3] In Particle Phonology, |a| indicates aperture. Again, the number of |a| particles is determined from the number of height contrasts in a system. For the three height system in (1), the highest vowel has no aperture particle, while the lowest has two.[4] Finally, in Clements' proposal in (1d), the feature [open] divides height into two registers, upper and lower, or [-open] and [+open]. This preliminary split creates a two height system. The upper and/or lower registers can then be subdivided, yielding systems with three or more heights. In the three height system in (1), the contrast between i and æ is represented as [-open1] and [+open1] respectively. The low vowel æ is [+open2] by default.

Before comparing the expression of raising and lowering in the binary and n-ary approaches, let us look at examples of these two processes, from Eastern Finnish and Southern Lappish respectively. As can be seen from (2), in both languages, long vowels are diphthongized. Eastern Finnish and Southern Lappish are the mirror image of one another; in the former, diphthongization raises the first mora of a long vowel one step, while in the latter, diphthongization lowers the second mora one step.

(2) *Eastern Finnish diphthongization* (Kiparsky 1968a,b):
e + e --> ie   ö + ö --> üö   o + o --> uo
æ + æ --> eæ   a + a --> oa

Southern Lappish diphthongization (McCawley 1973):
i + i --> ie   ü + ü --> üö   u + u --> uo
e + e --> eæ   o + o --> oa

2 Cf. McCawley (1973) who assigns zero to the lowest vowel.

3 However, Hayes maintains binary features for backness and rounding.

4 This is somewhat simplified. While true of a system such as that in (1), in a triangular inventory, e, o, and a all have one aperture particle; the mid vowels additionally contain tonality particles. See Schane (1984a,b) for details.

In (3) and (4), binary and n-ary accounts of diphthongization are given. The environments have been omitted for clarity. The rule under the binary approach is, needless to say, unsatisfactory. Eliminating the alpha-notation in (3a) in favor of '+' and '-' yields the two rules in (3b). First, the expansions of (3a) involve different structural changes. Focussing on Raising, when a low vowel raises to mid, the structural change involves the feature [low], but when the same mid vowel raises to high, the structural change involves the feature [high]. Second, the expansions in (3b) must be extrinsically ordered which makes their origin in (3a) somewhat dubious (see Saltarelli 1973): raising of mid to high must apply before raising of low to mid; and lowering of mid to low must apply before lowering of high to mid. Both problems stem from using two binary features to split up a single domain.

(3) *Binary approach:*

Raising:

a. $\begin{bmatrix} \text{-high} \\ \alpha\text{low} \end{bmatrix} \text{-->} \begin{bmatrix} \text{-}\alpha\text{high} \\ \text{-low} \end{bmatrix}$

Lowering:

$\begin{bmatrix} \alpha\text{high} \\ \text{-low} \end{bmatrix} \text{-->} \begin{bmatrix} \text{-high} \\ \text{-}\alpha\text{low} \end{bmatrix}$

b. *Low to mid:*
[+low] --> [-low]

High to mid:
[+high] --> [-high]

Mid to high:
[-high] --> [+high]

Mid to low:
[-low] --> [+low]

Under the n-ary approaches, however, where height is expressed as a single parameter, raising and lowering are unified processes. In the multivalued approach in (4a), a vowel of height *n* is raised or lowered by one degree. In Particle Phonology, an aperture particle is deleted or added as in (4b). And under Clements' proposal in (4c), for a vowel of [-open] degree *n*, *n* is raised or lowered by one.

(4) *N-ary approaches:*

	Raising:	*Lowering:*
a.	[n high] --> [n+1 high]	[n high] --> [n-1 high]
b.	delete |a|	add |a|
c.	[-open n] --> [-open n+1]	[-open n] --> [-open n-1]

While the n-ary approaches solve certain problems, they unfortunately create some new ones as well. Perhaps the first that comes to mind is that n-ary approaches cannot formally constrain the number of height contrasts found in languages. And yet, languages do not contrast more than four or five, depending on how one counts. While the height parameter could be limited to a maximum of degree four or five, this is unsatisfactory in the face of evidence from other domains which suggests that rules and constraints can only count up to two (see McCarthy & Prince 1986 for discussion).

In binary feature theory, a language with more than three heights requires an additional feature such as [tense] to accompany [high] and [low]. In most of the n-ary approaches, tense/lax contrasts are instead represented as additional contrasts in height.[5] I suggest that it is precisely because [tense] is not considered a feature separate from height that the n-ary approaches run into trouble. In particular, they predict that the three types of raising and lowering exhibited in (5) should all exist. What is found instead is that shifts occur in languages with three heights but not in languages with four or five heights, hence the labels preferred and dispreferred in (5).

(5) *Preferred:* / *Dispreferred:*

a. *Three-height:*		b. *Four-height:*		c. *Five-height:*	
i ↰	i ↲	*i ↰	*i ↲	*i ↰	*i ↲
e ↰	e ↲	e ↰	e ↲	ι ↰	ι ↲
ε, æ	ε, æ	ε ↰	ε ↲	e ↰	e ↲
		æ	æ	ε ↰	ε ↲
				æ	æ

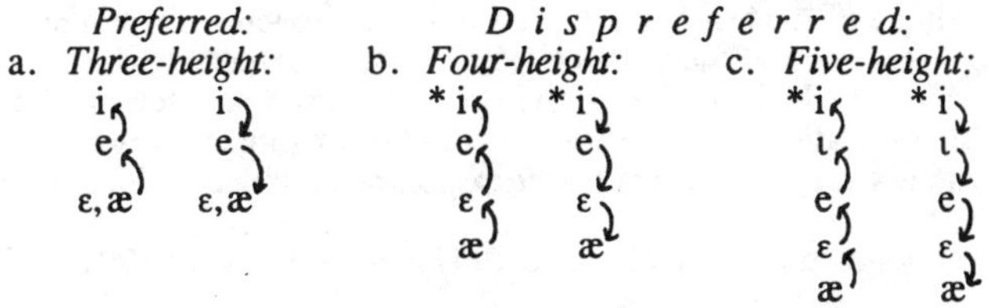

In other words, raising and lowering shifts are typically (if not always) restricted to languages in which vowels do not contrast for tense/lax. (Laxing apart from lowering will be discussed in section 5.)

Importantly, in (5a), I have written ε and æ on a single line because I analyze ε as [low] in four-height triangular systems. [tense] or some equivalent feature does not distinguish the mid and lower-mid vowels in such systems. This has earlier been proposed by, among others, Harris (1974) and Quicoli (1990) for Brazilian Portuguese, Capo (1985) and Clements (1989) for Ewe, Hyman (1988) for Esmibi, Goad (1991a) for Yoruba, and Rice & Avery (1991) for all such systems. Following Rice & Avery, I assume that the selection of [low] over [tense] is determined from the inventory of segments in a language. Specifically, [tense] only accompanies [low] in languages in which high vowels contrast for the feature. Compare in this regard (6a) and (6b).

(6)

a.			
high	i		u
mid	e		o
low	ε	a	ɔ

b.			
high tense	i		u
high	ι		υ
mid tense	e		o
mid	ε		ɔ
low		a	

As a consequence of these assumptions, the first stage of the Great Vowel Shift involves low raising to mid and mid raising to high and no reference at all to the value of [tense]; see (7).

(7) *Middle English* (Schane 1984b):

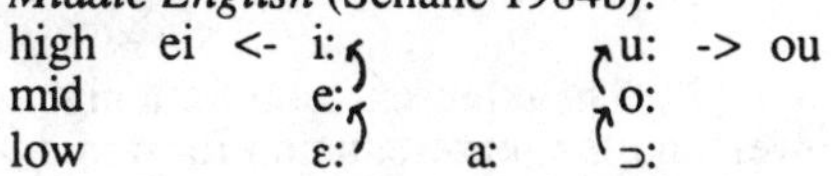

high	ei	<-	i: ↰		↱ u:	->	ou
mid			e: ↰		↱ o:		
low			ε:	a:	ɔ:		

The suggestion that lower mid vowels be treated as [low] is not a gratuitous solution to the restriction of raising and lowering to languages in which vowels do not contrast for [tense]. Importantly, raising and lowering in four height systems are limited to triangular inventories, precisely those systems where a conflation of

---

5 Ladefoged (1973) and Lindau (1978) do have a separate feature to mark tense/lax contrasts. However, since they both assume that the height feature has a maximim value of four, not three, the problem which follows holds of their proposals as well.

lower mid and low vowels is possible. Raising and lowering are absent from systems in which there is a contrast between ɛ and æ for instance; cf. (5b).

3. An alternative approach to height

Returning to the preferred and dispreferred shifts in (5), we are faced with a dilemma. The binary approach is too restrictive in that it cannot provide a unified account for raising and lowering at all. The n-ary approaches are too powerful in that the formal expression of the preferred shifts in (5a) extends to the dispreferred shifts in (5b) and (5c). To resolve this dilemma, I propose an alternative approach to height which: one, allows for a unified account of raising and lowering shifts in three height systems; and two, treats tense/lax contrasts with an additional feature, namely [atr].

Consider the geometry in (8) (cf. Goad 1991b, Rice & Avery 1991). (On [atr], see section 5.)

(8) *Geometry of height features (preliminary version):*

Vo
|
open
|
low

Vo is a vowel node for which true consonants are not specified and, in this way, bears some resemblance to the aperture node of Clements (1989) or to the Vocalic node of Rice & Avery (1991). Following Clements, I assume that Vo docks into the Supralaryngeal node or its equivalent. Dependents of Vo are [open] and [low]. I adopt the position that at least height features are monovalent and, because of this, [open] replaces [-high].

Representations for high, mid and low vowels are in (9). A high vowel appears as an unadorned Vo node, while a Vo node with a dependent [open] represents a mid vowel. A low vowel is represented as a mid vowel with an additional dependent [low]. A similar approach to height geometry appears in Rice & Avery (1991).

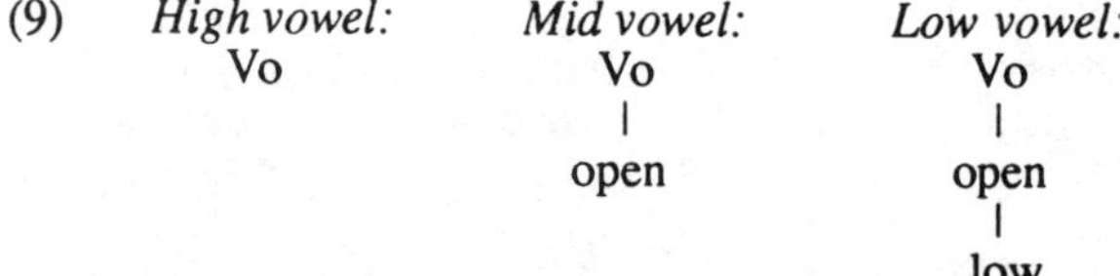

Features are in a subset relation in (9). The representation for a high vowel is contained within that for a mid vowel, and the representation for a mid vowel is contained within that for a low vowel. I argue that it is precisely this configuration which allows for a unified account of raising and lowering shifts.

To begin with raising, I suggest that such rules are formalized to delink the terminal dependent under Vo. In this way, the rule is defined by structure, not by content. Terminal delinking is illustrated in (10). Delinking [low] yields a mid vowel; delinking [open] yields a high vowel. Predictably, high vowels are themselves unaffected: there is no feature dependent on the Vo node to delink.

(10) *Raising:*

low to mid:
```
Vo --> Vo
 |      |
open   open
 ǂ
low
```

mid to high:
```
Vo --> Vo
 ǂ
open
```

It may appear that terminal delinking effects a result similar to that of angle brackets in SPE: delink [low] when [low] is present and otherwise delink [open]. Note, however, that it is entirely constrained by the configuration of features in (8).

A unified account of lowering involves the addition of a dependent as in (11). This is a single operation since, again, its output is completely constrained by the geometry. Vo projects [open] and [open] projects [low]. There is no other option.

(11) 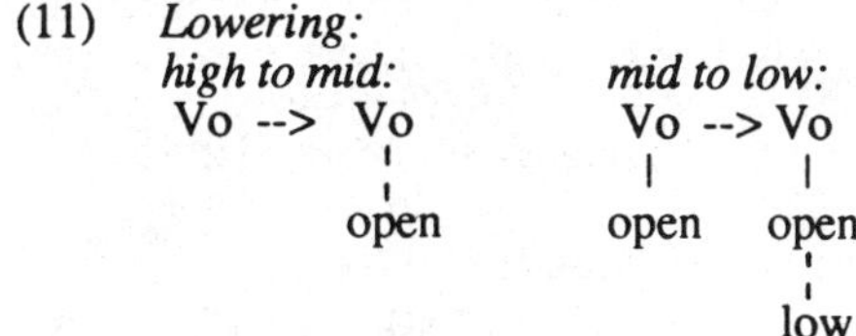

The operations in (10) and (11) are in accord with cross-linguistic observations about raising and lowering shifts, namely that without a segmental conditioning environment, raising is preferred to lowering. Under the analysis proposed here, raising results in a reduction of structure, while lowering adds complexity. The analysis of raising as a reduction of structure is also in accord with the fact that raising is weakening: it yields vowels which are less sonorous.[6]

4. Is Québec French a counter-example?

We have seen that the representations in (9) permit unified accounts of raising and lowering in three height systems. As raising and lowering in four height systems cannot be expressed as the simple delinking or addition of a dependent, these processes should be unattested or, at best, extremely rare. In this regard, we may look at Québec French which appears to present a problem for this claim.

According to Dumas (1981), in Québec French, the first mora of a long vowel is lowered one step, and the second mora is optionally raised: it may not raise at all, it may raise part way, or it may raise all the way to high. See (12).

(12) *Québec French* (Dumas 1981, Hayes 1990):

i: --> ei	ü: --> öü	u: --> ou
e: --> ɛi	ö: --> ɔ̈ü	o: --> ɔu
ɛ: --> ai	ɔ̈: --> aü	ɔ: --> ɑu
		ɒ: --> ɑu

6 The fact that raising often happens under stress does not preclude the label of 'weakening'. While it might appear that stress is a strengthening environment, in languages such as Russian, stressed vowel inventories are actually a subset of unstressed vowel inventories.

Focussing on lowering, the problem that Québec French provides is most apparent from (13), where only the alternations in the first mora of the long vowel are given. (13) bears a strong resemblance to the dispreferred shift in (5b) for which I cannot provide a unified account.

(13)
```
i        ü              u
e        ö              o
ɛ        ɔ̈              ɔ
a        a        ɒ ⟶  ɑ
```

It is precisely because of such cases that Hayes (1990) chooses to adopt Schane's (1984a,b) approach to height. For Hayes, then, diphthongization involves the addition of an aperture particle to the first mora of a long vowel. (The second mora, which raises variably, loses none, some, or all of its aperture particles.)

However, a closer look at the phonetics of Québec French vowels reveals that the lowering of the first mora can actually be treated as in (11), as the addition of a dependent. Naturally, this requires that Québec French be reanalyzed as a three-height system. The facts which lead to this conclusion are summarized in (14).

(14)
a. a --> ɒ word-finally and when long (Dumas 1981:17-18)
b. o and ɔ are 'auditivement identique[s]' (Dumas 1981:18)
c. o: ~ ɔ: --> ɒu, ɑu or au
   ɛ: --> ai or ɑi
   ɔ̈: --> aü or ɑü (Dumas 1981:18)
d. F2 values:
   a in Québec French = 1280 (Gendron 1966:93)
   a in European French = 1300 (Gendron 1966:93)
   æ in American English = 1660 (Ladefoged 1982:176)
   ɑ in American English = 1100 (Ladefoged 1982:176)

First, a and ɒ are not contrastive; rather, as noted in (14a), the latter is derived from the former in word-final position and when long. Second, when a backs and rounds to ɒ, it merges with ɔ. In other words, as noted in (14b), o and ɔ actually represent the same vowel quality.

While this eliminates the apparent contrast between a and ɒ, we must still contend with the fact from (12) that in diphthongization, the first mora of the low front vowels, ɛ and ɔ̈, surfaces as a, while the first mora of the low back vowel, ɒ ~ ɔ, surfaces as ɑ. Dumas notes in fact that when all of the low vowels are diphthongized, the quality of the first mora may vary in backness; thus the diphthongs in (14c) are all attested. It appears that the first mora of the lowest vowels, unable to lower to any further degree, instead loses its tonality and centralizes to a. Under certain phonetically determined conditions, a may then surface as back ɑ or as back and round ɒ.

There is alas one problem remaining. From the information in (14a) through (14c), we can conclude that there is only one contrastive low vowel in Québec French, a. Dumas (1981) and Walker (1984) regard this vowel as front. If this is indeed the case, Québec French is still a problem: a language with contrasts among four front unrounded vowels precludes an analysis of lowering as in (11). If a were instead centrally articulated, Québec French would have an inventory similar in relevant respects to that of Middle English (7) where lower-mid vowels are analyzed as low. Acoustic data from Gendron (1966) reveal precisely this, that a is actually centrally articulated. As can be seen in (14d), it has a second formant value of 1280, very close to the F2 value of European French and half way between the F2 values of American English æ and ɒ.

The information in (14) suggests a reinterpretation of Québec French diphthongization as in (15). It is then not a counterexample to the claim that lowering shifts are characteristic of languages with no more than three heights; cf (12).

(15)	i: --> ei	ü: --> öü		u: --> ou
	e: --> ɛi	ö: --> ɔ̈ü		o: --> ɔu
	ɛ: --> ai	ɔ̈: --> aü	a: --> ɔ: --> au	ɔ: --> au

This is most apparent from (16), where only the alternations in the first mora are given; cf. (13). [open] is added to Vo to yield a mid vowel from a high vowel, and [low] is added to [open] to yield a low vowel from a mid vowel.

(16)	i	ü		u	Vo
	e	ö		o	Vo--[open]
	ɛ	ɔ̈ ⟶	a	⟵ ɔ	Vo--[open]--[low]

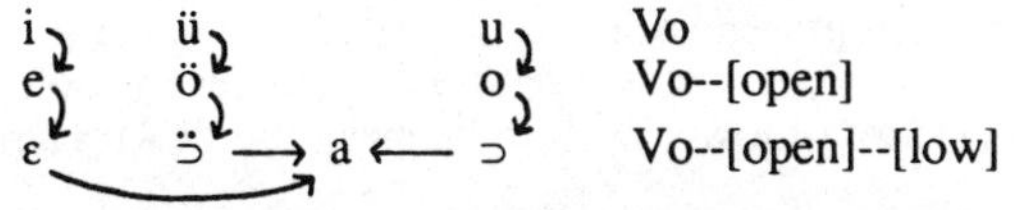

As a final note, the fact that the second mora of a low or mid vowel raises variably can be expressed as delinking at various points in the structure. In the case of a low vowel, raising to mid involves delinking of [low] as in (17a); raising to high involves delinking of [open] as in (17b); and, in cases where there is no raising, there is no delinking.

(17) *Raising of the second mora:*

a.	b.	c.
Vo	Vo	Vo
|	ǂ	|
open	open	open
ǂ	|	|
low	low	low

5. Laxing

We have seen that raising and lowering in three height systems involves the delinking or addition of a dependent. We can now look at laxing, which falls outside the scope of the preferred and dispreferred patterns in (5). We must first motivate the location of [tense], which I subsume under the feature [atr]. There is both phonological and phonetic motivation for this move.[7] Most notable is the fact that languages do not have [tense] nor [atr] contrasts among low vowels. This fact has a simple acoustic explanation. The frequency of the first formant inversely corresponds to the height of a vowel. a has an F1 value of about 700 Hertz.

7 Nonetheless, there is disagreement in the phonetics literature over the conflation of [tense] and [atr]. Compare Halle & Stevens (1969) and Perkell (1971) who argue in favor of it with Stewart (1967) and Lindau (1978, 1979) who argue against it.

Tensing or advancing a vowel results in a lowering of F1 by about 150 Hertz. Subtracting 150 from 700 leaves 550, precisely the F1 value of a mid vowel.

The result is that a vowel cannot be simultaneously [low] and [atr] (or [tense]): attaching [atr] to a low vowel yields a mid vowel. Formally, this suggests that [atr] and [low] are in complementary distribution. This is precisely the position I take, as can be seen from the revised configuration of features in (18). The slash indicates the complementarity between [low] and [atr].

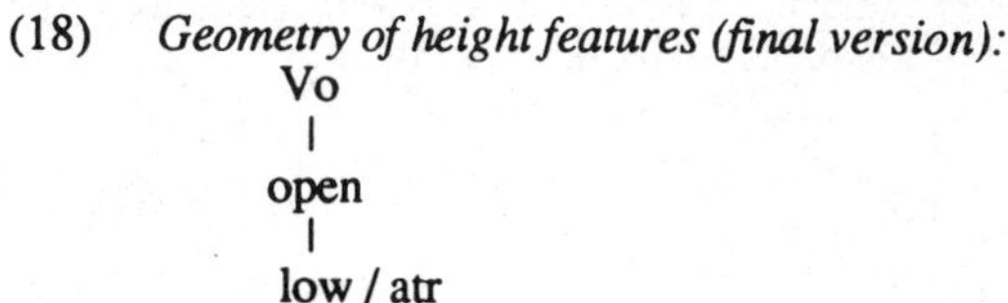

It is important to note that while [low] and [atr] occupy the same position in the geometry, they are not opposite values of one and the same feature. For instance, they are not subject to the same distributional constraints. While the linking of [low] to the Vo node must be mediated through the [open] tier, the linking of [atr] to Vo clearly need not be. The asymmetrical relationship between [low] and [atr] is most evident from (19) where representations for vowels in a language with the maximum five heights are given. These structures are independently motivated in Goad (1991a,b) from the behavior of low vowels in languages with Atr Harmony.[8]

(19)

High:	*Mid:*	*Low:*	*High atr:*	*Mid atr:*
Vo	Vo	Vo	Vo	Vo
	|	|	|	|
	open	open	|	open
		|	|	|
		low	atr	atr

At this point, we may question the lowering analysis provided for Southern Lappish and Québec French above. If lowering involves the addition of a dependent, why does a mid vowel not project [atr] instead of [low]? Recall from section 2 that the selection of features is determined from the inventory of segments in a language. In particular, [atr] is only selected if contrasts among vowels cannot be captured with [low] alone. In this way, the privileged articulatory correlate of the terminal feature in (18) is [low]. If lowering (not laxing) is restricted to three height systems, systems in which vowels do not contrast for [atr], this feature is simply not available.

To return to laxing, in a framework where all features are monovalent, [-atr] (as [-tense]) is not available. As such, laxing must be represented as the absence of tensing, as the delinking of [atr] from a tense vowel. Pasiego is somewhat more complex however. When a̲ laxes, it surfaces as a mid front lax vowel. Penny (1969:149) describes this vowel as 'very palatal (i.e., fronted and slightly raised, almost [ɛ])'. Alternations are in (20).[9]

---

8 Briefly, low vowels behave in either of two ways. One, they may be opaque to Atr Harmony. As [low] and [atr] occupy a single position in the geometry, [low] may prevent the association of [atr] and effectively block harmony. Two, low vowels may undergo Atr Harmony but raise to mid in the process. Because of the dependence of [low] on [open], the spreading [atr] may force the delinking of [low], yielding a mid vowel as the [atr] counterpart of a̲.

9 e̲ is neutral, a problem which is beyond the scope of the present discussion.

(20) *Pasiego* (Penny 1969, McCarthy 1984; see also Vago 1988):

i u
ι ʊ
(e) o
ε ɔ
a

Laxing in Pasiego can be analyzed as terminal delinking, as a reduction of structure. In this way, all specifications on the [atr]/[low] tier are delinked. Terminal delinking yields results in (21).[10]

(21)

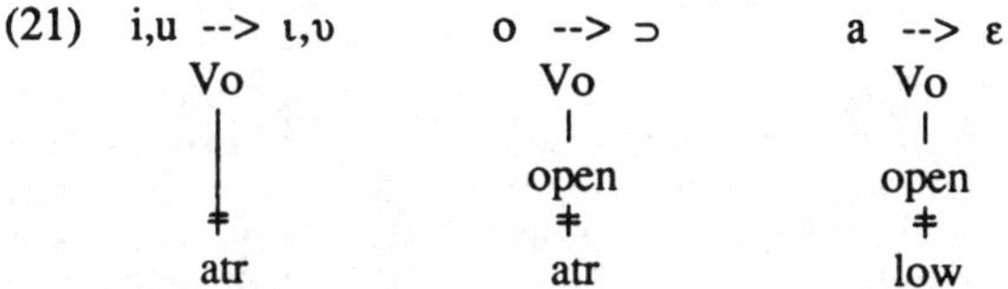

Finally, with the structures in (19), I will provide an account of Lund Swedish diphthongization.[11] Most accounts of Swedish opt for an n-ary approach to height (see Lindau (1978), Schane (1984a), Clements (1989), Hayes (1990). Yip's (1980) binary account, on the other hand, requires both angle brackets and alpha-notation.

Diphthongization is illustrated in (22).

(22) *Lund Swedish* (Clements 1989, Hayes 1990; on Malmö Swedish, see Bruce 1970, Lindau 1978, Schane 1984a, Yip 1980):

i: > ei	ü: > eü	ʉ: > eʉ	u: > eu
e: > εe	ö: > εö		o: > εo
ε: > æε			ɔ: > æo

As can be seen, I assume that the alternations represent two stages in the development of Swedish.This is in contrast to Hayes who argues that the process is still productive. He provides as evidence the following. First, educated speakers often produce monophthongs for diphthongs in formal speech. However, I would suggest that these alternations need not be related by rule; instead, speakers may have command of two dialects. Second, vowels are shortened before clusters, resulting in alternations such as those in (23) (from Hayes 1990:54):

(23)				
[veit]	'white'	vs.	[vit-t]	'white' (neut)
[lεed-a]	'lead' (inf)	vs.	[led-də]	'lead' (past)
[mæεt-a]	'measure' (inf)	vs.	[mεt-tə]	'measure' (past)

Hayes suggests that shortening precludes the application of diphthongization and, as a result, the underlying vowel surfaces. However, if these alternations are indeed due to a shortening rule, the rule can be formulated so as to delete the first half of a diphthong before consonant clusters. In this way, the forms to the left of the arrowheads in (22) need not be the current underlying representations.

10 For an analysis of fronting as an automatic consequence of the delinking of [low], see Goad (1991a).

11 This analysis of Lund Swedish diphthongization is taken from Goad (1991a).

In fact, the analysis I provide crucially requires that the process not be synchronic. It is also necessary that feature selection be determined on the basis of the inventory of segments in a language. Focussing on the front unrounded vowels, in (24) I propose height specifications for the two stages in (22). (I will comment on including ι at Stage 2 in a moment.)

(24)	*Stage 1:*		*Stage 2:*	
	i	Vo	i	Vo------------[atr]
			ι	Vo
	e	Vo--[open]	e	Vo--[open]--[atr]
			ε	Vo--[open]
	ε	Vo--[open]--[low]	æ	Vo--[open]--[low]

At Stage 1, Lund Swedish is a three-height system. As in Middle English and Québec French, lower mid vowels are analyzed as [low]. Stage 2 is characterized by the introduction of contrastive [atr]; the result is a five-height system. So, while at Stage 1, i and e are represented as Vo and Vo--[open] respectively, these same vowels at Stage 2 additionally require [atr] specifications to distinguish them from ι and ε. In addition, while ε is represented as [low] at Stage 1, once æ is introduced into the system at Stage 2, ε must be reanalyzed as [open].

Consistent with the representations in (24), diphthongization yeilds the results in (25).

(25)				
	i: > ιi	ü: > ιü	ʉ: > ιʉ	u: > ιu
	e: > εe	ö: > εö		o: > εo
	ε: > æe			ɔ: > æo

Two differences between (22) and (25) must be noted. First, regarding ε:, I assume that it diphthongizes to æe and not to æε.[12] This parallels the diphthongization of ɔ: to ao in (22). Second, and more importantly, I assume that the first half of the high diphthongs is ι and not e. This is not entirely unwarranted as these two vowels are acoustically quite similar and tend to merge diachronically. Further, Donegan (1978:214) points out that in the Malmö dialect of Swedish, which has a diphthongization process very similar to that in the Lund dialect, the first half of a diphthong may indeed vary. For example, she gives as the diphthongized counterpart of u: both ιu and eu.

Formally, I suggest that diphthongization involves the linking of [atr] to the second half of a long vowel as in (26).[13]

---

12 As is evident from a comparison of the diphthongization of low(er mid) vowels in (22) and (25), under any account, either the diphthongization of ε: or the diphthongization of ɔ: requires a patch-up rule.

13 I should mention that the representations in (26) for the stage immediately prior to the linking of [atr] violate the Obligatory Contour Principle. Here, I am only concerned with the quality of the vowels and not with the logistics of fission. For recent treatments of this problem, see Steriade (1987), Selkirk (1988), Clements (1989), Hayes (1990).

(26)

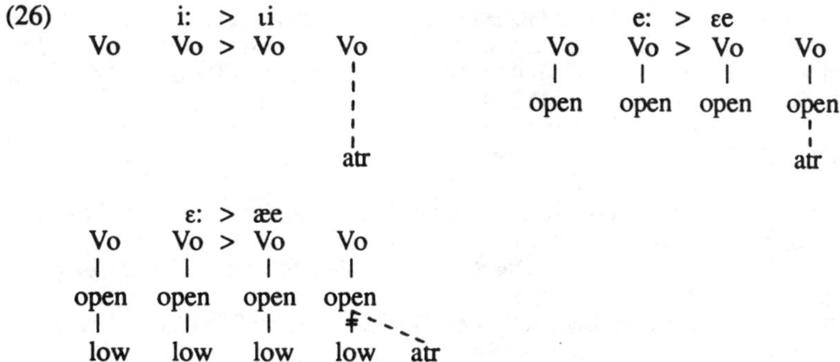

In the diphthongization of the high and mid vowels, [atr] simply links to the second Vo and Vo--[open] respectively. However, in the case of the low vowel, the linking of [atr] forces the simultaneous delinking of [low] as these features occupy the same position in the geometry; a mid [atr] vowel results. Regarding the first half of this diphthong, the 'lowering' of ɛ to æ results automatically: once [atr] is introduced at Stage 2, a [low] front vowel can only be interpreted as æ.

6. Summary

To summarize briefly, in response to typological observations about raising and lowering shifts, I have rejected the binary and n-ary approaches to height in favor of an alternative in which height is represented by three features in a subset relation. This allowed for a unified account of raising and lowering in three-height systems, as the delinking and addition of a dependent respectively. Next, in keeping with the view that tense/lax contrasts are marked by an additional feature [atr], I suggested that laxing is represented as the absence of tensing, as the delinking of [atr]. Finally, the complementarity between [atr] and [low] allowed for unified accounts of the more complex facts of laxing in Pasiego and diphthongization in Lund Swedish.

* I would like to thank Alicja Gorecka, Donca Steriade, Jean-Roger Vergnaud and the audience at WCCFL 11 for useful comments. All errors are my own. This research was supported by the Social Sciences and Humanities Research Council of Canada, doctoral fellowship no. 452-90-1256.

References

Bruce, G. 1970. Diphthongization in the Malmö Dialect. *Working Papers in Linguistics* 3:1-20. Lund University.

Capo, H.B.C. 1985. Vowel Features in Gbe. *Journal of West African Languages* 15:19-30.

Chomsky, N. & M. Halle 1968. *The Sound Pattern of English.* New York: Harper & Row.

Clements, G.N. 1989. On the Representation of Vowel Height. Ms., Cornell University.

Contreras, H. 1969. Simplicity, Descriptive Adequacy, and Binary Features. *Language* 45:1-8.

Donegan, P. 1978.*On the Natural Phonology of Vowels*. Doctoral Dissertation, Ohio State University. Published 1985 by New York: Garland.

Dumas, D. 1981. Structure de la diphtongaison québécoise. *Canadian Journal of Linguistics* 26:1-61.

Gendron, J.-D. 1966. *Tendances phonétiques du français parlé au Canada.* Québec: Les Presses de l'Université Laval.

Goad, H. 1991a. Dependency and Complementarity in Vowel Geometry. *The Linguistic Review* 8:1-24.

Goad, H. 1991b. [atr] and [rtr] are Different Features. *Proceedings of WCCFL* 10:163-173.

Halle, M. 1977. Tenseness, Vowel Shift and the Phonology of Back Vowels in Modern English. *Linguistic Inquiry* 8:611-625.

Halle, M. & K.P. Mohanan 1985. Segmental Phonology of Modern English. *Linguistic Inquiry* 16:57-116.

Halle, M. & K. Stevens 1969. On the Feature 'Advanced Tongue Root'. *Quarterly Progress Report* 94:209-215. MIT Research Laboratory of Electronics.

Harris, J.W. 1974. Evidence from Portuguese for the 'Elsewhere Condition' in Phonology. *Linguistic Inquiry* 1:61-80.

Hayes, B. 1990. Diphthongisation and Coindexing. *Phonology* 7:31-71.

Hyman, L.M. 1988. Underspecification and Vowel Height Transfer in Esimbi. *Phonology* 5:255-273.

Kiparsky, P. 1968a. Metrics and Morphophonemics in the Kalevala. *Studies Presented to Professor Roman Jakobson by his Students*, ed. C.E. Gribble, 137-148. Cambridge, Mass: Slavica Publishers.

Kiparsky, P. 1968b. How Abstract is Phonology? Indiana University Linguistics Club. Published 1973 as Phonological Representations. *Three Dimensions of Linguistic Theory*, ed. O. Fujimura, 1-136. Tokyo:TEC Co.

Ladefoged, P. 1966. An Attack on the Number Two. *UCLA Working Papers in Phonetics* 4.

Ladefoged, P. 1973. *Preliminaries to Linguistic Phonetics*. University of Chicago Press (1st edition 1971).

Ladefoged, P. 1982. *A Course in Phonetics*. New York: Harcourt, Brace, Jovanovich (1st edition 1975).

Lindau, M. 1978. Vowel Features. *Language* 54:541-563.

Lindau, M. 1979. The Feature Expanded. *Journal of Phonetics* 7:163-176.

McCarthy, J.J. 1984. Theoretical Consequences of Montañes Vowel Harmony.

Linguistic Inquiry 15:291-318.

McCarthy, J.J. & A.S. Prince 1986. Prosodic Morphology. Ms., University of Massachusetts Amherst and Brandeis.

McCawley, J.D. 1973. On the Role of Notation in Generative Phonology. *The Formal Analysis of Natural Languages*, eds. M. Gross, M. Halle & M.-P. Schützenberger, 51-61. The Hague: Mouton.

Penny, R.J. 1969. Vowel-Harmony in the Speech of the Montes de Pas (Santander). *Orbis* 18:148-166.

Perkell, J.S. 1971. Physiology of Speech Production: A Preliminary Study of Two Suggested Revisions of the Features Specifying Vowels. *Quarterly Progress Report* 102:123-139. MIT Research Laboratory of Electronics.

Quicoli, C. 1990. Harmony, Lowering and Nasalization in Brazilian Portuguese. *Lingua* 80:295-331.

Rice, K. & P. Avery 1991. Segmental complexity and the Structure of Inventories. Talk Delivered at GLOW Workshop on the Acquisition of Phonology, University of Leiden.

Saltarelli, M. 1973. Orthogonality, Naturalness, and the Binary Feature Framework. *Issues in Linguistics*, eds. B.B. Kachru et al., 798-807. University of Illinois Press.

Schane, S. 1984a. The Fundamentals of Particle Phonology. *Phonology Yearbook* 1:129-155.

Schane, S. 1984b. Two English Vowel Movements: A Particle Analysis. *Language Sound Structure*, eds. M. Aronoff & R.T. Oehrle, 32-51. MIT Press.

Selkirk, E.O. 1988. A Two-Root Theory of Length. Talk Delivered at NELS 19.

Steriade, D. 1987. On Class Nodes. Ms., MIT.

Stewart, J.M. 1967. Tongue Root Position in Akan Vowel Harmony. *Phonetica* 16:185-204.

Vago, R.M. 1988. Underspecification in the Height Harmony System of Pasiego. *Phonology* 5:343-362.

Walker, D.C. 1984. *The Pronunciation of Canadian French*. University of Ottawa Press.

Wang, W. S.-Y. 1968. Vowel Features, Paired Variables, and the English Vowel Shift. *Language* 44:695-708.

Yip, M. 1980. Why Scanian is Not a Case for Multivalued Features. *Linguistic Inquiry* 11:432-436.

Modeling the Effects of Processing Limitations on the Acquisition of Morphology: The Less is More Hypothesis

BORIS GOLDOWSKY & ELISSA NEWPORT
University of Rochester

Children are better at learning a language than adults are. This is a surprising fact, and particularly so since compared to adults, children are quite limited in many ways, including perceptual and memory abilities—which would seem to be crucial for learning a language.

The LESS IS MORE HYPOTHESIS attempts to resolve this paradox. After we describe the hypothesis, we will present a model that shows how it can be applied to one particular domain: the learning of a morphological system.

Evidence for a critical period

The first to argue that children are in fact better at language learning was Eric Lenneberg (1967). He proposed this CRITICAL PERIOD HYPOTHESIS in 1967, but at that time there was very little direct evidence to support it. However, his arguments convinced other investigators to look for such evidence, and the hypothesis has since been confirmed by several studies, both of first and second language acquisition.

Susan Curtiss (1977, 1988) studied two subjects, Genie and Chelsea, who were deprived of normal language input as children. When they were later exposed to spoken English, neither was able to attain a command of morphology or syntax, although they were able to acquire vocabulary items and, in one of the cases, basic word order.

Elissa Newport and Ted Supalla (Newport 1988, 1990; Newport and Supalla 1992), and Rachel Mayberry and her colleagues (Mayberry and Fischer 1989; Mayberry and Eichen 1991) were able to study a larger population by testing deaf people who were exposed to American Sign Language, as their first language, at different ages. Even after many years of speaking ASL as

[1]This work was supported by NIH grant DC00167 to ELN and by an NSF Graduate Fellowship to BNG. We are grateful to Philip Resnik and to innumerable colleagues at the University of Rochester for helpful discussion. This paper was also presented at the Stanford Child Language Research Forum in April 1992.

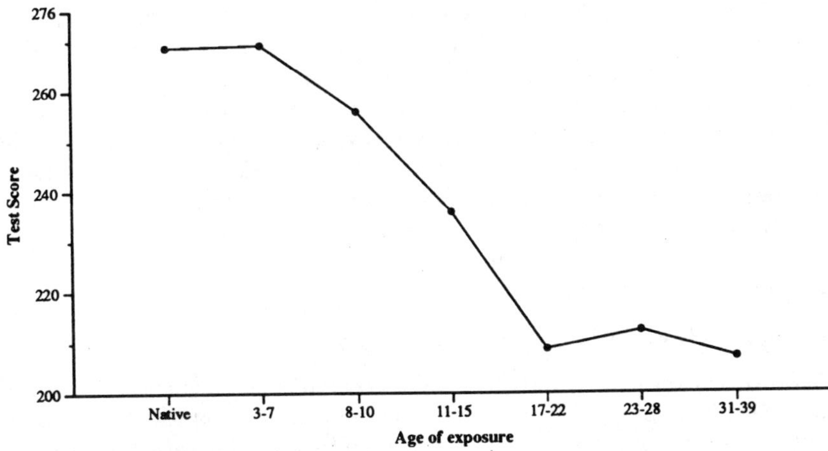

Figure 1: Language competence declines with age of initial exposure to a language: data from Johnson and Newport (1989)

their primary language, clear differences were found between native speakers, early learners, and late learners.

It is much easier, of course, to find populations of people who begin speaking a **second** language at different times in their lives. Jackie Johnson and Elissa Newport (Johnson and Newport 1989, 1991) administered tests of English syntax and morphology to immigrants to the United States who had moved here at varying ages, and found a very similar pattern to that observed for first-language learners of ASL. Comparable results have been obtained on other aspects of second language performance (Oyama 1976, 1978; Patkowski 1980; for reviews, see Krashen, Long, and Scarcella 1982 and Long 1990).

Figure 1, based on data from Johnson and Newport (1989), shows the general pattern found by all these studies.[2] Natives always achieve near perfect scores, but those who begin later do worse. The graph levels off at an ability that, although obviously well above chance, is much lower than that of the native speakers.

The first explanation that may come to mind is that humans have a specific LANGUAGE ACQUISITION DEVICE, and it is that device which decays over maturation in the manner of figure 1. This resolves the paradox of why children get worse at language learning while getting better at other cognitive tasks—but does so by making it into a mere coincidence.

In this paper we consider an alternative explanation, suggested by New-

[2]One difference between figure 1 and the results of most of these studies concerns the earliest non-native learners. While in most studies this group scores somewhat below natives, in the Johnson and Newport (1989) data (and therefore in figure 1), both the natives and the 3–7 group score at the ceiling of the test. Other than this, figure 1 does accurately reflect the findings across a large number of studies.

port (1984, 1988, 1990, 1991), called the LESS IS MORE HYPOTHESIS: that the child's language learning ability is neither a paradox nor a coincidence, but a consequence of the child's limitations—and conversely, that the adult's advantages in perception and memory are, in fact, no advantage at all.

Our research examines this hypothesis by constructing a computer simulation of the acquisition of morphology, in which we ask whether a device with limitations like a child's is in fact more capable of learning than is the same device without these limitations. In the present paper we present a brief overview of our results; for the larger body of mathematical and computational work, see Goldowsky and Newport (forthcoming).

Comparison of early and late acquisition

In order to show how limitations could be helpful in this domain, we first need to point out some characteristics of language as learned by children, and the differences between the way children and adults typically learn a language.

Native speakers make very few errors; they are characterized by extremely consistent use of the rules of the language. In the early stages of acquisition, when they do make mistakes, these tend to be errors of omission (leaving out a required element), overanalysis (segmenting a form into smaller pieces than it actually contains), or overgeneralization (using rules in situations where they do not apply, for example the classic childhood error of using *goed* instead of *went*).

Adult learners, in contrast, are characterized by variable and inconsistent use of rules; much of their behavior appears to be probabilistic. Furthermore, the types of errors they make are quite different: common are what have been termed STEREOTYPED PHRASES or FROZEN FORMS—relatively large chunks of language which have been memorized and are used in situations outside the range of their appropriateness (Wong-Fillmore 1979; Newport 1984, 1988; Newport and Supalla 1992; Dufour, Newport, and Medin 1990).

The Less is More Hypothesis

We can summarize these data by saying that children appear to concentrate on smaller bits and pieces of language—probably because they are incapable of perceiving or remembering a larger chunk all at once, so they are forced to use these small pieces. But it so happens that meaning in language tends to be carried by small pieces: a word, or a morpheme; and more complex meanings are made up out of combinations of these small pieces.

This, then, is the Less is More Hypothesis: that a child's limited perceptual and memory abilities may be an advantage, rather than a liability, in language acquisition, because they force the child to attend to those units that actually carry meaning.

The learning model

In order to demonstrate that this idea is workable, we will consider a simple model of the acquisition of morphological systems.

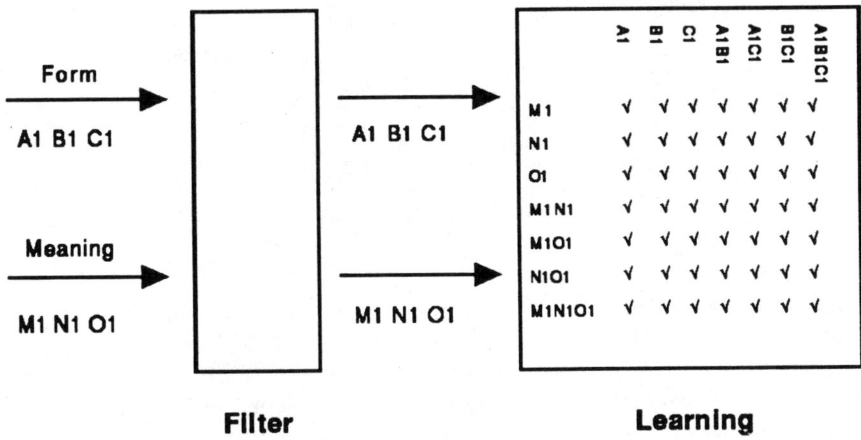

Figure 2: Structure of the model: adult version

The model uses a learning mechanism that is designed to be as uncontroversial and theory-neutral as possible; in fact, it just implements the basic computational problem of correlating the linguistic FORMS and MEANINGS that occur in the environment. This sort of correlation must be computed by any model that is trying to figure out which forms are associated with which meanings.[3]

We model the limitations of the child as resulting in restriction of the data available to this learning device; our manipulations are restricted to a so-called INPUT FILTER, which lies between the environment and the learning mechanism, and controls how much information is available to the learner. The focus of this work is what happens if there is a maturational change in this filter—or in other words, a maturational change in the ability to perceive or retain a complete word. (For evidence that such a maturational change occurs, see Kail 1984; Dufour et. al. 1990).

In any model that attempts to learn the mapping between forms and meanings, both must be available—so we provide as input to our learner pairs of a linguistic form (representing a word the learner hears) and a meaning (representing aspects of the meaning of that word that the learner infers from context). In our notation, words are made up of a number of FEATURES (which could be syllables, or segments—in any case, they are the smallest

[3]In the present work, in order to most clearly observe the effects of central importance (see below for the input filter), we have chosen to make the learning mechanism maximally simple, unbiased by either linguistic or cognitive constraints aside from those of the input filter, and identical for both the adult and child. By this means we can most cleanly reveal the effects of manipulating the filter itself. However, one's ultimate theoretical conception of language acquisition, as well as a more nearly correct simulation, might of course involve additional constraints within the learning mechanism. See the section 'Future Directions' for further discussion.

Form	Meaning
$A_{1,2,3}$	$M_{1,2,3}$
$B_{1,2,3}$	$N_{1,2,3}$
$C_{1,2,3}$	$O_{1,2,3}$

Figure 3: Example system: a simple morphology

units that will be considered to be possible morphemes). Each word has a number of SLOTS (labelled A,B,C), each with a set of mutually exclusive features (denoted 1,2,3). The meanings have a parallel scheme; they are made up of sets of semantic features (which could be actual semantic features, or simple concepts).

The learner's problem, then, is to figure out what the morphemes of the language are. Each morpheme will be a set of form features, and a set of meaning features which are the meaning of that form. In general, the only way to tell what means what in the language is to look for forms and meanings that consistently occur together. So the model makes a table of COOCCURRENCES, with form features and combinations of form features on one axis, and meaning features and combinations of them on the other axis. Each time a particular set of form features and a particular set of meaning features appear in the same input item, a mark is made in the cell of the table whose coordinates are those sets.

As an example, take the input item consisting of the form $A_1B_1C_1$ and the meaning $M_1N_1O_1$. How would the model deal with this? First, for simplicity, we will demonstrate it with no input filter, in other words using the adult version of the model. Figure 2 shows a schematic representation of the structure of the model and its behavior when exposed to this item. Since A_1 and M_1 both appear in the input, the model makes a mark in the cell A_1/M_1. Likewise, it makes marks in B_1/M_1, A_1B_1/M_1, B_1C_1/M_1N_1, and so forth (all the marks shown in figure 2)—all of these could conceivably be morphemes.

There is clearly a large number of hypotheses about what the morphemes of the language could be that are suggested by this single input item. In order to narrow down the possibilities, more data are needed. Therefore we give the model a stream of input items, which are constructed based on some assumed morphemes.

For example, one simple system is shown in figure 3; here each morpheme is made up of a single form and a single meaning feature, so that A_1 means M_1 (and those two always occur together if they occur at all), A_2 means M_2, and so forth.

Figure 4 shows the number of marks made in the table of cooccurrences after the model has been exposed to all the words in this system. In order to highlight the relationships between the magnitudes of the numbers in each cell

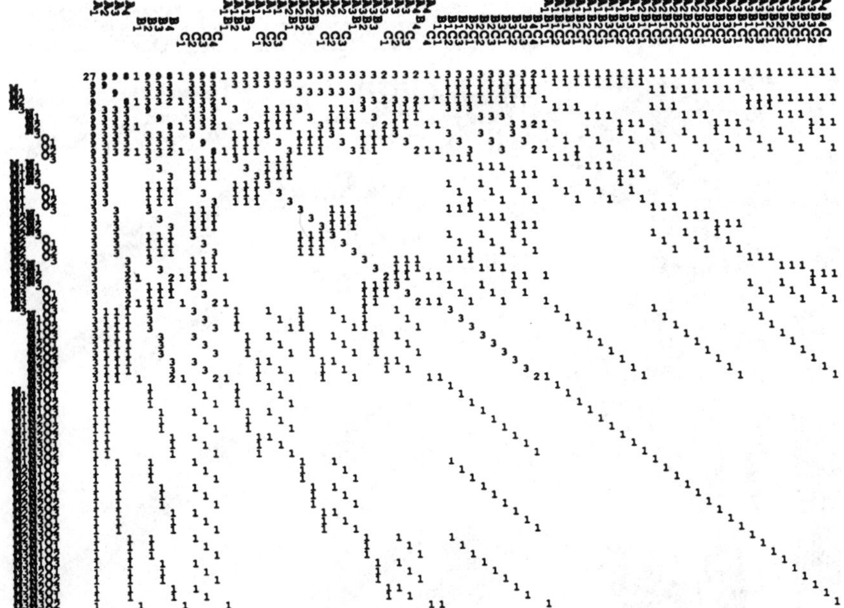

Figure 4: The model's table after being exposed to the system of figure 3.

and thus make the data more easily interpreted, we will from now on present such data in a graphical representation such as that in figure 5. These are the same data as in figure 4, but each nonempty cell is drawn as a dot whose area is proportional to the number and consistency of cooccurrences between its form and its meaning.[4]

There are several important features of this chart to notice. The large dots in the upper left-hand corner of the chart contains the mappings between single form features and single meaning features, which we call ONE-TO-ONE mappings. The lower right of the table contains HIGH-LEVEL mappings—that is, mappings between several form and several meaning features. The large dots along the diagonal in the one-to-one part of the table are the cells representing A_1/M_1 and the other actual morphemes of the language. The other large dots along the rest of the diagonal are cells like A_1B_1/M_1N_1—combinations of several morphemes, which although undeniably perfectly correlated, are redundant information. Everything off the diagonal is noise, chance cooccurrences that have nothing to do with meaning relationships.

It is clear that there is a lot of noise in this table. This is the problem

[4]See Goldowsky and Newport (forthcoming) for full details. In brief, consistency of cooccurrence is computed as a ratio of the number of form-meaning cooccurrences to the number of occurrences of each of the forms and the meanings.

Unfiltered

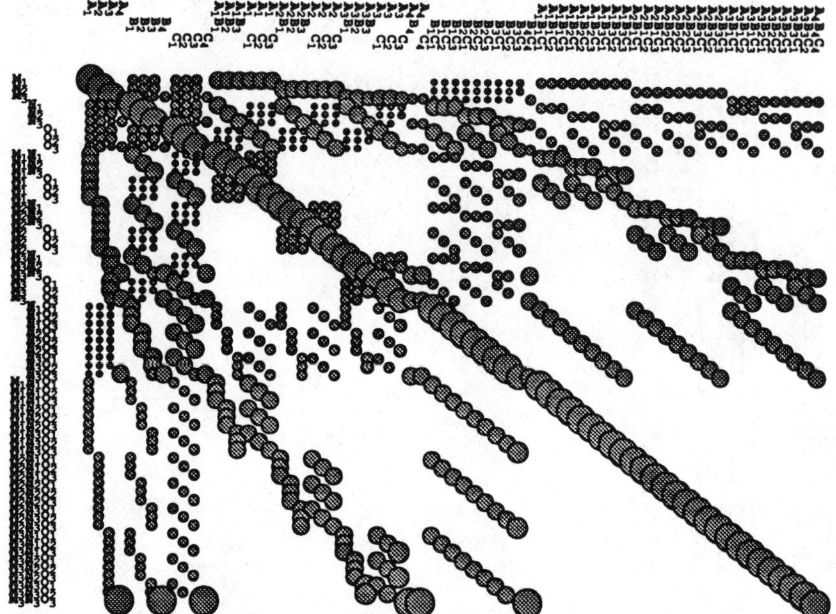

Figure 5: The data of figure 4 in graphical representation.

that Noam Chomsky and others have alluded to: the data available to a language learner support, to varying degrees, many different hypotheses about the underlying system (Chomsky 1965, 1981). This is a striking example that this is true even when the system to be learned is as simple as this one.

A table like that in figure 5, filled with noise and many alternative hypotheses about the nature of the system, will lead to inconsistent responding, as is found for late learners of a language. Our suggestion about late learners is thus that their inconsistent responding may be, at least in part, the outcome of encoding the actual input data without the child's limitations and constraints.

What, then, about the child learner? What will this picture look like if we restrict the model's data by imposing an input filter?

Figure 6 shows a filter that only allows through half of the features making up each word (with a word containing three features, like these, the filter lets through one feature 50% of the time, and two features the other 50% of the time). Which features are let through and which are deleted are **randomly** chosen. We believe this to be the most conservative reasonable assumption: in fact it is likely that children have biases about which parts of an utterance they attend to—for example they may be biased towards stressed syllables, ends of words, or the like—but whatever biases they have are no doubt helpful

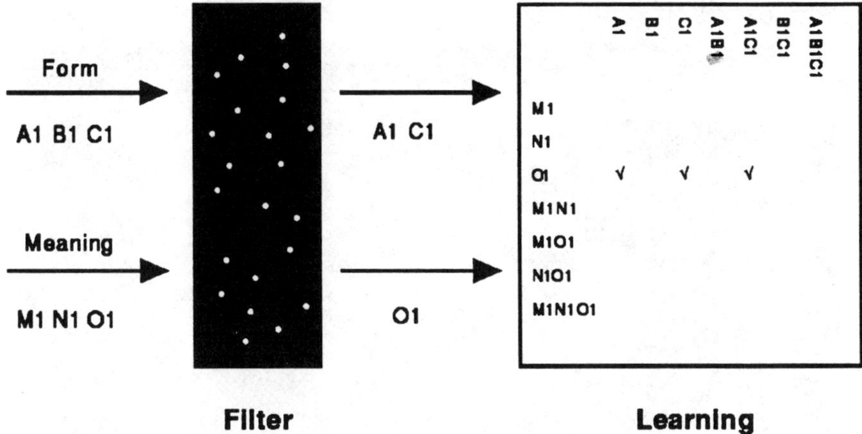

Figure 6: Structure of the model: child version

in orienting them to important parts. If we can show helpful effects of even a random filter, then a 'smart' filter will be even more helpful.[5]

So once again, we make marks in the table for all the cooccurrences—but since some of the data has been filtered out, there will be fewer marks made this time.

Figure 7 shows the table as learned by the child model. There are fewer large dots overall, which is simply the effect of having eliminated parts of the input; this effect we call DATA LOSS.

However, the data are not lost evenly: the upper left corner, containing the one-to-one mappings, retains more data than the rest of the table, since only small pieces of form and meaning can make it through the filter. Thus the model is forced to concentrate on smaller units, much as the child does. This effect we call DATA FOCUS.

What is the result of these effects, taken together? Recall that the real morphemes of the language are in the upper left corner of the table—so although the amount of good data (signal) is reduced by the filter, the noise is cut down much more, resulting in a cleaner table. The SIGNAL-TO-NOISE RATIO improves.

We have shown only one simple example system and one filter, but this system is not special. In fact it can be proven that even with other, more complex systems, there is **always** some particular size of filter that will produce optimal learning for that system. Far from being a liability, the child-like constraints we imposed on our learner turn out to be extremely useful in learning this system, and in fact any system.

You may still be wondering, however, what if there were a word in the system that did not break down into morphemes at all—or rather, a word

[5]See footnote 3 and the section 'Future Directions' for further discussion.

Filtered at 1.5

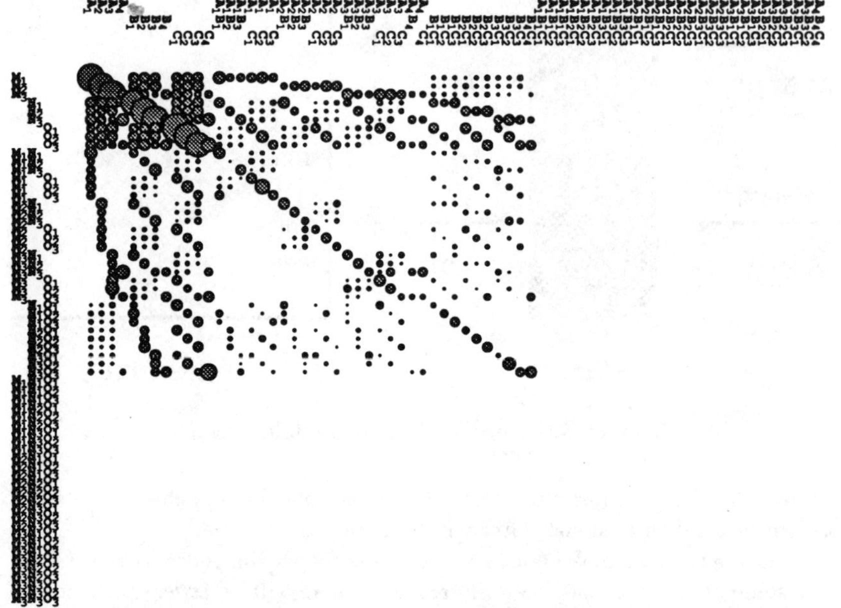

Figure 7: The table created by the child version of the model, exposed to the same language as figure 5.

that was made of exactly one morpheme, which contained more features than would fit through the filter? It seems that the learner could not learn this word, since it could not perceive it in its entirety.

In fact, there is such a word in the system used in the examples in this paper. As shown in figure 8, there is one word whose form is not predictable from its meaning—similar to examples such as irregular past tenses or plurals in English, or 'frozen' verbs of motion in ASL, or other exception words in morphological systems. As predicted, the child version of the model was unable to learn this word.

However, the child is not a static system, and does not learn language instantaneously. If we allow the model to mature—which means if we make the filter less and less restrictive over time—it will eventually learn this exception word as well.

Figure 9 shows what happens if, after the learner has reached the stage of figure 7, we allow it another stage of exposure to the system with a less restrictive filter. (In this case we allow the model a first stage, as before, with a filter set at one feature 50% of the time, and two features 50% of the time; but then we follow this with a second stage in which the filter is set at two features 50% of the time and three features 50% of the time.) Note how the

Form	Meaning
$A_{1,2,3}$	$M_{1,2,3}$
$B_{1,2,3}$	$N_{1,2,3}$
$C_{1,2,3}$	$O_{1,2,3}$

Except:

$A_4\ B_4\ C_4\quad M_3\ N_3\ O_3$

Figure 8: A morphology with one exception word

exception word stands out in this picture; it is the only high-level mapping that is worth learning—the only one not redundant with the morphemes learned at the earlier stage of development.[6]

More generally, allowing the child model to mature, and successively pass through filters of less restrictiveness, results in the child learner acquiring in later stages of acquisition a succession of more complex cooccurrences—but particularly and only those which are not predictable from morphemes already learned in earlier stages. In contrast, recall that the adult learner, who is modeled as receiving all of the data simultaneously, never learns any of these mappings as well.

Summary and Conclusions

We have shown that a limitation on the ability to perceive or remember the full complexity of linguistic input, as seems to occur in young children, may have unexpected benefits for the learning of morphology. If the child begins acquisition with a very restrictive input filter, it will obtain the optimally clean data for the smallest meaningful units in the language. Learning larger units will require a less restrictive filter; but, as we mentioned earlier, for **any** structure in the language there is a filter that produces optimal learning of that structure. If you start with very limited capabilities and then mature, you will have each size of filter in turn, and therefore have the chance to learn each structure in the language at the time appropriate for that structure—and you end up learning the entire language optimally.

In contrast, starting as an adult, you have no access to this kind of sequencing of the data, and as a result you are not guaranteed to learn anything at all optimally. Your language will be characterized by generally poor learning and inconsistency due to having many competing analyses of structures.

This is the way in which limitations can make the child's task in language learning a little bit easier, and therefore make the child, but not the adult, end up as a native speaker.

[6]Yet an additional stage of further exposure with an unrestrictive (adult-like) filter results in no appreciable change in the outcome.

Maturationally Filtered: 1.5 & 2.5

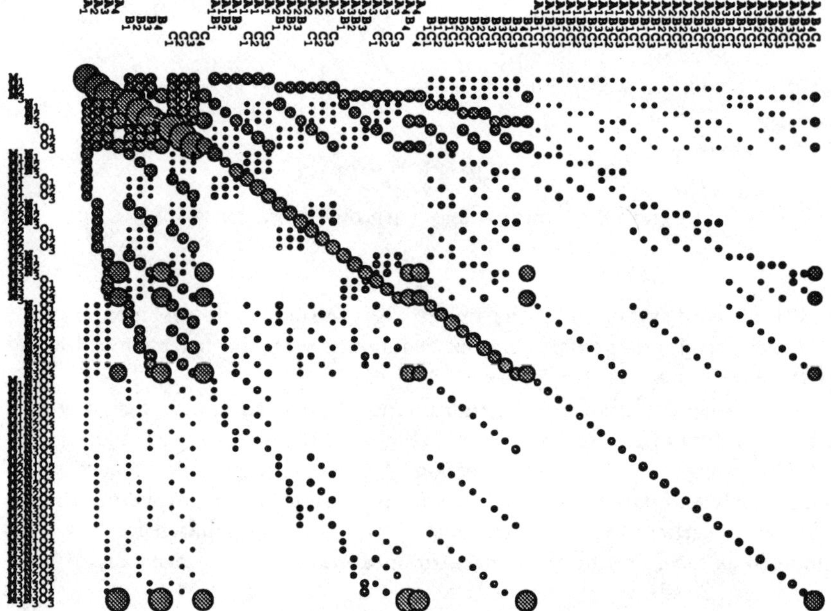

Figure 9: The table produced by the maturational version of the model: Figure 7 plus a second stage of learning with a less restrictive filter.

Future Directions

The purpose of the present work has been to show that one particular instantiation of the Less is More Hypothesis—a limitation on the extraction of input—will work correctly in the acquisition of morphology to account for the critical period phenomena with which we began. As we have shown, such a limitation will indeed produce superior learning. However, there remain several important directions for future research on our hypothesis.

First, our research has intentionally manipulated only one aspect of language learning, and has left others aside. However, a more realistic model of acquisition would employ additional constraints on learning, including such things as perceptual biases in the selection of input features (see Slobin 1973, 1985) and structural constraints particular to language (see Chomsky 1981). Our research raises the possibility that at least some of the additional constraints needed for an appropriate model of language acquisition may, like our own constraint, be ones in which the processing limitations of children improve the outcome of learning. For example, some of our research has investigated long term memory loss, with the outcome that imperfect memory results in improved rule learning. Some quite different research in the connectionist literature has found related outcomes (see, for example, Baum and Hausler 1989,

Hertz, Krogh, and Palmer 1991, and Elman 1991). Further empirical and modeling work is needed to determine the appropriate balance among these different types of constraints.

Second, our research has focused only on the acquisition of quite simple morphological systems. A greater challenge lies in considering the acquisition of syntax, where it has been customary to assume that specifically linguistic constraints will be needed to account for acquisition, and therefore where a maturational decay in such constraints would seem to be the most natural account of critical period effects. However, while we have not yet begun research in this area, the direction of some critical period effects here suggest that the problem might in fact be amenable to an approach like ours. In particular, Johnson and Newport (1991) have shown that late learners of English sometimes accept subjacency violations as grammatical. One approach to accounting for this pattern of results is to suggest that, as in the present work, late learners are less limited than early learners. Again, determining whether this less constrained linguistic behavior in late learners should be accounted for by a loss in linguistic principles, or rather by a loss of processing limitations, remains for future work.

Finally, our hypothesis suggests more generally that other areas of development might profitably be viewed from the perspective of potential advantages of limitations. Some time ago Turkewitz and Kenny (1982) suggested that one evolutionary advantage of protracted infancy might be to permit learning in certain domains to occur at a time when other abilities are quite limited. Our hypothesis is an instance of the kind they had in mind. However, relatively little research has considered the developmental consequences of the very primitive state in which the organism begins. Commonly, development is merely viewed as phenomenon in its own right. The results presented here, along with related work by us and others, suggest that it may profitably be viewed as a unique means through which adult behavior may emerge.

References

Baum, E. B. and D. Haussler. 1989. What Size Net Gives Valid Generalization? *Neural Computation* 1:151–160.

Chomsky, Noam. 1965. *Aspects of the Theory of Syntax.* Cambridge, MA: MIT Press.

Chomsky, Noam. 1981. *Lectures on Government and Binding.* Dordrecht: Foris.

Curtiss, Susan. 1977. *Genie: A Psycholinguistic Study of a Modern Day "Wild Child".* New York: Academic Press.

Curtiss, Susan. 1988. The Case of Chelsea: A New Test Case of The Critical Period for Language Acquisition. University of California, Los Angeles.

Dufour, Robert, Elissa L. Newport, and Douglas Medin. 1990. Adult-Child Differences in the Imitation of Gestures: The Less is More Hypothesis. Unpublished Manuscript, University of Rochester (NY).

Elman, Jeffrey L. 1991. Incremental Learning, or The Importance of Starting Small. Technical report, Center for Research in Language, University of California, San Diego.

Hertz, John, Anders Krogh, and Richard G. Palmer. 1991. *Introduction to the Theory of Neural Computation.* Studies in the Sciences of Complexity. Redwood City, CA: Addison-Wesley.

Johnson, Jacqueline S. and Elissa L. Newport. 1989. Critical Period Effects in Second Language Learning: The Influence of Maturational State on the Acquisition of English as a Second Language. *Cognitive Psychology* 21:60–99.

Johnson, Jacqueline S. and Elissa L. Newport. 1991. Critical Period Effects on universal properties of language: The Status of Subjacency in the Acquisition of a Second Language. *Cognition* 39:215–258.

Kail, Robert. 1984. *The Development of Memory.* New York: W. H. Freeman & Co., 2nd edition.

Krashen, Stephen D., M. Long, and R. Scarcella. 1982. Age, Rate, and Eventual Attainment in Second Language Acquisition. *Child-Adult Differences in Second Language Acquisition*, ed. Stephen D. Krashen, R. Scarcella, and M. Long. Rowley, MA: Newbury House.

Lenneberg, Eric H. 1967. *Biological Foundations of Language.* New York: Wiley.

Long, M. 1990. Maturational Constraints on Language Development. *Studies in Second Language Acquisition* 12:251–285.

Mayberry, R. and E. Eichen. 1991. The Long-Lasting Advantage of Learning Sign Language in Childhood: Another Look at the Critical Period for Language Acquisition. *Journal of Memory and Language* 30:486–512.

Mayberry, R. and S. Fischer. 1989. Looking Through Phonological Shape to Lexical Meaning: The Bottleneck of Non-Native Sign Language Processing. *Memory and Cognition* 17:740–754.

Newport, Elissa L. 1984. Constraints on Learning: Studies of the Acquisition of American Sign Language. *Papers and Reports on Child Language Developement* 23:1–22.

Newport, Elissa L. 1988. Constraints on Learning and their Role in Language Acquisition: Studies of the Acquisition of American Sign Language. *Language Sciences* 10:147–172.

Newport, Elissa L. 1990. Maturational Constraints on Language Learning. *Cognitive Science* 14:11–28.

Newport, Elissa L. 1991. Contrasting Conceptions of the Critical Period for Language. *The Epigenesis of Mind: Essays on Biology and Cognition*, ed. Susan Carey and R. Gelman. Hillsdale: Erlbaum.

Newport, Elissa L. and Ted Supalla. 1992. Critical Period Effects in the Acquisition of a Primary Language: I. The Influence of Maturational State on the Acquisitin of Complex Morphology in American Sign Language. University of Rochester.

Oyama, Susan. 1976. A Sensitive Period for the Acquisition of a Nonnative Phonological System. *Journal of Psycholinguistic Research* 5:261–285.

Oyama, Susan. 1978. The Sensitive Period and Comprehension of Speech. *Working Papers on Bilingualism* 16:1–17.

Patkowski, M. 1980. The Sensitive Period for the Acquisition of Syntax in a Second Language. *Language Learning* 30:449–472.

Slobin, Dan I. 1973. Cognitive Prerequisites for the Development of Grammar. *Studies of Child Language Development*, ed. C. A. Ferguson and Dan I. Slobin. New York: Holt, Rinehart & Winston.

Slobin, Dan I. 1985. Cross-Linguistic Evidence for the Language-Making Capacity. *The Cross-Linguistic Structure of Language Acquisition, vol. 2: Theoretical Issues*, ed. Dan I. Slobin. Hillsdale, NJ: Erlbaum.

Turkewitz, Gerald and Patricia A. Kenny. 1982. Limitations on Input as a Basis for Neural Organization and Perceptual Development: A Preliminary Theoretical Statement. *Developmental Psychobiology* 15:357–368.

Wong-Fillmore, Lily. 1979. Individual Differences in Second Language Acquisition. *Individual Differences in Language Ability and Language Behavior*, ed. Charles J. Fillmore, D. Kempler, and W. S-Y Wang. New York: Academic Press.

The Matter of Two High Front Rounded Vowels and the Feature Theory

ALICJA GORECKA
University of Southern California

1. Introduction

In this paper, I address the long standing question of the representation of /y/ and /ʉ/, the two high front rounded vowels that contrast in Swedish. I present arguments that in order to capture the phonology of these vowels, it is necessary to appeal to passive articulator features such as [palatal] and [velar], in addition to active articulator features such as dorsal and [back]. The two types of features are reconciled in a system for which I have argued in Gorecka (1989). Throughout the paper I refer to this system as the site/articulator model.

With respect to the high front rounded vowels of Swedish, I argue that in addition to the labial constriction, present in both vowels, the vowel transcribed as /y/ involves a palatal constriction, and the vowel transcribed as /ʉ/ involves a velar constriction, articulated with the fronted tongue body. Since the site/articulator model generates exactly these two varieties of front rounded vowels, to the extent to which these representations explain the phonology of /y/ and /ʉ/, I submit the facts of Swedish as an additional source of evidence for this model.

I further strengthen the argument, by showing that the analysis of /y/ and /ʉ/ I am proposing accounts not only for the facts of Swedish, but for virtually all documented cases of high front rounded vowels (HFRV's from here on).

It is often assumed, and this assumption is reflected in phonetics and phonology textbooks, that there exists only one HFRV a linguist should be concerned with. In the IPA system, this vowel is transcribed as /y/. While Swedish presents a problem for this assumption, because it contrasts TWO high front rounded vowels, the common view is that the vowel transcribed as /ʉ/ is an oddity not found outside of Scandinavian languages. The second high front rounded vowel of Swedish, the one transcribed as /y/ is considered to be the same as the HFRV's in other languages.

Phonetic and phonological evidence suggests that contrary to these views, the HFRV's in languages outside of Swedish fall into two categories: either they are, phonetically and phonologically, like the Swedish vowel transcribed as /y/, or like the

[1] I am grateful to Michael Kenstowicz for directing my attention to the facts of Swedish. I also want to thank Diana Archangeli, Morris Halle, Pat Keating, Joe Salmons, Tom Shannon, Donca Steriade, Jean-Roger Vergnaud, and WCCFL XI audience for their comments on various points discussed in this paper.

Swedish vowel transcribed as /ʉ/. Furthermore, neither one of the two vowels is particularly exotic, although the vowel of Swedish which is considered to be rare, namely /ʉ/, seems to occur more commonly in languages of the world.

This paper consists of two parts: In the first part, I discuss the phonological properties of the Swedish vowels, and I present an analysis of these properties, prefaced with a brief explanation of theoretical assumptions. In the second part, I turn to HFRV's outside of Swedish, and I show how these vowels align, both phonetically and phonologically, with the Swedish /y/ and /ʉ/.

2. The high front rounded vowels of Swedish

The /y/ and /ʉ/ of Swedish (segment inventory of Swedish, following Ruhlen (1975) and Fant (1971): p, b, f, v, m, t, d, s, n, l, r, ç, j, k, g, ŋ, i:, y:, ʉ:, u:, e:, ɛ:, ø, o:, ɑ:, ɪ, y, ɵ, e, ɛ, ø, ɔ, ʊ, a) present a problem for an SPE-based feature system, for two reasons: First, both vowels are front, rounded, high and tense. Given that in addition, Swedish has a high front unrounded vowel /i/, and a high back rounded vowel /u/, this leaves the theory unable to represent the underlying contrast between /y/ and /ʉ/. Second, the phonology of Swedish, as we shall see in a moment,[2] requires that /ʉ/ be grouped together with the front vowels, and with the back vowels at the same time. But outside of [round], the theory does not have a feature that would group together a back vowel and a front vowel if the two vowels are of the same height.

As reported by Fant (1971), Linell (1973), and others, the high long vowels in the language are pronounced as diphthongs that end in homorganic off-glides:

---

[2] In what follows, I discuss only the diphtongization of high vowels and the palatalization of velars. Sometimes the remaining reflexes of the umlaut and ablaut phenomena in Swedish are also brought up in the context of the discussion of /y/ and /ʉ/ (cf. Linell (1973)). I do not include the umlaut and ablaut facts in the present discussion, as there is a great deal of evidence that these are no longer productive rules of Swedish. First, the alternations attributed to these rules are found in a relatively small subset of Swedish lexicon (cf. Linell 1973,17). Second, in many cases, the phonological conditioning for the alternation has been lost, e.g., brʉn-bryna 'brown', fʉll-fylla 'fill', blud-bløda 'blood', etc. Third, it is impossible to predict the alternating counterparts for some of the vowels, as /o/ alternates with /ø/ and /ɛ/, /ø/ alternates with /o/ and /u/, and /ɛ/ alternates with /o/ and /ɑ/ in umlaut (Linell 1973):

(i) /ʉ/ - /y/; e.g., brʉn 'brown' (a.), bryna 'brown' (v.)
/u/ - /ø/; e.g., gruv 'rough', grøvre 'rough' (comp.)
/o/ - /ø/; e.g., son 'son', søner 'sons'
/o/ - /ɛ/; e.g., trong 'narrow', trɛngre 'narrow' (comp.)
/ɑ/ - /ɛ/; e.g., stad 'city', stɛder 'cities'

In view of the above, it is reasonable to interpret the small number of alternating forms as the reflexes of a phonological process which has ceased to be productive. Most likely, given the height alternation in addition to the backness alternation in the forms in (i), umlaut has ended before the sound changes which have shifted /ɑ/ to /o/, /o/ to /u/, and /u/ to /ʉ/.

(1) Diphtongization of long high vowels in Swedish:

i: --> i:j; y: --> y:j^{w}; ʉ: --> ʉ:β^{ɥ}; u: --> u:β^{w}

(Linell 1973)

The vowels /i/ and /y/ are produced with the palatal closing gesture, with added lip rounding in the case of /y/. Both /u/ and /ʉ/ are produced with the labial off-glide, which is transcribed as a voiced bilabial fricative. Clearly, the diphtongization process in Swedish divides the high vowels into two classes, one which contains /i/ and /y/, and one which contains /u/ and /ʉ/. Since both classes contain a [-back] and a [+round] segment, it is obvious that the traditional feature system cannot account for this pattern of diphtongization.

There have been proposals, due to Fant (1971), and Lindau (1978), to deal with the diphtongization facts in terms of features which refer to labial gestures. These proposals were prompted by thc fact that /y/ and /ʉ/ involve rather different types of rounding. While /y/ is sometimes characterized as involving labial protrusion, the /ʉ/ is considered to have the same type of extreme rounding as it is found in the back rounded vowels. Both Fant and Lindau have argued for the distinction labial vs. round in vowels, with some differences as to the exact specifications of these features in /y/ and /ʉ/.

While the proposals which appeal to different labiality features are capable of delivering the contrast between the two vowels, and can account for the natural class effects associated with diphtongization, they do not address another problem /y/ and /ʉ/ pose, this time, for the treatment of palatalization in Swedish:

(2) Palatalization facts (/k´/ represents a fronted velar):

çɛmpa	'struggle'	kɑmp	'struggle'
çyla	'cold', n"	kɑll	'cold', adj
çøld	'cold', n		
jiv(a)	'give'	gɑv	'gave'
šylla	'blame	sk´ʉl(d)	'blame', n
šymma	'obscure', v	sk´ʉm	'obscure', a

As shown in (2), palatalization in Swedish converts velars into palatal fricatives, and the cluster /sk/ into a palato-alveolar fricative. This process is triggered by all front vowels, except /ʉ/. Before /ʉ/ velars are fronted, but not palatalized.

Clearly, these facts cannot be handled with different labiality features. They cannot be handled within an SPE-based feature system either, since in such a system, the ability to trigger palatalization is attributed to the specification for [-back]. Since /ʉ/ is [-back], as demonstrated by the fact that it can trigger velar fronting, it ought to be automatically equipped with palatalizing properties.

Earlier proposals which have attempted to resolve the problem posed by the palatalization facts, either relied on abstract solutions, or appealed to new features. The abstract solution proposals, due to Kiefer (1970), and Hammarberg (1970) among others, posit the underlying representations which reflect the state of affairs in the language prior to the vowel shift which converted the high back rounded vowel into /ʉ/. There are obvious problems with such proposals: first, they place heavy demands on human learning capacity, after all, language learners do not have access to historical evidence; second, they are strictly language-specific. As we shall see, the /ʉ/ is not limited to Swedish, nevertheless, in languages outside of Swedish, it is associated with the same phonological properties as the Swedish vowel.

The proposals which appeal to new features, such as Fant's (1971) positing the feature [palatal] in addition to [back], or Linell's (1973) adding the feature [front], do deliver the palatalization facts. On such accounts, the feature responsible for palatalization is either palatal or front, and only the vowels which trigger palatalization bear the palatal or front specification. As to the reasons why these proposals have not been widely accepted, one could speculate that because they were based on a single, fairly rare phenomenon, they were not able to make the case for the new features sufficiently strong.

3. The solution

The representations which I propose for /y/ and /ʉ/, to some extent follow the insight of Fant (1971), in that they appeal to constriction location, or passive articulator features. The way in which my proposal differs from Fant's, is in the status I accord to such features. I assume, following the line I have taken in Gorecka (1989), that all speech sounds[3] are represented in terms of passive articulator features, in addition to being represented in terms of active articulator features.

On this view, the constriction gesture corresponds to the constriction node, and is defined by a pair of variables: the site and the articulator. These two are simply shorter names for the passive and active articulators respectively. A well-formed, fully specified representation contains the articulation component which conforms to the general schema shown in (3) :

(3)

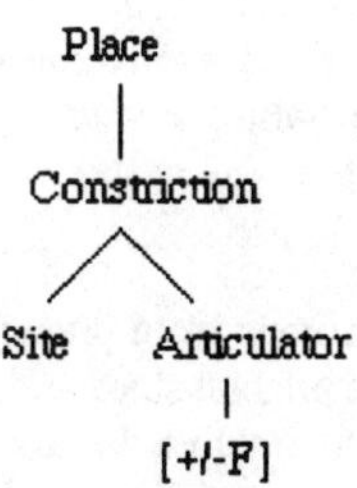

Site values: labial, anterior, palatal, velar, pharyngeal.
Articulator values: lower lip, coronal, dorsal, radical.

[3] With the possible exception of laryngeals, cf. Steriade (1986).

Consider examples of fully specified representations which follow this schema:

(4)

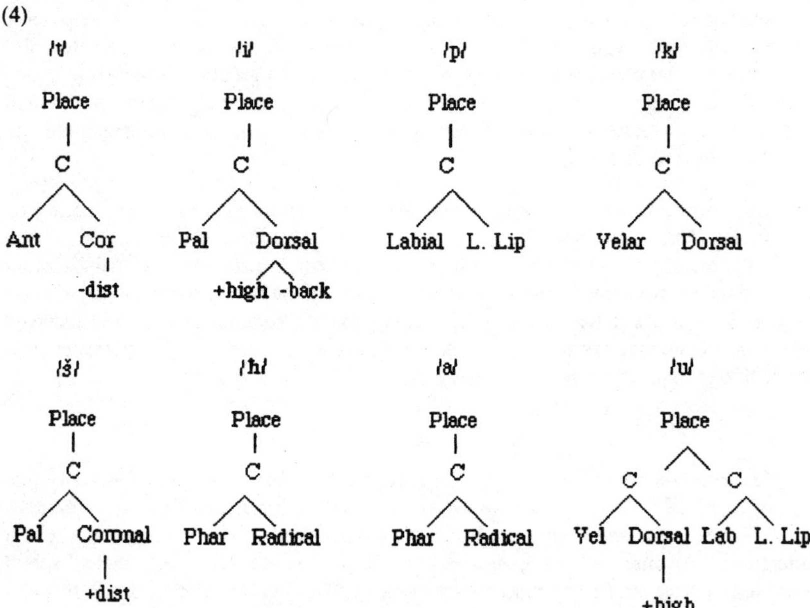

I have argued for this view of articulation on the basis of the phenomena which point to natural classes of sounds based on constriction location (palatal, velar, pharyngeal, etc.), in addition to the natural classes based on the active articulator (coronal, dorsal, etc.). Below I list several examples of the phenomena which motivate this proposal; for reasons of space, I limit these remarks to site features.

Arguments for the feature palatal site come from palatalization facts in languages all over the world. In palatalization, the trigger, a **dorsal** front vowel, and the output, most commonly, a **coronal** palato-alveolar, share only one articulatory property: the constriction location. In this case it is **the hard palate**. Feature systems which rely only or primarily on active articulator features, such as the system in Sagey (1986), cannot account for palatalization effects.

Support for the labial site comes from phenomena such as dissimilation in Zulu (Ziervogel and Venda which affects bilabial stops and fricatives, but excludes labiodentals. Since both labiodentals and bilabials involve the lower lip as an articulator, only the site feature, which in this case corresponds to the upper lip, could be viewed as the trigger of the OCP effect in Zulu and Venda.

The pharyngeal site is well motivated by the phenomena in which the low and lower mid vowels and the guttural sounds pattern as a natural class. Numerous examples of such phenomena are discussed in McCarthy's (1989) paper on gutturals.[4] Active articulator features are again of no use here, since the sounds that pattern together in these cases are produced either with the tongue body or the tongue root.

This is just a small sample of the phenomena which cannot be handled in terms of active articulator features, but are easily analyzed in terms of site features, simply because the sounds which produce the natural class effects in these phenomena share the same constriction location. For additional examples of such phenomena, as well as the data and the analyses, see Gorecka (1989).

The feature system just presented divorces the ability to trigger palatalization from the specification for [-back]. This is motivated by the following: there exist segments which must be specified as [-back], primarily because of their behavior in frontness harmonies, which have never been seen to trigger palatalization; these are the low front vowel and the fronted velar consonants (see Gorecka 1991). On the other hand, coronal sounds articulated in the palatal region, which could not be assumed to be [-back] (since [-back] is the tongue body feature), can trigger palatalization, as demonstrated by the palatalization of back vowels preceded by palato-alveolars in Slavic languages.

The view I take of the feature [-back] is that it reflects the fronted gesture the tongue body can execute regardless of the location of the constriction in which it is involved. I then predict that for every articulatory region at which the tongue body can constrict the vocal tract, there should be a [-back] dorsal segment. Assuming that the tongue body can form constrictions against the hard palate, the soft palate and the pharyngeal wall, there should be palatal, velar and pharyngeal vowels which are [-back]. Thus I predict that in addition to the high front vowel and the low front vowel, there should be a high front rounded vowel which would differ from /u/ only in its specification for [back]. This vowel should have similar phonological properties to the fronted velar consonants: it should be able to trigger or block fronting, and it should have no palatalizing properties.

I assume that rounding in such a vowel would be supplied by the same mechanism by which the back velar vowels are rounded, following to some extent the insight of Stevens, Keyser, and Kawasaki (1986), who attribute rounding in /u/-like vowels to feature enhancement.[5] There is independent support for this view: as mentioned earlier, the

---

[4] Note, however, that the feature pharyngeal enjoys a different status in the feature model McCarthy proposes.

[5] I depart from Stevens, Keyser, and Kawasaki's proposal to the extent that I assume that rounding enhances velarity, not backness. If backness were the feature requiring enhancement, we would expect greater numbers of rounded than unrounded back vowels for every degree of height. As it turns out, only the non-low back vowels (= velar vowels in my system) seem to require rounding. This generalization is based on the frequency of occurrence of back rounded and plain back vowels in the sample of 317 languages in Maddieson (1984): /u/: 253 vs. /ɯ/: 20; /ɔ/: 97 vs. /ʌ/: 4; but /ɒ/: 5 vs. /ɑ/: 22. These numbers show that while rounding is practically obligatory in velar vowels (/u/, /ɯ/, /ɔ/, and /ʌ/), it is rare in the low back vowels (/ɑ/ and /ɒ/), which lack the velar component. Furthermore, it is not the case that rounding is required in back vowels just in case there is a contrast with a corresponding [-back] vowel: out of 28 languages in Maddieson's sample,

rounding in /ʉ/ is characterized to be the same as the rounding in the high back vowel. This is accounted for if both vowels are rounded by the same mechanism.

On the assumption that labiality can be used contrastively, I predict that in addition to high front rounded vowels which are fronted velars, there should be high front rounded vowels which are rounded palatals. Unlike fronted velars, these vowels should have palatalizing properties. The two representations are shown in (5):

(5)

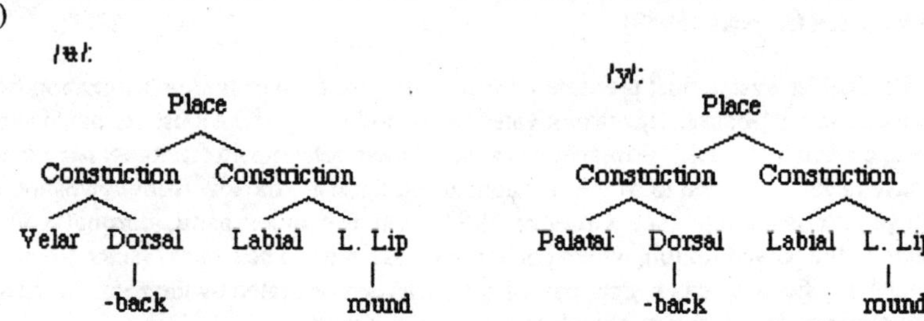

I now come to the point of this paper, which is that the two representations in (5) correspond to the two high front rounded vowels in Swedish: the fronted velar is /ʉ/; the rounded palatal is /y/. These representations account for the facts of Swedish as follows: /y/ is a palatal, therefore it triggers palatalization along with other palatal vowels in the language. For the same reason, when diphthongized, it slides towards a palatal glide. /ʉ/ is a fronted velar, which explains why it does not trigger palatalization, and why it does not diphthongize towards a palatal glide, but rather, patterns with the high back rounded vowel /u/ in this process. Finally, /ʉ/ triggers velar fronting, because it is [-back].

Palatalization of velars is analyzed as follows: the palatal constriction of the vowel spreads onto a velar consonant. The original articulation of the consonant is deleted. The rule is formalized in (6).

(6) Palatalization of velars:

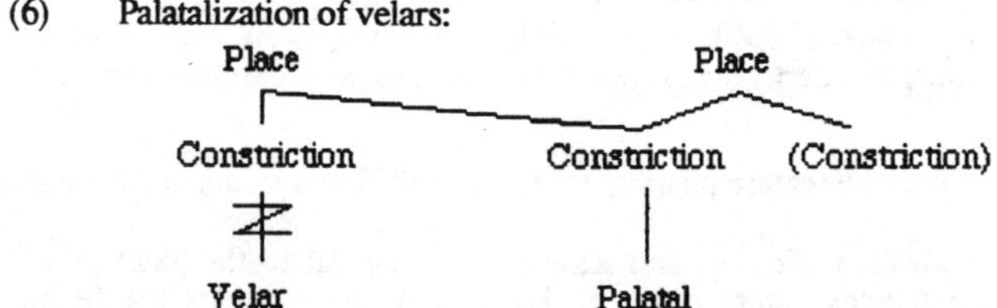

---

in which a [+back] non-low vowel lacks a [-back] counterpart, twenty five have rounded back vowels (note: excluded from this count are languages with asymmetries such as /ɛ/ vs. /o/ in the absence of /ɔ/ and /e/, or /i/ vs. /o/ in the absence of /u/ and /e/; if these asymmetries were included, they would raise greatly the number of languages with asymmetrical rounded back vowels). These data show that rounding in velar vowels does not necessarily serve the purpose of increasing the acoustic distance between [+back] and [-back] vowels.

In the case of velars preceded by /s/, there is additional process of assimilation to coronality, followed by cluster simplification.

Velar fronting is analyzed as the spreading of the dorsal node of a vowel onto the constriction node of a velar consonant.[6] It is formalized in (7):

(7) Velar fronting:

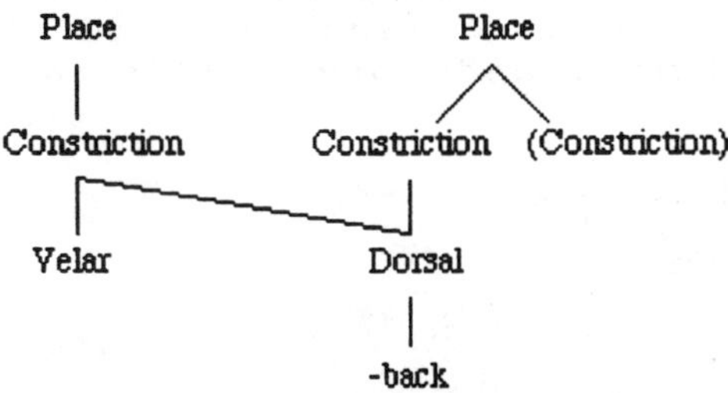

The analysis I have just proposed faces a potential problem: it treats the /ʉ/ of Swedish as a fronted velar, despite the fact that articulatorily, this vowel does not have a velar component. It's constriction is entirely palatal. While I am not prepared to solve it away, I would like to suggest that perhaps the problem is not that serious: as noted by Keating and Lahiri (1992), fronted velar stops, which, given the proposal I am making, are to be viewed as consonantal counterparts of /ʉ/, do not have the velar component either; they too are articulated against the hard palate. What Keating and Lahiri observe, however, is that the area of the hard palate against which fronted velar stops are articulated is towards the back of the hard palate, and it is not the same as the area against which true palatals are articulated. If it could be shown that fronted velar consonants and fronted velar vowels share the constriction location, the only remaining question would be why fronted velars have the constriction location shifted away from the soft palate.

In the literature on Swedish vowels I have not found a detailed analysis of the constriction locations in /y/ and /ʉ/. However, the acoustic data for the two vowels, shown in (8), suggest that /y/ ought to have a more anterior constriction than /ʉ/, given that its second formant is much higher than the second formant of /ʉ/. Since both vowels are rounded, this difference cannot be all due to the difference in labiality.

(8) Front rounded vowels in Swedish (the range in parentheses):

	F_1	F_2	F_3
/y/:	285 (236-360)	2065 (1806-2304)	2580 (2380-2747)
/ʉ/	277 (202-316)	1748 (1675-1823)	2221 (2120-2414)

(Linker 1982)

---

6 See Gorecka (1989, 1991) for arguments supporting this view of velar fronting.

Next, let us turn to high front rounded vowels outside of Swedish. The proposal I am making predicts that these vowels should fall into two categories: those which phonetically and phonologically pattern with the Swedish vowel /y/, and those which phonetically and phonologically are aligned with /ʉ/. I now proceed to show that this indeed is the case.

In (9) below, I have compiled acoustical data for high front rounded vowels from various languages. They are divided into two categories, based on the value of the second formant. I adopt the transcription practice employed in the literature on Swedish, and transcribe the vowels with the higher second formant as /y/, and the vowels with the lower second formant as /ʉ/.

(9) High front rounded vowels outside of Swedish:

(a) Vowels with F_2 of 1950 cps or more:

	F_1	F_2	F_3
Korean /y/ (Han 1963):	318	1959	unavailable
Cantonese /y/ (Linker 1982):	273 (208-396)	1986 (1800-2058)	2550 (2308-2765)
Mandarin /y/ (Svantesson 1984):	292 (210-380)	2040 (1820-2220)	2501 (2340-2670)
Canadian French /y/ (Gendron 1966):	250	2000	unavailable

(b) Vowels with F_2 of 1800 cps or less:

	F_1	F_2	F_3
French /ʉ/ (Linker 1982):	292 (227-465)	1761 (1531-1943)	2291 (2117-2695)
Finnish /ʉ/ (Linker (1982)):	344 (248-542)	1702 (1540-1953)	2270 (2115-2497)
Estonian /ʉ/ (Liiv and Remmel 1970):	255 (225-338)	1813 (1550-1950)	2172 (1850-2550)
German /ʉ/ (Jørgensen 1969):	242 (222-276)	1675 (1571-1840)	2059 (1925-2265)

Hungarian /ʉ/ (Magdics 1969):

284 (250-400)	1850 (1700-1900)	2529 (2500-2550)

Dutch /ʉ/ (Disner 1983)

305 (240-400)	1695 (1340-2100)[7]	2251 (1900-2900)

The data in (9) reveal that with the possible exception of Dutch (but see footnotes 7 and 9), high front rounded vowels do not take advantage of the available acoustic space, but rather, align with one or the other Swedish vowel.

Next, let us consider the phonology of these vowels. The prediction is that vowels in (9a), (with the higher second formant) should display palatalizing properties in languages with palatalization phenomena. The vowels in (9b), on the other hand, should be capable of triggering frontness harmony and velar fronting, but should never display palatalizing properties. This prediction is borne out by the facts, as shown below.

In the transition from Middle Chinese to Mandarin (segment inventory of Mandarin (Maddieson 1984): p, p^h, m, f, t, t^h, ts. ts^h, s, l, n, ʈʂ, $ʈʂ^h$, ʂ, ʐ, cç, $cç^h$, ç, j, k, k^h, ŋ, x, ɥ, w, i, y, u, ə, ʌ, a), the vowel which today aligns with the Swedish /y/ acoustically, patterned with the high front vowel in the palatalization of velars and dental fricatives:

(10) Palatalization of velars and dental fricatives in Mandarin:

<u>Middle Chinese</u>	<u>Mandarin</u>	
syan	çyan	'to declare'
ɣyan	çyan	'to hang'
tsiai	cçi	'sacrifice'
kiai	cçi	'to continue'

(Chen 1976)

While this is no longer a productive process in Standard Mandarin, there is a secret language based on the principle Fan-che, reported by Chao (1931), which does have a productive rule of velar palatalization. In this language, the original initial is appended with the final /-ai/, and the original final is prefixed with the voiceless velar stop. If the original final begins with either /i/ or /y/, the velar turns into a palatal affricate:

---

[7] There are two points to be made about the unusually broad F2 range of the Dutch vowel: (1) Even though the range begins at 1340 cps, in Disner's sample (the total of 34 measurements), the bulk of /ʉ/ tokens have F2 between 1540 and 1850. There are only two tokens in the sample with F2 below 1500: since these values are unusual for any front vowel, and since they are unrepresentative of the sample, perhaps they should not be viewed as representative of the vowel's acoustic properties. (2) There are six tokens in Disner's sample with the F2 of 1900 cps or more. In view of phonological evidence quoted in Zonneveld (1978), I am led to believe that there is dialectal variation in the language: while the majority of Dutch speakers produce /ʉ/, a small number produce /y/. See the footnote 9 for more discussion of this variation.

(11) Velar palatalization in the secret language Fan-che:

pu	-->	pai- ku	'cloth'	fu	-->	fai-ku	'mother'
cçy	-->	cçyɛ-cçy	'go'	çyan	-->	çyɛ-cçyan	'propaganda'
liŋ	-->	liɛ-cçiŋ	'order'	mɑ	-->	mai-kɑ	'mother'

(Chao 1931)

Next, in Korean (segment inventory of Korean (Maddieson 1984): p, pʰ, p', m, t, tʰ, t', s, s', n, l, č, čʰ, č', j, k, kʰ, k', ŋ, h, w, i, y, u, ɯ, e, ø, o, ʌ, æ, a, i:, y:, u:, ɯ:, e:, ø:, o:, ʌ:, æ:, a:), /y/ patterns with the high front vowel in the palatalization of dentals, as shown in (12):

(12) Palatalization in Korean:

sihəm --> śihəm	'exam'	əməni --> əməɲi	'mother'
talli --> taʎʎi	'to run'	sympʰjo --> śympʰjo	'comma'
čʰolyn --> čʰoʎyn	'rel. law'	ny --> ɲy	'who'

In Canadian French[8] (segment inventory of Canadian French (Walker 1984): p, b, m, f, v, t, d, s, z, n, l, š, ž, ɲ, k, g, ʀ, i, y, u, e, ø, o, ɛ, œ, ə, a, ɑ, ɛ̃, œ̃, ɔ̃, ɑ̃), /y/ patterns with /i/ in the assibilation of dentals:

(13) Assibilation in Canadian French:

tip --> tsip 'type' tyb --> tsyb 'tube'

(Walker 1984)

It is not clear to me why the output of this process is an alveolar, instead of a palato-alveolar or a palatal. At this point I can only speculate that perhaps alveolars are first palatalized before palatal vowels, and that assibilation applies to palatalized alveolars, rather than plain alveolars.

The vowels with F_2 in the range of 1700-1800 cps pattern both with the [-back] and with velar vowels. For example, in harmony processes in Finnish and Hungarian, they align with the front vowels. In Dutch, however (segment inventory of Dutch, Ruhlen 1975, Collins and Mees 1981): p, b, m, f, v, t, d, s, z, n, l, r, č, š, k, x, ŋ, i, ʉ, u, e:, ø:, o:, a:, ɪ, ɛ, ɑ, ɔ, ə), a vowel with these acoustic properties fails to pattern with other front vowels in the process of hiatus resolution. In this process, all front vowels (including the mid front rounded vowel) trigger insertion of the palatal glide, while the non-low back vowels trigger the insertion of the labio-velar glide. /ʉ/ patterns with /u/ and /o/ by triggering the insertion of the labio-velar glide, as shown below:

---

[8] I am grateful to Diana Archangeli for directing my attention to these facts.

(14) Hiatus resolution in Dutch:[9]

dija: mant	'diamond'	pa: rija:	'pariah'
bløje	'shy'	se: jul	'Seoul'
duwa: ne	'customs'	sa: mo: wa	'Samoa'
flʉwor	'fluor'	rʉwind	'ruin'

(Zonneveld 1978)

4. The summary

I've set out to show in this paper that a model of feature representation which reconciles passive and active articulator features makes accurate predictions about possible high front rounded vowels. I believe I have accomplished this goal by documenting the phonological effects that are predicted by the model.

One of the advantages of the the view of high front rounded vowels I have presented is that it eliminates all inconsistencies between the representations and the phonological patterning of these vowels. Consider the range of phonological effects associated with high front rounded vowels (in addition to the fact that two different phonetic types fall under HFRV label): without the representations I am proposing, and on the assumption that feature systems based on the SPE tradition are sufficient, one is forced to recognize only one representation associated with the HFRV label: a segment that is [+round, -back, +high]. But then, one must face a number of cases in which a high front rounded vowel patterns in a manner inconsistent with the assumed representation: it fails to trigger palatalization in a language with a palatalization process, it patterns with back vowels, even though it itself is [-back]. These problems do not arise within the model of segment representation I am advocating.

References:

Chao, Y.-R. 1931. Eight Varieties of Secret Language Based on the Principle of Fan-che. *Bulletin of the National Research Institute of History and Philology*, vol II, part 3:312-354.

Chen, M. Y. 1976. From Middle Chinese to Modern Peking. *Journal of Chinese Linguistics* 4:113-277.

---

9 Zonneveld (1978) reports that there are some speakers of Dutch who insert a palatal glide after the high front rounded vowel, if the vowel is stressed. Could this be related to the fact that some speakers of Dutch seem to produce /y/ rather than /ʉ/? Recall from footnote 7 that the sample on which I have based the acoustic data for Dutch included six tokens of a /y/-like vowel. It would be interesting to find out whether the speakers who insert a palatal glide after a stressed high front rounded vowel also happen to pronounce this vowel as /y/, not as /ʉ/.

Collins, B. and I. Mees 1981. *The Sounds of English and Dutch.* Hague: Leiden University Press.

Disner, S. F. 1983. *Vowel Quality. The Relation between Universal and Language-Specific Factors.* UCLA Working Papers in Phonetics No. 58, Los Angeles: University of California.

Fant, G. 1971. Notes on the Swedish Vowel System. In Hammerich, Jakobson, and Zwirner, (eds.) 259-268.

Gendron, J.-D. 1966. *Tendances Phonetiques du Français Parle´au Canada.* Québec: Les Presses de L'Université Laval.

Gorecka, A. 1989. *Phonology of Articulation.* Doctoral dissertation, MIT.

Gorecka, A. 1991. Palatalized Velars and the Representation of Front Vowels. Presented at WECOL 1991, Vancouver. To appear in the proceedings.

Hammarberg, R. 1970. Umlaut and Vowel Shift in Swedish. *Papers in Linguistics* 3:477-501. Champaign, Ill: Linguistic Research Inc.

Hammerich, L. L., R. Jakobson, and E. Zwirner, eds. 1971. *Form and Substance.* Copenhagen: Akademisk Forlag.

Han, M. S. 1963. *Acoustic Phonetics of Korean.* Technical Report No. 1. Los Angeles: University of California.

Jørgensen, H.-P. 1969. Die gespannten und ungespannten Vokale in der norddeutschen Hochsprache, mit einer spezifischen Untersuchung der Struktur ihrer Formantenfrequenzen. *Phonetica* 19:217-245.

Keating, P. and A. Lahiri, 1992. Articulatory and Acoustic Differences between Palatal and Velar Stops. Ms, UCLA and MPI.

Kiefer, F. 1970. *Swedish Morphology.* Stockholm: Skriptor.

Liiv, G. and M. Remmel 1970. On Acoustic Distinctions in the Estonian Vowel System. *Soviet Fenno-Ugric Studies* 6:7-23.

Lindau, M. 1978. Vowel Features. *Language* 54:541-562.

Linell, P. 1973. /ʉ/; On the Phonology of the Swedish Vowel System. *Studia Linguistica* 27:1-52.

Linker, W. 1982. *Articulatory and Acoustic Correlates of Labial Activity in Vowels: A Crosslinguistic Study.* UCLA Working Papers in Phonetics 56, Los Angeles: University of California.

Maddieson, I. 1984. *Patterns of Sounds*. Cambridge: Cambridge University Press.

Magdics, K. 1969. *Studies in the Acoustic Characteristics of Hungarian Speech Sounds*. Uralic and Altaic Series, vol. 97. Bloomington: Indiana University Publications.

McCarthy, J. 1989. *Guttural Phonology*. Ms. University of Massachusetts at Amherst.

Perkell, J. S. and D. H. Klatt, eds. 1986. *Invariance and Variability in Speech Processes*. Hillsdale, New Jersey: Lawrence Erlbaum Associates.

Ruhlen, M. 1975. *A Guide to the Languages of the World*. Language Universals Project, Stanford University.

Sagey, E. C. 1986. *The Representation of Features and Relations in Non-Linear Phonology*. Doctoral dissertation, MIT.

Steriade, D. 1986. Locality Conditions and Feature Geometry. *NELS 17*, GLSA. Amherst: University of Massachusetts.

Stevens, K. N., S. J. Keyser, and H. Kawasaki 1986. Toward a Phonetic and Phonological Theory of Redundant Features. In: Perkell and Klatt, eds. 426-449.

Svantesson, J.-O. 1984. Vowels and Diphthongs in Standard Chinese. *Lund University Department of Linguistics Working Papers* 27.

Walker, D. C. 1984. *The Pronunciation of Canadian French*. Ottawa: University of Ottawa Press.

Zonneveld, V. 1978. *A Formal Theory of Exceptions in Generative Phonology*. Dordrecht: Foris Publications.

Head Movement and the Licensing of Non-Thematic Positions

CAROLINE HEYCOCK & BEATRICE SANTORINI
Oakland University & Northwestern University

1. Introduction

Adopting an idea originally due to Fillmore (1968) and McCawley (1970), a number of syntacticians have recently argued in favor of the VP-Internal Subject Hypothesis—the view that clausal subjects are generated not in their superficial Spec(IP) position, but rather within a projection of the verb, like other arguments (Fukui 1986, Fukui and Speas 1986, Sportiche 1988, Koopman and Sportiche 1991, among many others).[1] According to this hypothesis, subjects occupy Spec(IP) at S-Structure because they raise into this position. Further, since Spec(IP) is never assigned a θ-role, it is expected to pattern together with A′-positions like Spec(CP) rather than with A-positions. As we discuss in Section 2.1, this expectation is confirmed straightforwardly in Yiddish, where the appearance in Spec(IP) of constituents other than the subject is clear evidence for its A′ character. However, in Section 2.2 we show that the availability of Spec(IP) in Yiddish as a landing site for nonsubjects is not completely general, for Spec(IP) is restricted to subjects in certain syntactic contexts—namely, when the inflected verb moves from I^0 to C^0, as it does in matrix questions and in some instances of long-distance extraction. In Section 3, we argue that this restriction follows from a general principle that nonthematic positions like Spec(IP) cannot be licensed before S-Structure, and hence that they are crucially affected by movement of the licensing head between D- and S-Structure. We show in Section 4 that our analysis is supported by synchronic and diachronic evidence from Yiddish and other verb-second (V2) languages. Finally, in Section 5, we briefly address the implications of our analysis for the nature of nonthematic positions in general.

[1] We would like to thank David Braun and Mikhl Herzog for their judgments on Yiddish, Bob Frank, Naoki Fukui and Anthony Kroch for helpful discussion, and the audience at WCCFL XI for their spirited response.

2. V2 in Yiddish

2.1 Spec(IP) as an A′-position

Yiddish, like most Germanic languages, is a V2 language—that is, the position preceding the inflected verb need not be occupied by the subject, but may instead be occupied by some other argument or by an adjunct, as long as the inflected verb occupies second position, as illustrated in (1):

(1) a. **Vayn** ken men makhn fun troybn oykh.
wine can one make from grapes also
'One can make wine from grapes also.'

b. **Hayntike tsaytn** kenen fil mentshn afile nit leyenen.
today's times can many people even not read
'Nowadays, many people can't even read.'

According to the most influential analysis of V2, originally proposed for Dutch and German by Thiersch (1978) and den Besten (1983), the inflected verb in a V2 clause moves to C^0 and some XP moves to Spec(CP), as sketched in (2):

(2) $[_{CP}\ XP_i\ [_{C'}\ V{+}Infl_j\ [_{IP} \ldots\ t_i \ldots\ t_j\ ]]]$

A major strength of this analysis is that it accounts straightforwardly for the absence of V2 subordinate clauses in Dutch and German. In these 'asymmetrical' V2 languages, whenever C^0 is occupied by a complementizer, the inflected verb must stay within IP. However, unlike Dutch and German, Yiddish is what we will call a 'symmetrical' V2 language—that is, it is V2 not only in main clauses, but in all types of subordinate clauses as well (Diesing 1988, 1990, Santorini 1989). This is illustrated in the examples from Vikner (1991, 82–92) given in (3) ((3a) = his (90d), (3b) = his (95a)):

(3) a. John bedoyert az **zayn bukh** hob ikh geleyent.
regrets that his book have I read
'John regrets that I read his book.'

b. Ikh veys nit farvos **in tsimer** iz di ku geshtanen.
I know not why in room is the cow stood
'I don't know why the cow stood in the room.'

The absence of a main clause/subordinate clause asymmetry in Yiddish means that Thiersch's and den Besten's analysis of V2 does not extend straightforwardly to this language.

In order to bring Yiddish into line with the standard analysis, it has been proposed that embedded clauses like those in (3) are instances of CP recursion. For example, Vikner (1991) would give the embedded clause in (3a) the structure in (4):

(4) Derived structure of (3a)—CP recursion analysis:
... [$_{CP1}$ [$_{C'1}$ az [$_{CP2}$ zayn bukh [$_{C'2}$ hob [$_{IP}$ ikh ...]]]]]

We reject a CP recursion analysis of embedded V2 in Yiddish for two reasons. Firstly, in languages like Frisian and Swedish, where CP recursion is independently motivated by word order facts, embedded V2 is restricted to embedded clauses that are asserted (de Haan and Weerman 1986, Holmberg 1986, Platzack 1986)—a restriction that does not hold in Yiddish (den Besten and Moed-van Walraven 1986, Diesing 1988, 1990, Santorini 1989). Secondly, in languages in which CP recursion is independently motivated, no extraction from recursive CPs is possible.[2] By contrast, Diesing (1990) has shown that nonsubject-initial subordinate clauses in Yiddish allow extraction. This is illustrated in (5) (Diesing 1990, 62, her (30)):

(5) Vemen$_i$ hot er nit gevolt
who(DAT) has he not wanted
[$_{CP}$ t_i [$_{C'}$ az **ot di bikher** zoln mir gebn t_i]]?
that *prt* the books should we give
'To whom did he not want us to give *these* books?'

From these two facts, we conclude that CP recursion is not the proper analysis for embedded V2 clauses in Yiddish.

Instead, following much recent work (Diesing 1988, 1990, Santorini 1989, Cardinaletti and Roberts 1991; cf. also Rögnvaldsson and Thráinsson 1990 and Kosmeijer 1991 for Icelandic), we propose to resolve the dilemma raised by the acceptability of embedded V2 clauses in Yiddish by adopting the VP-Internal Subject Hypothesis. Specifically, we assume that rather than moving into C^0, as in asymmetrical V2 languages, the inflected verb in Yiddish moves no further than I^0. Moreover, we assume that the subject in Yiddish may remain in its base-generated VP-internal position, receiving nominative case under government from I^0 (we discuss case-assignment in detail in Section 3.2). If the subject remains within VP, Spec(IP), as a vacant A′-position, is available for occupation by any other XP (movement of the subject itself to Spec(IP) is, of course, equally possible). Thus, we take the structure of (3a) to be as in (6):

(6) Derived structure of (3a)—verb movement to I^0 analysis:
... [$_{CP}$ [$_{C'}$ az [$_{IP}$ zayn bukh [$_{I'}$ hob [$_{VP}$ ikh ...]]]]]

[2] It might be proposed that extraction from recursive CPs is ruled out because the additional CP counts as a barrier for subjacency. However, the island effect of recursive CPs is unexpectedly strong for a subjacency violation. Holmberg (1986, 111) describes extraction from recursive CPs in Swedish as 'completely unacceptable', regardless of whether the lower Spec(CP) is occupied by the subject or some other constituent. However this strong unacceptability is to be explained, it strengthens the point that CP recursion is not the correct analysis for the Yiddish examples.

In sum, then, the proposal that V2 in Yiddish involves movement of the inflected verb to I^0 together with A′-movement of some XP to Spec(IP) accounts directly for the occurrence of V2 in both main and subordinate clauses.

2.2 Restrictions on Spec(IP)

While Spec(IP) is generally available as a landing site for A′-movement in Yiddish, it is striking that there are syntactic contexts where the only element that can move to Spec(IP) is the subject (cf. Vikner 1991, 97f.). One such context is matrix questions, where the verb moves from I^0 on into C^0, as illustrated by the contrast in (7):

(7) a. [$_{CP}$ Vemen$_i$ [$_{C'}$ zoln [$_{IP}$ **mir**$_j$ [$_{VP}$ t_j gebn t_i ot di bikher]]]]?
who(DAT) should we give *prt* the books
'To whom should we give *these* books?'

b. *[$_{CP}$ Vemen$_i$ [$_{C'}$ zoln [$_{IP}$ **ot di bikher**$_j$ [$_{VP}$ mir gebn t_i t_j]]]]?
who(DAT) should *prt* the books we give
Intended reading: as (7a)

Similarly, Spec(IP) must be occupied by the subject in subordinate clauses where the verb has moved on to C^0, as it may in long-distance extractions (Diesing 1990, 71–75). Thus, we find contrasts as in (8):

(8) a. Vemen$_i$ hot er nit gevolt
who(DAT) has he not wanted
[$_{CP}$ t_i [$_{C'}$ zoln [$_{IP}$ **mir**$_j$ [$_{VP}$ t_j gebn t_i ot di bikher]]]]?
should we give *prt* the books
'To whom didn't he want us to give *these* books?'

b. *Vemen$_i$ hot er nit gevolt
who(DAT) has he not wanted
[$_{CP}$ t_i [$_{C'}$ zoln [$_{IP}$ **ot di bikher**$_j$ [$_{VP}$ mir gebn t_i t_j]]]]?
should *prt* the books we give
Intended reading: as (8a)

Since both of the ungrammatical examples in (7b) and (8b) involve extraction past an A′-position (the Spec(IP) position), it might be proposed that their ungrammaticality is a consequence of Relativized Minimality (Rizzi 1990a): the element in Spec(IP), as an A′-element intervening between the extracted *wh*-phrase and its trace, would block antecedent government of the trace. However, Relativized Minimality does not account for the data presented here. Since the source of the ungrammaticality under this approach is the intervention of the element in the lower Spec(IP), the position of the inflected verb in the clause from which extraction takes place should be irrelevant, and the contrast between the unacceptable (8b) and the acceptable (5)—a sentence identical to (8b) except that the verb has remained in I^0 rather than moving on to C^0—is unexplained. In fact, the final version of the system of Relativized Minimality set out in Rizzi (1990a) requires antecedent government only in the case of extracted adjuncts. Thus, since argument traces needn't be antecedent governed, Relativized Minimality actually turns out not to bear on examples like (5) and (8b), both of which should violate only subjacency.

The type of extraction that is ruled out by Relativized Minimality is the extraction of an adjunct past an element in an A′-position, since traces of adjuncts violate the ECP unless they are antecedent governed. But contrary to this prediction, extracting an adjunct from a nonsubject-initial IP is possible in Yiddish, as shown in (9a).[3] Again, however, we find the same contrast that we observed between (5) and (8b): movement of the verb to the embedded C^0, as in (9b), gives rise to ungrammaticality.

(9) a. Ven/vu$_i$ hot er nit gevolt
when/where has he not wanted
[$_{CP}$ t_i [$_{C'}$ az [$_{IP}$ **ot di bikher**$_j$ zoln [$_{VP}$ mir leyenen t_j t_i]]]]?
that *prt* the books should we read
'When$_i$/where$_i$ didn't he want us to read *these* books t_i?'

b. *Ven/vu$_i$ hot er nit gevolt
when/where has he not wanted
[$_{CP}$ t_i [$_{C'}$ zoln [$_{IP}$ **ot di bikher**$_j$ [$_{VP}$ mir leyenen t_j t_i]]]]?
should *prt* the books we read
Intended reading: as (9a)

We conclude from the above discussion that Relativized Minimality fails to provide insight into the contrasts in (7) and (8), and that we must look elsewhere for an account of them.

3. Licensing of nonthematic positions at S-Structure

In this section, we present our solution to the puzzle raised by the contrasts in (7) and (8). To restate the puzzle: we have seen that what can fill Spec(IP) in Yiddish depends on the S-Structure position of the inflected verb: if the inflected verb is in I^0, Spec(IP) can be filled by any maximal projection, whether argument or adjunct, but if the inflected verb moves on to C^0, Spec(IP) can only be filled by the (nominative) subject.

To understand this restriction, it is necessary to consider the question of licensing. It is generally agreed that all positions in a well-formed syntactic structure must be licensed by any of various types of licensing relations. Three

[3]Not all Yiddish speakers accept long-distance extraction from nonsubject-initial clauses (cf. Vikner 1991, 118). The corresponding judgments in Icelandic, which we expect to pattern with Yiddish, vary as well: while Zaenen (1980) reports long-distance extraction from nonsubject-initial clauses to be ungrammatical, some speakers do accept it, regardless of whether it is an argument or an adjunct that is extracted (Höskuldur Thráinsson, pers. comm.; Iatridou and Kroch 1992).

of the most important are θ-assignment, predication, and case-assignment. θ-assignment takes place at D-Structure: in fact, the most restrictive view of D-Structure is that the only positions present at this level are those licensed by θ-assignment. Positions not licensed by θ-assignment may be licensed by predication. As established by Rothstein (1983) and Heycock (1991), this type of licensing holds at S-Structure. Since θ-positions are licensed at D-Structure, while the positions of subjects of predication are licensed at S-Structure, it follows straightforwardly that elements may move from positions licensed by θ-assignment to positions licensed by predication, but not vice versa. The third type of syntactic licensing mechanism is case-assignment. Case may be assigned both to thematic and to nonthematic positions. In this paper, we will assume that case can be assigned either at D-Structure or S-Structure. However, maintaining the strict view that D-Structure is a pure projection of θ-Structure, we propose that case-assignment cannot license D-Structure positions that are not licensed independently by θ-assignment. Consequently, case-assignment as an independent licensing mechanism becomes relevant only at S-Structure. The above discussion is summed up in the principle in (10):

(10) Nonthematic positions are licensed only at S-Structure.

As already mentioned, the fact that nonthematic positions are not licensed before S-Structure explains why licensed elements cannot move from a position licensed only by predication into a position licensed by θ-assignment. What has been overlooked, however, is the effect of moving the licensing element itself. Since licensing of nonthematic positions cannot take place before S-Structure, it is to be expected that, if a licensing head moves, it will license from its S-Structure position. This, we argue, is exactly what our data show.

3.1 Licensing of Spec(IP) by predication

We begin by considering the licensing of Spec(IP) in Yiddish when the verb has moved to I^0. As in any other V2 language, some maximal projection must move to the clause-initial position immediately preceding the inflected verb—which, following convention, we refer to as the topic position.[4] We assume that the topic position in V2 languages, whether Spec(IP) as in Yiddish or Spec(CP) as in German, is licensed (and required) because a constituent whose head is [+V] constitutes a syntactic predicate that must be saturated (Holmberg 1986, Taraldsen 1986, Rizzi 1990b, Heycock 1991). Thus, since V-to-I movement in Yiddish results in an I^0 that is [+V] at S-Structure, Spec(IP) is licensed by predication.

Notice that in V2 clauses in German, it is Spec(CP) that is licensed by predication, rather than Spec(IP) as in Yiddish. Given what we have said about the licensing of nonthematic positions, this follows straightforwardly from the fact that the inflected verb in a German V2 clause occupies C^0 at

[4]Yiddish also exhibits superficially verb-initial clauses; following Diesing (1990, 56), we assume that such clauses contain an empty operator in Spec(IP).

S-Structure. If we make the reasonable assumption that the relationship between licensing mechanisms and the positions licensed by them is a one-to-one relationship, then it follows that Spec(IP) in German cannot be licensed by predication, since Spec(CP) must be. More generally, we would expect that in Yiddish also, Spec(IP) can no longer be licensed by predication if the verb moves on from I^0 to C^0. Thus, while Spec(IP)—the position occupied by *ot di bikher*—is licensed by predication in (5), it is not so licensed in sentences like (7b) and (8b).

Clearly, however, there must be some way of licensing the position in question, since otherwise the acceptable (7a) and (8a) would incorrectly be ruled out on a par with their unacceptable (b) counterparts. The crucial distinction between the (a) and the (b) sentences in (7) and (8) is that Spec(IP) in the (a) sentences is occupied by a nominative NP. This is the clue to the solution we propose: namely, that when the inflected verb moves from I^0 to C^0, Spec(IP) is licensed not by predication, but by nominative case-assignment. Moreover, since Spec(IP) is a nonthematic position, it must be that nominative case is assigned from the S-Structure location of the case-assigner: that is, from C^0. In what follows, we outline an analysis of nominative case-assignment that is consistent with the considerations just discussed.

3.2 Nominative case-assignment

Following Rizzi (1990b), let us assume that just as lexical categories are defined in terms of combinations of the features [N] and [V], so functional categories are defined in terms of the features [C] and [I]. Specifically, Rizzi assumes that in addition to 'pure' C^0 ([+C ,–I]) and 'pure' I^0 ([–C, +I]), there exists a 'hybrid' head with the feature composition [+C, +I]. It is this hybrid category that acts as the head of V2 clauses in languages with a main clause/subordinate clause asymmetry like German. While Rizzi's discussion is restricted to such asymmetrical V2 languages, it can be extended to accommodate symmetrical V2 languages like Yiddish if we take the location of the highest [+I] category in a V2 clause to be subject to parametric variation (Diesing 1990, Kosmeijer 1991, Santorini 1992). Specifically, we assume that in asymmetrical V2 languages, the highest [+I] category is C^0 (which is therefore hybrid). In symmetrical V2 languages like Yiddish, on the other hand, the highest [+I] category is I^0 (we return directly to the status of languages like English, where I^0 is also the highest [+I] category, but which are non-V2).[5]

[5]Rizzi (1990b, 383) takes C^0 in German subordinate clauses to be [–I]; thus, for him, the highest [+I] category in subordinate clauses in asymmetrical V2 languages is I^0 rather than C^0. By contrast, we assume that C^0 is hybrid in asymmetrical V2 languages in both main and subordinate clauses (cf. Vikner 1991, 74f.). If the highest [+I] category in a clause assigns nominative case (see below), then Rizzi's analysis would lead us to expect nominative case-assignment in subordinate clauses to be parallel in German and Yiddish. Specifically, nonsubjects should be able to occupy Spec(IP) in subordinate clauses in German, contrary to what is true in main clauses. Although clause-initial nonsubjects are possible in German subordinate clauses, this turns out not to provide conclusive evidence in favor of Rizzi's analysis, since such word orders might also be derived by scrambling, which

We further assume that nominative case is assigned by the highest [+I] category of a (finite) clause under head-government, which we define as in (11); we adopt a first branching node definition of c-command, as in (12).[6]

(11) Definition of head-government:
 (i) X is a lexical head or is [+I],
 (ii) X c-commands Y,
 (iii) minimality is respected.

(12) Definition of c-command:
 X c-commands Y iff the node immediately dominating X dominates Y.

In Yiddish, the highest [+I] category in a V2 clause is I^0, which can therefore assign nominative case to the underlying subject position. As a result, Spec(IP) is available for other arguments or adjuncts to move into. In German, on the other hand, the highest [+I] category in a V2 clause is C^0. We assume that considerations of minimality prevent nominative case from being assigned to the underlying subject position, since I^0 is a closer potential head-governor. Nominative case must therefore be assigned to Spec(IP), since otherwise a well-formedness condition requiring a one-to-one relationship between case-assigners and case-receivers would not be met (Platzack and Holmberg 1990, 8). Nominative case-assignment in Yiddish clauses in which the inflected verb has moved to C^0 is parallel to the German case, and the same considerations of minimality force nominative case to be assigned to Spec(IP).

The question arises why Spec(IP) cannot be filled by nonsubjects in English, where I^0 is the highest [+I] category, just as it is in Yiddish. We propose to derive this difference between English and Yiddish from a separate parameter: namely, the composition of Agr (which we take to be a feature of Infl). Following Platzack and Holmberg (1990, 6), we distinguish between two types of Agr: a type that is [+N] and inherently nominative, and a type that is categorially neutral.[7] We take the morphological correlate of this distinction to be

is independently motivated. However, if the expletive topic *es* is taken to be barred from governed positions (cf. Kosmeijer 1991), then its parallel distribution in main and subordinate clauses—specifically, its unacceptability in post-C^0 positions—provides evidence in favor of our view.

[6]The definition of head-government in (11) is inspired by that proposed by Platzack and Holmberg (1990, 7), according to whom nominative case is assigned under head-government by a head containing the finiteness operator [+F] (cf. Pollock 1989). However, in Platzack and Holmberg's definition a head-governor must m-command, rather than c-command, its governee. Empirical justification of the c-command condition based on the distribution of empty and lexical expletives in Yiddish is given in Santorini (1991, 1992); cf. also Déprez (1989, 366–373), Koopman and Sportiche (1991, 229f.) and Rizzi (1990a, 30–32) for relevant discussion.

[7]It is worth noting that the distinction between nominative and neutral AGR is (roughly) equivalent in empirical coverage to the distinction made by Koopman and Sportiche (1991) between nominative case-assignment under Spec-head agreement and under head-government.

the presence of overt case-marking on full noun phrases (Santorini 1991 and references cited therein); specifically, we take Agr to be inherently nominative in languages with an overt morphological distinction between nominative and oblique case on full noun phrases, and neutral in languages without this distinction.[8] We can then state the distribution of subjects in terms of the licensing condition in (13).

(13) Licensing condition on Agr:
Agr must be identified as nominative.

In languages with inherently nominative Agr, the licensing condition in (13) is met trivially; in languages with neutral Agr, on the other hand, Agr must be identified under antecedent government (by being locally c-commanded by an antecedent bearing nominative case).[9] As a result, although we take nominative case to be assigned to the underlying subject position under government in both English and Yiddish, subjects must move to Spec(IP) in English in order to satisfy (13), but need not do so in Yiddish.[10] Independent diachronic evidence in favor of the analysis we have just presented, according to which the possibility of embedded V2 is related (among other things) to the presence of case morphology, comes from Old French, which lost case-marking on noun phrases (that is, the overt distinction between nominative and oblique case) at about the same time as the possibility of nonsubjects in Spec(IP) (Cardinaletti and Roberts 1991, 55–56).

3.3 Summary

To summarize this section: we have argued that the V+Infl complex can license the nonthematic position Spec(IP) in two ways: first, as the [+V] head of a predicate, it can license Spec(IP) via predication; second, as the [+I] source of nominative case, it can license Spec(IP) via case-assignment. Since nonthematic positions are not licensed until S-Structure, licensing in both of these cases is carried out from the S-Structure position of the V+Infl complex. Consequently, if the V+Infl complex occupies C^0, as it does in matrix questions and subordinate clauses with subject-verb inversion, Spec(IP) is no longer licensed by predication, as it would be if the verb had remained in I^0; instead it is licensed by nominative case-assignment from C^0.

An important consequence of our analysis is that head-movement of a licensor has strikingly different implications for the licensing of nonthematic and thematic positions. Note that head-movement of a transitive verb does not

[8]In this respect, our analysis diverges from that of Platzack and Holmberg (1990, 22–28), who attempt to relate the distinction between nominative and neutral Agr to features of subject-verb agreement morphology.

[9]The identification of Agr as nominative in languages with neutral Agr is not circular since the identifying noun phrase is assigned nominative case not by Agr, but by [+I].

[10]Once Agr has been identified as nominative in English, I^0 can move on to C^0, as it does in matrix questions and in complementizerless conditional clauses of the type *Had I known in time*, without violating (13).

affect the licensing of its complement: the object need not move to a position licensed by the verb at S-Structure. This is shown by the grammaticality of examples like (14), where the verb has moved to C^0, but the object remains within the VP, in the same position in which it was licensed by θ-assignment at D-Structure:

(14) [$_{CP}$ Farvos [$_{C'}$ leyenen$_i$ [$_{IP}$ zey$_j$ t_i [$_{VP}$ t_j t_i ot di bikher?]]]]
why read they *prt* the books
'Why do they read *these* books?'

4. Further synchronic and diachronic arguments

Having presented our analysis of the contrasts in (7) and (8), we now discuss further synchronic and diachronic evidence in favor of it. As we will show, our analysis has two important advantages over an alternative analysis of the same facts proposed by Diesing (1990).

4.1 Unified account of restriction on Spec(IP) position in Yiddish

Recall that under our analysis the licensing of Spec(IP) depends crucially on the S-Structure position of the licensing head. That is, if the inflected verb moves to C^0, Spec(IP) is licensed by nominative case-assignment and is therefore restricted to the subject, regardless of whether the clause in question is a main clause or a subordinate clause. Thus, we give a unified analysis of the constraints on filling Spec(IP) in both clause types.

Diesing (1990, 50ff.) offers a different account for the impossibility of a nonsubject immediately following the inflected verb in matrix questions in Yiddish. She takes matrix questions in Yiddish to be IPs: the *wh*-operator occupies Spec(IP) and the verb moves no further than I^0, as sketched in (15):

(15) [$_{IP}$ *wh*-XP [$_{I'}$ V+Infl [$_{VP}$ Subject ...]]]

Under her analysis, the contrast in (7) follows very simply because the position immediately following the inflected verb is the position where the subject is base-generated, rather than Spec(IP) as under our analysis. However, Diesing's account fails to generalize to the parallel contrast in embedded clauses illustrated in (8). This is because Diesing, like us, assumes that embedded finite clauses are uniformly CPs, and hence that inversion in these clauses involves movement of the embedded verb to C^0. As it stands, her analysis therefore predicts that inverted embedded clauses, in contrast to matrix questions, should allow the order in which a nonsubject immediately follows the verb. But as we have seen, this prediction is incorrect: the position immediately following the inflected verb is no more available to nonsubjects in embedded clauses with inversion than it is in matrix questions.

4.2 Cross-linguistic evidence from Old English and Old French

In addition to giving a unified account of the restrictions on filling Spec(IP) in main and subordinate clauses in Yiddish, our analysis has the further advantage of allowing us to maintain the generalization that matrix questions are CPs in all V2 languages—and specifically, in all symmetrical V2 languages. While we know of no evidence for this generalization in Yiddish that is independent of assumptions concerning government and nominative case-assignment, there is striking cross-linguistic evidence that matrix questions are CPs in other symmetrical V2 languages like Old English and Old French. As Pintzuk (1991) observes, unstressed pronouns and adverbs in Old English do not count for V2; in particular, they can precede the inflected verb in V2 declarative clauses. This is illustrated for unstressed object pronouns in (16) (Pintzuk 1991, 206, her (30a)):

(16) þin agen geleafa **þe** hæfþ gehæledne.
your own faith you has healed
'Your own faith has healed you.'

In questions, however, the inflected verb must precede any light elements, as shown in (17) (Pintzuk 1991, 239, (83)):

(17) Hu lomp **eow** on lade?
how happened you on journey
'How did you fare on the journey?'

Pintzuk derives the different position of light elements in V2 declarative clauses and questions by proposing that they precede I^0 in both clause types, and that the inflected verb moves to I^0 in V2 declarative clauses, but to C^0 in questions. It is this difference in the landing site of the inflected verb that results in the postverbal position of light elements in questions.

A parallel asymmetry is encountered in Old French, where clitic pronouns precede the inflected verb in V2 declarative clauses, but must follow it in questions. This phenomenon—known as the 'Tobler-Mussafia law' among traditional Romance scholars—is illustrated in (18) (Adams 1987, 103, her (2f)) and (19) (Adams 1987, 158, her (24b)):

(18) Tu **m'** as amé celéement et jou toi.
you me have loved secretly and I you
'You have loved me secretly and I, you.'

(19) Conois **la** tu?
know her you
'Do you know her?'

Recent generative analyses, among them Adams (1987) and Cardinaletti and Roberts (1991), derive the Tobler-Mussafia law just as Pintzuk derives the

Old English facts in (16) and (17): namely, by assuming that inflected verbs move to I^0 in declarative V2 clauses, but to C^0 in matrix questions.

4.3 Diachronic evidence

In addition to providing synchronic evidence that matrix questions are CPs, Old English and Old French also provide diachronic evidence to this effect. These languages went from being symmetrical V2 languages (Adams 1988, Hirschbühler and Junker 1988, Dupuis 1989, Pintzuk 1991), in which V2 is uniformly observed in embedded clauses,[11] matrix declarative clauses and matrix questions, to being residual V2 languages (Rizzi 1991), where V2 is observed only in matrix questions. If the landing site of the inflected verb in symmetrical V2 languages were identical in both V2 declarative clauses and V2 questions, as Diesing (1990) suggests for Yiddish, then the separate historical development of these clause types in the other symmetrical V2 languages would be unexpected (cf. Maling and Zaenen 1981, 260). By contrast, since we take the landing site of the inflected verb to differ in matrix declaratives and matrix questions, the diachronic divergence of these two clause types in symmetrical V2 languages provides strong evidence in favor of our analysis.

In summary, there is both synchronic and diachronic evidence that our analysis has two advantages over the one proposed by Diesing (1990): first, it gives a unified account of the restrictions on Spec(IP) in main and subordinate clauses in Yiddish, and second, it allows us to maintain the generalization that matrix questions are CPs in all V2 languages.

5. Theoretical implications

In this paper, we have argued on the basis of data from Yiddish (and other V2 languages) for a principle that nonthematic positions are licensed at S-Structure, and not before; that is to say, we have argued in favor of a strict conception of D-Structure as containing only positions licensed by θ-assignment. An important consequence of this view is that movement to nonthematic positions cannot be substitution, since substitution means moving into a position that has been licensed at a previous level. As long as the clausal subject position was conceived of as being generated at D-Structure regardless of the thematic properties of the verb—a violation of the Projection Principle sanctioned only by the stipulation that the [NP,S] position is obligatorily present at D-Structure (Chomsky 1981, 40f., Chomsky 1982, 9f.)—the idea of movement as substitution could be maintained. More recent work, however (Rothstein 1983, Stowell 1983, Heycock 1991), has shown that the requirement that clauses have a subject is only a special case of a general principle of predication, which is imposed on S-Structure rather than D-Structure.

[11]In addition to INFL-medial clauses, Old English also allowed INFL-final subordinate clauses, like modern Dutch and German (van Kemenade 1987, Pintzuk 1991), and INFL-final subordinate clauses are marginally attested in Old French as well (Adams 1988). The existence of synchronic variation between INFL-final and INFL-medial phrase structure is orthogonal to the present discussion.

Since movement of XPs cannot be substitution, it must be adjunction, and we therefore conclude that the positions that we have been calling specifiers throughout this paper are in fact adjoined positions. We are not the only ones to observe that the motivation for a structurally distinct specifier position is weaker than generally supposed. As Hoekstra (1991) points out, it is widely assumed that only specifiers can stand in a relation of agreement with a head, and this relation is often taken to be a reflex of the configurational relation between specifiers and heads. However, if we take agreement with a head to be the defining characteristic of the class of elements that have been called specifiers rather than a derived property, then we can simplify the theory of phrase structure because there is no need to stipulate an independent phrase-structure distinction between these elements and nonagreeing adjuncts.[12] In a similar vein, Heycock (1991, 226ff.) argues that restricting movement of XPs to adjunction allows us to simplify the θ-Criterion, since chains with other than tail elements in θ-positions are then ruled out without further stipulation.

Clearly, if the proposal that movement must be adjunction is correct, it will be necessary to uncover the principles constraining such adjunction. What principles will account for the possible and impossible orders of adjuncts? What exactly are the principles governing agreement? Addressing these issues lies beyond the scope of this paper, but we consider that the facts we have presented suggest that these will be important questions for future research.

References

Adams, Marianne Patalino. 1987. *Old French, null subjects and verb second phenomena.* Doctoral dissertation, UCLA.

Adams, Marianne Patalino. 1988. Embedded *pro*. *Proceedings of the 18th Annual Meeting of the Northeastern Linguistics Society*, eds. James Blevins and Julie Carter, 1–21.

Besten, Hans den. 1983. On the interaction of root transformations and lexical deletive rules. *On the formal syntax of the Westgermania*, ed. Werner Abraham, 47–131. Amsterdam: Benjamins.

Besten, Hans den and Corretje Moed-van Walraven. 1986. The syntax of verbs in Yiddish. *Verb second phenomena in Germanic*, eds. Hubert Haider and Martin Prinzhorn, 111–135. Dordrecht: Foris.

Cardinaletti, Anna and Ian Roberts. 1991. Clause structure and X-second. Ms., Università di Venezia and Université de Genève. To appear in: *Levels of representation*, eds. Wynn Chao and Geoffrey Horrocks. Dordrecht: Foris.

Chomsky, Noam. 1981. *Lectures in Government and Binding.* Dordrecht: Foris.

Chomsky, Noam. 1982. *Some concepts and consequences of the theory of Government and Binding.* Cambridge: MIT Press.

[12]Naoki Fukui (pers. comm.) has independently arrived at essentially the same conclusion.

Déprez, Viviane. 1989. *On the typology of syntactic positions and the nature of chains: Move α to the specifier of functional projections*. Doctoral dissertation, MIT.

Diesing, Molly. 1988. Word order and the subject position in Yiddish. *Proceedings of the 18th Annual Meeting of the Northeastern Linguistics Society*, eds. James Blevins and Julie Carter, 124–140.

Diesing, Molly. 1990. Verb movement and the subject position in Yiddish. *Natural language and linguistic theory* 8: 41–79.

Dupuis, Fernande. 1989. *L'expression du sujet dans les subordonnées en ancien français*. Doctoral dissertation, Université de Montréal.

Fillmore, Charles J. 1968. The case for case. *Universals in linguistic theory*, eds. Emmon Bach and R.T. Harms, 1–88. New York: Holt, Rinehart and Winston.

Fukui, Naoki. 1986. *A theory of category projection and its applications*. Doctoral dissertation, MIT.

Fukui, Naoki and Margaret Speas. 1986. Specifiers and projection. *MIT Working Papers in Linguistics* 8: 128–172.

Haan, Germen de and Fred Weerman. 1986. Finiteness and verb fronting in Frisian. *Verb second phenomena in Germanic*, eds. Hubert Haider and Martin Prinzhorn, 77–110. Dordrecht: Foris.

Heycock, Caroline. 1991. *Layers of predication: the non-lexical syntax of clauses*. Doctoral dissertation, University of Pennsylvania.

Hirschbühler, Paul and Marie-Odile Junker. 1988. Remarques sur les sujets nuls en subordonnées en ancien et en moyen français. *Revue québécoise de linguistique théorique et appliquée* 7: 63–84.

Hoekstra, Eric. 1991. *Licensing conditions on phrase structure*. Doctoral dissertation, University of Groningen.

Holmberg, Anders. 1986. *Word order and syntactic features in the Scandinavian languages and English*. Doctoral dissertation, University of Stockholm.

Iatridou, Sabine and Anthony S. Kroch. 1992. CP-recursion and Germanic verb-second. Ms., University of Pennsylvania.

Kemenade, Ans van. 1987. *Syntactic case and morphological case in the history of English*. Dordrecht: Foris.

Koopman, Hilda and Dominique Sportiche. 1991. The position of subjects. *Lingua* 85: 211–258.

Kosmeijer, Wim. 1991. The distribution of *það*: an argument against a generalized COMP analysis. *Papers from the 12th Scandinavian Conference of Linguistics*, ed. Halldór Ármann Sigurðsson, 182–193. Reykjavík: Linguistic Institute, University of Iceland

Maling, Joan and Annie Zaenen. 1981. Germanic word order and the format of surface filters. *Binding and filtering*, ed. Frank Heny, 255–278. Cambridge: MIT Press.

McCawley, James D. 1970. English as a VSO language. *Language* 46: 286–299.

Pintzuk, Susan. 1991. *Phrase structures in competition: variation and change in Old English word order*. Doctoral dissertation, University of Pennsylvania.

Platzack, Christer. 1986. COMP, INFL and Germanic word order. *Topics in Scandinavian syntax*, eds. Lars Hellan and Kirsti Koch Christensen, 185–234. Dordrecht: Reidel.

Platzack, Christer and Anders Holmberg. 1990. The role of AGR and finiteness in some European VO languages. Ms., University of Lund.

Pollock, Jean-Yves. 1989. Verb movement, Universal Grammar, and the structure of IP. *Linguistic inquiry* 20: 365–424.

Rizzi, Luigi. 1990a. *Relativized minimality*. Cambridge: MIT Press.

Rizzi, Luigi. 1990b. Speculations on verb-second. *Grammar in progress: A Festschrift for Henk van Riemsdijk*, eds. Marina Nespor et al., 375–385. Dordrecht: Foris.

Rizzi, Luigi. 1991. Residual verb second and the wh-criterion. University of Geneva Technical Reports in Formal and Computational Linguistics, No. 2.

Rögnvaldsson, Eiríkur and Thráinsson, Höskuldur. 1990. On Icelandic word order once more. *The syntax of Modern Icelandic*, eds. Joan Maling and Annie Zaenen, 3–40. Orlando: Academic Press.

Rothstein, Susan. 1983. *The syntactic forms of predication*. Doctoral dissertation, MIT.

Santorini, Beatrice. 1989. *The generalization of the verb-second constraint in the history of Yiddish*. Doctoral dissertation, University of Pennsylvania.

Santorini, Beatrice. 1991. Variation and change in Yiddish subordinate clause word order. Ms., Northwestern University. To appear in *Natural language and linguistic theory*.

Santorini, Beatrice. 1992. Two types of verb-second phenomenon in the history of Yiddish. To appear in *Diachronic aspects of the verb-second phenomenon*, eds. Adrian Battye and Ian Roberts. Cambridge: Cambridge University Press.

Sportiche, Dominique. 1988. A theory of floating quantifiers. *Linguistic inquiry* 19: 425–449.

Stowell, Timothy. 1983. Subjects across categories. *Linguistic review* 2: 285–312.

Taraldsen, Knut Tarald. 1986. On verb second and the functional content of syntactic categories. *Verb second phenomena in Germanic*, eds. Hubert Haider and Martin Prinzhorn, 7–25. Dordrecht: Foris.

Thiersch, Craig. 1978. *Topics in German syntax*. Doctoral dissertation, MIT.

Vikner, Sten. 1991. *Verb movement and the licensing of NP-positions in the Germanic languages*. Doctoral dissertation, Université de Genève (revised version).

Zaenen, Annie. 1980. *Extraction rules in Icelandic*. Doctoral dissertation, Harvard University.

Psych Verbs in Modern Greek

NORBERT HORNSTEIN & SPYRIDOULA VARLOKOSTA
University of Maryland at College Park

0. Introduction

Psych verbs of the "frighten" class are standardly analyzed as having an "inverted" argument structure (Belletti and Rizzi 1988, Grimshaw 1990). The S-structure (SS) syntactic object is argued to be higher in the thematic hierarchy than the SS syntactic subject. Recently, this analysis has been criticized (see Pesetsky 1991) and it has been argued that psych verbs pattern like other transitive verbs in that the SS object is also the D-structure (DS) internal argument and the SS subject is the DS external argument.

In this paper we present evidence from Modern Greek (MG) to support the former approach. The form of our argument is as follows: MG has a pronoun idhios "*he* ", which in its non-emphatic use must be bound by a 0-operator in the local SPEC CP. This binding does not obtain if idhios is in subject position. Nor does it hold for idhios in SS object position in psych verb constructions. Furthermore, idhios in the SS subject position in psych verbs does not pattern as a bound instance either. We account for these properties of idhios in psych verb constructions by assuming that the Experiencer raises at Logical Form (LF) to a position adjoined to IP thereby resulting in a configuration where idhios is not and

* We would like to thank Sara Rosen and Tim Stowell for helpful comments on an earlier draft of this paper.

cannot be operator bound.[1] We deduce this restriction by invoking a principle on A'-disjointness proposed by Aoun and Hornstein (1991), as well as, the Minimal Binding Requirement (MBR) proposed by Aoun and Li (1989).

1. Some background assumptions

The MG pronoun idhios has different properties depending on its grammatical function. The non-emphatic form of the pronoun, which appears in non-subject position, must have a binder but does not seem to obey the locality restrictions characteristic of anaphors. The following examples show that non-subject idhios must be free in its Governing Category (GC), unlike reflexives. However, in contrast to other pronouns, e.g., the MG pronoun ton "*him* ", it requires a sentence internal antecedent.

(1) O Yanis$_i$ theli o Vasilis$_j$ na voithisi ton eafton tou$*_{i/j}$
John wants Bill helps himself

(2) O Yanis$_i$ theli o Vasilis$_j$ na voithisi ton idhio$_{i/*j/*k}$
John wants Bill helps him

(3) * Thelo na dho ton idhio
(I) want see him

(4) O Yanis$_i$ theli o Vasilis$_j$ na ton$_{i/*j/k}$ voithisi
John wants Bill him helps

Furthermore, non-subject idhios cannot occur in embedded questions or relative clauses, though it can be found in noun complement constructions and adjuncts:

(5) *O Yanis$_i$ den kseri pjos aghapai ton idhio$_i$
John not knows who loves him

(6) *O Yanis$_i$ sinandise ton anthropo pou filakise ton idhio$_i$
John met the man who imprisoned him

(7) O Yanis$_i$ arnithike to gegonos oti i Maria aghapai ton idhio$_i$
John denied the fact that Mary loves him

(8) O Yanis$_i$ kharike otan i Maria filise ton idhio$_i$
John was pleased when Mary kissed him

In addition it licenses only sloppy identity interpretation under ellipsis and cannot tolerate split antecedents:

(9) O Yanis theli i Maria na voithisi ton idhio, ke o Vasilis episis
John wants Mary helps him and Bill too

---

1 Experiencer raising at LF has been proposed in Campbell and Martin (1989), Hermon (1984) and Stowell (1986). Our proposals though similar, differ in detail (see below).

a. John wants Mary to help John and Bill wants Mary
to help Bill (sloppy)

b.*John wants Mary to help John and Bill wants Mary
to help John (non-sloppy)

(10) O Yanis$_i$ ipe sto Vasili$_j$ oti i Maria aghapai tous idhious$_{*i+j}$
John told Bill that Mary loves them

Hornstein and Varlokosta (forthcoming) have shown that these properties of idhios follow from the assumption that non-subject idhios is A'-bound by a 0-operator residing in SPEC CP that is in turn identified by a c-commanding NP, which is idhios's semantic anchor.

(11) O Yanis$_i$ pistevi [$_{CP}$ 0$_i$ oti [$_{IP}$ o Vasilis$_j$ tha voithisi ton idhio$_{i/*j}$]]
John believes that Bill will help him

In (11) only Yanis can be the antecedent of ton idhio as it is the only NP that c-commands the SPEC CP position, the place where the 0-operator resides. The assumption that the 0-operator in MG must be identified by being bound by a c-commanding antecedent accounts for idhios's obligatory requiring a sentence internal antecedent as well as for the ungrammaticality of (12) and (13) in which the 0-operator is not c-commanded by a semantic antecedent.

(12) *[$_{CP}$ 0$_i$ [$_{IP}$ O Yanis$_i$ dhiavase [$_{NP}$ ena vivlio gia ton idhio$_i$]]]
John read a book about him

(13) ??[$_{CP}$ 0$_i$ [$_{IP}$ [$_{NP}$ Mia photographia tou Yani$_i$] athoose ton idhio$_i$]]
A picture John-Gen exonerated him

This accounts for why it is that further embedding improves (12) but not (13). In (14) the 0-operator is bound and thereby identified by a semantically appropriate antecedent. On the other hand, the semantic antecedent does not c-command the 0-operator in (15), thus yielding an unacceptable structure:

(14) O Yanis$_i$ nomizi [$_{CP}$ 0$_i$ oti [$_{IP}$ i Maria dhiavase ena vivlio
John thinks that Mary read a book

gia ton idhio$_i$]]
about him

(15) * [$_{CP}$ [$_{IP}$ [$_{NP}$ Mia photographia tou Yani$_i$] apedikse [$_{CP}$ 0$_i$ oti
A picture John-Gen proved that

[$_{IP}$ i Maria zouse me ton idhio$_i$]]]]
Mary lived with him

Furthermore, the unacceptability of (16) and (17) follow from the fact that the SPEC CP position is filled and so unavailable for the 0-operator which is required to bind idhios. On the other hand, in noun complement constructions (18) and adjuncts (19) the lower SPEC CP is unfilled and so a 0-operator can bind idhios from this position.

(16) *O Yanis$_i$ den kseri [$_{CP}$ pjos$_j$ 0_i [$_{IP}$ t_j aghapai ton idhio$_i$]]
John not knows who loves him

(17) *O Yanis$_i$ sinandise ton anthropo [$_{CP}$ pou$_j$ 0_i [$_{IP}$ t_j filakise ton idhio$_i$]]
John met the man who imprisoned him

(18) O Yanis$_i$ arnithike [$_{NP}$ to gegonos [$_{CP}$ 0_i oti [$_{IP}$ i Maria
John denied the fact that Mary

aghapai ton idhio$_i$]]
loves him

(19) O Yanis$_i$ kharike otan [$_{CP}$ 0_i [$_{IP}$ i Maria filise ton idhio$_i$]]
John was pleased when Mary kissed him

The inability to support split antecedents is explained assuming that the 0-operator must be uniquely bound for purposes of identification. These cases of idhios contrast sharply with those with idhios in subject position. These do not require a sentence internal antecedent, they can occur in embedded questions and relative clauses, they can support split antecedents and they don't require a sloppy identity interpretation.

(20) Den itan eki o idhios, alla me eksipiretise i gramateas tou
Not was there him but me helped the secretary his

(21) Mia photographia tou Yani$_i$ apedikse oti o idhios$_i$ zouse me ti Maria
A picture John-Gen proved that he lived with Mary

(22) O Yanis$_i$ den thimate [$_{CP}$ ti/pjo vivlio [$_{IP}$ agorase o idhios$_i$]]
John not remembers what/which book bought he

(23) O Yanis$_i$ sinandise ton anthropo [$_{CP}$ pou [$_{IP}$ o idhios$_i$
John met the man who he

iche filakisi]]
had imprisoned

(24) O Yanis nomizi oti o idhios ine o kaliteros ipopsifios
John thinks that he is the best candidate

ke o Vasilis episis
and Bill too

a. John thinks that John is the best candidate and Bill thinks that Bill is the best candidate (sloppy)

b. John thinks that John is the best candidate and Bill thinks that John is the best candidate (non-sloppy)

Hornstein and Varlokosta (forthcoming) account for the distribution of the two forms of idhios by assuming that the latter is not and cannot be 0-operator bound. They deduce this restriction by invoking (25), a requirement on A'-disjointness, proposed for bound pronouns in Mandarine Chinese (Aoun and

Hornstein 1991, Aoun and Li 1989) as well as for resumptive pronouns in Irish (McCloskey 1989)

(25) McCloskey (1989)
A'-Disjointness: A pronoun must be A'-free in the Least Complete Functional Complex (CFC) containing the pronoun and a subject distinct from the pronoun

According to this principle, structures like (26) are prohibited. This is because the minimal CFC which contains the pronoun and a subject distinct from the pronoun, will be the higher S. The pronoun is not A'-free in this domain since its antecedent (the 0-operator in SPEC CP) is contained within the higher S in violation of (25).

(26) O Yanis$_i$ pistevi [$_{CP}$ 0$_i$ oti [$_{IP}$ o idhios$_i$ ine o kaliteros ipopsifios]]
John believes that he is the best kandidate

The grammaticality of (26) and the appearance of idhios in the subject position is justified by the fact that this instance of the pronoun has none of the properties of bound idhios, as has been exemplified in (20) through (24). In fact, idhios in subject position has a focus reading and it functions like a standard pronominal element. [2]

2. Psych verbs

It was pointed out above that the binding requirement on the 0-operator binding non-subject idhios accounts for the ungrammaticality of sentences like (12) and (13):

(12) * [$_{CP}$ 0$_i$ [$_{IP}$ O Yanis$_i$ dhiavase [$_{NP}$ ena vivlio gia ton idhio$_i$]]]
John read a book about him

(13) ??[$_{CP}$0$_i$ [$_{IP}$ [$_{NP}$ Mia photographia tou Yani$_i$] athoose ton idhio$_i$]]
A picture John-Gen exonerated him

There seems to be an apparent counterexample to this account. (27) is an example of a subject sentence in MG and (28) is an example of a complex noun complement NP in subject position. In these examples the available COMP is the

2 In addition to the regular form of the pronoun idhios there also exists an emphatic version. This form of the pronoun receives a foccused interpretation, as observed in Iatridou (1986), and it functions syntactically like a regular pronoun rather than an anaphor even when in non-subject positions:

A: Thelis na dhis ton iatro i ti nosokoma tou?
(You)want to see the doctor or the nurse his

B: Thelo na dho TON IDHIO
(I) want to see HIM HIMSELF

For a more detailed analysis of the emphatic idhios, see Hornstein and Varlokosta (forthcoming).

matrix COMP. Thus, Yani should not be a possible antecedent for idhios, as it does not c-command this COMP.

(27) To oti i Maria aghapa to Yani$_i$ afora ton idhio$_i$
That Mary loves John concerns him

(28) To gegonos oti i Maria aghapai to Yani$_i$ afora ton idhio$_i$
The fact that Mary loves John concerns him

Nonetheless, both of these examples are perfectly grammatical in MG. There is, however, a further important characteristic of these constructions; they involve psych predicates instead of regular agentive predicates.

There are currently several different approaches to these constructions which analyze them as having an "inverted" argument structure (see Belletti and Rizzi 1988, Grimshaw 1990).In particular, Belleti and Rizzi (1988) argue that psych verbs deviate from verbs with agentive subjects in that there is no DS subject generated at all. Rather, the SS subject is derived (through NP-movement) from a position lower than the surface object (it is, in fact, adjoined to V'). On the other hand the surface object is, in fact, a structural VP subject since it is the most prominent theta-marked NP. Thus, on this account, (28) has the DS/SS/LF triad of phrase markers indicated in (29):

(29) a.[$_{IP}$ ec [$_{VP}$ [$_{V'}$ afora [$_{NP}$ to gegonos i Maria aghapai to Yani]] ton idhio]]

b.[$_{IP}$ [$_{NP}$ to gegonos i Maria aghapai to Yani]$_i$ [$_{VP}$ [$_{V'}$ afora t$_i$] ton idhio]]

c.[$_{CP}$ 0$_j$ [$_{IP}$ [$_{NP}$ to gegonos i Maria aghapai to Yani$_j$]$_i$ [$_{VP}$ [$_{V'}$ afora t$_i$] ton idhio]]

There is an intuition implicit in (29) which provides the beggining of an answer to our problem. This is reflected in the DS that Belletti and Rizzi (1988) assign to these sort of constructions , where the Experiencer is outside the V' projection. It is in essence an external argument. It seems, therefore, that in psych verb constructions, the post verbal NP is actually functioning like a subject. In English this is reflected in the peculiar binding facts that psych verbs manifest. Not only can the SS object bind a reflexive within a subject NP but the apparent subject NP cannot bind a reflexive in apparent object position.

(30) a. Naked pictures of himself$_i$ concern John$_i$
b. * John$_i$ concerns himself$_i$

There is further empirical evidence suggesting the DS prominence of the SS object. Despite being in SS object position, the psych verb cases of idhios pattern like the non-operator bound form. In other words, unlike the other instances of non-subject idhios, these instances can be discourse bound, they don't require a c-commanding antecedent, they can be embedded in the object position of a relative clause or an embedded question, they allow split antecedents and they permit a strict reading under ellipsis:

(31) Milise sto Yani$_i$. Afto to provlima afora ton idhio$_i$
Talk to John. This problem concerns him

(32) I idhiotiki zoi tou Yani$_i$ afora ton idhio$_i$
The private life John-Gen concerns him

(33) O Yanis$_i$ lini ta provlimata pou aforoun ton idhio$_i$
John solves the problems which concern him

(34) O Yanis$_i$ den kseri pja provlimata aforoun ton idhio$_i$
John not knows which problems concern him

(35) O Yanis$_i$ ipe sto Vasili$_j$ oti afti i ipothesi afora tous idhious$_{i+j}$
John told Bill that this matter concerns them

(36) O Yanis nomizi oti afto to provlima afora ton idhio
John thinks that this problem concerns him

ke o Vasilis episis
and Bill too

a. John thinks this problem concerns John and Bill thinks this problem concerns Bill (sloppy)

b. John thinks this problem concerns John and Bill thinks this problem concerns John (non-sloppy)

Furthermore, this use of idhios has an emphatic feel to it just like the subject instances with agentive verbs. If we were to assume that in psych verb constructions, the post verbal NP was indeed functioning as a subject, then principle (25) would prevent its being A'-bound by a 0-operator in the matrix COMP. One way to flesh this idea out would be to interpret the notion "subject" in (25) to be the most prominent argument in a CFC. In psych verbs the SS object functions as the most theta-prominent NP in the CFC and thus idhios in this position cannot be 0-operator bound.

A version of this view is in fact executed in Grimshaw (1990). The main difference between Belletti and Rizzi (1988) and Grimshaw (1990) is that what the former do in DS, Grimshaw does in the Lexicon at Lexical Conceptual Structure, a structured representation which represents prominence relations among a predicate's arguments. These relations are jointly determined by the theta-properties of the predicate (via the thematic-hierarchy) and by the aspectual properties of the predicate. According to Grimshaw (1990) the behaviour of psychological predicates can be understood as a result of a mismatch between their thematic-prominence and their other properties. More specifically, the Experiencer of psych verbs is the thematically most prominent argument despite the fact that it is realized in object position. It is not, however, the aspectually most prominent argument. The cause/theme argument, on the other hand, is aspectually but not thematically the most prominent argument and is, therefore, realized as a D-structure subject. Since no argument holds prominency on both dimentions, psychological predicates have no External Argument. It is the relative prominence of the Experiencer of psych verbs that accounts for the various distinct anaphoric facts in such constructions. Again under this view the SS object would function as the most theta-prominent NP in the CFC along the thematic tier and thus idhios in this position could not be 0-

operator bound if we interpret "subject " in (25) not structurally but as the most theta-prominent argument in the CFC.

We suspect, however, that a more structural approach will prove to be more empirically adequate. The reason is that derived subjects act as structural subjects with respect to (25), as (37), (38) and (39) indicate:

(37) O Yanis nomizi oti o idhios fenete na exei nikithi
John thinks that he appears to have been won

(38) O Yanis nomizi oti o idhios eftase arga
John thinks that he arrived late

(39) O Yanis nomizi oti o idhios siginite eukola
John thinks that he is moved easily

Bound *idhios* can not occur in these positions though thematically they are not prominent arguments of the predicate. In fact, in (37) *idhios* is not an argument of the verb *fenete* at all, but it is the raised argument of the embedded predicate *exei nikithi* .

In order to pursue a more structural approach, we could manipulate the Belletti and Rizzi (1988) account in several ways. Assuming binding of *idhios* by the operator takes place at LF, an LF representation like (29c) would not suffice to rule out the bound reading of *idhios* , as (29c) satisfies (25) since *idhios* is not a structural subject. One solution would be to assume that the Theme lowers back into its DS position at LF. This would yield an LF structure essentially the same as (29a). In this configuration, the Experiencer NP is structurally the most prominent argument in the CFC so (25) would come into play to block operator binding of the object *idhios*:

(40) [CP [IP t_i [VP [V' afora [NP to gegonos i Maria aghapai to Yani$_j$]$_i$] ton idhio$_j$]]

This approach, however, would result in another problem. Lowering of the Theme back to its DS position at LF would leave an unbound trace which would result in a violation of either the ECP or the Binding Theory. This suggests that a modified version of Belletti and Rizzi (1988) is not quite what we need.

This said, it is clear that a Belleti-Rizzi like story has one important advantage over Pesetsky's (1991) recent analysis. Pesetsky (1991) argues that psych verbs pattern just like regular agentive verbs in that the SS subject is also a DS external argument. This assumption renders it the most prominent argument in the CFC of the predicate and we are left with no way of explaining why it cannot be operator bound.

In sum, none of these three accounts yield unproblematic explanations of the distinct distribution of object *idhios* in psych verb constructions. What we need is a structural way of reflecting the "inverted" thematic relations of psychological predicates at LF. Before making a concrete proposal about how to do this, we would like to take a look at the behaviour of *idhios* in SS subject positions in psych verb constructions.

The distinct behaviour of *idhios* in SS object position in psych verb constructions would lead one to wonder what the behaviour of the pronoun is when it occupies the SS subject position in these sort of constructions. If the SS object in psych predicates is more thematically prominent than the SS subject, one might expect a SS subject instance of idhios to behave like an object, and thus to be bindable by a 0-operator.

This assumption, however, finds no empirical support. Idhios can occupy the SS subject position of psych verbs, but this is possible only when the pronoun has a focused contrastive reading as in (41):

(41) O Yanis nomizi oti O IDHIOS fovizi ti Maria ki ohi o adhelfos tou
John thinks that HE frightens Mary and not his brother

What is more interesting is the fact that in this position idhios does not exhibit the properties of a non-subject instance. In fact, it patterns like the subject instances, in that it can be discourse bound and it does not require a c-commanding antecedent:

(42) O IDHIOS fovizi ti Maria, ohi o adhelfos tou
HE frightens Mary not his brother

(43) I adhelfi tou Yani nomizi oti O IDHIOS fovizi
The sister John-Gen thinks that HE frightens

ti Maria ki ohi o pateras tous
Mary and not their father

Furthermore, it can occur in embedded questions and relative clauses, it allows split antecedents and it permits a strict reading under ellipsis:

(44) O Yanis den kseri pjon fovizi O IDHIOS ke pjon
John not knows who frightens HE and who

o adhelfos tou
his brother

(45) ? O Yanis sinandise ti gineka pou iche fovisi O IDHIOS
John met the woman who had frightened HE

ke ohi o adelfos tou
and not his brother

(46) O Yanis ipe sto Vasili oti I IDHII prepi na fovizoun
John told to Bill that THEY should frighten

ta paidia tous ke ohi i ginekes tous
their children and not their wives

(47) O Yanis nomizi oti O IDHIOS fovizi ti Maria, ke o Vasilis episis
John thinks that HE frightens Mary and Bill too

a. John thinks that John frightens Mary and Bill thinks that Bill frightens Mary (sloppy)

b. John thinks that John frightens Mary and Bill thinks that John frightens Mary (non-sloppy)

What does this indicate? It seems that neither the SS subject nor the SS object *idhios* can be 0-operator bound in psych verbs. The question is why not.

We suggest that the surface object of psychological predicates moves to a position adjoined to IP at LF. [3] Assuming this proposal, the LF representation of (29) would be (48) :

(48) $[_{CP}$ 0_i $[_{IP}$ ton idhio$_i$ $[_{IP}$ $[_{NP}$ to gegonos i Maria aghapai to Yani$_i$ $]_j$ $[_{VP}$ $[_{V'}$ afora t_j $]$ t_i $]]]]$

In this configuration *idhios* violates a version of (25). In particular, it violates the version of the A'-disjointness requirement proposed by Aoun and Hornstein (1991):

(49) A pronoun has to be A'-free in the least Complete Functional Complex containing this pronoun and a c-commanding subject.

According to (49), *idhios* in (48) should be A'-free in the Complete Functional Complex containing the pronoun and a c-commanding subject but in this domain there is no c-commanding subject.

With respect to the SS subject cases their LF representation would look like (50) :

(50) $[_{CP}$ 0_i $[_{IP}$ ti Maria$_j$ $[_{IP}$ o idhios$_i$ $[_{VP}$ $[_{V'}$ fovizi t_i $]$ t_j $]]]]$

Idhios in (50) is not in the domain of a subject again in violation of (49). Note that it is crucial for our purposes that the object not A-move to a higher "subject" position (i.e., a higher SPEC IP) as proposed in Campbell and Martin (1989) and Hermon (1984). The reason is that *ti Maria* would allow *idhios* in (50) to be operator bound, contrary to fact. [4]

There is another interesting fact about (50) which suggests that the object moves to an A'-position at LF. In this configuration *ti Maria* c-commands *o idhios* and, therefore, since we assume it occupies an A'-position it qualifies as a potential A'-binder for the pronoun *idhios*. Thus, (50) might also induce an A'-Binding Minimality effect, in the sence of Aoun and Li (1989) :

(51) Minimal Binding Requirement (MBR)
Variables must be bound by the most local potential antecedent (A'-binder).

---

3 For a similar proposal, see Zubizarreta (1992)

4 This proposal has one other interesting property. Grimshaw (1990) observes, (30b), repeated here as (i), is more accurately evaluated as ? than *.

(i) ? John concerns himself

Our account implies that (i) should be about as unacceptable as (ii), in which the anaphor is overtly topicalized.

(ii) ? Himself, John fears

We believe that this implication is correct and that (i) and (ii) are equally unacceptable.

According to the MBR, ti Maria is the first available A'-binder for o idhios and thus idhios cannot be 0-operator bound in this configuration. This gives us another reason for why SS subject idhios does not behave as a 0-operator bound pronoun. Hornstein and Varlokosta (forthcoming) show that the same Minimal Binding Requirement effect is obtained with bound idhios in regular agentive constructions when a wh-element intervenes between idhios and the 0-operator:

(52) ?* O Yanis$_i$ ipe [$_{CP}$ 0$_i$ oti [$_{IP}$ o Vasilis thimithike
John said that Bill remembered

[$_{CP}$ pjos$_j$ [$_{IP}$ t$_j$ filise ton idhio$_i$]]]]
who kissed him

In (52) the first potential A'-binder is pjos and this element interferes with the binding between the 0-operator and idhios. [5]

In fact, we have further empirical evidence that bound idhios is subject to minimality effects . If our proposal is correct, one would expect quantifiers to induce problems for the distribution of idhios, assuming Quantifier Raising at LF. In fact this prediction is born out by the data. There is a clear contrast between (53) and (54):

(53) * O Yanis$_i$ nomizi [$_{CP}$ 0$_i$ oti [$_{IP}$ kathenas$_j$ [$_{IP}$ t$_j$
John thinks that everyone

[$_{VP}$ aghapai ton idhio$_i$]]]]
loves him

(54) O Yanis$_i$ nomizi [$_{CP}$ 0$_i$ oti [$_{IP}$ o Vasilis [$_{VP}$ aghapai ton idhio$_i$]]]]
John thinks that Bill loves him

(53), unlike (54) involves raising of a quantifier in a position adjoined to IP, where it induces a minimality effect with respect to the binding of idhios. [6]

3. Conclusion

In this paper we argued that the "inverted" thematic relations of psychological predicates are hierarchically represented at LF. By making this assumption we derived the distribution of the pronoun idhios in psych verb constructions in MG. To do so we invoked a principle on A'-disjointness proposed

5 If the lowest IP in (52) was occupied by a psych predicate then the sentence would be grammatical, which is in accordance with our predictions.

6 There are some differences between no one and other quantifiers in their behavior with respect to the distribution of idhios. Thus, no one does not induce the minimality effect observed in (53) with respect to everyone. The same behaviour is also observed in the distribution of Negation. Thus, the negative marker den (=not) does not induce any minimality effect with respect to the binding of idhios. It is interesting to note that the morphological form of no one in MG is kanenas "*not one* ". If the indefinite can be bound by Negation and need not move at LF, we would expect no Minimal Binding Requirement effect. This view is consistent with the treatment of indefinites in Heim (1982).

by Aoun and Hornstein (1991), as well as, the Minimal Binding Requirement (MBR) proposed by Aoun and Li (1989).

References

Aoun, Joseph and Norbert Horstein (1991). "Bound and referencial pronouns", in *Logical Structure and Linguistic Structure*, C.T.J. Huang and R. May eds., Kluwer, Dordrecht

Aoun, Joseph and Audrey Li (1989). "Scope and constituency", *Linguistic Inquiry*, 20 : 141-172.

Belletti, Adriana and Luigi Rizzi (1988). "Psych-Verbs and theta-theory", *Natural Language and Linguistic Theory*, 6 : 291-352.

Campbell, Richard and Jack Martin (1989). "Sensation Predicates and the Syntax of Stativity", *Proceedings of WCCFL VIII.*, CSLI

Grimshaw, Jane (1990). *Argument Structure*, MIT Press, Cambridge, Mass.

Heim, Irene (1982). *The Semantics of Definites and Indefinites Noun Phrases*, Doctoral Dissertation, University of Massachusetts , Amherst

Hermon, Gabriella (1984). *Syntactic Modularity*, Dordrecht: Foris Publications.

Hornstein, Norbert and Spyridoula Varlokosta (forthcoming)." A Bound Pronoun in Modern Greek", *Natural Language and Linguistic Theory.*

McCloskey, James (1989). "Resumptive Pronouns, A' -Binding and Levels of Representation in Irish", ms., SRC-89-07.

Pesetsky, David (1991). "Experiencer Predicates and Universal Alignment Principles", MIT ms.

Stowell, Tim (1986). "Psych-Movement in the Mapping between D-Structure and LF" , paper given at Glow 1986, Girona.

Zubizarreta, Maria Luisa (1992). "The lexical encoding of scope relations among arguments", Syntax and Semantics, 26: 211-258.

The Complexity of Inducing a Rule from Data

MARK JOHNSON
Brown University

1 Introduction

This paper discusses the problem of identifying the conditioning context of a rule from two perspectives. As motivation it sketches an algorithm initially described in Johnson (1984) for inducing an ordered set of SPE-style phonological rules (Chomsky and Halle 1968) that account for the alternations in a set of surface phonological forms arranged in paradigm format. Then it abstracts away from the details of that algorithm, and uses the tools of computational complexity theory to characterize the computational complexity of two problems that occur as sub-problems of this and presumably most other rule discovery procedures.

The first problem asks if a rule exists that can account for data exhibiting a single alternation, i.e., if there is a rule such that this rule's context is satisfied in all of cases in which the rule must apply, and fails to be satisfied in all of the cases in which the rule does not apply. The second problem is similar to the first, except that in this case the answer is a rule with the minimum number of features. It turns out that the first problem can be answered in deterministic polynomial time, and hence is tractable in the technical sense, while the universal version (Barton, Berwick and Ristad 1987) of the second problem is NP-complete, and hence is intractable in the technical sense (assuming $P \neq NP$). The paper concludes with a discussion of these results and their implications for empiricist and rationalist models of language acquisition.

The discussion in this paper is stated in terms of the identification of the conditioning contexts for SPE-style rules because they are simple and familiar, but the results are far more general. It shows that while the problem of determining if there is some set of features that 'matches' all the members in a set *Pos* of 'positive examples' and does not match any member of another set *Neg* of 'negative examples' is tractable, the probem of finding the *minimal* set of features that distinguish *Pos* from *Neg* is in general computationally intractable.

* I would like to thank Motorola computer corporation for the donation of the 88k Delta computer used in this research.

2 A Phonological Rule Discovery Procedure

Johnson (1984) describes a procedure for discovering an ordered sequence of SPE-style phonological rules that account for certain types of phonological alternations in a data set given to it.[1] Specifically, it induces rules of the format $s_1 \rightarrow s_2 / C$, where s_1 and s_2 are segments, and C is a feature bundle identifying the contexts in which the rule applies. It does not attempt to generalize these rules to inputs and outputs specified with feature bundles (but this does not appear difficult to do). It also does not posit either insertion or deletion rules.

The procedure's input consists of a table in paradigm-format of surface phonological forms, and another table assigning each phonological segment a set of phonological features. (It's assumed that some other component of the language acquistion device has assembled these tables). Table 1 shows a typical paradigm-format input showing six alternations in Japanese surface forms.[2] Table 2 shows the assignment of features to segments given as input to the procedure.[3]

kak+u	*kai+ta*
tat+u	*tat+ta*
sin+u	*sin+da*
nom+u	*non+da*
tor+u	*tot+ta*
kog+u	*koi+da*
tob+u	*ton+da*

Table 1: A typical paradigm-format input (Japanese)

a	{ + *back*, + *low*, + *segmental*, + *voiced*, - *consonantal*, - *coronal*, - *high*, - *nasal* }
b	{ + *consonantal*, + *segmental*, + *voiced*, - *back*, - *coronal*, - *high*, - *nasal* }
d	{ + *consonantal*, + *coronal*, + *high*, + *segmental*, + *voiced*, - *back*, - *low*, - *nasal* }
g	{ + *back*, + *consonantal*, + *low*, + *segmental*, + *voiced*, - *coronal*, - *high*, - *nasal* }
i	{ + *high*, + *segmental*, + *voiced*, - *back*, - *consonantal*, - *coronal*, - *low*, - *nasal* }
k	{ + *back*, + *consonantal*, + *low*, + *segmental*, - *coronal*, - *high*, - *nasal*, - *voiced* }
m	{ + *consonantal*, + *nasal*, + *segmental*, + *voiced*, - *coronal* }
n	{ + *consonantal*, + *coronal*, + *nasal*, + *segmental*, + *voiced*, - *low* }
o	{ + *back*, + *segmental*, + *voiced*, - *consonantal*, - *coronal*, - *high*, - *low*, - *nasal* }
r	{ + *consonantal*, + *segmental*, + *voiced*, - *back*, - *coronal*, - *nasal* }
s	{ + *consonantal*, + *coronal*, + *segmental*, - *back*, - *low*, - *nasal*, - *voiced* }
t	{ + *consonantal*, + *coronal*, + *high*, + *segmental*, - *back*, - *low*, - *nasal*, - *voiced* }
u	{ + *back*, + *high*, + *segmental*, + *voiced*, - *consonantal*, - *coronal*, - *low*, - *nasal* }

Table 2: A typical segment-feature assignments input

---

[1] The procedure was first implemented at the University of California in San Diego in Franz Lisp on a VAX 11–750 (computer time provided courtesy of Jeff Elman); this implementation required approximately 1 hour to enumerate the rule systems generating the Japanese data presented here. It has been reimplemented on a Motorola Delta 88k in Prolog; this implementation requires 17 seconds to enumerate the same rule systems generating the same data.

[2] This data was kindly provided by Yuki Kuroda (p.c.).

[3] This feature assignment is for illustrative purposes only. In practice, a larger and more phonologically-realistic set of features is used. The implementation allows a more complex encoding which encodes syllable and morpheme structure as well.

Given these inputs, the procedure returns an underlying form for each row and column of the paradigm format input, and an ordered sequences of rules that when applied to these underlying forms yield the surface input. (In general it finds not just one solution but several, which it simply enumerates). For example, one of the solutions returned by the procedure when given the data in Tables 1 and 2 is displayed in Tables 3 and 4. Each entry in Table 4 actually abbreviates several rules, since any one of the rule contexts listed in each cell correctly conditions that alternation (e.g. the $m \rightarrow n$ rule is consistent with the data if it is conditioned by either a + *consonantal*, a + *coronal* or a + *back* following segment).

Stems:	*kak*	*tat*	*sin*	*nom*	*tor*	*kog*	*tob*
Suffixes:	*u*	*da*					

Table 3: Underlying forms for the data in Table 1 discovered by the procedure

$m \rightarrow n$ /	__ [+ *consonantal*]
	__ [+ *coronal*]
	__ [- *back*]
$b \rightarrow n$ /	__ [+ *consonantal*]
	__ [+ *coronal*]
	__ [- *back*]
$r \rightarrow t$ /	__ [+ *consonantal*]
	__ [+ *coronal*]
	__ [- *back*]
$d \rightarrow t$ /	[- *voiced*] __
$k \rightarrow i$ /	__ [+ *consonantal*]
	__ [+ *coronal*]
	__ [- *back*]
	__ [- *voiced*]
$g \rightarrow i$ /	__ [+ *consonantal*]
	__ [+ *coronal*]
	__ [- *back*]

Table 4: Ordered rules for the data in Table 1 discovered by the procedure

The procedure enumerates the rules in the reverse order in which they would be applied in a derivation. It relies on the fact that the conditioning context of the last rule to apply cannot be 'opaque', since no other rule can have applied to alter its context. The top-level structure of the discovery procedure is shown in Figure 1 (comments appear in parentheses).

If there are no alternating pairs of segments, return the data set and the reversed list of rules, otherwise:

Non-deterministically pick an alternation (say $m \sim n$).

(*Could all* ns *that alternate with* m *be derived by some rule* m → n / *C* ?)

Let *Pos* be the set of examples in which an *n* that alternates with an *m* appears. (*In Table 1, Pos* = { *#no_+da#* })

Let *Neg* be the set of examples in which an *m* appears on the surface. (*In Table 1, Neg* = { *#no_+u#* })

Determine if there is a rule context *C* such that *C* matches every context in *Pos*, and *C* does *not* match any context in *Neg*. If so, posit rule $m \rightarrow n / C$.

If there is such a context *C*, replace with an *m* every *n* that alternates with an *m* in the data, and repeat.

Figure 1: The top-level structure of the rule discovery procedure

The subprocedure for determining if there is a rule context *C* that matches every context in *Pos* and does not match any context in *Neg* is described and analysed below. At this point, all that is important is that if there is an effective procedure for doing this, then the procedure described in Figure 1 is also effective.[4]

3 Identifying a single rule's context

The discovery procedure in Figure 1 calls an auxiliary procedure to determine a rule context *C* such that *C* matches every example in *Pos* (i.e., the rule context matches all the of the phonological forms in which the rule applies), and *C* does not match any example in *Neg* (i.e., the rule context does not match any context in which the rule does not apply). Two versions of this problem are actually of interest.

- The EXISTENCE problem: does there exist a *C* such that *C* matches every example in *Pos* and none of the examples in *Neg*?
- The MINIMALITY problem: what is the 'simplest' *C* such that *C* matches every example in *Pos* and none of the examples in *Neg* (where 'simplest' is defined with respect to some 'evaluation metric')?

In order to analyse these problems further, it is necessary to specify more precisely what 'rule contexts', 'examples', and 'matching' are. In the rest of this paper, it is assumed that both rule contexts *C* and the examples in the sets *Pos* and

[4] The procedure in Figure 1 is non-deterministic, in that in general there will be several alternations in the data. But because the data set is finite, the number of alternations is also finite, and hence the non-determinism is also finite, and hence can be simulated by a deterministic algorithm in a standard fashion. Further, each (non-deterministic) iteration reduces the number of alternating pairs of segments in the data by one, and since the data set and hence the number of alternating pairs of segments are finite, eventually the procedure must terminate. Thus the procedure is effective.

$$\left\{\begin{array}{llll}
\langle -2,+\mathit{consonantal}\rangle & \langle -1,+\mathit{back}\rangle & \langle +1,+\mathit{consonantal}\rangle & \langle +2,+\mathit{back}\rangle \\
\langle -2,+\mathit{coronal}\rangle & \langle -1,+\mathit{segmental}\rangle & \langle +1,+\mathit{coronal}\rangle & \langle +2,+\mathit{low}\rangle \\
\langle -2,+\mathit{nasal}\rangle & \langle -1,+\mathit{voiced}\rangle & \langle +1,+\mathit{high}\rangle & \langle +2,+\mathit{segmental}\rangle \\
\langle -2,+\mathit{segmental}\rangle & \langle -1,-\mathit{consonantal}\rangle & \langle +1,+\mathit{segmental}\rangle & \langle +2,+\mathit{voiced}\rangle \\
\langle -2,+\mathit{voiced}\rangle & \langle -1,-\mathit{coronal}\rangle & \langle +1,+\mathit{voiced}\rangle & \langle +2,-\mathit{consonantal}\rangle \\
\langle -2,-\mathit{low}\rangle & \langle -1,-\mathit{high}\rangle & \langle +1,-\mathit{back}\rangle & \langle +2,-\mathit{coronal}\rangle \\
 & \langle -1,-\mathit{low}\rangle & \langle +1,-\mathit{low}\rangle & \langle +2,-\mathit{high}\rangle \\
 & \langle -1,-\mathit{nasal}\rangle & \langle +1,-\mathit{nasal}\rangle & \langle +2,-\mathit{nasal}\rangle
\end{array}\right\}$$

Table 5: The set of pairs encoding the example *no_+da*

Neg are sets of features, and a rule context C matches an example E iff $C \subseteq E$, i.e. if every feature in C also appears in E.[5] Both rule contexts and the examples in the sets *Pos* and *Neg* are encoded as sets of ordered pairs $\langle p,f \rangle$, where p is a non-zero integer indicating the 'offset' or relative position of feature f to the segment that the rule changes.

For example, the rule context [+ *voiced*] _ [+ *high*] is encoded as the set of pairs { ⟨−1, + *voiced*⟩, ⟨+1, + *high*⟩ }, and the example *no_+da* would be encoded as the set of pairs in Table 5. Since this rule context's features are a subset of the example's features, it matches the example.When rule contexts, examples and matching are defined in this way, the requirements that the rule context C must match every example in *Pos* and must not match any example in *Neg* are equivalent to the two following set-theoretic formulae.

1. $\forall P \in Pos, C \subseteq P$
2. $\forall N \in Neg, C \not\subseteq N$

Johnson (1984) describes an algorithm that computes the minimal C that simultaneously satisfy these formulae, to which the implementation-oriented reader is referred. The remainder of this paper takes a more abstract approach, and rather than analyse the properties of this or any other particular algorithm, it applies computational complexity theory to characterize the complexity of *any* algorithm that correctly answers the existence and minimality problems for this particular formalization.

4 The complexity of inducing a single rule's context from data

This section shows that the existence problem can be answered in deterministic polynomial time, whereas the minimality problem is NP-complete.

[5] There are two important things to note here. First, other definitions of matching are possible, e.g., based on unification, as in Shieber (1984) and Pollard and Sag (1989). Second, nothing here depends on features being binary valued, so the results presented below generalize to non-binary valued feature systems.

Before presenting the technical details of the proof, this section discusses in very general terms the goals of computational complexity theory. For a technical introduction see Garey and Johnson (1979), and for other linguistic applications of complexity theory see Barton, Berwick and Ristad (1987). Hopcroft and Ullman (1979) is a standard text covering automata theory, the Chomsky hierarchy, and computational complexity theory.

Many linguists will be familiar with the Chomsky hierarchy of classes of languages. This hierarchy classifies a language in terms of the type of machine that can recognize it. For example, every finite state language can be recognized by some finite-state automaton (i.e., a machine with a finite memory capacity), whereas every context-free language can be recognized by some push-down automaton (i.e., a machine with memory organized as a stack), and every context-sensitive language can be recognized by some linear-bounded automaton (i.e., a machine the size of whose memory is linearly related to the length of the string being recognized).

This classification tells us something about the architectural constraints on machines that recognize various classes of languages, but says little about the time or space resources that the machine consumes in recognizing a string.[6] For example, the language $a^nb^nc^n$ is a context-sensitive language but not a context-free language, and hence located fairly 'high' on the Chomsky hierarchy. But clearly it can be recognized in linear time and logarithmic space by checking the linear order constraints and that the numbers of *a*'s, *b*'s and *c*'s are equal. This is a case where the Chomsky hierarchy gives little insight into the inherent computational complexity of a problem.

Computational complexity theory attempts to abstract away from the details of architectures and algorithms, and identify the minimum time and space resources required by *any* algorithm and machine to answer a problem. There is a corresponding hierarchy of problems, ordered by the resources they require. Here only two classes in the hierarchy will be used: P, the class of problems that can be answered by a *deterministic* automaton in time (and hence space) bounded by some polynomial function of the length of its input, and NP, the class of problems that can be answered by a *non-deterministic* automaton in time (and hence space) bounded by some polynomial function of the length of its input.[7]

Currently, it is not known whether NP actually differs from P, i.e., if there is a problem in NP that is not also in P. However, the best known algorithms for solving problems in NP on deterministic machines require exponential time, and moreover there exists a large number of NP-complete problems, i.e., problems to

---

[6] It does tell us something, however. Because every finite-state language is also a deterministic finite-state language, every finite-state language can be recognized in deterministic linear time. Because every context-sensitive language can be recognized in linear space, it follows that every context-sensitive language is contained in PSPACE. Garey and Johnson (1979) mention that there are context-sensitive grammars which have PSPACE-complete recognition problems.

[7] In the definition of these classes the automata are usually taken to be Turing machines. However the classes of problems that can be answered in deterministic polynomial time and in non-deterministic polynomial time is the same for most uni-processor architectures.

which any problem in NP is translatable in deterministic polynomial time. Thus if P ≠ NP, then the NP-complete problems are not in P.

Given an NP-complete problem Q_1, a proof of the NP-completeness of another problem Q_2 can be established by showing (i) that any instance of Q_1 can be translated in deterministic polynomial time into an instance of Q_2 (i.e., there is a deterministic polynomial reduction of Q_1 to Q_2), and (ii) that Q_2 can be answered by a non-deterministic Turing machine in polynomial time. A large number of problems have already been shown NP-complete; Garey and Johnson (1979) list hundreds of the more important ones.

The classes P and NP are important because problems in P are generally regarded as 'tractible', i.e., amenable to actual implementation, whereas problems in NP are generally regarded as 'intractible', i.e., in general it is not possible to solve these problems exactly on any type of computing machine.

Two problems are now presented that abstractly correspond to the existence and minimality problems for the single rule context identification problem. The examples in the sets *Neg* and *Pos* are formalized here as sets of features in order to avoid reliance on assumptions about the nature of phonological representations. The problems' complexities remain the same if an example is formalized as a string of segments, and a segment-feature assignment table is provided as input to the procedure.

This formalization of the problems relies on there being an unbounded number of features, and that any combination of features can condition any alternation. This corresponds to the UNIVERSAL problem, where a language may have an arbitrary number of 'diacritic' phonetic features that interact in essentially arbitrary fashion. Imposing a finite bound on the number of possible features and on the number of distinct rule contexts that can condition an alternation simplifies these problems enormously, so that both are in P.

For technical reasons explained in Garey and Johnson (1979), the minimality problem is posed in terms of the existence of a context set C of size less than some constant K. (An algorithm that solves this latter problem can be used to determine size of the smallest context set C using binary search, and its witness could be used to identify the corresponding context C).

RULE CONTEXT EXISTENCE
INSTANCE: A finite set F (of feature pairs), and two sets *Pos* and *Neg* of subsets of F.
QUESTION: Does there exists a subset $C \subseteq F$ such that $\forall P \in Pos, C \subseteq P$, and $\forall N \in Neg, C \not\subseteq N$?

RULE CONTEXT MINIMALITY
INSTANCE: A finite set F (of feature pairs), two sets *Pos* and *Neg* of subsets of F, and a positive integer $K \leq |F|$.
QUESTION: Does there exists a subset $C \subseteq F$ with $|C| \leq K$ such that $\forall P \in Pos, C \subseteq P$, and $\forall N \in Neg, C \not\subseteq N$?

There is an algorithm that answers the existence problem in deterministic polynomial time. To see this, first note that C is bounded above by $C' = \bigcap Pos$. Then observe that if any subset C of C' satisfies $\forall N \in Neg, C \not\subseteq N$ then C' does also. Hence the rule context existence problem can be answered in deterministic polynomial time by first computing C' and then checking if $\forall N \in Neg, C' \not\subseteq N$.

The rule context minimality problem is clearly in NP, since a non-deterministic machine can simply 'guess' a set C of size K and then 'check' that it satisfies the constraints involving Neg and Pos. We show that it is NP-hard (and therefore NP-complete) via a reduction from HITTING SET, a problem already known to be NP-complete (Garey and Johnson 1979, page 222).

> **HITTING SET**
> INSTANCE: A set S of subsets of a finite set U, a positive integer $K \leq |U|$.
> QUESTION: Is there a subset $U' \subseteq U$ with $|U'| \leq K$ such that U' contains at least one element from each subset in S?

Given an instance of HITTING SET, we construct an instance of RULE CONTEXT MINIMALITY as follows. Let $F = U$, $Pos = \{ U \}$, and $Neg = \{ F - W \mid W \in S \}$. Clearly, $\forall N \in Neg, C \not\subseteq N$ just in case C contains at least one element from each subset of S, so the reduction is correct. The size of the rule context minimality problem is at most the square of the size of the hitting set problem, and it can be computed in deterministic polynomial time.

5 Conclusion

This paper has shown that the general problem of inducing even a single rule from a set of positive and negative examples is intractible (assuming P ≠ NP). This result seems to bear on the debate between rationalist and empiricist positions on language acquisition. The rationalist holds that the structure of a human language is essentially determined by the nature of the human mind, whereas the empiricist holds that the structure of a language is learned from the examples of it that the language learner is exposed to. There are several possible interpretations of this result.

One might take it as computational evidence for the rationalist position. As remarked above, the reduction relies on the unboundedness of the set of features that might potentially trigger the rule being learnt. If additional 'rationalist' constraints imposed a bound on this set—as a theory of 'universal grammar' might plausibly do—then the reduction would no longer go through, and finding even the minimal rule context that accounts for an alternation could be a computationally tractable problem

However, such a conclusion may be too strong. Although every NP-complete problem must contain 'intractible instances', some instances of an NP-complete problem may be easy, or even trivial, to decide. In fact, it can be the case that the *average* time complexity of an intractible problem grows relatively slowly with respect to problem size. To make the argument above stronger then, one might try to show that the minimal rule context problem was intractible even in the average case. But this might be hard to do, since it would require assumptions about the nature of the distribution of instances.

An empiricist could also weaken the assumption that the language learner is required to induce the minimal rule context, and claim that all that is necessary is that the language learner induce a rule whose context feature set is *approximately* minimal. Again, some intractible problems become tractable when weakened appropriately in this manner.

Finally, an empiricist might freely admit that the human language faculty in fact can put to use grammars which its grammar learning procedure cannot acquire. Such a grammar would never be learnt, therefore would never be spoken, and hence would never appear as input to a language learner. Thus 'performance constraints' on the grammar learning procedure would impose restrictions on the class of human languages. Functionally these constraints would appear to be similar to those posited by the rationalists, and it might be difficult to distinguish the two positions.

Bibliography

Barton, E., R. Berwick and E. Ristad (1987) *Computational Complexity and Natural Language*. The MIT Press.

Chomsky, N. and M. Halle (1968) *The Sound Pattern of English*. New York: Harper and Row.

Garey, M. and D. Johnson (1979) *Computers and Intractability, A Guide to the Theory of NP-completeness*. W.H. Freeman

Hopcroft, J. and J. Ullman (1979) *Introduction to Automata Theory, Languages and Computation*. Addison-Wesley.

Johnson, M. (1984) "A Discovery Procedure for Certain Phonological Rules", in *The Proceedings of the 10th International Conference on Computational Linguistics*, Stanford, California.

Pollard, C. and I. Sag (1989) *Information-based Syntax and Semantics, Volume 1*. CSLI Lecture Notes, Chicago University Press.

Shieber, S. (1984) *An Introduction to Unification-based Theories of Grammar*. CSLI Lecture Notes Series, Chicago University Press.

Shapes of the Generalized Trochee

RENÉ KAGER
University of Utrecht

1. Setting the stage

One major goal of metrical theory is to characterize the foot typology which adequately models the patterns of rhythmic alternation found in stress languages. In line with this research program, this paper[1] aims at the following three goals. Firstly, providing new empirical evidence for the foot parsing mode known as the generalized trochee (GT), which was originally proposed by Prince (1980), and was elaborated on by Hayes (1991). Secondly, narrowing down the set of empirically attested shapes of the GT. Thirdly, proposing a theory of two-layered foot parsing that rationalizes the attested variation in shape of the GT. This theory relies heavily on clash avoidance, and provides further evidence for the mora as a rhythmic unit apart from the syllable (cf. Prince 1983, Kager 1992a).

The asymmetric foot inventory of Hayes (1991) contains two types of trochaic feet, the SYLLABIC TROCHEE (1a) and the MORAIC TROCHEE (1b). Each of these characterizes one style of rhythmic alternation in trochaic stress systems:

(1) a. **Syllabic trochee:** Construct (* .)
σ σ

b. **Moraic trochee:** Construct (* .) or (*)
σ_μ σ_μ $\sigma_{\mu\mu}$

The syllabic trochee is indifferent to the weight of syllables that it organizes, i.e., it is QUANTITY INSENSITIVE. In contrast, the moraic trochee is QUANTITY SENSITIVE, since it demands that a bisyllabic foot consists of precisely two light syllables $[\sigma_\mu\sigma_\mu]$, and a monosyllabic foot of precisely one heavy syllable $[\sigma_{\mu\mu}]$.

Anyula (Kirton 1967) illustrates the syllabic trochee in its simplest form. It has no contrast of syllable quantity, and for this reason might be called 'trivially quantity insensitive'. Characteristically, it has a bisyllabic WORD MINIMUM, based on its foot, and a stress pattern which avoids adjacent stressed syllables, i.e., SYLLABLE CLASH. Syllabic trochees are assigned initially and finally.

---

1 This research was supported by the Linguistic Research Foundation, which is funded by the Netherlands organization for scientific research, NWO, grant no. 300-171-023. For comments on earlier versions of this paper, I wish to thank Janet Grijzenhout, Mike Hammond, Kristin Hanson, Bruce Hayes, Paul Kiparsky, Aditi Lahiri, Alan Prince, Harry van der Hulst, and Ellis Visch. (All of whom I exempt from responsibility for any errors or misconceptions.)

(2) a.
```
(*   .)
há.wu
```
'cloud'

b.
```
 .  (*   .)
ni.wán.ji
```
'animal flesh'

c.
```
(*   .)(*   .)
má.ru.wá.ra
```
'cousin'

d.
```
(*   .) . (*   .)
má.ru.wa.rá.la
```
'with the cousin'

In trisyllabic words (cf. 2b), the conflict between the initial and final foot seems to be resolved in favor of the latter.

Nunggubuyu (Hore 1981) constitutes a typical moraic trochee language. Stress is on all heavy syllables and on alternate light syllables. Again, the word minimum equals the minimal foot, which in this case is bimoraic. Another feature often found in moraic trochee systems is that syllable clashes are allowed to some extent, as can be seen in (3b,c).[2]

(3) a.
```
(*)
 –
yúul
```
'bushland'

b.
```
(*)    (*    .)  (*    .)
 –      ˘    ˘    ˘    ˘
ngàa.dhì.ya.rrí.nya
```
'tree species'

c.
```
 .  (*)  (*   .)(*)  (*   .)
 ˘   –    ˘   ˘   –    ˘   ˘
dhu.màa.mù.gu.nàa.mú.rra
```
'snake species'

When two adjacent syllables are stressed in Nunggubuyu, the first must be heavy, while the second may be either light or heavy. This signals that clash is defined as a pair of adjacent stressed moras, rather than syllables.

The notion of MORAIC RHYTHM can be represented by aligning each mora with a grid element (cf. Prince 1983), as in (4). Sonority factors designate initial moras of bimoraic syllables as strong, which under bipositional representation translates as trochaic internal prominence in bimoraic feet [$\sigma_{\mu\mu}$] (cf. Prince 1983, Kager 1992a). This has important external rhythmic consequences. In particular, a strong first mora of a heavy syllable, (e.g., *màa* or *nàa* in 4), does not clash with the first mora of a following syllable (*mù* and *mú*), since a weak mora intervenes:

(4)
```
 .  (*.)(*   .)(*.)(*   .)
dhu.màa.mù.gu.nàa.mú.rra
```

In Nunggubuyu, as in most other moraic trochee systems, the mora is the unit of foot parsing as well as rhythm (i.e., clash avoidance). Similarly, syllabic trochee systems such as Anyula, take the syllable as their unit of foot parsing and rhythm. This correlation between parsing units and rhythmic units was stated by Kager (1992a) as the RHYTHMIC UNIFORMITY HYPOTHESIS:

(5) **Rhythmic Uniformity Hypothesis**
Parsing units imply rhythmic units.

In this paper, I will focus on a third type of trochaic system, one which combines an underlying distinction of syllable quantity and syllable-based rhythm, the latter diagnosed by rhythmic alternation (and clash avoidance) based

2 Actually Nunggubuyu is bidirectional, main stress being assigned by a non-iterative moraic trochee at the right edge, and secondary stress by iterative moraic trochees from left to right. I also abstract away from two destressing rules (cf. Kager 1990).

on the syllable. To avoid syllabic clash, some syllabic systems even locate heavy syllables in unstressed positions of trochaic feet. These are referred to as *truly quantity insensitive*, or *quantity disrespecting* (cf. Hayes 1991), as distinct from 'trivially quantity insensitive' systems, which lack a weight contrast. Syllable-based rhythm and quantity insensitivity apparently diagnose the syllabic trochee as the relevant foot for such systems. But the situation is more complex. Hayes (1991) observes many systems where syllabic [σ σ] and moraic trochees [$\sigma_{\mu\mu}$] cooccur. This cooccurrence forms the empirical basis of the generalized trochee.

A simple example of a GT system is Pintupi (Hansen and Hansen 1969). It has a quantity contrast as well as syllable-based rhythm. As in many Australian languages, the vowel length distinction on which the quantity contrast is based is restricted to the initial syllable of the stem. For this reason, it is impossible to establish whether a heavy syllable may occupy a weak position in a foot [$\sigma_{\mu\mu}\sigma_{\mu\mu}$] or [$\sigma_{\mu}\sigma_{\mu\mu}$]. Still, syllabic trochees [$\sigma_{\mu\mu}\sigma_{\mu}$] are diagnosed by rightward alternation of secondary stresses, which follows the pattern of (6a), rather than (6b):

(6) a. [$\sigma_{\mu\mu}$ σ_{μ}][σ_{μ} σ_{μ}][σ_{μ} σ_{μ}] ... Syllabic trochee parsing
b. [$\sigma_{\mu\mu}$][σ_{μ} σ_{μ}][σ_{μ} σ_{μ}][σ_{μ} ... Moraic trochee parsing

Interestingly, there is also evidence for the moraic trochee [$\sigma_{\mu\mu}$] in the form of the bimoraic word minimum: all monosyllables in Pintupi contain long vowels.

To account for such 'mixed' systems Hayes suggests that trochaic systems may build syllabic and moraic trochees next to each other on the same iterative pass of foot construction. Formalizing this idea, Hayes proposes the GENERALIZED TROCHEE (GT), which is the net result of adding up all proper expansions of the syllabic trochee (1a) and moraic trochee (1b):

(7) **Generalized trochee**: Construct

(* .)	else	(*)
σ σ		$\sigma_{\mu\mu}$

Observe that the double-light expansion of the moraic trochee [σ_{μ} σ_{μ}] is subsumed under the bisyllabic foot [σ σ], so that essentially the GT is a foot type which includes all bisyllabic expansions of trochees, plus the monosyllabic heavy foot [$\sigma_{\mu\mu}$]. The latter is formed by default only, where no bisyllabic foot can be formed (i.e., in monosyllabic words and possibly at the end of the domain). This relationship reflects MAXIMALITY of foot parsing: whenever a string matches two expansions of a single foot scheme, the longest expansion is selected. In Pintupi, which has rightward parsing, this produces (6a) rather than (6b).

Observations on a number of other languages lead Hayes to hypothesize that the syllabic trochee (1a) may be completely eliminated as a foot type, since all languages with syllabic trochees either require a generalized trochee analysis, or else have no distinction of syllable quantity.[3] This so-called GENERALIZED TROCHEE HYPOTHESIS receives strong confirmation from a typological survey that I conducted on Australian languages, reported on in Kager (1992b).

Now consider Estonian (Hint 1973), the system for which Prince (1980) introduced an ancester of Hayes' generalized trochee. Estonian, as Pintupi, has a bimoraic word minimum, diagnosing the bimoraic trochee. But it is an even more telling example of a generalized trochee system because its distinction of quantity is unrestricted positionally, and all expansions of the GT are attested. Slightly

3 In a recent version of Hayes' manuscript, which came to my attention after presentation of this paper, the syllabic trochee has been redefined as the former GT, i.e., as [σ σ] or [$\sigma_{\mu\mu}$]. Hayes accordingly defines the degenerate foot as [σ_{μ}], so that [$\sigma_{\mu\mu}$] no longer counts as degenerate in a syllabic trochee system.

simplifying the Estonian stress pattern,[4] this may be described as follows. Main stress is initial, and secondary stresses fall on nonfinal odd-numbered syllables, counting rightward from the main stress, and disrespecting syllable quantity. Final syllables are stressed only if they are heavy, and when no stressed syllable precedes. That is, when rightward construction of bisyllabic trochees leaves one unfooted syllable at the edge of the domain, the only proper GT to be constructed is the monosyllabic heavy foot [$\sigma_{\mu\mu}$], as the degenerate foot [σ_{μ}] is excluded (cf. Prince 1980,532):

(8) a. (* .) (* .) (* .) .
$\sigma\ \sigma\ \ \sigma\ \sigma\ \ \sigma\ \sigma\ \ \sigma_{\mu}$

b. (* .) (* .) (* .) (*)
$\sigma\ \sigma\ \ \sigma\ \sigma\ \ \sigma\ \sigma\ \ \sigma_{\mu\mu}$

All (attested) iterative trochaic systems with syllabic rhythm and a free distinction of syllable quantity have this property of monosyllabic heavy feet at the edge of the domain where the iteration ends (cf. Kager 1992b).

For Estonian, it can be illustrated by the quantitative minimal pair of examples of (9a,b), where a difference in quantity of final syllables is reflected in a difference of stress. Example (9c) shows that a final syllable (even if it is heavy) is unstressed when the penult is stressed. This points to syllabic clash avoidance.[5] All examples are taken from Prince (1980).

(9)	a.	pí.mes.tà.va.le	'blinding (ill.sg.)'
	b.	pí.mes.tà.va.màit	'blinding (part.pl.)'
	c.	kín.nast	'glove (part.sg.)'

We actually find that in Estonian all predicted shapes of the GT are attested:

(10)	a.	[$\sigma_{\mu}\sigma_{\mu}$]	ré.ti.[lì.le]	'ladder (all.sg.)'
	b.	[$\sigma_{\mu\mu}\sigma_{\mu}$]	Ép.pet.[tùs.te].lè.ki	'lessons, too (all.pl.)'
	c.	[$\sigma_{\mu}\sigma_{\mu\mu}$]	pí.mes.[tà.vas].se	'blinding (ill.sg.)'
	d.	[$\sigma_{\mu\mu}\sigma_{\mu\mu}$]	vá.ra.[sèi.mat].tè.le	'earliest (all.pl.)'
	e.	[$\sigma_{\mu\mu}$]	pá.he.[mài]<t>	'worse (part.pl.)'

Considering the GT systems discussed so far, Pintupi and Estonian, there is every reason to believe that the GT parsing mode avoids syllabic clash, rather than mora clash. Of course, this is what we would expect from the Rhythmic Uniformity Hypothesis, since bisyllabic feet prevail under the GT parsing mode.

In the remainder of this paper I will analyze two more trochaic systems with distinctions of syllable quantity and (apparently) syllable-based rhythms. These systems, Finnish and Yindjibarndi, differ from those discussed earlier, however, in that they avoid mora clash as well as syllable clash. From the viewpoint of foot parsing, these systems seem to avoid particular shapes of the GT (Yindjibarndi avoids both L-H and H-H, and Finnish just L-H). Consequently they resist a straightforward analysis under the GT, whose bisyllabic expansion [$\sigma\sigma$] is blind to the internal structure of syllables parsed. I will propose an alternative two-layered theory, which allows optional access to moraic rhythm in syllabic parsing.

---

4 For expository purposes I abstract away from optional ternary alternation, as well as from the phenomenon of overlength. Prince (1980) and Hayes (1991) provide detailed analyses.

5 Overlong syllables, which are always stressed, may be followed by another stressed syllable.

2. Avoidance of $[\sigma_{\mu}\sigma_{\mu\mu}]$ trochees in Finnish

The first language to be discussed is Finnish, which is closely related to Estonian. Finnish, as Estonian, has strictly initial main stress, and secondary stress that alternates rightward. The secondary stress data on which my analysis is based are from the description by Kiparsky (1991a, p.c.).[6] According to this description, the binary alternation of secondary stresses becomes locally ternary in precisely one context. This is when a light syllable would be stressed directly before a heavy syllable. Here, the light syllable remains unstressed, and stress skips over to the heavy syllable. This produces a locally ternary pattern, as shown in (11i-l). Final syllables are stressed under the same conditions as in Estonian: they must be heavy, and may not follow a stressed syllable, cf. (11i).

(11)				
	a.	˘ ˘ ˘ ˘	ló.pe.tè.ta	'finish (negative)'
	b.	˘ ˘ - ˘ ˘	ló.pe.tèt.ta.va	'to be finished'
	c.	- - ˘ ˘	téu.ras.tà.mo	'slaughterhouse'
	d.	˘ ˘ - -	ló.pe.tèt.tiin	'one finished'
	e.	- - - ˘ - ˘	púo.lus.tèt.ta.vìs.sa	'defensible'
	f.	˘ - ˘ ˘ ˘ ˘	á.loit.tè.li.jà.na	'as a beginner'
	g.	˘ - ˘ ˘ ˘ ˘ ˘	ó.pet.tè.le.mà.na.ni	'as something I have been learning'
	h.	˘ - - - ˘	í.han.tèel.lis.ta	'idealistic (partitive)'
	i.	˘ ˘ ˘ -	ló.pe.te.tàan	'one finishes'
	j.	˘ - ˘ - ˘	rá.kas.tu.nèi.ta	'infatuated lovers'
	k.	˘ - ˘ - -	ló.pet.ta.jài.set	'concluding ceremonies'
	l.	˘ ˘ - ˘ ˘ - ˘	lú.e.tùt.te.lu.tèl.la	'to gradually cause to have been read'
	m.	˘ ˘ ˘ - ˘ ˘ ˘ ˘ ˘	ká.no.ni.sòi.ma.nà.ni.kò.han	'in a state of having been canonized by me, of course (essive sg.)'

Rephrasing the generalization in terms of trochaic feet we find that Finnish secondary stress avoids the light-heavy foot $[\sigma_{\mu}\sigma_{\mu\mu}]$, while all other predicted shapes of the generalized trochee are attested:[7]

(12)				
	a.	$[\sigma_{\mu}\sigma_{\mu}]$	ló.pe.[tè.ta]	'finish (negative)'
	b.	$[\sigma_{\mu\mu}\sigma_{\mu}]$	ló.pe.tèt.ta.va	'to be finished'
	c.	$[\sigma_{\mu}\sigma_{\mu\mu}]$	*Not attested*	
	d.	$[\sigma_{\mu\mu}\sigma_{\mu\mu}]$	ló.pe.[tèt.tii]<n>	'one finished'
	e.	$[\sigma_{\mu\mu}]$	ló.pe.te.[tàa]<n>	'one finishes'

Stress patterns of other GT languages show that Finnish is not unique in avoiding light-heavy trochees, as will be demonstrated below for two Australian languages, Yindjibarndi and Guugu Yimidhirr. Another example is Gooniyandi (McGregor 1990), which is analyzed in Kager (1992b).

From the viewpoint of the GT, avoidance of L-H feet is a mystery. Essentially the bisyllabic GT is a quantity insensitive foot, which predicts that the quantity of the syllables that are parsed is completely irrelevant. But for Finnish this is incorrect, since L-H feet are avoided. We now arrive at the (paradoxical)

---

6 Slightly different patterns of secondary stresses are reported by Harms (1960, 1964) and Carlson (1978).

7 The insight that Finnish avoids L-H trochaic feet is due to Kiparsky (1991a) and is also found in unpublished work by Hayes.

heart of the issue. Quantity insensitive stress systems which avoid syllable clashes must be based on syllabic feet; still some of these systems measure moraic quantity in avoiding L-H feet. How to reconcile these observations? In the next section, I will propose a two-layered theory of foot parsing which explains avoidance of L-H trochees as a clash avoidance effect on the mora layer.

3. A two-layered theory of foot parsing

My core hypothesis is that the GT effect derives from the hierarchical nature of the metrical representation. With Halle and Vergnaud (1987) and Kager (1992a) I assume that stress systems select either syllables, or moras as stressable elements. Here I propose to formalize this STRESSABLE ELEMENT PARAMETER by assigning foot parsing to one of two layers in the hierarchical metrical grid. This two-layered theory of foot parsing is summarized in the TWO-LAYER HYPOTHESIS:

(13) **Two Layer Hypothesis**
Foot parsing brackets together elements on one of two layers: the syllable layer, or the mora layer.

Under this theory the syllabic trochee is formalized as trochaic parsing on the syllable layer (14a), while the moraic trochee translates as trochaic parsing on the mora layer (14b). For expository purposes I depict foot bracketing around pairs of stressable elements, while prominences project over these elements:

```
(14) a.   *  .   *     .   *  .   *     .   *  .
         (σ  σ) (σ     σ) (σ  σ) (σ     σ) (σ  σ) . . .        σ layer
          |  |   |\    |   |  |\   |\    |\  |  |
          μ  μ   μμ    μ   μ  μμ   μμ    μμ  μ  μ  . . .       μ layer

     b.   σ  σ   σ     σ  σ   σ     σ     σ     σ  σ  . . .    σ layer
          |  |   |\    |  |   |\    |\    |\    |  |
         (μ  μ) (μμ)  (μ  μ) (μμ)  (μμ)  (μμ)  (μ  μ)  . . .   μ layer
          *  .   *.    *  .   *.    *.    *.    *  .
```

How do we derive the 'GT effect' that monosyllabic heavy feet occur in syllabic systems precisely in those cases where no bisyllabic feet can be constructed? Borrowing terminology from Prince and Smolensky's (1992) HARMONIC THEORY, we may describe this as follows: the constraint that heavy syllables are stressed is subordinated to that of foot bisyllabicity. Thus, quantity reasserts itself wherever bisyllabicity makes no claims. As a first step towards formalization in a two-layered theory, I propose that universally at the mora layer all mora pairs that form heavy syllables are bracketed as bimoraic constituents, regardless of the layer at which directional foot parsing applies. I will call this principle QUANTITY SENSITIVITY, after Prince (1983).

(15) **Quantity Sensitivity**
In systems with distinctions of syllable quantity, mora pairs that form heavy syllables are bracketed into bimoraic constituents.

The internal prominence of $[\sigma_{\mu\mu}]$ moraic constituents depends on sonority factors. Normally it is trochaic as sonority tends to decline between both moras of heavy syllables (cf. Prince 1983). Kager (1992a) argues that this intrinsic trochaic prominence of heavy syllables rhythmically conditions foot parsing in iambic systems, and, more generally, explains many rhythmic asymmetries between trochaic and iambic systems. As shown above for Nunggubuyu it also explains the directional asymmetries in clash avoidance in moraic trochee systems.

I will now formalize the 'GT effect' in the two-layered theory. The intuitive idea is that the scansion at the parsing layer is dominant, but if that scansion is left underspecified, (part of) the scansion may be read off the other layer. To formalize the default realization of bimoraic constituency at syllable layer, I propose a universal principle of HARMONIC CONSTITUENT COPYING:

(16) **Harmonic Constituent Copying**
Constituency is copied from one layer to another, provided that no conflicting scansions arise.[8]

Consequently, a heavy syllable that remains unfooted at syllable layer (because of bisyllabic minimality) will still be interpreted as a foot because of its intrinsic status as a bimoraic constituent on the mora layer. In pure moraic systems, all all moraic feet will be copied to the (empty) syllable layer.

Assuming this two-layered theory, let us now return to the stress pattern of Estonian, abstracting away from optional ternarity and overlength. The analysis contains parametric specification of the following: (a) the layer at which foot parsing takes place (here, syllable layer), as well as the dominance of feet (trochees) and the directionality (from left to right), (b) the layer at which rhythmic conditions are observed during parsing, in particular clash avoidance (here, syllable layer), and (c) the location of primary stress (here, the initial foot):

(17) Two-layered analysis of (simplified) Estonian
- a. Parsing: construct trochees from left to right on the syllable layer.
- b. Rhythm: avoid clash on the syllable layer.
- c. Word Layer: End Rule Left.

When I discuss Finnish and Yindjibarndi below, it will become fully clear why the layers of parsing and rhythm must be distinguished.

For expository reasons, I will use different symbols to indicate the source of constituents. That is, '[*.]' indicates an intrinsic moraic constituent due to QS (15), '{* }' a constituent copied from another layer by HCC (16). Finally, '#' indicates a strong position on the mora layer that is induced by a strong position on the syllable layer dominating it. (The principle behind this will be discussed below.) This results in the representations of (18):

(18)
```
a.  (*                 )       b.  (*                    ) ER
    (*   . ) (*   .)  .            (*   . ) (*   .) {*  } σ
     #  [*.] {#   .}  .             #  [*.] {#   .} [*.]  μ
    pí.mes.tà.va.le                pí.mes.tà.va.màit
```

Summarizing, the GT effect is derived by constructing trochees on the syllable layer, and by copying monosyllabic heavy feet from the mora layer into the syllable layer where no conflicting bracketings arise.

We now return to Finnish, which as I mentioned differs minimally from Estonian in disallowing light-heavy feet under secondary stress. As I will show the intrinsic trochaic nature of heavy syllables gives a rhythmic explanation of the avoidance of L-H feet, based on moraic clash avoidance. Of course, this provides further evidence for the mora as a rhythm unit. From the hierarchical nature of the

8 The ban against conflicting scansions may not need stipulation, as it is apparently an instantiation of the general principle of structure preservingness.

multi-layered grid, interaction between adjacent grid layers may be expected. The main source of interaction between layers is a well-established principle of grid structure, the CONTINUOUS COLUMN CONSTRAINT (CCC, cf. Prince 1983, Hayes 1991):

(19) **Continuous Column Constraint**
If a syllable forms a rhythmic beat on a given level, it must also form a rhythmic beat on all lower levels.

The CCC entails that whenever syllabic parsing produces a strong position on the syllable layer, a prominence is induced on the mora layer. When a L-H trochee is constructed at the syllable layer, a strong position is induced at the mora layer below the initial light syllable. This induced prominence clashes with the intrinsic mora prominence of the second syllable of the L-H foot. This is shown in (20a). In contrast no mora clash arises in a double heavy foot (cf. 20b), since the second (weak) mora of the initial syllable rhythmically separates both mora prominences:

```
(20) a.  (*   . )    σ layer        b.  (*    . )    σ layer
          # [*.]     μ layer            [*.][*.]     μ layer
          |  |                           |   |
          |  Intrinsic prominence        |   Intrinsic prominence
         Induced prominence             Intrinsic prominence
```

Crucially it takes a two-layered representation of foot structure, in a hierarchical grid, to make reference to the intrinsic mora prominence of a syllable that is not stressed itself. Intrinsic moraic prominences condition foot parsing from a layer hidden below the syllabic parsing layer.

Having identified the rhythmic trigger of L-H avoidance I now go on to formalize avoidance itself. I adopt a proposal from Prince (1983), Van der Hulst (1991), Kager (1992a), and Lahiri (1992), which I will call RHYTHMIC SKIPPING:

(21) **Rhythmic Skipping**
To avoid clash, directional foot parsing may skip one stressable element.

Rhythmic skipping is related to the WEAK LOCAL PARSING mode of ternary systems in Hayes (1991), which skips a syllable after every foot constructed. From a survey of ternary systems (Estonian, Pacific Yupik, Winnebago, and others), Hayes concludes that skipped syllables must be light. Interestingly, a two-layered theory explains why heavy syllable skipping is generally impossible. On the mora layer, heavy syllables are simply not stressable elements, hence ineligible for skipping. On the syllable layer, the need for rhythmic heavy syllable skipping never arises, since the proper rhythmic distance between stresses is encoded in the bisyllabic parsing foot itself. If a heavy syllable would be skipped by weak local parsing, its unfooted position would be automatically filled in by Harmonic Constituent Copying of a monosyllabic heavy foot from the mora layer, thereby cancelling the effect of skipping.

I now return to Finnish to illustrate this theory. First the fact must be accounted for that main stress is strictly initial, even in words that start with a L-H sequence. I adopt Hayes' (1988) proposal that the word layer of Finnish is constructed prior to the foot layer, an option called TOP-DOWN GRID CONSTRUCTION.[9] Consequently the location of the main stressed syllable becomes

9 Similar proposals are made by Van der Hulst (1984), Lahiri and Van der Hulst (1988), and Kager (1989).

independent of the output of directional foot parsing, and main stress is strictly initial. The Continuous Column Constraint (19) guarantees that the initial syllable is strong on subordinated grid layers. The complete two-layered analysis is stated below:

(22) Two-layered analysis of Finnish
 a. Word Layer: End Rule Left.
 b. Parsing: construct trochees from left to right on the syllable layer.
 c. Rhythm: avoid clashes on the syllable AND the mora layer.

We find that both Finnish and Estonian construct feet at the syllable layer, hence avoid syllabic clash as predicted by Rhythmic Uniformity. The difference is that Finnish, but not Estonian, measures the implied rhythm at the mora layer.[10]

The analysis of Finnish is illustrated in (23). (23a) shows the correct parsing of a word that contains a light-heavy sequence. At syllable layer, the syllable *lu* is skipped in order to avoid clash on the mora layer. If skipping had not taken place, the structure of (23b) would have arisen, in which the mora *lu* (its prominence induced by syllabic parsing) clashes with the strong first mora of the bimoraic foot *tel* (which is due to Quantity Sensitivity):

```
(23) a.  (*                  )   b.    (*                  )
         (* .)(*   .) . (*  .)         (* .)(*   .)(*   .) .
         {# .}[*.] .  . [*.] .          #    [*.] .  # [*.] .
         lú.e.tùt.te.lu.tèl.la   NOT  *lú.e.tùt.te.lù.tel.la

     c.  (*            )         d.    (*          )
         (*  . ) . (*  . )             (*  .)(*  .) .
          # [*.] . [*.] .              {#  .}[*.] .  .
         ló.pet.ta.jài.se<t>           ló.pe.tèt.ta.va

     e.  (*          )           f.    (*          )
         (*  .) . {* }                 (*  .)(*  . )
         {#  .} . [*.]                 {#  .}[*.][*.]
         ló.pe.te.tàa<n>               ló.pe.tèt.tii<n>

     g.  (*                              )  i.  (*                )
         (*  .)(*  . ) . (*  .)(*  .)           (*  . )(*     . ) .
         {#  .} . [*.] . {#  .}{#  .}            # [*.][*.] [*.] .
         ká.no.ni.sòi.ma.nà.ni.kò.ha<n>         í.han.tèel.lis.ta
```

Additional evidence for the claim that light-heavy feet are avoided in Finnish comes from Savo dialects (Skousen 1972, Kiparsky 1991a), where initial [σ_μ $\sigma_{\mu\mu}$] is repaired into [$\sigma_{\mu\mu}$ $\sigma_{\mu\mu}$] by gemination, e.g., */mi.tään/* => [*mít.tään*] 'anything'. In my theory, this reduces to moraic clash resolution. We thus find that mora clashes are both avoided and repaired in Finnish. Avoidance is implemented in skipping during foot parsing, and repair in initial gemination.

---

10 Kiparsky (1991a) bases his analysis of Finnish on the unificationist idea that sequences with iambic quantity [$\sigma_\mu\sigma_{\mu\mu}$] trigger iambic prominence. This may account for local ternarity, e.g., [*ló.pe*][*te.tàan*], but it is rather unclear how syllable clash avoidance is to be expressed in this analysis. E.g., what principle causes parsing to avoid *[*ká.no*][*ni.sòi*][*mà.na*][*nì.ko*].*han*? If rhythmic skipping were to be assumed this would miss an important generalization, namely that both effects (L-H avoidance and rhythmic skipping) are reactions on clash, either at the mora layer or the syllable layer.

An alternative analysis of Finnish, based on the moraic trochee, was suggested to me by Aditi Lahiri (p.c.). Assuming moraic trochees, avoidance of L-H feet follows from the bimoraic foot. A L-H sequence is parsed as an unfooted light syllable plus a bimoraic foot. In (24), light syllables that remain unfooted in this context are underlined. Avoidance of syllable clashes is built into the analysis by rhythmic skipping. A syllable, light or heavy, is skipped to avoid syllable clash (i.e., after every heavy syllable). In (24), skipped syllables appear in boldface:

```
(24)  a.   (*                          )
           (*  .) . (*)  . (*  .) (*  .)
            ˘  ˘  ˘  –   ˘  ˘   ˘  ˘  ˘
           ká.no.ni.sòi.ma.nà.ni.kò.ha<n>

      b.   (*                  )    c.   (*              )
           (* .) (*)  .  . (*)  .        (*  .) (*)   .
            ˘  ˘  –   ˘  ˘  –   ˘         ˘  ˘   –    –
           lú.e.tùt.te.lu.tèl.la         ló.pe.tèt.tii<n
```

The major similarity between this analysis and mine is rhythmic skipping. However, Lahiri's analysis crucially allows skipped syllables to be of any weight. This runs into Hayes' (1991) observation, discussed above, that syllables skipped by weak local parsing must be light. The second problem of heavy syllable skipping in a moraic parsing mode is that it violates Quantity Sensitivity (15), i.e., the intrinsic stress of bimoraic syllables. Relaxing QS would entail the loss of explanation of all 'intrinsic stress' phenomena observed by Kager (1992a).

One might try to preserve QS in a moraic trochee analysis by translating heavy syllable skipping as a destressing rule. Destressing would then affect the righthand of two syllables in clash, applying iteratively from left to right. However, this analysis produces misparsings in strings of light syllables lying to the right of a heavy syllable, e.g., *[ká.no].ni.[sòi].[mà.na].[ní.ko].ha<n>* (and *[ká.no].ni.[sòi].ma.na.[ní.ko].ha<n>* after destressing). This shows that foot parsing itself includes a syllable clash avoidance mechanism.

4. Syllabic clash avoidance in Yindjibarndi

The third system which I will discuss is Yindjibarndi (Wordick 1982), which shows an interesting interaction between stress and a process of long vowel breaking. The long vowels are /aa, ii, uu, oo/. Wordick (1982,40) describes the process of long vowel breaking as follows: '... long vowels, especially high ones, may be pronounced either as part of a single syllable consisting of two morae or as part of two different ones, i.e., with one mora in each.' Long vowel breaking is optional in some contexts, but obligatory in others, depending on metrical conditions to be discussed below. I will tentatively formulate the rule as in (25).

(25) **Long Vowel Breaking**

```
 σ             σ σ
 |\            | |
 μ μ    =>     μ μ
 \ /           \ /
  H             H
```

Wordick (1980, 17-18) provides two arguments against treating long vowels as (underlying) sequences of two identical short vowels. Firstly '... the long vowel *oo* cannot be pronounced with medial breaking, ... and in fact there is no short *o* in the language'. Secondly, long vowels behave as tautosyllabic in the allomorphy of the objective suffix, which is sensitive to the number of syllables in the base, e.g., monosyllabic */thaa+u/* 'mouth (obj.)', and */mii+u/* 'limb (obj.)', versus bisyllabic */thara+yi/* 'mouth (obj.)', */tyi.a+yi/* 'chair (obj.)'. Yindjibarndi apparently has a bimoraic word minimum.

Let us now take a first look at the stress pattern of the language:

(26)	*I. Words without long vowels in even-numbered syllables*			
	a.	˘ ˘ ˘	wílarrà	'moon'
	b.	˘ ˘ -	pángkarrìi	'go (infinitive)'
	c.	- ˘ ˘	káarrwarà	'loincloth'
	d.	˘ ˘ ˘ ˘	párnrturràrna	'Venus'
	e.	˘ ˘ - ˘	ngúnhungkìiri	'they'
	f.	- ˘ - ˘	káarrwan^{y}t^{y}àangu	'slip, slide (infinitive)'
	II. Words with long nonhigh vowels in even-numbered syllables			
	g.	˘ -	t^{y}arráarn	'frog'
	h.	- -	páarnpaarn	'mulga parrot'
	i.	˘ - ˘	purnngáarri	'cyclonic cloud'
	j.	˘ - ˘ -	ngurnáapurràa	'approximately towards him'
	III. Words with long high vowels in even-numbered syllables			
	k.	˘ -	pírri.ì *or* pirríi	'match'
	l.	- -	máapu.ù	'mob (objective)'
	m.	˘ - ˘	páli.ìrri *or* palíirri	'blue-tongue lizard'
	n.	- - ˘	káayu.ùrru	'southward'
	o.	˘ - -	mártu.urràa	'twilight'
	p.	- - -	máapu.urràa	'in the general direction of the group'

The generalizations are as follows. Firstly, in words that have no long vowels in even-numbered syllables (cf. 26a-f) stresses fall as predicted under the rightward GT, with binary alternation. Secondly, final degenerate feet [σ_μ] are allowed, under syllabic clash avoidance, (cf. 26a,c,l). Thirdly, in words where long vowels are underlying in even-numbered syllables, these never surface in weak positions. Two strategies occur to avoid surface weak heavy syllables. One, which we already know from Finnish, is skipping a light syllable before a heavy syllable, so as to stress the latter. In Yindjibarndi skipping also applies to initial sequences of a light plus a heavy syllable (cf. 26g,i,j,k,m). Interestingly, the second way of avoiding unstressed heavy syllables is breaking up long vowels in even-numbered syllables, producing two light syllables. In (26k-p) dots indicate the separated halfs of broken vowels. Breaking competes or alternates with light syllable skipping in sequences of light-heavy (cf. 26k,m,o). But breaking is obligatory in sequences of heavy syllables, the second of which avoids being parsed as the weak syllable of a double-heavy trochee (cf. 26l,n,p). An isolated example occurs of an even-numbered syllable with a nonhigh long vowel, cf. (26h).

In the descriptive vocabulary of the GT, Yindjibarndi seems, at the surface at least, to require all but two predicted expansions of the GT:

(27)				
	a.	[$\sigma_\mu \sigma_\mu$]	[wíla][rrà]	[pírri][ì]
	b.	[$\sigma_{\mu\mu} \sigma_\mu$]	[káarrwa][rà]	[káayu][ùrru]
	c.	[$\sigma_\mu \sigma_{\mu\mu}$]	*Not attested*	
	d.	[$\sigma_{\mu\mu} \sigma_{\mu\mu}$]	*Marginally attested*, cf. [páarnpaarn]	
	e.	[$\sigma_{\mu\mu}$]	[pángka][rrìi]	

Apparently Yindjibarndi requires a set of GT expansions that is a subset of that of Finnish, as one more shape of the bisyllabic GT is missing, the double heavy foot. That is, at the surface no heavy syllables may occupy weak positions in feet. Parsing apparently requires the heavy-light foot $[\sigma_{\mu\mu}\sigma_{\mu}]$, which points to syllabic foot parsing. But under a syllabic analysis, the quantity sensitivity of Yindjibarndi (which disallows heavy syllables in weak positions), cannot be expressed. It is this property that distinguishes Yindjibarndi from Finnish.[11] Therefore I take the mora to be the parsing unit. With parsing at mora layer, avoidance of L-H feet (cf. *purnngáarri*, instead of **púrnngaarrì*) becomes a simple matter of parsing, since L-H is not a proper moraic trochee. In addition to the mora, the syllable must be a rhythm unit, for three reasons. Firstly, final degenerate feet occur under strict syllable clash avoidance, e.g. *purnngáarri* 'cyclonic cloud', not **purnngáarrì*. Secondly, words with no long vowels in even syllables follow the pattern *káarrwarà* 'loincloth', instead of **káarrwàra* (hence $*[\sigma_{\mu\mu}][\sigma_{\mu}\ \sigma_{\mu}]$). Thirdly, the output of long vowel breaking conforms to it, cf. *káayu.ùrru* 'southward', instead of **káayù.urrù*. Avoidance of syllabic clash is implemented by switching the rhythm parameter to 'on' for the syllable layer, cf. (28b):

(28) Two-layered analysis of Yindjibarndi

- a. Parsing: construct trochees from left to right on the mora layer. Final degenerate feet are allowed.[12]
- b. Rhythm: avoid clash on the mora layer AND the syllable layer.
- c. Word Layer: End Rule Left.

Harmonic Constituent Copying copies moraic trochees to the syllabic layer, where the syllabic rhythmic effects of moraic parsing are measured. Moras are skipped to avoid syllabic clashes, as shown in (29b,e,f). (Vowel sequences that are the result of breaking have been underlined.)

```
(29) a.  (*                  ) b.  (*              )   Word
         {* }    .    {* }   .     {* }      . {*}     σ
         [*.]    .    [*.]   .     [*.]      . (*)     μ
         káarr.wanY.tYàa.ngu       káarr.wa.rà

     c.  (*              ) d.  (       *          )   Word
         {*    .}.  {* }             .  {* } .  {* }   σ
         (*    .).  [*.]             .  [*.] .  [*.]   μ
         már.tu.u.rràa             ngu.rnáa.pu.rràa

     e.  (*             )   f.  (*              )     Word
         {* } .{*     .}        {* } . .  {* }         σ
         [*.] .(*     .)        [*.] . .  [*.]         μ
         káa.yu.ù.rru           máa.pu.u.rràa
```

Under this analysis the function of Long Vowel Breaking becomes fully clear: the rule serves to satisfy the no-syllable-clash condition on the Yindjibarndi[13] foot

11 The foot required, the quantity sensitive syllabic trochee $[\sigma\ (\sigma_{\mu})]$ (cf. Hayes 1980), is dubious. Hayes (1991) convincingly shows that it should be eliminated from the theory.

12 As shown by Hayes (1991), Kager (1992a), and Kiparsky (1991b), word final degenerate feet need not be due to foot parsing proper, but can be derived in various other ways.

13 Other moraic trochee systems avoid syllabic clash by destressing, instead of breaking. This is the case in Ngiyambaa (Donaldson 1980), Wargamay (Dixon 1981), Nyawaygi (Dixon 1983), and to some extent in Nunggubuyu (Hore 1981), all Australian languages.

parsing mode. Breaking occurs precisely where otherwise a syllable clash would arise from mora layer parsing or from the juxtaposition of two long vowels. Light syllables in the output of vowel breaking are parsed regularly, including rhythmic skipping in (29c,e). That is, breaking may well apply in tandem with foot parsing.

5. Factoring out the rhythmic dimensions of trochaic foot parsing

On the basis of the systems discussed it can be concluded that rhythmic units are partly predictable from parsing units (cf. the Rhythmic Uniformity Hypothesis). Estonian and Finnish parse syllables, hence avoid syllable clash, while Nunggubuyu and Yindjibarndi parse moras, hence avoid mora clash. But languages may select a supplementary rhythmic unit different than that of foot parsing. This option is instantiated by Finnish and Yindjibarndi, where clash avoidance is switched to 'on' for both layers. These languages minimally differ in their parsing units, which captures their differences of quantity (in)sensitivity. Finnish parses syllables (and by the RUH avoids syllable clash), but also avoids mora clash (hence *[$\sigma_{\mu}\sigma_{\mu\mu}$]). Since syllables are parsing units, heavy syllables are allowed in weak positions of feet. Yindjibarndi parses moras (and by the RUH avoids mora clash), but also avoids syllable clash (hence *[$\sigma_{\mu\mu}$][$\sigma_{\mu}\sigma_{\mu}$]). Since moras are parsing units, heavy syllables are disallowed in weak positions of feet. This two-by-two arrangement of possibilities can be represented as in (30):

(30)

Language	Parsing unit	Rhythmic unit
Estonian	Syllable	Syllable
Finnish	Syllable	Syllable *plus mora*
Nunggubuyu	Mora	Mora
Yindjibarndi	Mora	Mora *plus syllable*

6. A puzzle: Guugu Yimidhhir

Finally, I will discuss a system that apparently poses problems to both the GT and the two-layered theory, but which as I will argue is still analysed more adequately under the latter theory. It is another Australian language, Guugu Yimidhirr (Haviland 1979). Its stress pattern is exemplified in (31):

(31)				
	a.	˘ ˘ ˘ ˘ ˘	márr.bu.gàn.bi.gù	'still in the cave'
	b.	- ˘ ˘ ˘	búu.rra.yày.gu	'still in the water'
	c.	˘ - ˘ ˘	ma.gíil.ngay.gù	'just branches'
	d.	- - ˘ ˘	búu.rráay.bì.gu	'still in the water'

The following generalizations are due to Haviland (1979,41-43). Firstly, length contrasts are restricted to the first two syllables. Secondly, in words starting with L-L and H-L (cf. 31a,b), main stress is initial, with an alternating secondary stress pattern, avoiding syllable clash. Thirdly, in words that start with L-H (cf. 31c), main stress is on the second syllable, with an alternating secondary stress pattern, again avoiding syllable clash. Fourthly, in words that start with H-H (cf. 31d), main stress is on both heavy syllables, and alternating secondary stress resumes on the third syllable, with double syllable clash. The puzzle resides in the resumption of rhythmic alternation after a heavy syllable. While this respects syllabic clash avoidance in (31b) and (31c), it violates it twice in (31d).

In order to get a hint of the foot employed, it proves useful to examine the prosodic morphology of the system. Interestingly, Guugu Yimidhiir has bisyllabic reduplication, regardless of weight. This diagnoses the syllabic trochee [σ σ].

(32) a. $[\sigma_\mu\sigma_\mu]$ yimi=yimidhirr 'this same way again'
b. $[\sigma_\mu\sigma_{\mu\mu}]$ gadhii=gadhii 'very far away'

But assuming syllabic trochees, we run into an apparent counterexample to the Rhythmic Uniformity Hypothesis, since (32d) contains two syllable clashes. This odd property may be captured in a syllabic analysis by the stipulation that the phonetic stresses are read off the mora layer, rather than the syllable layer:

(33) A two-layered analysis of Guugu Yimidhirr
a. Parsing: construct trochees from left to right on the syllable layer. Final degenerate feet allowed.
b. Rhythm: avoid clash on the syllable layer *and* the mora layer.
c. Phonetically interpret the *mora* layer.

As usual, mora clash avoidance accounts for initial skipping (cf. 31c). See (34):

```
(34) a.  (*    .)(*   .)(*)     b.  (*     .)(*   .)  σ
         {#    .}{#   .}{#}         [*.]  . {#   .}  μ
         márr.bu.gàn.bi.gù          búu.rra.yày.gu

     c.   . (*     .) (*)       d.  (*   . ) (*  .)  σ
          . [*.]   .  {#}           [*.] [*.] {#  .}  μ
         ma.gíil.ngay.gù            búu.rráay.bì.gu
```

This analysis captures the puzzling pattern of clash avoidance of the system.

7. Conclusion

I have demonstrated that stress systems may avoid clashes with respect to either moras, syllables, or both. Units of rhythm are partly predictable from units of foot parsing, but languages may opt to include an additional rhythmic unit. The second result is deriving the GT effect from a two-layered theory of foot parsing, which has three advantages. Firstly, it rationalizes the L-H avoidance effect as mora clash avoidance. Secondly, it explains why skipping is restricted to light syllables. Thirdly, it breaks down the rhythmic variation between trochaic systems with distinctions of quantity into two dimensions, parsing layer and rhythmic layer.

References

Carlson, L. 1978. *Stress in Finnish*. Unpublished manuscript, MIT.

Dixon, R.M.W. 1981. Wargamay. *Handbook of Australian Languages*, vol. II., eds. R.M.W. Dixon and B.J. Blake, 1--144. Amsterdam: John Benjamins.

Dixon, R.M.W. 1983. Nyawaygi. *Handbook of Australian Languages*, vol. III., eds. R.M.W. Dixon and B.J. Blake, 431--525. Amsterdam: John Benjamins.

Donaldson, T. 1980. *Ngiyambaa: The Language of the Wangaaybuwan*. Cambridge: Cambridge University Press.

Halle, M., and J.R. Vergnaud. 1987. *An Essay on Stress*. Cambridge: MIT Press.

Hansen, K.C., and L.E. Hansen. 1969. Pintupi phonology. *Oceanic Linguistics* 8:153--170.

Harms, R.T. 1960. Stress and Juncture in Finnish. *American Studies in Uralic Languages* (Indiana University Publications, Uralic and Altaic Series, vol. 1), 7--12. Bloomington: Indiana University.

Harms, R.T. 1964. *Finnish Structural Sketch*. (Indiana University publications, Uralic and Altaic series, vol. 42). Bloomington: Indiana University.

Haviland, J.B. 1979. Guugu Yimidhirr. *Handbook of Australian Languages*, vol. I., eds. R.M.W. Dixon and B.J. Blake, 27--180. Amsterdam: John Benjamins.

Hayes, B. 1980. *A Metrical Theory of Stress Rules*. Bloomington: Indiana University Linguistics Club.

Hayes, B. 1988. Ternary Stress Assignment in Finnish, Estonian, and Other Languages. Paper presented at the Generative Phonology Workshop, Leiden, September 23, 1988.

Hayes, B. 1991. *Metrical Stress Theory: Principles and Case Studies*. Unpublished manuscript, UCLA.

Hint, M. 1973. *Eesti Keele Sonafonoloogia* I. Tallinn: Eesti NSV Teaduste Akadeemia.

Hore, M. 1981. Syllable Length and Stress in Nunggubuyu. *Work Papers of SIL-AAB, Series A*, No. 5.

Kager, R. 1989. *A Metrical Theory of Stress and Destressing in English and Dutch*. Dordrecht: Foris.

Kager, R. 1990. *Strict Binarity and Destressing Rules*. Unpublished manuscript, Stanford University.

Kager, R. 1992a. Alternatives to the Iambic-Trochaic Law. To appear in *Natural Language and Linguistic Theory*.

Kager, R. 1992b. Are There Any Truly Quantity Insensitive Systems? To appear in *Proceedings of the 18th Annual Meeting of the Berkeley Linguistics Society*.

Kiparsky, P. 1991a. Quantity Sensitivity and the Nature of Templatic Parsing. Paper presented at the *17th Annual Meeting of the the Berkeley Linguistics Society*.

Kiparsky, P. 1991b. *Catalexis*. Unpublished manuscript, Stanford University and Wissenschaftskolleg zu Berlin.

Kirton, J.F. 1967. Anyula Phonology. *Pacific Linguistics Series A*, No. 10, (Papers in Australian Linguistics, No. 1), 15--28.

Lahiri, A. 1992. The Germanic Foot in Metrical Theory. Paper presented at the University of Amsterdam, February 1992.

Lahiri, A., and H. van der Hulst. 1988. On Foot Typology. *Proceedings of the North Eastern Linguistics Society* 18 (Vol. 2), 286--299. Amherst: GLSA.

McGregor, W. (1990). *A Functional Grammar of Gooniyandi*. Amsterdam: John Benjamins.

Prince, A. 1980. A Metrical Theory for Estonian Quantity. *Linguistic Inquiry* 11:511--562.

Prince, A. 1983. Relating to the Grid. *Linguistic Inquiry* 14:19--100.

Prince, A., and P. Smolensky. 1992. Optimality: Constraint Interaction in Generative Grammar. Paper presented at the 11th *West Coast Conference on Formal Linguistics*, UCLA, February 26, 1992.

Skousen, R. 1972. On Capturing Regularities. *Papers from the Eighth Regional Meeting of the Chicago Linguistics Society*, eds. P.M. Peranteau et al., 567-577. Chicago: Chicago University Press.

Van der Hulst, H. 1984. *Syllable Structure and Stress in Dutch*. Dordrecht: Foris.

Van der Hulst, H. 1991. *The Book of Stress*. Unpublished manuscript, University of Leiden.

Wordick, F.J.F. 1982. *The Yindjibarndi Language*. (Pacific Linguistics, Series C, No. 71.)

Unaccusativity and 'Inner' Aspect

WILLIAM MCCLURE
Cornell University

In this paper, I present a general theory of aspect and explore some of its syntactic consequences. My theory of aspect incorporates the insights of David Dowty's (1979) semantic analysis, although it differs from Dowty's in three major respects. First, instead of Dowty's interval semantics, I use a situation-based semantics much like that used by Terence Parsons (1990). Second, I give a situation-based definition for activity verbs, something Dowty does not provide for his DO operator, and third, I present a hypothesis for how this general semantics is syntactically encoded. Specifically, I define a mapping from my aspectual semantics into two aspectual functional categories, which appear between IP and VP, and which I have called OUTER and INNER ASPECT. I conclude by discussing some of the syntactic consequences of this hypothesis, especially in connection with unaccusativity.

In a tradition dating from Aristotle and institutionalized by Vendler (1967), verb phrases can be divided into one of four aspectual classes: achievements and accomplishments; states and activities, with achievements and accomplishments characterized by inherent conclusions, while states and activities are characterized by their open-endedness. Examples of each class are given in (1). Verbs such as 'die' and 'build a house' are TELIC; they both involve an inherent end or point of change, while 'stink' and 'run' are ATELIC states and activities, respectively. Neither stinking nor running is characterized by a well-defined end or point of transformation.

(1) Aspectual Types (Dowty 1979, and many others)

Telic		Atelic	
Achievements	Accomplishments	States	Activities
die	build a house	stink	run
break a window	destroy a city	belong	push a cart
sneeze	swim to Hawaii	seem	swim
recognize	write a paper	love school	write papers

In addition, there is a general division along the lines of controllability. The accomplishments and activities in (1) seem necessarily to involve an agent driven process. Someone must be alive and in control to run or to build a house, while a rock may break a window, and sneezing is certainly not a scripted event. In fact, however, the role of control is not clear. Obviously a person may break a window just as easily as a rock, and rivers flow (an activity) as well as erode away (an accomplishment) without awareness. Rolling and spinning are further examples of often non-controlled activities.

It is proposed by Dowty that the four aspectual verb classes in (1) are derived from underlying stative forms by means of the aspectual operators BECOME and DO in combination with the connective CAUSE. Semantically, Dowty's operators are defined as outlined in (2). A state α BECOMEs when it comes into existence. Although Dowty's definition is given in terms of interval semantics, its intuitive meaning is obvious, and BECOME is in some sense a pair of states, before and after the moment of change. CAUSE is somewhat more abstract, but at its most basic level, one event CAUSEs another when the absence of the first entails the absence of the second. The full semantics for CAUSE as given by Dowty actually involves counterfactuals, and I will not address the nature of causation in this paper except to comment on the theta-roles assigned by the CAUSE operator. Finally, in Dowty's theory, DO turns out to represent mainly the volitionality of the subject. It means that the subject is a sentient being, theoretically in control of the course of events. As a result, DO does not have an interval semantic or model theoretic definition. Unlike BECOME, it is not clear that DO can be thought of as a situation or as a set of situations, and as such, it is left to play a minor role in Dowty's theory.

(2) BECOME $(\alpha) = 1$ iff $\neg\, \alpha$ then α

CAUSE $(\alpha, \beta) = 1$ iff $\neg\, \alpha$ --> $\neg\, \beta$

DO (x, α (x)) --> volitional (x)

In Dowty's aspectual calculus, every verb may therefore be characterized by an underlying state and one or more of the aspectual operators. An achievement such as 'die' is represented as in (3). 'Dead' is a state. 'BECOME dead' means 'to die'. Examples of the other three classes are also listed in (3) both intuitively and with the more formal representation of intensional logic. States are basic so no operators are incorporated into their representation . All of the knowledge contained in a state is available by looking at the world at a single point of time. A state is therefore represented by a possible situation. Activities, however, entail a DOing, by somebody, of something like running or swimming, while accomplishments are the most complex. Intuitively, the accomplishment listed in (3) entails that Jeff DO something and that this something CAUSE, or result in, the BECOMEing of something else. CAUSE sets up the connection between Jeff's activity and the creation of a house. It says that without the activity this particular outcome will not be realized. Other kinds of outcomes include the BECOMEing of a book or the BECOMEing of being in a particular location.

(3) Jack dies = BECOME dead (J) = BECOME (^dead (J))

John stinks = stink (J) = ^stink (J)

Jill runs = DO run (J, run (J)) = DO (J, ^run (J))

Jeff builds a house = DO build (J, build (J)) CAUSE BECOME built (house) = CAUSE((^DO(J, ^build(J))) (^BECOME(^built (house))))

The various operators in Dowty's representations are then used to explain a host of aspectually related phenomena in syntax including the distribution of adverbials, causative constructions, and the behavior of the progressive. In the semantics I will propose, I hope to be able to incorporate these results wholesale while providing the basis for a systematic account of the increasingly strong evidence for a relationship between aspect and syntax as observed by Tenny (1987), Grimshaw (1990), and Travis (1991) among many others.

My semantics differs from Dowty's in that I use situation-based definitions for Dowty's operators, and I give a situation-based definition for DO. I propose that a DOing is in fact a kind of change characterized by a particular aspectual structure. In particular, I argue that DO is composed of a collection of BECOMEings.

Along the lines of Parsons (1990) and Higginbotham (1985), in my semantics, I assume that verbs are predicates of eventualities with arguments fed in locally under government by means of theta-roles. This means that all verbs have the general event structure outlined in (4) where the stative verb 'stink' is predicated of the eventuality 's' for stative with 'Jack' assigned the role of Theme. Consistent with Dowty, in this representation, 's' stands for a possible situation. In (4) then, 'Jack stinks' is the set of situations 's' such that 's' is a stinking situation and Jack is the theme of the situation.

(4) General Eventuality Structure
Verb = V (e)
NP + Verb = V (e) & Th (NP, e)

Jack stinks = {s | stink (s) & Th (s, Jack)} = λs (stink (s) & Th (Jack, s))

Returning then to the definitions in (2), recall that a BECOMEing can be intuitively represented as a pair of states, the state before and the state after a point of change. The change is in fact defined by the two situations, and BECOME can always be thought of as a pair of situations. The DO operator is then a set of these BECOMEings. Dowty has basically equated the DO operator with volitionality, but I believe that activities can in fact be represented by particular sets of changes. Specifically, an activity always contains the iteration of a single event. When Jill runs, she must take many steps, and if Picasso were still painting he would be making many strokes with his brush. An activity is therefore a collection of events. It is crucial, however, that this set of events be centered on a particular protagonist. A collection of steps will not form an activity unless all of the steps are taken by a single individual. This individual is generally identified as the agent, and its theta-role is assigned by the DO operator.

If this is true, it is then possible to characterize the aspectual structure of DO in terms of repeated BECOMEings which are themselves composed of states. These aspectual structures are summarized in (5) and their logical types are summarized in (6). Given that states are basic, achievements are represented by pairs of states, and activities are represented by open-ended sets of pairs of states.

(5) Aspectual structures

states = s, a situation
achievements = <s s'>
activities = {<s s'> <s' s"> <s"s'"> <s'"...}

(6) Aspectual types

BECOME : sets of states	-->	sets of pairs of states
DO: sets of becomings	-->	sets of sets of becomings having the same protagonist

In (7), I give more formal definitions of the complete semantics for each aspectual class in terms of Parson's definitions. Example (7a) is repeated from (4). A stative like 'Jack stinks' is a collection of situations where stinking is true of Jack. Example (7b) represents an achievement. 'Josh dies' is a collection of pairs of states where some state is true of Josh in the initial state and Josh is dead in the final state. Example (7c) represents an activity. Remember that an activity is a relation between an individual and a set of achievements. Here, running is predicated of Jill because Jill is the protagonist of each change. She is the one stepping from place to place. The achievements define movement from one location to the next. Further, for an activity it is necessary to say that all changes are spatio-temporally connected. Intuitively, this means that while Jill is moving about, there can be no gaps in her path. Her steps can be smooth and orderly if she happens to running or they can be unpatterned if she is slam-dancing, but they must connected one after the other and they must not have an end. Accomplishments are then defined similarly to activities except they do have a final state.

(7) Aspectual definitions (approximate)

a. States

Jack stinks = λe (stink (e) & Th (Jack, e))

b. Achievements

Josh falls = BECOME (λe [fallen (e) & Ex (Josh, e)])

= $\{\alpha \mid \exists$ s s', α = <s s'> &

λe [fallen (e) & Ex (Josh, e)] (s') &

$\neg\, \lambda e$ [fallen (e) & Ex (Josh, e)] (s) & s then s'$\}$

c. Activities

Let A be a set of becomings. Then:

Jill runs = DO (A)

= $\{\beta \mid \beta$ is a subset of A & the members of β are spatio-temporally connected & have X as a protagonist$\}$

Now, I will turn to the mapping of this semantics into a particular syntactic structure. In the spirit of Travis (1991), I would like to propose that aspect is projected as two functional heads in the manner of (8), where I have labelled the two functional heads AP_{outer} and AP_{inner}. DO and CAUSE are mapped into the outer position while BECOME is mapped into the inner position. Paralleling the treatment of negation in Pollock (1989), these aspectual projections are licensed only when the relevant aspectual operator is present. The verbal head is then interpreted as an incomplete form of the verb which incorporates the aspectual operators through head to head movement.

This mapping of three operators into two positions then explains observed restrictions on the structure of aspect. DO and CAUSE both represent a relationship between an individual and a set of situations, and it never seems to be the case that DO or CAUSE operate on each other, while both may operate on BECOME. Further, BECOME never operates on DO or CAUSE. A structure such as (8) with two aspectual nodes, and not a possible three, accounts for these observations in the simplest fashion. The existence of restrictions on aspectual operators of this kind has been observed quite widely in the literature (Dowty 1979, among others) My point is simply that by adopting the mapping hypothesis in (8), they can be reduced to standard X-bar theoretic accounts of co-occurrence restrictions in general in terms of subcategorization or semantic selection. So, for example, DO is defined as a relation between individuals and achievements; it therefore selects only AP_{inner} which is predicated of the NP in specifier of AP_{outer}, the projection headed by DO.

(8) Basic aspectual projection

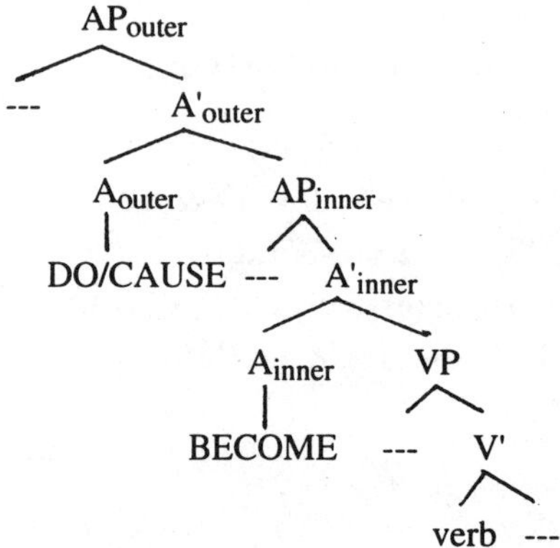

Further, since I have assumed that arguments are fed in via theta roles locally under government, all arguments must be realized as low as possible, with the subject occurring in Spec of VP for states and achievements, or in Spec of AP_{outer} whenever a DO or CAUSE operator is realized since these operators both must assign their theta-role locally. The direct object is always generated as the complement of the verb. The structure in (8) is therefore consistent with the VP-Shell Hypothesis and could be extended to include indirect objects. Further, simple unaccusative and unergative sentences can be represented as in (9), where I take the standard view that in unaccusative structures the D-structure direct object moves into the S-structure subject position, here into Spec of IP. This movement is motivated by some version of Burzio's generalization or whatever principle derives its effects. No external theta role is assigned, so accusative case is also not assigned and therefore the object must move into and through the Spec of VP before getting case in Spec of IP.

(9) Stative unaccusative 'A dollar suffices' Stative unergative 'Joan stinks'

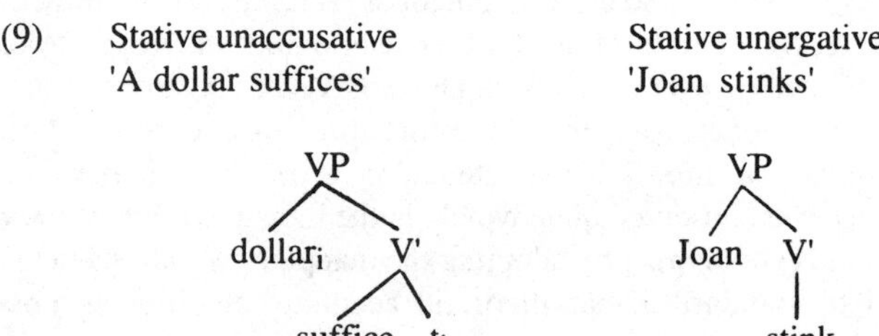

With these assumptions, all of which are straightforward variants of independently motivated hypotheses, we now have a general theory of aspect which can account for the various aspect-related phenomena discussed by Dowty and others. Let us now consider verbs of each aspectual class.

Looking at (9) again, I assume, following Dowty, that states are aspectually impoverished, and all arguments of the VP are realized locally. In the intransitive case, if the single argument is realized in object position, the verb will be unaccusative.

In (10), BECOME does not assign a theta-role to the Spec position. Hence, it is essentially a raising predicate which operates on a state. Again, all arguments of the VP are realized locally, with the initial state meaning something like 'in a sneezed state'. This state is predicated of Jill, and then the subject raises, and a state preceding Jill's sneezed state is paired with the final state, creating an achievement possibly meaning something like <'breathing ragweed', 'in a sneezed state'>

(10) Achievement
'Jill sneezes'

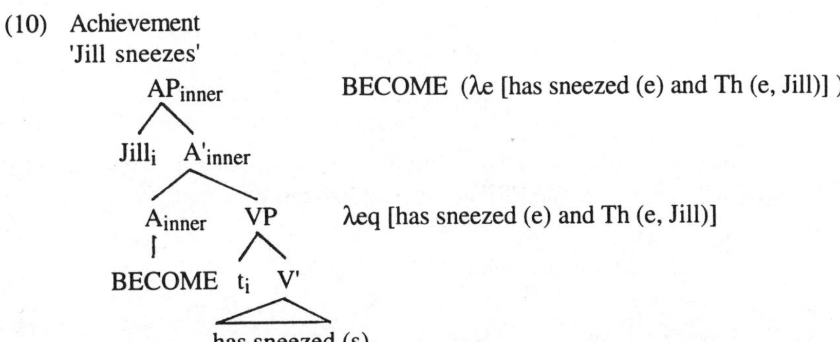

In (11), DO is a two place relation between an individual and an achievement with the agent realized in the Spec of AP_{outer}, while the achievement and its argument are realized below VP. All arguments are therefore realized locally since Spec of AP_{outer} is assigned its own theta-role. Both DO and the lower predicate assign a theta-role. The subject is base generated in the Spec of AP_{outer}, from where it moves into Spec of IP to receive Case. The Spec of VP is also a theta-position but it is Caseless. Hence it can only be filled by PRO. This fits well with the intuition that DO has an equi or control semantics. PRO in Spec VP would, however, occur in a governed position, which might be problematic under traditional assumptions. One way out could be to assume that the BECOME operator is not a governor and that PRO could escape from the governed position by moving into Spec of AP_{inner}. Other relevant options are discussed by Diesing (1990), and Kayne (1990) offers the proposal that PRO is governed.

(11) Activity
'Jack runs'

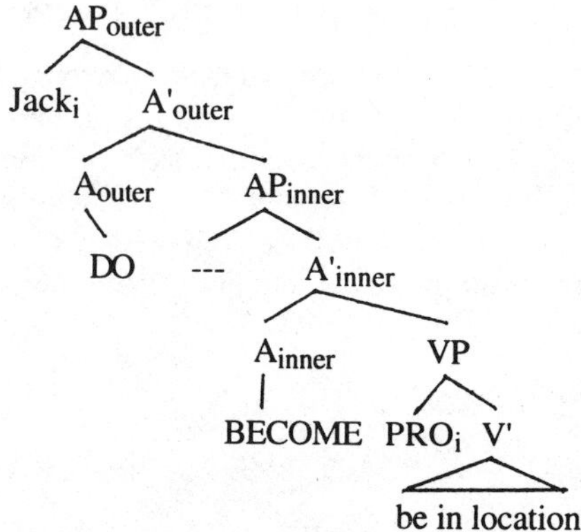

Finally, an example of an accomplishment sentence is shown in (12), although I will not discuss CAUSE at any length in this paper.

(12) Accomplishment
'Jack broke the window (himself)'

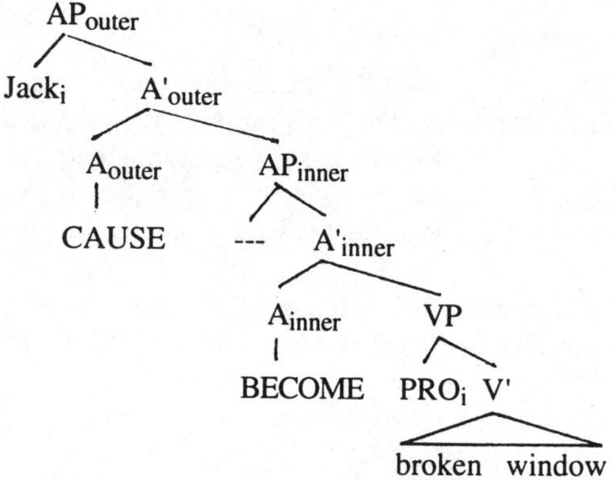

Now, given the general theory of aspect and the syntactic mapping which I have outlined, several strong predictions are made about the aspectual semantics of certain syntactic configurations. First, all intransitive activities will be unergative. This is the strongest prediction made by my theory, and it follows from the fact that the semantics for DO assigns a theta-role which it must discharge locally. DO can assign the agent-role only to a subject generated in Spec of AP_{outer}. A potentially unaccusative activity would have a structure like (13). It would require a direct object which moves into Spec of IP giving us the conditions for unaccusativity as well as a fully realized DO operator. If such a structure were realized, the direct object would in fact be able to move as far as Spec of AP_{inner} but it would not be able to move into the upper subject position because that would be a case of improper NP-movement. Moving the direct object into Spec of AP_{outer} would require moving something already with a theta-role into a thematic position. The structure in (13) is therefore ruled out for a reason similar to (14) where the NP cannot be raised into a position where it would receive a second theta-role. Note that this is not the case with achievements because the BECOME operator does not assign a theta-role of its own. The direct object of an unaccusative achievement is always free to raise into Spec of the inner AP position.

(13) Unaccusative activity (not possible)

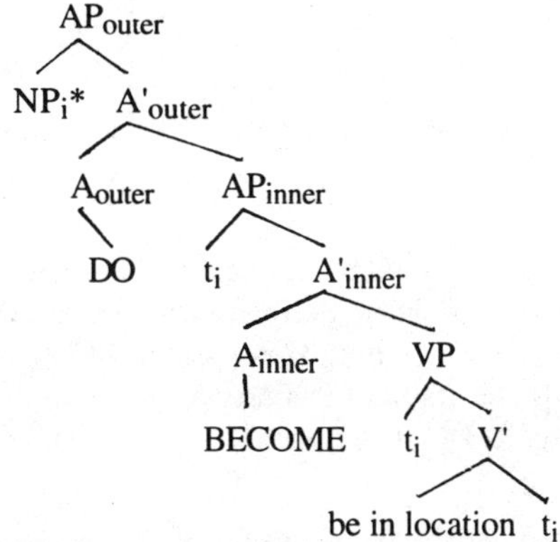

(14) Illegal NP-raising: e believes John to have left -->
*$John_i$ believes t_i to have left

Second, this theory predicts that only states and achievements can be unaccusative. The stative cases will look like (15) with a single argument assigned to the object position before moving into the subject position.

In (16), achievements may be unaccusative because the BECOME operator functions as a raising verb assigning no theta-roles of its own. The single argument of an intransitive achievement may raise through BECOME into the Spec of the inner AP from either the subject or the object position. Again, if it originates in the object position, the sentence will be unaccusative.

(15) (repeated from 9)

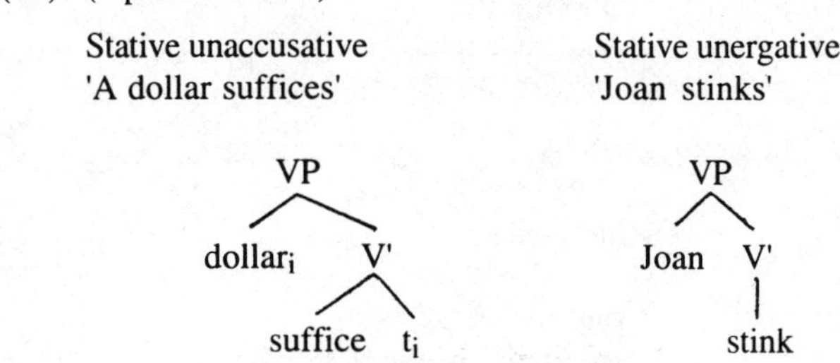

(16) Achievement unaccusative 'Jack died' | Achievement unergative 'Jill sneezed'

AP_{inner}
Jack$_i$ A'_{inner}
A_{inner} VP
BECOME t$_i$ V'
dead t$_i$

AP_{inner}
Jill$_i$ A'_{inner}
A_{inner} VP
BECOME t$_i$ V'
sneeze

In Italian, these predictions are born out exactly. Unaccusatives are always states or achievements and never activities. Further, facts similar to these have been noted by a number of researchers including Centineo (1986), Van Valin (1987), and Tenny (1987), and while the Italian facts are the most well-known, similar observations have been made in Dutch (Zaenen 1988) and Japanese (Tsujimura 1989).

In Italian, the simplest indicator of unaccusativity is the use of the past auxiliary *essere* 'be'. Typical stative unaccusatives include *appartenere* 'belong' while telic events include *morire* 'die' and *partire* 'depart'. These and other unaccusatives are listed in (17). They all take *essere* as their past auxiliary, and they all contrast directly with verbs like *piangere* 'cry' which is an atelic activity and selects *avere* 'have'. Examples of unergative verbs from each class are listed in (18). While states and achievements may be unaccusative or unergative, there are, to my knowledge, no activities which select *essere*. Given the standard conception of unaccusativity, this is exactly what the theory predicts.

(17) Unaccusative verbs (selecting *essere*)

Stative	Achievement
appartenere 'belong'	morire 'die'
sembrare 'seem'	partire 'depart'
piacere 'like'	sparire 'disappear'

(18) Unergative verbs (selecting *avere*)

Stative	Achievement	Activity
puzzare 'stink'	starnutire 'sneeze'	correre 'run'
	imbrogliare 'cheat'	rotolare 'roll'

Particularly striking is the case of a verb like *correre* 'run'. In English it is clearly an activity while in Italian it can take either past auxiliary. While one would expect running generally to be an activity in Italian as well, the theory I have presented predicts that the unaccusative case must be a state or an achievement. The stative interpretation is clearly ruled out so one would expect the unaccusative version of *correre* to be an achievement. This is in fact the case as is shown in (19a&b). Running is in fact generally an activity, but the auxiliary changes to reflect the aspectual shift when an endpoint is present or implied. (19a) therefore has the structure given in (20) while (19b) has the structure given in (21). (19c&d) illustrate the aspectual mismatch when the auxiliaries do not vary in this respect.

(19) Auxiliary shift with *correre* 'run'

Atelic	Telic
a. J **ha** corso per un ora	b. J **è** corso (al magazzino) in un
minuto	
J ran for an hour	J ran (to the store) in a minute

but

c. ??J **ha** corso in un minuto	d. ??J **è** corso per un ora

(20) (repeated from 11)

Activity
'Jack runs'

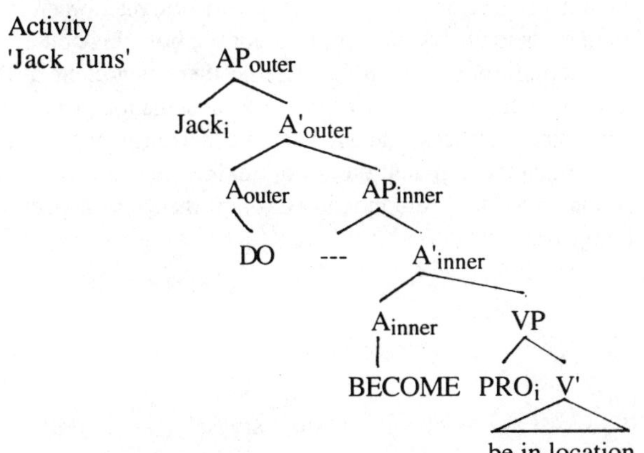

(21) Achievement
'Jack runs to the store'

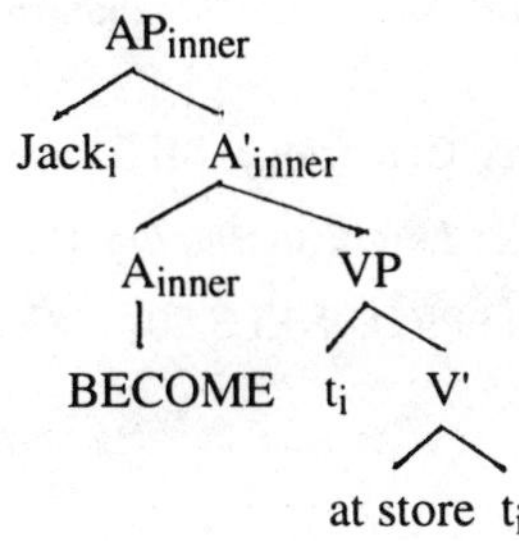

Further cross-linguistic evidence for this analysis is presented in McClure (1990) where apparent unaccusative mismatches between Dutch and Italian are shown to be apectually different. Thus the unaccusative *arrosire* 'blush' is an achievement in Italian while the unergative *blozen* 'blush' is in fact an activity in Dutch. From an aspectual point of view, there is no mismatch at all. I would take a similar approach in investigating verbs such as *flow* or *rain*. While speakers of English will generally assume that these verbs are activities, in many languages (e.g. Russian) they pattern as unaccusatives. My analysis predicts that in such languages, these verbs should be either stative or achievement-like, although it may be that control also has a role to play in the determination of unaccusativitiy in certain languages.

To conclude, I have argued for a general theory of aspect which is encoded in syntax through a specific mapping onto two aspectual functional categories. At this point, this theory is supported by the unaccidental correlation between unaccusative verbs and particular aspectual classes. Unaccusatives are states or achievements but never activities. My theory might of course turn out to be quite wrong, but some principled relationship between aspectual structure and grammatical relations must exist because the correlations noted in Italian and other languages are general and quite strong. Notice that my theory attempts to explain these facts not by reducing unaccusativity to a purely semantic phenomenon as, for example, Van Valin attempts to do. At present I do not see how this could be done within an explicit truth-conditional semantics. While there is a clear difference between achievements and activities, it is hard to see what semantic criterion might divide states into two disinct classes. Clearly such a criterion is not aspectual in nature. Instead, I believe that the explanation lies in linking unaccusative structures as they are currently conceived to a semantically explicit theory of aspect. In this paper, that is what I have tried to do.

References

Centineo, Giulia. 1986. A Lexical Theory of Auxiliary Selection in Italian. *Davis Working Papers in Linguistics* 1.

Diesing, Molly. 1990. *The Syntactic Roots of Semantic Partition.* Amherst: University of Massachusetts Dissertation.

Dowty, David. 1979. *Word Meaning and Montague Grammar.* Dordrecht: Reidel.

Grimshaw, Jane, 1990. *Argument Structure.* Cambridge: MIT Press

Higginbotham, James. 1985. On Semantics. *Linguistic Inquiry* 16.

Kayne, Richard. 1990. Romance Clitics and PRO. NELS 20.

McClure, William. 1990. A Lexical Semantic Explanation for Unaccusative Mismatches. In Dziwirek, Farrell, & Mejias-Bikandi, eds. *Grammatical Relations*. Stanford: CSLI.

Parsons, Terence. 1990. *Events in the Semantics of English*. Cambridge: MIT Press

Pollock, J.-Y. 1989. Verb Movement, UG, and the Structure of IP. *Linguistic Inquiry* 20.

Tenny, Carol. 1987. *Grammaticalizing Aspect and Affectedness*. MIT Dissertation.

Travis, Lisa. 1991. Derived Objects, Inner Aspect, and the Structure of VP. McGill University ms.

Tsujimura. 1989. Unaccusative Mismatches in Japanese. ESCOL 1989.

Van Valin, Robert D. 1987. The Unaccusative Hypothesis vs. Lexical Semantics: Syntactic vs. Semantic Approaches to Verb Classification. *Proceedings of NELS 17*, vol II.

Vendler, Zeno. 1967. *Linguistics in Philosophy*. Ithaca: Cornell University Press

Zaenen, Annie. 1988. Unaccusativity in Dutch: An Integrated Approach. Unpublished ms. Xerox-PARC and CSLI-Stanford.

The Nature of the Stage/Individual-Level Distinction and its Syntactic Reflex: Evidence from Spanish

ERRAPEL MEJÍAS-BIKANDI
University of California, San Diego

0. Carlson (1977, 1980) distinguishes between predicates that assign properties to individuals (INDIVIDUAL-LEVEL predicates) and predicates that assign properties to "stages", spatiotemporal slices, of individuals (STAGE-LEVEL predicates). Diesing (1988, 1989, 1990) and Kratzer (1989) argue that in German and English, the grammatical subject of individual-level predicates is generated outside the VP, whereas the grammatical subject of stage-level predicates is generated within the VP. In this paper, I present evidence from Spanish supporting Diesing's and Kratzer's insight that there is a correlation between the type of predicate and the structural position of the subject at some level of representation. In particular, I will argue that in Spanish, as in English and German, subjects of individual-level predicates must be generated in Spec(I), whereas subjects of stage-level predicates may be generated under some projection of V. However, I will propose that subjects of individual-level predicates show a distinctive syntactic behavior not by virtue of being subjects of individual-level predicates, but by virtue of being LOGICAL SUBJECTS in a PREDICATION. Under this proposal, the relevant distinction is not between predicates that are individual-level and predicates that are stage-level, but between sentences that represent predications and sentences that represent NON-PREDICATIONAL DESCRIPTIONS, and the relevant generalization

[1] I would like to thank Raúl Aranovich, Kathy Carey, Aintzane Doiz-Bienzobas, Gorka Elordieta, Rich Epstein, Jon Franco, Mary Hare, Yuki Kuroda and Maura Velázquez for their comments on earlier drafts of this paper. Usual disclaimers apply.

is the following: logical subjects in predications are generated in Spec(I).[2]

The argumentation will proceed as follows. In the first section, I motivate an analysis under which the distribution of the different readings (existential or generic) of an indefinite NP of the form *un/a N* 'a N' in Spanish is predicted by the structural position of the indefinite at S-structure. This is an extension of Diesing's analysis of bare plurals in German and English (cf. Diesing 1988, 1989). This analysis provides us with a test that indicates the structural position of an indefinite NP: if the indefinite is existential, it must be within the VP at S-structure, if the indefinite is generic, it must be outside the VP at S-structure. In the second section, I show that indefinite NPs that are subjects of individual-level predicates must be interpreted as generic, whereas indefinite NPs that are subjects of stage-level predicates may be interpreted as generic or as existential. I will take this as evidence that subjects of individual-level predicates must appear outside the VP at S-structure, whereas subjects of stage-level predicates may appear within the VP at this level of representation. In order to account for these facts, I propose an analysis under which subjects of individual-level predicates are generated in Spec(I), whereas subjects of stage-level predicates are generated within the VP. This analysis is shown to be independently motivated by some word order constraints on sentences with individual-level predicates, constraints that do not hold on sentences with stage-level predicates. In section 3, I examine the contrast between the indicative and the subjunctive mood in certain contexts in Spanish. I show that subjects of verbs in the indicative mood, whether the predicate is stage-level or individual-level, have properties similar to subjects of individual-level predicates. In other words, I will show that stage-level predicates, when they are realized by a verb in the indicative mood, also require that the subject be generated in Spec(I). The significance of this finding is the following. Subjects of a particular set *P* of predicates are claimed to be generated in Spec(I). For English and German, this set *P* has been claimed to consist of individual-level predicates. However, in Spanish, stage-level predicates that are expressed in the indicative mood also belong to *P*. Consequently, the relevant distinction for characterizing *P*, at least in Spanish, cannot be the distinction between stage-level and individual-level predicates. How then may we characterize *P*? An answer to this question is given in section 4. For this purpose, I introduce the distinction between the notions predication and description. I claim that both individual-level predicates and verbs in the indicative mood appear in sentences that must represent predications. Thus, *P* consists of predicates of sentences that

[2] For a discussion of the notions logical subject, predication and non-predicational description see, among others, Kuroda 1972a, 1972b, 1979, 1992. A predication, as defined by Kuroda, is the intentional object of a categorical judgement, which is in turn a particular cognitive act. On the other hand, a non-predicational description is the intentional object of a thetic judgement. A sentence is said to represent a predication or a description. The logical subject of the predication is the expression that denotes the entity of which a property is predicated. The logical subject may be the same as the grammatical subject, but this is not necessarily the case. This notion of predication should not be confused with the notion of predication which appears, for instance, in Williams (1980), where predication is a syntactic process that creates predicate structures.

represent predications, and the generalization is that the logical subject in a predication is generated in Spec(I).

1. Diesing (1988, 1989) claims that the different readings (generic or existential) of the bare plural in English can be predicted by the structural position of the bare plural at D-structure. In this section, I will first summarize Diesing's analysis. After that, I will show how such an analysis can be extended into Spanish.

1.1. Diesing claims that material outside the VP at LF appears in the RESTRICTIVE CLAUSE in the logical representation, whereas material inside the VP is part of the NUCLEAR SCOPE. In the absence of an overt quantifier, variables in the Restrictive Clause are bound by a default quantifier *Gen* (generic). Free variables in the Nuclear Scope are bound by an existential quantifier, the result of a process of EXISTENTIAL CLOSURE. Bare nouns introduce variables in the logical representation. A bare noun that is generated in Spec(I) appears outside the VP at LF and is part of the Restrictive Clause in the logical representation. Consequently, the corresponding variable is bound by *Gen*, and the generic reading is obtained. This is illustrated in (1), where only a generic interpretation of the bare noun 'lions' is possible:

(1) a. Lions have manes
b. $[_{IP}$ Lions$_i$ $[_{VP}$ PRO$_i$ have manes]]
c. *Gen* [x is a lion] $\exists y$ mane(y) & has(x, y)

Under Diesing's analysis, the syntactic representation of (1a) is (1b), and the corresponding logical representation (1c). The subject in (1b) is generated in Spec(I), and it is coindexed with a PRO in Spec(V).[3] The bare NP appears in Spec(I) at LF, and is part of the Restrictive Clause in the logical representation in (1c), where the corresponding variable is bound by the default quantifier *Gen*. Consequently, we obtain only a generic reading of (1a).

Consider now a case where a bare noun is generated in Spec(V). This NP must move to Spec(I) in order to receive Case. However, following May (1985), Diesing assumes an analysis under which a NP that is raised to Spec(I) can be lowered to Spec(V) at LF for the purposes of interpretation. Consequently, it may be part of the Nuclear Scope in the logical representation and the corresponding variable may be bound by $\exists$. This is illustrated in (2), where an existential reading of the bare noun is possible:

---

[3] An apparent problem with this analysis is that PRO in (1b) appears in a governed position, Spec(V). I will not discuss this problem here, and will just assume that PRO can appear in Spec(V) as long as Spec(V) is Case-less (cf. Williams 1980).

(2) a. Cows are in my backyard
b. [$_{IP}$ Cows$_i$ [$_{VP}$ e_i are in my backyard]]
c. $\exists x$ cow(x) & in-my-backyard(x)

The syntactic representation of (2a) is (2b) and (2c) is the corresponding logical representation. In (2b), the subject is generated in Spec(V) and moves to Spec(I) in order to receive Case. This bare noun is lowered to Spec(V) at LF. Material within the VP at LF appears in the Nuclear Scope in the logical representation. Thus, the corresponding variable is bound by the existential quantifier (the result of Existential Closure), as in (2c), and the existential reading of (2a) is obtained.[4] In this section, I will adopt Diesing's analysis to account for the distribution of the different readings (generic or existential) of indefinite NPs of the form*un/a N* 'a N' in Spanish. As we saw above, under this analysis, different semantic interpretations of a subject are the result of different structural positions of the subject at the relevant level of representation. In English, the relevant level of representation is LF. However, Diesing claims that for German, S-structure is the relevant level to determine the interpretation of the subject. This difference between English and German is due to the claim that subjects in German do not need to appear in Spec(I) at S-structure in order to receive Case. Spanish is similar to German in this respect. It has been claimed that subjects in Spanish need not appear in Spec(I) at S-structure (cf. Groos and Bok-Bennema 1986, Contreras 1987, Mejías-Bikandi 1992). Consequently, if we adopt Diesing's analysis for Spanish, we predict that the structural position of the indefinite subject at S-structure will determine its interpretation. In other words, in the logical representation, material outside the VP at S-structure is going to form the Restrictive Clause, whereas material inside the VP at S-structure is going to be part of the Nuclear Scope. I wi!l examine now whether this analysis can be adopted for Spanish.

1.2. Indefinite NPs of the form *un/a N* 'a N' are ambiguous between an existential and a generic reading, as sentence (3) shows:[5]

(3) *Un tren llega con retraso*
'A train (generic/existential) arrives/is arriving late'

Sentence (3) can be interpreted as a general statement about trains (generic

[4] This analysis predicts that there should be a generic reading of (2a). Diesing (1988) claims that such a generic reading is indeed possible, although pragmatically odd.

[5] There is an additional non-generic reading of (3) that I will not consider. Under this additional reading, the indefinite *un tren* `a train' is interpreted like the NP *uno de los trenes* `one of the trains'. This reading presupposes that a particular set of trains is under consideration, out of which the speaker singles out a particular train. It is interesting to notice that this additional non-generic reading has the same distribution as the generic reading.

reading), or as a statement about a particular train (existential reading). The analysis I would like to adopt claims that the position of the indefinite at S-structure determines its interpretation as generic or existential. This claim makes at least two predictions for Spanish: i) a postverbal indefinite subject must be existential, and ii) a preverbal indefinite subject that is separated from the verb by a 'scarcely'-type adverb must be generic. I will examine in detail why these predictions are made and whether they are in fact borne out.

The grammatical subject in Spanish may generally appear postverbally. The standard claim is that in those cases the subject is within the VP at S-structure. Since a postverbal subject is within the VP at S-structure, then, according to the analysis proposed, an indefinite postverbal subject must be existential. This prediction is borne out, as sentence (4) shows. The indefinite subject in (4) cannot be interpreted as generic:

(4) *Llega un tren con retraso*
Arrive a train late
'A train (existential) is arriving late'

Consider now the second prediction made by the analysis. 'Scarcely'-type adverbs have been argued to appear in the Spec(V) position in Spanish (Zagona 1988). Consequently, the presence of a 'scarcely'-type adverb between the verb and the preverbal subject may be taken as an indication that the subject appears outside the VP at S-structure. An indefinite subject outside the VP at S-structure must be part of the Restrictive Clause in the logical representation, and consequently, must be generic. Again, the prediction is borne out. Contrast (5) and (6):

(5) *Un hombre lava platos*
'A man (existential/generic) is washing/washes dishes'

(6) *Un hombre apenas lava platos*
'A man (generic) hardly (ever) washes dishes'

In (5), the indefinite can be interpreted as generic or existential. When the 'scarcely'-type adverb *apenas* 'hardly' appears between the subject and the verb, as in (6), the indefinite cannot be interpreted as existential.

The two predictions made by adopting Diesing's analysis for Spanish are borne out: when the subject is shown independently to be inside the VP at S-structure, the indefinite subject is interpreted as existential; when the indefinite subject is shown to be outside the VP at S-structure, it is interpreted as generic. Notice further that this analysis, together with the assumption that preverbal subjects in Spanish may appear in Spec(I) or Spec(V),[6] predicts the ambiguity of sentences such as (3) and (5). Under this assumption, (3) and (5) are structurally ambiguous. Their semantic ambiguity is the result of this structural ambiguity. When the subject of (3) and (5) is in Spec(I) at S-structure, we obtain the generic reading. When the subject of (3) and (5) is in Spec(V) at S-structure, we obtain the existential reading.

The analysis proposed above correctly predicts the distribution of the readings of indefinite NPs in Spanish. For this reason, I will adopt this analysis for Spanish. The claim is that the surface position of an indefinite subject is going to determine its interpretation as existential or generic. An indefinite subject within the VP at S-structure will be interpreted as existential. An indefinite subject outside the VP at S-structure will be interpreted as generic. Once this analysis has been independently motivated, the different readings of indefinite NPs can be used as a test that indicates the structural position of the subject in cases where the surface form does not make it obvious. In the next section, I show that subjects of individual-level predicates differ from subjects of stage-level predicates with respect to certain phenomena. This difference in behavior will be accounted for by claiming that subjects of individual-level predicates are generated in Spec(I) and must appear in Spec(I) at S-structure, whereas subjects of stage-level predicates are generated within the VP and may remain there at S-structure.

2. In this section, I will consider two manifestations of the stage/individual-level distinction in Spanish. The goal is twofold. First, I want to examine whether subjects of individual-level predicates show distinctive properties. Second, I want to examine whether those distinctive properties, if any, can be explained by claiming that the structural representation of sentences with individual-level predicates is different from the structural representation of sentences with stage-level predicates.

2.1. In Spanish there are two copular verbs that translate as 'be' in English, *ser* and *estar*. Stage-level adjectives appear with *estar*, whereas individual-level adjectives appear with *ser*.[7] Thus, adjectives such as 'intelligent', 'tall' and 'trustworthy' appear with *ser*, as in (7), whereas adjectives such as 'sick', 'bored' and 'tired' appear with *estar*, as in (8):

(7) *Juan es inteligente/alto/fiable*
'John is intelligent/tall/trustworthy

---

6 Mejías-Bikandi (1992) provides motivations for this assumption.

7 I do not wish to claim that all the uses of *ser* and all the uses of *estar* can be explained by appealing to the stage/individual-level distinction. The claim is simply that stage-level adjectives appear with *estar* and individual-level adjectives appear with *ser*.

(8) *Juan está enfermo/aburrido/cansado*
'John is sick/bored/tired'

A second manifestation of the stage/individual-level contrast is the distinction between the present continuous (stage-level) and the present habitual (individual-level) tenses. This is illustrated in (9) and (10):[8]

(9) *Juan está bebiendo vino*
'John is drinking wine'

(10) *Juan bebe vino*
'John drinks wine'

Not surprisingly (cf. Carlson 1977), indefinite NPs that are subjects of individual-level predicates must be interpreted as generic, as (11) and (12) show:

(11) *Un científico es inteligente*
'A scientist (generic) is intelligent'

(12) *Un hombre bebe vino*
'A man (generic) drinks wine'

On the other hand, indefinite NP subjects of stage-level predicates may be interpreted as existential, as in (13) and (14), or generic:

(13) *Un científico está enfermo*
'A scientist (existential) is sick'

(14) *Un hombre está bebiendo vino*
'A man (existential) is drinking wine'

If, as we concluded in the preceding section, the interpretation of an indefinite subject is an indication of its structural position, then it must be the case that the subject in (11) and (12) is in Spec(I) at S-structure, since it cannot be interpreted as existential. On the other hand, the indefinite in (13) and (14), in its existential interpretation, must be within the VP at S-structure. Therefore, the S-structure of (12) and (14) must be as in (12') and (14') respectively:[9]

---

[8] Sentence (10) is ambiguous in Spanish between an interpretation similar to (9) and a habitual reading. I will only be concerned with the habitual, generic reading of (10).

[9] I am leaving aside the question of where the subject is generated in Spanish, whether in Spec(V), Spec(I) or postverbally under a projection of V.

(12') [$_{IP}$ Un hombre [$_{VP}$ bebe vino]]
(14') [$_{IP}$ [$_{VP}$ Un hombre está bebiendo vino]]

The data in (11)-(14) show that in Spanish, the subject of individual-level predicates must be outside the VP at S-structure, whereas the subject of stage-level predicates may be within the VP at S-structure. As a preliminary account of the difference in the structural position of the subject in sentences (11)-(14), I propose adopting Diesing's analysis for Spanish. The proposal is the following:[10]

Proposal A (preliminary):
In Spanish, subjects of individual-level predicates are generated in Spec(I) (and appear in Spec(I) at S-structure). Subjects of stage-level predicates are generated within the VP.

In the next section I will show how this proposal *A* will provide an explanation for some word order constraints on individual-level predicates in Spanish. This will be taken as independent evidence for *A*.

2.2. Subjects in Spanish may generally appear postverbally, as in (4). However, subjects of individual-level predicates cannot appear postverbally. Thus, sentences (15) and (16), as declarative sentences, are unnatural:

(15) ??*Es (Pedro) inteligente (Pedro)*
Is (Peter) intelligent (Peter)
'Peter is intelligent'

(16) ??*Bebe (Pedro) vino (Pedro)*
Drinks (Peter) wine (Peter)
'Peter drinks wine'

On the other hand, subjects of stage-level predicates may appear postverbally, as (17) and (18) show:

(17) *Está (Pedro) enfermo (Pedro)*
Is (Peter) sick (Peter)
'Peter is sick'

(18) Está (Pedro) bebiendo vino (Pedro)
Is (Peter) drinking wine (Peter)
'Peter is drinking wine'

---

[10] Note that this proposal does not make explicit exactly where within the VP subjects of stage-level predicates are generated. For the purposes of the analysis, it is crucial to assume only that they are generated somewhere within the VP.

As we saw in section 1, postverbal subjects are generally assumed to be within the VP at S-structure. Consequently, the data in (15)-(18) follow given *A* above. Since subjects of individual-level predicates must appear in Spec(I) at S-structure, they cannot appear postverbally within the VP. This constraint does not hold with stage-level predicates, since their subjects are not required to be in Spec(I) at S-structure.

To summarize, I have shown that subjects of individual-level predicates must be interpreted as generic when they are indefinite and cannot appear postverbally, whereas subjects of stage-level predicates may appear postverbally and may be interpreted as existential when indefinite. This contrast is taken to show that individual-level predicates, and not stage-level predicates, require that the subject appear outside the VP at S-structure. To account for this fact, an analysis was proposed according to which subjects of individual-level predicates are generated in Spec(I), whereas subjects of stage-level predicates are generated within the VP. This conclusion is similar to Diesing's and Kratzer's analyses of the stage/individual-level contrast in English and German. Consequently, the data and analysis in this section provide additional evidence for the claim that the distinction between stage-level and individual-level predicates is structurally manifested. In the next section, I show that subjects of verbs in the indicative mood (whether the predicate is stage-level or individual-level) also show the same properties as subjects of individual-level predicates: that is, they must be interpreted as generic when indefinite and may not appear postverbally. These data will raise the following question: what do individual-level predicates have in common with stage-level predicates in the indicative mood?

3. Several linguistic contexts in Spanish allow the use of either the indicative or the subjunctive mood in a complement clause. This is illustrated in (19), where the negative matrix clause *no es cierto* 'it is not the case' allows the use of the indicative or the subjunctive in the complement clause:

(19) a. *No es cierto que Pedro trabaja para la OTAN*
'It is not the case that Peter works-IND for NATO'

b. *No es cierto que Pedro trabaje para la OTAN*
'It is not the case that Peter works-SUBJ for NATO'

An indefinite subject of a verb in the indicative mood is most naturally interpreted as generic, whereas this is not the case when the verb is in the subjunctive mood, as the contrast between (20) and (21) shows:[11]

---

[11] The indefinite subject in (21) is non-specific. In the intended interpretation, this indefinite is existential in the sense that it is non-generic. A generic interpretation of the indefinite subject in (21) is also possible.

(20) *No es cierto que un hombre trabaja en casa*
'It is not the case that a man (generic) works-IND in the house'

(21) *No es cierto que un hombre trabaje en casa*
'It is not the case that a man (existential) works-SUBJ in the house'

Similarly, the verb of the complement cannot appear in sentence initial position when it is in the indicative mood, but it may precede the subject when it is in the subjunctive mood. This is illustrated in (22) and (23):

(22) ??*No es cierto que trabaja (Pedro) en casa (Pedro)*
It is not the case that works-IND (Peter) in the house (Peter)
'It is not the case that Peter works in the house'

(23) *No es cierto que trabaje (Pedro) en casa (Pedro)*
It is not the case that works-SUBJ (Peter) in the house (Peter)
'It is not the case that Peter works in the house'

Sentences (20)-(23) show that subjects of verbs in the indicative mood behave like subjects of individual-level predicates: they are interpreted as generic when indefinite and they cannot appear postverbally.[12] This cluster of properties was accounted for in the case of individual-level predicates by the proposal in *A*, according to which subjects of individual-level predicates are generated in Spec(I) and appear in Spec(I) at S-structure. It would be natural to propose a similar account of the properties of verbs in the indicative mood, that is, subjects of verbs in the indicative mood, but not of verbs in the subjunctive mood, must be generated in Spec(I). However, this poses a problem for the generalization proposed in *A*. Verbs in the indicative mood are not necessarily interpreted as individual-level predicates, since stage-level predicates may appear in the indicative mood too, as (24) shows:

(24) *No es cierto que Pedro está enfermo*
'It is not the case that Peter is-IND sick'

Moreover, the subject in (24) shows properties similar to other subjects of indicative verbs. Thus, a postverbal subject results in an unnatural sentence:

---

12 A member of the audience pointed out to me the fact that in some complements in the indicative mood, the apparent subject must be postverbal and be interpreted as existential when indefinite. These are sentences such as (i) *No creo que hay un hombre en casa* 'I do not believe that there is-IND a man in the house'. I will informally call the kind of complements exemplified by (i) "impersonal", and will restrict the discussion to complements that are not "impersonal".

(25) ??*No es cierto que está Pedro enfermo*
It is not the case that is-IND Peter sick
'It is not the case that Peter is sick'

Also an indefinite existential subject produces an awkward result:

(26) ?? No es cierto que un hombre está enfermo
'It is not true that a man (existential) is-IND sick'

The generalization in *A* was made in terms of the stage/individual-level distinction. Consequently, *A* cannot account for (25) and (26), where the subject of a stage-level predicate behaves like subjects of individual-level predicates. In order for *A* to account for the fact that subjects of verbs in the indicative mood also require that the subject be generated in Spec(I), *A* must be modified in such a way that the crucial distinction is not between stage-level and individual-level predicates.

To summarize, I have argued that: i) subjects of individual-level predicates must appear in Spec(I) at S-structure, ii) subjects of verbs in the indicative mood (whether stage-level or individual-level) must also appear in Spec(I), since they share the relevant properties with subjects of individual-level predicates. Let me point out here the significance of (i) and (ii). It has been claimed that certain predicates have a particular property *Q*. *Q* is the property of causing the subject to appear in Spec(I) at some level of representation. *Q* was thought to be a property of a particular class of predicates: individual-level predicates. This reduces to saying that individual-level predicates have property *Q* by virtue of being individual-level predicates. However, the data in this section show that in Spanish, stage-level predicates in the indicative mood also have property *Q*. Consequently, what I considered to be a structural manifestation of the stage/individual-level distinction in Spanish may in fact be the structural manifestation of some other distinction. The question that arises is this: how can we define the class *P* of predicates that have property *Q*? *P* must be defined so as to include not only individual-level predicates, but also stage-level predicates realized by verbs in the indicative mood. Obviously, this definition cannot be made in terms of the stage/individual-level distinction of predicates. In the next section, I will address the problem of how to define *P*. In order to do this, I will introduce the notions of predication and non-predicational description.

4. In the previous section, we saw that a class *P* of predicates requires that the subject be generated in Spec(I). We also saw that *P* cannot be characterized as consisting only of individual-level predicates. In this section, I will introduce the distinction between the notions of predication and description. I will make the following proposal: *P* consists of predicates of sentences that represent predications. In other words, and informally, *P* consists of predicates of predications.

Kuroda (1992) claims that a sentence such as (27) is ambiguous between a reading as a predication and a reading as a description:

(27) *Juan está leyendo un libro*
'John is reading a book'

As a predication, the speaker who utters (27) is attributing a property to the individual denoted by the expression 'John', in this case, the property of reading a book. Under this reading, the interpretation of (27) conforms to the subject/predicate distinction of Aristotelian logic and 'John' is the logical subject of the predication. As a description, the speaker that utters (27) is not really saying something about the individual denoted by 'John'; rather, s/he is just describing a particular event or state of affairs, that John is reading a book. Under this interpretation, 'John' in (27), in spite of being a grammatical subject, is not a logical subject. As a description, sentence (27) does not conform to the Aristotelian subject/predicate distinction. Kuroda (ibid.) further distinguishes between generic and specific sentences. Specific sentences denote particular events located in space-time. Generic sentences do not relate to any specific situation. Notice that it must be the case that individual-level predicates appear in generic sentences, whereas stage-level predicates appear in specific sentences. Since generic sentences never make reference to specific events, generic sentences must always represent predications. On the other hand, specific sentences may represent either descriptions or predications, as in (27). Individual-level predicates appear in sentences that always represent predications (generic sentences), then individual-level predicates are always predicates in predications. However, stage-level predicates appear in sentences that can represent predications or descriptions (specific sentences). Consequently, stage-level predicates may or may not be predicates of predications. The discussion above points out an asymmetry between individual-level and stage-level predicates: individual-level predicates are always predicates of a predication, whereas stage-level predicates may or may not be predicates of predications. I will claim that this asymmetry is what causes the different structural manifestations of these two types of predicates. Furthermore, this asymmetry will also help us explain why in some cases stage-level predicates behave like individual-level predicates.

4.1. Let us first examine Diesing's proposal to account for the different syntactic behavior of subjects of individual-level predicates and subjects of stage-level predicates in English. Diesing (1989) assumes that the canonical subject position in English is Spec(V). The verb assigns a canonical θ-role of agent, etc. to Spec(V). However, the INFL of individual-level predicates (but not the INFL of stage-level predicates) assigns the θ-role of 'having the property x' (x being the predicate in question) to Spec(I). Consequently, the subject of individual-level predicates, but not the subject of stage-level predicates, is generated in Spec(I). When the subject is generated in Spec(I), Spec(V) is occupied by a PRO coindexed with the subject. This PRO receives the cannonical θ-role assigned by the verb to the subject position. Under this analysis, the structure of a sentence such as (28), where the predicate is individual-level, is as in (28'):

(28) 'Peter drinks wine'

(28') [$_{IP}$ Peter$_i$ INFL [$_{VP}$ PRO$_i$ drinks wine]]
|__θ_| |__θ'_|

In (28') INFL assigns the θ-role 'has the property x' to 'Peter', and the verb assigns the θ'-role 'agent' to the coindexed PRO. As a result, 'Peter' in (28) is interpreted both as the agent of the action of drinking wine and also as having the property of drinking wine. Notice that this interpretation is the interpretation that (28) receives also by virtue of representing a predication: the speaker attributes to the individual denoted by 'Peter' the property of drinking wine. This suggests that what makes INFL assign a θ-role to Spec(I) in (28) is not the fact that the predicate is an individual-level predicate, but rather that the predicate in (28) is the predicate of a predication. Following up on this idea, I propose the following modification of Diesing's analysis for Spanish:

Proposal B- θ-role Assignment in Predications:
In sentences that represent predications, INFL assigns the θ-role 'having the property x' to Spec(I).

4.2. I will examine now in some detail the consequences of the modification proposed in *B*. Since individual-level predicates always represent predicates of predications, the subject of individual-level predicates will always be generated in Spec(I). Consequently, with respect to individual-level predicates, the principle in *B* is empirically equivalent to *A* (Diesing's proposal). However, *B* makes a prediction that *A* does not make: since stage-level predicates may represent predicates of predications, stage-level predicates will on some occasions show properties similar to individual-level predicates. Notice that this is what the data in section 3 showed, that on some ocassions stage-level predicates also require the subject to be generated in Spec(I). Consequently, the principle in *B* allows us to give an account of the fact that stage-level predicates realized by verbs in the indicative mood behave like individual-level predicates with respect to certain relevant properties. Such an account relies on the assumption that, in linguistic contexts such as the ones illustrated in (19), complements in the indicative mood must represent a predication. Under this assumption, the semantic difference between (19a) and (19b), or at least part of the semantic difference, is that in (19a) the speaker is denying that a particular property applies to the individual denoted by the expression 'Peter', whereas (19b) is ambiguous: the speaker may be denying that a property applies to the individual denoted by

'John', or the speaker may be denying that a particular state of affairs holds. If complements in the indicative mood always represent predications, then, assuming *B*, the INFL of verbs in the indicative mood assigns a θ-role to Spec(I), whether the predicate is stage-level or individual-level. However, the INFL of verbs in the subjunctive mood may or may not assign a θ-role to Spec(I), depending on whether the complement is interpreted as a predication or as a description.[13]

To summarize, I have proposed that, in predications, INFL assigns a θ-role to Spec(I). As a result, the subject of individual-level predicates will always be generated in Spec(I), whereas the subject of stage-level predicates may be generated in Spec(I) or within the VP, depending on whether or not the stage-level predicate represents the predicate of a predication. This explains why on some occasions stage-level predicates show properties similar to individual-level predicates. The analysis relies on the assumption that the notions predication/description play a role in the semantic distinction between (19a) and (19b). Under this analysis, a sentence such as (27), with a stage-level predicate, is structurally ambiguous in Spanish. The structural ambiguity reflects in turn a semantic ambiguity. As a predication, the representation is as (27'); as a description, the representation is as (27"):[14]

(27') $[_{IP}$ Juan$_i$ $[_{VP}$ PRO$_i$ está leyendo un libro]]
(27") $[_{IP}$ $[_{VP}$ Juan está leyendo un libro]]

Consider, on the other hand, a case such as (28) above, where the predicate is individual-level. There is only one possible representation of (28), the one in (28'), since individual-level predicates are always predications.

5. Conclusions. In this paper I have studied the structural encoding in Spanish of two semantic distinctions: the distinction between stage and individual-level predicates, and the distinction between the notions of predication and non-predicational description. I have claimed that subjects in sentences that represent predications are generated in Spec(I). It entails from this claim that subjects of individual-level predicates are always generated in Spec(I) and that subjects of stage-level predicates may be generated in Spec(I) or within the VP. The claim hinges on the assumption that the notions of predication and description play a role in the characterization of the semantic difference between

---

[13] The assumption is that complements in the indicative must represent predications, whereas complements in the subjunctive mood may represent predications or descriptions. I will not try to independently motivate this assumption here. Notice, however, that such an assumption is not inconsistent with native intuitions regarding pairs of sentences such as (19a) and (19b).

[14] For the purposes of this discussion, I will assume, without further motivation, that Spec(V) is the canonical subject position in Spanish. However, as pointed out above, this assumption is not crucial for the analysis here; it is crucial only that the canonical subject position in Spanish is somewhere within the VP.

complements in the indicative mood and complements in the subjunctive mood in Spanish. This paper is significant in that it shows that the semantic notions of predication and description are relevant in accounting for the structural properties observed in some Spanish sentences. Furthermore, this paper suggests that what has been claimed to be structural manifestations of the stage/individual-level distinction in languages such as German or English may in fact be structural manifestations of the predication/description distinction.

References:

Carlson, Greg N. 1977. The English Bare Plural. *Linguistics and Philosophy* 1:413-457.

Carlson, Greg N. 1980. *Reference to Kinds in English*. Garland: New York.

Contreras, H. 1987. Small Clauses in English and Spanish. *Natural Language and Linguistic Theory*, 5:225-243.

Diesing, Molly. 1988. Bare Plural Subjects and the Stage/Individual Contrast. In *Genericity in Natural Language*, ed. by Manfred Krifka.

Diesing, Molly. 1989. *Bare Plural Subjects, Inflection and the Mapping to LF*. Unpublished ms., University of Massachusettes, Amherst.

Diesing, Molly. 1990. *The Syntactic Roots of Semantic Partition.*. PhD dissertation, University of Massachusettes, Amherst.

Groos, A. and Reineke Bok-Bennema.. 1986. The structure of the sentence in Spanish.*Generative Studies in Spanish Syntax*, ed by Ivonne Bordelois, Heles Contreras and Karen Zagona. Dordrecht: Foris.

Kratzer, Angelika. 1989. Stage and Individual Level Predicates. *Papers on Quantification*, NSF Grant Report, Department of Linguistics. University of Massachusettes, Amherst.

Kuroda, S.-Y. 1972a. Anton Marty and the Transformational Theory of Grammar. *Foundations of Language* 9:1-37.

Kuroda, S.-Y. 1972b. The Categorical and the Thetic Judgment: Evidence from Japanese.*Foundations of Language* 9:153-185.

Kuroda, S.-Y. 1979. *Grammatical Generative Studies in the Japanese Language*. 1965 MIT PhD dissertation. Published by Garland Publishing Co., New York: Garland.

Kuroda, S.-Y. 1992. Cognitive and Syntactic Bases of Topicalized and NontopicalizedSentences in Japanese. *Japanese Syntax and Semantics*. Collected papers\fR. Dordrecht: Kluwer.

May, Robert. 1985. *Logical Form*. Cambridge: MIT Press.

Mejías-Bikandi, Errapel. 1992. *The VP-internal Subject Hypothesis and Spanish Sentence Structure*. Paper presented at LSRL XXII, University of Texas at El Paso.

Williams, Edwin. 1980. Predication. *Linguistic Inquiry* 11:203-238.

Zagona, Karen. 1988. *Verb Phrase Syntax*. Dordrecht: Kluwer.

Morphological Marking Misses the Head

PHILIP MILLER
Ohio State University

One of the classical criteria for determining the Head of a phrase is that it is the primary locus for morphological marking on that phrase.[1] This is embodied in linguistic theories by principles such as the Head Feature Convention (HFC) of GPSG. In this paper I present a series of cases where lexically attached morphological marking appears in non-Head positions on the basis of linear order, viz., on the first or last item of a phrase. The central data discussed are the English possessive marker *'s*, the Tongan definitive accent, and the French demonstrative enclitics *-ci* and *-là*. I propose that this type of lexically realized phrasal inflection is accounted for by EDGE features (which can be FIRST or LAST) that are subject to the Edge Feature Principle (cf. Lapointe 1990, Miller 1992a) and to specific LP statements. I show how this analysis of phrasal inflection accounts for certain types of haplology phenomena which are unaccounted for under postlexical cliticization or syntactic movement analyses.

1. Introduction

The typical situation for the morphological exponence of a feature associated with a phrasal node is that the Head of the phrase is marked for the feature in question. This property is embodied by mechanisms such as the Head Feature Convention (HFC) of Gazdar et al. 1985 (henceforth GKPS). Secondary morphological marking may also occur on certain non-Head items in the phrase by agreement with the Head. This property is accounted for by the Control Agreement Principle of GKPS and similar mechanisms in other theories. The situations which I will be discussing in this paper are crucially different. Namely, I will be analyzing cases where the item of the phrase which receives the morphological mark is

[1]I would like to thank Chris Barker, Donka Farkas, Aaron Halpern, Brian Joseph, Andreas Kathol, Bob Levine, Michael Moortgat, Yves-Charles Morin, Dorian Popescu, Geoffrey Pullum, Hilary Sachs, Peter Svenonius and Arnold Zwicky for comments and discussion. This material was also presented at the Ohio State University and at CSLI, Stanford University. I would like to thank the audiences for their comments. Author's address: Center for Cognitive Science / 208 Ohio Stadium East / 1961 Tuttle Park Place / Columbus, OH 43210-1102. E-mail: pmiller@shs.ohio-state.edu.

determined by linear ordering within the phrase, rather than by Head status or Agreement. More specifically, I will be interested in cases where the morphological mark for a feature is realized on the first or the last item of the phrase. The morphological marking can be either affixal or processual, and is assumed to be lexically (rather than postlexically) realized. These phenomena have been called *phrasal inflection* (or *affixation*) and *edge inflection*; (cf. Poser 1985; Zwicky 1987; Lapointe 1990; Miller 1992a; Anderson 1992; Halpern and Miller in prep). I will briefly illustrate this notion with respect to the English possessive marker *'s* and the Tongan Definitive Accent (TDA).

It is well known that the English possessive marker *'s* appears on the last lexical item of a possessive NP. Thus, it is the linear ordering of items within the NP that determines on which lexical item the exponence of the feature POSS, associated with the NP phrasal node, is realized.

(1) a. $[_{NP}$ The boy's] talk was good.
    b. $[_{NP}$ The boy with blond hair's] talk was good.
    c. *$[_{NP}$ The boy's with blond hair] talk was good.

Similarly, Tongan indicates a certain type of definiteness on an NP by a prosodic process which consists in shifting the accent from the penultimate mora of a word (the default case) to the final mora (cf. Churchward 1953 §§2.15ff, 4.11ff, 33; Poser 1985; Anderson 1992 pp.212-15; the details of the semantics are not of interest to us here, cf. Churchward for discussion).

(2) a. ?i he fále *in a house* (specific indefinite interpretation)
    b. ?i he falé *in the house*

What makes the Tongan Definitive Accent (TDA) relevant to our present concerns is that the stress shift marking definiteness occurs on whatever word happens to be the final item of the definite NP. This is illustrated in the following examples, taken from Churchward §2.1.6).

(3) a. ?i he falé. *in the house*
    b. ?i he fale akó *in the school building*
    c. ?i he fale ako fo?oú *in the new school building*

I will argue, following Poser (1985) and Zwicky (1987), that both of these phenomena should be analyzed as lexically realized inflection on the last item of a phrase rather than as the result of postlexical cliticization of a separate syntactic formative to the last item. I am assuming that a postlexical clitic is a syntactic word which lacks the appropriate prosodic properties to be a word at the prosodic level, and which is consequently postlexically and postsyntactically attached (cliticized) to an adjacent word by a prosodic operation of stray adjunction (cf. Anderson 1992). For the case of an example like (1b), the structure in tree 1 represents a phrasal inflection analysis whereas that in tree 2 represents the *'s* as a postlexical clitic. The discussion of the precise mechanisms which produce the type of path for the feature PM illustrated in tree 1 is postponed to section 2.

Tree 1

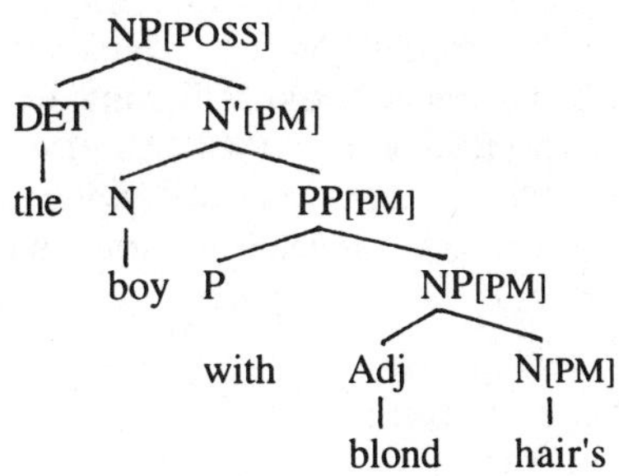

Tree 2

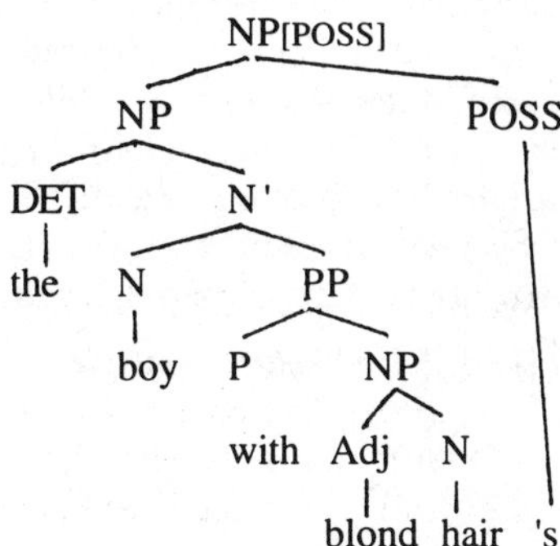

This position raises two central issues. First, what criteria are relevant to deciding that these are cases of lexically realized inflection, rather than postlexical cliticization? It should be noted that criterion A of Zwicky and Pullum (1983) ('Clitics exhibit a low degree of selection with respect to their hosts while affixes exhibit a high degree of selection with respect to their stems'), also known as the 'promiscuous attachment' criterion, goes against the position taken here. This is because the final word of an NP in English or Tongan can be of a variety of categories (essentially due to the fact that NPs are not head final in these languages). Consequently, morphological marking on the last word results in promiscuous attachment. Second, what types of syntactic mechanisms can account for such patterns of marking? Specifically, in tree 1, how can the presence of POSS on the NP node trigger inflection on the word *hair*? Clearly, it is difficult to interpret such marking as the result of an agreement phenomenon. Linear ordering has never been suggested as a basis of choice for agreement targets. Furthermore, if the marking of the last item in examples such as (1b) and (3b, c) were the result of agreement with the Head, it would be expected that the Head noun would also carry respectively the possessive and the definiteness features. But, in that case, we would expect that the NP would be marked for these features in two different places, in examples such as (1b) and (3b, c), namely, both on the last item and on the Head. Indeed, as shown by (1a) and (3a), the Head nouns do have inflected forms for these features. In what follows, I will address the questions of the appropriate criteria for assigning lexically attached phrasal inflection status and propose a syntactic mechanism, the Edge Feature Principle (EFP), to account for it.

2. The Edge Feature Principle

Elaborating on proposals by Nevis (1985), Poser (1985), Zwicky (1987), Lapointe (1990), I will be proposing a solution based on feature percolation in the GKPS style, as illustrated in tree 1 above. The problem can be divided into two parts. First, it is necessary to ensure that a path is established between the phrasal node bearing the relevant feature and some terminal node within the phrase, which will be inflected for the corresponding morphological mark. This is the job of the

Edge Feature Principle (EFP). Second, we must be able to specify that the node in question can be either the first or the last. This will be taken care of by LP rules.

The EFP can be informally stated as in (4) (a technically precise definition is given in the appendix. See Miller 1992a, 122ff. and Halpern and Miller ms. for more extensive discussion). In the definition, the feature T is a TRIGGERING feature. The feature E is an EDGE feature, or MORPHOLOGICAL MARKING feature, which will cause the lexical node on which it appears to be inflected, ensuring the exponence of the triggering feature on that node.

(4) *Edge Feature Principle*
- (i) If a node has T then one of its daughters has E;
- (ii) if a node has E, then its mother has T or E;
- (iii) if a node has E, then one of its daughters has E.

By clause (i) of the EFP, the presence of a triggering feature T on a node forces the instantiation of the corresponding EDGE feature E on one of its daughters. For clause (i) to be able to do its job, the grammar must provide a list of pairs defining which EDGE feature corresponds to each triggering feature. Clause (ii) of the EFP governs the 'upward percolation' of EDGE features. It requires that if an EDGE feature appears on a daughter in a local tree, then it must appear on the mother. There is one case where this requirement is relaxed, namely if the mother category bears a triggering syntactic feature corresponding to the EDGE feature under discussion. In that case, the EFP is satisfied whether upward percolation stops (the default case) or whether it continues through the node in question (this possibility is the central point on which the EFP and the Foot Feature Principle (FFP) of GKPS differ; it plays a crucial role in accounting for the haplology phenomena to be discussed below). Finally, clause (iii) governs the 'downward percolation' of EDGE features. It requires that if an EDGE feature appears on the mother node in a local tree, it must also appear on one of the daughters. This clause prevents an EDGE feature from 'getting lost' on the way down to a terminal node.

The functioning of the EFP can be illustrated with respect to tree 1. POSS is the triggering feature. It is the feature which is syntactically and semantically relevant (it is semantically potent in the sense of GKPS, p. 223ff.). PM (POSS Marking) is the EDGE feature which is triggered by POSS. The presence of PM on the lexical node dominating *hair's* is responsible for it appearing inflected with *'s*.[2]

In order to account for the fact that PM must follow a rightmost path to a terminal node, it is assigned to the class of LAST features, which are subject to the LP rule (5a). The similar LP rule (5b) for FIRST features ensures that the exponence of a triggering feature which triggers a FIRST feature will be realized on the first item of the phrase.

(5) a. X < LAST
    b. FIRST < X

Separating triggering features from morphological marking EDGE features has a number of advantages. First, it avoids a paradox pointed out for the analysis

[2]I am assuming that both POSS and PM are unary valued features.

of Zwicky (1987) by Lapointe (1990).[3] If POSS and PM were the same feature, subject to (5a), then we would incorrectly predict that the possessive NP should follow its sister N'. Second, it allows for a distinction between the status of features which can be semantically potent, and features which are responsible for morphological exponence, which are never semantically potent. Third, it provides an account for the fact that different syntactic features can trigger the same types of exponence, and for the fact that certain haplology phenomena can occur between such triggered morphological marks (cf. section 4).

3. Distinguishing postlexical cliticization from phrasal inflection

Let us now review various criteria that allow a distinction to be made between phrasal inflection and postlexical clitic status. Before doing this, let me briefly point out that the EFP type analysis of phrasal inflection just discussed makes Criterion A of Zwicky and Pullum (1983), quoted above, irrelevant. Indeed, the EFP provides a mechanism that specifically allows for the lexical realization of morphology on items of different categories, as illustrated in the case of the English possessive.

1. Arguments from phonology and morphology.

If lexical phonological rules can apply to the unit formed by the morphological mark and the stem, then the mark is a lexically realized inflection rather than a postlexical clitic. The justification of this criterion follows immediately from the definition of lexical phonological rules. The alternative is to have the lexical phonological rule exceptionally apply postlexically. Similarly, if the realization of the mark depends on the morphological structure of the host, it must be an instance of lexically realized inflection. Indeed, the bracketing erasure convention of Lexical Phonology (cf. Kiparsky 1982), and similar principles of other lexicalist frameworks, make the internal structure of a word invisible to postlexical processes. It should be noted that these types of arguments only carry weight if one assumes the lexicalist hypothesis. Weaker assumptions about the syntax/morphology interface — such as those espoused by current post-*Barriers* GB theory — make them invalid. We will discuss arguments of this type both for the English possessive marker and for the TDA.

2. Processual vs. affixal realization of the morphological mark.

In the case of the English possessive marker, phrasal inflection is realized as a case of phrasal affixation. In the case of Tongan, however, the TDA is realized processually, by a stress shift (cf. Poser 1985 and Anderson 1992, 213-215 for evidence that this cannot be reinterpreted as affixation of a melodically unattached moraic position). Processual realization is a widespread property within morphology. However, it is not clear how postlexical cliticization could be made to account for processual realization. Consequently, if the mark is realized processually, it is an instance of phrasal inflection, not of postlexical cliticization.

[3]Lapointe proposes a different solution to this paradox. However, his proposals raise a number of technical problems. Cf. Miller 1992a, pp.114ff.

3. Haplology.

If in cases where one would expect two occurrences of the morphological mark under investigation because of the syntactic structure, only one occurrence is found, then the mark is an instance of phrasal inflection rather than of postlexical cliticization. Indeed, nothing in the prosodic nature of postlexical cliticization would lead us to expect this type of haplology: one would simply expect a sequence of two occurrences of the clitic. On the other hand, it will become clear below how the phrasal inflection analysis via the EFP directly predicts the relevant types of haplology.

These three types of criteria are those that will be central to the discussion in this paper. Other criteria are also relevant. In Miller 1992a and 1992b, I argue in favour of two criteria based on repetition of morphological marks in coordinate structures:

(6) a. If an item must be repeated on each conjunct in a coordinate structure it is a lexically realized inflectional mark, not a PLC.
b. If an item may not be repeated on each conjunct in a coordinate structure, then it must be a PLC, and cannot be a lexically realized inflectional mark.

Other criteria can also be found in Zwicky and Pullum 1983, based on the presence of arbitrary gaps, morphophonological idiosyncrasies, interaction with syntactic rules and ordering between affixes and clitics. I will not discuss these criteria further here.

4. The English possessive marker *'s*

4.1. Phonological and morphological evidence for phrasal inflection status

As pointed out by Zwicky (1987), the English possessive marker exhibits a haplology phenomenon with Z ending words on the condition that the Z ending is a morphological mark (e.g., the plural marker or the 3rd person singular marker as in (7b) and (7d) below respectively), and not part of the stem (as in (7a) and (7c)). Note also that the presence of plural marking not realized by a Z (as in (7c)) does not lead to haplology.[4]

(7) a. the goose's egg — */s/, /sɪz/
b. the hens' eggs — /z/, */zɪz/
c. the geese's eggs — */s/, /sɪz/
d. the hen that sings' eggs — /z/, */zɪz/

If one accepts the central tenets of the lexicalist hypothesis, these haplology data give us crucial evidence that the possessive marker must be lexically attached. Indeed, if it were attached by postlexical cliticization (or syntactic movement), accounting for these data would entail a violation of the principle in (8):

(8) The morphological structure of a word should not be visible for syntactic or postlexical rules or conditions.

---

[4]Zwicky (1987) uses the notation 'Z' to note the different allomorphs [s], [z] and [ɪz] of the plural, the 3rd pers.sg., and the possessive.

4.2. Haplology between possessive markers

Zwicky (1987) shows that a haplology effect appears in cases where one would expect more than one occurrence of the possessive marker on a word, due to the syntactic structure. Consider example (9) which exhibits a 'locative possessive' (*at Harry's*) in final position within a larger standard possessive NP (*the people at Harry's*). Instead of the two occurrences of Z, that one might expect, only a single occurrence appears.

(9) The people at Harry's hats (*Harry's's [zɪz])

This phenomenon is automatically accounted for given the feature percolation solution provided above, as shown in the structure assigned to (9).

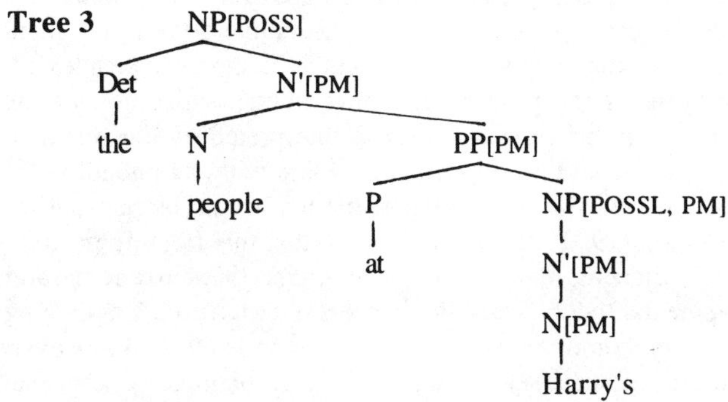

I assume that the feature PM, which marks the locative possessive, is triggered by a separate triggering feature POSSL (this assumption is necessary to account for the specific semantics of the locative possessive, which is obviously different from that of the standard possessive. See Barker 1991 on the semantics of possessives). The haplology is then automatically accounted for given the EFP and the GKPS framework. The node N' dominating *Harry's* is specified as carrying the feature PM both by clause (i) and by clause (iii) of the EFP, since its mother has both the triggering feature POSSL and the marking feature PM. But, given the GKPS definition of categories as partial functions, this cannot result in doubly marking the N' node for PM. The double requirement is satisfied by a single specification for the feature PM. This case provides us with an example of the type promised above, where the same morphological marking feature (PM) is triggered by two different triggering features (POSS and POSSL), and haplology can be observed between the resulting morphological marks. Without the distinction between triggering features and marking features, one would either have to say that the features driving the locative possessive and the standard possessive are different, which would satisfy the semantics but fail to account for the haplology, or that the features are the same, accounting for the haplology but not for the semantics. Note that the formulation of clause (ii) of the EFP, which allows a marking feature on a daughter if the mother has the triggering feature or the marking feature,[5] is central to this account. This is the aspect of the EFP which crucially distinguishes it from the Foot Feature Principle (FFP). Indeed, it allows one morphological mark to satisfy the demands of more than one triggering feature. If one attempted to account for the instantiation of EDGE features by the FFP, this would not be possible, barring modifications of the FFP that would be disastrous for the treatment of long distance dependencies (viz., they would incorrectly allow one gap to correspond to multiple fillers).

5. The Tongan Definitive Accent

5.1. Phonological and morphological evidence for phrasal inflection status

Poser (1985) extensively argues that the accent placement characterizing the TDA must be a lexical process. Specifically, Poser shows that accent placement must precede a phonological rule of syllable fusion which he shows to be a lexical rule. Furthermore, because of the processual nature of the realization of the inflection, it is not clear a priori how it could be interpreted as the result of cliticization at all. One idea would be to postulate a clitic with, as phonological representation, a melodically unattached mora position that would be relevant for accent placement. Anderson (1992, 213-15) points out that this floating position should be attached to adjacent melodic material under the current default assumptions of autosegmental theory, resulting in a stress shift **and** a lengthening of the final vowel if it is monomoraic. No such lengthening is attested however. Furthermore, Anderson discusses a set of cases in Tongan phonology where an empty position does in fact get attached to adjacent melodic material, showing that the default assumptions can be considered to be at work in Tongan.

5.2. Tongan Definitive Accent Haplology

In the line of the above proposals for the analysis of the English possessive marker, I propose that the TDA is the morphological realization of a LAST feature DEFM on the final element of an NP. The feature DEFM is a morphological marking feature triggered by the presence of a semantically potent feature DEF on the NP node. Such an analysis leads to the prediction that if an NP marked for DEF is final within a larger NP also marked for DEF, a haplology phenomenon similar to that observed for the English possessive in example (9) should occur. In fact, Churchward (1953, 279) explicitly describes situations of this type, and indicates that the relevant haplology is possible.

(10) a. Ko e hā [$_{NP}$e ?uhinga na?e ?ita ai ?a [$_{NP}$e faiakó] kiate aú]?
is the what the reason Past angry prt SM the teacher with me
Why was the teacher angry with me?
b. Ko e ha [$_{NP}$e ?uhinga na?e ?ita ai kiate au ?a [$_{NP}$e faiakó]]?

In (10a) and (10b), a complex definite NP has an embedded definite NP within it. If the embedded NP is not final within the larger NP, both exhibit the stress shift as

[5]Note that it is crucial that this is an inclusive *or*.

shown in (10a). If the embedded NP is final within the larger NP, then a single realization of the stress shift on the final word can make both NPs definite as in (10b). Note that (10b) is actually predicted to be triply ambiguous under this analysis: it results if either the embedded NP or the larger NP are definite (i.e., have the feature DEF) or if both are. For the reasons mentioned above in comparing the EFP with the FFP, the haplology reading is impossible under Poser's suggestion to treat the feature driving the TDA (/def in Poser's analysis) as a FOOT feature, but immediately falls out if it is treated as a LAST feature, by mechanisms entirely parallel to those accounting for (9).

6. The French demonstrative enclitics *-ci* and *-là*

A similar haplology phenomenon also occurs for the French demonstrative enclitics *-ci* and *-là*, which I propose to treat as instances of phrasal inflection, rather than as postlexical clitics. These items can appear on the last word of an NP with the demonstrative determiner *ce*, as illustrated in the following examples.[6]

(11)	a.	Cette fille-ci	*this girl*
	b.	Cette grande fille-ci	*this big girl*
	c.	*Cette grande-ci fille	
	d.	Cette fille intelligente-ci	*this intelligent girl*
	e.	*Cette fille-ci intelligente	

In Miller 1992a, I analyze *-ci* and *-là* as being respectively the morphological realization of the feature specifications +L-PROX and –L-PROX, where L-PROX is a LAST feature. L-PROX is triggered by the semantically potent feature PROX[7] which an FCR restricts to occurring on demonstrative NPs. As in the case of the English possessive and the TDA, examples can be constructed where a demonstrative NP is embedded within a larger demonstrative NP. The relevant aspects of the structures for these NPs are given in trees 4 and 5 (it is beyond the scope of this paper to motivate the details of these structures; see Miller 1992a for extensive justification).

(12)	a.	Ce garçon de cette ville-ci	*This boy from this town*
	b.	*Ce garçon de cette ville-ci-ci	
	c.	*Ce garçon de cette ville-ci-là	

Tree 4 NP[+PROX]

NP — N — ce-garçon

NP[+PROX, +L-PROX] — N[+L-PROX] — de-cette-ville-ci

Tree 5 NP[+PROX]

NP — N — *ce-garçon

NP[–PROX, +L-PROX] — N[+L-PROX, –L-PROX] — de-cette-ville-ci-là

---

[6]The facts are somewhat more complex than is indicated here. See Miller 1992a, 273ff., 289ff. for a more detailed discussion. The semantic effect of *-ci* and *-là* is proximal vs. distal (the demonstrative *ce* being neutral in this respect).

[7]Note that clause (i) of the full version of the EFP given in the appendix accounts for the fact that the triggering feature PROX transmits its value + or – to the triggered feature L-PROX.

As expected, the NP (12a) is triply ambiguous: the proximal reading can be assigned to the higher NP, to the embedded NP or to both. The interpretation where *-ci* realizes the exponence of +PROX present both on the higher NP and on the lower NP is shown in tree 4, which exhibits the same type of merging of paths of LAST features, leading to the haplology effect, as in tree 3 for the English possessive marker haplology. If, on the other hand, *-ci* was a postlexical clitic, there would be no reason to expect the haplology under this reading. One would incorrectly expect to get two occurrences of the the morpheme as in (12b). Indeed, there is nothing about (12b) that could lead us to believe that it is prosodically ill-formed. (12a), on the other hand, would be predicted to be ambiguous only between a proximal reading for the higher NP or the embedded NP but not both at the same time. Finally, the phrasal affix analysis correctly predicts that (12c) cannot be generated. Indeed, in order to generate it (and in order for the EFP to be satisfied), it would be necessary for the feature L-PROX on the node directly dominating *ville* in tree 5 to be marked both for the values + and –, which is impossible given the definition of categories as partial functions. Once again, the postlexical cliticization analysis has no obvious way to avoid generating (12c).

To my knowledge, there is no clear evidence from phonology either supporting or arguing against the lexically attached phrasal inflection status proposed here for *-ci* and *-là*. For instance, it is not clear that one could construct an argument based on the fact that strings like *garçon-ci* are stressed on *-ci* rather than on the final syllable of *garçon.* Indeed, the question of whether stress is determined at the level of the morphological word or at a more inclusive prosodic level can only be decided on the basis of numerous auxiliary hypotheses.

7. Further perspectives on non-Head morphological marking

In this section, I would like to briefly review further cross-linguistic data which can be argued to be instances of non-Head morphological marking. In my thesis, I provide extensive arguments based on syntax, morphology and phonology that in French, the determiners and the prepositions *à*, *de* and *en* should be analyzed as phrasal inflections on the NP, driven by FIRST features. The case of Welsh soft mutation can also be argued to be an instance of processually realized phrasal inflection driven by a FIRST feature (cf. Zwicky 1984).[8]

The definite articles in Rumanian, Macedonian and Bulgarian provide further interesting evidence, showing that, in some cases, the notions of first and last lexical item in the phrase are not sufficient to account for the locus of non-Head morphological marking. Consider the following data from Rumanian:[9]

---

[8]See Anderson (1992, 215) for arguments against Lieber's (1987) proposal to analyze soft mutation as the result of the affixation of [+Voice, +Continuant].

[9]The Rumanian data reported here are being studied in independent work, within this perspective, by Aaron Halpern, Peter Svenonius (cf. Svenonius ms.) and myself. For an analysis of the Rumanian, Bulgarian, and Macedonian data cf. Halpern 1992.

(13) a. prietenul *the friend*
b. bunul prieten vs. *bun prietenul *the good friend*
c. *foartele bun prieten vs. foarte bunul prieten vs. * foarte bun prietenul *the very good friend*

As shown in (13a), the definite article in Rumanian is realized as a suffix (*-ul* or *-le* in the masc. sg.). If the noun is preceded by an adjective, the suffix must appear on the adjective (13b). If however, the prenominal adjective is itself modified by the adverb *foarte*, then the suffix must appear on the adjective (13c). These data are compatible with the EFP, but it is clear that the LP statement (5b) will be insufficient to account for cases like (13c). The Rumanian data, and the somewhat similar data from Bulgarian and Macedonian, show that further investigation is needed of the possible loci for non-Head morphological marking (cf. Halpern 1992 and Svenonius 1992 for concrete proposals). It should also be noted that the linear ordering of the determiner affix *after* the first word of the NP makes it impossible to analyze it as the result of postlexical cliticization interpreted as a purely prosodic phenomenon (see however Sadock 1991, e.g., 117, for an alternative perspective).

Finally, a still more challenging case can be taken from certain Amharic data (cf. Halefom 1990, Svenonius 1992). In Amharic, definiteness is indicated by a suffix that occurs on the Head of the leftmost phrase in the NP. Moreover, the suffix may be repeated on the Heads of other prenominal phrases. Accounting for such multiple occurrences of morphological marking for the same feature on a phrase will require further rethinking of the principles which control the directionality of percolation of the marking features.

8. Head movement and affix lowering analyses

Up to this point, I have only discussed analyses in terms of postlexical cliticization and phrasal affixation for the range of data presented here, ignoring possible post-*Barriers* type analyes in terms of Head movement (cf. e.g., Baker 1988) or affix lowering (cf. e.g., Chomsky 1991). My position is that, in the absence of compelling evidence in favour of the contrary position, general metatheoretical principles disfavour the less restrictive and less modular conception of the syntax/morphology interface embodied in post-*Barriers* style analyses (cf. Zwicky and Pullum 1986 for more general argumentation in favour of restrictive interfaces between modular components of grammar). Moreover, two empirical arguments against such analyses can be made with respect to the data discussed here. First, the existence of processually realized phrasal inflection, as in the cases of the TDA and Welsh soft mutation, is hard to reconcile with the essentially affixal approach which characterizes Head movement and affix lowering approaches. Second, the haplology phenomena discussed above are just as problematic for these approaches as for postlexical cliticization. The very concrete approach to the interaction of syntax and morphology, advocated by Baker, claiming that certain aspects of affix ordering can be directly accounted for by the ordering of syntactic movement, gives us no reason to expect the type of haplology discussed above. On the contrary, that approach leads to a strong expectation that there should be multiple occurrences of the relevant morphological marks.

Appendix

Definition: *Edge Feature Principle* (EFP)

Let Φ_r be the set of projections from r, where $r = C_0 \rightarrow C_1, \ldots, C_n$, and let g_k be a syntactic feature triggering the morphological marking EDGE feature f_k.

Then, $\phi \in \Phi_r$ meets the EFP on r if and only if for all pairs (g_k, f_k)

(i) if $[g_k, v] \in \phi(C_0)$ then $\exists C_i$, $1 \leq i \leq n$, such that $[f_k, v] \in (\phi(C_i))$; and

(ii) $\forall C_i$, $1 \leq i \leq n$, if $[f_k, v] \in \phi(C_i)$ then $[g_k, v] \in \phi(C_0)$ or $[f_k, v] \in \phi(C_0)$; and

(iii) if $[f_k, v] \in \phi(C_0)$, then $\exists C_i$, $1 \leq i \leq n$, such that $[f_k, v] \in \phi(C_i)$.

References

Anderson, S. 1992. *A-morphous Morphology.* Cambridge University Press.

Baker, M. 1988. *Incorporation. A Theory of Grammatical Function Changing.* Chicago: Chicago University Press.

Barker, C. 1991. *Possessive Descriptions.* Doctoral dissertation, University of California, Santa Cruz.

Chomsky, N. 1991. Some notes on economy of derivation and representation. In R. Freidin, ed. Principles and Parameters in Comparative Grammar. Cambridge, MA: MIT Press.

Churchward, C.M. 1953. *Tongan Grammar.* Oxford University Press.

Gazdar, G., Klein, E., Pullum, G. K. and Sag, I. A. 1985. *Generalized Phrase Structure Grammar.* Oxford: Basil Blackwell.

Halefom, G. 1990. Head movement triggered by weak functional heads. *Proceedings of the Ninth West Coast Conference on Formal Linguistics.*

Halpern, A. 1992. The Balkan definite article and pseudo-second position. *Proceedings of the Berkeley Linguistic Society.*

Halpern, A. and P. Miller. 1992 (ms). English possessives and the syntax of morphological features. Department of Linguistics, Stanford University/Center for Cognitive Science, Ohio State University.

Kiparsky, P. 1982. Lexical Morphology and Phonology. *Linguistics in the Morning Calm.* Seoul: Hanshin Publishing Co., 3-91.

Lapointe, S. 1990. EDGE features in GPSG. *Proceedings of the 26th Regional Meeting of the Chicago Linguistic Society* (to appear).

Lieber, R. 1987. *An Integrated Theory of Autosegmental Processes.* Albany: State University of New York Press.

Miller, P. 1992a. *Clitics and Constituents in Phrase Structure Grammar.* New York: Garland. (Doctoral dissertation, University of Utrecht, 1991.)

Miller, P. 1992b. Postlexical cliticization vs. affixation: Coordination criteria. *Proceedings of the 28th Regional Meeting of the Chicago Linguistic Society* (to appear).

Nevis, J. 1985. *Finnish Particle Clitics and General Clitic Theory.* New York: Garland. (Ohio State University PhD thesis, also *OSU WPL* 33.)

Poser, W. 1985 Cliticization to NP and Lexical Phonology. *Proceedings of WCCFL* 4, UCLA, 262-272.

Sadock, J. 1991. *Autolexical Syntax.* Chicago: Chicago University Press.

Svenonius, P. 1992. The structure of the Norwegian NP. Paper read at the 9th Conference on Comparative Germanic Syntax. Ms., University of California, Santa Cruz.

Zwicky, A. 1984. Welsh soft mutation and the case of object NPs. *Proceedings of the Chicago Linguistic Society* 20: 387-402.

Zwicky, A. 1987. Suppressing the *Zs*. *Journal of Linguistics* 23, 133-148.

Zwicky, A. and Pullum, G. 1983. Cliticization vs. Inflection: English *n't*. *Language* 59.3, 502-513.

Zwicky, A. and Pullum, G. 1986. The Principle of Phonology-Free Syntax: Introductory Remarks. *OSU WPL* 32, 63-91.

Statives, Perfectives and Accusivity: The Importance of Being HAVE

MÁIRE NOONAN
McGill University

1.0. Introduction.

This paper illustrates a theory of structural Case that views accusativity as a configurational rather than a lexical property, resulting from syntactic geometry and not from lexical feature specifications on verbs. To this end, I compare two languages, Irish and English, showing that an investigation of Irish stative and perfective structures helps us understand how verb types determine syntactic geometry, and how syntactic geometry in turn determines patterns of structural Case marking. My main proposal here is that, universally, stative and perfective verbs are unaccusative. The surface difference between English and Irish is related to the presence and absence, respectively, of a lexical entry HAVE, a property that is independently attested in the grammars of English and Irish.

1.1. Statives.

A striking fact about Irish is that it appears to have no stative transitive verbs — that is, psychological state verbs equivalent to such English verbs as *know, love,* and *fear.* As a first pass, this observation can be stated as a filter ruling out stative verbs that take two NP arguments:

(1) * V NP NP (word order reflects Irish VSO order)
[stative]

The form that psychological state predicates typically do take in Irish is that of nominal constructions, as shown in (2).

* I would like to thank Joseph Aoun, Mark Baker, Ilan Hazout, Anna Szabolcsi, Benjamin Shaer, Dominique Sportiche, Tim Stowell, and Lisa Travis, for helpful questions, comments or suggestions. Special thanks to Benjamin Shaer for editorial help, and to Máire Ní Chiosáin for supplying many of the Irish data. The research for this paper was supported by grants from FCAR (#91-ER-0578) and SSHRC (#410-90.523).

(2) a. Tá gaeilge ag Fliodhais.
is Irish at Fliodhais
'Fliodhais knows Irish.'

b. Tá eagla roimh an bpúca ag Ailill.
is fear before the Puca at Ailill
'Ailill fears the Puca.'

c. Tá meas ar Meadhbh ag Ailill.
is respect on M. at Ailill
'Ailill respects Meadhbh.'

This contrasts with languages like English, German, and French, which contain stative transitive verbs such as those in (3).

(3) a. John loves/hates/fears Mary.
b. Hans liebt/haßt/fürchtet Maria.
c. Jean aime/déteste/craint Marie.

Since the missing verbs in Irish form a natural class (namely statives), it is unlikely that the differences between (2) and (3) arise from an accidental gap in Irish, and more likely that they represent a systematic grammatical difference between Irish and certain other languages. Given a 'principles and parameters' approach to language variation, as suggested by Chomsky (1979, 1981) and others, there are two basic ways to account for a syntactic difference like that described above: one is that the attested difference itself constitutes a primitive difference between languages; and the other is that it can be derived from more basic differences. An analysis along the lines of the first approach might see this difference in the form of statives as a primitive one, reflecting a choice between mapping stative predicates onto the category VERB, as in English (and thus expressing them as ordinary transitive verbs in the syntax), and mapping them onto the category NOUN or ADJECTIVE, as in Irish. In such an analysis, the relevant parameter simply represents the possible choices that languages may make in realising certain concepts syntactically, where the setting of the parameter itself is of a coincidental nature. It thus resembles, for example, the head-initial/head-final parameter, which (to my knowledge) is neither reducible to any more basic features of the grammar nor has marked and unmarked settings. An analysis along the lines of the second approach, representing the null hypothesis, might view both languages as underlyingly the same, except that one has some 'special' property, which on the surface obscures its similarity with the other, i.e., the null case. Crucially, the existence of this 'special' feature must have syntactic reflexes independent of the feature originally attested, and thus be established by empirical considerations. It is the latter possibility that I will explore here, whereby the cross-linguistic variation in the realisation of stative predicates, as illustrated in (2)-(3), is best explained by positing one of the two languages — namely Irish — as directly reflecting some basic property of UG, and the other — English — as the diverging language. The relevant property of UG will be used to explain another, hitherto unrelated difference between Irish and English, involving perfective constructions, to be described below.

1.2. The case of participles.

In English and many other languages, the past perfective and the passive participles are identical in form. However, they do differ in behaviour, since the passive participle does not permit an accusative object, while the past perfective participle does, as demonstrated by sentences like (4):

(4) She has painted her door bright red.

This in itself is a surprising fact that should be accounted for. Even more surprisingly, the perfective participle in Irish IS passive in form, even though it receives a perfective reading. This is illustrated in (5):[1]

(5) a. * Tá Sean déannta é.
aux S. do(participle) it (acc.)

b. Tá sé déannta ag Seán.
aux it(nom.) do(participle) at Seán
'Sean has done it.'

The direct object raises to subject position in order to be licensed by nominative Case, while the subject is marked with the preposition *ag*. In this way Irish resembles Hindi, where, as Mahajan (1990) has shown, perfective verbs also do not assign Case to their objects and therefore trigger an ergative Case pattern. Again, as a first pass, I will capture this generalisation with a filter:

(6) * V NP NP
[perfective]

Notice that (6) is related straightforwardly to Case theory; (1), however, is not necessarily so.[2] I will nevertheless maintain as a working hypothesis that stative verbs do not appear in Irish because they would not assign Case to their internal arguments, and thus relate (1) and (6) under a uniform Case-theoretic account.

Summing up the two observations: we find accusative stative and perfective verbs in English but not Irish. At this point there are two options available: either English constitutes the unmarked case, and some property of Irish (and Hindi) prevents accusativity with perfectives and statives; or Irish is the null case, and some property of English allows perfective participles and statives to surface as accusative verbs. I choose the latter option, which I formulate as (7):

(7) Stative and perfective verbs are unaccusative.

---

[1] I have purposefully used a sentence with a pronominal object, since nominative and accusative Case marking in Irish appears only on pronouns.

[2] It should be noted here that there are also no intransitive stative verbs in Irish; my analysis will also capture this fact (see section 3 below). My analysis also carries over to stative verbs generally (e.g. *entail, surround*). A potential problem for my analysis are perception verbs (e.g. *see, hear*), which do exist as transitive verbs in Irish. However, these can be shown to pattern with achievement verbs, which are present in the Irish lexicon, and thus do not fall under the generalisation made in this paper (see Noonan 1993b).

I choose this option for several reasons. The first is that Irish constitutes a subset of English, since (i) the class of possible verbs in Irish is more restricted (no statives), and (ii) the morphological identity of passive and perfective participles in English (and the attested unaccusativity of perfectives in Irish and Hindi) suggests that there exists only one participle in English, and that this is always unaccusative.[3,4] The second reason is more intuitive and concerns the fact that, while English contains numerous instances of highly conflated verbs such as *shelve* (meaning 'put on a shelf'), Irish typically expresses semantic relations in a very transparent way syntactically; one might say it wears its lexical structure on its sleeve. The third and final reason is to see where this hypothesis takes us, in particular whether it leads us to a deeper understanding of the phenomena of accusativity and ergativity. The remainder of the paper explores the hypothesis from this perspective, first by establishing the structural conditions on accusativity (section 2), and then by answering two questions: (i) why (7)? and (ii) why do languages like English exhibit the accusative stative and perfective structures that they do? (sections 4-5).

2.0. Syntactic projection and accusativity.

Until now, the claim that stative and perfective verbs do not assign accusative Case has been entirely stipulative. Ideally, we want to derive this claim from some common property of stative and perfective verbs. Before doing so, however, we need to explain the conditions on accusativity, since without such an explanation, we cannot even begin to search for a reason why stative and perfective verbs would be unaccusative. So let us address this issue presently.

2.1. Burzio's Generalisation.

There exists a well-known correlation between accusativity and verb types, commonly referrred to as Burzio's generalization (hereafter BG). This is stated in (8) (Burzio 1986, 185).

(8) V assigns accusative Case iff it assigns an external theta role

Note that (8) is not an explanation, but only an observation of a general correlation between two properties. Moreover, the correlation is an odd one, as it combines two properties that belong to different modules of the grammar — Case theory and Theta theory — the connection between which is somewhat obscure. In fact, there is evidence that the phenomena of accusative Case assignment and argument structure are often disjoint: in ECM constructions, a matrix verb can assign accusative Case to an NP that is the subject of the embedded clause, i.e., an NP that is not its internal argument. It is, however, quite clear that structural accusative Case is constrained by geometric notions such as c-command and government. Thus, assuming that BG is correct, we would like the presence of an external

---

[3] The issue of aspectual differences between passives and perfectives will not be addressed here. It has frequently been argued that Irish constructions like (5b) are aspectually always perfective.

[4] See Fabb (1984) and Cowper (1989), who also identify perfective participles with passive ones, based on their morphological identity.

argument to have a geometric reflex from which accusativity falls out directly. In what follows, I will present and develop an idea outlined in Sportiche (1990), which pursues precisely this line of reasoning.

2.2. Deriving BG.

Under a Larsonian phrase structure approach, VPs may have considerably different syntactic realisations depending on the number of arguments a verb has. This follows from the 'single argument hypothesis' (Larson 1988), according to which a verb with more than two arguments projects syntactically as two VP layers. Let us make the stronger claim that a verb projects every NP argument with its own VP shell. This is captured by the following condition:

(9) **Condition on Argument Projection (CAP)**
NPs are always projected into a specifier position of the verb by which they are selected.

(9) states that if a verb assigns more than one NP argument (i.e., an internal and an external argument) it must project two VP layers in order for each NP to be projected into a specifier position. The tree structures below illustrate the geometric reflex of the presence of an external argument. The observation that only those verbs that project like (10a) assign accusative Case suggests that the upper VP layer is in some way responsible for accusativity.[5]

(10) a. transitive: b. unaccusative:

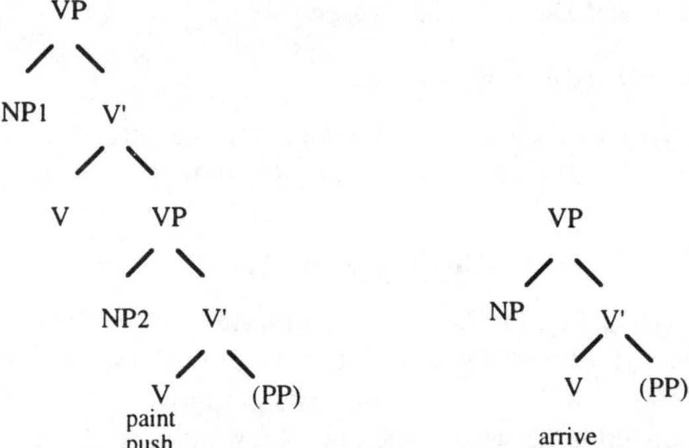

This approach to VP structure can be related to Case theory through the assimilation of the mechanism of accusative Case licencing to that of nominative Case checking, taking it to be a checking device under a spec/head configuration in a functional category (Chomsky 1990; Johnson 1991; Mahajan 1990; Sportiche 1990; Travis 1991). Crucially, I will assume with Sportiche (1990) and Travis (1991) that the

[5] As it turns out, (9) is not strong enough: we need to assume that unergative verbs like *laugh,* (which like unaccusatives assign only one NP argument) project a double layer VP, since it can be shown that these verbs can license an accusative NP (cf. *Mary laughed herself silly).* We therefore need to say that whenever a verb assigns an external argument, a double layer VP is projected (see Sportiche 1990). This will follow independently from the analysis in section 3.

Case-checking category for accusative Case is within the double layer VP. We can now formulate the following condition on accusativity:

(11) **Condition on Accusativity:**
Accusative Case occurs whenever a functional Case checking category is governed by a verb at D-structure.[6]

(11) essentially states that all instances of accusative Case result from an ECM-type configuration. The tree below illustrates the checking mechanism of accusative Case.[7]

(12)

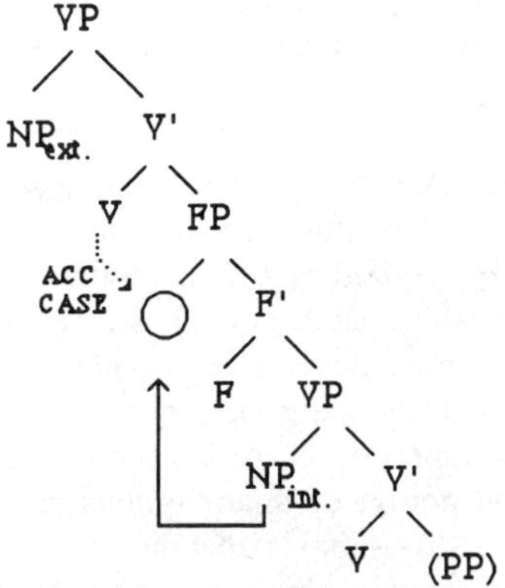

Under this approach, the claim made above that stative and perfective verbs are unaccusative implies that these types of verbs do not project a double-layered VP into the syntax. In the following sections, I will pursue this conjecture, beginning with a discussion of stative predicates.

---

[6] The clause 'at D-structure' is added for the following reason: in languages with verb-movement to INFL (like V2 languages or French; see Emonds (1978), Pollock (1989) amongst others), at S-structure, the verb governs the internal NP argument in a projection like (10b). Sportiche (1990) avoids this problem by assuming that V-to-I movement is an adjunction operation, so that INFL, rather than V, governs the position in unaccusatives. Although this constitutes an alternative solution, it conflicts with an analysis like that of Rizzi and Roberts (1989), who argue that V-to-I is a substitution process and I-to-C movement an adjunction process. Thus, for me, the availability of accusative Case is determined at D-structure.

[7] The dotted line does not imply that the verb 'assigns' accusative Case to Spec/FP, but rather that it 'determines' it: accusative Case is no longer assumed to be 'assigned' by verbs, but to be 'checked' by the head of the functional category, and 'determined' by the structural position of the verb vis-à-vis Spec/FP at D-structure. For the present purposes, I remain agnostic as to the precise identity of FP. See Noonan (1992), Johnson (1990), Travis (1991) for various proposals. Note that ECM verbs, such as *believe*, govern Spec/IP — a Case-checking functional category — at D-structure and thus provide accusative Case. However, see Sportiche (1990) for evidence from binding that embedded subjects in ECM constructions undergo raising to object position. I leave this issue open here.

3.0. Syntactic projection of statives.

A common assumption about the syntactic projection of arguments is that stative psych verbs project their EXPERIENCER argument in a hierarchical fashion as the external argument, so that verbs like *love* project in the same manner as verbs like *hit,* namely as a double layer VP (differing only in that the specifier of the upper VP layer bears the role EXPERIENCER rather than AGENT).[8] In the spirit of the theory of accusativity sketched above and hypothesis (7) that universally transitive stative verbs do not exist per se, I will challenge this view and argue that experiencers are not mapped onto the position of external argument — in other words, that stative predicates **do not** project a double layer VP into the syntax. I shall motivate this claim by developing an idea from Hale and Keyser (1990).

3.1. Hale and Keyser (1990).

Hale and Keyser (henceforth H&K) (1990) pose the following questions about theta theory: (i) why are there so few theta roles? and (ii) can we derive the Uniformity of Theta Assignment Hypothesis (henceforth UTAH), according to which 'identical thematic relationships between items are represented by identical structural relationships between those items at the level of D-structure' (Baker 1988a, 46)? This is their idea in a nutshell: the answer to (i) is related to the limited inventory of lexical categories (namely V, N, A, P), and the answer to (ii) is that UTAH can be derived from the notion of unambiguous projection in Lexical Relational Structure (henceforth LRS) — that is, that theta roles are unambiguously derived from the way in which arguments are projected in relation to each other onto lexical syntactic trees. Crucial for us here is their claim that the double VP template as in (13) represents the canonical LRS expression of a causal relation: the upper verb is viewed as an empty 'abstract causative verb' whose specifier is interpreted as the agent/causer of the event, whereas the lower VP corresponds to the notion of change of state, and its specifier to the AFFECTED PATIENT or THEME:

(13)

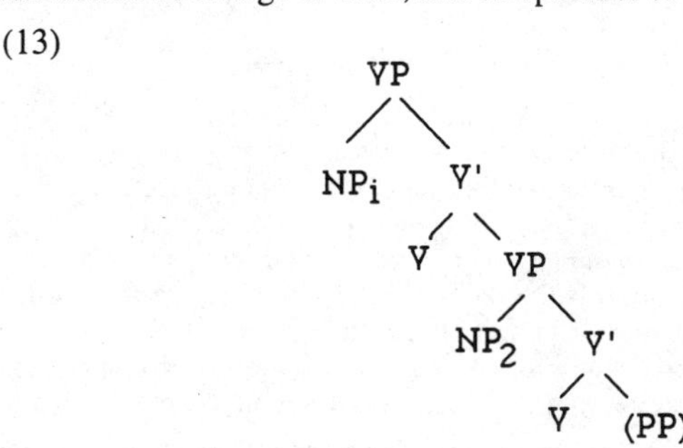

[8] For arguments for and against the view that experiencer NPs are projected as external arguments, see e.g. Grimshaw (1990) and Carrier-Duncan (1985), and e.g. Belletti and Rizzi (1988), Baker (1988b), and Campbell and Martin (1989), respectively. Note that any strict interpretation of UTAH (Baker 1988a) would deny syntactic mapping of arguments according to a theta hierarchy.

I shall adopt this idea, but assume (13) to be the syntactic representation of a given causation event, rather than just a LRS.[9] This view is also compatible with the kind of event semantics developed in Pustejovsky (1988). He argues that the event structure of verbs is constructed from subevents: for example 'accomplishment verbs' in the sense of Vendler (1967) are composed of two subevents, a 'process' and a '(resulting) state'.[10] This goes nicely with the view that a double layer VP corresponds to a causation event: we might say that the upper layer corresponds to the subevent 'process' and the lower one — in fact the functional category within the two VP layers — to the notion 'resulting state'.[11]

3.2. Syntactic projection of statives.

According to this view of double layer VP projections, the syntax of statives cannot be as in (13), since they do not denote causation events. This derives my earlier claim that experiencer arguments are not mapped onto the external argument position, as Grimshaw (1990) and others have claimed. We can now account for the observation that Irish has no stative transitive verbs: (13) is not a syntactic template compatible with statives; however, it is the necessary configuration for the availability of accusative Case. Thus, Irish (i.e., the null case) is accounted for; here, stative predicates are projected as predicate nominal constructions, where the experiencer NP is marked by preposition *ag:*

(14) á eagla roimh an mbúca ag Ailill.
is fear before the Puca at Ailill
'Ailill fears the Puca.'

3.3. HAVE

Let us now look at English, which, unlike Irish, exhibits a broad set of stative transitive verbs, like *love, know, respect, hate, envy,* and *fear*. Having demonstrated that statives do not project as (transitive) verbs, we must now show that English possesses some special mechanism to permit statives to surface as transitive verbs, despite the universal projection procedures outlined in the preceding section. What might this mechanism be? Note that most of the stative verbs listed above can be paraphrased by a possessive construction involving the main verb *have*:

(15) a. Kathleen **has** knowledge of many little things.
b. Hannah **has** little respect for her sisters.
c. John **has** too much love for himself.
d. Ben **has** enough hate to wipe out a small village.

---

[9] For further details, see H&K (1990). Since I assume (13) to be a syntactic representation, I take the relevant functional Case-checking projection to be within the two VP layers (see section 2).

[10] See also Grimshaw (1990).

[11] However, this notion has to be refined in order to accommodate eventive unaccusative verbs such as *arrive*.

Let us assume that these constructions reflect the basic representation of stative predicates, and that along with an overt verb *have,* there can also be an abstract (i.e., empty) HAVE. The verbal counterparts of the periphrastic constructions in (15) derive from an incorporation process: abstract HAVE incorporates a nominal element. Thus, a verb like *fear* is abstractly represented as HAVE *fear.* The difference between English and Irish can now be explained as follows: the ability of statives to surface as accusative verbs in English derives from a lexical property, namely the existence of the verb HAVE in the lexicon of English but not Irish. Crucially, HAVE is more than just a lexical item that one language has and another lacks. I suggest we rather think of it as a 'lexical function', that permits a structural relationship to be established between an NP and a predicate clause, like a predicate NP, in such a way that it results in accusativity.[12] I suggest that HAVE projects an NP argument into its specifier and takes a PredP as its sister. As such, it satisfies the structural condition on accusativity (11): a verb governing the specifier of a Case checking category at D-structure. The lexical entry of HAVE is as follows: [13]

(16) HAVE: V, [NP, PredP]

Crucial for my analysis is that HAVE is not a raising verb (the reason for which will become clear in section 4).[14] The tree diagram below illustrates the process: a nomi-nal element like *fear* incorporates into the verb HAVE, and the internal argument of the predicate NP raises to Spec/PredP and is checked for accusative Case in that position.

---

[12] In fact, my theory predicts that statives are unable to surface not only as transitive verbs, but as verbs period. Not surprisingly, we also do not find intransitive stative verbs in Irish.

[13] Note, however, that we need to ensure that in sentences like (i)a the subject of HAVE is coreferential with the person who loves, and thus to distinguish these sentences from those like (i)c:

(i) a. John has a deep love for his work.

b. John loves his work.

c. John has Mary's love.

This might be captured by means of a notion of predicate coindexation (to be discussed in section 4 below). See Noonan (1993b)

[14] As such it differs from Tremblay (1990), who claims that *have* is a Case-assigning copula. This is incompatible with the present account, which seeks to derive the ability of *have* to assign Case from the syntactic geometry that it determines. See Campbell (1989, 48ff.) for arguments against a raising analysis of *have.*

(17)

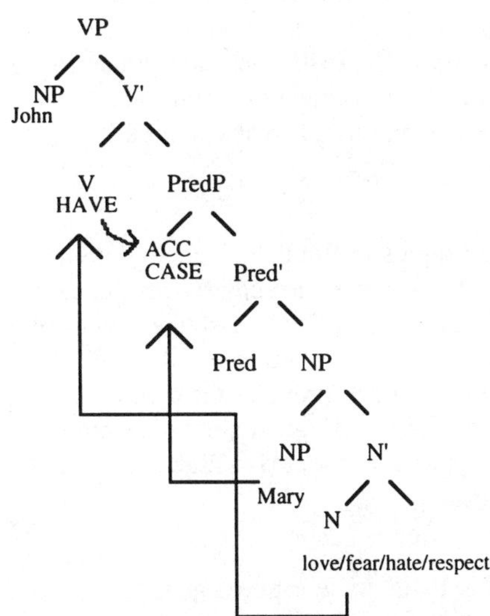

4.0. Syntactic projection of perfective verbs.

In section 1, I proposed that perfectives are unaccusative. This proposal was motivated by (i) the identical morphology of the unaccusative passive and the perfective participle in English and other languages, and (ii) the cross-linguistic observation that perfective verbs do not license an accusative object NP, triggering an ergative pattern. As with statives, we can derive this conjecture by maintaining that perfectives do not project a double layer VP into the syntax, thus failing to provide the necessary structural configuration that outputs accusative Case. But what prevents the upper layer containing the external argument from being projected in perfectives? The explanation for the failure of statives to project two VP layers, namely that only verbs denoting causation events project in that way, does not carry over to perfective and passive participles. I propose a different motivation in this case: this is that the participle morphology heads a projection which is placed within the double layer VP,[15] and that the verb, upon incorporating into this projection, loses its categorial status as a verb and becomes in some way adjectival.[16] As a result, the derived ambiguous categorial status of the verb participle prevents it from assuming the empty V-position of the upper VP, as this position requires a 'pure' verb to fill it. By not moving into the upper V-slot, the lexical verb fails to license the upper VP layer; and as this layer cannot remain empty, a representation in which a participle projects an upper layer VP crashes, while one in which only the lower

[15] This is assumed in Sportiche (1990), based on participle agreement in French. See also Travis (1991b), who assumes that the functional category within the double layer VP is Aspect (which is not unrelated to what is being suggested here).

[16] It has been suggested that the participle loses its categorial feature [+V]. This carries over to the perfective participle in my approach.

level is projected survives. However, under the latter option, we lack the proper structural configuration for accusative Case — hence the unaccusativity of passive and perfective participles. The Irish case is accounted for: the object NP, in order to receive Case, must move to subject position, where it is licensed by nominative Case; while the external argument is realised in a PP.

4.1.0. Auxiliary *have*.

What about participles in English, French and German? In these languages, even though passive participles are clearly unaccusative, perfective participles appear to maintain their accusativity. I suggest that this is not so, and that the availability of Case is due to properties of auxiliary *have*. In section 3, we established that main verb *have* provides the necessary configuration for accusative Case. Evidence from Hiberno-English perfective constructions, as given in (18), suggests that auxiliary *have* also seems to function as an ECM verb:

(18) a. I have the books read.
b. She has her dinner eaten.

This is precisely what I will argue happens generally: auxiliary *have* provides accusative Case in perfectives.[17] Furthermore, I maintain that it is not coincidental that auxiliary *have* and main verb *have* both assign Case: they are both a part of the same lexical function, the HAVE-function. In this way, we can relate the accusativity of statives and perfectives in English. However, the procedure in perfectives is slightly different from statives, in a way to be made explicit in the following section. The gist of my proposal is that auxiliary *have* rescues the upper layer VP in a perfective construction from crashing by functioning as a 'filler' of the higher verb slot. This process is illustrated in (19):

---

[17] Auxiliary *have* and accusative Case in perfectives have previously been related (see Fabb 1984, Cowper 1989, Roberts 1987, among others). Fabb and Roberts assume that the morpheme-*en* needs to receive Case. In passives, it receives Case from the verb, forcing the object to raise to subject position; in perfectives, however, -*en* receives Case from *have;* as a result the verb is free to assign its Case to the direct object. This analysis is incompatible with my own, which maintains that participle verbs never license accusative Case. See also Baker, Johnson and Roberts (1990). Incidentally, my proposal is also not compatible with their and Jaeggli's (1986) view that -*en* receives the external theta role. Under my view, -*en* represents a morpheme heading its own projection; as a head it is a category that receives neither a theta role nor a structural Case. Thus the observation from German that impersonal passives are possible only with verbs that assign an external theta role needs to be derived differently. I argue elsewhere (Noonan 1993a) that this observation can be derived from properties of the passive modal *werden,* which this language uses to form verbal passives.

(19)

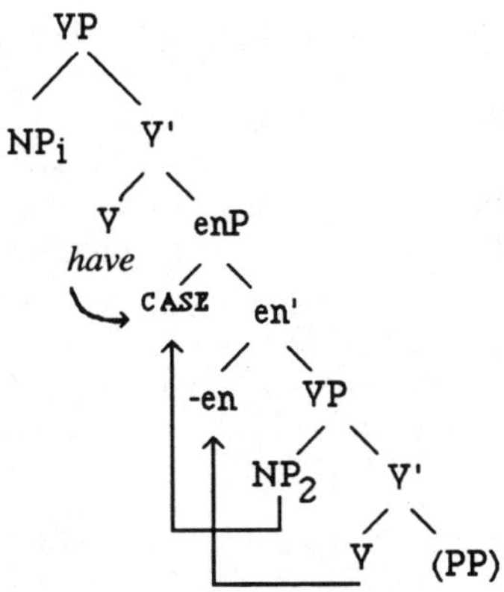

Going back to Irish perfectives, this possibility is not available, since the HAVE-function is missing from its lexicon: Irish not only lacks main verb *have* (see section 3) but also auxiliary *have*. The only auxiliary that it contains is *bí,* which corresponds to English *be* in its unaccusativity.[18] The crucial question now is: how precisely is auxiliary *have* to be characterized, and how is it to be distinguished from *be?* What we need is for *have,* but not *be,* to result in a syntactic projection like that shown in (19). The answer lies in different lexical entries: while *have* selects its own NP argument, *be* selects only a small clause or PredP. Specifically, I propose that auxiliary *have* has the same entry as main verb *have* (see (16)), except for being obligatorily coindexed with the PredP it selects (a point to which I will return):

(20) a. *have:* aux-v, [NP_i $PredP_i$]
b. *be:* aux-v, [PredP]

An important stipulation in the hypothesis to be outlined shortly is the following:

(21) **Condition on Argument Projection** (extended version)
a. Single arguments and NPs must be projected into the specifier of the head that selects them.
b. NPs are always projected into a specifier position of the verb by which they are selected.

(21)a states that if a verb has only one argument, it maps it into its specifier position. (21)b (repeating the result of the original version of CAP in (9)), states that

[18] I should mention here that there are languages without an auxiliary corresponding to *have*, which nevertheless seem to exhibit accusative perfective and stative structures. One such language is Arabic. However, this language, unlike Irish, has an aspectual system; aspect might thus accomplish the same function as *have* in English (thanks to Joseph Aoun for pointing this possi-bility out to me). Old Irish is another language without a lexical item like *have*, but with transi-tive stative verbs. Crucially, however, these verbs are deponent, bearing inflection for middle rather than active voice, unlike ordinary transitive verbs. See Noonan (in preparation) for an analysis.

if it has two — one an NP and the other a PP or PredP — it maps the NP into its specifier and the remaining one into its sister complement position; and if it has more than one NP it must project two VP layers in order for each NP to be projected into a specifier position. (21)a is equivalent to saying that an argument-taking head cannot have an empty specifier. What follows from the lexical specification (20)a in conjunction with the CAP is that the selection by *have* of an NP argument permits the PredP to appear as a sister complement, thus providing the relevant configuration for accusativity (i.e., a verbal head governing the specifier of a Case-checking projection at D-structure). Auxiliary *be*, on the other hand, is unaccusative, since it selects only a PredP, and is forced (by CAP) to project it into its specifier position, thus being unable to provide the required structural configuration for accusative Case.[19]

4.1.1. Predicate coindexation.

I will refer to the process of coindexing the NP argument of auxiliary *have* with the PredP in the lexical entry (20) as PREDICATE COINDEXATION. What I want to express by this notion is that *have* + verb form one complex predicate: *have* functions as an 'overlay' on the double layer VP, which, crucially, is projected by the verb's own argument specification. The verb itself, however, cannot license the upper layer on its own (as it is unable to license the higher VP carrying participle morphology). *Have* rescues the upper VP from crashing by functioning as a place filler; *have* is thus an auxiliary verb in the true sense: it 'helps' the verb maintain its two VP layers.[20] However, the reason why it can function as such (and the way in which it is different from auxiliary *be,* which cannot accomplish the same) is its lexical entry as main verb *have.* The difference between main verb and auxiliary *have,* expressed through the notion of predicate coindexation, lies in the fact that it cannot add an argument in the same way that main verb *have* can. In the next section, I will discuss the ramifications of this proposal for languages like English, which uses *have* as an auxiliary in perfectives with unaccusative verbs, i.e., verbs that do not project two VP layers.

4.1.2. *Have* with unaccusatives.

Note that with *have* acting as an accusative auxiliary, we run the danger of predicting the availability of accusative Case in a perfective construction with an

---

[19] Perhaps existential *be* permits the projection of an existential expletive *there* into its specifier, thus satisfying the structural configuration for Case. This, then, would be the source of constructions like *there were three men killed* or *there is a unicorn in the garden.* See Travis (1991a), who suggests an analysis — based on insights from Ritter (1988) — along these lines; and Lasnik (1988) for evidence that *be* assigns Case to the NP (as opposed to the NP receiving Case by being in a chain with the expletive *there*). This might also be the source of the French existential *il y a* construction, as well as the Southern German *es hat,* where auxiliaries *avoir* and *haben* ('have') take an expletive in their specifier.

[20] My proposal resembles those of Campbell (1989) and Cowper (1989) in saying that *have* takes its own argument position in terms of c-selection but that theta marking is accomplished through complex predicate formation. It also has some resemblance to the concept of 'argument transfer' within the theory of light verbs as developed by Grimshaw and Mester (1988).

unaccusative verb — that is, of predicting a contrast in (22), where (a) should be ungrammatical and (b) should be, if not grammatical, at least considerably better.

(22) a. * Jack often arrives himself in tricky situations.
     b. * Jack has arrived himself in a tricky situation

If *have* takes its own NP argument (see (20)), then the subject *Jack* in (22)b would be the argument of *have*, and *himself* would be the argument of *arrive*, and in a structural position to receive accusative Case. Clearly, this prediction is wrong: (22) (a) and (b) are equally ill-formed.[21] The properties atttributed to auxiliary *have* in the preceding section exclude this prediction: the notion of predicate coindexation in its lexical entry implies that its ability to take its own NP argument is parasitic upon the verb's projecting an NP.[22] The lexical entry for the *have* that occurs with unaccusatives in English (which I refer to as *have2)* is thus as follows:

(23) *have2:* aux-v, [PredP]

Note that structurally, *have2* is just like auxiliary *be* (see (20)b). As a result, the PredP it takes is projected into specifier position. This is desirable, since languages like Italian and German seem to lack *have2* altogether and use the auxiliary corresponding to *be* in its place (thus, *have2 = be).* In these languages, auxiliary *have* can only have a lexical entry as in (20)a — that is, it always needs to be licensed by a verb projecting an upper layer. English has generalised *have* to serve as the auxiliary whenever a perfective occurs.

4.1.3. Word order.

Amongst the things yet to be addressed is the question of word order in Standard English (henceforth SE): even though the hypothesis that perfective auxiliary *have* acts as an ECM verb explains the Hiberno-English (henceforth HE) data in (18), SE word order presents a problem, since here the object does not seem to raise to receive Case from *have.* If the object does raise, then the interpretation cannot be that of a perfective as in HE, but must be that of a causative, where the specifier of *have* is interpreted as distinct from the agent of the participle verb.

(24) I have my door painted. ('I' cannot be painter)

This can be worked out by assuming (i) that the object NP in SE perfectives undergoes movement to its Case position at LF (so that the word order of SE at LF is identical to HE perfectives), or (ii) that the participle verb adjoins to the V *have,*

---

[21] It is important to compare the constructions in (24) with unergative verbs, which can appear in precisely the constructions given in (22), if these are licensed by a PP or extent modifier:

(i) He laughed himself silly.

(ii) She can drink him under the table.

Constructions like (i) and (ii) are possible precicely because the verb *laugh,* assigning an external theta role, projects an upper VP layer, and thus has the ability to assign accusative Case (see n. 5).

[22] This result might relate to data presented in Miyagawa (1989), who shows that the Japanese light verb *suru* cannot appear with an ergative nominal as its object NP.

without actually incorporating into it.[23,24] I will choose the latter option and maintain that, in SE, the participle must adjoin to auxiliary *have* as a result of predicate coindexation. If the participle does not adjoin and we find the word order of (24), *have* in SE must be interpreted as a main verb, specifically as causative main verb.[25] In HE, since adjunction of the participle to auxiliary *have* is not obligatorily, (24) is ambiguous beween a causative and an auxiliary reading.

5.0. Possessives.

Since Irish lacks the HAVE-function in its lexicon, we expect possessive constructions in this language not to surface as transitive possessive verbs. This is confirmed by the data: the theme raises to receive nominative Case and the possessor appears with the preposition *ag* — the same preposition that appears with the experiencer NP in statives and with the 'demoted agent' in perfectives. In English, these same arguments appear as the subject of *have*. This is illustrated in the two paradigms below:

(25)	a. Irish:	poss:	Tá carr ag Seán	**tá** NP		**ag** NP[26]
		stative:	Tá eagla ag Seán	**tá** NP		**ag** NP
		perf:	Tá an doras dunte ag S	**tá** NP Vpart		**ag** NP
	b. <u>English</u>:	poss:	Seán has a car	NP ***have***		NP
		stative:	Seán has fear of lions	NP ***have***		NP
		perf:	Seán has closed the door	NP ***have***	V_{part}	NP

---

[23] A third way would be by permitting *have* to 'transmit' its Case-assigning ability to the participle (see Cowper (1989) amongst others for this suggestion). I do not consider this possibility here, since the present proposal departs from the view of 'Case marking ability' as a feature specification on verbs.

[24] Under this second hypothesis we have to allow for head movement to excorporate the head *have* in the case of subj.-AUX inversion. This hypothesis might find supporting evidence from Spanish, where participles invert together with the auxiliary in inversion constructions (see Torrego 1984).

[25] However, there are other interesting constructions, where the NP in the specifier of *have* is obligatorily coindexed with a pronoun in a PP of its complement clause:

(i) a. $John_k$ had his computer die on him_k.

b. $Bill_k$ had his partner cheat on him_k.

c. $John_k$ has money on him_k.

In this case, the subject of *have* is usually interpreted as an experiencer. See Ritter and Rosen (1990), and Noonan (in preparation) for discussion.

[26] However, the construction differs from the *etre à* construction in French in that the latter describes a relation of ownership. The difference manifests itself in the predicative character of the NP occurring with *have* and in the occurrence of a definiteness effect (see Campbell (1989) on predicate NPs and definiteness):

(i) *? I have the house.

(ii) ? J'ai cette maison.

(iii) Tá an teach agam.

We might think of the *ag* on the subject in Irish as an ergative marker. In this sense, Irish is a split ergative language, where the split occurs in statives and perfectives.

5.1. Conclusion.

In this paper, I have argued that, as the null hypothesis, stative and perfective predicates do not surface as accusative verbs, deriving this from (i) a view of accusativity as a configurational rather than lexical property, and (ii) a theory of syntactic argument projection. Crucial to my argument are the claims (i) that verbs project their event semantic structure into the syntax, and (ii) that specifiers of lexical heads cannot remain empty. The unaccusativity of statives and perfectives was shown to derive from their inability to project a double layer VP into the syntax. Moreover, it was shown that HAVE in English (as well as German, French, and other languages) can 'simulate' a double layer VP[27] with the kinds of predicate types under discussion, thus providing the syntactic geometry necessary for accusativity. I view the HAVE-function as one possible tool which permits statives and perfectives to surface as transitive structures. However, my proposal does not exclude other means that languages might exploit to arrive at the same result.[28]

References

Baker, M. 1988a. Incorporation: Towards a Theory of Grammatical Function Changing. University of Chicago Press.

Baker, M. 1988b. On the Theta Roles of Psych Verbs. Ms., McGill University.

Baker, M., K. Johnson and I. Roberts. 1990. Passive Arguments Raised. *Linguistic Inquiry* 20: 219-252.

Belletti, A. and L. Rizzi. 1988. Psych-Verbs and θ-Theory. *Natural Language and Linguistic Theory* 6: 291-352.

Burzio, L. 1986. *Italian Syntax: a Government and Binding Approach.* Dordrecht: Reidel.

Campbell, R. 1989. The Grammatical Structure of Verbal Predicates. Ph.D. diss., UCLA.

Campbell, R. and J. Martin. 1989. Sensation Predicates and the Syntax of Stativity. In E. J. Fee and K. Hunt (eds), *Proceedings of WCCFL 8.* Stanford Linguistics Association.

Carrier-Duncan, J. 1985. Linking of Thematic Roles in Derivational Word Formation. *Linguistic Inquiry* 16: 1-34.

Chomsky, N. 1979. Principles and Parameters in Syntactic Theory. In N. Hornstein and D. Lightfoot (eds), *Explanation in Linguistics.* London: Longman.

Chomsky, N. 1981. *Lectures on Government and Binding*. Dordrecht: Foris.

---

[27] However, I argue in Noonan (1993b) that the double layer VP created by *have* does not behave exactly like that associated with a causation event, but that its upper layer has the properties of the lower layer in a 'causation VP'. In other words, the specifier of HAVE has properties analogous to an 'inner subject' rather than an outer one. This behaviour is shared by achievement verbs, which I also discuss there.

[28] See fn. 18.

Chomsky, N. 1990. Class lectures, MIT.

Cowper, E. 1989. Perfective [-en] is Passive [-en]. In E. J. Fee and K. Hunt (eds), *Proceedings of WCCFL 8*. Stanford Linguistics Association.

Fabb, N. 1984. *Syntactic Affixation.* Ph.D. diss., MIT.

Emonds, J. 1978. The Verbal Complex V-V' in French. *Linguistic Inquiry* 9.

Grimshaw, J. 1990. *Argument Structure*. MIT Press; Boston.

Grimshaw, J and A. Mester. 1988. Light Verbs and θ-Marking. *Linguistic Inquiry* 19: 205-232.

Hale, K. and J. Keyser. 1990. Categories and Projections. Ms., MIT.

Jaeggli, O. 1986. Passive. *Linguistic Inquiry* 17: 587-622.

Johnson, K. 1991. Positions of Objects. *Natural Language and Linguistic Theory* 9: 577-636.

Larson, R. 1988. On the Double Object Construction. *Linguistic Inquiry* 19: 335-393.

Lasnik, H. 1991. Case and Expletives: Notes Towards a Parametric Account. In R. Freidin (ed.), *Comparative Syntax*: Princeton Workshop II.

Mahajan, A. 1990. *The A/A-Bar distinction and movement theory.* Ph.D. diss., MIT.

Miyagawa, S. 1989. Light Verbs and the Ergative Hypothesis. *Linguistic Inquiry* 20: 659-668.

Noonan, M. 1992. *Case and Syntactic Geometry.* Ph.D. diss., McGill University.

Noonan, M. 1993a. Impersonal Passives in German: A Reply to Baker, Johnson, and Roberts. Ms., University College Dublin.

Noonan, M. 1993b. Properties of subjects of stative predicates. Ms. University College Dublin

Pollock, J.-Y. 1989. Verb Movement, Universal Grammar, and the Structure of IP. *Linguistic Inquiry* 20: 365-424.

Pustejovsky, J. 1988. Event Semantic Structure. Ms., Brandeis University.

Ritter, E. 1988. Existentials, Posessives, and Locatives in Hebrew. Ms., Université du Québec à Montréal.

Ritter, E and S. Rosen. 1990. Causative have. NELS XXI, Université du Québec à Montréal.

Roberts, I. 1987. The Representation of Implicit and Dethematized Subjects. Foris: Dordrecht.

Sportiche, D. 1990. Movement, Agreement and Case. Ms., UCLA.

Torrego, E. 1984. On Inversion in Spanish and Some of Its Effects. *Linguistic Inquiry* 15:103-129.

Travis, L. 1991a. Notes on Case and Expletives: a Discussion of Lasnik's Paper. In R. Freidin (ed). *Comparative Syntax:* Princeton Workshop II.

Travis, L. 1991b. Derived Objects, Inner Aspect and the Structure of VP. NELS XXII.

Tremblay, M. 1990. Possession and Datives: Binary Branching from the Lexicon to Syntax. Ph.D. diss., McGill University.

Vendler, Z. 1967. *Linguistics in Philosophy.* Ithaca: Cornell University Press.

Double-Object Small Clauses and Reanalysis in Icelandic Passives

KJARTAN OTTÓSSON
University of Maryland at College Park

In this paper,[1] I argue for a GB analysis of double object constructions in Icelandic in terms of SMALL CLAUSES, a variation of argument Small Clauses as in *I consider [John a liar].* Such a generalised Small Clause approach can account for the commonly discussed facts of double objects in English as well as in Icelandic, and because it generalises independently needed devices, it should be preferred to the powerful device of empty verbal heads proposed by Larson (1988), for reasons of parsimony. Jackendoff's (1990) ternary branching analysis is at a disadvantage because it has to stipulate left-to-right directionality for binding and has no account for the fact that the direct object is more closely linked to the verb than the indirect object. Crucially, the Small Clause approach provides a natural way, a process of reanalysis, to account for the facts of passivisation of double objects in Icelandic, as well as for the phenomenon of 'Inversion', which moves the direct object to the left of the indirect object. These facts are problematic for the empty verb analyses, on the other hand.

1. Adapting Larson's proposal to Icelandic, with rare prepositional variants

Before proceeding, it must be pointed out that the 'Larsonian' analyses that have been proposed for Icelandic double objects differ from Larson's (1988) original proposal in that they do not assume a prepositional source for 'dative-shifted' variants. A 'Dative Shift' alternation cannot be posited for Icelandic.

[1] I am indebted to Norbert Hornstein for valuable comments and discussion of this topic, and to Jóhannes G. Jónsson for comments. I would also like to thank the audience at WCCFL and at University of Maryland, where some of this material was presented. A somewhat fuller discussion of many of the issues can be found in Ottósson (1991).

Prepositional variants like *give the book to Mary* are rare in that language and tend to have an idiosyncratic meaning (cf. Ottósson 1991, 78), as illustrated in (1)-(2).

(1) *Jón gaf bókina til Maríu
John gave the-book to Mary

(2) Jón gaf bókasafn sitt til háskólans
John donated library SELF's to the-university

On the other hand, there are many case marking patterns for the 'dative-shifted' type. The common case combinations are listed in (3)-(5). The most common pattern by far is the dative-accusative pattern in (3), where the indirect object has lexical dative, and the direct object has structural accusative. The other case combinations all involve LEXICAL CASE on the direct object. In (4), we see structural accusative on the indirect object, and lexical dative or genitive on the direct object. In (5), we see lexical dative on the indirect object, lexical dative or genitive on the direct object.

(3) Indirect object: lexical case, direct object: structural case
DAT-ACC Jón gaf Maríu bókina
John gave Mary(D) the-book(A)

(4) Indirect object: structural case, direct object: lexical case
a ACC-DAT Þeir leyndu Ólaf sannleikanum
they concealed Olaf(A) the-truth(D)
b ACC-GEN Jón bað mig bónar
John asked me(A) a-favour(G)

(5) Indirect object: lexical case, direct object: lexical case
a DAT-DAT Jón skilaði Maríu bókinni
John returned Mary(D) the-book(D)
b DAT-GEN María óskaði Ólafi alls góðs
Mary wished Olaf(D) everything(G) good(G)

In view of the near-absence of prepositional variants to double objects in Icelandic, those who have adapted Larson's approach to that language have departed from him in not assuming a prepositional source for the 'dative-shifted' type. The most detailed adaptation is the insightful treatment by Falk (1990), who uses the structure shown in (6).

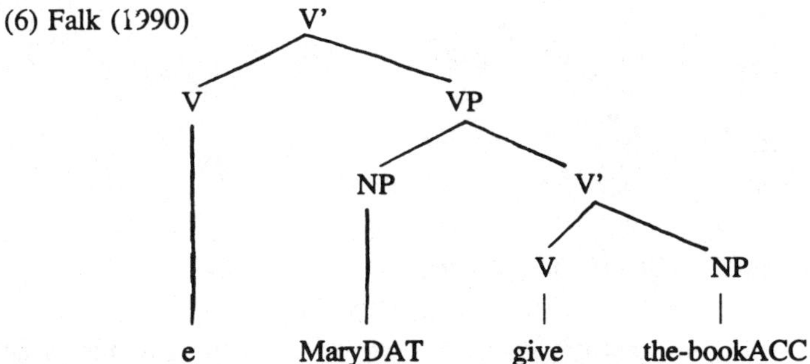

Holmberg's (1991) proposal is quite similar, but Sprouse (1989) assumes that it is the lower verbal head that is empty, so his proposal is closer to some Small Clause analyses. In (6), the surface order indirect object - direct object is base-generated in a verb phrase headed by the ditransitive verb, which obligatorily raises to the position of an empty verb which subcategorises for the lower VP.

In what follows, I will first discuss briefly the basic ideas behind generalising the Small Clause phrase structure to double objects (sections 2 and 3), and then I will turn to the facts specific to Icelandic.

2. The assumed structure for double objects and typical Small Clauses

The phrase structure I am assuming for double objects is the one shown in (7). It has obvious similarities to Stowell's (1981) analysis of Small Clauses and to Kayne's (1984) analysis of (some) double objects, cf. Holmberg (1986). The present approach to double objects is quite close to that of Hellan (1991), who analyses them as what he calls a GROUP, which is 'a phrase whose constituent parts have independent argument functions within the same argument complex'.[2] As indicated in (7), I assume that the phrase structure for typical argument Small Clauses is the same, but the crucial difference is that these latter involve a predication relation between NP_1 and NP_2 (cf. Hellan 1991, 84f).

[2] An analysis of Icelandic double objects in terms of Small Clauses is hinted at by Kayne (1984, 200, 202).

(7)

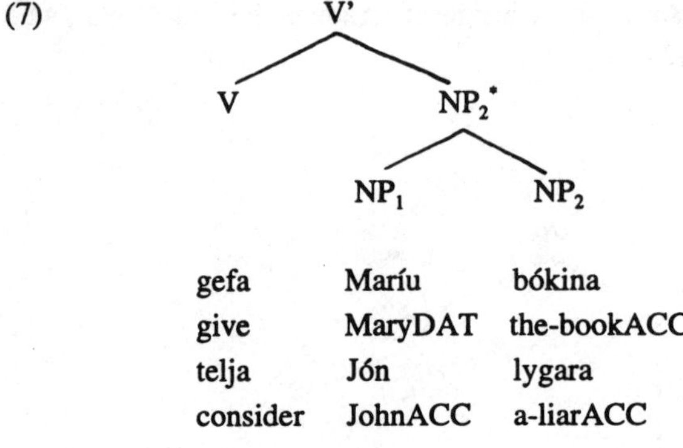

I use the label NP_2^* to identify the upper projection, which is of the same projection level as the lower one. The labelling makes it explicit that the direct object is the head of the Small Clause, whereas the indirect object is a base-generated adjunct, or a SPECIFIER in a loose sense. This configuration reflects the closer semantic links of the verb to the direct object than to the indirect object. The verb often forms an idiom with the direct object only, e.g., *give x the finger*. Assuming the structure in (7), this falls under the same generalisation as e.g., *pull x's leg*, that the verb forms an idiom with the head of its complement, leaving out the specifier.

This is a rather peculiar phrase structure, with the head of the Small Clause a maximal projection and that head projecting even further. However, it is hard to avoid this structure for typical argument Small Clauses. As is well known, specific verbs select the category of the head of its Small Clause, as illustrated in (8)-(9).

(8)a I consider John a liar
b *I consider John off my ship

(9)a *I expect John president
b I expect John off my ship

Consider can take an NP Small Clause head but not a PP Small Clause, while the converse is true for *expect*. This means that the highest projection of the Small

Clause, which is the only projection the verb can see, must be of the same category as the head.[3]

3. Binding asymmetries and how the Small Clause analysis handles them

We now turn to the well-known asymmetries discussed Barss and Lasnik (1986) between the indirect and the direct object. Two types of these asymmetries are illustrated for Icelandic in (10)-(11).

(10)a Ég sýndi Jóni sjálfan sig (í speglinum)
I showed JohnDAT himselfACC (in the-mirror)
b *Ég sýndi sjálfum sér Jón (í speglinum)
I showed himselfDAT JohnACC (in the-mirror)

(11)a Ég sýndi hverjum manni móður sína /hans
I showed each man$_i$DAT mother SELF's$_i$ /his$_i$
b *Ég sýndi móður sinni /hans hvern mann
I showed mother SELF's$_i$ /his$_i$ each man$_i$

In (10), we see that the indirect object can bind a direct object reflexive. By contrast, the direct object cannot bind the indirect one, as shown in (10b). In (11), we see that a quantified NP can bind the direct object, which can be a pronoun or a reflexive in Icelandic.

In the phrase structure that I am assuming for double objects, i.e., (7), the indirect object and the direct object mutually c-command each other, if we define C-COMMAND simply in terms of first branching node. Therefore, we have to refine the definition of c-command slightly to cover these structures. I suggest that this be done by incorporating the concept of EXCLUSION from *Barriers* (Chomsky 1986). We then get the modified definition of c-command in (12), with the addition underlined.

---

[3] This selection cannot be accounted for straightforwardly if Small Clauses of this type are seen as projections of Infl or Agr. If these SCs are analysed as Agreement Phrases, there is the additional problem that there is no grammatical phi-feature agreement between Noun Phrases, as seen e.g., in *I consider these secretaries an asset to the company*. The agreement there often is, like in *I consider these men liars*, must be semantic in nature. At the same time, the head of such NP Small Clauses is clearly a full NP (or DP), as it can take the whole range of determiners, specifiers etc. as standard argument NPs can.

(12) Modified definition of c-command

α c-commands β iff α excludes β and every branching node that dominates α dominates β

(α excludes β if no segment of α dominates β)

SEGMENT is defined as a specific projection level of a category (cf. Chomsky 1986, 7, 92), so that for example N' and NP do not qualify as segments of the same projection.

If we look at the structure in (7), we see that the direct object NP_2 does not exclude the indirect object NP_1 because there is a segment of the direct object, namely NP_2^*, which dominates the indirect object. Because the direct object does not exclude the indirect object, it does not c-command it. The indirect object NP_1 on the other hand, has no further projection which could dominate the direct object, so that the indirect object indeed excludes and c-commands the direct object. This achieves asymmetrical binding between the two objects. Insofar as sentences like (13) are acceptable, this refinement of c-command, like the proposed phrase structure for DOs, is independently required for typical Small Clauses.[4]

(13) As for now, I consider the men themselves

Thus we have so far not introduced anything new for direct objects that is not required for typical Small Clauses.[5]

4. Case assignment and argument licensing in Icelandic

We move now to the specifically Icelandic part of this paper. The Small Clause analysis helps explain the fact that Icelandic indirect objects can always passivise, but direct objects only when they have structural case. I argue that this is because indirect objects are not licensed in their base-generated Small Clause specifier position and so are forced to move. Before looking at these facts, it is necessary to look at the way in which lexical NPs are assigned case in Icelandic and how they are licensed.

---

[4] In most cases where the specifier of a typical Small Clause binds into the head, the bindee is embedded within the head, so mutual c-command of head and specifier would not cause problems. However, in examples like (13), possible in a make-believe play, the specifier must asymmetrically c-command the head.

[5] As Edward Keenan has reminded me, double objects cannot usually be moved as a constituent. The same is true for typical Small Clauses, as is well known. This may be due to the unusually loose attachment of the specifier/adjunct to the head, which would then have to be reflected in the top node (NP^*, PP^*, etc.).

The case assignment mechanisms must allow lexical as well as structural case to be assigned to either the indirect or direct object. Lexical or inherent case is linked to a specific argument place in the lexical entry of the verb, and must therefore be present already in the projection from the lexicon into the syntax at D-structure. Lexical case can only be assigned under ADJACENCY. This can be linear adjacency between the verb and the NP, for example for indirect objects. Adjacency may also involve sisterhood. In that case, a projection of the lexically case-marked NP (NP_2^* for the direct object) can be the sister of the verb in a strict sense. This is a straightforward assumption, given the mediating role of the NP_2^* projection in theta-marking of the direct object.

Structural case assignment, by contrast, can be long-distance in Icelandic. Thus the assignment of structural accusative to the specifier of a double-object Small Clause (in accusative-lexical case combinations) is straightforward; it parallels accusative assignment to a downstairs specifier in typical Small Clauses and is even more local than for the subjects of Exceptional Case Marking complements. Structural case assignment to the head of a double Object Small Clause (in dative-accusative combinations) is also straightforward; it too has parallels in ECM complements and typical Small Clauses.

Now, case assignment is not sufficient to license a lexical NP, as is especially clear in Icelandic. Here, a lexical NP is barred from many S-structure positions where it can get structural case long-distance. In formalising this insight, I will follow Sigurðsson (1991) who uses the term PROPER HEAD GOVERNMENT for the additional licensing mechanism. That appellation is not entirely happy, as Rizzi (1991) uses the same term for something different; Falk (1990) has a proposal about ARGUMENT LICENSING which is similar to that of Sigurðsson. Refining Sigurðsson's definition a little (Ottósson 1991, 85--87), I assume that the parametric specification of Proper Head Government for Icelandic is as given in (14).

(14) Proper Head Government (Argument Licensing) in Icelandic:

> α properly head governs β iff α locally governs β, α being an Agr-containing Infl or a lexical head capable of assigning structural case or (direct) theta-role to β

I will return to the restriction to direct theta-role shortly. According to (14), a proper head governor for a verbal object is a lexical head, that is, a verb or verb trace capable of assigning case or theta-role to that object. Local government is taken here to mean government by the closest eligible governor. Lexical heads properly head govern only under strict c-command, i.e., a head does not govern its specifier.

Let us see how this works for a few cases. The object of a garden variety transitive verb is licensed both by the structural case assignment potential of the verb and its theta-marking capability. Passivisation deprives the verb of its ability to assign structural case, but it retains its capability to assign a theta-role to its object, so that it can still be licensed. Thus the passive verb can license its object in its base-generated complement position, with nominative assigned long-distance from Infl, as illustrated in (15).

(15) Það var keypt einhver bók
there was bought some book(N)

There are further cases where licensing by theta-role assignment and licensing by case assignment are dissociated. Take Exceptional Case Marking constructions, like in (16).

(16) Ég tel [Jón vera lygara]
I believe John(A) [to] be a-liar(A)

(17) Ég tel [Jón lygara]
I consider John(A) a-liar(A)

Here, the downstairs subject, which is the specifier of IP, is licensed solely by structural accusative assignment from the verb, which does not assign theta-role to that subject. Specifiers of typical Small Clauses, as in (17) above, are licensed in the same way.

Turning now to the double objects, the indirect object specifier is licensed by structural case marking, as the observant reader will already have realised. The direct object head is licensed by theta-marking from the verb. Here, the restriction to direct theta-marking becomes important. I think it is natural to assume that a lexical head can only license one NP by theta-assignment because this accords with the strictly local nature of Proper Head Government. The one NP licensed by theta-assignment is then bound to be the directly theta-marked object.

If we passivise ECM constructions, the downstairs subject cannot stay in situ, even if indefinite. It must raise, as shown in (18a-b).

(18)a Jón er talinn vera lygari
John(N) is believed [to] be a-liar(N)
b *Það er talinn einhver vera lygari
there is believed someone(N) [to] be a-liar(N)

(19)a Ólafur er talinn lygari
Olaf(N) is considered a-liar(N)
b *Það er talinn einhver lygari
there is considered someone(N) a-liar(N)

This is because the passivised verb cannot assign structural case, which was its only means of licensing the downstairs subject position. The same thing happens in typical Small Clauses, as shown in (19a-b) above.

5. Why direct objects cannot passivise

We are now ready to look at the passivisation of ditransitive verbs. As illustrated in (20)-(22), the indirect object can always be promoted to passive subject. In (20a), a dative indirect object is promoted, and also in (22a), while in (21a), a structurally case-marked object is promoted. By contrast, the direct object can only be passivised when it has structural case as in (20b), not when it has lexical case as in (21b) and (22b).

(20) Indir. obj.: lexical case, dir. obj.: structural case
a Maríu var gefin bókin
Mary(D) was given the-book(N)
b Þessi bók var gefin Maríu
this book(N) was given Mary(D)

(21) Indir. obj.: structural case, dir. obj.: lexical case
a María var svipt ökuskírteininu
Mary(N) was deprived the-driver's license(D)
b *Ökuskírteininu var svipt María
the-driver's license(D) was deprived Mary(N)

(22) Indir. obj.: lexical case, dir. obj.: lexical case
a Maríu var skilað peningunum
Mary(D) was returned the-money(D)
b *Peningunum var skilað Maríu
the-money(D) was returned Mary(D)

I argue that passivisation of the direct object is generally excluded, and that the special mechanism of reanalysis allows structurally case-marked direct objects to passivise. To exclude passivisation of direct objects, we can straightforwardly generalise from the passivisation of ECM constructions and typical Small Clauses that we just discussed. The indirect object must move in the passive because it is not licensed in its base-generated specifier position. The passive verb is unable to assign structural case, so the indirect object must move up to a place where it can be licensed, more specifically to a Spec-VP position locally governed by Agr-containing Infl, or to Spec-IP. Note that the indirect object specifier is not licensed by theta-marking from the verb because it is indirectly theta-marked, and only direct theta-marking counts for licensing.

6. Reanalysis allows passivisation of structurally case-marked direct objects

To explain the fact that structurally case-marked direct objects can passivise, I invoke a mechanism of REANALYSIS which can only apply when the direct object has structural case. This process applies in the projection from the lexicon into D-structure, somewhat similar to syntactic passivisation. This reanalysis is illustrated in (23), with A showing its input and B its output.

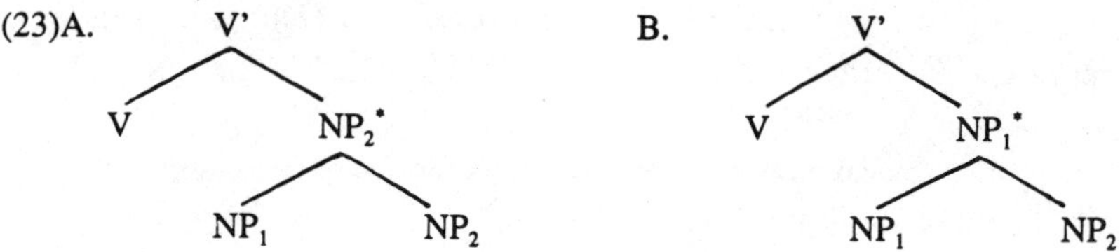

Note in (23A), that the only thing which distinguishes between the head and the specifier is which one projects further up. If NP_1 is allowed to project instead of NP_2, as in (23B), it in effect becomes the head of the Small Clause, now NP_1^*. Thereby NP_1 can be licensed, exceptionally, by the theta-role assigning property of the passive verb. Its reanalysis as head makes it eligible as the one NP that is licensed by theta-marking. This in turn allows NP_1 to stay in situ, while it forces NP_2 to move up, because it is no longer licensed by theta-marking.

The reanalysis has quite detrimental consequences for the former head position, and this provides the key to the question why only structurally case-marked direct objects can passivise. After the reanalysis, the former head position is a specifier position of sorts, but it is deviant in that it is on the opposite side of the Small Clause from the verb which selects it. Lexical case cannot be assigned to this position because the adjacency condition on lexical case assignment, discussed in section 4, is violated. A specifier on the opposite side of a Small Clause is neither linearly adjacent to the verb, nor is it a sister of the verb via a higher (NP*) projection. Now, it will be recalled that lexical case must be assigned already at D-structure and cannot be picked up later in the derivation. This means that reanalysis cannot be applied to a verb with a lexically case-marked direct object because reanalysis would preclude any licit derivation.

Note that this kind of reanalysis cannot be duplicated by empty verb analyses like that illustrated in (6). Such analyses can only commute the roles of NP_1 and NP_2 by switching the positions of the two NPs, and this in turn requires two subcategorisation frames for the verb. Under a subcategorisation approach however, it is entirely unexpected that passivisation of structurally case marked direct objects is restricted in that it is sensitive to specific verbs, focussing properties and definiteness of the direct object (Ottósson 1989). This is not surprising under a reanalysis approach on the other hand, given the sensitivity to such factors of another process dependent on reanalysis, namely Inversion, discussed in the next section. Even more importantly, a subcategorisation approach affords no non-stipulative means to exclude passive of lexically case-marked direct objects.

7. Inversion

The second phenomenon which the proposed reanalysis helps account for is that called INVERSION by Holmberg (1991). This is a process which moves a direct object to the left of an indirect object, as illustrated in (24b), compared to (24a). Just like direct object passives, Inversion is only possible for verbs with an accusative direct object. It is impossible to invert the other case combinations, as illustrated in (24c-d).

(24)a Jón gaf konunginum ambáttina
John gave the-king(D) the-maidservant(A)
b Jón gaf ambáttina konunginum t
John gave the-maidservant(A) the-king(D)
'John gave the maidservant to the king'
c *Jón skilaði ambáttinni konunginum t
John returned the-maidservant(D) [to-] the-king(D)
d *Jón svipti ambáttinni konunginn t
John deprived [of-] the-maidservant(D) the-king(A)

One crucial property of Inversion is that the inverted direct object can bind into the indirect object, as illustrated in (25).[6]

(25)a Ég gaf ambáttina$_i$ konungi sínum$_i$ t
I gave the-maidservant(A) king(D) SELF's
'I gave the maidservant to her king'
b *Ég gaf ambáttina sína$_i$ konunginum$_i$ t
I gave the-maidservant SELF's the-king
'I gave his maidservant to the king'
c Ég gaf konunginum$_i$ ambáttina sína$_i$
I gave the-king maidservant SELF's
'I gave the king his maidservant'

This binding indicates that the moved object lands in an A-position c-commanding the indirect object which stays put. It may be assumed that reanalysis is required in order to provide the required configuration for this binding, more specifically an A-position, which is a secondary Small Clause specifier. A further plausible motivation for the reanalysis requirement on Inversion is that a head cannot adjoin to its own projection, as the moved object would do in the absence of reanalysis. The reanalysis requirement explains why only verbs with structurally case-marked, i.e., accusative, objects can undergo Inversion. This is because verbs with a lexically case-marked head cannot undergo reanalysis as just discussed for direct object passives. Again, empty verb analyses cannot reduplicate this, as such analyses cannot accommodate the proposed reanalysis.

Under empty verb analyses, one is forced to assume, with Falk (1990) and Holmberg (1991), that Inversion structures are base-generated. Several facts speak against such an assumption, however. First, as illustrated in (26a), inverted direct objects cannot undergo Heavy-NP Shift, unlike base-generated indirect objects as in (26b).[7] The reflexive possessive in the shifted NP in (26b) shows that the latter comes from a position c-commanding the non-shifted object from the left. (I take

[6] As discussed by Webelhuth (1989), a direct object scrambled to the left of an indirect object in German can also bind into the indirect object, and the focus conditions on the objects involved are similar to Inversion in Icelandic. Webelhuth argues that the landing site in the German case is a position exhibiting properties of both A-positions and A'-positions.

[7] It may be hard to distinguish Inversion from Heavy-NP Shift in individual cases, as the order of the objects is the same. However, an adverbial at the right edge of VP may intervene in Heavy-NP Shift, and indirect objects moved by Heavy-NP Shift must meet heaviness requirements that are stricter than the focus requirements for indirect objects left behind by Inversion.

the mild deviance of (26b) to reflect a preference for the reflexive to follow rather than precede its antecedent.)

(26)a *Ég gaf t unnusta sínum$_i$ [stúlkuna sem allir
I gave fiancé SELF's the-girl that all
strákarnir voru á höttunum eftir]$_i$
the-boys were out after

b ?Ég gaf t unnustu sína$_i$ [piltinum sem hafði beðið
I gave fiancée SELF's the-boy who had waited
óþreyjufullur í mörg ár]$_i$
impatient for many years

Although it is not clear to me exactly why inverted structures cannot undergo Heavy-NP Shift, the base-generation analysis has no way to distinguish the Inversion structures from the others.

A second indication that Inversion is derived comes from its sensitivity to focus properties of the inverted object as well as to those of the object which stays in place. The inverted object must apparently be unfocussed (often definite), or at least not more focussed than the unmoved object, as illustrated in (27)-(28).

(27)a Ég mun gefa bókina einhverju bókasafni t
I will give the-book(A) some library(D)

b ??Ég mun gefa bók einhverju bókasafni t
I will give a-book(A) some library(D)

c Ég mun gefa hana einhverju bókasafni t
I will give it(A) some library(D)

(28)a *Ég mun gefa einhverja bók bókasafninu t
I will give some book(A) the-library(D)

b *Ég mun gefa einhverja bók bókasafni t
I will give some book(A) a-library(D)

(29)a *Jón gaf einhverjar bækur háskólanum t
John gave some books(A) the-university(D)

b Jón gaf einhverjar bækur til háskólans
John donated some books(A) to the-university(D)

Focus restrictions of the kind just described are generally not found in base-generated structures. In particular, there are no such restrictions in the few prepositional variants there are to double-object verbs in Icelandic, as illustrated in (29).

Now one may ask, if the reanalysis process is available to make the indirect object the head of a double-object Small Clause, why then cannot the direct object bind freely into the indirect object in the active? The answer is, I assume, that a head turned specifier by reanalysis may no longer be argument-licensed in situ. Such a specifier cannot be licensed by theta-assignment of course, and it cannot be licensed by structural case assignment either because a specifier on the opposite side of a Small Clause from a verb is too far from it for that sort of local licensing. Therefore, reanalysis must always be followed by some movement to ensure a licit S-structure.

8. Extending the argument to other languages

In concluding, it is natural to ask whether the reanalysis argument can be extended to languages other than Icelandic. A full discussion of this question would lead too far in the present context. However, it may be pointed out that indirect objects are generally more easily passivised than direct objects in languages such as the Mainland Scandinavian languages and English. We may then wonder whether the facts of Argument Licensing (Proper Head Government) are similar in crucial respects in these languages to the facts discussed here for Icelandic. Alternatively, and perhaps more likely, a RELATIVISED MINIMALITY account, in the spirit of Vikner (1990), might be developed for these languages and possibly Icelandic as well. In either case, the reanalysis proposed here is relevant, a mechanism not available to empty verb analyses.[8]

According to Vikner (1990, 4-10--14), the direct object cannot A-move across another A-element, the indirect object. This is based on Rizzi's (1991) argument that an A-moved element must antecedent-govern its trace, so that the moved element can form a chain with the trace and thus, inherit its theta-role. An intervening A-element, that is, one c-commanding the trace but not the moved NP, would violate relativised minimality, one of the conditions for antecedent government. The process of reanalysis proposed here would circumvent this minimality violation by switching the c-command relations of the indirect and

[8] Vikner (1990, 4-12f) adopts a suggestion by Rizzi, that direct object passives in Norwegian are made possible by reanalysing the two verbal heads in (6) as part of the same verb. As the indirect object is now governed by the same governor as the direct object, it is assumed not to count as an intervening specifier. I find this proposal rather unclear, and if it were to be adapted to Icelandic, it would not help explaining Inversion, in particular the binding capability of the inverted direct object.

direct object. Because the direct object c-commands the indirect object after reanalysis, the indirect object no longer interferes with its A-movement. This approach gives an intuitively appealing way to account for the differences in direct object passivisation between Danish, Norwegian and Swedish, discussed by Vikner (1990) and Falk (1990). Direct object passives are always ungrammatical in Danish, but sometimes grammatical in Norwegian and Swedish. This may (cf. Vikner) be connected to the presence of certain reanalysis processes, such as the one underlying pseudo-passives, in Norwegian and Swedish but not in Danish. It may be argued that direct object passives are a marked construction, learned by positive evidence. Although it seems unlikely that the various processes of reanalysis can be reduced to a single parameter setting, one reanalysis involving verbal arguments may support another in acquisition.[9]

Finally, it should be kept in mind that one of the major motivations for Larson's (1988) empty verb analysis was the UNIFORMITY OF THETA-ASSIGNMENT HYPOTHESIS (UTAH) proposed by Baker (1988). This principle, in the relativised form assumed by Larson (1990, 601), states that identical thematic relationships are represented by identical relative hierarchical relations between the items at D-structure. Larson achieves these D-structure syntactic relations, in particular, the lower position of the Goal relative to the Theme, by assuming that the indirect object originates in a prepositional phrase which is the sole sister of the lowest verbal head and is subsequently adjoined to the left of the direct object. However, although both Holmberg (1991), Falk (1990), and Vikner (1990) adopt Larson's empty verbal heads, none of them subscribes to a transformational relationship between ('dative-shifted') double objects and prepositional variants in the Mainland Scandinavian languages in view of its empirical and conceptual difficulties (see in particular the criticism of Falk 1990, 70--73). The prepositional variants are about as frequent in these languages, though, as they are in English. One problem with Larson's analysis is his assumption that the verb has closer semantic links to the indirect object than to the direct object, which does not fit well with facts such as the idiom formation discussed in 2. Generally speaking, semantic determination of syntactic projection appears to have limited applicability when it comes to prepositional arguments (Dowty 1991). Even among bare-NP arguments, however, there seem to be cross-linguistically rather many indeterminacies, and even exceptions, with respect to the regular projection rules,

---

[9] The fact that direct object passives are ungrammatical in standard English while pseudo-passives are quite common does not militate against this view, as it is more likely that additional parametric differences enter into the picture in English than in the mutually quite similar Mainland Scandinavian languages.

as established without consideration of the UTAH. Recalcitrant cases include (Dowty 1991) verbs like *receive* and *undergo*, psych-verbs, and verbs of possession (e.g., the transitive counterparts of *own* and *belong to* in Icelandic). If (relativised) UTAH or similar principles, strictly enforced, cannot be taken as support for a Larsonian analysis of double objects, this adds to the vulnerability of that approach to more properly syntactic arguments, such as those presented here.

References

Baker, Mark. 1988. *Incorporation: A Theory of Grammatical Function Changing*. Chicago: University of Chicago Press.

Barss, Andrew & Howard Lasnik. 1986. A Note on Anaphora and Double Objects. *Linguistic Inquiry* 17:347--354.

Chomsky, Noam. 1986. *Barriers*. Linguistic Inquiry Monographs, 13. Cambridge, Mass.: MIT Press.

Dowty, David. 1991. Thematic proto-roles and argument selection. *Language* 67:547--619.

Falk, Cecilia. 1990. On Double Object Constructions. *Working Papers in Scandinavian Syntax* 46:53--100.

Hellan, Lars. 1991. The phrasal nature of double object clusters. *Issues in Germanic Syntax*, ed. Werner Abraham, Wim Kosmeijer & Eric Reuland, 67--92. Berlin - New York: Mouton de Gruyter. [Also in Working Papers in Scandinavian Syntax 42, 1988].

Holmberg, Anders. 1986. *Word Order and Syntactic Features in the Scandinavian languages and English*. Stockholm: Department of General Linguistics, University of Stockholm.

Holmberg, Anders. 1991. On the Scandinavian double object construction. *Papers from the Twelfth Scandinavian Conference of Linguistics*, ed. Halldór Á. Sigurðsson, 141--152. Reykjavík: Linguistic Institute, University of Iceland.

Jackendoff, Ray. 1990. On Larson's Analysis of the Double Object Construction. *Linguistic Inquiry* 21:427--456.

Kayne, Richard. 1983. *Connectedness and Binary Branching*. Dordrecht: Foris.

Larson, Richard K. 1988. On the Double Object Construction. *Linguistic Inquiry* 19:335--391.

Larson, Richard K. 1990. Double Objects Revisited: Reply to Jackendoff. *Linguistic Inquiry* 21:589--632.

Ottósson, Kjartan G. 1989. The Anticausative Middle and Other Voices of Modern Icelandic. MS, University of Maryland at College Park.

Ottósson, Kjartan G. 1991. Icelandic Double Objects as Small Clauses. *Working Papers in Scandinavian Syntax* 48:77--97.

Rizzi, Luigi. 1991. *Relativized Minimality*. (Linguistic Inquiry Monographs, 16.) Cambridge (Mass.): MIT Press.

Sigurðsson, Halldór Á. 1991. Icelandic Case-marked PRO and the Licensing of Lexical Arguments. *Natural Language and Linguistic Theory* 9:327--363.

Sprouse, Rex A. 1989. *On the Syntax of the Double Object Construction in Selected Germanic Languages.* Princeton Ph. D. dissertation.

Stowell, Timothy. 1981. *Origins of Phrase Structure.* MIT Ph.D. dissertation.

Vikner, Sten. 1990. *Verb Movement and the Licensing of NP-Positions in the Germanic Languages.* Doctoral thesis (draft version), Université de Genève.

Webelhuth, Gert. 1989. *Syntactic Saturation Phenomena and the Modern Germanic Languages.* University of Massachusetts Ph.D. dissertation.

SigmaP and Hungarian

CHRISTOPHER PIÑÓN
Stanford University

Since the advent of Pollock 1989, functional projections have played an ever increasing role in syntactic analysis.[0] In the standard theory of functional features in the *Barriers* framework, the feature bundles [±Tns, ±Agr] and [±Wh] project from heads to I(nfl)P and C(omp)P, respectively (Chomsky 1986). Pollock 1989, noting the internal heterogeneity of the feature bundle [±Tns, ±Agr], proposed that each feature be taken as a category in its own right and project according to X' theory, thereby yielding T(ense)P and AgrP, respectively. In the same article, he also argues for a Neg(ative)P, embodying the claim that English *not* and French *ne* head their own projections as well.[1] Whereas Chomsky 1986 posits two functional projections, Pollock 1989 concludes with four.

In this paper, I want to address the question of what justifies a functional projection more generally and question the status of NegP as a independent projection in particular. In §1., after reviewing current assumptions, I propose a strong condition on functional projections in terms of the 'identifiability' of the specifier, head, and complement positions. In particular, identifiability of the specifier entails that the specifier of each functional projection be distinguishable from others with respect to some salient property. Given this condition, I ask whether NegP can be justified as a projection in its own right. In §2., I argue on the basis of Hungarian that NegP is non-distinct from TP, i.e., NegP forms a composite projection with TP which I call the Σ(igma) Phrase (borrowing a notion from Laka 1990[2]). In §3., I review Pollock's (1989) and Zanuttini's (1990a, 1990b) explicit arguments for NegP, concluding that they constitute necessary but not sufficient motivation for such a projection. I then argue that the ΣP hypothesis not only can be extended to Romance but can also account more successfully for certain head movement facts.

[0] This work was supported by a Dorothy Danforth Compton graduate fellowship. Many thanks to Cleo Condoravdi, Gillian Ramchand, and Elizabeth Traugott for valuable comments and to Tibor Laczkó for checking my Hungarian.

[1] For Pollock, *ne* (like *not*) is the head of NegP, *pas* its specifier. Rizzi (1990, 17-18), not fully embracing the NegP approach, has *ne* cliticize to Agr° and requires that both *not* and *pas* be A'-specifiers of some projection. For *pas* at least, he takes the relevant projection to be TP. Chomsky 1989, in contrast, assumes that both *not* and *pas* head a NegP.

[2] Laka 1990 introduces ΣP as a projection for negative and 'emphatic' elements in Basque, English, and Romance. The central difference between her approach and mine is that she posits an IP independent of ΣP: the latter is not a tense projection. The view I will articulate is that they are effectively the same projection.

ΣP is a composite functional projection containing (minimally) tense and (optionally) negation.[3] As such, it replaces TP. The essential difference between Hungarian and Romance in this regard is that [Spec, ΣP] is an A'-position in the former and an A-positon in the latter. The negative marker, when a head, projects not to NegP, but rather with the [+tense] head to ΣP.

1. Functional projections

In the current Government-Binding (GB) approach to phrase structure with functional projections, a NegP exists insofar as the negative marker is a head of category Neg°, i.e., a functional head projects to a full X' projection of the same type. In this section, I propose a stronger (more empirically testable) condition on functional projection-hood in terms of standard X' theory. The essence of this condition is that a functional projection should have not only a characteristic head and complement type, but also an identifiable specifier type. Given this condition, I will later claim that full motivation for NegP as a projection of its own is lacking.

Speas 1990 hypothesizes that there is one rule of the base, the 'Project Alpha' rule. She states it as follows (p. 43):

(A) PROJECT ALPHA: 'A word of syntactic category *X* is dominated by an uninterrupted sequence of *X* nodes.'

Speas then proceeds to define both 'maximal projection' and 'minimal projection' in terms of being either the highest or lowest in a projection sequence. To wit (p. 44):

(B) Maximal Projection: $X = X^{max}$ iff $\forall G$ which dominate X, $G \neq X$.
Minimal Projection: $X = X^{\circ}$ iff X dominates a word.

Thus, the maximal projection is the highest X node in an uninterrupted sequence of X nodes, and the minimal projection is the lowest (a terminal node). For Speas, the licensing of complements and specifiers is dependent on the properties of the head. For example, a specifier position is projected iff the head assigns a 'Kase feature'[4] leftward to that position; otherwise it is not (p. 112). In sum, Speas claims (p. 114) that 'functional heads must have grids which specify what sort of complement they take, and specify the Kase features that they have.'

In this connection, we can ask what the grid of the negative marker looks like. In particular, does it assign a Kase feature to its specifier? Although Speas allows that a particular functional head of category X° may not be a Kase assigner (cf. [-Wh] vs. [+Wh]), generally there is always at least some member of category X° which is a Kase assigner. The NegP hypothesis has the characteristic that there is a single member of the category Neg°, hence if this category contains a Kase assigner, we do not have far to search. Suppose, then, that we interpret Speas in the strongest form, i.e., as saying the following:[5]

(C) PROJECT ALPHA for a functional element of category X° ↔ at least one member of X° both selects a complement and is a Kase assigner.

---

[3]In this paper, I remain agnostic about the role of Agr. My analysis is compatible with Agr either projecting to AgrP or constituting another feature specification in Σ°.

[4]A Kase feature is a type of abstract agreement feature, such as [+Wh] or Case: the Spec/head relation is thus an agreement relation. Heads may or may not assign a Kase feature. The complementizer *that* ([-Wh]) does not, hence its specifier position is not projected. In contrast, the [+Wh] element does, hence its specifer position is both projected and filled with a Wh-phrase.

[5]I am aware that Speas does not actually phrase her thesis in this way. But since I am interested in strong possible motivation for NegP, I seek a strong but reasonable condition on functional projections.

In current X' theory, Ernst (1991, 1) diagnoses the 'Obligatory Functional Category Hypothesis', a hypothesis which he rejects in his paper.

(D) 'All zero-level functional elements of category F take a complement and project to a maximal projection FP.'

In the standard approach, (D) entails that if the negative marker belongs to category Neg, it will project to NegP and hence will have both a complement and a specifier. This is because to be an XP means that X° has a complement and that X' has a specifier. In contrast to Speas's theory, the full projection is a property of the phrase structure, and not of the head.

If NegP exists, then its structure according to (D) is that shown in (E).

(E) NegP schema

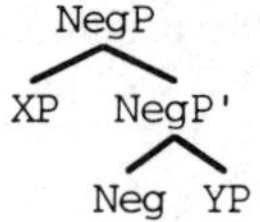

Minimally, it includes a specifier (XP) and a complement (YP), its location in the tree depending on the dominance ordering among the functional projections. If a principle like (D) is correct, then strong support could be adduced for it by arguing that the FP projected from a functional element F° does indeed contain both the specifier and complement predicted to exist. In terms of NegP, then, the issue is not only whether Neg° exists, but also whether XP and YP can be identified. If they can, then this would constitute fairly solid evidence for the existence of NegP. I state this condition as follows:

(F) NegP $\leftrightarrow$ (i) Neg° selects a complement YP and (ii) NegP' has an identifiable[6] specifier XP.

As with (C), (F) establishes a strong condition on NegP. Of course, one may consider either (C) or (F) to be too strong, preferring the weaker statement in (A) or (D). I cannot argue with this preference; if accepted, the matter simply becomes a theory-internal one, and it is difficult to see what would count as evidence against either (A) or (D).[7] Therefore, for the sake of argument I retain the strong variants (C, F), for either of these has a more testable basis than (A, D). For concreteness, I will henceforth refer only to (F) and the task will be to evaluate NegP proposal with respect to it.

2. ΣP in Hungarian

Facts from Hungarian indicate that a generalization is missed if NegP is postulated. Specifically, the A'-character of [Spec, NegP] is not distinguishable from the A'-nature of the specifier of some more general projection. Thus, by the condition (F)

---

[6]Clearly, much depends on what I mean by 'identifiable' here. The idea is that [Spec, NegP] should exhibit some property which distinguishes it from other specifiers. For example, [Spec, CP] is distinguishable from [Spec, IP] in that it is the landing site of Wh-phrases, whereas the latter is the position to which nominative Case is assigned. The question is whether [Spec, NegP] also has some such distinguishing property.

[7]Ernst (1991, 8-9), who also rejects (D), points out that if *not* is a head in English, then it does not count as a potential (intervening) head governor for head movement, in violation of Rizzi's (1990) Relativized Minimality. (Cf. *Mary has not left*, where *has* has moved from Agr° past *not* to T°.) This is a theory-internal argument that (C) is problematic.

of the previous section, the postulation of NegP is not fully justified and the negative marker is to be analyzed as an element of this more general projection. Adopting the essential insight (but not the accompanying details) of Laka 1990, I call this latter projection ΣP, a projection for focus and negation. Negation does not constitute a syntactic category in its own right (Laka (1990, 86)).

Hungarian contains a wealth of preverb-verb combinations, many partially or fully lexicalized, which are subject to tmesis (lit. 'cutting') in the syntax. Some examples of these are given in (1) ('PV' abbreviates 'preverb').

(1) *be·fejez* 'finish', *le·fordít* 'translate', *meg·ismer* 'recognize', *ki·javít* 'correct'

The conditions for the tmesis of such complex verbs play a vital role in the argument for ΣP. I now review these conditions.

(i) In neutral affirmative sentences, the PV immediately precedes the simple (preverb-less) verb; in negative sentences it does not. The negative marker *nem* in Hungarian is obligatorily preverbal.

(2) Sentence negation

a. Mari le·fordította a cikket.
Mary PV-translated the article
'Mary translated the article'

b. *Mari fordította le a cikket.
Mary translated PV the article

c. Mari *nem* fordította le a cikket.
Mary NEG translated PV the article
'Mary didn't translate the article'

d. *Mari *nem* le·fordította a cikket.
Mary NEG PV-translated the article

(2b) is bad because the PV must precede the simple verb in a neutral affirmative sentence. (2c, d) show that the PV follows and cannot precede the verb when *nem* is present.

(ii) A focussed phrase having the exhaustive listing interpretation similarly induces separation of the PV (focus indicated in bold italics).

(3) Exhaustive listing-focus predication

a. ***Mari*** fordította le a cikket.
Mary translated PV the article
'It is Mary who translated …
… the article'

b. ****Mari*** le·fordította a cikket.
Mary PV-translated the article

(iii) The *csak*-phrase, being a focussed constituent, also induces separation.

(4) *csak*-focus ('only'-phrase)

a. ***Csak Mari*** fordította le a cikket.
only Mary translated PV the article
'Only Mary translated the article'

b. ****Csak Mari*** le·fordította a cikket.
only Mary PV-translated the article

(iv) Wh-phrases, since they are inherently focussed items, require separation.[8]

(5) Wh-focus

a. ***Ki*** fordította le a cikket?
who translated PV the article
'Who translated the article?'

b. ****Ki*** le·fordította a cikket?
who PV-translated the article

[8] I assume the result that Wh-phrases do not occupy [Spec, CP] in Hungarian. See É. Kiss 1987 for details.

(v) 'Exclusive' adverbs (broadly characterizable as 'contrastive') also effect tmesis of the complex verb (cf. Kiefer (1967, §1.5.), É. Kiss (1987, 90)).[9]

(6) <u>'Exclusive' adverbs</u>
(*nehezen*, 'with difficulty', *ritkán* 'rarely', *lassan* 'slowly', etc.)
a. Mari *hiába* fordította le a cikket.
Mary in-vain translated PV the article
'Mary translated the article in vain'
b. *Mari *hiába* le·fordította a cikket.
Mary in-vain PV-translated the article

The data in (2-6) clearly support the view that the negative marker *nem* patterns with focussed phrases in requiring tmesis of the complex verb. If a NegP is postulated to account for the facts in (2), then the similar behavior of focus in the non-negative sentences (3-5) is not explained in an analogous way. On the other hand, if we postulate a special focus projection for Hungarian, as Brody 1990 does, then we do not expect the negative marker to induce tmesis as well. I propose that this parallel between focus and the negative marker can best be captured in an analysis which makes use of the ΣP projection, a projection which houses both types of items.

The essential ingredients of my analysis are as follows. I assume that lexical items are inserted fully inflected, consequently the verb does not 'pick up' its tense and agreement morphology in the syntax; rather, such morphology is 'checked' in the appropriate position (Chomsky 1991). Following É. Kiss 1990 and Brody 1990, I do not postulate an independent IP in Hungarian; in my analysis, ΣP effectively fills this role. The basic order of phrases in the preverbal field in Hungarian is such that topics precede quantified phrases which in turn precede focus (É. Kiss 1987, Brody 1990). Since it is beyond the scope of this paper to present a full analysis of word order, I limit myself to a consideration of ΣP, the 'post-quantifier field' in Hungarian. I analyze the ΣP as an optional functional projection, dominating the VP, as shown in (7).[10]

(7) SigP = ΣP

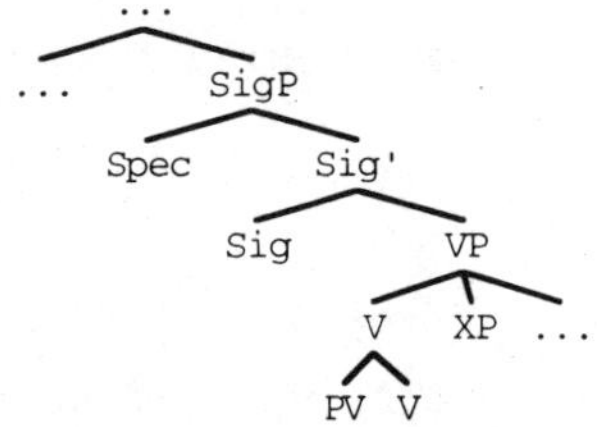

[Spec, ΣP] is an A'-position, licensed as all specifiers are, by the head of the projection (Speas 1990). In Chomsky's (1991) terms, [Spec, ΣP] is not 'L-related' to Σ° in that the specifier does not stand in a local 'agreement' relation with the head Σ°. This specifier position is inherently associated with a Σ FEATURE,

[9]'Exclusive' adverbs are not canonical instances of focus, hence I do not write them in bold. They are in some sense inherently 'contrastive', but unlike true focussed items, they do not necessarily trigger the 'eradicating' prosody noted by Kálmán et al. 1989, whereby phrases following the focussed constituent are all reduced in stress. This is another reason why a focus projection would be too narrow a construct.

[10]Following É. Kiss 1987, I assume (though not crucially) that Hungarian is non-configurational in the sense that the VP has no distinguished position for the subject.

which is roughly like a [+focus] or [+contrastive] feature marking. The essence of ΣP is that it is a composite projection whose feature structure accommodates (minimally) both [+tense] and [+neg]. The structure of Σ° is given in (8), where the left branch is optional.

(8) Head of ΣP

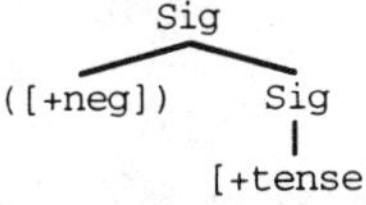

It is evident that ΣP is like TP in that it contains an obligatory [+tense] head. Nevertheless, it cannot be identified with TP for two reasons. First, and most obviously, Σ° can also be marked as [+neg]. This would be unexpected if ΣP were actually the same as TP, for the negative marker is not of category T°. Second, and crucially, ΣP is an optional projection even if the verb itself is inflected as [+tense], i.e., I assume that there is the option of checking the morphological features of the verb in V° as well. The optionality of ΣP is a feasible hypothesis precisely because [Spec, ΣP] is not L-related to and therefore does not stand in an agreement relation with the verb. (This contrasts with the situation in Romance, to be considered later, where [Spec, ΣP] is L-related to the head (hence an A-position) and is therefore effectively obligatory.) If ΣP were merely TP, then its optional character in Hungarian would be unexpected.

To see how this analysis gets off the ground, consider the structures assigned to the examples in (2-6).

(9) a. Structure for (2a) b. Structure for (2c)

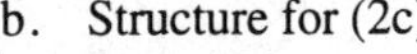

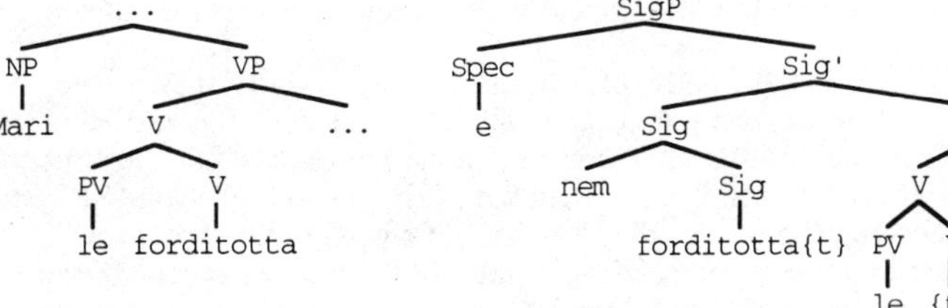

c. Structure for (3a) d. Structure for (4a)

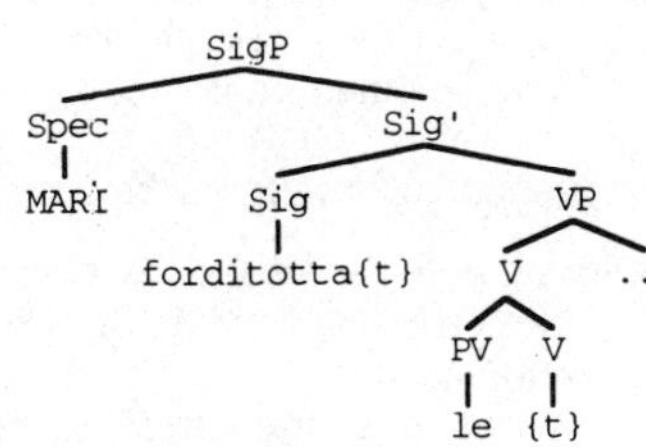

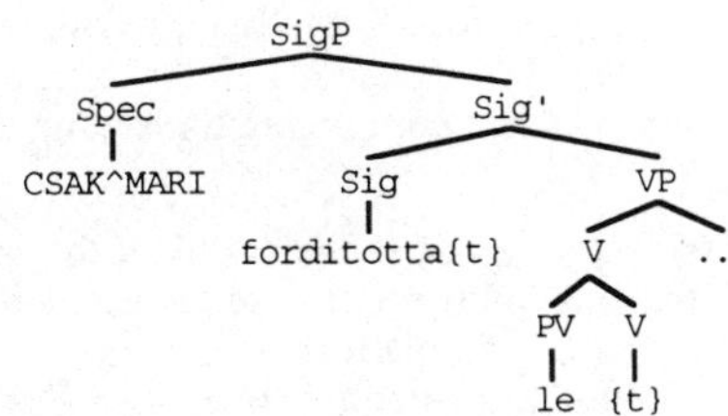

e. Structure for (5a) f. Structure for (6a)

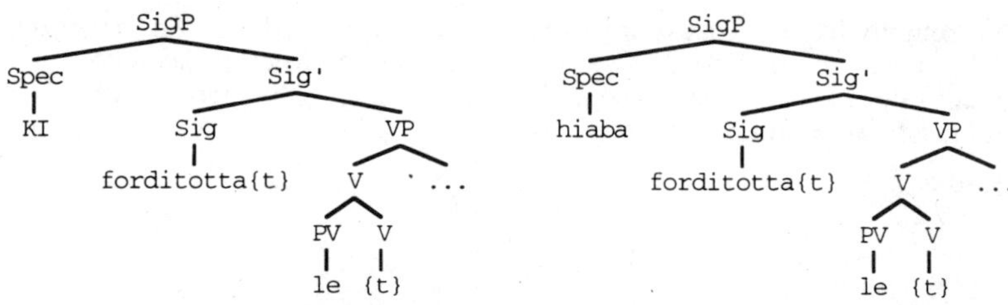

In (9a), ΣP is not projected, since it need not be. The verb is drawn from the lexicon fully inflected, hence it does not have to move to $\Sigma°$ to 'pick up' its inflectional morphology. Of course, this entails that the [+tense] feature of the verb be 'checkable' in V° when there is no ΣP. Assuming that [+tense] can be generated in at most one head position, the statement in (10) ensures that the respective head position is permitted to be V°. Thus, if ΣP is projected, there is really no option, for [+tense] must appear in $\Sigma°$ (cf. (8)). On the other hand, if ΣP is not projected, then (10) in effect has to be chosen so as to ensure feature 'checking'.

(10) [+tense] optionally in V°

V
|
([+tense])

In (9b), ΣP is projected as a consequence of the negative marker in its head. The specifier position remains empty (alternatively, it is not projected, cf. Speas 1990), as nothing forces it to be filled. Since ΣP is projected, [+tense] must be present in $\Sigma°$, hence the verb must move to this position to have its feature checked. If the verb remains in the VP, checking fails, and the structure is ruled out (cf. (2d)).

Why, then, is (2b) bad? Its structure is essentially that of (9b), with the difference that the negative marker is absent. But nothing forces the negation anyhow, and it is clear that checking of [+tense] is successful. Strictly speaking, then, (2b) is grammatical. The problem with (2b) lies in how such V-PV structures are interpreted in Hungarian: they cannot have perfective aspect (É. Kiss (1987, §2.3.4.). Thus, (2b) is rejected in isolation, but it becomes acceptable in a context which forces a progressive aspect reading:

(11) <u>(2b) as progressive aspect</u> (''' indicates heavy stress)
Mari (épp) 'fordította 'le a 'cikket, amikor a postás csengetett.
Mary (just) translated PV the article when the postman rang
'Mary was just completing translating the article ...
... when the postman rang the bell'

The interpretability of sentences like (2b) depends a lot on both the local context and the semantics of the complex verb in question. Nevertheless, the structures themselves are grammatical, as is predicted by the present account.

ΣP is also projected in the remaining structures of (9). In each case, the specifier position is filled by an item which receives a focus or contrastive interpretation. The verb must consequently raise to $\Sigma°$ so that its [+tense] feature can be checked; ungrammaticality results if it does not do so, as (3b, 4b, 5b, 6b) show.

A straightforward prediction of this analysis in which the negative marker occupies $\Sigma°$ is that the specifier position should be fillable even in the presence of *nem*. This expectation is borne out, as seen in (12). Here, ΣP is fully articulated.[11]

(12) Focus in specifier; *nem* in head
Mari *nem* fordította le a cikket.
Mary NEG translated PV the article
'It is Mary who didn't translate the article'

Another prediction of the present account crucially depends on the feature [+tense] being generated in Σ°. Suppose that the verb is drawn from the lexicon inflected with a suffix specified as [-tense]. If ΣP is projected, then the verb has to raise to have its tense feature checked. But if the verb is equipped with a suffix marked as [-tense], then checking should fail once the verb moves to Σ°. This means that ΣP should be incompatible with a verb specified as [-tense]. To test this, consider the 'adverbial participle' as exemplified in the absolute construction.[12]

(13) [+tense] of Σ° is incompatible with [-tense] of adverbial participle
a. A cikket le·fordítva, Mari sokkal jobban meg·értette az elméletet.
the article PV-translated Mary much better PV-understood the theory
'Having translated the article, Mary understood the theory much better'
b. *A cikket *nem* fordítva le, Mari rosszul értette meg az elméletet.
the article NEG translated PV Mary poorly understood PV the theory
'Having not translated the article, Mary poorly understood the theory'
c. ****A cikket*** fordítva le, Mari sokkal jobban meg·értette az elméletet.
the article translated PV Mary much better PV-understood the theory
'Having translated ***the article***, Mary understood the theory much better'
d. ****Csak a cikket*** fordítva le, Mari sokkal jobban meg·értette az...
only the article translated PV Mary much better PV-understood the...
'Having translated ***only the article***, Mary understood the theory much better'
e. *A cikket *nehezen* fordítva le, ...
the article with-difficulty translated PV
... Marinak nem sikerült meg·értenie az elméletet.
Mary-to NEG succeeded PV-understand the theory
'Having translated the article with difficulty, ...
... Mary didn't manage to understand the theory'

The ungrammaticality of (13b-e) provides striking confirmation of the ΣP hypothesis. For if the adverbial participle is specified as [-tense], then checking of this feature against [+tense] will fail after verb movement to Σ°, with the consequence that ΣP cannot be projected in an absolute construction. But if ΣP is not projected, then [Spec, ΣP] is not present, and neither the (syntactic) negative

---

[11]While (9b-d) are all compatible with the negative marker present, as expected, (9e) is not, i.e., **Mari hiába nem fordította le a cikket* '*Mary in vain didn't translate the article'. An independent condition, valid in both Hungarian and English, requires that the 'exclusive' adverb have narrow scope with respect to the negative marker, i.e., *Mari nem fordította le hiába a cikket* 'Mary didn't translate the article in vain'.

[12]The designation 'adverbial participle' is my translation of the Hungarian term *határozói igenév*. The unit is similar to (but not the functional equivalent of) a past participle. The feature system that I presuppose for tense is $\frac{[+\text{tense}]\ \frac{[+\text{finite}]}{[-\text{finite}]}}{[-\text{tense}]}$, where both indicative and subjunctive affixes are subtypes of [+finite] and the participial ending *-va/ve* is marked as [-tense].

marker, focus, nor an 'exclusive' adverb can appear in that clause. This is exactly what is expected in the present analysis, where [+tense] occupies $\Sigma°$.[13]

Note that (13b) becomes grammatical if we insert the negative marker between the PV and the simple verb. This appears to contradict the claim that ΣP is not projected in such clauses.

(14) (cf. (13b))
A cikket le *nem* fordítva, Mari rosszul értette meg az elméletet.
the article PV NEG translated Mary poorly understood PV the theory

Although (14) may appear to be a counterexample, I claim that this *nem* is a morphological negative marker. Independently, there must be a morphological rule which places *nem* between the PV and simple verb before derivational suffixation applies:

(15) a. a [le *nem* fordított] cikk
the PV NEG translated article
'the untranslated article'

b. a vonat [meg *nem* érkezése]
the train PV NEG arrival-POSS
'the train's non-arrival'

The negated adverbial participle in (14) can have the same basic derivation as the deverbal adjective and nominal in (15a, b), whatever the preferred analysis of the latter is. In any case, examples like (14) appear to have an alternative explanation.

To summarize, I have argued that Hungarian has a ΣP projection whose specifier is an A'-position and whose head is a complex feature structure including [+tense] and (optionally) [+neg]. ΣP is optionally projected, with the consequence that the verb raises only when ΣP is projected. I have also argued that ΣP cannot be identified with TP, for the negative marker is not of category T° and TP is not an optional projection in tensed clauses.

Brody 1990 claims that Hungarian has an optional F(ocus)P, projected whenever a focussed constituent is needed. In his account, the verb raises to the head F° to assign a focus feature to the specifier as a species of Spec/head agreement. The main difficulty with this conception is that it is too narrowly construed. Negative sentences like (2c) or those in the progressive aspect like (11) do not appear to have a focussed constituent. If ΣP is Brody's FP, then the inversion-inducing behavior of *nem* is quite puzzling, for the (sentential) negative marker is not commonly assumed to be a focus formative, hence it would not fill the head of FP. If so, then Brody requires a different treatment of negation (perhaps via NegP), and the claimed parallel with tmesis is not straightforwardly captured. I conclude that ΣP is not inherently a focus projection.

ΣP satisfies the criterion for functional projections given in (F) of the previous section. [Spec, ΣP] is identifiable by virtue of its A'-character, and its head is a feature structure containing [+neg] and [+tense], selecting a VP complement. If, on the other hand, we postulate both a NegP and a TP for Hungarian, their specifiers would be effectively indistinguishable, and so by (F) we would have to conclude that a single projection is present.[14]

3. About NegP

In §2., I have argued that NegP in Hungarian is indistinguishable from a more general projection ΣP. This claim is supported both empirically and by the strong criterion (F) on functional projections. In this section, I review the major

---

[13](13b-e) remain bad even if the adverbial participle remains in the VP, thus appearing after the PV. This is because [+tense] in $\Sigma°$ is never checked against the verb's tense feature, and so the derivation crashes when [+tense] remains unrealized after SPELL-OUT (cf. Chomsky 1991).

[14]I assume that nominative Case is assigned in the VP by the verb (É. Kiss 1987).

arguments for NegP and conclude that they constitute necessary but not sufficient motivation for NegP. Finally, I argue that the ΣP hypothesis, if extended to Romance, can even account for certain data better than the NegP analysis. With regard to NegP, the central difference between Hungarian and Romance is that [Spec, ΣP] is a A'-position in the former and an A-position in the latter.

3.1. Pollock's legacy

It is reasonable to speculate that the widespread popularity of NegP is due in large part to the influence of Pollock 1989. Note, however, that Pollock himself is quite cautious, stating (p. 421, fn. 50) that 'languages could differ precisely in that some could have a NegP and others ... a purely adverbial Neg.' In the same place he even suggests that '[i]n other languages Neg might be a specifier of Tense.' Yet if languages can differ in this way, then we should ask what factor(s) might determine the presence of NegP in a given language.

(16) a. Baker's analysis

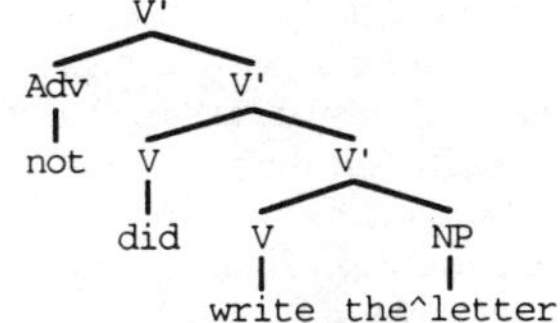

Put another way, the issue is whether there are criteria for distinguishing the more traditional 'adverbial Neg' hypothesis from the newer NegP one. The traditional view is that the negative marker of predicate negation is adjoined to and thereby has scope over the VP by surface structure (cf. Klima 1964, McCawley (1988: v. 2, chap. 17)). Both Baker 1991 and Ernst 1991 pursue versions of this traditional view, arguing that Pollock's NegP in English is both unneccessary and undesirable. Baker, for example, would advocate a D-structure like that in (16a) for *[Laura] did not write the letter*, whereas Pollock would propose the one in (16b). For Baker, certain special verbs like *do* must raise past *not*; for Pollock, *do* raises past *not* to T°, independent of whether *not* is present. As shown in (16a, b), the salient difference between the two analyses is whether *not* is a head or not.

(16) b. Pollock's analysis

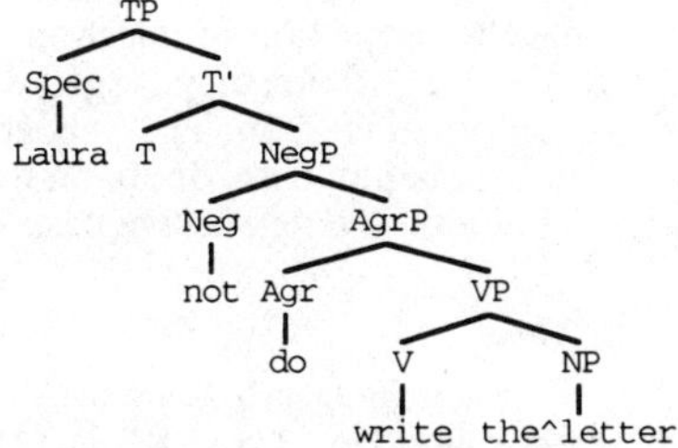

Why does Pollock postulate a NegP for English and French? The idea is that NegP is an inherent barrier, blocking the raising of Pollock's 'empty *do*' verb 'Ø' to T° in English, thereby ruling out **Laura Ø$_i$ not t$_i$ left* (cf. *Laura never left*; *Laura left*), and preventing the raising of [-finite] verbs to T° in French (cf. the contrast *Ne pas regarder la télévision .../*Ne regarder pas la télévision ...*). As the empty verb 'Ø' is not lexical, it cannot L-mark the NegP and thus cannot render it transparent for antecedent government. The blocking of movement for [-finite] verbs can be viewed as a Minimality effect of the intervening Neg head.[15]

I do not intend to engage in a detailed criticism of Pollock's analysis. Both Baker and Ernst argue against the NegP approach for English, maintaining that the data can be satisfactorily analyzed without such a phrasal projection. They find the '*not* as head' claim unconvincing. In addition, my point is simply that neither Pollock nor Chomsky 1989 (following him) has any use for the [Spec, NegP] position. Indicative of this is that it is typically left out of their representations, having no special role or property (e.g., see Pollock, p. 397). And yet if this is correct, then strong independent motivation for NegP, as would be required by (F) of §1., is lacking. The specifier of *not* is not identifiable in English.

French is less straightforward in this regard. If Pollock is correct, then *pas* is the specifier, and *ne* the head, of NegP. We might suppose, then, that *pas* is licensed by virtue of standing in this Spec/head relation to *ne*. While this idea is attractive, it is hard to verify directly, for *ne* always raises to T° by S-structure.[16] Thus, it is not obvious that *pas* actually is in [Spec, NegP] as opposed to some other position (e.g., either in another specifier position or in the head of Chomsky's (1989) NegP). Moreover, the NegP hypothesis would fare better if the other '*forclusifs*', i.e., polarity items dependent on *ne* like *rien* 'nothing', *plus* 'anymore' *personne* 'nobody', etc., behaved just like *pas*. If this were so, then it might be argued that all such items are licensed as NegP specifiers of *ne*. However, as Pollock makes clear at various points, this is not the situation. The *forclusifs* cannot have a uniform treatment even with the postulation of NegP.[17]

Whatever the merits of Pollock's particular comparative analysis of English and French, I conclude that it does not suffently justify the existence of NegP. Quite simply, insofar as the negative markers *not* and *pas* induce barrierhood behavior in certain contexts, Pollock requires that they head a NegP. If these markers were adverbial Negs, the barrierhood behavior would be unexpected. Thus, on the basis of Pollock, I state the following condition.

(17) NegP ↔ the negative marker creates a barrier for movement (in some context)

If such negative markers interfere with movement, then they must be given expression in the vocabulary that the GB theory of movement makes reference to. This vocabulary includes the notion 'maximal projection' but excludes construction-specific references (e.g., to a negative marker).

Nevertheless, accepting the left side of the condition in (17) may require a leap in faith, for what we are actually allowed to conclude is only that the negative marker is a head element of some projection. That the projection in question is really NegP is an unwarranted conclusion, given (F) of §1. To justify NegP, we should argue (as Pollock does not) that NegP is really distinct from TP. Indeed, the fact that French *ne* consistently ends up in TP at S-structure casts doubt on the validity of this distinction. Therefore, I conclude that unless a persuasive case is

---

[15]Cf. Rizzi 1990. Alternatively, [-finite] morphology is 'opaque' in French, hence the verb cannot raise to T°. For [-finite] sentences with imperative force, though, Pollock clearly invokes the head status of *ne* (p. 402).

[16]Pollock (p. 414, fn. 43): '... I am tacitly assuming that Tense will have to include a variety of different positions, one for tense itself, of course, but also others for subject and object clitics and one for negative clitics like French *ne*.'

[17]See Pollock (§6.3.) for details. It is not even the case that *ne* is always base generated as the head of NegP. For example, the polarity items *point* 'not', *plus* 'anymore', and *guère* 'hardly' are actually specifiers of a VP-initial adverbial phrase with *ne* as a head. It is not clear whether there is also a NegP present in such clauses.

made to the contrary, they are not distinct. (17) is too strong even if the negative marker is a head element.

3.2. Zanuttini on NegP

Zanuttini (1990a, 1990b) takes a fresh perspective on NegP, arguing for the following two theses:

(18) a. NegP → TP
b. In Romance, the preverbal negative marker heads a NegP, whereas the postverbal negative marker does not.

The content of (18a) is that Neg° always selects TP, whereas (18b) states that only a preverbal negative marker projects a NegP. In other words, the following deduction is said to be valid.

(19) preverbal negative marker → NegP → TP

The basic empirical contrast that Zanuttini seeks to explain is exemplified in (20) (from Zanuttini (1990a, 518)):

(20) <u>Italian</u>
a. Maria *non* ha parlato molto.
Mary NEG has talked much
'Mary hasn't talked much'

<u>Piedmontese</u>
b. Maria a l'ha *nen* parlà tant.
Mary cl has NEG talked much
'Mary hasn't talked much'

In Italian the negative marker precedes the inflected verb, while in Piedmontese it follows it. This is the surface difference to be accounted for.

The observation that Romance splits into those languages with a preverbal negative marker and into those with a postverbal one is not new (e.g., see Posner 1985, Schwegler 1988). Zanuttini's new twist on the old observation is to claim that this surface variation in the position of the negative marker correlates with the presence vs. absence of a structural NegP. Specifically, she offers three pieces of evidence in support of this thesis (cf. (18b)).

(21) a. The *postverbal* negative marker overlaps in its distribution with certain adverbs; the *preverbal* negative marker does not.
b. The *postverbal* negative marker can also occur to the left of the complementizer of a dependent clause; the *preverbal* negative marker cannot.
c. The *postverbal* negative marker does not interfere with head movement; the *preverbal* negative marker does.

(21a) is a classic syntactic distribution argument. For both Romance and Hungarian, the preverbal negative marker clearly has a distinguished distribution, a fact which any theory needs to account for. Zanuttini captures this by hypothesizing that the negative marker heads its own projection, the NegP. The postverbal negative marker, on the other hand, has a distribution which overlaps with that of certain sentential adverbs (Zanuttini (1990a, 519)), hence it is not a head but rather an adverb in some adjoined position. While this evidence does lead to the conclusion that there are two types of negative markers, it is not sufficient to establish NegP. In particular, it does not rule out the possibility that the preverbal negative marker appears in another projection, e.g., ΣP.

(21b) is also an argument based on distribution. The reasoning is that the adverbial nature of the postverbal negative marker allows it to adjoin to a number of projections, including CP. The head nature of the preverbal negative marker, in contrast, renders it particularly selective of its complement—not just any one will do. Again, while this is a real difference between the two negative markers, it falls short of requiring the postulation of NegP, for the hypothesis that the preverbal (but not the postverbal) negative marker is in a more general projection like ΣP would also account for these facts.[18]

These two pieces of distributional evidence that Zanuttini adduces suggest that she would support the following statement:

(22) NegP ↔ the negative marker has a unique distribution and selects its complement (a TP in Romance)

What is attractive about (22), when contrasted with (17), is that the conditions for NegP are now at least more firmly empirically grounded. In principle, it is straightforward to determine whether the negative marker has a unique distribution and selects for a particular type of complement. Note, however, that Zanuttini makes no use of [Spec, NegP], thereby satisfying only half of the requirement on functional projections given in (F). Indeed, it is unclear whether [Spec, NegP] has any identifiable function in the Romance languages with preverbal negative markers. Thus, when measured by these strong criteria, the projection NegP is itself not fully motivated.

What about the third piece of evidence in (21c)? Here we revisit (17), the barrierhood behavior of the negative marker. Specifically, Zanuttini claims that it is the preverbal negative marker which interferes with verb or clitic movement. Consider her examples:

(23) Piedmontese (Zanuttini (1990a, 521-522))

a. A-m lo da *nen.*
CL_{subj}-CL_{dat} CL_{acc} gives NEG
'He/she won't give that to me'

Italian

b. *Maria parla *non.*
Mary talks NEG
'Mary doesn't talk'

c. Posso parlar*ti.*
can talk-to-you
'I can talk to you'

d. *Ti*$_j$ posso parlare e_j.
to-you can talk

e. Posso *non* parlar*ti.*
can NEG talk-to-you
'I can not talk to you'

f. ??*Ti*$_j$ posso *non* parlare e_j.
to-you can NEG talk

The Piedmontese negative marker in (23a) does not prevent the verb and clitics from moving past to its left. Although Zanuttini is not explicit about the structure involved, if we accept Kayne's (1991) view on the matter, then *nen* is in [Spec, TP], and the (finite) verb and clitics move past to a higher AgrP. Since *nen* is not a head, no blocking effect for head movement is observed. (23b) shows that no such leftward movement is possible in Italian, an indication of *non*'s head status.

(23c) and (23d) are straightforward examples of non-raising and raising of the pronominal clitic, respectively. (23e, f), then, are the crucial examples.[19] (23e) is acceptable because the finite verb starts out in a higher projection and so does not have to raise past *non*. (23f), in contrast, is bad (or at least much worse) because the pronominal clitic *ti*, claimed to be a head, has moved past the head *non* and a Minimality effect results.[20]

---

[18]The issue of how constituent negation should be analyzed comes to mind, for very often the same negative marker is used in both sentence and constituent negation. I leave this matter open.

[19]The contrast is originally due to Kayne. See Pollock (p. 421, fn. 50) for similar examples.

[20]If the negative marker is inert for government, then Minimality is not relevant. Zanuttini (1990a, 522) actually characterizes the blocking effect in another way. If the negative marker, not being a lexical category, lacks the ability to L-mark its complement, then this complement phrase will act as a barrier to antecedent government by the moved clitic. In either characterization, the crucial point is that *non* is a head.

Given the contrast exhibited in (23e, f), the question is whether the NegP hypothesis is crucial to explaining it. The interference effect could also be captured by the claim that *non* is a head in ΣP, the hypothesis already suggested (see below). Thus, invocation of NegP is a possible but clearly not critical hypothesis.

More generally, we might wonder whether Zanuttini's NegP must always engage in barrier-like behavior for clitic movement. Some data from other Romance languages in Posner (1985, 179-180) cast doubt on this view.

(24) Modern Leonese (Posner's (14))
a. porque lo *non* veia
because him not he-saw
'because he didn't see him'

Old Spanish (Posner's (15i))
b. que la *non* pierda
that her not he-should-lose
'that he shouldn't lose her'

Old Portugese (Posner's (15ii))
c. que o irmão lhe *não* queria revelar
that the brother to-him not wished to reveal
'which his brother didn't want to let him know'

The clitic has moved past the preverbal negative marker in all of these examples. If the preverbal negative marker projects a NegP, then it is not obvious why clitic movement is not blocked here. Naturally, the facts in (24) may have an alternative explanation,[21] but for the present it appears that the preverbal negative marker, even if a head, does not interfere with head movement in such examples. The sporadic blocking effects of NegP surely do not suffice to establish its existence.

I conclude that Zanuttini is correct about the preverbal negative marker in Romance being a head element as opposed to an adverbial one. Nevertheless, if the justification of functional projections is taken seriously (cf. (F)), then she may also overstate her case for NegP. There is no distinction, as far as I can determine, between the properties of [Spec, TP] and that of [Spec, NegP].[22] And insofar as this is true, then we have reason to think that only a single projection is present.

3.3. ΣP in Romance

Suppose that Romance also has ΣP, differing from ΣP in Hungarian in that [Spec, ΣP] of the former is an A-position, i.e., the position in which nominative Case is checked. It follows that ΣP will be effectively obligatory in Romance, for if ΣP is not projected, then nominative Case will not be checkable and the derivation will crash. In principle, though, ΣP is optional in Romance as well, and I assume that it is not necessarily projected when nominative Case does not need to be checked, e.g., with dependent infinitives (cf. (23d)). As in Hungarian, Σ° is a complex feature structure, containing at least [+tense] and (optionally) [+neg].

[21]For example, if these 'clitics' are actually NPs, then these would not be instances of head movement.

[22]Stevens 1991 postulates a NegP in Spanish to account for a difference in scopal behavior between negative and positive quantifiers, arguing that only clauses with the former have a NegP. Although the matter clearly warrants closer scrutiny, the fact that negative quantifiers do not share certain semantic properties with positive quantifiers does not *ipso facto* justify the presence of a syntactic NegP. See Laka (1990, §3.4.3). for a discussion similar to Stevens'.

(25) Structure for (24c)

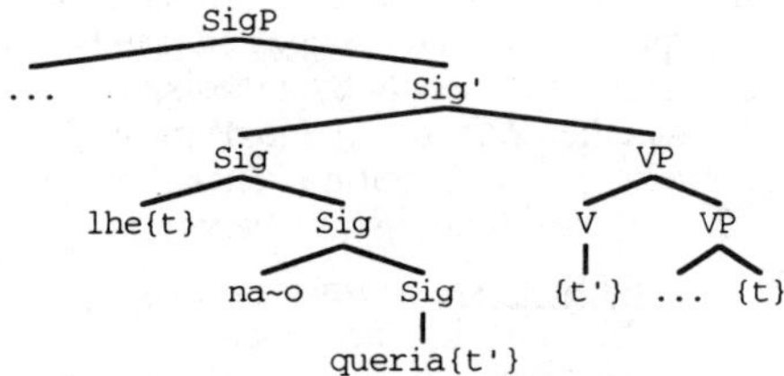

I believe that the ΣP hypothesis is more successful than Zanuttini's in analyzing examples like (24c), assuming that clitic movement is involved. The salient difference between Zanuttini's approach and mine is that where she has the two functional projections NegP and TP, I have only ΣP. Her TP cannot be L-marked by the negative marker and therefore creates a barrier for (head) movement. Thus, when the clitic moves out of TP into NegP, as in (24), the result is (incorrectly) predicted to be ungrammatical. In my approach, however, the clitic moves only out of the VP and not out of ΣP, the former being L-marked by the raised verb in Σ°. Thus, no barrier is crossed, unlike in Zanuttini's account. Neither does any potential head governor intervene, thereby respecting Relativized Minimality (Rizzi 1990). The relevant structure for (24c) is given in (25).

(26) Structure for (23f)

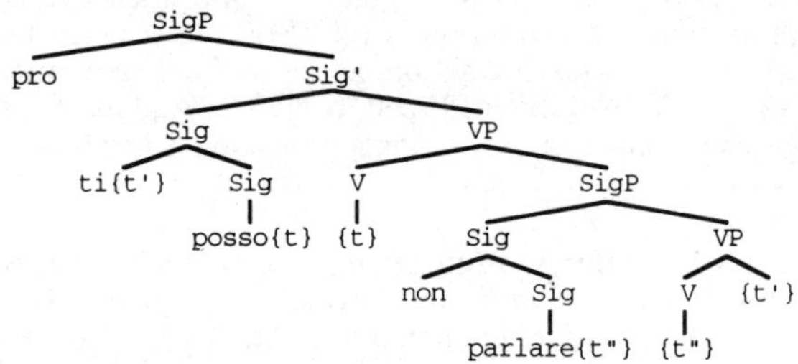

If the examples in (24) are analyzed in this way, then we may ask whether (23f) is still ruled out. Here, the negative marker appears between the auxiliary *posso* and the main verb *parlare*. For Zanuttini, both NegP and TP intervene between the two verbs, whereas only ΣP does for me. Her analysis is essentially the same: the clitic raises out of the lower TP barrier, a prohibited move. This (now correctly) predicts that long clitic movement over *non* in (23f) will be prohibited.

In my analysis, this result is also predicted, though, unlike Zanuttini, I cannot invoke barrierhood in my explanation. Consider (26), the basic structure I attribute to (23f). The lower VP is L-marked by the raised infinitive *parlare*, voiding its barrierhood. Analogously, both the lower ΣP and the higher VP are L-marked by the auxiliary *posso*, hence they are also not barriers. Therefore, the clitic *ti* does not move through a barrier on its way to the higher Σ°. Nonetheless, a Minimality violation does occur, for the lower Σ° *non parlare* is a closer potential antecedent governor than *posso* for the clitic.[23] The lower head governor thus 'intervenes' and the derivation is ruled out.

[23]Rizzi (1990, 7): 'Z is a typical potential antecedent governor for Y, Y in an X°-chain = Z is a head c-commanding Y ' Note that (25) crucially does not have an intervening head governor.

Zanuttini's analysis, while accounting for (23f), incorrectly rules out (24) precisely because she posits two functional projections where I posit one. I have argued that it is this difference, the essence of the ΣP hypothesis, that is critical.

4. Conclusion

Two central theses emerge from this paper. The first is that NegP does not constitute a functional projection in its own right. Instead, there is a composite projection ΣP which includes both negation and tense. This conclusion is warranted not only by the theoretical prerequisite in (F), but also by data from Hungarian and Romance. The second thesis is that [Spec, ΣP] can be either an A'-position (Hungarian) or an A-position (Romance). This difference accounts for the optional nature of ΣP in Hungarian and its near obligatory character in Romance.

References

Baker, C. L. 1991. The syntax of English *not*: the limits of core grammar. *Linguistic Inquiry* 22: 387-429.

Brody, Michael. 1990. Remarks on the order of elements in the Hungarian focus field. In I. Kenesei (ed.) 1990, 95-121.

Chomsky, Noam. 1986. *Barriers*. Cambridge: The MIT Press.

Chomsky, Noam. 1989. Some notes on economy of derivation and representation. *MIT Working Papers in Linguistics,* vol. 10: 43-74.

Chomsky, Noam. 1991. A minimalist program for linguistic theory. Ms., MIT.

Ernst, Thomas. 1991. The phrase structure of English negation. Ms., University of Delaware.

Kálmán, C. György, László Kálmán, Ádám Nádasdy, Gábor Prószéky. 1989. A magyar segédigék rendszere [The Hungarian auxiliary system]. *Általános Nyelvészeti Tanulmányok* 17: 49-103.

Kenesei, István, ed. 1990. *Approaches to Hungarian*, vol. 3. Szeged: JATE.

Kenesei, István. 1992. Functional categories in Finno-Ugric. Ms., University of Szeged, Hungary.

Kiefer, Ferenc. 1967. *On emphasis and word order in Hungarian*. Bloomington: Indiana University Publications.

É. Kiss, Katalin. 1987. *Configurationality in Hungarian*. Dordrecht: D. Reidel Publishing Company.

É. Kiss, Katalin. 1990. Against treating Hungarian as a V-second language. In I. Kenesei (ed.) 1990, 29-63.

Kayne, Richard S. 1991. Romance clitics, verb movement, and PRO. *Linguistic Inquiry* 22: 647-686.

Klima, Edward S. 1964. Negation in English. *The structure of language*, Jerry A. Fodor, Jerrold J. Katz (eds.), 246-323. Englewood Cliffs: Prentice-Hall, Inc.

Laka, Itziar. 1990. *Negation in syntax: on the nature of functional categories and projections*. Doctoral dissertation, MIT.

McCawley, James D. 1988. *The syntactic phenomena of English,* vol. 2. Chicago: The University of Chicago Press.

Pollock, J.-Y. 1989. Verb movement, universal grammar, and the structure of IP. *Linguistic Inquiry* 20: 365-424.

Posner, Rebecca. 1985. Post-verbal negation in Non-standard French: a historical and comparative view. *Romance Philology* 39: 170-197.

Rizzi, Luigi. 1990. *Relativized Minimality*. Cambridge: The MIT Press.

Ross, Haj. 1984. Inner islands. *Proceedings of BLS* 10: 258-265.

Schwegler, Armin. 1988. Word-order changes in predicate negation strategies in Romance languages. *Diachronica* 5: 21-58.

Speas, Margaret J. 1990. *Phrase structure in natural language*. Dordrecht: Kluwer.

Stevens, Alison. 1991. The structure of negative quantified sentences in Spanish. to appear in *Proceedings of CLS* 27, *Parasession on negation.*
Zanuttini, Raffaella. 1990a. Two types of negative markers. *Proceedings of NELS* 20: 517-530.
Zanuttini, Raffaella. 1990b. On the relevance of tense for sentential negation. Ms., presented at the Time Conference at MIT, U. of Pennsylvania/U. of Geneva.

Verb Second, Negation, and Minimality in Danish

CHARLOTTE REINHOLTZ
University of Southern California

0. Introduction

The principal issue addressed in this paper is the interaction between Verb Second (V2) and negation. The paper focusses on Danish, and the problem under investigation is illustrated in (1).

(1) a. Peter troede [at den film$_j$ havde$_i$ Maria t_i set t_j].
(Peter thought that that film had Maria seen)
"Peter thought that that film, Maria had seen."

b. *Peter troede **ikke** [at den film$_j$ havde$_i$ Maria t_i set t_j].
(Peter thought not that that film had Maria seen)
"Peter didn't think that that film, Maria had seen."

Example (1a) illustrates an environment where Danish ordinarily allows V2, namely in the complement of a non-wh-selecting verb. Example (1b) introduces the problem; when negation appears in the upstairs clause, V2 is no longer allowed to apply in the embedded clause.

The chief problem in accounting for the contrasting judgements for (1a vs b) lies with the absence of any element inside the embedded clause of (1b) which would interfere with the application of V2.

V2 involves movement of the finite verb to a position immediately before the subject. In declaratives and Wh-questions, this is accompanied by A'-movement, placing respectively a Topic- and Wh-phrase immediately before the fronted verb. This is illustrated with examples from Danish in (2).

(2) Da. a. Den film$_j$ har$_i$ [Maria aldrig t_i set t_j]
(that film has Maria never seen)
"That film, Maria has never seen."

b. Hvad$_j$ har$_i$ [Maria aldrig [$_{VP}$ t$_i$ set t$_j$]]?
(what has Maria never seen)
"What has Maria never seen?"

V2 is obligatory in matrix clauses, but only exceptionally so in embedded contexts,[1] where occurrences of V2 are restricted, though not uniformly so across Germanic V2 languages. In the case of Danish, V2 is restricted in interrogative selecting contexts and a number of operator initial contexts, as well as in negated contexts such as (1b).[2] The standard treatment links such restrictions on embedded V2 to the presence of a complementizer. The working assumption is that V2 involves finite verb movement into Comp, and therefore is blocked when Comp is lexically filled. The classical case in point comes from German, where lexical complementizers and V2 cannot cooccur.

(3) Ge. a. *Peter glaubt [$_{CP}$ dass diesen Film$_i$ hat$_j$ [$_{IP}$ Maria nie t$_i$ gesehen t$_j$]]
(Peter thinks that this film has Maria never seen)
"Peter thinks that this film, Maria has never seen."

b. Peter glaubt [$_{CP}$ dass [$_{IP}$ Maria nie diesen Film gesehen hat]]
(Peter thinks that Maria never this film seen has)
"Peter thinks that Maria has never seen this film."

c. Peter glaubt [$_{CP}$ diesen Film$_i$ hat$_j$ [$_{IP}$ Maria nie t$_i$ gesehen t$_j$]]
(Peter thinks this film has Maria never seen)
"Peter thinks this film, Maria has never seen."

The only head position before the subject is Comp. When this contains a lexical complementizer *dass* 'that', finite verb movement into Comp is blocked. Hence the ungrammaticality of (3a), but not (3b,c), where Comp contains just one element; in (3b) a complementizer, and in (3c) a fronted verb.

The reason why this line of approach will not account for the contrast in (1) is that in Danish, an initial complementizer *at* 'that' must be present, not

---

[1] E.g., in appositive clauses appearing to the right of a Topic-phrase, as in (i). Such appositives differ from subordinate clauses in disallowing topicalization, ordinarily a requirement when V2 applies in embedded context. When finite verb movement does not apply within the appositive clause, the sentence is out (see i b).

(i) Den bog mumlede Peter har jeg ikke læst.
(That book mumbled Peter have I not read)

(ii) *Den bog Peter mumlede har jeg ikke læst
(that book Peter mumbled have I not read)

[2] This point, to which we shall return in Section 2, applies to Mainland Scandinavian in general. For details regarding embedded V2 restrictions across Germanic V2 languages, see the V2 literature listed under References. The present discussion focusses on Danish.

absent, when V2 applies in embedded context.[3] Thus, the only bad sentence in (4) below is the embedded V2 clause in (4c), which has no initial complementizer.

(4) Da. a. Peter tror [at $\underline{\text{den film}}_j$ $\underline{\text{har}}_i$ Maria aldrig t_i set t_j].
(Peter thinks that that film has Maria never seen)
"Peter thinks that that film, Maria has never seen."

b. Peter tror [at Maria aldrig har set den film].
(Peter thinks that Maria never has seen that film)
"Peter thinks that Maria has never seen that film."

c. *Peter tror [$\underline{\text{den film}}_j$ $\underline{\text{har}}_i$ Maria aldrig t_i set t_j].
(Peter thinks that film has Maria never seen)
"Peter thinks that film, Maria has never seen."

This cooccurrence of [-wh] complementizers and V2 is a completely regular and grammaticalized characteristic of subordinate clauses. Provided an initial *at* is present, V2 is allowed in a wide variety of [-wh] selecting expressions, including psyche expressions *frygte* 'fear', volitionals *forlange* 'demand', and expressions of certainty *sikker* 'sure'.

(5) Pia {frygtede/forlangte/var sikker på} [at hver dag skulle de løbe to mil]
(Pia {feared/demanded/was sure on} that each day should they run two miles)
"Maria {feared/demanded/was sure} that every day they must run two miles."

We thus have a situation where lexical complementizers and V2 systematically co-occur in embedded contexts, indicating the presence of some non-lexical category between Comp and the subject position, which provides a landing site for the fronted verb and a preceding topic phrase. For present purposes, we shall identify this simply as a Functional Phrase (FP), to indicate that we are dealing with a functional, not a lexical category:[4]

(1a) Peter troede $[_{CP}$ $[_{C'}$ at $[_{FP}$ den film$_j$ $[_{F'}$havde$_i$ $[_{TP}$ Maria t_i set t_j]]]]]
(Peter thought that that film had Maria seen)
"Peter thought that that film, Maria had seen."

---

[3] [-wh] complementizers, which can usually be dropped in Danish, must be present when non-selected material appears before the subject position, e.g., 'if' or V2 material:

(i) a. Peter mente *(at) hvis det regnede ville han aldrig vinde løbet.
(Peter believed *(that) if it rained would he never win the-race)

b. Peter frygtede *(at) den sag ville de aldrig blive enige om.
(Peter feared *(that) that case would they never agree on)

[4] Commonly identified as a recursive CP, FP is a hybrid category as far as its contents (which includes a variety of non-selected complementizer material as well as V2 material) are concerned, and an A'-category as far as the behaviour of Topic phrases is concerned; these display a long range of properties traditionally associated with A'-movement: unbounded movement, sensitivity to island effects, creation of parasitic gap support, etc.

This leaves us with negation as the only key to the forced absence of V2 in (1b).

(1b) Peter troede ikke [$_{CP}$ [$_{C'}$ at [$_{FP}$<u>den film</u>$_j$ [$_{F'}$<u>havde</u>$_i$ [$_{IP}$Maria t_i set t_j]
(Peter thought not that that film had Maria seen)
"Peter didn't think that that film, Maria hadn't seen."

Being stationed in the matrix clause, *ikke* 'not' is in no position to interfere with movement inside the embedded clause below it. Moreover, negation does not in fact block crossing applications of V2. Thus (6), where negation appears inside the embedded V2 clause, is grammatical.

(6) Peter troede [$_{CP}$ [$_{C'}$at [$_{FP}$ <u>den film</u>$_j$ [$_{F'}$<u>havde</u>$_i$ [$_{IP}$ Maria ikke t_i set t_j]
(Peter thought that that film had Maria not seen)
"Peter thought that that film, Maria hadn't seen."

This completes an introduction to the problem at hand. The following two sections present evidence for an account in terms of operator selection, and a Minimality Condition on Operator Binding. Initial motivation for this approach comes from the behavior of Negative Polarity Items, to which we turn next.

1. Negative Operator Selection

When an embedded clause is introduced by a negated matrix verb, it becomes a licensing environment for Negative Polarity Items (NPIs). Thus the complement of 'thought not' is not only an environment where V2 is prohibited, but also a licensing environment for an NPI like *nogetsomhelst* 'anything at all'.

(7) Maria troede **ikke** [at Peter havde set **nogetsomhelst**].
(Maria thought not that Peter had seen anything-at-all)
"Maria didn't think that Peter had seen anything at all."

This is significant, firstly because there is a contrast between clauses which contain an NPI licensing element, and clauses introduced by an NPI licensing expression. The latter disallow V2 (see 8b), the former do not (see 8a).

(8) a. Maria troede [at derfor havde Peter **ikke** sagt **nogetsomhelst**]
(Maria thought that therefore had Peter not said anything-at-all)
"Maria thought that therefore Peter hadn't said anything at all."

b. *Maria troede **ikke** [at derfor havde Peter sagt **nogetsomhelst**]
(Maria thought not that therefore had Peter said anything-at-all)
"Maria didn't think that therefore Peter had said anything at all."

Secondly, V2 is also ruled out in the complement of other matrix expressions which create NPI licensing in a following embedded clause. Expressions which have this property include verbs and adjectives with morphological negation (see

9d-f) and certain expressions with no overt element of negation (see 9g-i), as well as verbs and adjectives accompanied by sentential negation (see 9a-c).

(9) a. *Peter mente **ikke** [at [den film havde [Maria set]]]
(Peter believed not that that film had Maria seen)
"Peter didn't believe that that film Maria had seen."

b. *Peter påstod **ikke** [at [den film havde [Maria set]]]
(Peter claimed not that that film had Maria seen)
"Peter didn't claim that that film Maria had seen."

c. *Peter var **ikke** sikker på [at [det ville [Maria gøre hver dag]]]
(Peter was not certain on that that would Maria do every day)
"Peter wasn't certain that that Maria would do every day."

d. *Det er **u**muligt [at [den film har [Maria set før]]]
(it is impossible that that film has Maria seen before)
"It is impossible that that film, Maria has seen before."

e. *Peter var **u**lykkelig over [at den bil_j $skulle_i$ [han t_i vaske t_j]]
(Peter was unhappy over that that car should he wash)
"Peter was unhappy that that car he had to wash."

f. *Peter be**nægtede** [at [den film havde [han set]]]
(Peter denied that that film had he seen)
"Peter denied that that film he had seen."

g. *Peter **fortrød** [at [den film havde [han set]]]
(Peter regretted that that film had he seen)
"Peter regretted that that film, he had seen."

h. *Peter var **overrasket** over [at [den film havde [Maria set]]]
(Peter was surprised over that that film had Maria seen)
"Peter was surprised that that film Maria had seen."

i. *Jeg **tvivler** på [at [den film har [Maria set]]]
(I doubt on that that film has Maria seen)
"I doubt that that film, Maria has seen."

The ability to create NPI licensing in a clausal complement is illustrated for 'not sure of', 'impossible', and 'surprised in (10a-c).

(10) a. Maria var **ikke** sikker på [at Peter **nogensinde** havde set filmen].
(Maria was not sure on that Peter ever had seen film-DEF)
"Maria wasn't sure that Peter ever had seen the movie."

b. Det er **u**muligt [at de har opdaget **nogetsomhelst**].
(it is impossible that they have discovered anything-at-all)
"It is impossible that they have discovered anything at all."

c. Maria var **overrasket** over [at Peter **overhovedet** var kommet].
(Maria was **surprised** over that Peter at-all was come)
"Maria was surprised that Peter had come at all."

The clausal complements of expressions like those in (9) and (10) are unusual, not only in disallowing V2, but also from an NPI licensing point of view. NPI licensing is ordinarily a clause bound phenomenon, requiring the presence of an m-commanding element such as negation inside the clause the NPI occupies.[5] For this reason, it has been proposed, amongst others by Progovaç (1988) and Laka (1990), that in cases like (10), NPI licensing involves an abstract negative operator inside the embedded clause. The working assumption is that certain expressions, notably those with an element of negation, require the presence of such an operator initially in a clausal complement:[6]

(11) Maria var **ikke** sikker på [$_{CP}$ at[**Op**] Peter **nogensinde** havde set filmen]
(Maria was not sure on that Peter ever had seen film-DEF)
"Maria wasn't sure that Peter ever had seen the film."

Before detailing the evidence for this analysis, we need to consider the conditions under which negation licenses NPIs in its own clause. In such cases, NPI material must be m-commanded by negation. This condition is met in (12a,b), where negation licenses the occurrence of an NPI in object position, and in Spec-NegP. Both of these positions are m-commanded by negation.

(12) a. Måske havde Maria [$_{NegP}$ **ikke** [$_{VP}$ spist **nogetsomhelst**]].
(maybe had Maria **not** eaten anything-at-all)
"Maybe Maria hadn't eaten anything at all."

b. Måske havde Maria [$_{NegP}$ **overhovedet ikke** [$_{VP}$ spist fisken]].
(Maybe had Maria at-all not eaten fish-DEF)
"Maybe Maria hadn't eaten the fish at all."

Outside the m-command of negation, NPI licensing is not provided. To see this, we need to look at *nogen af hundene*, which is ambiguous between 'some' and

---

[5] For instance, 'what' licenses an NPI in its own clause, but not in a following embedded one:

(i) a. Hvad spiste Peter overhovedet?
(what ate Peter at-all)
b. *Hvad mener de [at Peter overhovedet spiste]?
(what believe they that Peter at-all ate)

[6] See also Laka (1990) for evidence that Basque has overt negative complementizers.

'any of the dogs'.[7] The 'any' reading requires NPI licensing. This is available in (13a), where the phrase is in object position, but not in (13b,c), where the phrase is in subject and Topic position, outside the m-command domain of negation.

(13) a. Heldigvis havde tigeren [$_{NegP}$ **ikke** [$_{VP}$ spist **nogen af hundene**]].
(luckily had tiger-DEF not eaten **any** of dogs-DEF)
"Luckily the tiger had not eaten **any** of the dogs."

b. Heldigvis havde **nogen af hundene** **ikke** spist det giftige kød.
(luckily had **some** of dogs-DEF not eaten the poisoned meat)
"Luckily some of the dogs had not eaten the poisoned meat."

c. **Nogen af hundene**$_i$ havde tigeren **ikke** spist t_i.
(**some** of dogs-DEF had tiger-DEF not eaten)
"Some of the dogs, the tiger had not eaten."

With these facts in mind, consider now the readings available in (14).

(14) a. Maria mente **ikke** [$_{CP}$ at[**Op**] tigeren havde spist **nogen af hundene**]
(Maria believed not that tiger-DEF had eaten **any** of dogs-DEF)
"Maria didn't believe that the tiger had eaten **any** of the dogs."

b. [$_{CP}$ at[**Op**] tigeren havde spist **nogen af hundene**]$_i$ mente Maria ikke t_i.
(that tiger-DEF had eaten **any** of dogs-DEF believed Maria not)
"That the tiger had eaten **any** of the dogs, Maria din't believe."

The phrase *nogen af hundene* allows an 'any' reading, not only in (14a), where its clause appears in complement position, but also in (14b), where its clause appears in Topic position where it is not m-commanded by matrix negation. This is precisely what we expect if the 'any' reading is licensed by a negative operator appearing within the topicalized clause.

If we owe the 'any' readings in (14) to a negative operator appearing initially in the embedded clause, we should also expect the reading to disappear when the phrase *nogen af hundene* is extracted out of its clause, and hence outside the m-command domain of the negative operator. This turns out to be correct.

(15) **Nogen af hundene**$_i$ mente Maria **ikke** [$_{CP}$ at[**Op**] tigeren havde spist t_i]
(**some** of dogs-DEF believed Maria not that tiger-DEF had eaten)
"**Some** of the dogs, Maria didn't believe that the tiger had eaten."

[7] Danish NPs appearing in subject position must be definite, and those in Topic position specific. Unambiguous NPIs like 'anything at all' meet neither of these requirements.

Similarly, if we owe the 'any' readings in (14-15) to a negative operator initially in the embedded clause, we should also expect an 'any' reading to be available when *nogen af hundene* appears in subject position, this being a position the operator m-commands. This too is correct. When *nogen af hundene* appears in subject position in (16), it yields an 'any' reading.

(16) Pia mente ikke [$_{CP}$ at[**Op**] **nogen af hundene** havde spist det forgiftede kød]
(Pia believed not that **any** of dogs-DEF had eaten the poisoned meat)
"Pia didn't believe that **any** of the dogs had eaten the poisoned meat."

When the embedded clause is topicalized (see (17)), the 'any' reading is still available. This points, once again, to the presence of a negative operator initially in the clausal complement of 'believed not'.

(17) [$_{CP}$ at[**Op**] **nogen af hundene** spiste det dårlige kød]$_i$ mente Pia ikke t_i.
(that **any** of dogs-DEF ate the bad meat believed Pia not)
"That any of the dogs ate the bad meat, Pia didn't believe."

Evidence for negative operator selection also comes from the existence of expressions which create NPI licensing in a clausal complement but fail to do so in their own clause.[8]

(18) a. *Maria fortrød **nogetsomhelst**
(Maria regretted anything-at-all)
"Maria regretted anything at all."

b. Maria fortrød [$_{CP}$ at[**Op**] hun havde gjort **nogetsomhelst**].
(Maria regretted that she had done anything-at-all)
"Maria regretted that she had done anything at all."

'Anything at all' is ungrammatical in (18a), where it is m-commanded by 'regret'. This is a clear indication that 'regret' cannot itself license an NPI. The clause introduced by 'regret' in (18b) nevertheless licenses 'anything at all'. Once again, this speaks for the need to recognize negative operators, for which expressions like 'regret' select, as an independent source of NPI licensing.

This completes a presentation of the evidence for negative operator selection. The representation for an embedded clause introduced by a negative operator selecting expression is given in (19).

(19) Maria fortrød [$_{CP}$ at[Op_i] [$_{FP}$ [$_{TP}$ hun T_i havde gjort **nogetsomhelst**]]].
(Maria regretted that she had done anything-at-all)
"Maria regretted that she had done anything at all."

---

[8] This point comes from Progovaç (1988).

To satisfy selectional requirements, the operator in (19) must be in CP. That the operator is placed in the head - rather than Specifier - is taken here to be the null assumption. Unless it is visibly associated with a phrasal constituent, for instance an NP, we do not assume that negation occupies anything other than a head position.[9] When the operator coincides with an overt complementizer *at* 'that', the complementizer assumes the negative value provided by the operator. This is possible because *at* 'that' does not, properly speaking, carry any positive feature specification (negative or interrogative).[10] As a quantifier, the operator must also bind something to avoid vacuous quantification. Given that it takes logical scope over the entire clause, I will assume that the position the operator binds is the pivotal point of this domain, here identified as Tense. The relationship between Operator and Tense is one of binding; it involves c-command and coindexation, but not movement.

2. A Minimality Condition on Operator Binding

In the preceding section, we saw that negated matrix verbs and adjectives, together with a number of expressions with a morphological or semantic element of negation, select for the presence of an abstract negative operator. We also saw that V2 is ruled out in the clausal complement of just such expressions. This provides us with a difference between our initial problem sentence in (1b), and its grammatical counterpart in (1a):

(1) a. Peter troede $[_{CP}$ at $[_{FP}$ den film$_j$ havde$_i$ $[_{TP}$ Karen t_i set $t_j]]]$
(Peter thought that that film had Karen seen)
"Peter thought that that film Karen had seen."

b. *Peter troede **ikke** $[_{CP}$ at$[Op_i]$ $[_{FP}$den film$_j$ havde$_i$ $[_{TP}$Karen T_i t_i set $t_j]]]$
(Peter thought not that that film had Karen seen)
"Peter didn't think that that film Karen had seen."

I would like to propose that V2 is ruled out in the embedded clause in (1b), not because verb movement is blocked, but because the presence of a fronted verb blocks operator binding. The proposal is that we are observing the effects of a minimality condition stated in terms of 'potential antecedent', a concept developed in recent works of Aoun and Li (1990;1992), and Rizzi (1990).

(20) **Minimality Condition on Operator Binding (MCOB)**
An abstract operator must be the minimal potential antecedent c-commanding the element it binds.

---

[9] Similarly, CP material is not, as a rule, analysed as occupying Spec-CP unless it also binds a phrasal position, e.g., NP, PP, etc.

[10] The claim is that [-wh] is not a feature value, but the absence of one. Lasnik and Saito (1984) make a similar point, that [-wh] complementizers are semantically empty.

When a fronted verb appears in F, as in (1b), it is the minimal potential antecedent for Tense. The operator in Comp, therefore, fails to meet the minimality condition in (20); it is not the minimal potential antecedent for the element it binds. Once operator binding fails, the sentence is necessarily ill-formed; as a quantifier, the operator must bind something - otherwise we get vacuous quantification. If the operator is deleted, we avoid vacuous quantification. However, the embedded clause will then fail to meet selectional requirements; 'thought not' being an expression which requires the presence of an abstract operator in its complement.[11]

On this account, we make three predictions. Firstly, we expect all those expressions which select for a negative operator to disallow V2 in their clausal complements. This we have already seen to be true (see 9a-i). Secondly, we expect minimality effects to be strictly local. The examples in (21) show that this is also correct.

(21) Maria troede ikke ...
(Maria thought not ...
"Maria didn't think ...

a. *[$_{CP}$ at[Op] [$_{FP}$ den bil havde$_j$ [$_{TP}$ Bo T$_i$ indset [$_{CP}$ at hun kunne reparere]]
that that car had Bo realized that she could repair)
that that car Bo had realized that she could repair."

b. [$_{CP}$ at[Op$_i$ [$_{FP}$ [$_{TP}$ Bo T$_i$ havde indset [$_{CP}$at den bil kunne hun reparere]]]]
that Bo had realized that that car could she repair)
that Bo had realized that that car she could repair."

The negated matrix verb selects for a negative operator in its clausal complement, which is the higher of the two successively embedded clauses. Only when V2 applies in this clause, as in (21a), do we get a minimality effect: The fronted verb appears under F, between the abstract operator in Comp, and the Tense node it binds, giving rise to a violation of the MCOB. Example (21b) is well-formed, since the fronted verb in the lower of the two embedded clauses does not interfere with operator binding of the Tense node in the higher of the two clauses.

Finally, we also predict that V2 is ruled out in the complement of a negative operator selecting expression when it applies without an accompanying Topic phrase. This too turns out to be correct, as shown in (22).

[11] Notice that the operator cannot bind the Tense morphology on the fronted verb, since this is incorporated into, and minimally governed by the verb, a lexical category distinct from Tense.

(22) *Maria fortrød [$_{CP}$ at[**Op**] [$_{FP}$ havde [$_{TP}$ hun T_i t_i set den film]]].
(Maria regretted that had she seen that film)
"Maria regretted that she had seen that terrible film."

Before we continue to look at some further evidence for an MCOB, notice that verb movement into Tense does not place the verb in a position where it c-commands the Tense node, and so cannot give rise to MCOB violations. This is important because although Danish has no visible verb movement into Tense, we cannot rule out the possibility that clause medial adverbs and negation appear above Tense,[12] in which case V-to-Tense would cause no visible difference in word order.[13]

Also notice that German *glauben*, otherwise capable of introducing an embedded V2 clause, can no longer do so when negated.

(23) a. Maria glaubt [diesen Film_i hat_j Peter t_i gesehen t_j]]
(Maria thinks this film has Peter seen)
"Maria thinks that this film Peter has seen."

b. *Maria glaubt **nicht** [diesen Film_i hat_j Peter t_i gesehen t_j T]]
(Maria thinks not this film has Peter seen)
"Maria doesn't think that this film Peter has seen."

This is as predicted under the MCOB. *Nicht glauben* 'not believe' is a negative operator selecting expression, as shown in (24).[14]

(24) Maria glaubt **nicht** [$_{CP}$ dass[$\mathbf{Op}_i$] Peter **überhaubt** die Film gesehen T_i hat]
(Maria thinks not that Peter at-all the film seen has)
"Maria doesn't think that Peter has seen the film at all."

Evidence for the proposed MCOB also comes from the behavior of conditionals. It is commonly assumed, for instance in Lycan (1984), that

---

[12] See Platzack (1986) for a proposal to this effect.

[13] Assuming that the verb appears under Tense in the Spanish inversion structures below, we then correctly predict this word order to be productive in matrix contexts, and in the complement of a negated matrix verb:

(i) a. Creo que ha salido Juan.
(I-think that has left John)
b. No creo que ha salido Juan.
(NEG I-think that has left John)

[14] Notice that this prediction holds regardless of whether the negative operator is in Comp, as I have argued, or in Spec-CP. In the latter case, the application of V2 will give rise to an MCOB violation. The same point applies to the Danish cases discussed above. In the former case, finite verb movement into Comp would be blocked by the presence of the negative operator in Comp.

conditional clauses contain an initial operator which quantifies over the clause.[15] Like negative operators, conditional operators also license NPIs. On the analysis I am assuming, a conditional clause would thus have the representation in (25), where *hvis* 'if', marks the presence of a conditional operator in Comp, and Tense, the pivotal point of the clause, is bound by this operator.

(25) a. [$_{CP}$ Hvis[Op$_i$] [$_{FP}$ [$_{TP}$ Peter T$_i$ (**nogensinde**) har læst den bog]]], ...[16]
(if Peter ever has read that book)
"If Peter has (ever) read that book, ..."

If conditional clauses have the representation in (25), we should expect V2 to be ruled out in this environment: A fronted verb under F would function as the minimal potential antecedent for Tense, and thus give rise to an MCOB violation.[17] Example (26a) shows that V2 is indeed ungrammatical in this environment, and (26b) that the effect is strictly localized. This is as predicted under the MCOB.

(26) a. *[$_{CP}$ Hvis[Op$_i$] [$_{FP}$ den bog <u>har</u>$_j$ [$_{TP}$ Peter T$_i$ t$_j$ læst]]]
(if that book has Peter read)
"If that book Peter has read, ..."

b. [$_{CP}$ Hvis[Op$_i$] [$_{FP}$[$_{TP}$ Pia T$_i$ siger [$_{CP}$at [$_{FP}$ den bog <u>har</u>$_j$ [$_{TP}$ hun t$_j$ læst]]]]]]
(if Pia says that that book has she read)
"If Pia says that that book she has read, ..."

Conditionals are also allowed in embedded contexts, and in these cases, the conditional marker *hvis* 'if' is not placed in Comp; rather it appears under the functional category F below Comp, which contains a complementizer *at* 'that'.

(27) Det er muligt [$_{CP}$ at [$_{FP}$ hvis[Op$_i$] [$_{TP}$ Pia T$_i$ har læst bogen]]], ...
(it is possible that if Pia has read book-DEF)
"It is possible that if Pia has read the book, ..."

This provides us with an independent scenario for testing the assumption that conditional mood involves binding of Tense by a conditional operator in Comp.

---

[15] Note I am using the term operator not in the sense of overt A'-movement by a Topic or Wh-phrase, but in the sense of an abstract operator element.

[16] The bracketed NPI 'ever' is included to illustrate that this is an NPI licensing environment.

[17] V1 word order, sometimes used for conditionals in older Danish, is also ruled out in this context (see (ii). The example in (i) is taken from Lollesgaard (1920,93).

(i) Dræpær han man ... tha bøtæ ...
(kills he man ... then pays ...)

(ii) *Hvis dræber han nogen ... så bøder ...
(if kills he somebody ... then pays ...)

If this is the case, we should expect an MCOB violation to arise in (28) below, and this turns out to be correct.

(28) *Det er umuligt [$_{CP}$ at[Op$_i$] [$_{FP}$ hvis[Op$_j$] [$_{TP}$ Pia T$_{j/*i}$ har læst bogen]]]
(it is impossible that if Pia has read book-DEF)
"It is impossible that if Pia had read the book, ..."

In (28), 'impossible' selects for a negative operator in its clausal complement. The presence of 'if' under F signals the presence of a conditional operator which also binds Tense. As a result, we get an MCOB violation; the negative operator in Comp is not the minimal potential A'-antecedent for Tense, and the sentence becomes ill-formed. The sentence in (29) below shows that the effect is strictly localized, as predicted under the MCOB: When 'if' appears in the lower of two embedded clauses, and the abstract negative operator appears in the higher of the two embedded clauses, the resulting sentence is fine.

(29) Det er umuligt [$_{CP}$ at[Op$_i$] [$_{FP}$ [$_{TP}$ Maria T$_i$ har sagt
(it is impossible that Maria has said
"It is impossible that Maria has said

[$_{CP}$ at [$_{FP}$ hvis[Op$_j$] [$_{TP}$ Peter T$_j$ læste bogen]]]]]] ....
that if Peter read book-DEF) ....
that if Peter read the book, ..."

In the preceding, we have seen that V2 is ungrammatical in two operator initial environments, and that conditional operators are themselves capable of inducing a minimality effect. We have also seen that these effects are strictly localized. These are precisely the properties we would expect under the proposed MCOB. The remainder of this section discusses the possibility of extending the MCOB to account for the forced absence of V2 in embedded interrogatives.

Bresnan (1972) notes that the interpretation of of embedded wh-phrases differs from that of matrix wh-phrases in being determined by the content of the upstairs clause, often yielding readings unlike those afforded by matrix interrogatives; e.g., asking for permission, or instructions, or simply imposing on the reading of an embedded clause an interrogative or dubitative aspect inherent in the verb or adjective introducing it. This would be the case of e.g., 'ask', whose behavior resembles that of 'regret' in several respects. 'Ask' does not provide an interrogative reading in its own clause, but selects for a wh-marked clausal complement. Similarly, 'ask' does license an NPI in its own clause, while its clausal complement is an NPI licensing environment.

(30) a. *Peter havde **overhovedet** spurgt [om Maria kunne svømme]
(Peter had at-all asked if Maria could swim)
"Peter had asked at all if Maria could swim."

b. Peter havde spurgt [om Maria **overhovedet** kunne svømme]
(Peter had asked if Maria at-all could swim)
"Peter had asked if Maria could swim at all."

As Bresnan observes, the complement of 'ask' is more accurately characterized as a semantically open complement. This suggests the presence of an operator which quantifies over the clause with existential force, yielding this "open" reading.

If wh-selection involves selection for such an operator, the MCOB can be extended straightforwardly to account for the forced absence of V2 in (31a,b).

(31) a. *Maria spurgte [$_{CP}$ om[**Op**] [$_{FP}$ den film$_j$ havde$_i$ [$_{TP}$ Peter t_i set t_j]]]
(Maria asked if that film had Peter seen)
"Maria asked if that film Peter had seen."

b. *Maria spurgte [$_{CP}$ hvad$_j$ [**Op**] [$_{FP}$ havde$_i$ [$_{TP}$ Peter T t_i set t_j]]]
(Maria knew what had Peter seen)
"Maria didn't know what had Peter seen?"

The interrogative matrix verb in (31a,b) selects for the presence of an interrogative operator initially in a clausal complement. As a quantifier, the interrogative operator must bind something to avoid vacuous quantification. Given that it takes scope over the entire embedded clause, I will assume the position the operator binds is the pivotal point of the clause, here identified as Tense. As in previous cases, binding involves c-command and coindexation, but not movement. The operator is in Comp, either overtly as in (31a), where its presence is marked by *om* 'if', or covertly as in (31b), where Spec-CP contains a Wh-phrase. As in the case of negative and conditional operators, an MCOB violation occurs when a fronted verb appears under F between an abstract interrogative operator in Comp and the Tense node it binds; not being the minimal potential antecedent for Tense, the abstract operator cannot properly bind Tense, and we get vacuous quantification, or in case the abstract operator is subsequently deleted, a failure to satisfy selectional requirement. Hence the ungrammaticality of (31a,b) above.[18]

As predicted under the MCOB, the effect is strictly local. Thus (32) below is perfectly well-formed; V2 in the lowest embedded clause will not interfere with operator binding of the Tense node in the higher of the two embedded clauses.

[18] Notice that on this account we correctly predict that English V-to-Tense and subject-auxiliary inversion will behave differently. V-to-Tense cannot give rise to MCOB violations, and so applies symmetrically in matrix and embedded questions. Subject-auxiliary inversion, on the other hand, places the finite verb above Tense, and so is asymmetrical, applying in matrix clauses, but not embedded interrogatives.

(32) Maria spurgte $[_{CP}$ om[**Op**$_i$] Peter T_i vidste
(Maria asked if Peter knew
"Maria asked if Peter knew

$[_{CP}$ at $[_{FP}$ den film$_k$ havde$_j$ $[_{TP}$ byrådet censureret]]]]
that that film had town-council-DEF censored)
that that film the town council had censored."

3. Conclusion

The object of this paper has been to provide a principled account of the forced absence of V2 in embedded clauses introduced by a negated matrix verb. The principal virtue of this restriction is that it is inexplicable in terms of a lack of landing sites. This forces us to recognize that matrix material can and will play a role in determining whether V2 can apply in embedded context. In the preceding, I have presented evidence to show that this phenomenon results from the combined effects of operator selection and a Minimality Condition on Operator Binding. We have seen that the MCOB accounts for the initial problem at hand, as well as for the forced absence of V2 in several other operator initial environments. In addition, we have seen that the MCOB accounts for the localized nature of these minimality effects. Moreover, we have seen that operators are themselves capable of inducing a minimality effect.

REFERENCES

Aoun,J. and A.Li. 1989. Scope and Constituency. *Linguistic Inquiry* **20.2**

den Besten, H. 1977. On the Interaction of Root Transformations and Lexical Deletive Rules. *Gröninger Arbeiten zur Germanistischen Linguistik*, Vol.**1-3**.

Bresnan, J. 1972. *Theory of Complementation in English Syntax*. Doctoral Dissertation, MIT. Cambridge, Massachussetts.

Haider, H. 1985. V-Second in German. *Verb Second Phenomena in Germanic Languages*. Haider, H. & M. Prinzhorn (eds.), Foris, Dordrecht.

Hellan, L. and K. Koch Christensen (eds). *Topics in Scandinavian Syntax*. Reidel, 1986.

Holmberg, A. 1986. *Word Order and Syntactic Features in the Scandinavian Languages and English*. Doctoral Dissertation, University of Stockholm. Stockholm, Sweden.

Holmberg and Platzack 1988. On the Role of Inflection in Scandinavian Syntax. *Working Papers in Scandinavian Syntax* **42**. Lund, Sweden.

Hyams, N. 1991. *Clausal Structure in Early Grammars: A Crosslinguistic Perspective*. ms. UCLA. Los Angeles, California.

Kempchinsky, P.M. 1986. Romance Subjunctive Clauses and Logical Form. Doctoral Dissertation, UCLA. Los Angeles, California.

Koopman, H. 1984. *The Syntax of Verbs*. Foris, Dordrecht.

Laka, M.I. 1990. Negation in Syntax: On the nature of functional categories and projections. Doctoral Dissertation, MIT. Cambridge, Massachussetts.

Lasnik, H. & M.Saito. 1984. On the Nature of proper Government. *Linguistic Inquiry* **15.2**.

Lollesgaard, J. 1920. *Syntaktiske Studier over det ældste danske Skriftsprog*. Nykøbing F Stiftstidendes Bogtrykkeri, Nykøbing, Denmark.

Lycan, W.G. 1984. A Syntactically Motivated Theory of Conditionals. *Midwest Studies in Philosophy* IX.

Platzack, C. 1985. The Position of the Finite Verb in Swedish. Haider & Prinzhorn op. cit.

Platzack, C. 1986. COMP, INFL, and Germanic Word Order. *Topics in Scandinavian Syntax*, op. cit.

Platzack, C. & A. Holmberg. 1989. The Role of AGR and Finiteness. *Working Papers in Scandinavian Syntax* **43**, pp.51-76.

Progovaç, L. 1988. A Binding Approach to Polarity Sensitivity. Doctoral Dissertation, USC. Los Angeles, California.

Reinholtz, C. 1990. Verb-Second in Mainland Scandinavian: A Reanalysis. *Proceedings of the 9th West Coast Conference on Formal Linguistics*. Stanford Linguistics Association. Stanford, California.

Rizzi, L. 1990. *Relativized Minimality*. Linguistic Inquiry Monograph Sixteen, MIT Press, Cambridge, Massachussetts.

Sanchez, L. 1987. Topicos sobre el Subjuntivo. Dissertation, PUCP. Lima, Peru.

Schwartz, B. and S. Vikner 1989. All Verb Second Clauses are CPs. *Working Papers in Scandinavian Linguistics* **46**. University of Lund. Lund, Sweden.

Taraldsen, K.T. 1985. On Verb Second and the Functional Content of Syntactic Categories. Haider and Prinzhorn op. cit.

Thrainsson, H. 1985. V1, V2, V3 in Icelandic. Haider & Prinzhorn op. cit.

Thrainsson, H. 1986. On Auxiliaries, AUX, and VPs in Icelandic. Hellan and Koch Christensen op. cit.

The Acquisition of Referentially Dependent Items and Their Development

TETSUYA SANO
University of California, Los Angeles

In this paper, I propose a theory of the acquisition of referentially dependent items. By 'referentially dependent item' (RD item), I mean a lexical item which is less referential than a name, that is, a lexical item which may be bound by a name (e.g. *he*[1] and *himself*). (This is different from Reinhart and Reuland (1991) who treat pronominals as referentially independent).

The task for children is to determine which item obeys which Binding Condition. For example, the child must learn that *himself* obeys Binding Condition A. Evidently, this information is not innately given. Then, the question to be answered is (1), and there are two difficulties, as stated in (2).

(1) How can a child come to know which lexical item α obeys which Binding Condition(s)?

(2) PROBLEM 1: There is no negative evidence.
PROBLEM 2: Some input data are ambiguous.

First, children have no access to negative evidence. For instance, there is essentially no way for children to learn that '*John$_i$ hit him$_i$*' is impossible. Second, some input data are ambiguous because the Domain in which Binding Conditions apply may vary. This is exemplified by the pair in (3).

(3) a. [John$_i$ thinks [that Mary hates him$_i$]]
b. [John$_i$-ga [Mary-ga zibun$_i$-o kiraida to] omotteiru]
NOM NOM self ACC hate that thinking

(3b) is a Japanese equivalent of (3a). Although they are structurally identical as

* The earlier version of this paper was presented at UC Irvine in spring, 1991. For comments and discussion on this version, I am grateful to Michael Dukes, Nina Hyams, Dominique Sportiche, Ed Stabler, Tim Stowell, Takeru Suzuki, Anna Szabolcsi, Ken Wexler, among others. None of them should be assumed to be in full agreement with my conclusions, and all the remaining errors are mine. I thank Jonathan Mead for editorial help.

[1] In referring to pronominal expressions, I will use male-gender forms when forms of different genders are possible. This is just for expository reasons.

far as relevant matters are concerned, *him* obeys Binding Condition B and *zibun* 'self' obeys Binding Condition A. Thus, it is impossible for children to acquire *him* or *zibun* to be pronominal or anaphor, respectively, on the basis of data in (3) alone. Whatever the mechanism of acquisition, either Japanese children or English children will wrongly identify the item, if they rely on (3) alone. In this way, ambiguous data as in (3) are problematic for acquisition of RD items.

In this paper, I will address the question in (1) and attempt to solve the problems in (2). I will leave aside the question of how to set the Binding Domains, which are to be determined for each RD item after lexical acquisition. (It may take place either by Parameter setting, as in Wexler and Manzini 1987, etc. or by LF head movement, as in Chomsky 1986, etc.). I will argue that the acquisition of RD items proceeds by elimination, so that it dispenses with negative evidence. Also, I will restrict the class of 'triggering data', the data with which children acquire the relevant items, so that ambiguous data such as (3) will be excluded from the class of triggers. The acquisition theory I propose has some consequences for grammatical development, as we will see.

1. Principles of UG

In this section, I introduce my assumptions about the Principles of UG which are related to referential dependencies.

1.1. Binding Conditions

Binding Conditions A and B are defined as in (4).

(4) Binding Conditions
(A) An anaphor must be bound in its Domain.
(B) A pronominal must be free in its Domain.

(5) β is a CFC for α if β is a maximal projection containing both a subject and a lexical category governing α (cf. Chomsky 1986,169)

Although I assume that the notion Domain is defined in terms of CFC (cf. (5)), I will not attempt to formulate its precise definition, as I do not distinguish long-distance binding of an anaphor from local binding. Both locally-bound anaphors and long-distance anaphors are 'anaphors' in the sense that they must be bound in their Domain. Consequently, my assumptions on Binding Conditions are very simple.

I assume that Condition C (cf. Chomsky 1981) does not belong to UG. As Lasnik (1986) points out, there are languages which allow a name to be bound by the same name, for instance, Thai, Vietnamese, and Japanese. See (6) for Thai examples.

(6) a. cɔɔn_i chɔɔp cɔɔn_i
John likes John
b. cɔɔn_i khít wâa cɔɔn_i chàlaàt
John thinks that John is-smart (from Lasnik 1986)

Instead of Condition C, I adopt Condition D in (7), which allows (6) but not (8).[2]

(7) Condition D: (cf. Lasnik 1986, Huang 1988)
A less referential expression may not bind a more referential one.

(8) a. *He_i hit $John_i$.
b. *He_i thinks that Mary likes $John_i$.

1.2. Coreference Condition

So far, I have discussed only binding, but in some cases, coreference is said to be possible even when two NPs have different indices (cf. Reinhart 1983, etc.).

(9) a. Everyone has finally realized that Oscar is incompetent. Even he_i has realized that $Oscar_j$ is incompetent. (Evans 1980)
b. That must be John. At least, he_i looks like him_j. (Chien and Wexler 1990)

Coindexing between *he* and *Oscar* in (9a) and between *he* and *him* in (9b) is blocked by the Binding Conditions. However, the two NP's may corefer in the specified contexts in (9).

When there is no special context, such coreference with contraindexing is impossible as in (10).

(10) a. *He_i has realized that $Oscar_j$ is incompetent.
b. *He_i looks like him_j.

It is not easy to precisely define a condition which allows (9) and disallows (10). To simplify the discussion, I informally state it as the Coreference Condition in (11) and assume that any condition which deals with coreference is virtually equivalent to it.

(11) Coreference Condition (Informal definition):
When possible, use coindexing to corefer (except for some special cases like (9)).

1.3. Strong Continuity

There are various positions on the status of Grammatical Principles in language development. As Klein (1982), Hyams (1983), Pinker (1984), and others argue, the most parsimonious assumption is that principles of grammar are operative

---

[2]It will be necessary to assume Condition D instead of Condition C in explaining a developmental fact in language acquisition (cf. section 5). However, as Tim Stowell (p.c.) has pointed out to me, we do seem to need Condition C to rule out English equivalents of (6). There are several ways I can think of to escape this conflict. Here I mention only one of them, namely, Condition D holds universally and Condition C is parametrized: English has it, but Thai does not. To explain the developmental facts (cf. section 5.), I must assume that English children start out with Condition D only, and somehow later obtain Condition C. As a matter of fact, Radford (1990) has data which suggests that English children do not obey Condition C during early stages of acquisition.

throughout development (i.e., Continuity). Here I argue for a strong version of Continuity as in (12).

(12) Strong Continuity: Children know and obey all innate conditions in any component of grammar (including pragmatics) throughout development.

Some studies in language acquisition attempt to loosen the Continuity Assumption in various ways, in order to explain developmental delays. This is what I attempt to avoid, in order to maintain the most parsimonious position as long as it is tenable. For this matter, it seems that even though some conditions (e.g., the Coreference Condition) are pragmatic, it should not make any difference. To the extent that some condition is innate, the most parsimonious assumption is that it holds throughout the course of development. I will later show that it is possible to explain the reported developmental delays related to binding and coreference while maintaining Strong Continuity.

As for the Binding Conditions, I take the position that children both know and obey all of them, namely Condition A, B, and D from the beginning. This is different from Grimshaw and Rosen (1990), who argue that children know but fail to obey Condition B until the age of six.

Also, I assert that the Coreference Condition is active throughout development, unlike Chien and Wexler (1990) who claim that children lack it until about six years of age. Their claim raises two problems. First, consider the very early stage of development in which children do not yet know that *himself* is an anaphor. If they lack the Coreference Condition, they can assign either choice of indices in (14) to (13). In other words, without the Coreference Condition, *John* and *himself* can corefer in both representations in (14).

(13) John is touching himself. (situation: John is touching his own body.)

(14) a. John_i is touching himself_i.
b. John_i is touching himself_j.

But then, they cannot identify *himself* as an anaphor on the basis of (13), as it can be free in the representation (14b).[3] Also, if (14b) is possible for (13), it

---

[3]Ken Wexler (p.c.) suggested a way out of this problem: children rely on an example like (i) alone in identifying *himself* as an anaphor, and exclude (13) from triggering data because of its ambiguity.

(i) No one_i is touching himself_i.

According to this idea, something which can never be bound by a quantifier cannot be identified as an anaphor or as a pronominal, as there is no trigger for the identification. Thus, it is predicted that such an item should have the same referentiality as a name and behave like a name in binding. Japanese third person 'pronoun' *kare* is such an item; it cannot be bound by a quantifier (cf. (32)). Contrary to what the idea above predicts, it is different from a name in referentiality. While *kare* cannot bind a name (hence the ungrammaticality of (ii)), a name can bind the same name in Japanese (hence the grammaticality of (iii)), which has Condition D but not Condition C.

(ii) *Kare_i-ga [Taro_i-ga kasikoi to] omotteiru.
he NOM NOM smart that thinking

wrongly predicts that children at an early stage would allow *himself* to be unbound, as in '**Himself left*'.[4] Therefore, I claim that children from the beginning know and obey the Coreference Condition, to make it impossible for children to have (14b) for (13).

2. Inventory of Referentially Dependent Items

In this section, I define the feature combinations of RD items, as in (15). I assume three features [A], [B], and [R] to make the necessary distinctions (cf. Lasnik 1986). The features [A] and [B] represent whether an item obeys Condition A and B, respectively. The feature [R] indicates whether an item is as referential as a name or not. The inventory of feature combinations is given in (15), which will be revised later without changing the basic properties.

(15) Inventory of feature combinations (1st version)

[0A, 0B, +R]: name, English epithet (initial values)
[-A, +B, -R]: pronominal, Thai epithet
[+A, -B, -R]: anaphor

unlearnable combination: (*)[+A, +B, -R]
impossible combination: *[-A, -B, -R] (cf. (16))

A name is [0A, 0B, +R]. Two things should be noted here. First, I assume this combination to be the initial setting for all nouns. Second, I assume that the values for [A] and [B] are underspecified in this case.[5]

According to the acquisition theory to be presented, the combination [+A, +B, -R] is not learnable. This might be a correct prediction if there is no lexical counterpart of PRO, but I leave it as an open question.

I exclude [-A, -B, -R] from the inventory of possible combinations by

---

(iii) Taro$_i$-ga [Taro$_i$-ga kasikoi to] omotteiru.
NOM NOM smart that thinking

In order to derive this fact, it is necessary that children identify *kare* in (iv) as bound and thus as referentially dependent, even though the antecedent is not a quantifier. Therefore, the suggested wayout cannot be compatible with my proposal as a whole.

(iv) Taro$_i$-ga [kare$_i$-ga kasikoi to] omotteiru.
NOM he NOM smart that thinking
'Taro thinks that he is smart'

[4]McDaniel et al. (1990) report that there are children who accept sentences like '*Himself left*' in judgement tasks. As they argue, they could be treating the unbound *himself* as emphatic pronouns in which case the sentence is probably irrelevant to Condition A. Moreover, these children are older than 4, and they demonstrate in other tasks that they already know that *himself* obeys Condition A.

[5]One might wonder if the initial setting could alternatively be [-A, -B, +R] (I thank Nina Hyams for bringing this to my attention). With [-A, -B, +R] as the initial combination, when the child acquires *himself*, he would have to reconfirm [-B] by receiving positive evidence, in order to arrive at [+A] by elimination (cf. section 4 for the process). (The same kind of reconfirmation is necessary for the acquisition of *he*, too). Thus, even without underspecification, [-B] and [reconfirmed -B] should be distinguished, to make the acquisition feasible. Therefore, the alternative would be a notational variant of the underspecified initial setting. So as to capture the intuition that the features [A] and [B] are irrelevant for [+R] items, I have proposed that their values are underspecified at first.

proposing a Condition on Referentially Dependent Items (CRDI) (16).

(16) Condition on Referentially Dependent Items (CRDI)
An item which is less referential than a name, namely an item with the feature [-R], must obey either Condition A or Condition B.

The facts of Thai epithets support CRDI (16). In Thai, epithets can be bound non-locally, as in (17), hence they are [-R] and they are subject to Condition B, as in (18).

(17) cɔɔn$_i$ khít wâa ?aybâa$_i$ chàlaàt.
John thinks that the nut is-smart

(18) *cɔɔn$_i$ chɔ̂ɔp ?âybâa$_i$.
John likes the nut (from Lasnik 1986)

3. Theory of Acquisition

Here I introduce my assumptions about the mechanisms for the acquisition of RD items. Children should be able to accomplish the acquisition without running into the two problems in (2). My strategy to escape PROBLEM 2 in (2) is to restrict the set of triggering data so that those ambiguous data such as (3) will be excluded. The first step is to assume (19).

(19) Indeterminacy Hypothesis
Given only non-triggering data, a child does not make any decision as to the form of his grammar.

Then, I have to specify what the triggering data are for the acquisition of RD items. This is given in (20).

(20) Triggers (for the acquisition of RD items)
A sentence S is a trigger for the acquisition of a feature [-X] for a lexical item α in S iff the derivation of S violates Principle(s) of UG when α is taken as [+X].

The definition (20) excludes ambiguous data from the trigger (See Roeper and Weissenborn 1990 and Wu 1992 for similar ideas about Parameter setting). Moreover, together with the CRDI (16), definition (20) solves the no-negative-evidence problem, PROBLEM 1 in (2). In the next section, I will explain how this solution works using concrete examples.

4. The Acquisition of RD Items by Elimination

4.1. Anaphors

First, let's consider anaphors such as *himself* and *zibun*. They are [+A, -B, -R]. Their feature-values are acquired by just one type of example, such as (21) or (22).

(21) [$_{IP}$ John$_i$ [$_{VP}$ hit himself$_i$]]

(22) [$_{IP}$ John$_i$-ga [$_{VP}$ zibun$_i$-o nagutta]]
NOM self ACC hit
'John hit himself'

(23) The acquisition of *himself*

	[+R]	->	([-R])	->	([-B, -R])	->	[+A, -B, -R]
		⇑		⇑		⇑	
Trigger:		(21)		(21)			
Conditions:		D+inference		B		CRDI(16)	

Take *himself*, for example. At first, children assume the initial value [+R] for *himself*. (Features with [0] values are omitted in (23) and hereafter to save space). The switch to [-R] is done by Condition D plus a little inference. Since in (21) *John* and *himself* are coindexed and yet they are different words, one of them must be referentially dependent on the other. As *himself* is bound by *John*, Condition D would be violated if *John* were less referential than *himself*. Thus, children learn that *himself* is less referential than a name, and switch it to [-R].

Also, example (21) tells children that *himself* is [-B], because it is bound by *John* and there can be no CFC which includes *himself* and excludes *John*, as a CFC must include a subject. (This point remains even if we adopt the VP-internal subject hypothesis). In other words, (21) certainly violates Condition B if *himself* were [+B], and so it is a trigger for [-B], as it satisfies the definition of triggering data in (20).

Now that the child has got [-B, -R] for *himself*, he is forced to assign [+] to the feature [A] to satisfy the CRDI (16). Thus, without ambiguous data such as (3), and without negative evidence, children can correctly set the feature values for *himself* at [+A, -B, -R]. The acquisition of *zibun* works in exactly the same way. (I assume that the difference as to locality can be acquired somehow, after the lexical acquisition).

4.2. Pronominals

The acquisition of pronominals is more complicated than the acquisition of anaphors, because pronominals require two separate kinds of input sentences, for instance, (24) and (25). Below, I explain what this means exactly, using *he* as an example.

(24) He is tall.

(25) John$_i$ thinks that he$_i$ is smart.

(26) The acquisition of *he*

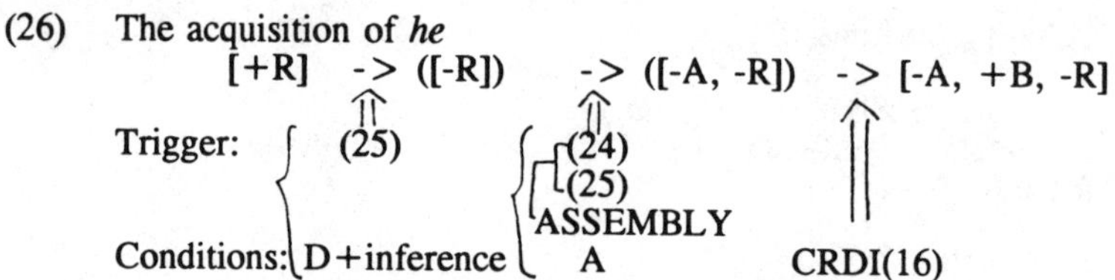

Unlike the case of *himself*, the switch to [-R] for *he* is not easy; there is no single input which guides children to the correct conclusion. At first, children take the initial value [+R] for *he*.

In order to acquire [-R] for *he*, children need examples in which *he* is bound, namely (25) or (27).

(25) $John_i$ thinks that he_i is smart.

(27) $John_i$ has his_i book.

Note that [0A, 0B, -R] is not a legitimate combination, as it violates Strong Continuity (if it applies to lexicon, too). Thus, children cannot take it as an intermediate combination after receiving (25) alone. Moreover, given (25) alone, children cannot tell whether *he* is [-A] or [-B], as its Binding Domain cannot be set until *he* is acquired (cf. Lexical Parametrization Hypothesis in Wexler and Manzini 1987).

Turning to the feature [A], recall that its value is initially underspecified. (24) or (28) could in principle tell children that *he* is [-A], but not necessarily, for they do not violate any UG conditions with the initial setting [+R] (cf. Finer 1987).

(24) He is tall.

(28) That is $John_i$. Do you know him_i?

That is, unless children know that *he* is [-R] beforehand, (24) or (28) cannot trigger any change, and *he* remains as [+R]. Crucially, [0A, 0B, -R] is illegitimate, as mentioned above. Therefore, it is impossible for children to acquire *he* in a few separate steps as follows: first switch from [+R] to [-R] on hearing (25), change it to [-A, -R] on hearing (24), and arrive at [-A, +B, -R] by CRDI.

What children have to do to identify *he* to be a pronominal is ASSEMBLE (24) with (25). ASSEMBLY is defined in (29).

(29) ASSEMBLY: compute derivations for a sentence inconjunction with another sentence

Of course, this never means that children must memorize sentences. What they do in ASSEMBLING (24) with (25) is check the referential dependency of *he* in (24) while knowing that it may be bound, as in (25). When this is done, *he* must be [-R] because of (25), and *he* must be [-A] because of (24). (24) would violate Condition A with *he* as [-R, +A], since there can be no Binding Domain larger than the matrix CP (cf. Huang 1982, 345). Therefore, children switch the initial [+R] to [-A, -R], and, to satisfy CRDI (16), they conclude that *he* is [+B].[6]

5. Development

The theory of acquisition which has been presented has direct consequences for real-time language development. With respect to binding and coreference, there are two major developmental facts to be accounted for. First, children allow (30) even at the age of six (cf. Otsu 1981, Jackubowicz 1984, Chien and Wexler 1990). Second, children successfully reject (31) earlier than (30), between the ages of 5 and 6 (cf. Chien and Wexler 1990, etc.).

(30) (*)John is touching him. (situation: John is touching himself)

(31) *Every bear is touching him. (situation: Every bear is touching himself)

Previous studies explain these results by arguing either that children do not have knowledge of Condition B or the Coreference Condition, or that they know them but are unable to use them for some reason (cf. Chien and Wexler 1990, Grimshaw and Rosen 1990).[7] These proposals contradict my assumption of Strong Continuity. I will posit an alternative account and supportive evidence for it.

5.1. Delay of Condition B effects

Let's consider the delay of (30) first. Grimshaw and Rosen (1990) argue that the delay occurs because children do not obey Condition B at first. Chien and Wexler (1990) attribute the delay to the lack of Coreference Condition. They argue that it is with the indexing in (30'b), but not with the one in (30'a), that young children allow coreference between *John* and *him* in (30). According to their assumptions, children lack the Coreference Condition before age 6, thus (30'b) is grammatical for them. Both of these accounts argue against Strong Continuity.

---

[6]Adopting LF head movement of long-distance bound anaphors (cf. Chomsky 1986), there is an alternative account of the acquisition. If they know that *him* does not undergo LF head movement. Children could acquire *him* as a pronominal with one type of example such as (i).

(i) John$_i$ thinks that Mary likes him$_i$.

The proposal hinges on the assumption that children are able to differentiate what undergoes LF head movement from what does not, which is not obvious. Although it has been suggested that the difference follows from morphological complexity, lack of features, etc., no such approach seems to work without exceptions. Also, Hestvik (1990a, b) argues for LF movement of pronouns. Thus, the proposal above depends on something indefinite. In contrast, I do not think that there are exceptions to the claim that what appears in the context of (21) is an anaphor and what appears in the context of both (24) and (25) is a pronominal. On these grounds, I prefer to maintain the proposal in the text. (I thank Ed Stabler for discussion on this)

[7]Jakubowicz (1984) argues that the developmental delay with (30) occurs because children at first treat *he* as an anaphor. There are empirical problems with this account, as argued by Wexler and Manzini (1987).

(30)' a. John$_i$ is touching him$_i$ (*John* and *him* corefer)
b. John$_i$ is touching him$_j$ (*John* and *him* corefer)

In contrast, I claim that the delay happens because ASSEMBLY cannot take place until a certain age, say six (cf. footnote 9). Recall that neither (24) nor (25) alone completes the acquisition of *he*. When and only when they ASSEMBLE (24) with (25), they acquire the correct values for *he*. It is reasonable that the acquisition of *he*, which requires ASSEMBLY, shows a developmental delay as compared with the acquisition of *himself*, which is done without ASSEMBLY (cf. 4.2.).

5.2. Delay of Condition B effects in Referential Binding

Let's next consider the delay with (30) in comparison with (31). It is reported that children correctly reject examples such as (31) at ages between 5 and 6, when they wrongly accept (30).

(30) (*)John is touching him. (situation: John is touching himself)

(31) *Every bear is touching him. (situation: Every bear is touching himself)

(30)' b. John$_i$ is touching him$_j$ (*John* and *him* corefer)

Chien and Wexler (1990) attribute the difference in children's behavior with (30) and (31) to the fact that *John* is referential but *every bear* in (31) is not. Recall that they assume children before 6 do not have the Coreference Condition. Thus, young children can accept (30) with indexing in (30'b), as mentioned before, but such coreference with contraindexing is impossible for (31), since *every bear* has no reference. As this is against Strong Continuity, again, (even though the Coreference Condition could belong to pragmatics), I propose an alternative account.

I argue that the difference is due to the nature of *he* as non-variables in early childhood. There are two types of pronominal elements (cf. Montalbetti 1984): those that can be construed as bound variables, and others that cannot be so construed. I distinguish them by a feature [V]. For example, Japanese *kare* is an example of [-V], as it cannot be bound by a quantifier irrespective of locality (cf. Saito and Hoji 1983, Hoji 1989, etc.). Thus, (32a), as well as (32b) is ungrammatical.

(32) a. *Minna$_i$-ga [Taro-ga kare$_i$-o semeta to] omotteiru.
everyone NOM NOM he ACC blamed that thinking
'everyone$_i$ thinks that Taro blamed him$_i$'
b. *Minna$_i$-ga kare$_i$-o semeta.
everyone NOM he ACC blamed
'everyone$_i$ blamed himself$_i$'

Given the feature [V], I revise the inventory (15).

(15)' Inventory of feature combinations (revised)
[0A, 0B, +R, -V]: name, (initial values)
[-A, +B, -R, -V]: pronominal *kare*,[8] [-V] epithet
[-A, +B, -R, +V]: pronominal *he*, [+V] epithet
[+A, -B, -R, +V]: anaphor *himself*, *zibun*

unlearnable combination: (*)[+A, +B, -R]
impossible combination: *[-A, -B, -R]

The initial value of the feature [V] is [-]. Until children receive positive evidence like (33), *he* is still [-V] for them. This explains the time-lag related to (30) and (31). When *he* is [+R, -V], children reject (31) but not (30). This proposal predicts that (33) will be rejected by those children who reject (31) and accept (30).

(33) Every bear$_i$ is thinking that John is touching him$_i$.

The results reported in Chien and Wexler (1991) seem to be compatible with this prediction. Thus, children at the ages between 5 and 6 accept examples like (33) only 59% of the time with a matching picture, although they accept control examples like (34) 97% of the time with a matching picture.

(34) Every bear is thinking that John is touching Pinocchio.

The ages between 5 and 6 are exactly when children are reported to reject (31) and accept (30). This supports my claim that it is because *he* is [-V] for them that children reject (31) between 5 and 6.

6. Conclusion

To conclude, I have proposed a theory of the acquisition of RD item which has the following advantages: i) it circumvents the two problems in (2), ii) it explains the two developmental delays associated with RD items while preserving Strong Continuity.

Finally, I mention the following additional merit of my proposal: there is a principled reason that the Condition B effect emerges later than the Condition A effect. I have argued that the delay is found because young children cannot ASSEMBLE, which is necessary for the acquisition of *he*, but not for *himself*. That is, I have made the developmental delay follow from the relative complexity of lexical acquisition. According to this account, it should never be

---

[8] I am not sure if *kare* has [+B]. To me, local binding of *kare* is quite ok, and there are Japanese speakers who agree with me.

(i) (??)Taro$_i$-ga kare$_i$-o nikundeiru.
NOM he ACC hating
'Taro hate him'

The weakness of Condition B effects with *kare* seems to be correlated with its [-V] value.

the case that effects of the Condition B emerges earlier than those of Condition A. By contrast, accounts which assume that children lack/disobey Condition B or the Coreference Condition are stipulative in specifying a particular condition which children do not know/obey. Why can't it be Condition A that children disobey or lack at first? Thus, my account is more motivated than previous ones in this respect.[9]

References

Chien, Yu-Chin., and Wexler, Ken. 1990. Children's Knowledge of Locality Conditions in Binding as Evidence for the Modularity of Syntax and Pragmatics. *Language Acquisition* 1:225--95.

Chien, Yu-Chin., and Wexler, Ken. 1991. Children's Knowledge of Pronouns as Bound Variables. Presented at Child Language Research Forum, Stanford University.

Chomsky, Noam. 1981. *Lectures on Government and Binding*. Dordrecht: Foris.

Chomsky, Noam. 1986. *Knowledge of Language: Its Nature, Origin, and Use*. New York: Praeger.

Evans, Gareth. 1980. Pronouns. *Linguistic Inquiry* 11:337--362.

Finer, Dan. 1987. Comments on Solan. *Parameter Setting*, eds. Tom Roeper and Edwin Williams, 211--9. Dordrecht: Reidel.

Grimshaw, Jane., and Rosen, Sara T. 1990. Knowledge and Obedience: The Developmental Status of the Binding Theory. *Linguistic Inquiry* 21:187--222.

Hestvik, Arild. 1990a. *LF-movement of Pronouns and the Computation of Binding Domains*, Doctoral Dissertation, Brandeis University.

Hestvik, Arild. 1990b. LF-movement of Pronouns. *Proceedings of the North Eastern Linguistic Society* 20.

Hoji, Hajime. 1989. Kare. To appear in R. Ishihara and C. Georgeopolous, eds. *Interdisciplinary Approaches to Language: in Honor of Prof. S.-Y. Kuroda*, eds. R. Ishihara and C. Georgeopolous, Dordrecht: Reidel.

Huang, James C.-T. 1982. *Logical Relations in Chinese and the Theory of Grammar*, Doctoral Dissertation, MIT.

Huang, James C.-T. 1988. Comments on Hasegawa's Paper. *A Japanese Syntax Workshop: on empty categories*, eds. Mineharu Nakayama and Wako Tawa. Connecticut College.

Hyams, Nina. 1983. *The Acquisition of Parametrized Grammars*. Doctoral Dissertation, CUNY.

Jakubowicz, Celia. 1984. On Markedness and Binding Principles. *Proceedings of the North Eastern Linguistic Society* 14.

Klein, Sharon. 1982. *Syntactic Theory and the Development of Grammar*.

[9] Probably, I will have to assume maturation of ASSEMBLY, to explain why it takes time for children to begin doing it. But my point is this: with ASSEMBLY, there is a reason to expect that something which involves it emerges later than something which does not, because the former is more complicated. Moreover, maturation of ASSEMBLY does not violate Strong Continuity, as it is not a condition.

Doctoral Dissertation, UCLA.

Lasnik, Howard. 1986. On the Necessity of Binding Conditions. *Essays on Anaphora*, H. Lasnik 1989. Dordrecht: Kluwer.

McDaniel, Dana., Cairns, Helen S., and Hsu, Jennifer R. 1990. Binding Principles in the Grammars of Young Children. *Language Acquisition* 1, 121--139.

Montalbetti, Mario M. 1984. *After Binding: On the Interpretation of Pronouns*. Doctoral Dissertation, MIT.

Otsu, Yukio. 1981. *Universal Grammar and Syntactic Development in Children: Toward a Theory of Syntactic Development*. Doctoral Dissertation, MIT.

Pinker, Steven. 1984. *Language Learnability and Language Development*. Cambridge, Mass: Harvard University Press.

Radford, Andrew. 1990. The Syntax of Nominal Arguments in Early Child English. *Language Acquisition* 1:195-223.

Reinhart, Tanya. 1983. *Anaphora and Semantic Interpretation*. London: Croom Helm.

Reinhart, Tanya., and Reuland, E. 1991. Reflexivity. ms. Tel Aviv/Groningen.

Roeper, Tom., and Weissenborn, Jugen. 1990. Making Parameters Work. *Language Processing and Language Acquisition*, eds. Lyn Frazier and Jill de Villiers, 147--62. Dordrecht: Kluwer.

Saito, Mamoru., and Hoji, Hajime. 1983. Weak Crossover and Move Alpha in Japanese. *Natural Language and Linguistic Theory* 1:245--59.

Wexler, Ken., and Rita, Manzini. 1987. Parameters and Learnability in Binding Theory. *Parameter Setting*, eds. Tom Roeper and Edwin Williams, 41--76. Dordrecht: Reidel.

Wu, Andy. 1992. A Computational Approach to 'Intake' Ordering in Syntactic Acquisition. *Proceedings of the West Coast Conference on Formal Linguistics* 11. Stanford: CSLI. (This volume.)

On Subject-Verb Constituency: Evidence from Athapaskan Languages

LESLIE SAXON & KEREN RICE
University of Victoria & University of Toronto

Following the work of Kuroda (1988), Sportiche (1988), Fukui and Speas (1986), Koopman and Sportiche (1991), and many others, it is widely accepted that subject NPs occur in D-structure within the maximal projection VP. Investigations of 'free inversion' in Italian have yielded analyses (for example, Burzio 1986,33, Belletti 1988) in which the derived subject is adjoined to VP. Recently the possibility has also been raised, particularly in connection with the origins of basic VSO word order, that subjects occur in a hierarchical position lower than either [Spec, VP] or a position adjoined to VP: Choe 1986 proposes that the D-structure subject position in Berber is sister to V; Chung 1990 argues that derived subjects in Chamorro may occur adjoined to any projection of V; Woolford 1991 shows that similar analyses can be supported for Jacaltec, Niuean, and Breton. These works thus share the view that subjects in some VSO languages may occur as sisters to V, hierarchically as low as, or lower than, direct objects. Chung (1990) has made a similar suggestion for the SVO language Italian. Discussing some data problematic for Burzio (1986), she suggests that the position of inverted subjects in Italian may in fact involve adjunction of the subject to verbal constituents smaller than VP.

We will argue in this paper that some Athapaskan languages with basic SOV word order also give evidence of permitting subject NPs as sisters to V, evidence entirely parallel to that noted in the studies of basic VSO and SVO languages. In this context, such a finding for SOV languages is, on the one hand, entirely expected. On the other hand, however, the finding is unexpected. For basic SVO languages, and for those basic VSO languages considered to be derived from underlying SVO structures, derived subject positions within VP are commonly thought to follow from a requirement that the verb (or V+I constituent) canonically

*This work was supported by Social Sciences and Humanities Research Council of Canada Research Grant no. 410-90-0946 and by a Dean's Grant (University of Victoria) to the first-named author. This work grew out of a larger project initially reported on at the Athapaskan Linguistics Conference, UCSC, July 1991. We are very grateful to the audience there and to the WCCFL audience, especially Pam Munro, Ed Keenan, and Tim Stowell. We would like to thank Chad Thompson for help with Koyukon, and Paul Agbedor, Tom Hukari, Alana Johns, Jim Kari, S.-Y. Kuroda, Tadao Miyamoto, Chiharu Uda, and Suying Yang for leads and very helpful suggestions and discussion. Errors are our own.

govern both the subject and direct object NPs, with the consequence that the verb precedes both NPs. In a basic SOV language, the verb canonically governs both subject and direct object in either the SOV or OSV order; hence, no justification for movement can arise from this source. We propose, following standard views of Athapaskan word order, and also discussion by Chung (1990) of VSO orders in the underlyingly VOS language Chamorro, that the alternative word orders have their origins in information structure. Word orders in which subject precedes object are preferred when the subject is more topical than the object.

Our conclusions provide strong support for two subject positions in the two Athapaskan languages of Alaska that we treat. As we are arguing that the hierarchically lower subject position is actually within V', and hence is emphatically an internal argument, our conclusions at the same time present a challenge to Burzio's generalization. By this generalization, structures lacking an external argument are not expected to surface as transitives. Yet this is exactly what we propose.

The Athapaskan evidence to be presented comes from facts of idioms, noun incorporation, word order, verbal agreement, and binding.

1. Evidence that subjects are V'-internal

In the first section of the paper, we will explore evidence that the subject in Ahtna and Koyukon is underlyingly internal to V'. Evidence for this comes from two sources, the existence of transitive subject idioms in addition to what might pretheoretically be called VP idioms, and the existence of incorporated transitive subjects. The crosslinguistic rarity of such phenomena argues that transitive subjects in these languages are generated lower in the structure than they are in languages lacking such possibilities.

1.1. Idioms

Koyukon and Ahtna, in common with all Athapaskan languages we have knowledge of, have idioms of a type considered rare (Marantz 1984,27): 'subject idioms' based on transitive verbs in which the direct object is the free element.[1] Three examples from Ahtna are given below.

---

[1]Marantz (1984,313), on information from Ken Hale, cites Navajo as a language having 'a great number ... of subject idioms (with free object positions)'. Besides the transitive subject idioms shown in the text, 'subject idioms' based on intransitive verbs are numerous in Athapaskan languages too--though Marantz (1984,30) is of the opinion that their usefulness in arguments about structural relations is limited by the fact that 'subjects' of intransitives may derive from deep subject or deep object positions, given the existence of unaccusative predicates. Three examples from Ahtna of intransitive 'subject idioms' are given below.

(i) Ba kaltlok'e. (Kari 1990,355)
3-for events-are-brittle
'S/he is lucky' (lit. 'events are brittle for him/her')

(ii) Neniic uyighiyaa. (Kari 1990,422)
happiness 3-in-went
'S/he became happy' (lit. 'happiness went into him/her')

Ahtna

(1) Naał sdzełghaen. (Kari 1990,213)
sleep 1sDO-start-to-kill
'I am getting sleepy' (lit. 'sleep is starting to kill me')

(2) C'eyuuni sizkat. (Kari 1990,232)
ghost 1sDO-slapped
'I have a birthmark' (lit. 'a ghost slapped me')

(3) Naał stniłts'aax. (Kari 1990,401)
sleep 1sDO-opened
'I yawned' (lit. 'sleep opened me')

If we follow Marantz in assuming a structure-based semantics, Ahtna idioms like those above argue that at some level of structure subject + verb are contained within a single constituent. The crosslinguistic rarity of subject idioms suggests that the relevant level of structure is an underived one, and smaller than VP; hence, that subject and verb are D-structure sisters within V'.

Subject idioms are not the only idioms found in these languages; also plentiful are 'VP idioms' of the type exemplified in English by *kick the bucket*, or *take X to the cleaners.*

Ahtna

(4) Hnae dadeł'aen. (Kari 1990,85)
word 3S-does
'S/he is articulate' (lit. 's/he does words')

(5) Kezbaen. (Kari 1990,101)
3S-swam-ashore
'S/he went broke playing cards' (lit. 's/he swam ashore')

(6) I'eł natxetnaas. (Kari 1990,288)
3OO-with 3S-works-again
'He flirts with her' (lit. 'he is working again with her')

(iii) Bikay'teztset. (Kari 1990,383)
3-for-Indef-reached
'S/he got startled' (lit. 'something reached for him/her')

Crosslinguistic evidence in Athapaskan suggests that the verbs in (ii) and (iii) are among the group that would be considered unergative. (See Rice 1991 on the unaccusative hypothesis for Athapaskan languages.)

Paul Agbedor (p.c.) informs us of the existence of 'subject idioms' in the Kwa language Ewe, for example, *vuvɔ lé X* 'cold catches X; X has a cold', and *dɔ wu X vevie* 'hunger killed X much; X was very hungry'. Ewe has the basic word order SVO. Under our assumptions, examples like these potentially support the postulation of two subject positions in Ewe clause structure.

(7) Kentinaasyoł. (Kari 1990,443)
ashore-2sDO-will-1sS-chase
'I will bluff you' (lit. 'I will chase you ashore')

If idioms of this type are defined over the syntactic unit VP, and if 'gaps' as in *take X to the cleaners* are possible in VP idioms, it is unclear why subject idioms do not exist in English, under the assumption that English subjects originate within VP. Postulating a difference between English and Ahtna in the underlying position of subjects helps to account for the observed difference between the two languages in idiom inventory. In particular, it is our view that Ahtna subjects originate within V', whereas their counterparts in English originate outside of V'.

1.2. Noun Incorporation

Noun incorporation is a fairly productive process in some Athapaskan languages. Both Ahtna and Koyukon permit the incorporation not only of direct objects, but also of subjects in transitive clauses. Examples of incorporated subjects in each of Ahtna and Koyukon are given below. (The incorporated subject is underlined in the examples.)

(8) **Ahtna** (data from Kari 1990)

a.	Tetayiniłtaen.	'S/he drowned' (lit. 'water carried him underwater')
b.	Łiyiz'ał.	'A dog bit him/her (once)'
c.	Nic'ałts'iidiłt'ak.	'The wind lifted it up'
d.	Kanaałsghiłt'ak.	'I fell asleep' (lit. 'sleep moved me up')

(9) **Koyukon** (data from Axelrod 1990)

a.	Haatsehyedeełtaanh.	'S/he went away crying' (lit. 'tears carried him/her off')
b.	Kk'oełts'eeyhyeedzoyh.	'The wind is moving them around'
c.	Notenhyetaatłgheł.	'(The cracking of) ice scared him/her back off'

Though in most of these cases the incorporated subject is very clearly non-agentive, it is equally clearly a transitive subject in each case. The sentences in (8) and (9) include pronominal (or equally possibly, nominal) direct objects, and are built on transitive verbs, several of them verbs morphologically derived with the transitivizer prefix ł-.

Such incorporations are considered rare, and indeed are predicted to be impossible under the usual pair of assumptions, that a noun incorporated into a verb must be lexically governed by the verb, and that a subject is not so governed (Baker 1988). If, as we propose, the subject NP in these Athapaskan languages is lexically governed by the verb--being a sister to the verb--the incorporation of subjects is not unexpected. It is then just as expected as the incorporation of direct objects, also found in Ahtna and Koyukon, for instance in the examples below.

(10) **Ahtna** (data from Kari 1990)
a. Nixałnitaan. 'He stopped the sled'
b. Ketl'anitsaes. 'Put your rear against it'
c. Łukon'dałt'aał. 'He is carrying a torch (fire) around'

(11) **Koyukon** (data from Axelrod 1990)
a. Tots'eeyhgheetonh. 'S/he launched the boat'
b. Beyeekkaaghestleyh. 'I stuck my foot in it'
c. Neehaałnee'onh. 'S/he set a trap'

1.3. Summary

So far we have argued that the existence of transitive subject idioms and incorporated subjects suggests that the subject and the direct object both are V'-internal and both bear the same relationship to the verb, being lexically governed by the verb.[2]

2. The hierarchical relation of subject and direct object

Given that both the subject and the direct object are lexically governed by the verb in Ahtna and Koyukon, the question arises of what hierarchical relation exists between the two NPs. In this section we present a simplicity argument based on word order which supports the view that the direct object NP precedes the subject NP. We examine some suggestive facts of inflectional morphology but conclude that they are not relevant to our present concerns. Binding facts clearly suggest a mutual c-command relation between the subject and the direct object. Adopting the assumption that structures are binary-branching, we conclude that all of the evidence is best accounted for with a structure in which subject + verb form a constituent V' which has the direct object NP as its sister, as in the tree in (12).

(12)

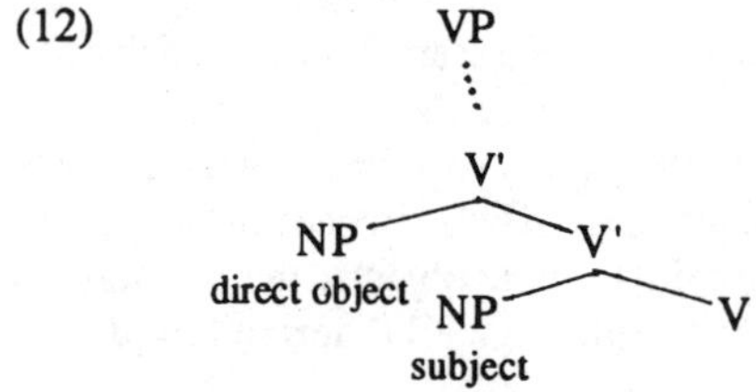

2.1. Word order

SOV is considered by Athapaskanists to be the unmarked word order in Athapaskan languages. This is illustrated in the examples below from Ahtna.

[2] As pointed out to us by Ken Hale, our analysis is apparently in conflict with the proposals of Hale and Keyser 1992.

Ahtna

(13) Sta' 'inn nen'ta teni kughił'aen'. (Kari 1990,85)
1s-father pl land-in trail 3pS-had
'My father's people had a trail out in the country'

(14) Tsaani 'unii uke' hwt'aene na'es. (Kari 1990,88)
grizzly hind 3-foot all 3S-trample
'The grizzly bear tramples its entire hind foot'

(15) Tselc'utsaey kuggaedi ldaeł. (Kari 1990,146)
dragonfly mosquito 3S-eat-pl O
'The dragonfly is eating mosquitoes'

(16) Xał tsiitl' naghaldza'. (Kari 1990,168)
sled snow 3S-become-stuck
'The sled got embedded in the snow'

However, SOV is not the only possible word order in Ahtna and Koyukon: OSV word order is also found, as in (17)-(19).

Ahtna

(17) Udaghos tuu k'endezc'et'. (Kari 1990,125)
3-gunwales water 3S-reach
'Water reaches its gunwales'

(18) Xał łts'ii datiił. (Kari 1990,217)
club wind 3S-move-sticklike O
'The wind is blowing the club'

(19) Nyuu' ggas nighilaa. (Kari 1990,266)
2s-clothes dirt 3S-reached
'Dirt got on ('reached') your clothes'

Morphological evidence based on the distribution of agreement clearly indicates that the objects in these examples are not in a dislocated position. If a direct object NP occurs in a position where it is lexically governed by the verb, it triggers no overt agreement. If it is dislocated, agreement is overt. The verbs in examples (17)-(19) are unmarked for direct object agreement; hence, the direct object NPs in them are in undislocated positions.

Ahtna and Koyukon thus allow both SOV and OSV word orders. It has been argued that when SOV order is found, the subject is topical (see, for instance, Thompson 1989). Topicality is important throughout the Athapaskan family: the well-known animacy hierarchy in the Apachean Athapaskan language Navajo (e.g. Hale 1973, Frishberg 1972, Witherspoon 1977) has been argued to be correctly viewed as a topicality hierarchy, with topical NPs occupying clause-initial position (Thompson 1989a). Assuming that the specifier position in IP is reserved for topical subjects, an argument exists for the structure shown in (12), where the direct object precedes the subject, over one in which the order of arguments is reversed. According to (12), SOV order is derived from the underlying OSV order by the 'raising' of topical subjects. Since subjects are so often topical (see discussion in Thompson 1989a), the word order SOV appears to be unmarked. Suppose now that the underlying word order in Ahtna and Koyukon were SOV. It would be difficult to derive the order OSV; an anlysis would require that the subject 'lower' (or, alternatively, that the object 'raise') just in case the subject were non-topical. The OSV orders seen in (17)-(19) would have no plausible source. Simplicity thus argues in favour of the structure in (12), with the direct object preceding the subject.[3]

2.2. Non-evidence from inflectional morphology

One set of facts which might appear to lend weak support to our claim concerns morpheme order in the verb. The agreement prefixes in the verb in Athapaskan languages occur in the order oblique object - direct object - subject. This is shown in the examples in (20) from Ahtna and (21) from Koyukon.

(20) **Ahtna**

a. beydiises 'I struck it against it once' (Kari 1990,300)
b- oblique object, y- direct object, i- subject

b. nasghilbaeł 'swim me towards land' (Kari 1990,101)
s- direct object, i- subject

c. hwtaydesbes 'he spread it out on it' (Kari 1990,106)
hw- oblique object, y- direct object, Ø subject

d. uc'oosdaet 'I bought something from him' (Kari 1990,240)
u- oblique object, c'- direct object, s- subject

e. uyii tay'dghastsiy 'I stretched something in it' (Kari 1990,393)
u- oblique object, y'- direct object, s- subject

(21) **Koyukon**

a. begh yooghskkett 'I bought it from him' (Thompson 1989a:45)
b- oblique object, y- direct object, s- subject

b. betl'o yens'oyh 'I am giving it to him/her' (Thompson 1989a,46)
b- oblique object, y- direct object, s- subject

The linear order of affixes in these verbal forms matches the linear order of NPs in (12). This might be interpreted as evidence for the underlying order IO--DO--S

---

[3]The example in (i) contains a dislocated object NP.

(i) Bill too deyeeloh. (Thompson, p.c.)
water DADO-got
'Bill drowned' (lit. 'water got Bill')

The presence of the direct object agreement form y- in the verb indicates that the object in this sentence ('Bill') has been dislocated. The objects in (17)-(19) are not dislocated, as argued in the text, as no overt agreement marker is present.

proposed. However, Rice 1990 and Speas 1991 argue for Slave and Navajo respectively that this order of morphemes reflects not the base-generated structure within VP but the structure associated with functional projections external to VP, in which the [Spec, IP] position c-commands all other argument positions. (See the trees below in (27)-(29).) Rice and Saxon 1991 further argues that Slave and Navajo differ from Koyukon and Ahtna precisely in relation to possible surface positions of subject NPs. The order of inflectional elements, then, is not relevant to the central issue we are discussing.

2.3. The facts of binding

The facts of binding provide very strong evidence for the position of the subject inside V', and for its hierarchical relationship with the direct object position. The essential fact of interest is that anaphors in Ahtna and Koyukon are licensed as subjects. At some level of structure, then, direct and oblique objects c-command the subject. A topical subject, however, can never have the form of an anaphor: this follows if a topical subject occupies the [Spec, IP] position as we have argued in section 2.1, unilaterally c-commanding every other position within IP. A topical subject can license anaphors in non-subject positions.

From the description just given it follows that simple transitive clauses and other clauses containing two or more NPs will have a form in which an anaphor in an object positon is licensed by a topical subject in [Spec, IP], and another form in which an anaphor appears as a nontopical subject, licensed by a c-commanding direct or oblique object. Contrasting sets of examples like this are shown in (22)-(26), all involving the 'disjoint anaphor' (Saxon 1984). The disjoint anaphor has a limited distribution in all Athapaskan languages, occurring only in the context of a clause-mate third person from which it is disjoint (Rice and Saxon 1991). In the Apachean and Mackenzie branches of the family, the disjoint anaphor occurs only in non-subject positions. In Alaska, in contrast, it may occur as a subject, but only in the context of a clause-mate third person.

(In Koyukon and Ahtna, the presence of the disjoint anaphor--an empty category--is observable in the agreement form y-/i-. Third person pronominal agreement takes the form b-/u- for non-subjects, and zero for subjects. In the glosses, 'DA' stands for disjoint anaphor.)

Koyukon

(22) a. Yeneeł'aanh. (Thompson 1989a,40)
DA-3S-see
'He is looking at him(DA)'

b. Beyeneeł'aanh. (Thompson 1989a,40)
3DO-DA-see
'He(DA) is looking at him'

(23) a. Yegh neeneeyo. (Thompson 1989a,40)
DA-to 3S-walk up
'He walked up to him (DA)'

b. Begh neeyeeneeyo. (Thompson 1989a,41)
3OO-to DA-walk up
'He(DA) walked up to him'

(24) a. Yetl'o yegheełtaanh. (Leer 1990)
DA-to DA-3S-gave
'He gave it (DA) to her/it(DA)'

b. Yetl'o beyegheełtaanh. (Leer 1990)
DA-to 3DO-DA-gave
'It (DA) gave him to her/it(DA)'

c. Betl'o yeyegheełtaanh. (Leer 1990)
3OO-to DA-DA-gave
'It(DA) gave him (DA) to her'

Ahtna

(25) a. Inał'aen. (Kari 1990,86)
DA-3S-see
'He is looking at it/him(DA)'

b. Biinał'aen. (Kari 1990,96)
3DO-DA-see
'It(DA) is looking at him'

(26) a. I'eł na'idyaa. (Kari 1990,419)
DA-with 3S-return
'He returned with him(DA)'

b. U'eł yayaał. (Kari 1990,419)
3OO-with DA-walk
'He(DA) is walking with him'

The sets of examples above mean essentially the same thing, differing in topicality: in contrast with the (a) examples, the subject in the (b) examples is non-topical (Thompson 1989, Leer 1990, Kari 1990). In each pair, the (a) example contains a direct or oblique object represented by the disjoint anaphor, while in the (b) example the *subject* is a disjoint anaphor. This description is most easily verified in the intransitive clauses (23) and (26), where oblique object agreement is marked on the postposition and subject agreement is marked on the verb, and in (24c), where the transitive verb in a ditransitive construction shows disjoint anaphor agreement for both direct object *and* subject. Limiting our attention to the Koyukon simple transitive clause in (22) for reasons of exposition, (22a) has the structure shown in (27), (22b) the structure shown in (28). (We abstract away from V-I movement.)

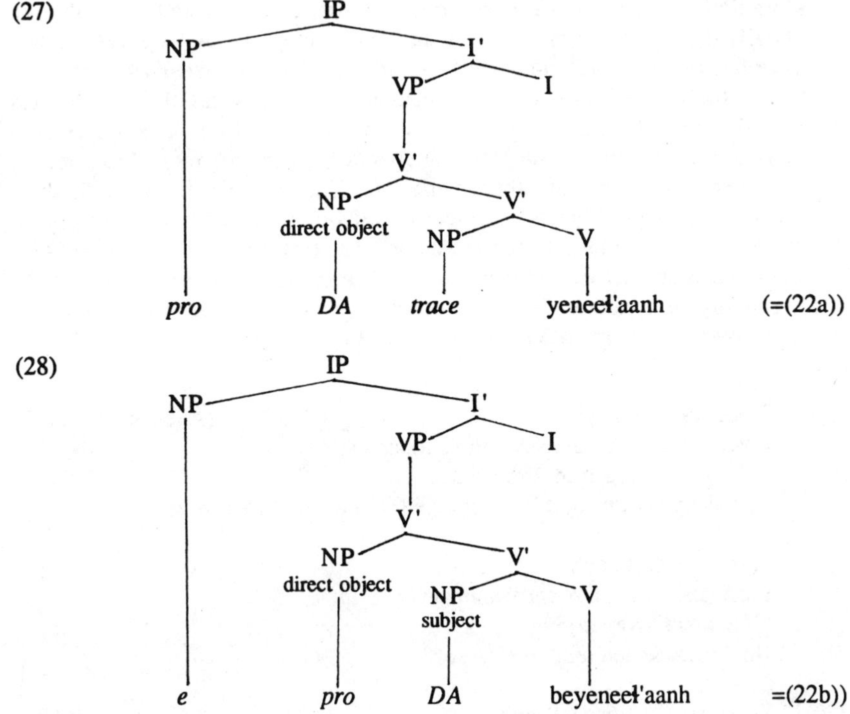

The disjoint anaphors are licensed in these structures because they are c-commanded at S-structure by a disjoint third-person clause-mate.

In (28) it is not the case simply that the direct object c-commands the subject: the two NPs are in a relation of mutual c-command. The prediction can be made therefore that in this structure the subject NP in its base position might license a disjoint anaphor in direct object position. In this case, the sentence would have the structure shown in (29).

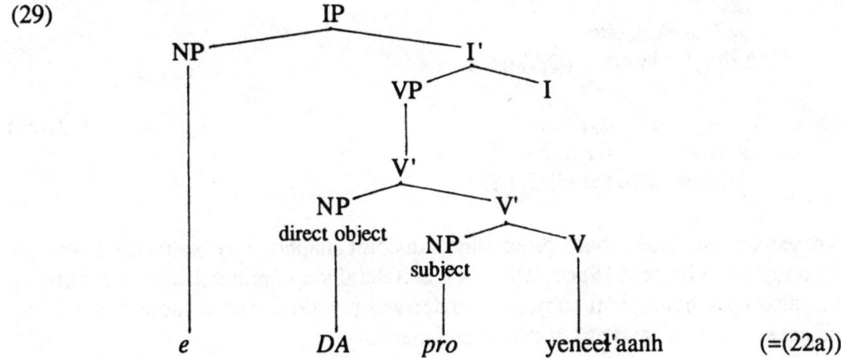

This prediction seems to be borne out. Notice that (27) and (29), though structurally distinct, yield the identical surface form, (22a). As is expected, this sentence has two interpretations. In the interpretation associated with structure (27), the subject is topical; in the interpretation associated with (29), the subject is nontopical. Support for the validity of this contrast comes from facts of anaphora in clauses which contain subjects independently known to be nontopical: incorporated or nontopical nonhuman subjects. The examples in (30)-(35) show that such nontopical subjects can license a disjoint anaphor as direct object. Examples (30), (31) and (34) contain incorporated subjects; (32), (33) and (35) contain subjects characteristically nontopical. We analyse all of the sentences (30)-(35) as having the structure (29). (The questionable status of (32) and (33) will be addressed once a bit more data has been examined.)

Koyukon

(30) Nonobełyeeten'oyh. (Axelrod 1990,185)
down-again-sleep(beł)-DA-move round O
'S/he is nodding from drowsiness'
(lit. 'sleep is causing it [his/her face](DA) to go down repeatedly')

(31) Haatsehyedeełtaanh. (Axelrod 1990,185)
away-tears(tseh)-DA-carry animate O
'S/he went away crying'
(lit. 'tears carried him/her(DA) off')

(32) ? Deneege yeneeł'aanh. (Thompson 1989b)
moose DA-see
'The moose is looking at him/her(DA)'

(33) ? Ses yelaatłghaanh. (Thompson 1989b)
bear DA-killed
'The bear killed him/her(DA)'

Ahtna

(34) Łiyiz'ał. (=(8b))
dog-DA-Perf-bite
'A dog bit him/her (DA) once'

(35) Ts'ax dyilaak. (Kari 1990,427)
sickness DA-afflicted
'Sickness afflicted him(DA)'

These examples show that a direct object disjoint anaphor may be licensed not only by a topical subject in [Spec, IP] which unilaterally c-commands the direct object, but also by a nontopical subject in underived position, where subject and direct object stand in a relation of mutual c-command.

The question arises of whether the position of the subject can ever be verified empirically when one or more of the NPs in the clause is an empty category. It can be. In the Koyukon examples in (36) and (37), 'John' is the subject, and a distinct third person is the direct object. In this context, given that Koyukon has both a third person disjoint anaphor and a third person pronominal, it is predicted that either one could function as direct object. This prediction is upheld, to a point. Example (36), in which the disjoint anaphor occurs as a direct object, is ambiguous, but (37) with the pronominal as direct object, is not.

Koyukon

(36) John yeneeł'aanh. (Thompson 1989b and p.c.)
DA-see
i. 'John (topic) is looking at him/her(DA)'
ii. 'John (nontopic) is looking at him/her(DA)'

(37) John beneeł'aanh. (Thompson 1989b and p.c.)
3DO-see
i. * John (topic) is looking at him/her'
ii. John (nontopic) is looking at him/her'

As the glosses indicate, when 'John' is nontopical, and by our analysis occupies the D-structure subject position, the direct object can take the form of either an anaphor as in (36ii) or a pronominal as in (37ii). When 'John' is topical, however, and occupies [Spec, IP] position, only the disjoint anaphor is grammatical as in (36i) and (37i). The contrast between unilateral c-command of the object by the subject (as in structure (27)) and mutual c-command (as in structure (29)) seems to be responsible for the facts in (36) and (37). These data provide unusual evidence for the postulation of two subject positions in Koyukon, and these examples taken together with what we saw earlier strongly support our view that D-structure subject and direct object positions c-command each other.

The examples in (38)-(40) complete the Koyukon paradigms for nontopical subjects begun in (30)-(33).

Koyukon

(38) Hʉgho'ełts'eeyhbeetenaatltsonh. (Axelrod 1990:186)
wind('ełts'eeyh)-3DO-tire
'The wind tired him/her out'

(39) Deneege beneeł'aanh. (Thompson 1989b)
moose 3DO-see
'The moose is looking at him/her'

(40) Ses belaatłghaanh. (Thompson 1989b)
bear 3DO-killed
'The bear killed him/her'

Examples (32) and (33) are slightly less acceptable than (39) and (40). We attribute the difference in acceptability to a Gricean or Reinhartian pragmatic principle: examples (32) and (33) are potentially structurally ambiguous, while examples (39) and (40) are not. Thus the use of the latter examples will be more felicitous.

With this discussion of the disjoint anaphor, we mean to have given evidence to strengthen the position we were led to by the facts of idioms and incorporation: that the subject and direct object NPs both occupy base positions inside V', and consequently stand in a relationship of mutual c-command.

What of other binding facts? If the disjoint anaphor can appear as a subject in Ahtna and Koyukon, the same might be expected of the reflexive anaphor. This is not the case. However, it is our view that this fact follows from independent considerations in the grammars of these languages. As is true in many languages, the antecedent for a reflexive must be animate in Ahtna and Koyukon (as well as in other Athapaskan languages we have knowledge of). As animate (or especially, human) subject NPs usually raise to canonical subject position [Spec, IP], being topical, the structural contexts for reflexive subjects will not arise. Examples like those in (41)-(43) therefore occur, but not examples in which the subject is a reflexive.[4] (The underlined d- in (41)-(43) is the reflexive agreement element.)

Ahtna

(41) Nadnolk'ii'. (Kari 1990,257)
cust-Refl-2pS-cool
'You cool yourselves customarily'

(42) Denehduudle' tahwnal'aen. (Kari 1990,86)
Refl-eye lashes among-3S-see
'He is peering through his eyelashes'

(43) Deyadahwdult'aen'de. (Kari 1990,85)
Refl-2pS-identify verbally
'You should identify yourselves verbally'

2.4 Summary

Ahtna and Koyukon provide clear evidence from subject idioms and noun incorporation that underived subjects in these languages are lexically governed by the verb just as direct objects are. There is evidence too, from idioms, noun incorporation, and anaphora, that subject and direct object NPs c-command each other at the level of D-structure. Facts of word order are suggestive that at the underived level the direct object NP precedes the subject NP.

3. Conclusions

3.1. On precedents

Our conclusion that subject + verb form a constituent in some Athapaskan languages is not without precedent. Choe 1986, using evidence from 'subject

[4] Parallel data in Koyukon is not currently available to us.

idioms' and facts of cliticization and noun morphology, argues that at D-structure verb + subject form a syntactic unit in the VSO language Berber. Chung 1990, arguing that Chamorro has the basic word order VOS, shows with coordination facts that verb + subject form a constituent at a derived level of structure in that language. In this context, it is entirely to be expected that the conclusions of these studies should be validated elsewhere, for instance in the class of languages with basic SOV word order. We should not be surprised either if Chung's notes on the potential for VSO word orders in the SVO languages Italian (p.581) and Rumanian (p.615) yielded a similar conclusion.

Our finding--on one hand--is not unexpected; however, on the other hand, for a number of reasons it leads to a reexamination of the source of this constituency and the motivations suggested previously for the 'subject lowering' by which it may be derived. Choe (1986) argues that the VSO word order in Berber follows from requirements of uniform directionality of L-marking which cannot be satisfied in an SVO word order. The strict requirement for VSO order in Berber, contrasting with alternative SVO order available in a language like Irish, is correlated with the fact that all Berber verbs are inflected. If inflected V within VP rather than the category I assigns nominative case in Berber, then consistent VSO word order will be predicted. Attempting to extend Choe's account to Athapaskan, we observe that the OSV order we have proposed for Ahtna and Koyukon also indicates uniform directionality of L-marking. But so would SOV order. Thus no justification for D-structure OSV over SOV order can be found in considerations of directionality. We observe, however, that Athapaskan--like Berber and also Chamorro--lacks uninflected verbs. We will follow Choe in taking this property as a prerequisite for verb + subject constituency.

Chung (1990), in arguing that VSO is an alternative to underlying VOS in Chamorro, likewise cannot appeal to directionality of government to motivate the adjunction of subject to a verbal category. Chung suggests instead that SO versus OS order in Chamorro can be linked to information structure. Though Chamorro SO orders derive from subject lowering, and Ahtna and Koyukon SO orders derive from subject raising to [Spec, IP], both derivations result in the subject NP preceding the direct object NP, evidently reflecting some universal word-order preference (Greenberg 1963). It is our view, expressed earlier in section 2.1, that subject-initial word order in Athapaskan correlates with subject topicality. Subjects which are likely to be topical--human subjects, for instance--almost invariably occupy clause-initial position. In the absence of a topical subject, the OSV word order of the base emerges.

In suggesting that surface SOV order is derived, our account follows much work on VP-internal subjects (Sportiche 1988, Kuroda 1988). In particular, our claim that [Spec, IP] is a position for topical subjects recalls the very similar proposals of, among others, Diesing 1990 on Yiddish, and Guilfoyle, Hung, and Travis (to appear) on Malayo-Polynesian languages.

3.2. Further implications

These findings about Ahtna and Koyukon provide very clear support to any view in which two notions of subject are distinguished, whether the two notions are defined wholly in terms of phrase structure (such as [Spec, VP] and [Spec, IP]) as in Kuroda 1988 or Koopman and Sportiche 1991, or are more explicitly dependent on argument structure ('logical subject' and 'external argument') as in Grimshaw 1990 or Bresnan and Kanerva 1989.

A problematic element of our analysis is the lack of asymmetry in it between subject and object: these NPs are both lexically governed by the verb and stand in a relation of mutual c-command. The problems are most easily discussed in light of concrete analyses which must be found in other domains of Ahtna and Koyukon grammar. Notice that the structure we have argued for entails the existence of transitive unaccusative predicates, something predicted to be impossible under 'Burzio's generalization'. If nominative case is available for the subject along the lines of Choe's (1986) suggestion for Berber, the only 'problem' is a case for the direct object. If transitivity can be defined independently of unaccusativity, this difficulty can be resolved also. (Marantz 1991 on 'Case and licensing' has an interesting analysis of 'Burzio's generalization' which we might adopt.)

Ahtna and Koyukon passives pose another kind of potential difficulty. If passivization depends on the existence of an external argument, and if external argument is defined configurationally, it is predicted that passivization does not exist in these languages. In fact, passivization exists in both. Examples of passives are provided in the (b) examples in (44)-(47).

Koyukon

(44) a. Yeetots'eeyh. (Thompson 1989a:166)
'S/he will pinch him/her (once)'

b. Eetodets'eeyh.
'S/he will be pinched (once)'

(45) a. Yeneeł'aanh. (Thompson 1989a:47)
'S/he is looking at him/her'

b. Neenla'aanh. (Thompson 1989a:48)
'You are being watched'

Ahtna

(46) a. Inezga'. (Kari 1990:180)
'S/he overcooked it'

b. Nestga'.
'It got overcooked'

(47) a. Hnaa gha ninłtaen. (Kari 1990:329)
work for 3DO-Pf-1sS-pick up
'I hired him for a job'

b. Hnaa gha nisteltaen.
work for 1sDO-Pf-Psv-pick up
'I got sent for a job'

The asymmetry which the existence of a process of passivization entails is evidently not a structural asymmetry in Koyukon and Ahtna. If passivization is a lexical process in these languages, the asymmetry presupposed by thematic hierarchies would appear to be the asymmetry tapped by the process. This and other considerations quite strongly favour a lexical treatment of such processes in Athapaskan languages.

While an analysis with external subjects offers a ready account of these kinds of data in many languages, it is our view that such an analysis of the facts of Koyukon and Ahtna is untenable, and that the alternative analysis that we have sketched here must be pursued.

References

Axelrod, Melissa. 1990. Incorporation in Koyukon Athapaskan. *International Journal of American Linguistics* 56:179-195.

Baker, Mark. 1988. *Incorporation*. University of Chicago Press, Chicago.

Belletti, Adriana. 1988. The case of unaccusatives. *Linguistic Inquiry* 19:1-34.

Bresnan, Joan and Jonni Kanerva. 1989. Locative inversion in Chichewa: A case study of factorization in grammar. *Linguistic Inquiry* 20:1-50.

Burzio, Luigi. 1986. *Italian Syntax*. Reidel, Dordrecht.

Choe, Hyon-Sook. 1986. An SVO analysis of VSO languages and parametrization: A study of Berber. *NELS* 16:75-93.

Chung, Sandra. 1990. VP's and Verb Movement in Chamorro. *Natural Language and Linguistic Theory* 8:559-619.

Diesing, Molly. 1990. Verb movement and the subject position in Yiddish. *Natural Language and Linguistic Theory* 8:41-79.

Frishberg, Nancy. 1972. Navajo object markers and the great chain of being. *Syntax and Semantics*, volume 1, ed. Charles Li. Academic Press, New York.

Fukui, Naoki and Margaret Speas. 1986. Specifiers and projections. *MIT Working Papers in Linguistics*, volume 8, p. 128-172.

Greenberg, Joseph. 1963. Some universals of grammar with particular reference to the order of meaningful elements. In *Universals of Language*, ed. by Joseph Greenberg, MIT Press, pp. 73-113.

Grimshaw, Jane. 1990. *Argument Structure*. MIT Press.

Guilfoyle, Eithne, Henrietta Hung, and Lisa Travis. To appear. Thematic subjects and structural subjects in Malayo-Polynesian languages. *Natural Language and Linguistic Theory*.

Hale, Kenneth. 1973. A note on subject-object inversion in Navajo. In *Issues in Linguistics: Papers in Honor of Henry and Renee Kahane*, ed. B. Kachru et al., University of Illinois Press, Chicago.

Hale, Ken and Jay Keyser. 1992. On argument structure and the lexical expression of syntactic relations. Ms, MIT.

Kari, James. 1990. *Ahtna Athabaskan Dictionary*. Alaska Native Language Center, Fairbanks.

Koopman, Hilda and Dominique Sportiche. 1991. The position of subjects. *Lingua* 84:211-258.

Kuroda, S.-Y. 1988. Whether we agree or not: A comparative syntax of English and Japanese. *Lingvisticae Investigationes* 12:1-47.

Leer, Jeff. 1990. The Tlingit anaphoric system and the typology of voice systems. Presented at the Athapaskan Linguistics Conference, Vancouver, British Columbia.

Marantz, Alec. 1984. *On the nature of grammatical relations.* MIT Press, Cambridge.

Marantz, Alec. 1991. Case and licensing. Presented at the Eastern States Cconference on Linguistics.

Rice, Keren. 1990. The structure of the Slave (Northern Athapaskan) verb. Presented at the workshop on Lexical Phonology, University of Washington.

Rice, Keren. 1991. Intransitives in Slave (Northern Athapaskan): Arguments for unaccusatives. *International Journal of American Linguistics* 57:51-69.

Rice, Keren and Leslie Saxon. 1991. A structural analysis of **y-* in Athapaskan. Paper presented at the Athapaskan Linguistics Conference, Santa Cruz, California, July 1991.

Saxon, Leslie. 1984. Disjoint anaphora and the binding theory. *Proceedings of the West Coast Conference on Formal Linguistics* 3:242-251.

Speas, Peggy. 1991. Functional heads and the Mirror Principle. *Lingua* 84:181-214.

Sportiche, Dominique. 1988. A theory of floating quantifiers and its corollaries for constituent structure. *Linguistic Inquiry* 19:425-449.

Thompson, Chad. 1989a. *Voice and obviation in Athabaskan and other languages.* Doctoral dissertation, University of Oregon.

Thompson, Chad. 1989b. Pronouns and voice in Koyukon Athapaskan: A text-based study. *International Journal of American Linguistics* 55:1-24.

Witherspoon, Gary. 1977. *Language and Art in Navajo Culture.* University of Michigan Press, Ann Arbor.

Woolford, Ellen. 1991. VP-internal subjects in VSO and nonconfigurational languages. *Linguistic Inquiry* 22:503-540.

The Irish and Other Mutations

KARI SWINGLE
University of California, Santa Cruz

1.0 Introduction

Stem-initial consonants in Irish 'mutate' in various morphosyntactic environments. For example, a verbstem-initial /k/ mutates to /x/ in past tense forms *caith* [ka:] 'spend' → *chaith* [xa:] 'spent'; a feminine nounstem-initial /k/ mutates to /x/ after the definite article *comharsa* [korsə] 'neighbor' → *an chomharsa* [ə xorsə] 'the neighbor'.

The alteration of an initial /k/ to /x/ exemplifies the Irish mutation system referred to in traditional grammars as LENITION. In (1) is the complete set of Irish consonants that occur stem-initially underlyingly together with the form each consonant takes in lenition-triggering environments.[1] The prime notation, C′, represents a palatalized consonant, a consonant with no diacritic (except for the palatal glide /j/ and true velars) is velarized.[2]

*I am particularly grateful for comments from and (often long) discussions with Junko Itô, Bill Ladusaw, Jim McCloskey, Louise McNally, Armin Mester, and Nancy Stenson. This work was partly funded by a University of California Santa Cruz faculty senate grant awarded to Junko Itô and by the UCSC Syntax Research Center.

This paper is dedicated to Nancy Stenson, who taught me Irish and introduced me to linguistics.

[1] In most, if not all, previous analyses of Irish lenition, the velarized bilabials /b/ and /m/ are cited as leniting to /v/; the palatalized coronal /d′/ and palatalized velar /g′/ as leniting to /ɣ′/ (O'Dochartaigh 1978, Massam 1983, Gussmann 1986, Ní Chiosáin 1991, and my own analysis in the presentation of this paper). The glide variants cited in (1) as basic, if acknowledged at all, are typically attributed to some low-level (and optional) phonetic process independent of lenition. As Jim McCloskey (personal communication) points out, however, this is, strictly speaking, a misrepresentation of the facts (albeit convenient in that it allows for an overall simpler account of the lenition of stops). A survey of representative dialect monographs (de Bhaldraithe 1945, Breatnach 1966, Wagner 1959) reveals that 1) the segment /ɣ′/ is not found in any Irish dialect and 2) although the glides /w/ and /j/, both underlying and derived, have (labial and palatal) fricative variants, these variants have a highly restricted distribution, occurring only in onset clusters before the coronal sonorants n(′), l(′), and r(′). The fricative variants are generally viewed in the monographs as deriving from the glides via a 'hardening' process. This seems to me correct. I will adopt the view that the hardening of the glides /w/ and /j/ is a low-level, non-structure preserving process governed by sonority considerations.

[2] For presentational clarity in the derivations below, I follow Ní Chiosáin 1991 and others in recognizing both palatalized and velarized laryngeals, h/h′, in the segment inventory of Irish. In fact, however, there is little evidence for assuming the existence of /h′/ either in the Irish inventory or as the lenited form of a palatalized voiceless coronal. Instead, all voiceless coronals palatalize to /h/ (Breatnach 1967, de Bhaldraithe 1945, O Cuív 1975, Sommerfelt 1922, Wagner 1959). A minor revision to the analysis below, removing palatalization from a lenited voiceless coronal in observance of Structure Preservation will handle this fact.

(1)	p	p′	b	b′	m	m′	k	k′	g	g′	t	t′	d	d′	s	s′	n	n′	l	l′	r	f	f′
	↓	↓	↓	↓	↓	↓	↓	↓	↓	↓	↓	↓	↓	↓	↓	↓	↓	↓	↓	↓	↓	↓	↓
	f	f′	w	v′	w	v′	x	x′	γ	j	h	h′	γ	j	h	h′	n	n′	l	l′	r	∅	∅

As seen here, the lenition of a consonant means different things for different consonants. Noncoronal stops lenite to continuants, coronal obstruents lenite to continuants with a simultaneous change in place of articulation, coronal sonorants do not lenite,[3] and f(′) is deleted. The immediate goal of this paper is to present a unified affixational account of the set of alterations which comprise the Irish lenition system.

An affixational account of Irish lenition or, indeed, of any mutation system clearly cannot involve simple concatenation of strings of segments. The derivation of the past tense form *chaith* [xa:] 'spent' from the stem *caith* [ka:], for example, cannot be accomplished by simply adding a segment or string of segments to the stop-initial stem. Two basic questions which must be addressed by any affixational account of mutation are: 1) Why is there no overt evidence of an affix in mutated forms, where by 'overt evidence' I mean a phonetically realized segment or string of segments not properly belonging to the stem? and 2) What causes the alteration of a stem segment? The latter question here requires refinement; the refinement necessary becomes apparent upon a consideration of the term 'mutation' itself.

Not all morphosyntactically conditioned segment altering processes are mutations. An example of one that is not is a Chaha process discussed in McCarthy 1983 where a rightmost noncoronal consonant is labialized in verbs whose direct object is third person masculine singular; e.g., *nædæf* 'sting' → *nædæf*^{w} 'sting him'. What distinguishes this segment altering process of Chaha from mutation systems like Irish lenition is the acceptable alteration of **non-edge** segments. Chaha labialization applies to the rightmost noncoronal consonant in a verbstem, regardless of whether this segment is an edge segment or not; e.g., *nækæs* 'bite' → *næk*^{w}*æs* 'bite him'. In contrast, morphosyntactically conditioned segment altering processes properly classified as mutations are exactly those processes whose application is restricted to edge, morpheme-initial or morpheme-final, position (Ultan 1970, Lieber 1987).

Irish lenition is properly classified as a mutation system because only stem-initial segments are targeted for alteration. If a stem does not have an initial leniting segment, then lenition simply does not apply. The past tense form of *leacaigh* [l′akə] 'flatten', for example, a stem which begins with a segment immune to lenition, is *leacaigh* [l′akə] 'flattened' and not *[l′axə] where the second segment from the left has been lenited. The second of the two questions posed above, then, can be revised as follows: What causes the alteration of an edge (and only an edge) segment in the stem? It is this question that has gone unanswered in

[3] The set of coronal sonorants given in (1) is simplified. Irish in fact has a three-way distinction for coronal laterals and nasals: L, L′, l′ and N, N′, n′ where the sounds represented by capital letters have been described as 'more obstruent-like' (O'Dochartaigh 1978) or 'more tense' (Massam 1983) than the corresponding sounds represented by lower-case letters. Historically, L′ and N′ lenited to l′ and n′ respectively. In the analysis of lenition to be presented here, these mutations may be handled as instances of sonority-induced changes from [-cont] to [+cont] (cf. section 3.0); however, as the mutation of L′ and N′ is extremely rare in Modern Irish (cf. Gussmann 1986), it will not be further dealt with here.

previous affixational accounts of mutation systems.[4]

Rochelle Lieber, in a series of works including Lieber 1983 and Lieber 1987, was the first to explicitly propose that mutation systems like Irish lenition be treated as affixational phenomena. In Lieber's treatment of mutation, the mutation-inducing element is analyzed as a feature-sized affix, a floating autosegment, which links to a targeted stem segment to effect its mutation. One account of Irish lenition along these lines is Massam 1983 where, ignoring some details, the lenition of an initial segment is derived via the linking of a floating [+cont] autosegmental affix, exemplified for the lenition of /k/ in (2).

(2) [+cont] - - - - STEM
k → [x]

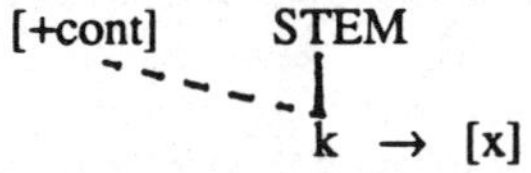

Clearly, such an analysis cannot straightforwardly handle the entire range of facts in (1) nor does it claim to. Such an analysis does, however, purport to account for the basic stop to continuant alteration characteristic of Irish lenition and it is this claim that I want to call into question.

While floating autosegment analyses of mutation phenomena account directly for the absence of any overt segmental affix in the mutated forms of stems, they do not provide a satisfactory account for the strict peripherality of segment alteration. Consider the [+cont]-linking analysis of Irish lenition. Under this analysis, the linking of [+cont] to stem-initial segments exclusively can be ensured only by a stipulation that states, roughly: link the lenition affix [+cont] to a stem-initial consonant if possible; otherwise, do not link. What is odd (and suspicious) about such a stipulation is not the fact that it provides an algorithm for the linking of a floating autosegment but the fact that this algorithm makes specific mention of the linear position of the targeted segment. Allowing a mapping algorithm to specify the linear position of a target in this way is not licensed by autosegmental theory and for good reason: it is simply not the case that the mapping of autosegments to segmental hosts is governed in any way by the linear order of segments. There are no known cases of autosegmental affixation, for example, where an autosegment is systematically mapped to the third segment of a stem.

True cases of floating autosegment affixation involve the mapping of an autosegment to a stem via an algorithm in accordance with universal mapping principles. The direction of the mapping can be specified (left-to-right or right-to-left) and, if necessary, restrictions can be placed on the kinds of segments which serve as acceptable targets for linking. Examples of floating autosegment affixation are well-attested, originating with McCarthy's 1983 analysis of agreement processes in Chaha. The Chaha labialization process noted above, for example, is analyzed in this work as the right-to-left mapping of a [+labialized] autosegmental affix to noncoronal consonants. Other instances of floating

[4] A recent non-affixational account of Irish lenition is Ní Chiosáin 1991. In this work, lenition is analyzed as a complex process involving three independent operations: Spirantization (a [+cont] feature fill-in rule) to account for the stop-to-continuant alteration, Coronal Debuccalization (a [coronal]-delinking rule like the one proposed below) to account for the lenition of coronal obstruents, and a rule of /f/ Deletion.

An earlier non-affixational account of Irish lenition is Gussmann 1986 where (roughly) the stop-to-continuant alteration is analyzed as the spreading of [+cont] from the second segment of a stem to the first, the lenition of coronals is handled by a feature changing rule, and the lenition of f('), by a deletion rule.

autosegment affixation include Japanese mimetics (Mester and Itô 1989) and numerous cases discussed in Cole 1987. Characteristic of floating autosegment affixation is the routine linking of an autosegment to nonperipheral stem segments (cf. the Chaha example above). It is this fact that makes floating autosegment analyses of mutation phenomena--strictly peripheral effects--untenable.

The view to be adopted and advocated here is that mutation phenomena are segment-altering processes triggered upon the affixation of a rooted or anchored autosegment or set of autosegments.[5] Like floating autosegment analyses of mutation, this line of analysis accounts for the absence of overt segmental addition to a stem by identifying the mutation affix as subsegmental; i.e., the anchored featural content of such an affix is insufficient to merit full segment status.[6] Unlike floating autosegment analyses, however, an anchored autosegment analysis of mutation accounts directly for the peripherality of such processes by identifying the featural content of the affix as anchored to a root node, not as floating.

The idea that strictly peripheral segment-altering processes involve the affixation of an anchored autosegment or autosegments is not a new one. Itô and Mester (1986) analyze Japanese Rendaku, a process in which the initial segment of the second member of a compound is voiced, as affixation of an anchored [voice] autosegment with subsequent voicing assimilation of the adjacent initial stem segment. Fusion processes, where the root node of an anchored autosegmental affix merges (under feature compatibility) with an adjacent root node of the stem, are discussed in Steriade 1991. Unnoted to date, however, are cases of anchored autosegment affixation which trigger dissimilatory processes in an adjacent stem segment. This gap is troubling since anchored autosegments, for the very reason that they have a root node, should participate in the full range of phenomena that fall under the heading 'adjacency effects' (Prince 1984).

The claim of this paper is that Irish lenition fills in this gap. Irish lenition is analyzed here as a set of dissimilatory processes triggered upon the prefixation (and syllabification) of a morpheme consisting of the anchored features [-cont] and [cor]. The stop to continuant alteration is analyzed as a sonority driven repair process that operates on derived [-cont] [-cont] onset sequences. Loss of coronality in the lenition of coronal obstruents is analyzed as a repair process operating on derived [cor] [cor] onset sequences in accordance with the Obligatory Contour Principle (Leben 1973, McCarthy 1979, 1981, 1986). The realization of certain lenited consonants as glides and the realization of the lenited velarized voiced coronal as a velar fricative are attributed to subsidiary processes governed by Structure Preservation; the former attributed to a process of primary to secondary place demotion, following Ní Chiosáin 1991; the latter, to a process of secondary to primary place promotion of the kind discussed in Clements 1991.

---

[5] I am indebted to Armin Mester (personal communication) for pointing out the relationship between the analysis of Irish lenition to be presented below and previous analyses employing anchored autosegment affixation. It was Armin's suggestion that all such phenomena properly fall under the rubric 'mutation'.

[6] This may be too strong. It is conceivable that some mutation systems involve full segment affixation where the ultimate non-realization of such an affix is due to syllabification constraints.

2.0 Preliminaries

The complete inventory of Irish consonants and glides is given in (3). Segments in parentheses are segments that do not occur in initial position underlyingly and hence are not subject to mutation.

(3)

	labial	alveolar	palatal	velar	labiovelar	laryngeal
stop	p p′	t t′		k k′		
	b b′	d d′		g g′		
fricative	f f′	s s′		(x) (x′)		(h) (h′)
	(v′)			(γ)		
nasal	m m′	n n′		(ŋ) (ŋ′)		
liquid		l l′				
		r (r′)				
glide			(j)		(w)	

All Irish consonants except the nonpalatalized velars (and glides) are either palatalized or velarized and this distinction is contrastive: e.g., *bó* [bo:] 'cow' vs. *beo* [b′o:] 'alive', *tubh* [tu:] 'touch' vs. *tiubhaigh* [t′u:] 'thicken'.

I assume the feature geometry in (4) for the representation of Irish segments where manner of articulation features are directly linked to the root node and place features, as well as [lateral] and [nasal], are privative (Clements 1985, Sagey 1986, Schein and Steriade 1986, McCarthy 1988). I follow Ní Chiosáin 1991 in recognizing a distinct secondary place node for Irish and adopt the proposal of Clements 1991 concerning the location of this node in the tree structure and its dependents. In Clements's structure, consonant and vocoid (vowel and glide) features are identical. The primary place features of consonants are linked directly to CPlace; secondary articulation and vocoid place features are linked to VPlace, which is itself linked to CPlace, with palatalization represented by linking to VPlace [coronal] and velarization, by linking to VPlace [dorsal].

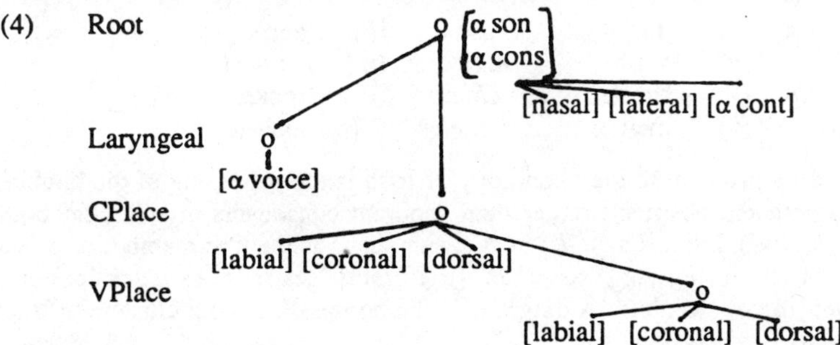

The degree of specification of Irish consonants is an issue largely independent of the analysis to be presented here. I will assume for the purposes of this analysis that all features are fully specified at the point where lenition applies, although nothing in the analysis crucially hinges on this assumption.

3.0 Sonority-driven [-cont]-delinking

In (5) is repeated the set of facts to be accounted for.

(5)	p	p′	b	b′	m	m′	k	k′	g	g′	t	t′	d	d′	s	s′	n	n′	l	l′	r	f	f′
	↓	↓	↓	↓	↓	↓	↓	↓	↓	↓	↓	↓	↓	↓	↓	↓	↓	↓	↓	↓	↓	↓	↓
	f	f′	w	v′	w	v′	x	x′	γ	j	h	h′	γ	j	h	h′	n	n′	l	l′	r	Ø	Ø

Let me state at the outset that the lenition of f(′) will remain mysterious here; this analysis, like all previous analyses of Irish lenition, must resort to handling the lenition of f(′) via a separate rule of f(′)-deletion. That said, let us begin by examining the stop to continuant alteration, which characterizes the lenition of noncoronal stops, exemplified in (6) with past tense verb formation.

(6)a.	*pós*	[p]	'marry'	*phós*	[f]	'married'
	pioc	[p′]	'pick'	*phioc*	[f′]	'picked'
b.	*báigh*	[b]	'drown'	*bháigh*	[w]	'drowned'
	bearr	[b′]	'shave'	*bhearr*	[v′]	'shaved'
c.	*caith*	[k]	'spend'	*chaith*	[x]	'spent'
	ciúnaigh	[k′]	'quieten'	*chiúnaigh*	[x′]	'quietened'
d.	*gortaigh*	[g]	'hurt'	*ghortaigh*	[γ]	'hurt (past)'
	gearr	[g′]	'cut'	*ghearr*	[j]	'cut (past)'
e.	*mol*	[m]	'praise'	*mhol*	[w]	'praised'
	meas	[m′]	'think'	*mheas*	[v′]	'thought'

The lenition of a noncoronal stop results in a segment of increased sonority. This observation, together with the view that lenition involves the affixation of anchored featural content, suggests that this alteration is triggered by the creation of a sonority sequencing violation upon prefixation of the leniting affix.

That sonority sequencing is the principle governing the lenition of noncoronal stops is further suggested by the fact that m(′) but not n(′) or l(′)--all sonorant noncontinuants by standard accounts--undergoes a change in continuancy.

(7)a.	*nasc*	[n]	'tie'	*nasc*	[n]	'tied'
	nigh	[n′]	'wash'	*nigh*	[n′]	'washed'
b.	*labhair*	[l]	'speak'	*labhair*	[l]	'spoke'
	leáigh	[l′]	'melt'	*leáigh*	[l′]	'melted'

An outstanding problem in the phonology of Irish is the patterning of the bilabial nasal m(′) with the obstruent rather than sonorant consonants in syllabification. For example, m(′), but not n(′), l(′) or r(′), can occur as the first member of a two consonant onset cluster; e.g., *mriathán* [m′r′i:ra:n] 'sea-rods', *mléach* [m′l′e:x] 'grist', *mná* [mna:] 'women'. A diagram of the permissible onset clusters in Irish is given in (8).[7]

[7] Three comments are in order concerning the diagram of Irish onsets in (8). First, there is some dialectal variation as regards the onset cluster mn; in general, the southern Irish dialects have this cluster, while the Northern and Western dialects do not-- orthographic mn in these dialects is pronounced [mr]: *mná* [mra:] 'women'.

Secondly, a general though not absolute constraint on consonant clusters in Irish is agreement in secondary place of articulation (see Ó Siadhail 1989 for discussion).

Thirdly, although there are initial sp(′), s(′)t(′), s(′)k(′), and sm(′) clusters in Irish, (but not s′p(′) or

(8)

C1 → C2 ↓	p(′)	b(′)	t(′)	d(′)	k(′)	g(′)	f(′)	s	s′	m(′)	n(′)	l(′)	r(′)
n(′)			+		+	+		+	+	+			
l(′)	+	+	+	+	+	+	+	+	+	+			
r(′)	+	+	+	+	+	+	+	+		+			
m(′)													

Various proposals for formally handling the obstruent-like behavior of m(′) have been put forth, including the classification of m(′) as a nonsonorant (Rogers 1972, O'Dochartaigh 1978)[8] and the underspecification of m(′) for the feature [sonorant] (Ní Chiosáin 1991). For the purposes of this analysis, which, if either, of these proposals is best adopted is a side issue. What is important here is the fact that the bilabial nasal is to some degree less sonorant than the coronal nasal and lateral, enough so that it is subject to a change in continuancy in lenition-inducing environments.

The trigger for the spirantization of noncoronal stops is analyzed here as the prefixation of the leniting affix which consists (in part) of a root node linked to [-cont]. When this prefix is syllabified into a stem whose initial consonant is a noncontinuant obstruent or m(′), an unacceptable sequence of onset segments arises and is obligatorily 'repaired' by spirantizing the second segment, the stem-initial consonant. The spirantization operation can be formalized in a number of ways. I will treat it as a delinking operation, where [-cont] is delinked as necessary in observance of sonority.[9] [+cont], I assume, is later filled in by default.[10]

(9) [-cont]-delinking: delink [-cont] in accordance with sonority

The lenition of noncoronal stops, then, proceeds as diagrammed in (10) (with irrelevant parts of the feature geometry omitted). Note that spirantization of the bilabial nasals is accompanied by a loss of nasality,[11] presumably in accordance

s′m(′)), I assume such sonority-violating clusters are not true complex onsets but rather consist of an extrasyllabic fricative plus a single onset consonant. Justification for including sm(′) clusters in this set comes from the behavior of such clusters in lenition-triggering environments, seen below in section 5, data set (21).

[8] In O Dochartaigh (1978), the bilabial nasal is not treated as a 'nonsonorant', precisely, but as a segment with the same degree of sonority as voiced fricatives, represented configurationally within the framework of dependency phonology.

[9] The OCP is not identified as the trigger for [-cont]-delinking in light of McCarthy 1988 and Yip 1989, where it is demonstrated that the OCP is largely irrelevant to processes affecting manner of articulation and major class features. For this reason, in addition, I assume that prefixation of the leniting affix to a [-cont] coronal sonorant-initial stem, which results in a sequence of two instances of the feature [-cont], is not problematic. Either the OCP does not hold here or such sequences undergo automatic fusion upon Tier Conflation (cf. Yip 1988).

[10] The re-linking of [-cont] can be formally precluded in a number of ways. The most straighforward of these is to assume that sonority sequencing is enforced at all levels of the derivation for onset clusters; hence an unacceptable cluster that arises upon affixation will remain unacceptable unless (permanently) fixed. Alternatively, we might invoke the Relinking Condition of Pulleyblank 1986 which explicitly precludes the re-linking of a feature that has been delinked by rule.

[11] This statement needs some qualification. While it is generally the case that the lenition of m(′) results in a loss of nasality, there appear to be instances where nasality is retained: Ní Chiosáin (1991; p.24), citing de Bhaldraithe 1945 and O'Siadhail 1989, notes '...labial glides and fricatives that are derived from underly-

with Structure Preservation, there being no nasal fricatives (or glides) in the inventory of Irish.

(10) the mutation of noncoronal stops: sonority-driven [-cont]-delinking

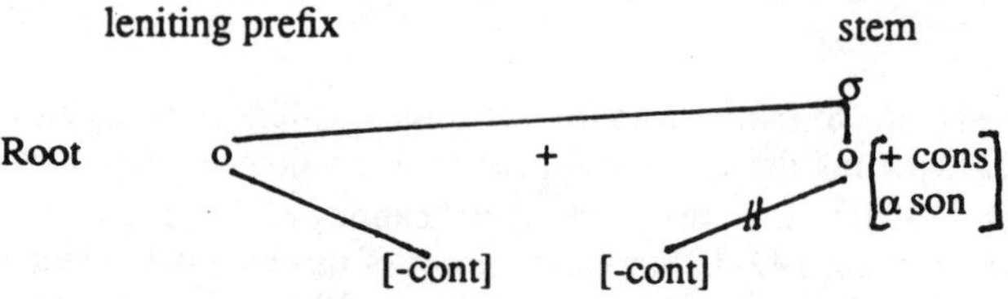

3.1 The lenition of /b/, /m/, and /g′/: primary place demotion

Application of [-cont]-delinking to the velarized voiced labials /b/ and /m/ produces the velarized fricative /v/. Application of [-cont]-delinking to the palatalized voiced velar /g′/ produces the palatalized fricative /ɣ′/. As seen in (3), these fricatives are not part of the Irish inventory and, as seen in (1), these fricatives are not the lenited forms of /b/, /m/, and /g′/. /b/ and /m/ lenite to /w/; /g′/ lenites to /j/. To handle this fact, I assume a process of Glide Formation which applies to the output of [-cont]-delinking in these cases, this further alteration required by Structure Preservation to create acceptable Irish segments from unacceptable ones.

Ní Chiosáin 1991 proposes to handle the gliding of /v/ and /ɣ′/ via a primary-to-secondary place demotion process which induces a simultaneous change in major class features from [+cons, αson] to [-cons, +son].[12] Given the feature geometry assumed here, and again omitting irrelevant details as well as the changes in [cons] and [son], this operation will proceed as illustrated in (11). In (11a) is the demotion of [labial] to VPlace. As this node already dominates [dorsal], the end result of demotion is the labiovelar glide /w/. In (11b) is the demotion of [dorsal] to VPlace. Here, the VPlace is linked to [cor], where the palatalization of the underlying segment is represented. As [cor] and [dorsal] are incompatible features, equivalent, roughly, to [-back] and [+back], respectively, the linking of [dorsal] to VPlace is precluded and [dorsal] demotion ultimately results in the deletion of primary [dorsal], producing the palatal glide /j/.

(11)a. /b/, /m/ → /w/ b. /ɣ′/ → /j/

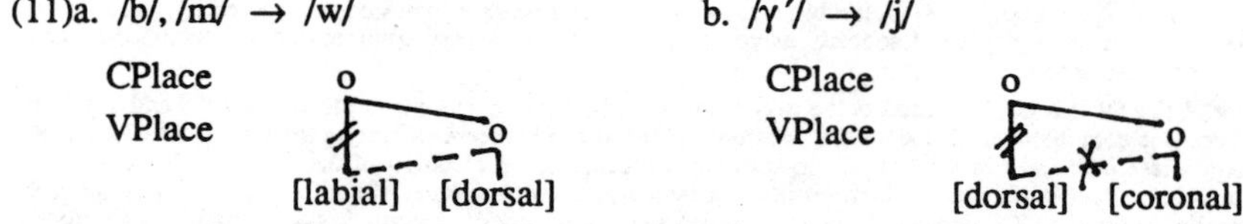

ing labial nasals are commonly weakly nasalized by older speakers of the western dialect of Irish'; O'Dochartaigh (1978; fn. 6) writes, '...the phonetic nasality of the segment [lenited m(′)] shows a strong tendency to be reduced in most dialects--either disappearing entirely or being realized as nasality on the surrounding vowel segments.'

[12] Glide Formation in Ní Chiosáin 1991 is viewed as an optional operation in contrast to the view here that Glide Formation is obligatory as required by Structure Preservation.

4.0 OCP-driven [coronal]-delinking

Like the noncoronals, the coronal stops, t(ʹ) and d(ʹ), undergo [-cont]-delinking upon affixation of the leniting prefix; however, matters are complicated here by a simultaneous change in place of articulation for these segments: the voiced stops /d/ and /dʹ/ lenite to a velar fricative and palatal glide, respectively, and the voiceless stops /t/ and /tʹ/, like the coronal fricatives /s/ and /sʹ/, lenite to /h/ and /hʹ/.

(12)a.	*tosaigh*	[t]	'begin'	*thosaigh*	[h]	'began'
	tiubhaigh	[tʹ]	'thicken'	*thiubhaigh*	[hʹ]	'thickened'
b.	*dúisigh*	[d]	'wake up'	*dhúisigh*	[ɣ]	'woke up'
	diúl	[dʹ]	'suck'	*dhiúl*	[j]	'sucked'
c.	*salaigh*	[s]	'dirty'	*shalaigh*	[h]	'dirtied'
	siúil	[sʹ]	'walk'	*shiúil*	[hʹ]	'walked'

Compelling support for the anchored autosegment approach to an analysis of mutation is the fact that disparate alteration processes can be attributed to a common source. What makes this possible, of course, is the availability of a root node in the mutation-inducing affix to which more than one feature may be anchored. In the case of Irish lenition, the mutation of coronal obstruents can be derived by assuming that the leniting prefix consists of a root node linked to CPlace [coronal] as well as to [-cont].

(13) The leniting prefix

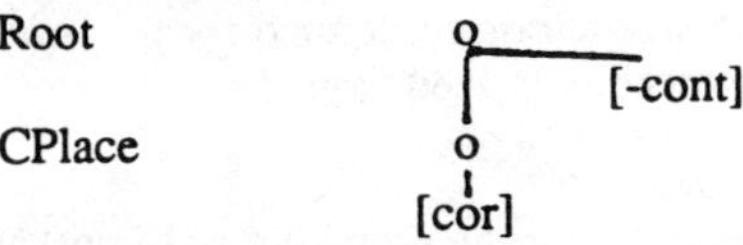

With this proposal, the lenition of coronal obstruents is derived via the delinking of their primary place node to correct an OCP violation arising as a result of the affixation of the leniting prefix. This rule, formalized in (14), is properly viewed as a process of onset dissimilation.[13]

(14) [coronal]-delinking

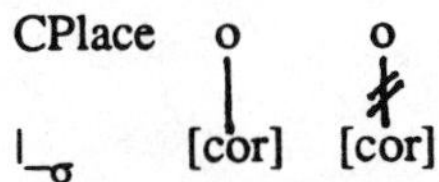

Application of [coronal]-delinking, together with [-cont]-delinking for the stops, is shown in (15).

[13] Viewing [coronal]-delinking as restricted to onsets allows for initial clusters consisting of an extrasyllabic coronal followed by a coronal stop, s(ʹ)t(ʹ) (cf. fn.6).

(15) the mutation of coronal obstruents: OCP-triggered coronal-delinking

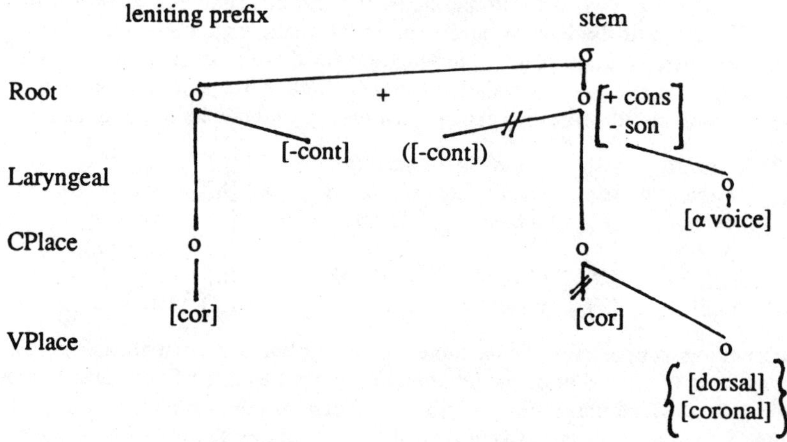

For the voiceless coronals s(ʹ) and t(ʹ), the delinking operations produce a primary placeless voiceless continuant, h(ʹ), as is correct. The lenition of the palatalized voiced coronal stop is also correctly derived via the delinking of [-cont] and [cor], provided we assume an automatic change in major class features from [+cons, -son] to [-cons, +son]; the lenited form of this consonant being the palatal glide /j/ (cf. (11b)). The only coronal obstruent whose correct lenited form is not derived via [-cont]- and [cor]-delinking is the voiced velarized stop /d/.

4.1 Secondary place promotion

Consider the representation of this segment after the delinking of [-cont] and [cor] in (16) where the default feature [+cont] has been added (cf. fn.9).

(16)

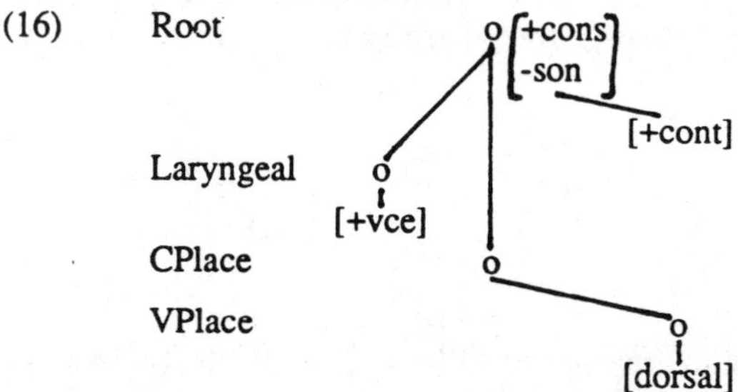

It is not clear what segment the configuration in (16) would represent other than a velar glide /ɰ/, assuming an appropriate amendment of the root node features. Whatever segment this is, it is neither in the inventory of Irish nor the lenited form of /d/.

The voiced velarized coronal /d/ lenites to the velar fricative /ɣ/. We can obtain this result straightforwardly from the representation in (16) via a promotion of VPlace [dorsal] to CPlace. This promotion operation is formalized in (17) as a tree pruning operation, where [α place] signifies any of the features [labial], [coronal], or [dorsal], and the place nodes are unlabelled, their identification being structurally determinable: CPlace is the node dominating [α place] that is immediately dominated by the root node; VPlace is the node dominating [α place] that is itself immediately dominated by a daughter of the root. Note that this rule must be restricted to apply only when necessary to 'fix' a segment not in accordance with Structure Preservation to prevent its applying to acceptable vocoids and h(ʹ).

(17) Secondary Place promotion (in accordance with Structure Preservation)

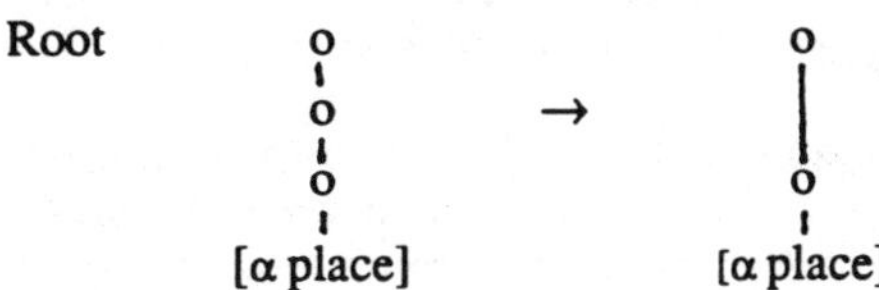

Application of this rule to the structure in (16) produces the velar fricative /ɣ/, as required.

(18)

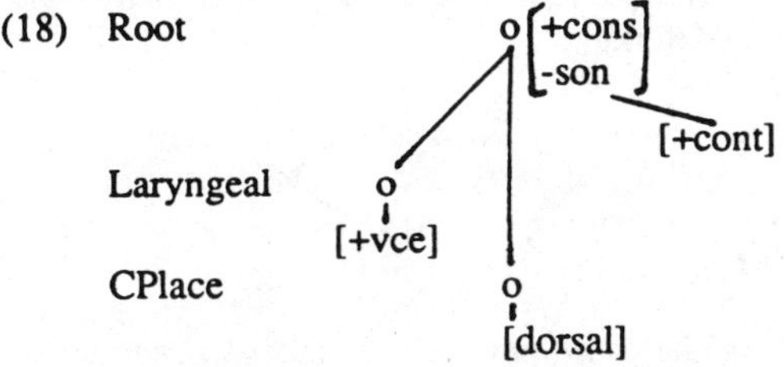

The elegance of this account of the lenition of /d/ is due in large part to our adoption of the feature geometry proposed in Clements 1991 and thus lends substantial support to this proposal as well as to the claim made in that work that promotion processes of the type seen here are operative in natural language.[14]

4.2 Coronal sonorants

A potential embarrassment for the analysis of Irish lenition presented to this point is the behavior of coronal sonorants in lenition-triggering environments. Recall that these segments undergo no change; the past tense form of *roinn* [ri:n] 'divide', for example, is identical to the base form, *roinn* [ri:n] 'divided' (see also (7)). Application of [coronal]-delinking, therefore, must somehow be prevented from applying to these segments.

The obvious and simplest way out of this dilemma is to assume that sonorants

[14] The 'hardening' of the glides /j/ and /w/ discussed in fn.1 might also be viewed as a promotion process triggered not by Structure Preservation, but by sonority considerations. In the case of the palatal glide, whose place feature is a VPlace [coronal], promotion of [coronal] to CPlace to create a (voiced) palatal fricative seems quite straightforward and can be accomplished via the 'tree-pruning' operation proposed in (17). In the case of the hardening of the labiovelar glide, however, matters are slightly complicated as this segment has two VPlace features, [dorsal] and [labial], only one of which, [labial], can be permitted to promote in order to correctly derive a velarized labial fricative. This type of promotion could not be treated as a 'tree-pruning' operation, perhaps indicating that the rule in (17) is too simple or perhaps indicating the need to recognize more than one kind of VPlace promotion operation (cf. Clements 1991 for a discussion of various promotion processes).

are unspecified for (CPlace) [coronal] at the point where [coronal]-delinking applies. Coronal sonorants, then, would not undergo [coronal]-delinking because there would be no [coronal] to delink. This solution, unfortunately, appears to be unavailable, given the persuasive arguments in Ní Chiosáin 1991 for the underlying specification of [coronal] for both obstruents and sonorants in Irish. An alternative explanation, therefore, is needed.

A certainly relevant fact is the acceptability of coronal obstruent + coronal sonorant onset clusters in Irish (cf. (8)). The acceptability of such clusters entails a shared primary place node in order to satisfy the OCP and this observation in turn suggests an explanation for the failure of coronal sonorants to undergo [coronal]-delinking.

Suppose that an OCP-violating [cor] [cor] sequence arising upon prefixation of the leniting affix can be corrected in one of two ways: either via [coronal]-delinking, as in the cases we have seen to this point, or via coronal fusion (19), with the choice determined by the syllabification constraints of Irish. As coronal + coronal sonorant clusters are well-formed onsets in Irish, the latter operation applies to sonorant-initial stems. As coronal + coronal obstruent clusters are ill-formed Irish onsets, coronal fusion is not possible in obstruent-initial stems, and the second instance of [cor] subject to delinking.

(19) coronal fusion

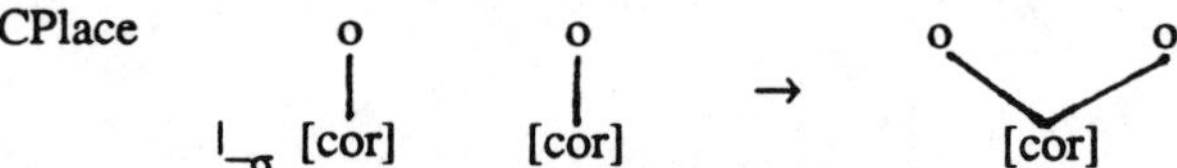

With the addition of coronal fusion, the 'non-lenition' of coronal sonorants is accounted for and our analysis of Irish lenition essentially complete.

5.0 Syllabification of the leniting prefix

The analysis of Irish lenition developed here crucially depends on the so far unjustified assumption that the leniting prefix is syllabified into the initial onset of a stem. This assumption is necessary, of course, to motivate the application of [-cont]-delinking, [coronal]-delinking, and coronal fusion, rules which make crucial reference to properties of the syllable: sonority sequencing in the case of [-cont]-delinking, onset cluster constraints in the cases of [coronal]-delinking and fusion. As the leniting prefix is subsegmental and hence not phonetically realizable, it is conveniently difficult to argue against this assumption. There is, however, evidence to believe that this assumption is correct. Consider the data in (20) and (21).

(20)					
a.	*glan*	[glan]	*ghlan*	[ɣlan]	'clean'/'cleaned'
b.	*bris*	[b′r′is′]	*bhris*	[v′r′is′]	'break'/'broke'
c.	*snámh*	[sna:]	*shnámh*	[hna:]	'swim'/'swam'
d.	*sleáigh*	[s′l′a:]	*shleáigh*	[h′l′a:]	'spear'/'speared'

(21)a. *stuáil*	[stua:l′]	'stow'/'stowed'	*[htua:l′]
b. *sciob*	[s′k′ib]	'snatch'/'snatched'	*[h′k′ib]
c. *smaoinigh*	[smi:n′ə]	'think'/'thought'	*[hmi:n′ə]

In (20) are the past tense forms of verbs whose initial onset is a sonority-observing cluster. Lenition in these forms applies as before. In (21) are the past tense forms of verbs with initial sonority-violating clusters. These forms are identical to the base forms--specifically, the initial s(′) does not mutate to h(′) as it does in (20c) and (20d). This contrast can be explained by assuming that the leniting prefix has been syllabified in (20), but not in (21), due to the intervening presence of an extrasyllabic consonant, /s/ or /s′/. Given that the rules of [-cont]-delinking, [coronal]-delinking and coronal fusion apply within a syllable, it follows that if the leniting prefix is not syllabified into a stem, these rules will be inapplicable. The set of facts above, then, are precisely as this analysis predicts and validate the assumption that the leniting prefix is syllabified when possible.

6.0 Conclusion and speculation

Let me begin this conclusion with a summary of what has been accomplished in the sections above. Beginning with the observation that floating autosegment analyses are inappropriate to accounts of strictly peripheral phenomena--i.e., mutations--we showed that, with the exception of the lenition of f(′), the array of facts characterizing the Irish lenition system reduced to a set of dissimilatory processes triggered upon the prefixation of a subsegmental affix consisting of the anchored features [-cont] and [cor]; a welcome result, given that the participation of anchored autosegmental affixes in dissimilatory processes had heretofore gone unnoted, although predicted to exist by autosegmental theory. Furthermore, an anchored autosegment analysis of Irish lenition proved to be uniquely successful in providing a unified account of the lenition of noncontinuants and the lenition of coronals, insofar as it identifies a common trigger, the subsegmental prefix, for both sets of alterations; a result which lends substantial support to the view that such subsegmental affixes exist and to the theory which predicts their existence. Finally, the feature geometry of Clements 1991 was shown to facilitate a surprisingly simple account of the lenition of certain consonants to glides, (Ní Chiosáin's (1991) primary place (CPlace) demotion), and of the lenition of /d/ to /γ/, analyzed here as involving, in part, a VPlace promotion process of the type described in Clements's work.

Let me end this discussion with an intriguing set of facts and some speculation as to their relevance. Throughout this paper, the data presented to exemplify Irish lenition have been (almost) exclusively restricted to past tense verb forms. Although lenition is triggered in many other morphosyntactic environments, past tense verb formation is particularly interesting because it is the only lenition-triggering environment where an overt prefix appears on vowel- and f(′)-initial stems. The prefix that appears here is a coronal stop.

(22)a.	*aontaigh*	[intə]	*d'aontaigh*	[dintə]	'agree'/'agreed'
b.	*uachtaigh*	[uəxtə]	*d'uachtaigh*	[duəxtə]	'will'/'willed'
c.	*fág*	[fa:g]	*d'fhág*	[da:g]	'leave'/'left'
d.	*foghlaim*	[foləm′]	*d'fhoghlaim*	[doləm′]	'learn'/'learned'

Given the proposal that the featural content of the leniting prefix is [-cont] and [cor], these data are striking, and it is tempting to identify the prefixed /d/ in these examples as the leniting prefix itself. Alternatively, of course, one could attribute the appearance of an overt coronal stop prefix in (22) to coincidence and regard these forms as doubly prefixed; once by the past tense prefix /d/ (deleted before consonant-initial stems), and again by the leniting prefix.[15] At present, it is not clear to me which of these analyses is preferable. Let me sketch, however, how an analysis of the former type might proceed in a way compatible with the overall analysis of Irish lenition proposed in this paper.

If one pursues the possibility that the overt prefix in (22) is the leniting prefix itself, a number of questions arise, including 1) What, precisely, permits the realization of the leniting prefix in (22)? 2) Why /d/? 3) Why doesn't an overt prefix show up in other lenition-triggering environments; for example, on vowel- and f(′)-initial feminine nounstems after the definite article?[16]

(23)a.	*cearc*	[k′ark]	*an chearc*	[ə x′ark]	'hen'/'the hen'
b.	*aois*	[i:s′]	*an aois*	[ən i:s′]	'age'/'the age'
c.	*iníon*	[in′i:n′]	*an iníon*	[ən′ in′i:n′]	'daughter'/'the daughter'
d.	*folc*	[folk]	*an fholc*	[ən olk]	'flood'/'the flood'
e.	*feoil*	[f′o:l′]	*an fheoil*	[ən′ o:l′]	'meat'/'the meat'

The latter two questions appear to require the same answer and that is that Irish has not one but (at least) two leniting prefixes, both of which consist of the anchored features [-cont] and [cor], (and hence trigger the same dissimilatory processes in adjacent tautosyllabic consonants), but only one of which consists solely of these features. That is, suppose that in all lenition-triggering environments except past tense verb formation, the prefix which occurs is the one posited above in (13). Suppose, in contrast, that the leniting prefix of past tense verb formation, plausibly identifiable as the past tense morpheme itself, consists of the anchored feature [+voice], in addition to the features [-cont] and [cor], and has a root node specified as [+cons, -son]. The addition of the features [+voice], [+cons], and [-son] to the representation in (13) would identify this second leniting prefix as a voiced coronal stop, as required.

Note that if no specification for a secondary place feature is added to the representation of this new leniting prefix, it is feasible that this prefix, like the first, can be viewed as subsegmental, given the Irish consonant inventory, where all consonants, except the nonpalatalized velars, have a secondary place of

[15] This analysis of the data in (22) was suggested to me, at different times, by Armin Mester, Bill Ladusaw, and Jim McCloskey.

[16] Note that the final consonant of the definite article appears only before vowel-initial stems (compare (23a) and (23b-e)). Note also that this consonant is a coronal nasal. With few exceptions, the final consonant of the word or clitic preceding a lenited form is coronal and realized only before vowel-initial stems. This fact may prove significant upon further investigation.

articulation. Viewing the leniting prefix of past tense verb formation as subsegmental appears to be necessary in order to account for the absence of an overt prefix in the past tense forms of consonant-initial verbstems; in particular, in the past tense forms of coronal sonorant-initial verbstems (cf. section 4.2) in light of the fact that d(ʹ)r(ʹ) and d(ʹ)l(ʹ) are acceptable onset clusters in Irish(cf. (8)). If this is correct, and the past tense leniting prefix is subsegmental because of its lack of a secondary place specification, we would expect its appearance only under the circumstance that a secondary place specification was somehow made available to it. The availability of such a specification is precisely what distinguishes vowel- and f(ʹ)-initial stems from consonant-initial stems in lenition triggering environments.

To see this, consider first the lenition of f(ʹ)-initial stems. Recall that the lenition of f(ʹ) corresponds to a deletion process (cf. (1)). Not all of f(ʹ) is deleted, however; specifically, the secondary place specification of the underlying segment is retained and appears on a preceding consonant. Compare the past tense forms in (24) with those in (22c) and (22d) (see also (23d) and (23e)).

(24)a.	*feall*	[fʹa:l]	*d'fheall*	[dʹa:l]	'betray'/'betrayed'
b.	*feoigh*	[fʹo:]	*d'fheoigh*	[dʹo:]	'wither'/'withered'

In (24), the prefixed coronal stop is palatalized as is the underlying stem-initial consonant in contrast to the forms in (22c) and (22d), where both prefix and underlying segment are velarized. It appears that the deletion of f(ʹ) in lenition-triggering environments serves to 'free up' a secondary place of articulation feature which can associate to a preceding place node; when that preceding place node belongs to the leniting prefix of past tense verb formation, the end result of this association is the creation of a full-fledged phonetically realized segment, /d/ or /dʹ/.

Finally, consider the data in (25).

(25)a.	*íoc*	[i:k]	*d'íoc*	[dʹi:k]	'pay'/'paid'
b.	*iompaigh*	[umpə]	*d'iompaigh*	[dʹumpə]	'turn'/'turned'

Here we have additional past tense forms of vowel-initial stems. Note that whereas the prefixed /d/ in (22a) and (22b) is velarized, the prefix in these examples is palatalized. Note, furthermore, that the palatalization or velarization of this prefix is not predictable in terms of the place features of the stem-initial vowel; compare (22a) with (25a), (22b) with (25b). To account for facts like those in (22a,b) and (25) (as well as (23b), (23c)), Ní Chiosáin 1991, elaborating on a proposal made in Gussmann 1986, proposes that all vowel-initial stems in Irish are in fact consonant-initial; in specific, that all vowel-initial stems have an initial 'consonant' onset consisting of a consonantal root node linked solely to a secondary place specification; in our terms, VPlace [coronal] or [dorsal]. This VPlace feature can associate to a preceding place node via a spreading operation, as proposed in Ní Chiosáin 1991 or, perhaps, via a fusion operation. However this association is accomplished, the end result is again the creation of a full fledged segment, /d/ or /dʹ/, when the preceding place node is that of the leniting prefix proposed for past tense verb formation.

To conclude, while this analysis of past tense verb formation in Irish is sketchy, and can only be regarded as speculative at this point, it appears to be a viable one. Whether it is correct or not, and, more generally, whether it is appropriate to recognize one or more than one leniting prefix in Irish, are questions that depend, in large part, on the appropriate morphosyntactic characterization of the full range of lenition-triggering environments and on the appropriate characterization of the process by which a leniting prefix is introduced into a morphological or syntactic structure. These issues, I leave for future work.

References

Breatnach, Risteard B. 1967. *The Irish of Ring, Co. Waterford*. Dublin: Dublin Institute for Advanced Studies.

Clements, George N. 1985. The geometry of phonological features. *Phonology Yearbook* 2: 225-252.

Clements, George. N. 1991. Place of articulation in consonants and vowels: a unified theory. ms. [to appear in *L'Architecture et la Géométrie des Représentations Phonologiques*, eds. B. Laks and A. Rialland. Paris: Editions du C.N.R.S.]

Cole, Jennifer. 1987. *Planar phonology and morphology*. Doctoral dissertation, MIT, Cambridge, Mass.

de Bhaldraithe, Tomás. 1945. *The Irish of Cois Fharraige, Co. Galway*. Dublin: Dublin Institute for Advanced Studies.

Gussmann, Edmund. 1986. Autosegments, linked matrices, and the Irish lenition. *Linguistics across historical and geographic boundaries, vol. 2*, eds. D. Kastovsky and A. Szwedek, 891-907. Amsterdam: Mouton de Gruyer.

Itô, Junko and R. Armin Mester. 1986. The phonology of voicing in Japanese: theoretical consequences for morphological accessibility. *Linguistic Inquiry* 17:49-73.

Leben, William R. 1973. *Suprasegmental phonology*. Doctoral dissertation, MIT, Cambridge, Mass. [Published, New York: Garland, 1979.]

Lieber, Rochelle. 1984. Consonant gradation in Fula: an autosegmental approach. *Language Sound Structure*, eds. Mark Aronoff and Richard Oehrle. Cambridge, Mass.: MIT Press.

Lieber, Rochelle. 1987. *An integrated theory of autosegmental processes*. Albany: State University of New York Press.

Massam, Diane. 1983. Phonological and morphological aspects of Irish lenition. ms. MIT, Cambridge, Mass.

McCarthy, John. 1979. *Formal problems in Semitic phonology and morphology*. Doctoral dissertation, MIT, Cambridge, Mass.

McCarthy, John. 1981. A prosodic theory of nonconcatenative morphology. *Linguistic Inquiry* 12: 373-413.

McCarthy, John. 1983. Consonantal morphology on the Chaha verb. *Proceedings of the West Coast Conference on Formal Linguistics* 2:176-88.

McCarthy, John. 1986. OCP effects: gemination and antigemination. *Linguistic Inquiry* 17: 207-263.

McCarthy, John. 1988. Feature geometry and dependency: a review. *Phonetica* 43:84-108.

Mester, R. Armin, and Junko Itô. 1989. Feature predictability and underspecification: palatal prosody in Japanese mimetics. *Language* 65:258-294.

Ní Chiosáin, Máire. 1991. *Topics in Irish Phonology*. Doctoral dissertation, University of Massachusetts Amherst.

O'Cuív, Brian. 1975. *The Irish of West Muskerry, Co. Cork*. Dublin: Dublin Institute for Advanced Studies.

O'Dochartaigh, Cathair. 1978. Lenition and dependency phonology. *Eigse* 17:457-494.

O'Donaill,Niall. 1977. *Foclóir Gaeilge-Béarla*. Dublin: Richview Browne & Nolan Ltd.

O'Siadhail, Mícheál. 1989. *Modern Irish: grammatical structure and dialectal variation*. Cambridge: Cambridge University Press.

Prince, Alan S. 1984. Phonology with tiers. *Language Sound Structure* eds. Mark Aronoff and Richard Oehrle, 234-244. Cambridge, Massachusetts: MIT Press.

Pulleyblank, Douglas. 1986. *Tone in lexical phonology*. Dordrecht: Reidel.

Rogers, H. 1972. The initial mutations in Modern Scots Gaelic. *Studia Celtica*. 7:63-85.

Sagey, Elizabeth. 1986. *The representation of features and relations in non-linear phonology*. Doctoral dissertation, MIT, Cambridge, Mass.

Schein, Barry and Donca Steriade. 1986. On geminates. *Linguistic Inquiry* 17:691-744.

Sommerfelt, Alf. 1922. *The Dialect of Torr, Co. Donegal*. Christiania.

Steriade, Donca. 1991. Closure, release, and nasal contours. ms. UCLA.

Ultan, Russell. 1970. Some sources of consonant gradation. *Stanford University Working Papers in Linguistics Universals*, no.2.

Wagner, Heinrich. 1959. *Gaeilge Theilinn*. Dublin: Dublin Institute for Advanced Studies.

Yip, Moira. 1988. The OCP and phonological rules: a loss of identity. *Linguistic Inquiry* 19: 65-99.

Yip, Moira. 1989. Feature geometry and cooccurrence restrictions. *Phonology* 6: 349-374.

Auxiliary Coalescence in Chicheŵa: Mismatch Not Required

WHITNEY TABOR
Stanford University

Recent work on the phonology of units larger than the word has resulted in a number of theories which allow 'mismatch' between the prosodic and syntactic constituent structures of utterances (see, among others, Selkirk (1980), (1984), (1986), Nespor and Vogel (1982), Chen (1985), Myers (1987), (1989), Kanerva (1990a), (1990b)). In fact, the two kinds of constituent structure usually coincide. To predict this pervasive coincidence, mismatch theories generally posit a mapping which generates prosodic structure from information about syntactic structure. My purpose here is to point out that if there is an empirically accurate approach which does not require mismatch and is otherwise no more complicated than the mismatch approach, then, to minimize complexity of description, the mismatch approach should be cast aside in favor of this unistructural account. I will consider a particular phenomenon—an auxiliary coalescence alternation in the Nkhotakota dialect of Chicheŵa—for which a mismatch account is tempting. Indeed Myers (1987) and (1989) has proposed a mismatch account of a closely related phenomenon in Chishona. Nevertheless, I will argue that there is a more elegant characterization in which prosodic and syntactic units coincide.

Chicheŵa auxiliary coalescence is illustrated in (1) and (2).

(1) Long-form auxiliary:	A-na-*yés-á*	ku-túng-á	mǎ-dzi.
	3rd-PAST-try-FV	INF-draw-FV	6-water
	'(S)he tried to draw water' (FV = 'final vowel')		

(2) Coalesced auxiliary (CA):	A-na-*yés-ó*-túng-á	mǎ-dzi.
	3rd-PAST-try-O-draw-FV	6-water
	'(S)he tried to draw water'	

Many thanks to Sam Mchombo, who generously gave his time in order to provide the data and to Joan Bresnan who has given me frequent advice throughout the development of the paper. Thanks also to Andrew Garrett, Sharon Inkelas, Paul Kiparsky, Will Leben, Stanley Peters, and Peter Sells for helpful comments on various drafts. This work was supported in part by NSF BNS 89-19880.

When certain auxiliary verbs ending with the final vowel, *-a*, are followed by an infinitive complement whose verb is in initial position and begins with the infinitive-marker *ku-*, there is an alternative way of expressing the same meaning in which the morpheme sequence, *-a ku-* is replaced by the single morpheme *-o-*.[1] It is tempting to think of this alternation as involving mismatch because there is clear evidence that (1) involves three syntactic terminals corresponding to the hyphen-groups in the word-by-word gloss; moreover, the syntax of (2) is very similar to the syntax of (1); but the phonology of (2) strongly suggests that the phonological words are the hyphen-groups shown in (2); thus the syntactic constituency of (2) would seem to be at odds with its phonological constituency. But I will argue that this appearance is deceptive.

The structure of the paper is as follows. First I consider the hypothesis that long-forms and coalesced forms are related by a simple postlexical rule—one that operates without exception in a phonologically specified environment. I give evidence that this hypothesis is untenable. Next, I consider Hayes's (1990) theory of 'Precompiled Phonology'. This approach also turns out not to be suited to the coalescence facts. Third, I consider a mismatch proposal based on the model of Selkirk (1986) and inspired by Myers' Chishona work. This proposal has only a few empirical difficulties but is undesirable because of the complexity of the mismatch mapping. I show in the final section that there is an empirically adequate alternative account, 'Morphosyntactic Divergence', in which the phonological words and the syntactic terminals in the coalescence structure coincide.

1. A Postlexical Rule?

Four observations make it tempting to claim that long forms and coalesced forms are related by a simple postlexical rule.

First, CAs occur most often in fast speech and it is impossible to pause immediately after uttering a CA. These facts suggest that coalescence may be a fast-speech phenomenon and therefore a postlexical process.

Second, there is a lexicon-wide rule of tone reduction, Chichewa's version of the wide-spread Bantu process called 'Meeusen's Rule', which fails to apply at the juncture between a CA and the following verb stem. Kanerva (1990a) has argued for the following formulation of tone reduction (p. 25):

(3) Tone Reduction in Chichewa (lexical): $\begin{matrix} \mu & \mu & & \\ | & | & & \\ \mathrm{H} & \mathrm{H} & \rightarrow & \emptyset \end{matrix}$

Independent evidence indicates that the underlying forms of the verb root, *kond-* 'love' and the coalescence morpheme are as shown in (4). The notation in figure (4) is meant to indicate that each morpheme places a high tone on

[1] For convenience of description I will use the term Coalesced Auxiliary (CA) to refer to the unit consisting of a verb stem followed by the coalescence vowel, *-o-*—e.g., *yes-o-* in example (2).

(4) 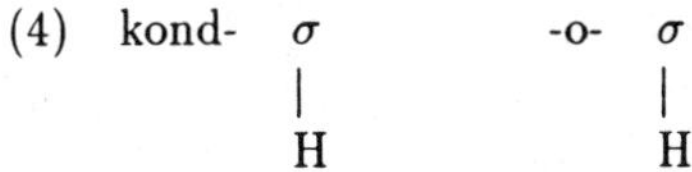

the immediately following syllable. Since the concatenation of *kond-*, *-o-*, and any verb stem in the lexicon results in the juxtaposition of the high tone from *kond-* and the high tone from *-o-*, we should expect Meeusen's rule to apply. However, it doesn't as example (5) shows.

(5) Nd-a-kond-ó-phíká maûngu.
1st-PERF-love-O-cook pumpkins
'I have loved to cook pumpkins.'

Here, *-phika* 'cook' is a underlyingly toneless verb stem. The high tone on the final vowel of *-phika* is the result of a postlexical rule of tone doubling (see Kanerva (1990a), 60).

The third observation which might prompt us to treat coalescence as a simple postlexical rule is that CAs can be stacked up unboundedly. (6) is an example with three CAs in a row. Examples with four or more are awkward, though not impossible.

(6) ti-na-*yénér-ó-yamb-ó-fún-ó-*-dy-a ma-pwetekere
1stPl-PAST-must-O-begin-O-want-O-eat-FV 6-tomato
'We had to begin to want to eat tomatoes.'

Since it is sometimes thought that recursion is limited to syntax, these observations might be taken to indicate that CAs are generated by a syntactic rule.

Finally, some coordination data also seem to support the simple postlexical rule hypothesis. When the complement of a long-form auxiliary is a coordinated infinitive complement, there is an alternative construction in which the auxiliary is coalesced with the verb of the first coordinand of the complement:

(7) Ti-na-fún-á ku-dy-á mbûzi ndí kú-mw-á mowa.
1stPl-PAST-want-FV INF-eat-FV goat and INF-drink-FV beer
'We wanted to eat goat and to drink beer.'

(8) Ti-na-*fún-ó*-dy-á mbûzi ndí kú-mw-á mowa.
1stPl-PAST-want-O-eat-FV goat and INF-drink-FV beer
'We wanted to eat goat and to drink beer.'

If the coalesced forms are derivationally related to the long forms, then these examples suggest that the process occurs after coordination. Since in Chicheŵa, coordination is plausibly a syntax-only rule, these data also seem to argue for the postlexical rule hypothesis.

Nevertheless, two further observations make it seem unlikely that coalescence is a simple postlexical rule. First, the degree of segmental mutation involved is extreme: a consonant is eliminated and the resulting adjacent vowels mutate and become a single vowel. Such radical phonetic distortion is unheard of in the domain of postlexical phonology.

Moreover, there is a clear syntactic constraint on the occurrence of coalescence. And yet a simple postlexical rule should not be sensitive to syntactic structure. To describe the constraint, I must give some background information on the nature of auxiliary verbs in Chicheŵa. It turns out that the language employs two kinds of auxiliaries, which I will call 'Transitive Auxiliaries' (TAs) and 'Intransitive Auxiliaries' (IAs), respectively. The two types differ on five syntactic properties which are cataloged in (9). Supporting data are given in the Appendix.

(9)

Property	TAs	IAs
take ordinary noun complements	yes	no
allow nominal modifiers on complement	yes	no
passivize	yes	no
take an object marker	yes	no
allow ellipsis of complement	no	yes

These contrasts indicate a structural account in which TAs take an NP complement while IAs take a VP complement.[2] Illustrations of these analyses are given in (10) for *zond-a* 'hate', a typical TA, and *yener-a* 'must', a typical IA.

(10)

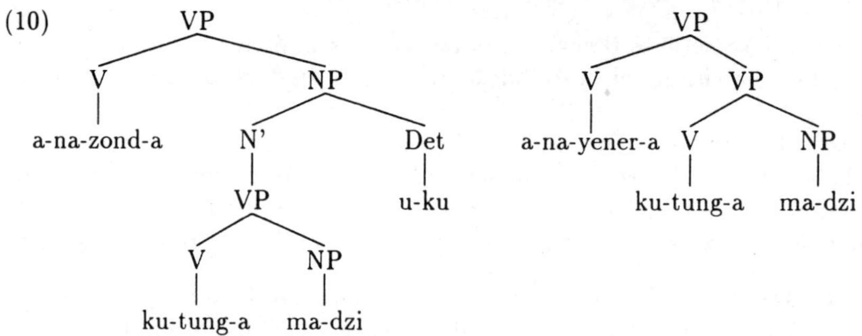

'(S)he hated this drawing of water.' '(S)he had to draw water.'

Now it is possible to describe the conditions on coalescence. Precisely the constructions in which an IA takes a VP complement have an alternative coalesced form. Constructions involving TAs and, in fact, all other constructions involving a surface segmental sequence of the form [aku] fail to undergo coalescence.[3,4] This contrast is shown in (11) and (12).

[2]See Bresnan and Mchombo (1990) and Tabor (1991) for detailed arguments.

[3]It should be noted, though, that certain qualificative constructions provide motivation for a lexical phonological rule, [aku] → [o] (see Watkins (1937), 11, 107–8).

[4]There are a number of forms which show all the positive indications of being TAs as

(11) TA: Banda á-ma-zónd-a ku-lúk-á madengu.
Banda 3rd-HAB-hate-FV INF-weave-FV (6)basket
'Banda hates weaving baskets.'

* Banda á-ma-*zónd-ó*-lúk-á madengu.
Banda 3rd-HAB-hate-weave-O-FV (6)basket
LIT: 'Banda hates weaving baskets.'

(12) IA: Banda á-ma-yés-á ku-lúk-á madengu.
Banda 3rd-HAB-try-FV INF-weave-FV (6)basket
'Banda tries to weave baskets.'

Banda á-ma-*yés-ó*-lúk-á madengu.
Banda 3rd-HAB-try-O-weave-FV (6)basket
'Banda tries to weave baskets.'

Simple postlexical rules are not supposed to have exceptions. In particular, they are not supposed to be sensitive to syntactic structure. Thus, these data indicate that the coalesced constructions cannot be treated as the result of applying a simple postlexical rule to the long-form constructions.

2. Hayes' (1990) Precompiled Phonology?

Assuming that syntax and phonology have to interact in some way, it is desirable to propose a theory in which the interaction is as simple as possible. A desirable hypothesis, notes Hayes (1990), is that

> I. Syntax has phonological effects only insofar as it determines phonological phrasing [p. 85]

where 'phonological phrasing' is as defined as in Nespor and Vogel (1982), Selkirk (1980), (1984), (1986), Hayes (1989), and others. But in his 1990 paper, Hayes points out a number of phenomena which appear to be violations of this constraint and he offers an addendum to the theory which is designed to take care of these cases: the mechanism of 'Precompiled Phonology'. The 'mismatch' proposal which I consider in the next section is consistent with Hypothesis I. But before turning to this account and arguing that it too is inadequate, let me address the question of whether coalescence is, in fact, one of the special cases for which Precompiled Phonology is designed.

A vowel-length alternation in Hausa provides a good example of what Precompiled Phonology is for: verb-final long vowels are shortened precisely in case they immediately precede a full NP object (see Hayes (1990), 93–5). Hayes's proposal is to generate verbs with both long and short vowels in the

well as the one positive indication of being an IA. Examples are *-konda* 'love' and *-funa* 'want'. Moreover, such forms participate in coalescence. But these forms do not prove the tests inconsistent. For example, if *kond-* takes a complement with a nominal modifier, then neither complement ellipsis nor coalescence is possible with that example. This suggests treating such forms as lexically ambiguous.

lexicon and attach a feature to each form which allows the syntax to distinguish appropriately between them. Thus, what looks like a phonological process operating postlexically is analysed instead as a case of lexical allomorphy.

There is an obvious way of applying the precompilation mechanism to the case of the auxiliary constructions in Chichewa̭. We can assume that both IA-constructions and CA-constructions are biclausal and that a feature generated in the lexicon ensures that only an IA can take a VP complement that is headed by a infinitive verb and that only a CA can take a VP complement that is headed by a bare verb stem ((13)-(14)):[5]

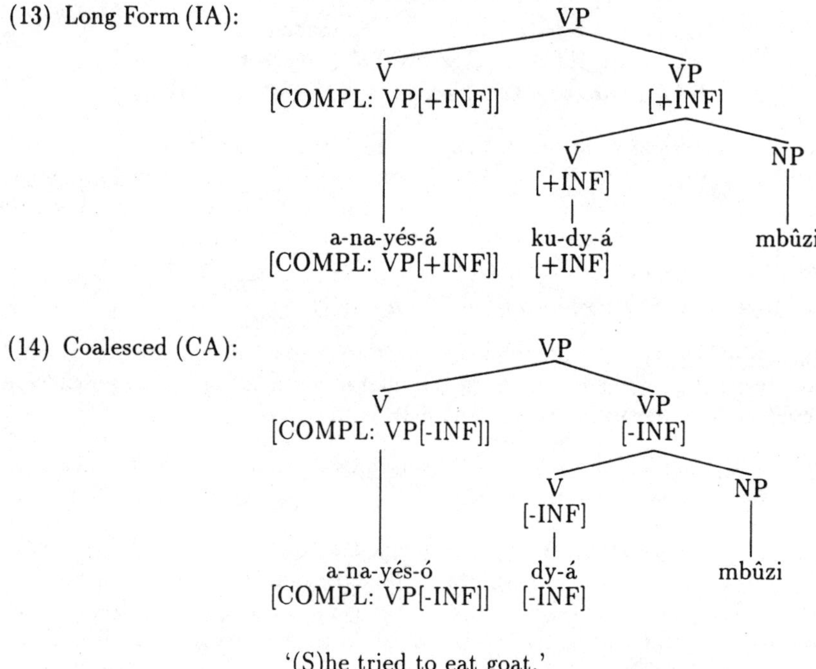

'(S)he tried to eat goat.'

On the face of it, such a proposal has several advantages: the failure of Meeusen's Rule is guaranteed for the CA constructions since there is a syntactic boundary separating the CA from the following verb stem; unbounded sequences of CAs are expected since CAs are generated by a potentially-recursive syntactic rule; the major segmental mutation involved in the alternation is also expected since allomorphic variation tolerates greater phonological divergence than simple postlexical variation; the syntactic restriction of coalescence to IAs is expected since allomorphic alternations are typically syntactically controlled.

[5]Here, I assume that syntactic terminals correspond to phonological words—i.e., that this is not a 'mismatch account'. If one permits mismatch in the Precompiled framework, the most natural result is a proposal that is virtually identical to the proposal which I critique in the next section. Therefore, I'll not review that option here.

Nevertheless, certain additional data argue against using the Precompiled approach for this phenomenon. The essential problem is that CAs, even in combination with preceding inflectional morphology, do not behave like full phonological words and nor do verb stems. Yet, on the above Precompiled account, these units are claimed to have passed through and exited the lexicon.[6]

For example, Chicheŵa has a disyllabicity requirement which results in the epenthesis of an initial [i] to a content word which has reached the end of the lexicon. The imperative *Idya* 'Eat!' of the monosyllabic verb stem *-dya* illustrates (cf. Kanerva (1990a), 38–44). The Precompiled analysis of CA constructions (14) implies that epenthesis should apply to the verb stem immediately following the CA. And yet it does not:

(15) * A-na-yés-ó idya nkhûku
3rd-PAST-try-O eat chicken
LIT: '(S)he tried to eat chicken'

Moreover, Chicheŵa has a clitic morpheme, *-nso* 'also', which can appear to the right of any verb in the language including an IA:

(16) A-na-yés-á(-nsó) kú-túng-á(-nsó) mă-dzi.
3rd-PAST-try-FV-also INF-draw-FV-also 6-water
'(S)he also tried to draw water.'

There is no reason, on the Precompiled approach, to expect this clitic not to appear to the right of a CA since a CA is also a type of verb. And yet it fails to:

(17) *A-na-yés-ó-*nsó*-túng-á mă-dzi.
3rd-PAST-try-O-also-draw-FV 6-water
'LIT: (S)he also tried to draw water.'

Finally, with an appropriate supporting context, it is possible to drop the VP complement of an IA (this is an instance of the construction referred to as 'complement ellipsis' in the preceding section):

(18) Q: A-na-yés-á ku-gôn-a kŏdi?
3rd-PAST-try-FV INF-sleep-FV INTERR
'Did (s)he try to sleep?'
A: Ĭnde, a-na-yés-á ku-gôn-a.
yes 3rd-PAST-try-FV INF-sleep-FV
'Yes, (s)he tried to sleep.'
A: Ĭnde, a-na-yês-a.
'Yes, (s)he tried.'

The Precompiled approach would lead us to expect the complement of a CA to be omissible in a similar fashion. And yet it is not:

[6]I thank Sharon Inkelas for pointing out this implication of the Precompiled account.

(19) Q: A-na-yés-ó-gôn-a kŏdi?
A: Ĭnde, a-na-yés-ó-gôn-a.
A: * Ĭnde, a-na-yês-o.
Q: Did (s)he try to sleep?
A: Yes, (s)he tried to sleep.
A: LIT: Yes, (s)he tried.

Thus three pieces of evidence argue against the claim that there is a phonological word boundary immediately to the right of a CA. Since the Precompiled account depends on this assumption, I suggest that the account is not suitable for the generation of Chichewa coalesced forms.[7]

3. Syntax/Prosody Mismatch?

I noted at the beginning that Myers (1987 and 1989) proposes a 'mismatch' analysis of a Chishona construction that is very similar to the Chichewa CA construction. His approach follows the end-based domain theory of phonological phrasing proposed in Selkirk (1986). Unfortunately, his analysis makes no distinction between IAs and TAs for it treats all infinitive phrases as NPs. For this reason, it has problems with the five distinctions between Chichewa IAs and TAs which I noted in Section 1 above. Bresnan and Mchombo (1990) and Tabor (1991) have cataloged these problems. What I will do here is consider an alternative analysis which also employs Selkirk's formalism and is inspired by Myers' Chishona model but which makes an appropriate distinction between IAs and TAs. This analysis, which I will refer to as the 'Coalescence = Prosodic Rebracketing' (C = PR) analysis, is shown in (20) and (21). Here, TA constructions and IA constructions receive the analyses proposed in Section 1 above. CA constructions and IA constructions have the same syntax but they have different prosodic constituencies. The syntactic units are shown by the tree structures in each diagram. The prosodic units at the level of the phonological word are shown by the curly brackets around the sequences of terminal nodes. Note that the analysis of CA constructions involves a mismatch between syntactic and prosodic constituency.

I noted at the beginning that it is desirable for a theory which posits distinct constituencies for syntax and prosody to propose some kind of mapping between them. The mapping proposed by Selkirk (1986) works as follows. Each morphemic category in the language gets classified as being of the type 'full' or the type 'functional'. Phonological word domains are then defined by an algorithm which scans the speech stream either from right to left or from

[7]One could rescue the Precompiled approach from the criticism that it incorrectly predicts epenthesis by assuming that the word-units in examples like (14) are in fact, *a-na-yes o-dya mbuzi*. But under this parse, clitic placement is still impossible after the auxiliary element and nor can the auxiliary terminate a phrase. Moreover, the claim that *a-na-yes* is a word is surprising given that, except for syllabic nasals, virtually all syllables in the language end in a vowel (cf. Watkins (1937),10; Kanerva (1990a) refers to 'a few ideophones' which are also exceptions but does not identify them (p. 31)).

(20)

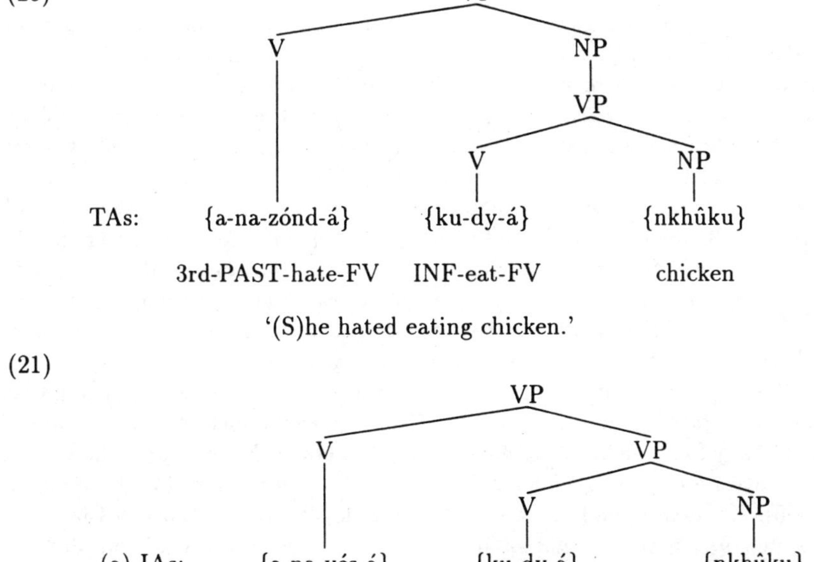

3rd-PAST-hate-FV INF-eat-FV chicken

'(S)he hated eating chicken.'

(21)

VP
V VP
V NP

(a) IAs: {a-na-yés-á} {ku-dy-á} {nkhûku}
(b) CAs: {a-na-yés-ó- -dy-á} {nkhûku}

3rd-PAST-try-FV (INF-)eat-FV chicken

'(S)he tried to eat chicken.'

left to right and places a domain-edge just 'after' each full category. For example, Myers (1989) proposes that the functional categories in Chishona are 'P, [Noun] Class, INFL, and AuxV' and that scanning proceeds from left to right (p. 36). To get the above-pictured C = PR account of Chicheŵa auxiliary verb constructions, we must assume that TAs, IAs, main verb stems, and noun stems are full categories while noun-class markers, subject markers, tense markers, and CAs are functional. Also in Chicheŵa scanning must proceed from left to right. The different bracketings of the IA and CA constructions then follow from the contrasting classification of IAs and CAs.

A great advantage of this proposal is that it handles all the observations which foiled the Precompiled approach. In particular, we do not expect epenthesis of a vowel before a monosyllabic main verb in a CA-construction because the main verb does not by itself form a phonological word. Nor do we expect a CA to be able to occur utterance-finally if we adopt the Strict Layer Hypothesis (cf. Selkirk (1984) and others) which requires that at each phonological level there must be exhaustive parsing into the phonological units of that level. Since CAs are not final in the phonological word, they cannot be final in the utterance. We also predict that clitics like *-nso* 'also' will fail to appear immediately to the right of a CA since clitics can attach only to full phonological words.

But the proposal has a number of problems which make it undesirable in the long run. The reader may have noticed a slight awkwardness in the characterization of Chicheŵa's full and functional categories: it is not quite accurate to say that each 'morphemic category' in the language gets classified as full or functional; instead a superordinate type must be defined: the set consisting of the verb stems (including TAs, IAs, CAs, and main verb stems) and all other morphemes in the language which are not parts of verb stems.[8] It is then the members of this set which get classified as full or functional. The identification of this set is not without independent motivation: it is essentially what people think of as the output of the derivational morphology. But given the fuzziness of the distinction between derivation and inflection generally, it is discomforting to have to use it as a crucial pylon of the theory.

Although I will not be able to offer an improvement, it is worth noting that there is a related difficulty with clitics like *-nso* 'also' which may appear to the right of any full verb in the language (see (16) above): Myers (1987) shows that such clitics form a phonological word with the preceding verbal material (p. 134–6); Kanerva (1990a) shows that the same situation obtains in Chicheŵa (pp. 160–9). Since the clitics are not part of the derivational morphology, they are not correctly handled by the device of defining the full/functional partition on the output of the derivational morphology. Instead Myers (1987) must follow Nespor and Vogel's (1982) account of Italian and propose a rule of 'prosodic reanalysis' which incorporates a clitic into the preceding phonological word after the phrasing algorithm has performed its scan. Clearly it would be preferable not to have to employ such a stipulative device.

Also, some additional coordination data present a problem for the C = PR account. I noted in Section 1 above that when the complement of an IA consists of the coordination of two infinitive phrases, then the IA can coalesce with first infinitive verb (e.g., (7)-(8)). However, if a complex auxiliary is formed by coordinating two IAs, then it is not possible to coalesce the second IA with a following infinitive complement ((22)-(23)).

(22) A-na-yénér-á ndipo a-na-fún-á ku-dy-á nkhûku.
3rd-PST-must-FV and 3rd-PST-want-FV INF-eat-FV chicken
'He had to and, moreover, he wanted to eat chicken.'

(23) * A-na-yénér-á ndipo a-na-*fún-ó*-dy-á nkûkhu.
3rd-PST-must-FV and 3rd-PST-want-O-eat-FV chicken
'He had to and, moreover, he wanted to eat chicken.'

The C = PR account cannot easily account for this contrast in the way coalescence interacts with coordination. One may assert that the impossibility of (23) stems from a prohibition against coordination of different categories

[8] Verb stems are morphologically complex for they consist of a verb root, optional derivational morphology, and a final vowel.

since, in order to have the reading shown, (23) would have to involve coordination of a full category (IA) with a functional category (CA). However by the same logic, the grammatical sentence, (8) would involve coordination of a VP headed by a bare verb stem with a VP headed by an infinitive verb. This hardly seems more desirable, especially since the hypothetical imperative construction which would have this form is ungrammatical:

(24) * Vin-a ndi ku-mw-a mowa!
dance-FV and INF-drink-FV beer
'Dance and drink beer!'

Finally, I suggest that the most damning property of the C = PR account is the complexity of the mechanism it employs. If there is an account which has comparable empirical accuracy and comparable complexity in other regards but for which the mapping between syntactic and prosodic constituent structure is simpler than the end-based phrasing algorithm, then such an account should be preferred. In the next section, I argue that such an account exists.

4. Solution: Morphosyntactic Divergence

The solution I propose may appropriately be called 'Morphosyntactic Divergence': instead of treating IA and CA constructions as syntactically identical, IA constructions are given the analysis presented in Section 1 while CA constructions are treated as monoclausal:

(25) IAs: CAs:

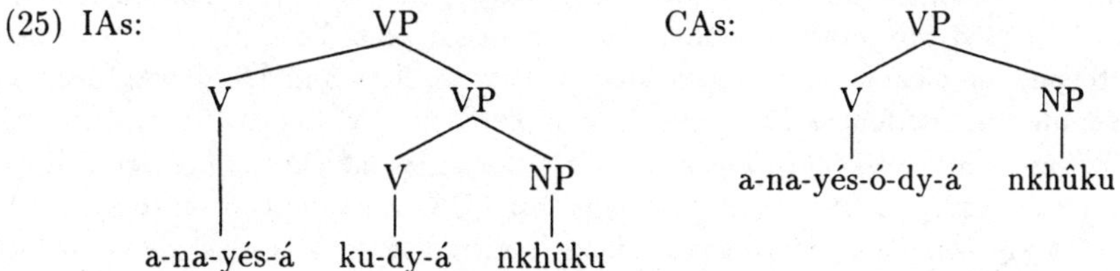

TA constructions also receive the analysis proposed for them in Section 1. A key feature of the CA analysis is the claim that there is an additional position in the verbal morphology in which the CAs appear.

This set of structural claims makes correct predictions about all of the data so far examined. The coordination structure (23) is not generated because there is no way of coordinating the elements *a-na-yénér-á* and *a-na-fún-ó* since the latter is not a syntactic formative. Of course, it is necessary to explain why example (8), repeated below, is good:

(8) Ti-na-*fún-ó*-dy-á mbûzi ndí kú-mw-á mowa.
[1stPl-PAST-want-O-eat-FV goat$_S$] [and$_{Conj}$] [INF-drink-FV beer$_S$]
'We wanted to eat goat and to drink beer.'

It cannot be treated as coordination of infinitive VPs under the scope of the element *ti-na-fún-ó* since this element is not a syntactic formative (and nor are there two infinitive VPs) on the Divergence account. But there is evidence that this construction is properly treated as the S coordination indicated in the square-brackets in the word-by-word gloss. It turns out that the ordinary way of getting the semantics of VP-coordination under the scope of subject and tense information is as shown in example (26).

(26) Ti-na-dy-á mbûzi ndí kú-mw-á mowa.
[1stPl-PAST-eat-FV goat$_S$] [and$_{Conj}$] [INF-drink-FV beer$_S$]
'We ate goat and drank beer.'

(26) requires us to permit coordination of an infinitive phrase with a fully inflected S. We can view the infinitive marker *ku-* as an anaphoric element which inherits the inflectional features of the preceding S. In (26), these inflectional features include subject-class and tense information. In (8), these inflectional features include subject-class, tense, and the modality information expressed by the CA.[9]

The failure of epenthesis to occur before a monosyllabic main verb following a CA is predicted on the Divergence account if we assume that the disyllabicity requirement is not imposed until all the inflectional morphology is added to the verb stem. The fact that subject and tense markers also block epenthesis provides evidence for this assumption. The failure of CAs to host clitics is predicted because a CA is always strictly inside a phonological word and clitics can be assumed to attach only to whole phonological words.[10] The impossibility of placing a CA in utterance-final position follows from the assumption that an utterance must be syntactically well-formed; hence it must be exhaustively parsed into morphological words; hence it must be exhaustively parsed into phonological words. The contrast between TAs and IAs is captured as proposed in Section 1: TAs take NP complements; IAs take VP complements. The possibility of generating any number of adjacent CAs is predicted if we make the morphological rule that generates CAs a recursive rule (e.g., **subV → CA subV**). Contrary to the intuition referred to, in Section 1 above, recursive morphological rules must be allowed in Universal Grammar to handle the compounding facts of many languages. The failure of Meeusen's Rule, though surprising, is not theoretically problematic: Meeusen's rule is a lexical rule and lexical rules are known to be able to have exceptions.[11] Finally, the major

[9]I assume that example (24) above is bad because the inflectional features of the imperative mood are degenerate and thus can't support *ku-*.

[10]I would like be able to claim that the syntax/prosody line-up assumption can be extended to clitics—this would avoid the need for a stipulative 'prosodic reanalysis' rule like that proposed by Nespor and Vogel (1982) for Italian and by Myers (1987) for Chishona. On this view, a clitic would combine with a syntactic host to form a syntactic unit and this unit would also be the domain for the application of any phonological rules associated with the host/clitic combination. I do not yet have enough data to confirm or disconfirm this hypothesis, so I won't pursue the matter here.

[11]I have not yet discovered any other exceptions to the rule in Chicheŵa, but Myers (1987, 137) notes that coalescence-structures are similarly exceptional in Chishona and he presents three independent cases of failure of the rule in a draft of a paper on Chishona INFL (Myers 1992).

segmental difference between an IA construction and the corresponding CA construction is also expected since the two construction-types are not related by transformation but only by the sharing of certain lexical formatives.[12]

Moreover, some additional data provide an especially persuasive argument in favor of the Divergence hypothesis. It turns out that there is a set of directional/adverbial morphemes in the language which behave like CAs in all respects so far mentioned except that these morphemes are not plausibly derived from verbs. Examples are the morphemes *ka-* 'go' and *ngo-* 'only', illustrated in (28) and (29).

(28) A-na-*ká*-túng-á mă-dzi.
3rd-PAST-go-draw-FV 6-water
'(S)he went to draw water.'

(29) A-ná-*ngo*-túng-á mă-dzi.
3rd-PAST-only-draw-FV 6-water
'(S)he only drew water.'

These morphemes always appear immediately after the tense marker and before the verb stem (or the object-marker, if it is present), and they show the same restrictions as CAs with regard to epenthesis, utterance-final positioning, and clitic-placement. It is clear that *ka-* and *ngo-* are not derived from verb stems because the corresponding IA constructions are ungrammatical:

(30) * Ti-ku-k-á ku-dy-á nkhûku.
1stPL-PRES-K-FV INF-eat-FV chicken
LIT: 'We are going to eat chicken.'

(31) * A-na-ng-á/ó ku-túng-á mă-dzi.
3rd-PAST-NG-FV INF-draw-FV 6-water
LIT: '(S)he only to draw water.'

[12]When I gave this paper as a talk, a member of the audience pointed out that it would be unprecedented if I were to claim that Chicheŵa contains a type of lexical item that is only used in fast speech. The Divergence Hypothesis would be making this claim if it is the case that CAs can only occur in fast speech. However, having discussed the matter more fully with Sam Mchombo I have come to believe that coalescence is not a fast-speech-only phenomenon after all. Sam is perfectly happy to pronounce coalescence expressions slowly. He can also pause at the end of the verb and before a PP complement as in:

(27)
A-na-yés-ó-lémb-á [PAUSE] pa mwáala.
3rd-PAST-try-O-write-FV on (3)rock
'(S)he tried to write on a rock.' (rock receives inscription)

This pause cannot be a phrase-final pause because it does not condition the phrasal rules of Penultimate Lengthening and Retraction (cf. Kanerva (1990a), 55–9). I am assuming that true fast-speech does not tolerate pauses except phrase-finally.

These directional/adverbial elements seem to be morphological auxiliary elements which appear in precisely the position which the Divergence hypothesis assigns to the CAs. In other words, this position is independently needed as a part of the morphological description of the language. Therefore, using it to generate CAs does not require adding any mechanism to the grammar.

In sum, the Divergence hypothesis covers all the data so far considered and employs a simpler structural framework than the Mismatch account. Therefore, Mismatch is not required; Divergence is preferable.

Appendix: TAs vs IAs

Ordinary Noun Complements:

(32) TA: Á-ma-zónd-á ng'ona
3rd-HAB-hate-FV (10)crocodiles
'(S)he hates crocodiles'

(33) IA: * A-ku-yénér-á ng'ona
3rd-PRES-must-FV (10)crocodiles
'LIT: '(S)he must crocodiles'

Nominal Modifiers on Complement:

(34) TA: Tí-ma-zónd-á ku-pínd-á njingá u-ku
1stPl-HAB-hate-FV INF-bend-FV (10)bicycle this-15
'We hate this bicycle bending.'

(35) IA: * A-ku-yénér-á ku-pínd-á njingá u-ku
1aSM-PRES-must-FV INF-bend-FV (10)bicycle this-15
LIT: '(S)he must this way of bending bicycles' [Bresnan & Mchombo (1990), 23.40c]

Passivization:

(36) TA: Ku-dy-á nkúkhú kw-ákó kú-ma-kond-édw-a (ndí Bánda).
15INF-eat-FV chicken 15-your 15-HAB-love-PASSV-FV by Banda
'Your way of eating chicken is loved (by Banda)'

(37) IA: * Ku-dy-á nkhúkú kwá-kó kú-ma-yes-édw-a (ndí Bánda).
15INF-eat-FV chicken 15-your 15-HAB-try-PASSV-FV by Banda
LIT: 'Your way of eating chicken is tried to by Banda'

Replacement of Complement by Object Marker:

(38) TA: A-na-zónd-á ku-bwêr-a ndí kú-dy-á nkúkhú y-ăthu.
1aSM-PAST-hate-FV INF-come-FV and 15INF-eat-FV (9)chicken 9-our
'(S)he hated to come and eat our chicken'
A-na-ku-zônd-a.
1aSM-PST-15OM-love-FV
'(S)he hated it (e.g., coming and eating our chicken).'

(39) IA: A-na-yénér-á ku-bwêr-a ndí kú-dy-á nkhúkú y-ăthu
1aSM-PST-must-FV INF-come-FV and INF-eat-FV (9)chicken 9-our
'(S)he had to come and eat our chicken'
* A-na-ku-yénêr-a.
1aSM-PST-15OM-love-FV
LIT: '(S)he had to it.'

Ellipsis of Complement:

(40) TA: A: Kapatuka wa-∅-nyoza ku-ímbá û-ku.
Kapatuka 3rd-IMMFUT-hate INF-sing this-15
'Kapatuka hates this singing.'

B: S-a-∅-*(ku)-nyôza ngati Shéíla á-lî-po.
Neg-3rd-IMMFUT-OM-hate if Sheila 3rd-BE-LOC
'He doesn't hate *(it) if Sheila's around.'

(41) IA: A: Kapatuka s-á-∅-yénérá ku-píndá zóvâla.
Kapatuka Neg-3rd-IMMFUT-must INF-bend (10)clothes
'Kapatuka doesn't have to fold laundry.'

B: Á-∅-yénérá ngati Shéíla á-lî-po.
3rd-IMMFUT-must if Sheila 3rd-BE-LOC
'He has to if Sheila's around.'

References

Bresnan, J., and S. Mchombo. 1990. What's in a word? On the syntax of Bantu noun class prefixes. Ms., Stanford University.

Chen, M. 1985. The syntax of phonology: Xiamen tone sandhi. Ms., University of California, San Diego.

Hayes, B. 1989. The prosodic hierarchy in meter. In P. Kiparsky and G. Youngman (Eds.), *Rhythm and Meter*. Orlando: Academic Press.

Hayes, B. 1990. Precompiled phrasal phonology. In S. Inkelas and D. Zec (Eds.), *The Phonology-Syntax Connection*, 85–108. The University of Chicago Press.

Kanerva, J. M. 1990a. *Focus and Phrasing in Chicheŵa Phonology*. New York: Garland Press.

Kanerva, J. M. 1990b. Focusing on phonological phrases in Chicheŵa. In S. Inkelas and D. Zec (Eds.), *The Phonology-Syntax Connection*, 145–62. The University of Chicago Press.

Myers, S. P. 1987. *Tone and the Structure of Words in Shona*. PhD Dissertation, University of Massachusetts.

Myers, S. P. 1989. The phonological word in Bantu. Ms., School of Oriental and African Studies.

Myers, S. P. 1992. The morphology and phonology of INFL in Bantu. Ms., University of Texas at Austin.

Nespor, M., and I. Vogel. 1982. Prosodic domains of external sandhi rules. In H. van der Hulst and N. Smith (Eds.), *The Structure of Phonological Representations, Part I*, 225–255. Dordrecht: Foris.

Selkirk, E. 1980. Prosodic domains in phonology. In M. Aronoff and M. L. Kean (Eds.), *Juncture*, 107–129. Saratoga, California: Anma Libri.

Selkirk, E. 1984. *Phonology and Syntax: The Relation between Sound and Structure*. Cambridge: MIT Press.

Selkirk, E. 1986. On derived domains in sentence phonology. *Phonology Yearbook* 3.

Tabor, W. 1991. Rule frequency and syntactic innovation. Ms., Stanford University.

Watkins, M. H. 1937. *A Grammar of Chichewa*. Vol. 24 of *Language Dissertations*. Philadelphia: Linguistic Society of America.

Verb Movement and Tense Specification in Japanese

SATOSHI TOMIOKA
University of Massachusetts at Amherst

1. Introduction

Case Marking in Japanese has been one of the central issues for generative grammarians working on the language. Particularly, some complications arise in the so-called 'multiple nominative' construction, which presents a challenge to our common hypothesis that grammatical variations across languages are to be reduced to parameterization of Universal Grammar. One parametric explanation for this phenomenon is found in Takezawa (1987), which claims that nominative Case assignment in Japanese is realized under head government by [+tense] INFL, although the question of why an infinite number of Cases can be assigned is not directly addressed.[1] In order to justify his claim, Takezawa shows various cases where a tense morpheme is absent and nominative Case is not available. One such case is the ECM construction, as shown in (1).

---

* I would like to thank the following individuals for their comments and criticisms: Elena Benedicto, Hagit Borer, Mürvet Enç, Kyle Johnson, Tohru Noguchi, Barbara Partee and Paul Portner. The earlier version of this paper was presented at the University of Wisconsin-Madison in January, 1992, and I am grateful to the audience, particularly Hui-i Kung, and Soon Hyuck Park, who provided me with Korean examples. Among the audience at WCCFL, Takako Aikawa, Joseph Aoun, Jonathan Bobaljik, Vivienne Déprez and Hajime Hoji are acknowledged for their useful comments. Special thanks to Pat Deevy for the last minute proof reading. All the remaining errors are mine.

[1] For convenience, we will use the term 'assignment' for nominative Case in Japanese. In the framework of generative grammar, there seems to be implicit agreement on the biunique relationship between a Case assigner and assignee. Even in the case of multiple objects, it is generally believed that a verb cannot assign more Cases than the number of its arguments. As for nominative Case in Japanese, it might not be desirable to call this process 'assignment' since it is in principle possible to have an infinite number of nominative-marked NPs in a single clause. Thus, 'licensing' would be more appropriate term. Saito (1985) claims that nominative Case in Japanese is inherent Case that is not assigned by any syntactic element. This wording is, however, quite misleading because inherent Case is thought to be 'Theta related', but the fact is that Japanese nominative Case does not discriminate in terms of θ-roles. As Dubinsky (1991) notes, what Saito means by 'inherent' should be paraphrased as 'default', (see also Terada 1987 for relevant discussion), and if it is the case, Saito's claim is not far from our position.

(1) a. John-wa [$_{CP}$ Mary-no yokogao-ga utukusi-i to] omo-tta
John-top Mary-gen silhouette-nom pretty-imperf Comp think-perf
'John thought that Mary's silhouette was pretty.'

b. John-wa Mary-no yokogao-$_1$o [$_{CP}$ pro$_1$ utukusi-i to]
John-top Mary-gen silhouette-acc pretty-imperf Comp
omo-tta
think-perf
'John thought that Mary's silhouette was pretty.'

c. John-wa [$_{SC}$ Mary-no yokogao-o/*-ga utukusiku] omo-tta
John-top Mary-gen silhouette-acc/*-nom pretty-ϕ think-perf
'John thought of Mary's silhouette pretty.'

In (1c), the NP *Mary-no yokogao*, 'Mary's silhouette', cannot be marked for nominative in a small clause which contains no tense morpheme.[2]

Takezawa also discusses some instances in which controlled PRO is obligatory in non-finite contexts. Examples in (2) illustrate his discussion.

(2) a. Hanako-ga Taroo$_1$-ni [$_{CP}$ [$_{IP}$ *zibun$_1$-ga/PRO$_1$ ik]]-ase-ta
Hanako-nom Taroo-dat *self-nom go-cause-perf
'Hanako made Taroo go.'

b. Hanako-ga Taroo-ni$_1$ [$_{CP}$ [$_{IP}$ *zibun$_1$-ga/PRO$_1$ i-tte]] moraw-ta
Hanako-nom Taroo-dat *self-nom go-ing receive-perf
'Hanako had Taroo go.'

c. Hanako$_1$-ga [$_{CP}$ [$_{IP}$ *zibun$_1$-ga/PRO$_1$ miruku-o
Hanako-nom *self-nom milk-acc
kai]]-ni it-ta
buy -dat go-perf
'Hanako went to buy milk.'

d. Boku$_1$-ga [$_{CP}$ [$_{IP}$ *zibun$_1$-ga/PRO$_1$ iki]] tak-atta
I -nom *self-nom go want-perf
'I wanted to go.'

In all cases in (2), the embedded CP is tenseless and nominative Case fails to be assigned.

Although Takezawa's generalization is quite robust and seems to hold in many cases, there are some instances in which tensed INFL is absent but nominative Case assignment is still possible. One such construction is 'tenseless conjunction'. An example is shown in (3).

(3) a. Chris-ga Pat-o korosi, Terry-ga kane-o uba-tta
Chris-nom Pat-acc kill-ϕ Terry-nom money-acc steal-perf
'Chris killed Pat, and Terry stole the money.'

---

[2] Throughout this paper, we use 'ϕ' to indicate absence of a tense morpheme.

b. Chris-ga Pat-o korosi, Terry-ga kane-o uba-u
Chris-nom Pat-acc kill-ϕ Terry-nom money-acc steal-imperf
'Chris will kill Pat, and Terry will steal the money.' OR
'Chris kills Pat, and Terry steals the money.'

The problematic fact for Takezawa's analysis is that the subject in the first conjunct is marked nominative, despite the absence of a tensed INFL.

This paper sets as its goal to account for (3) while maintaining Takezawa's generalization. Pursuing this direction, we will also face some interesting questions concerning the syntax and semantics of tense, especially the relationship between the presence/absence of a tense morpheme and temporal interpretations. The examples in (3) show that temporal dependency holds between the conjuncts, namely the first conjunct is understood to have the same tense as the second conjunct.[3] If any account for nominative Case assignment is provided under Takezawa's generalization, in which the [+tense] feature plays a crucial role, it should also provide an explanation for the temporal dependency between the conjuncts we have just observed.

In the following section, we will briefly discuss our basic assumption concerning the syntactic structure of the tenseless conjunction. More concretely, we will eliminate the possibility that it is subordination rather than coordination. Section 3 will show that the tenseless conjunction is not VP-conjunction but IP-conjunction. Subsequently, we will argue that the subject NP in the tenseless conjunct receives nominative Case under head government by the tensed INFL in COMP, adopting a recent proposal by Whitman (1991) that a verb string vacuously moves to COMP in Korean and Japanese. We will also see how the temporal dependency follows from our assumption that V moves to COMP. Conditions for tense-specification will be formulated so as to account for both nominative Case assignment and temporal interpretations in the tenseless conjunction. The last section is devoted to the discussion of a problem that arises from our analysis, namely the Coordinate Structure Constraint.

2. Conjunction or Adjunction?

So far we have been referring to a construction like (3) as 'conjunction' without providing any direct evidence. In fact, in the earlier stage of this paper, it was pointed out by some that (3) might be a case of subordination. Since it is

---

[3] Korean manifests the same effect, as shown below.

(i) Terry-ka New York-ey ka-ko, Robin-i Boston-ey ka-ssta
Terry-nom New York-to go-ϕ-and Robin-nom Boston-to go-perf
'Terry went to New York, and Robin went to Boston.'

(ii) Terry-ka New York-ey ka-ko, Robin-i Boston-ey ka-n-ta
Terry-nom New York-to go-ϕ-and Robin-nom Boston-to go-imperf
'Terry will go to New York, and Robin will go to Boston.'

crucial in the following discussions to assume that it is coordination, this question should be addressed.

One interesting comparison is the absolute construction in English, discussed by Stump (1985).[4] Some of the examples are shown below.

(4) a. Being a master of disguise, John would fool anyone.
b. Dinner being ready, the guests moved into the dining room.

These examples show striking similarity with our examples in Japanese: (i) the first clause lacks a tense morpheme, (ii) the first clause seems to be temporally dependent on the second. Nonetheless, we argue that the Japanese construction in question is fundamentally different from the English absolute construction. Stump claims that there must be a certain relation between the first and second clauses, such as Cause/Result, if...then, when..., after... etc. Although the Japanese examples do allow some of those relations, it is well-known that such relations can also be found in the coordinate structure. What is crucial for our purpose is not that the Japanese 'tenseless conjunction' allows such relations between conjuncts but that the English absolute construction requires such relations whereas the Japanese case doesn't. In this sense, it mimics the coordination more than the absolute construction.[5]

Another piece of evidence for coordination comes from an asymmetry in anaphor binding. As (5ab) show, the Japanese anaphor *zibun* in a subordinate clause can take the subject of the main clause as its antecedent, whereas (5c) suggests that it is not possible in the tenseless conjunction.

(5) a. Zibun$_1$-no kodomo-ga sotugyoo-si-ta node, Terry$_1$-wa
self-gen child-nom graduate-perf because Terry-top
yorokonde-iru
pleased-imperf
'Because self's child graduated, Terry is pleased.'

---

[4] I am grateful to Mürvet Enç for referring me to Stump's work.

[5] Another rather subtle difference comes from relative scope of the adjuncts. Consider (i).

(i) a. Having long arms, standing on the chair, John could touch the ceiling.
b. ?? Standing on the chair, having long arms, John could touch the ceiling.

It is noted by Stump that the interpretations of the adjuncts can vary in terms of what kind of predicates are involved (i.e., individual or stage level predicates.) Generally speaking, individual predicates prefer the reading of Cause/Result whereas stage level predicates the temporal readings, such as when..., or after... There seems to be a restriction on the relative scope of the adjuncts, as seen in (i). There is no such restriction in the Japanese construction.

b. Zibun$_1$-no kodomo-ga kaer-u-toki, Terry$_1$-wa
self-gen child-nom return-imperf-time Terry-top
kuukoo-e mukae-ni ik-u
airport-to pick up-dat go-imperf
'When self's child returns, Terry goes to the airport to pick him/her up.'

c. *Zibun$_1$-no kodomo-ga Pat-o korosi, Terry$_1$-ga
self-gen child-nom Pat-acckill-ϕ Terry-nom
kane-o uba-tta
money-acc steal-perf
'Self's child killed Pat, and Terry stole the money.'

To sum up our discussion in this section, the examples presented above strongly imply that the Japanese construction in question behaves like coordination, rather than subordination, both semantically and syntactically.

3. Against 'VP-Conjunction' Analysis

Assuming the construction in question is coordination, what kind of solutions are available? The sentences in (3) may well be analyzed as conjunctions of VPs, assuming the claim by various scholars (Kitagawa 1986, Kuroda 1986 and Koopman and Sportiche 1988 among others) that the subject is base-generated inside a verbal projection and the subject can remain there at S-structure receiving Case in some languages. If this claim is correct, both subject NPs in (4ab) are in SPEC of VP and assigned Case under government by the [+tense] INFL, as shown in (6). Since the two VPs share one INFL, the matching of tense between the conjuncts follows automatically.

(6)

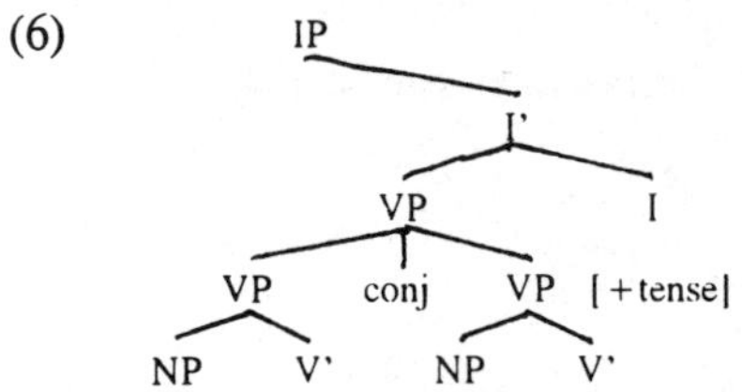

Nonetheless, this analysis does not seem to correctly capture various facts concerning this construction. First, each of the conjuncts can have its own sentential modifier, as shown in (7).

(7) Chris-ga kitto Pat-o korosi, Terry-ga tabun
Chris-nom surely Pat-acckill-ϕ Terry-nom perhaps
kane-o uba-tta
money-acc steal-perf
'Surely Chris killed Pat, and perhaps Terry stole the money.'

Travis (1988) argues that sentential adverbials are licensed by INFL and projected somewhere in the I-projection (i.e., adjoined to I, I' or IP). If her analysis is correct, (7) must be analyzed in a way that each of the conjuncts has its own I-projection, and that the subjects are in SPEC of IP since they precede the adverbs.

In addition, a tenseless conjunction can contain so-called 'focus NPs' that bear nominative Case, as in (8).

(8) Natu-ga biiru-ga umaku, fuyu-ga atukan-ga
summer-nom beer-nom tasty-ϕ winter-nom hot sake-nom
uma-i
tasty-imperf
'It is in summer that beer tastes good and in winter that hot sake tastes good.'

It is also possible to topicalize conjunct-internally, as illustrated in (9).

(9) Pat$_1$-wa Chris-ga t_1 korosi, kane$_2$-wa Terry-ga t_2 uba-tta
Pat-topic Chris-nom kill-ϕ money-topic Terry-nom steal-perf
'Pat, Chris killed t, and the money, Terry stole t.'

The exact position of a focused NP or a topicalized phrase still remains as a debatable question: IP adjunct, SPEC of CP and SPEC of TopicP seem to be possible candidates.[6] Notice, however, that we do not have independent evidence yet that those positions can be VP-internal. Therefore, these data strongly suggest that the conjuncts are most likely to be IPs or some projections higher than VPs.

Another problem with the 'VP-Conjunction' analysis is raised in connection with temporal adverbs. Contrary to our previous examples, the first conjunct can be interpreted to have an independent tense when a temporal expression is present.[7]

(10) Kinoo Chris-ga kaeri, asita Pat-ga kaer-u
yesterday Chris-nom return-ϕ tomorrow Pat-nom return-imperf
'Chris returned yesterday, and Pat will return tomorrow.'

If the two conjunct shared the same tense, namely the imperfect, (10) should be ruled out, as is (11).

(11) *Kinoo Chris-ga kae-ru
yesterday Chris-nom return-imperf
'*Chris returns yesterday.'

---

[6] See Saito (1985) and Hoji (1985) for the relevant discussion.

[7] Unlike Japanese, Korean does not allow this 'tense mismatch', as illustrated in (i).

(i) *Ecey Terry-ka New York-ey ka-ko, onul Robin-i Boston-ey ka-n-ta
yesterday Terry-nom New York-to go-ϕ-and, today Robin-nom Boston-to go-imprf
'Yesterday Terry went to New York, and today Robin will go to Boston.'

This contrast will be discussed in section 5.

Based on these facts, we conclude that the construction we are dealing with is a conjunction of IPs, containing a null INFL in the first conjunct. Abandoning the 'VP-Conjunction' analysis, we are now back to the questions posed earlier: (i) How is nominative Case realized in the first conjunct that lacks a tense morpheme? (ii) Why is the tenseless conjunct understood to have the same tense as the second conjunct? (iii) Why can it have an independent tense when a temporal expression is present?

4. Nominative Case

Let us first address the question of how nominative Case is assigned. First of all, we assume, following Whitman (1991), that V moves to COMP in Japanese, and that the [V+I] in COMP head-governs both subject NPs in SPEC of IP, as schematized in (12).

(12)

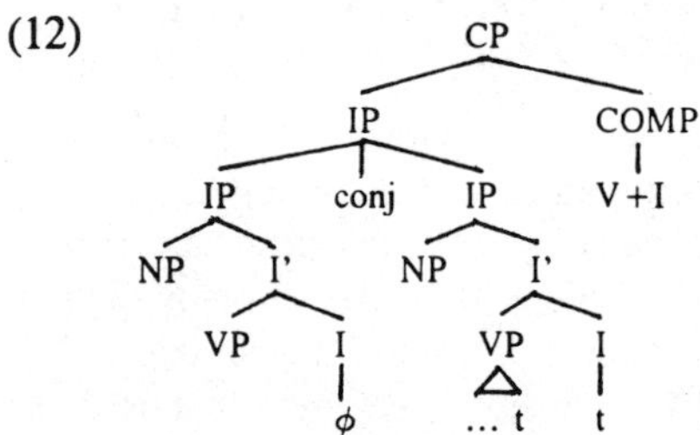

For the definition of head government, we adopt Whitman's (1991) definition, which is a modified version of Rizzi (1989).

(13) X head governs Y iff:

- (i) X is a lexical category
- (ii) X c-commands Y
- (iii) no barrier intervenes
- (iv) Relativized Minimality is respected

There are a couple of technical problems to be addressed. One of them is whether or not the coordination is transparent for head-government. Chomsky (1986) suggests that a 'conjunction is a (possibly somewhat defective) governor of its conjuncts.' (Chomsky 1986, 87) This view is reconsidered by Woolford (1987) in her discussion of the conjunction of small clauses, such as (14).

(14) They consider [$_\alpha$[$_\alpha$ Bob intelligent] and [$_\alpha$ Tom competent]]
(= (15) in Woolford 1987)

Woolford suggests that the Case marking in (14) can be accounted for either by assuming that α is not a maximal projection so that it cannot be a barrier, or by what she calls 'indirect Case marking' (i.e., the conjunction inherits the Case assigning property from the verb and reassigns Cases to the NPs under government). Although we do not commit ourselves to the theory of 'indirect

Case marking', we follow Chomsky's and Woolford's insight that the conjunction is transparent to head-government.

The second question concerns the [tense] feature of the null INFL in the first conjunct. Can it ever be [+tense] so that it assigns nominative Case? As shown in (15), the first conjunct can have a so-called 'double nominative' predicate.

(15) Chris-ga nihongo-ga hanas-e, Pat-ga kankokugo-ga
Chris-nom Japanese-nom speak-can-ϕ Pat-nom Korean-nom
yom-e-ru
read-can-imperf
'Chris can speak Japanese, and Pat can read Korean,'

If the nominative-marked object can receive Case inside the VP, as claimed by Terada (1987), Yoshida (1990) and others, then the null INFL must be involved in Case-marking since the overt INFL in COMP does not head-govern the object NP inside VP. Thus, we conclude that the null INFL in (15) does bear the [+tense] feature and consequently is capable of assigning Case. Now it must be explained how it receives the [+tense] feature despite the absence of tense morpheme. We will discuss this question in the following section.

5. Conditions for Tense Specification

As we have seen, there are two phenomena to be explained concerning the temporal interpretations of the tenseless conjunct: the temporal dependency between the conjuncts and the peculiar behavior of temporal adverbs. Moreover, the null INFL in the first conjunct is [+tense] so that it participates in nominative Case marking. The behavior of temporal adverbs is particularly obscure since it is not always the case that they succeed in specifying a null INFL for tense. For example, as (16) shows, the tense morpheme is obligatory in a root clause, regardless of the presence of a temporal adverb.

(16) *Chris-ga kinoo kane-o nusumi.
Chris-nom yesterday money-acc steal-ϕ
'Chris stole money yesterday.'

Also impossible is a nominative-marked NP in an infinitival clause, again regardless of the presence of a temporal adverb, as shown in (17).

(17) Boku$_1$-ga [$_{CP}$ [$_{IP}$ *zibun$_1$-ga/PRO$_1$ asita iki]] ta-katta
I -nom *self-nom tomorrow go want-perf
'I wanted to go tomorrow.'

Since we assume, as well as Whitman, that V moves to COMP in an embedded clause, if the null INFL in the infinitival clause receives the [+tense] feature from the temporal adverb, we would expect nominative Case to be available, which is apparently a wrong prediction.

What we formulate in (18) are the conditions which specify a null INFL for [+tense], discriminating a null INFL in the tenseless conjunct from other null INFLs that are unspecifiable for [+tense].

(18) Conditions for Tense Specification
 a. An INFL has a [+tense] feature iff:
  i) it bears a tense morpheme or
  ii) it is tense-specified
 b. An INFL is tense-specified iff:
  i) it is licensed and
  ii) it is tense-bound
 c. An INFL is licensed for tense specification iff it is head-governed by a tense morpheme.
 d. X tense-binds Y iff:
  i) X is a potential tense-binder
  ii) X c-commands Y and
  iii) X is coindexed with Y
 e. Potential tense-binders are a [+tense] INFL, temporal adverbs and temporal PPs.

An INFL has a [+tense] feature by virtue of containing a tense morpheme. For a null INFL to be specified for [+tense], on the other hand, it must satisfy (18b): both the licensing condition and the identification condition. The licensing condition is determined in terms of head-government by a tense morpheme, as stated in (18c). In the identification condition (18d), we adopt the view first proposed by Partee (1973), and defended and developed by Enç (1981, 1987) that tense in natural language is better characterized as a referring expression. Assuming this view, we also argue that tense is identified in a fashion similar to other referring expressions; namely via binding. (18e) lists potential tense-binders for Japanese, but what can count for a potential tense-binder varies across languages. As we have seen in footnote 7, Korean, which has similar constructions, does not have temporal adverbials that can be tense-binders, whereas Japanese does.

Let us see now how the conditions in (18) produce desirable results for our previous problems. In the tenseless conjunction, we have claimed that the [V+I] in COMP head-governs both of the conjoined IPs since the conjunction is transparent to head-government, and we adopt (19), originally claimed by Belletti and Rizzi (1981).

(19) If X^0 head-governs YP, it head-governs Y^0.

Since the IP headed by a null INFL is head-governed by the tense morpheme in COMP, the null INFL is licensed for tense specification. The identification condition will be satisfied either by a temporal adverb as in (10) or by a tensed V in COMP, both of which c-command the null INFL.

In (16) and (17), the null INFLs are not licensed for tense specification since in both cases, they fail to be head-governed by a tense morpheme. (16) simply contains no tense morpheme at all, and in (17), the tense morpheme is prevented from head-governing the null INFL by the VP, which we assume to be a barrier. Thus, a null INFL in those cases cannot be specified for [+tense] in spite of the presence of temporal adverbials.

6. A Remaining Problem: Coordinate Structure Constraint

One problem our analysis has is that the movement of V to COMP in the tenseless conjunction violates the Coordinate Structure Constraint (henceforth, CSC). At this point, we are not ready to provide a fully articulated explanation for this problem but will make some suggestions for its potential solution.

Instances of so-called 'Across-the-Board' rule application (henceforth, ATB) still remains as a residue of other syntactic principles. Many of the studies devoted to this problem focus on the movement of Wh-phrases (e.g., Williams 1977), and very little attention has been paid to the movement of AUX in those cases. Consider (20) and (21).

(20) a. What did Chris buy and Pat throw away?
b. Where is Chris walking and Pat jogging?

(21) a. *What did Chris buy and Pat threw away?
b. *Where was Chris walking and Pat was/is/be jogging?
c. *What did Chris buy and Pat will throw away?

They show a striking similarity with the Japanese tenseless conjunction in terms of the temporal dependency between the conjuncts: the second conjunct cannot have an independent tense and it necessarily has the same tense as the first conjunct. Interestingly, if there is no AUX to COMP movement, the situation is completely reversed; the second conjunct must have an independent tense even when it is the same as the first conjunct, as shown in (22).

(22) a. I wonder what Chris bought and Pat threw away.
b. *I wonder what Chris bought and Pat throw away.
c. I wonder where Chris was walking and Pat was jogging.
d.?*I wonder where Chris was walking and Pat jogging.
e. I wonder who Chris hates and Pat will marry.

There is more than one way to interpret these data. Suppose that the ATB rule applies to AUX to COMP movement as well as Wh-movement. It requires the two AUXs to be identical so that the ATB rule applies. The 'tense mismatch' seen in (21) blocks the ATB rule application, which ultimately produces an ungrammatical sentence. However, unlike the 'tense mismatch', the 'agreement mismatch' seems to play no role in blocking the ATB rule application, as shown in (23).[8]

(23) a. ?Who do you hate and Mary love?
b. ???Who do you hate and Mary loves?

---

[8] Native speakers' judgements for (23ab) are rather subtle although everyone agrees that (23c) shows a sharp contrast with the other two.

c. *Who does you hate and Mary love?

To maintain the view that the ATB rule also applies to AUX to COMP, it is necessary to make the following stipulations: i) the ATB rule is sensitive to the 'tense mismatch' but not to the 'agreement mismatch' ii) if the agreements of the conjuncts do not match, the AUX in COMP always agrees with the subject of the first conjunct, as the contrast between (23a) and (23c) shows.

We suggest that some other explanation is possible in terms of the tense specification analysis we have developed here. Under our analysis, (20a) has the structure illustrated in (24).

(24)

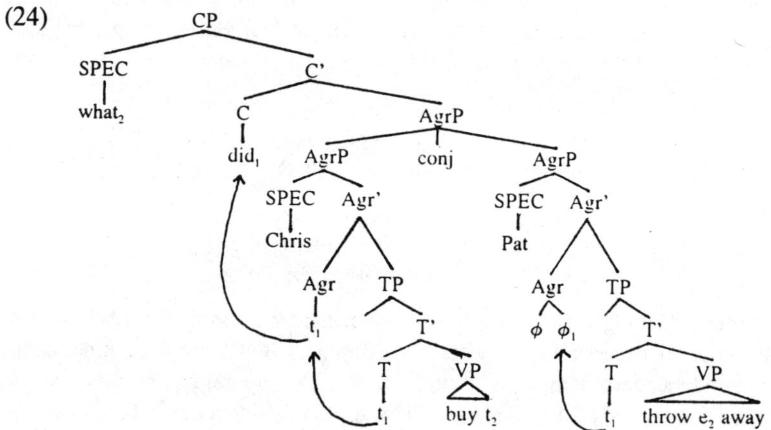

In (24), the tensed AUX, which we assume to be generated in T^0, moves to COMP via Agr^0 and binds the null T^0 in the second conjunct via c-command and coindexation. The null T^0 is not, however, head-governed by COMP in its original position and consequently undergoes X^0 movement to the null Agr^0 so as to be head-governed by COMP.[9] In this manner, all the conditions for the tense specification are met so that a null T is allowed in the second conjunction.

Next question is why an overt T is prohibited in this position, as seen in (21). To incorporate this fact into our analysis, we formulate a condition to restrict an overt T as in (25).

(25) Anti-government Requirement for Tense
An overt tense cannot be head-governed by another tense morpheme.

As briefly mentioned in footnote 10, the T^0-to-Agr^0 movement is independently required, and if the second conjunct has an overt tense morpheme, it ends up

---

[9] We assume that this 'T^0-to-Agr^0' movement is, in fact, independently needed, as claimed by Laka (1990). Laka proposes Tense C-command Condition (TCC), in which T^0 must c-command all the functional heads. Chomsky (class lecture) also takes this view, arguing that for the Φ features of $AgrS^0$ to be activated, T^0 must move to $AgrS^0$ by LF.

being head-governed by the tensed AUX in COMP, which results in a violation of (25). This requirement amounts to saying that an overt and a null T be in complementary distribution, and this prediction seems to be empirically correct. As for the contrast between (23ab), let us say that an overt agreement morpheme also signals the presence of an independent tense.[10] Thus, the presence of an agreement morpheme in the second conjunct would violate (25) although it remains unexplained why the contrast between (23ab) is not as sharp as we predict.

Notice, however, that our analysis of tense and agreement in the ATB extraction implies that X^0-movement does not obey the CSC. The main purpose of this paper is not to challenge the relevance of the CSC, but we would like to point out that the nature of this constraint in grammar has been questioned for independent reasons. For example, Munn (1991) and Bahloul and Harbert (1992) argue in favor of a binary structure for coordination. Although their analyses will not be discussed any further nor implemented in our analysis, we acknowledge this direction of research as a promising one.

7. Conclusion

We have argued that some problems in Takezawa's generalization of nominative Case assignment can be solved under the 'V-to-COMP' movement analysis and the conditions for tense specification developed here. Our analysis also has desirable consequences in temporal interpretations of tenseless clause and the distribution of [+tense] null INFLs.

References

Aoun, Josef. 1985. *The Syntax of Anaphora*. Cambridge: MIT Press.

Aoun, Josef. 1986. *Generalized Binding*. Dordrecht: Foris.

Bahloul, Maher and Wayne Harbert 1992. Agreement Asymmetries in Arabic. Paper presented at *WCCFL* 11, UCLA.

Belletti, Adriana and Luigi Rizzi 1981. The Syntax of *ne*: Some Theoretical Implications. *The Linguistic Review* 1:117-154.

Chomsky, Noam. 1986. Barriers. Cambridge: MIT Press.

Dubinsky, Stanley. 1991. Case-motivated Movement to Non-argument Positions: Evidence from Japanese. paper presented at *The Southern California Japanese/Korean Linguistics Conference*. University of California at Santa Barbara.

Enç, Mürvet. 1981. *Tense without Scope: An Analysis of Nouns as Indexicals*, Doctoral dissertation, University of Wisconsin-Madison.

Enç, Mürvet. 1987. Anchoring Conditions for Tense. *Linguistic Inquiry* 18.4:633-658.

Enç, Mürvet. 1990. On the Absence of the Present Tense Morpheme in English. ms. University of Wisconsin-Madison.

---

[10] This assumption is contrary to the proposals made by Johnson (1990) and Enç (1990) that English lacks present tense.

Hoji, Hajime. 1985. *Logical Form Constraints and Configurational Structures in Japanese*. Doctoral dissertation, University of Washington.

Johnson, Kyle. 1990. On the Syntax of Inflectional Paradigm. ms. University of Wisconsin-Madison.

Kitagawa, Yoshihisa. 1986. *Subjects in Japanese and English*, Doctoral dissertation, University of Massachusetts at Amherst.

Koopman, Hilda. and Dominique Sportiche 1988. Subjects. ms. UCLA.

Kuroda, Shige-yuki 1988. Whether We Agree or Not. in Poser, W. (ed.) *Japanese Syntax*, CSLI, Stanford University.

Laka, Itziar. 1990. *Negation in Syntax: On the Nature of Functional Categories and Projections*. Doctoral dissertation. MIT.

Munn, Alan. 1991. Across-the-board Gaps are Parasitic. paper presented at *NELS* 22, University of Delaware.

Partee, Barbara. 1973 Some Structural Analogies between Tenses and Pronouns in English. *Journal of Philosophy* 70:601-609.

Rizzi, Luigi. 1989. *Relativized Minimality*. Cambridge: MIT Press.

Saito, Mamoru. 1985. *Some Asymmetries in Japanese and Their Theoretical Consequences*, Doctoral dissertation, MIT.

Stump, Gregory. 1985. *The Semantic Variability of Absolute Constructions*. Dordrecht: Reidel Publications.

Takezawa, Koichi. 1987. *A Configurational Approach to Case-Marking in Japanese*, Doctoral dissertation, University of Washington.

Terada, Michiko. 1987. Unaccusativity in Japanese. *Proceedings of NELS 17* :619-640 Graduate Student Association, University of Massachusetts at Amherst.

Travis, Lisa. 1988. The Syntax of Adverbs. in *McGill Working Papers in Linguistics: Special Issue on Comparative German Syntax*. 280-310, McGill University.

Whitman, John. 1991. String Vacuous V to COMP," paper presented at *GLOW*, University of Leiden, Holland.

Williams, Edwin. 1977. Across-the-board Rule Application. *Linguistic Inquiry* 9.1:31-44.

Woolford, Ellen. 1987. An ECP Account of Constraints on Across-the-board Extraction. *Linguistic Inquiry* 18.1:166-171.

Yoshida, Tomoyuki. 1990. Case Marking and Verb Movement in Japanese. *Cornell Working Papers in Linguistics* 9.

Nominal Affixes and Case to Specifer in DP

DANIEL VALOIS
UQAM, Université de Montréal

0. Introduction

In Valois (1991a, 1991b, 1991c) I argued that drawing a strict parallel between the structure of Noun Phrases and clauses provides a straightforward account of a number of syntactic phenomena concerning the internal syntax of Noun Phrases, both language internally and cross-linguistically. In this paper, I will address one of these issues, namely CASE assignment. More specifically, I will argue that Case in Noun Phrases is structural and is assigned to the SPECIFIER canonically governed by the (first potential) Case assigning head. The analysis will be cast in a framework in which each DP-internal argument is contained in an independent projection of the θ-marking head (cf. Sportiche 1990), and in which EVENT NOMINALS are derived by syntactic (V-)movement to a nominalizing affix (Murasugi 1989, Hazout 1990, Picallo 1990). I will further propose that: (i) all nominal affixes select an XP complement; and (ii) when combined with a lexical head, Case and external θ-role assignment is a joint property of both the affix and the head it attaches onto. The consequences of this proposal are that: (i) I derive, via Case Theory, Grimshaw's (1990) observation that prenominal genitive objects in English are not compatible with the event reading of a derived nominal; (ii) assuming that the Visibility Condition holds of clauses (Stowell 1981), it is predicted that sentential complements to nouns are impossible in some languages, while some other languages allow them; and (iii) we will see why the direct object gets accusative Case in gerunds, while it gets genitive Case in ing-nominals (Abney 1987). The paper will be organized as follows: In section I, introduce the notion of layered structures for both clauses and Noun Phrases; in section 2, I draw a parallel between the structure of periphrastic clauses and event nominals, while addressing the issue of prenominal objects. In section 3, I discuss -ing nominals and show how the claim that Case is assigned to Spec accounts for the fact that complements

* I would like to thank Dominique Sportiche, Tim Stowell, Hilda Koopman, and Anna Szabolcsi for comments on the issues presented here, as well as the WCCFL 11 audience. I also acknowledge the support of the Social Sciences and Humanities Research Council of Canada (grants #756-91-0243 and #091-29-028), and of the FCAR (grant #091-28-532).

receive different cases. Finally, in section 4, I discuss the absence of sentential complements with event nominals, and argue that the contrast between nouns and verbs with respect to their ability to select sentential complements follows from the absence of expletive pronouns in Noun Phrases.

1. Layered structures (Sportiche 1990)

Expanding on an idea of Larson (1988), Sportiche (1990) argues for the structure of VP shown in (1), where both the internal and the external arguments of the verb are projected in an independent maximal projection of V. An important feature of (1) is that the direct object Case position is the specifier of the lower VP:

```
(1)                 VP*
                   /   \
              Spec       V*'
               |        /   \
             ext.     V*      VP
             arg.     |      /   \
                      e   Spec     V'
                                  /  \
                       Case     V     XP
                      position
                                    int. arg.
                                 not Case position
```

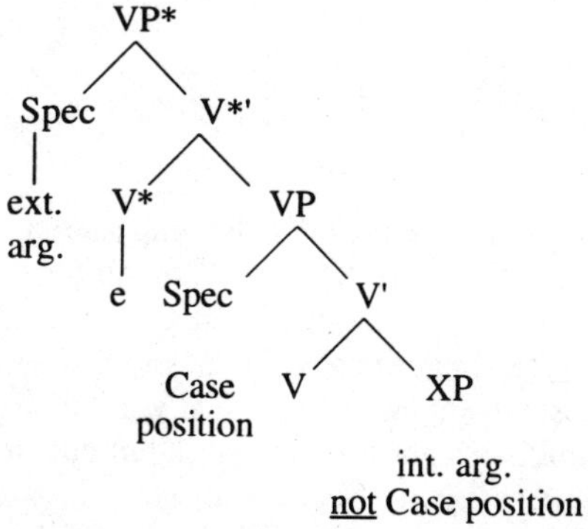

As we will see below, the structure in (1) is motivated by the theoretical claim that agreement positions coincide with Case positions. Given my theoretical stand that the internal structure of Noun Phrases is similar to that of clauses, I have argued (op. cit.) for the argument structure in (2) for Noun Phrases (Sportiche 1990):[1]

```
(2)              NP*
                /   \
           Spec       N*'
                     /   \
           ext.    N*      NP
           arg.    |      /   \
                   e  Spec      N'
                               /  \
                   Case      N     XP
                  position
                                int. arg.
```

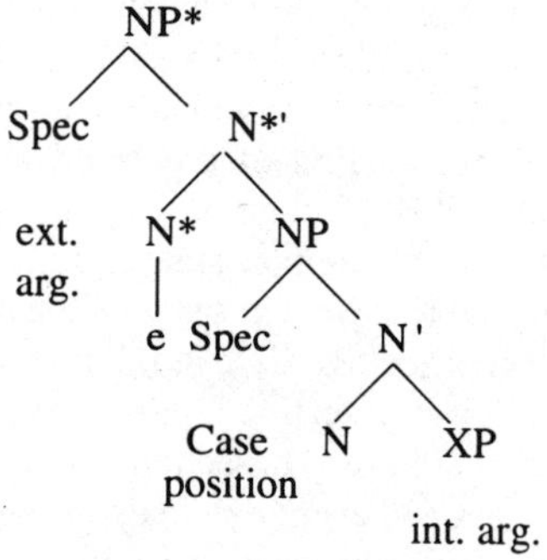

There are two underlying premises to the parallel between the two structures in (1) and (2): (i) nouns assign structural Case, and (ii) there is no process of of-insertion, i.e., the complement of picture in (3) below is a DP, not a PP (of being a

[1] In case a possessor is also projected in Romance, it appears outside of the argument structure.

Case marker; see Valois 1991c for details). To illustrate the process, the noun in (3) moves up to the head of NP*, and assigns Case to the DP object which has itself moved to the Spec, NP position.

(3) Jack's picture$_k$ [$_{NP}$ [$_{DP}$ of Jill]$_i$ [$_{N'}$ t_k t_i]]

The above structure (omitting functional categories above NP*; see (6b)), I claim, constitutes that of both underived and result nominals. I would now like to draw a further parallel between clauses and Noun Phrases, more specifically between the structure of compound tense clauses and event nominals.

2. Compound tense and event nominals

The structure proposed by Sportiche for compound tense clauses is shown in (4), where the past participle affix (the head of $I_{p(articiple)}$P) has both the property of taking an internal (VP) complement, and of discharging the external θ-role of the verb (when combined with it) in two distinct I_pP layers:

(4) [$_{CP}$ C [$_{AgrP}$ Agr [$_{TP}$ [$_T$ a] [$_{I_pP*}$ Spec [$_{I_p*'}$ Jean I_p* [$_{I_pP}$ Spec [$_{I_p'}$ Case position [$_{I_p}$ -é] [$_{VP}$ [$_V$ mang-] [$_{DP}$ des pommes]]]]]]]]]

Here, the verb moves up to the past participial morphology, and the newly formed complex moves up to Ip* in order to both discharge the external θ-role of the verb and assign Case to the direct object in Spec, IpP. A structure such as (4), where the Case/agreement (A-)position is inside the projection containing the internal argument, provides a straightforward account of French past participle agreement, since the direct object is able to move to Spec, IpP as an instance of A-movement without causing a violation of the Specified Subject Condition. There, it both gets Case and triggers specifier-head agreement with the past participle:

(5) Les pommes (fem./plur.) qu'il a mangées (fem./plur.).
'The apples that he ate'

That affixes have thematic and Case properties has already been argued in a number of analyses of passive constructions, where it is claimed that the passive morpheme -en both absorbs Case assignment to the direct object by the verb, and prevents it from assigning its external θ-role.

Returning to nouns, it is well known that certain derived nominals (such as observation) may denote either the result or the process of an action (Milner 1982, Zubizarreta 1987, Grimshaw 1990, among others), each type of nominal being subject to a different range of syntactic phenomena (Grimshaw 1990). In Valois (1991c) I adopted the idea that event nominals are derived syntactically through movement of the verb to a nominalizing affix taking a VP complement (cf. Murasugi 1989, Hazout 1990, Picallo 1990 for similar proposals). I also argued that this affix has Case and thematic properties: it forces Case assignment to the object, and it discharges the external θ-role of the noun. The structure of event nominals I argued for is shown in (6b), where No(un)P is the projection of the affix, and NumP is a functional projection containing the number features of the noun[2] (see Ritter 1990, Carstens 1991, Picallo 1990):

(6) a The doctor's observation of the patient.

b

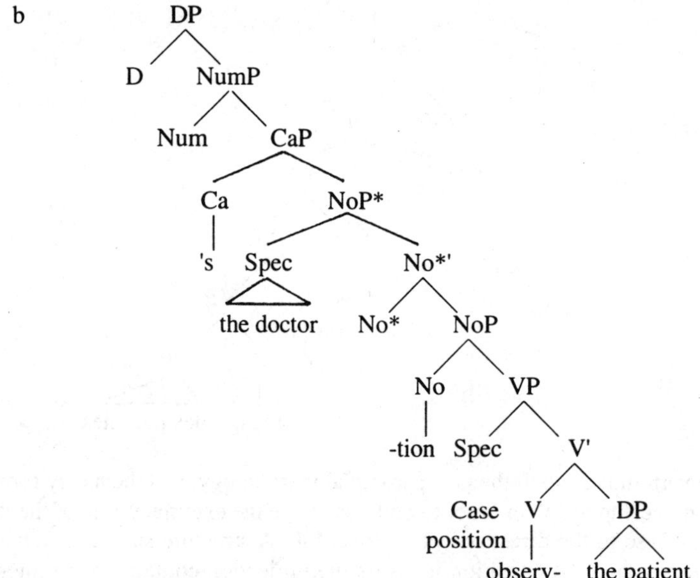

[2] Actually, I argued in my dissertation that the determiner is in fact the head of an XP which is generated in Spec, NumP, and which further cliticizes onto D. Nothing hinges on this here.

In (6b), the verb moves up to the nominalizing affix in No^0.[3] Then, the verb+affix complex assigns Case to the right to the direct object in Spec, VP, and the external θ-role is discharged in Spec, NoP* after the V+affix complex has moved to No*. Furthermore, the 's morpheme projects (to Ca(se)P) in English, and the subject moves to Spec, CaP and gets Case from 's by specifier-head agreement (Abney 1987).

Taking such a position predicts that the direct object cannot be omitted when the noun denotes an event (Lebeaux 1984, Safir 1987, Grimshaw 1990). This is because the VP must contain the direct object in a clause, as shown in (7):

(7) *The doctor observed __.

Note finally that discharging the external θ-role in Spec, NoP* (rather than within the VP) makes the right prediction with respect to the position of referential adjectives in English, i.e., those adjectives which may receive the external θ-role of a noun (Kayne 1984, Cinque 1990):

(8) The Japanese invasion of China.

If the external argument were projected inside VP, i.e., lower than the noun, (8) would not be derivable without some other stipulation. Furthermore, generating the subject of both nouns and verbs inside VP could not explain why only nouns may take AP external arguments. Here, we just need to say that only nominal affixes can discharge an adjectival external θ-role.

I now turn to the first consequence of our proposal, i.e., the absence of prenominal objects with event nominals.

2.1. Absence of prenominal objects in event nominals (Grimshaw 1990)

Grimshaw (1990) claims that the internal argument of an event nominal cannot appear in the prenominal position (cf. (9)), while it can with result nominals (cf. (10)).[4] This can be seen in (9) where the presence of the adjunct modifiers in three hours and frequent force the event reading of observation:

---

3 In fact, it is hard to see how it could be otherwise, since it is the nominal affix which 'changes' the category of a verb into a noun. If Affix-hopping were responsible for attaching the affix onto the verb, the newly formed complex would still be headed by V.

4 It seems that judgements differ significantly regarding the absence of prenominal objects with event nominals, many people having no difficulty accepting them. This is consistent with a Case-Theoretic (rather than a semantic) approach to Grimshaw's observation: good cases of prenominal objects could simply be attributed to the fact that, for some speakers, the nominalizing affix does not force Case to be assigned to a direct object. As a result, the object is free to move to the Spec, CaP position without violating the conditions on chain formation. In fact, Hungarian is a clear case of the opposite: in both event and result nominals objects can only appear in prenominal position. This means that the nominalizing affix not only does not force Case assignment, but that it does not even make it possible. This means that, when both an agent and a theme are projected, the second argument must be "adjectivalized".

(9) a *The patient$_i$'s observation t_i in three hours.
b *The frequent patient$_i$'s observation.
c The/The doctor's observation of the patient in three hours.

This is straightforward under the system presented here if we make the assumption that the verb+affix complex assigns Case obligatorily. Then, the direct object may not further move to Spec, CaP, since if it did, it would be receiving Case twice (once from the V+affix complex, once from 's), in violation of the conditions on chain formation (Chomsky 1981, Sportiche 1983, Chomsky 1986).

As opposed to event nominals, result nominals allow prenominal objects, as illustrated in (10), where the Noun Phrase is the subject of a predicate which induces a result interpretation:

(10) The patient's observation is now complete.

Here I will adopt Picallo's (1990) idea that result nominals are not derived syntactically. As a consequence, the nominalizing affix is not syntactically present to force Case assignment to the object, and Case to the complement may either be realized in object position or prenominally, just as with underived nominals (Chomsky 1986):

(11) a A picture of John.
b John's picture.

3. -ing nominals

In his dissertation, Abney (1987) proposed an analysis of ing-nominals which is in many ways similar to some aspects of the analysis of event nominals presented in the previous section, in that he argues for a syntactic derivation of ing-nominals. Abney also proposes that the nominalizing morpheme -ing is generated in different places within the DP. I will argue that, in addition to unifying the various types of ing-nominals with derived nominals, a modification of Abney's analysis provides good support for the claim that Case to the direct object in event nominals is assigned to the specifier canonically governed by the first potential Case assigning head.

Abney distinguishes three types of -ing nominals, two of which are illustrated below;[5] the (a) examples represent what Abney labels -ing-of nominals and the (b) examples Poss-ing gerunds:

It is not clear how to reconcile these differences in Grimshaw's analysis, since it relies on the fact that nouns are not proper θ-markers. In (i) the trace does not receive the θ-role that event nominals must discharge, while (ii) shows that θ-role transmission is not possible through a preposition (cf. (ii)):

(i) The patient$_i$'s observation t_i.
(ii) *The patient$_i$'s observation of.

[5] I leave aside the third construction discussed by Abney, i.e. Acc-ing nominals, which, for our purposes is just like Poss-ing nominals.

(12) a John's reading of the book.
b John's reading the book.

(13) a John's (*having completely) read of the book.
b John's having completely read the book.

Examples (12) and (13) highlight two important properties which distinguish the two types: (i) the object is marked for genitive in -ing-of nominals, while it is accusative in Poss-ing gerunds; and (ii) only Poss-ing gerunds allow both auxiliaries and adverbs to occur. Abney proposes that this is accounted for if the structure of both nominals differ in that the -ing morpheme attaches to N in the first case, while it selects a VP complement in the second case. Reinterpreting Abney's proposal, I propose that -ing selects a complement in both cases, and that (12) and (13) reflect the fact that the complements is a VP in -ing-nominal, while gerunds select an Asp(ect)P complement (see Carstens & Kinyalolo 1988, Kinyalolo 1990, Travis 1992 for AspP). This is illustrated in (14):

(14) ing-nominal (ing-of)

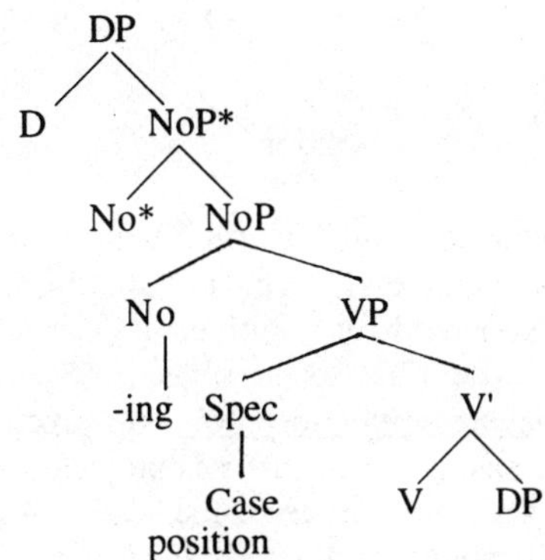

(15) Poss-ing gerund

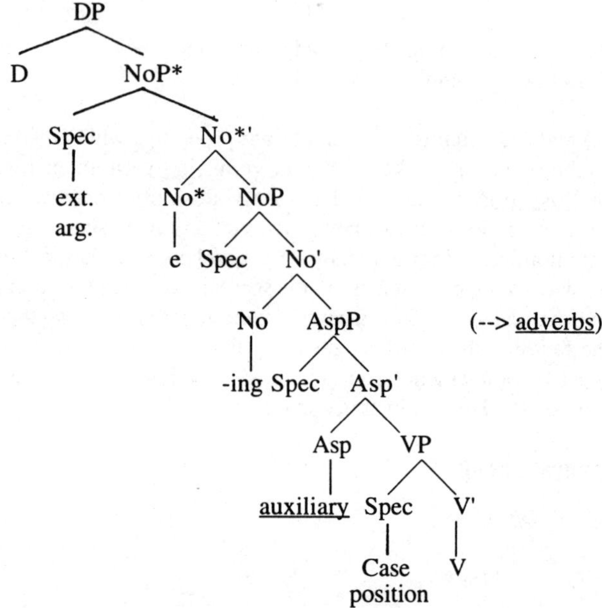

In (12a)/(14), the verb moves up to the nominalizing affix. As is the case with event nominals, the object gets Case not from the verb under V', but in Spec, VP from the V+affix complex. Hence, it is marked for genitive. In (12b)/(15), the verb moves to Asp^0, and assigns accusative Case to the object in Spec, VP. As for periphrastic gerunds (e.g., John's having written the book), the structure is slightly more complicated: once again, the past participle affix is projected in the syntax, and takes an VP complement (cf. (4)). The auxiliary is the head of AspP, and, as it is the case in clauses, it obligatorily moves up (Emonds 1978, Pollock 1990), here to -ing. Finally, the verb moves up to the participial morphology and assigns accusative Case to the direct object in Spec, VP. This is schematized in (16):

(16)

```
DP
 D   NoP*
      Spec   No*'
      ext.   No*   NoP
      arg.   e     Spec   No'
                          No     AspP
                          -ing   Spec   Asp'
                                        Asp    IpP
                                        hav-   Spec   Ip'
                                                      Ip    VP
                                                      -en   Spec   V'
                                                            Case   V      DP
                                                            position writ- the book
```

4. Sentential complements

Stowell (1981) pointed out that the event reading of an English derived nominal is not available when the complement is a tensed clause:[6]

(17) The announcement that the position had been filled was a surprise.

The claim is that in (17) the sentential complement is necessarily interpreted as an adjunct modifier to a result nominal. This is clearly seen if a modifier which forces

---

[6] Infinitival complements appear to constitute counterexamples to this claim (cf. Stowell 1981):

(i) Their attempt to climb the mountain.

However, Grimshaw argues that nouns such as *attempt* which take infinitival complements behave more like result nominals (in her terms, 'simple event nominals') than event (or 'complex event') nominals in many respects (cf. also Zucchi 1988). For instance, Grimshaw observes that *attempt* cannot be modified by the aspectual adjectives *frequent* or *constant*, which are only compatible with event readings:

(ii) *Their frequent/constant attempt to climb Mount Everest.

the event reading appears inside the Noun Phrase. In this case, the phrase is ungrammatical:

(18) *The constant announcement that the job had been filled.

Stowell argues that the unavailability of the event reading in (17) is a consequence of two interacting factors: first, in order to receive a θ-role, arguments must be Case-marked; but, then, following Vergnaud (1977), he argues that nouns are not Case assigners. As a result, the CP in (17) cannot be an argument (of-insertion being disallowed for clauses as a result of the Case Resistance Principle).

For her part, Grimshaw proposes a somewhat similar account of the ungrammaticality of (18). She claims that the reason why the event reading is not possible is that nouns are 'defective' θ-markers (see also Emonds 1985), and that, as a result, they require a preposition to transmit their θ-role. Since DPs, but not CPs, may be preceded by a preposition, the CP in (17) cannot receive a θ-role, and since event nominals obligatorily project their argument structure, a θ-Criterion violation ensues.

Aside from conflicting empirical evidence (see discussion of (28) below), neither account is tenable under the analysis presented in this paper. First, I have argued that nouns are Case-assigners, and second, unlike Grimshaw, I proposed that of-NPs are DPs, not PPs, i.e., that of is merely a Case-marker. But the claim that Case to the direct object is assigned to specifier provides an interesting account of both the ungrammaticality of (18) and sentence (28). The structure of (17) would be like (19) if CP were in complement position:

(19)

```
DP
├── D
└── NoP*
    ├── No*
    │   └── e
    └── NoP
        ├── Spec
        └── No'
            ├── No
            │   └── -ment
            └── VP
                ├── Spec
                │   └── Case position
                └── V'
                    ├── V
                    │   └── announce
                    └── CP
                        └── that the position has been filled
```

After the verb raises to the affix, the CP must get Case from the newly formed noun in order to satisfy the Visibility Condition. I claim that the problem with (19) is that the CP cannot receive Case at all, because it cannot get Case by moving to the Case position.[7] This can be seen as an instance of Stowell's Case Resistance Principle, which prevents clauses to be in a position where they would be Case-marked directly. As a result, the CP cannot be interpreted as a complement.

Under this approach, we must now explain why the clausal counterpart to (17) is grammatical. In other words, if CPs cannot move to Spec, VP to get Case (and hence be visible for θ-role assignment), we must explain why it is that verbs can nonetheless take sentential complements:

(20) They mentioned to the candidate that the position had been filled.

To account for this asymmetry between nouns and verbs, I will capitalize on a crucial difference between Noun Phrases and clauses: the possibility of containing expletive pronouns. As opposed to Noun Phrases (see below), clauses can contain expletive pronouns. We also know that these expletives can, under certain analyses, transmit nominative Case to a clausal complement of a non-Case assigning verb:

(21) It seems/is believed [that Nick will go back to Scotland].
|______Case_______↑

Similarly, Sportiche (1990) proposes that accusative Case in French is assigned through transmission from an expletive in the specifier corresponding to the Case position of a transitive verb:[8]

(22) Jeanne a donné ses livres.
'Jeanne gave her books'

(23) $[_{IpP}$ ext. θ-role $[_{Ip'}$ $[\text{donn}_i\text{-é}]_k$ $[_{IpP}$ pro t_k $[_{VP}$ DP t_i]]]]
|_________↑ |_________↑
Case Case transmission

This, he claims, explains why, in sentences such as (22), past participle agreement is not triggered with postverbal objects, even though the Case position (which is the same as the agreement position) is in a specifier-head relation with the participial morphology.

---

[7] In fact, Giorgi & Longobardi (1991) show that clauses cannot even transit through specifiers. If they could, step-by-step extraction through specifier should be possible on a par with DP extraction. The contrast in the Italian sentences in (i) shows that it is not:

(i) a Una guerra, [di cui]$_i$ non so valutare la probabilità t_i, sarebbe catastrofica.
a war, of which I cannot evaluate the probability, would be catastrophic

b *Una guerra, [che si sia la quale]$_i$ non so valutare la probabilità t_i ...
a war, that there will be which I cannot evaluate the probability ...

[8] Of course, this option is not possible in Noun Phrases since they do not allow expletives, forcing the object to move to the Case position (see discussion of (25)).

Similarly then, it is logical to say that the CP complement in (20) receives Case from pro in Spec, VP:[9,10]

(24) They [$_{VP}$ mentioned$_k$ [$_{VP}$ pro t_i [$_{V'}$ [$_{CP}$ that the position had been filled]$_i$]]]
|___Case____↑ |__Case transmission____↑

Now, it is well known that Noun Phrases in English do not allow expletive pronouns to occur (cf. Clark 1989 for an account):

(25) a There were discussed many problems.
b *There's discussion of many problems.
c It appears that Jack is missing.
d *It's appearance that Jack is missing.

As a result, the Case transmission process is not available for the CP in Noun Phrases such as (17). Since the CP cannot move to the Case position either, it cannot be Case-marked at all, hence it cannot be a complement.

Interestingly, this analysis makes the prediction that if a language allows expletives to occur inside Noun Phrases, event nominals should be able to have sentential complements. Hungarian is just such a language.

As discussed by Szabolcsi (1983, 1987, 1990), a noun complement can either receive nominative Case in a postnominal position (in the specifier of an inflectional head) or dative Case in the predeterminer position (Spec, DP).

(26) [$_{DP}$ a [$_{NP}$ Mari-ø INFL vendég-e-ø]]
the Mary-nom guest-poss-3sg

---

9 This means that another explanation must be provided for the fact that clauses always appear on the right periphery of VP in English:

(i) I said to Norma that she had a good idea.

Stowell (1981) proposes that the relative order of the complements in sentences such as (i) is the result of his Case Resistance Principle which forces the CP complement to move out of the Case position to a peripheral position in VP. Since in our case the clause does not start out in a Case position, we must say that (i) is the result of some other process.

10 It is tempting to say that the sentence in (i) represents a case of overt realization of the expletive (see Authier 1991):

(i) They mentioned it to the candidate that the position has been filled.

As pointed out to me by Beatrice Santorini, we would then have to explain why extraction is only possible when the expletive is null:

(ii) What did they mention that they filled?
(iii) *What did they mention it that they filled?

See Kiss (199o) for a possible account.

(27) Mari-nak a vendég-e-ø
Mary-dat the guest-poss-3sg

Kenesei (1991) observes that, parallel to clauses, Case to sentential complements in DP can be realized through an expletive (see also Kiss 1990):

(28) a Péter megcáfolt-a az-t [$_{CP}$ hogy a szabály érvényes]
Peter refuted-3sg it-acc that the rule valid
'Peter refuted that the rule was valid'

b an-nak a megcáfol-ás-a [$_{CP}$ hogy a szabály
it-dat the refut-ation-3sg that the rule

érvényes]
valid
'The refutation that the rule is valid'

Example (28b) illustrates a case where the sentential complement remains in its base position and receives Case through an expletive in Spec, DP. Here, the event reading is possible, as is shown by the occurrence of a temporal adjunct inside the Noun Phrase:[11, 12]

(29) an-nak a két órán belül való megcáfol-ás-a
it-dat the two hours within being refut-ation-3sg

[$_{CP}$ hogy a szabály érvényes]
that the rule valid
'The refutation that the rule is valid in two hours'

This contrast between English and Hungarian strongly suggests that the prohibition on sentential complement in event nominals is due to structural factors.

5. Conclusion

I have argued that Case in Noun Phrases is assigned to the specifier canonically governed by the head. This proved to have a number consequences with respect to Case-related syntactic phenomena in Noun Phrases. Perhaps the most important consequence of the analysis is that it provides a syntactic account of the absence of prenominal objects and of sentential complements in event nominals. With respect to the latter, it was shown that the fact that sentential complements receive Case through an expletive pronoun in Spec, VP not only accounts for the difference between clauses and Noun Phrases, but also provides a

[11] Thanks to Anna Szabolcsi for pointing this out to me.

[12] Kiss (1990) points out that extraposition of the complement clause is only optional.

solution to cross-linguistic differences concerning the ability of event nominals to select sentential complements.

REFERENCES

Abney, Steve. 1987. *The English Noun Phrase in its sentential aspect*. Ph.D. dissertation, MIT.

Authier, Jean.-Marc. 1991. V-governed expletives, Case Theory, and the Projection Principle. *Linguistic Inquiry* 22:721-40.

Carstens, Vicki. 1991. *The morphology and syntax of Determiner Phrases in Kiswahili*. Ph. D. dissertation, UCLA.

Carstens, Vicki & Kasangati Kinyalolo. 1989. On IP structure: Tense, Aspect, and Agreement. Paper presented at GLOW 12, Utrecht, The Netherlands.

Chomsky, Noam. 1981. *Lectures on Government and Binding*. Dordrecht: Foris.

Chomsky, Noam. 1986. *Knowledge of language*. New York: Praeger.

Cinque, Guglielmo. 1990. Agreement and Head-to-Head Movement in the Romance Noun Phrase. Paper presented at the *XXth Linguistic Symposium on Romance Languages*, University of Ottawa.

Clark, Robin. 1989. Structured θ-grids and the syntax of nominals. Ms. Université de Genève.

Emonds, Joseph. 1978. The verbal complex V'-V in French. *Linguistic Inquiry* 9:151-75

Emonds, Joseph. 1985. *A unified theory of syntactic categories*. Dordrecht: Foris.

Giorgi, Alessandra & Giuseppe Longobardi. 1991. *The syntax of Noun Phrases: Configuration, parameters and empty categories*. Cambridge University Press.

Grimshaw, Jane. 1990. *Argument structure*. Cambridge, MA: MIT Press.

Hazout, Ilan. 1990. *Verbal nouns: Theta-theoretic studies in Hebrew*. Ph. D. dissertation, University of Massachusetts, Amherst.

Kayne, Richard. 1984. *Connectedness*. Dordrecht: Foris.

Kenesei, István. 1990. Expletives in DP. In J. Payne (ed.), *Proceedings of the Manchester Colloquium on Noun Phrases*.

Kinyalolo, Kasangati 1990. *Syntactic dependencies and the Spec-Head Agreement Hypothesis in KiLega*. Ph. D. dissertation, UCLA.

Kiss, Katalin. 1990. Why noun-complement clauses are barriers. In Grammar in progress: GLOW essays for Henk van Riemsdijk. Dordrecht: Foris.

Larson, Richard. 1988. On the Double Object Construction. *Linguistic Inquiry* 19:335-91.

Lebeaux, David. 1984. Nominalizations, argument structure, and the organization of grammar. Ms. University of Massachustts, Amherst.

Milner, Jean-Claude. 1982. *Ordres et raisons de langue*. Paris: Le Seuil.

Murasugi, Kumiko. 1989. The derivation of derived nominals. Ms. MIT.

Picallo, Carme. 1990. Nominals and nominalization in Catalan. Ms. Universitat Autonoma di Barcelona.

Pollock, Jean-Yves 1989. Verb movement, Universal Grammar and the structure of IP. *Linguistic Inquiry* 20:365-424.

Ritter, Elizabeth. 1990. TWO functional categories in Noun Phrases: Evidence from Modern Hebrew. Ms. UQAM.

Safir, Kenneth. 1987. The syntactic projection of lexical thematic structure. *Natural Language and Linguistic Theory* 5:561-601.

Sportiche, Dominique. 1983. *Structural invariance and symmetry in syntax*. Ph. D. dissertation, MIT.

Sportiche, Dominique. 1990. Movement, agreement, and Case. Ms. UCLA.

Stowell, Timothy. 1981. *Origins of phrase structure*. Ph. D. dissertation, MIT.

Szabolcsi, Anna. 1983 The possessor than ran away from home. *Linguistic Review* 3: 89-102.

Szabolcsi, Anna. 1987. Functional categories in the Noun Phrase. In I. Kenesei, (ed.), *Approaches to Hungarian* vol. 2.

Szabolcsi, Anna. 1990. Noun Phrases and Clauses: Is DP Analogous to IP or CP?. In J. Payne (ed.), *Proceedings of the Manchester Colloquium on Noun Phrases*.

Travis, Lisa. 1991. Derived objects, inner Aspect, and the structure of VP. Paper presented at *NELS 22*, University of Delaware.

Valois, Daniel. 1991a. The internal syntax of DP and adjective placement in French and English. *NELS 21*:367-80.

Valois, Daniel. 1991b. Functional categories and Case In DP. *GLOW Newsletter*.

Valois, Daniel. 1991c. *The internal syntax of DP*. Ph. D. dissertation, UCLA.

Vergnaud, Jean-Roger. 1977. Formal properties of phonological rules. In R. Butts & J. Hintikka (eds.), *Basic problems in methodology and Linguistics*. Dordrecht: Reidel.

Zubizarreta, María-Luisa. 1987. *Levels of representation*. Dordrecht: Foris.

Zucchi, Alessandro. 1988. The syntactic and semantic status of the by-phrase. *NELS 19*:467-84.

Adverbs of Quantification, Conditionals, and Presupposition Accommodation

KAI VON FINTEL
University of Massachusetts at Amherst

Introduction

So-called donkey-sentences like the one in (1) raise many important issues for the syntax and semantics of natural language.[1]

(1) If a farmer owns a donkey, he often beats it.

Intuitively, (1) can be understood as claiming that many pairs of a farmer and a donkey that he owns are such that he beats it. Two questions arise immediately: (i) How is it possible for (1) to make this claim about many farmer-donkey pairs when on the surface we only see two indefinite noun phrases in the *if*-clause and a frequency adverb in the matrix clause? (ii) How are the farmer and donkey pronouns in the matrix clause bound, when their potential antecedent binders, the indefinites, are buried in the subordinate clause?

The by now standard account of donkey sentences was pioneered by David Lewis (1975), Hans Kamp (1981), and Irene Heim (1982). The main ingredients are: (i) Indefinites are not existential quantifiers as traditional logic maintained; instead they are interpreted as restricted free variables. (ii) These variables can be bound by an "adverb of quantification" (Lewis' term), such as *often* in (1); these adverbs are unselective binders which can bind all free variables in their scope. (iii) The donkey pronouns are also bound by this

For helpful comments and suggestion I would like to thank Paul Portner, Hotze Rullmann, Barbara Partee, Sue Tunstall, and the audience at WCCFL XI. Research on this paper has been partially supported by the National Science Foundation under Grant No. BNS 87-19999 (Principal Investigators: Emmon Bach, Angelika Kratzer, and Barbara Partee). The title of the paper differs slightly from the title it had when it was just a little abstract. At some not so distant point I plan to discuss the relation between focus and scrambling, which was supposed to be part of this paper.

[1]The clearest exposition of the issues involved can be found in Irene Heim's dissertation (1982).

unselective binder. (iv) *If*-clauses in general serve to supply the domain of the unselective quantifier.

Our example donkey-sentence (1) will then receive the logical form and the paraphrase in (2).

(2) a. $\text{Often}_{x,y}$ [a farmer(x) ∧ a donkey (y) ∧ x owns y] [x beats y]
   b. "Many pairs x,y such that x is a farmer, y is a donkey, and x owns y are such that x beats y".

There are at least two alternative approaches on the market: Dynamic Montague Grammar (Groenendijk and Stokhof 1991, Chierchia 1991) and the situation-based account (Berman 1987, Heim 1990). An important goal would then be to find new data to evaluate the performance of the three theories. What kind of data could there be? Henriette de Swart (1992) and Cleo Condoravdi (1992) both discuss types or uses of indefinite NPs that had not been considered before in the donkey literature. My goal in this paper is to start expanding the coverage to other conditional clause-types beyond the usual *if/when*-clauses. In particular, I will present data concerning the availability of donkey-binding with indefinites in *unless*-clauses.

This paper is merely a start. While I will sketch an arguably plausible explanation of the data within the situation-based approach, a detailed comparison with possible accounts within the other theories will have to wait for a future occasion. Also, I will concentrate mainly on *unless*-conditionals although it would be desirable to extend the discussion to other conditionals (*only if, even if, if and only if*) and other adverbials (especially *although* and *because*).

This then is the organization of what's to come: (i) the crucial data about *unless*-conditionals and donkey-binding are presented; (ii) the situation-based approach to adverbial quantification is sketched; (iii) the meaning of conditionals is discussed; (iv) the first set of data will be explained; (v) the second set of data will be explained once a mechanism of presupposition accommodation is implemented; (vi) some general speculations on conditionals, adverbials, and quantifiers are ventured.

The Data: Donkey Binding and 'Unless'-Conditionals

The first observation is that in general the possibility of donkey-anaphora seems severely limited with *unless*-clauses.

(3) a. If a farmer owns a donkey, he often beats it.
   b. *Unless a farmer owns a donkey, he often beats it.

(4) a. If anyone objects, I will talk to him.
   b. *Unless anyone objects, I will talk to him.

A fact that I will suggest is just another instance of the unavailability of donkeys with *unless* is that *unless* does not allow a *then*-correlate in the main clause.

(5) a. If it rains tomorrow, (then) I won't leave.
b. Unless it rains tomorrow, (*then) I won't leave.

Our theory should not be too successful in deriving the illformedness of donkeys with *unless*, however. There are actually types of examples where donkey-binding is well-formed even with *unless*-clauses, as (6) illustrates.[2]

(6) a. Unless a farmer is RICH, he shouldn't beat his donkeys.
c. Unless you {*own / √OWN} a donkey, you shouldn't beat it

The challenge for the general theory of donkey-anaphora and for the semantics of conditional clauses then is to explain (i) the general unavailability of donkey-binding and of a *then*-correlate in *unless*-clauses and (ii) the possibility of donkey-binding in special circumstances. In this paper, I will concentrate on demonstrating that the data can be captured in a situation-based approach to adverbial quantification that assumes that donkey pronouns are disguised definite descriptions. Ultimately, this account should be compared with possible treatments in alternative frameworks. But the fact that the data presented here are new to the discussion in donkey science should be justification enough for this venture.

The Situation-Based Account of Adverbial Quantification

The standard account of donkey-sentences sketched in the introduction breaks with tradition in many respects: especially with its new type of unselective binding and the unorthodox view of indefinites as introducers of free variables rather than as existential quantifiers. A more conservative approach treats the adverb as quantifying over one variable only: events, times, or situations, states of affairs, circumstances, conditions, whatever we want to call it.[3] Such an account also rescues the traditional intuition that indefinite noun phrases have existential force. The most sophisticated version of this line of research is represented by Berman (1987) and Heim (1990) who suggest that adverbs of quantification quantify over situations. They adopt the framework of situation semantics developed by Angelika Kratzer (1989) to handle problems of counterfactual reasoning. There situations are parts of possible worlds and propositions are reconstructed as sets of situations (intuitively, those situations in which the proposition is true).

Modulo the interpretation of the pronouns and some refinements, this gives (1) the logical form in (7).

---

[2]Capitals indicate pitch accent on a syllable.

[3]An early proposal along these lines was made by Greg Stump (1981, 1985).

(7) a. Often_S [$_S$ a farmer owns a donkey] [$_S$ he beats it]
b. "Many situations in which there is a farmer and there is a donkey that the farmer owns are such that he beats it."

What can we do with the pronouns in the matrix clause? The situation-based approach takes recourse to the theory of pronouns as disguised definite descriptions (Cooper 1979, Evans 1980). Let me be non-committal as to any specific implementation of the E-type approach (for some discussion of the choices see Heim 1990 and Chierchia 1991). The logical form for (1) is then amended to (8).

(8) a. Often_S [$_S$ a farmer owns a donkey] [$_S$ the farmer beats the donkey]
b. "Many situations in which there is a farmer and there is a donkey that the farmer owns are such that the farmer beats the donkey."

One last modification has to be made. In her dissertation, Heim had argued very forcefully against the E-type construal of donkey pronouns using among others her now famous sage plant example, a conditional version of which is given in (9).

(9) If someone buys a sage plant here he usually buys eight others with it.

The problem of course is that there won't be a unique sage plant that the definite description hidden in the E-type pronoun can felicitously refer to. The situation-based account has an answer to this problem. Berman 1987 suggested to have the adverb quantify solely over the minimal elements in the set of situations supplied as its first argument. The quantificational adverb *always*, for example, will take two sets of situations and will demand that all the miminal situations in the first set are part of a situation in the second set. The new paraphrases for the sage-plant example and for our stock example are given in (10).

(10) a. "Most of the minimal situations in which someone buys a sage plant here are part of a larger situation in which that someone buys eight other sage plants with the one in the minimal situation."
b. "Many of the minimal situations in which there is a farmer and there is a donkey that the farmer owns are are part of a larger situation in which the farmer beats the donkey."

The Semantics of Conditionals

Since we plan to integrate all sorts of conditionals into the picture, we need to be clear about what conditionals are doing in adverbially quantified sentences. The conventional wisdom is that *if*-clauses provide the domain of quantification, they restrict the adverb of quantification. I would like to spell this out in a way that can be extended to account for other types of conditionals.

Let us adopt a suggestion by Mats Rooth (1985, 1989, 1991) who argues that the first argument of an adverb of quantification is a free variable C that can be restricted in various ways: explicitly by an *if*-clause, or implicitly by accommodating presupposed material.

Slightly more technical, we will say that adverbs of quantification denote a relation between sets of situations. For example, *always* will denote the subset relation (modified to allow for Berman's minimality trick). The first argument of the adverb is a free variable C over sets of situations. The second argument of the adverb is supplied by the matrix clause minus the adverb. The general schema for the interpretation of adverbially quantified sentences with a restrictive *if*-clause is given in (11). Example (1) is now analyzed as in (12).

(11) **if** R Q [C] [M] (to be revised)
= Q [C ∩ R] [M]
= Q-many of the minimal situations in C ∩ R are part of a situation in M.

R:	the antecedent proposition used to restrict C
Q:	the interpretation of the adverb of quantification
C:	the set of currently relevant circumstances
M:	the interpretation of the main clause minus the adverb

(12) a. [**if** (∃x ∃y (farmer(x) owns donkey(y))], **many** [C] [the farmer beats the donkey].

b. "Many of the minimal situations in the set of currently relevant situations in which there is a farmer and there is a donkey and the farmer owns the donkey are part of a larger situation in which the farmer beats the donkey."

The Meaning of 'Unless'

Next we will have to specify what exactly the other kinds of conditionals (*unless*, *only if*, *even if*) mean. The idea will be that while *if*-clauses operate on the quantifier domain C by intersecting with it, other conditionals perform other set-theoretical operations. What about *unless* under this perspective? In numerous textbooks and grammars we can find the traditional view that *unless* is equivalent to *if...not*. A typical example like (13a) is paraphrased by (13b).

(13) a. I will leave *unless* Bill calls soon.
b. I will leave *if* Bill does*n't* call soon.

Taken together with the semantics for *if* as marking a restrictive operator on the domain of an adverbial quantifier, this would suggest that *unless* is a subtractive or exceptive operator on quantifiers. Something along the lines of (14) seems called for. The example in (13a) then gets a paraphrase as in (15)

(14) **unless** R, Q [C] [M] (to be revised)
= Q [C - R] [M]

(15) "All of the minimal situations in the set of currently relevant situations except the ones in which Bill calls soon are part of a larger situation in which I leave." (modulo modality and tense)

In von Fintel (1991) I discussed in some detail the advantages of this approach to the meaning of *unless*, which can be traced back to Geis (1973) and in fact to perceptive lexicographers.[4] I argued there not only that *unless* is an operator on quantifier domains, but also that there is an additional implicature on top of the meaning in (14): the *unless*-clause states the only exception to the quantified proposition. The *except*-paraphrase almost captures that ingredient. As far as I can see, this uniqueness implicature does not interact with donkey-binding, which is why I will ignore this complication here.

No Donkeys

What can we say now about the data presented at the beginning? Why do *unless*-clauses not allow donkey anaphora? It is important to realize at this point that within the situation-based account the availability of donkey-binding is not a question of syntactic or semantic scope. Instead, the operative question is: *Is there an appropriate entity in the antecedent situation to refer back to?* Consider now the contrast in (4), repeated here.

(4) a. If anyone objects, I will talk to him.
b. *Unless anyone objects, I will talk to him.

Take (4a). The donkey pronoun *him* in the main clause is interpreted as an E-type pronoun, as a disguised definite description, something like *the man who objects*. This interpretation meshes successfully with the meaning of the rest of the sentence, which as a whole can be paraphrased as "All of the minimal situations in which someone objects are part of a larger situation in which I will talk to the man who objects". The analysis for (4b) will be something like (16).

(16) a. **all** (C-{s| ∃x (x objects in s)}) (‖ I talk to the one who objects ‖)
b. "All of the minimal situations in the set of currently relevant situations except the ones in which someone objects are part of a larger situation in which I talk to the one who objects".

This is patently nonsensical. In a situation where no one objects there is no objector to talk to. More precisely, the E-type pronoun carries an existence presupposition: simply that in each of the cases considered there exists a man who objects. The *unless*-clause on the other hand removes exactly those situations where there is an objector from the domain of quantification. The presupposition of the E-type pronoun therefore cannot be fulfilled. (4b) then is deviant because of a presupposition failure.

---

[4]The main gloss in the OED entry on *unless* reads: "Except, if…not".

No 'Then'

Why do *unless*-clauses not allow a *then*-correlate in the main clause? Consider (5) again.

(5) a. If it rains tomorrow, (then) I won't leave.
    b. Unless it rains tomorrow, (*then) I won't leave.

I think this is just another instance of the unavailability of donkey-binding across the non-*if*-complementizers. Assume *then* is a kind of grammaticized donkey pronoun picking up the antecedent situation (meaning something like "in that case", for a similar suggestion cf. Haiman 1978). Then the same lines of argumentation as in the previous section will assure that there is some kind of anomaly in the ungrammatical examples in (5).

But if all *then* wants is some situation to refer back to, why can't it just pick one from somewhere in the context, or why can't it just pick one from the remaining elements in C? This is where it becomes important to have an explicit theory of the way E-type anaphors find their antecedent. Heim (1990) discusses the fact that E-type pronouns are not entirely pragmatic in their resolution of reference as shown by classic examples like **Every husband hates her*. Heim proposes an LF approach where the antecedent is copied and adjoined to the pronoun which makes the necessity of a linguistic antecedent part of the E-type theory. For the time being I will subscribe to this (see however the criticisms and an alternative approach involving a new type of co-indexing in Chierchia 1991).

Note how the account of the behavior of *then* suggested here denies the notion, common especially among logicians, that *then* is a mere syntactic particle without any semantic content. That this cannot be quite right is shown fairly dramatically by the contrast in (17), attributed by Geis (1985) to Davis.

(17) a. If you open the refrigerator, it won't explode.
     b. If you open the refrigerator, then it won't explode.

Sabine Iatridou (1991) proposes that *then* in a statement of the form "If **p**, then **q**" induces a presupposition that the negation of **p** implies the negation of **q**. She later amends this to a presupposition that the negation of **p** is compatible with the negation of **q**. One of her examples is (18).

(18) If Quayle runs, then the Republicans will lose. #In fact, if Quayle doesn't run, the Republicans will still lose.

An important task for future research will be to see whether the conception of *then* as an E-type or donkey pronoun and Iatridou's presuppositionality account can be unified.

Conditionals and Presupposition Accomodation

Having successfully explained why there cannot be any donkey-pronouns picking up entities introduced in *unless*-clauses, we now have to turn to the data in (6), repeated here.

(6) a. Unless a farmer is RICH, he shouldn't beat his donkeys.

b. Unless you {*own / √OWN} a donkey, you shouldn't beat it.

What's going on? Here we do have well-formed donkey anaphora with *unless*-clauses. How come?

A Focus-Savvy Story

Here's my story. What is the difference between the cases where donkey anaphora is unavailable and those where it is o.k.? Let us meditate on the specific contrast in (19).

(19) Unless you {*own / √OWN} a donkey, you shouldn't beat it.

Why should stress on the verb make it possible that the object is available as an antecedent for a donkey pronoun? After all, *unless* will still remove all the situations where you own a donkey. Where is the donkey that *it* refers back to?

The intuition I will develop is that the focus on the verb signals that we are contemplating alternative relations between you and a donkey (cf. de Hoop 1992), and we are saying that none of those except the ones that are owning relations entitle you to beating it. The donkey will exist in all the situations considered. Hence the donkey pronoun is licit.

Sketch of an Implementation

Can we make this intuition a little more precise? What we need is an explicit theory of focus and presupposition. What I will try to do here is adapt Mats Rooth's system (1985, 1989, 1991) to the situation semantics for adverbs of quantification.

The input to the semantics from the syntax in the case of the sentence in (19) with verb focus will be as in (20).

(20) [unless [you [own]$_F$ a donkey]] [shouldn't [you beat it]]

The focus feature F on the verb will be used to compute the presupposition of the complement of *unless*. Following Rooth, we interpret the sentence [you [own]$_F$ a donkey] twice: (i) we give it its normal semantic value $[\![\ ]\!]^o$, i.e. in our framework, the set of situations in which there is a donkey that you own; (ii) we give it a second semantic value, its focus value $[\![\ ]\!]^p$, which is the set of all propositions of the form 'you R a donkey' where R is any binary relation. By taking the union of that set we get a set of all those situations which contain you R-ing a donkey. That set can be taken to be the presupposition of the complement of *unless*.

The intuition sketched above now was that the domain of quantification is restricted to exactly these situations, the ones which contain you and some donkey and some relation between the pair of you. And then we subtract all those situation where you own the donkey. But every situation that's left will still contain you and a donkey and so the donkey anaphora will still work.

We have modified the semantics for *unless* given earlier in (14) in such a way as to allow the donkey anaphora in the special focus cases. The proposal under consideration is seen in (21).

(21) **unless** $[\![R]\!]^o$ Q [C] [M]
= $Q[(C \cap [\![R]\!]^p) - [\![R]\!]^o][M]$

The domain of quantification free variable C is first restricted (by intersection) to those situations in the presupposition of the complement of *unless*. And then we subtract the situations described by the complement of *unless*.

Relevant Contrasts

The alert reader will have spotted a problem with the story just told. If we consider all possible binary relation between a person and a donkey there will be lots and lots of those and in particular many that do not entail the existence of the donkey. For example, this is a binary relation between me and a donkey: "living in the same century as an artist who painted a picture of". This problem is discussed in by Rooth (1991). The existential quantification over alternatives has to be restricted to a set of relevant contrasts to the focussed material. For our stock example, that means that the domain of quantification will be all those situations that contain you standing in an owning-type relation (borrowing/leasing/renting/etc.) to a donkey. From now on, I will assume that $[\![\ ]\!]^p$ is the set of relevant contrasts, however that is computed.

A Generalization to Other Conditionals

The question we must address now is whether the proposal in (21) is an ad hoc solution to the peculiar behavior of *unless* or whether it is just an instance of a general scheme of how we interpret conditionals. Does the semantics of *if* have to be focus-conscious, too?

There are suggestions in the literature that say yes. The question arises in the context of the so-called 'proportion problem', which is a serious problem for the unselective binding approach to donkey anaphora. The crucial observation is that there is a prominent reading of (22) that does not quantify over farmer-donkey pairs but over donkey-owning farmers. The empirical test consists in judging whether a very rich farmer owning hundreds of donkeys would tip the balance. The consensus is that there is a reading where it doesn't matter how many donkeys a farmer owns: we are just quantifying over donkey-owners.

(22) If a farmer owns a donkey, he is happy.

The problem is of course that any unselective approach would have the higher operator bind both indefinites in the restrictive *if*-clause, thus predicting that (22) is counting farmer-donkey pairs. A way of selecting the correct quantifiees is needed.

There are quite a variety of ideas on the market on how to deal with this selection problem. Kratzer (1989) and Diesing (1990) suggest that only indefinites that can be scrambled outside the VP can be captured. Chierchia (1991) appeals to a process of topic-selection, so far unreduced to other mechanisms. All of these bear a close relation to focus phenomena. Let me sketch how a focus-sensitive semantic rule for conditionals along the lines of (21) would fare with the proportion problem.

Within a situation-based approach, the task boils down to finding a principled way of deriving the set of situations specified in (23), from Heim (1990), as the domain of quantification.

(23) $\{s: \exists x[x \text{ is a farmer in } s \;\&$
$$\exists s'[s \leq s' \;\&\; \exists y[y \text{ is a donkey in } s' \;\&\; x \text{ owns } y \text{ in } s']]]\}$$

The minimal situations in the set of situations in (23) will contain a farmer and not much else. All of them will be extendable into bigger situations containing donkeys that the farmer owns. Any of the farmers quantified over will therefore be donkey-owners. But the number of donkeys owned plays no role for the evaluation of the quantified statement. The desired farmer-donkey asymmetry is achieved. Heim (1990) derives (23) via syntactic manipulations at LF. Can we get the same result by using the focus story?

Let's assume, maybe not too recklessly, that there is focus on the verb phrase in the asymmetric reading of (22). The input to the semantics therefore will be (24).

(24) If a farmer [owns a donkey]$_F$, he is happy.

Try this on for size. The presupposition value for the complement of *if* will be all the situations containing a farmer where the farmer has some property in the contrast class of donkey-owning. Now, we could say that this set is pared down further by making sure that all these situations are **part** of a situation where the farmer owns a donkey. This will weed out all the non-donkey-owning farmers. But the domain of quantification are still just situations with a farmer and some property. This will mean that the adverb will in fact quantify over farmers, The proposal in (25) is what we seem to need. Sentence (22) under the asymmetric reading will be interpreted as in (26).

(25) **if** $[\![R]\!]^o$ Q [C] [M]
$= Q\,[\,(C \cap [\![R]\!]^P) \cap \{s \mid \exists s'(s' \geq s \;\&\; s' \in [\![R]\!]^o)\}\,]\,[M]$

(26) "All of the minimal situations in the set of currently relevant situations in which there is a farmer with some property of the donkey-owning type and which are part of a situation in which there is a farmer who owns a donkey are part of a larger situation in which the farmer is happy."

We have a problem now. The unfocussed existential quantifier *a farmer* from the *if*-clause will be interpreted twice, once in $[\![R]\!]^P$ and once in $[\![R]\!]^o$, Note the double occurrence of "there is a farmer..." in the paraphrase in (26). There is no guarantee that we are talking about the same farmer. In effect, any farmer will be in the domain of quantification as long as there is one donkey-owning farmer in the world. How can we make sure that only donkey-owning farmers are considered? Heim had no problems with this, since in her LF-approach there was no second occurrence of the existential quantifier. Instead, there was a trace interpreted as a bound variable. The more purely semantic account that we are pursuing here has no such option.

What we need is a relation between the farmer-situations quantified over and the farmer-donkey-owning situations that is stronger than the mere part-of relation. Within the machinery of situation semantics there is in fact such a stronger relation. Not only can we say that a proposition is true in a situation ($s \in p$), but we can also construct a notion of a situation being a fact that makes a proposition true, which is somewhat stronger. Building on that notion we can then use a more selective part-of relation which does the right thing for our problem. Angelika Kratzer (1990, 1991) gives the definition in (27).

(27) *Facts that make propositions true*
If s is any situation and p any proposition, then s is a fact that makes p true iff for all s' such that $s' \leq s$ and $s' \notin p$, there is an s" such that $s' \leq s'' \leq s$, and s" is a minimal situation in which p is true.

Essentially, this definition ensures that a fact that makes a proposition true does not contain any situation that doesn't contribute to the truth of the situation, it doesn't contain any irrelevant stuff. That is what we needed. The non-donkey-owning farmers do not contribute to the truth of "there is a farmer who owns a donkey". So they can be filtered out. The amended semantics for *if* is given in (28) and sentence (23) gets the paraphrase in (29).

(28) **if** $[\![R]\!]^o$ Q [C] [M]
$= Q[(C \cap [\![R]\!]^P) \cap \{s \mid \exists s'(s' \geq s \,\&$ s' is a fact that makes $[\![R]\!]^o$ true$)\}]$ [M]

(29) "All of the minimal situations in the set of currently relevant situations in which there is a farmer with some property of the donkey-owning type and which are part of a larger situation which is a fact that makes it true that there is a farmer who owns a donkey are part of another larger situation in which the farmer is happy."

We have now successfully mimicked Heim's situation-based approach to the proportion problem in a way that uses focus-induced presupposition accommodation rather than LF-maneuvers.[5]

Back to 'Unless'

The focus-sensitive semantics for *unless* formulated earlier in (21) did not make reference to the elaborate notion of a fact making a proposition true. Can we harmlessly incorporate this into the meaning of *unless* in order to achieve a uniform schema for the interpretation of conditionals? Is (30) adequate?

(30) **unless** $[\![R]\!]^o$ Q [C] [M]
$= Q[(C \cap [\![R]\!]^P) - \{s \mid \exists s'(s' \geq s \,\&$ s' is a fact that makes $[\![R]\!]^o$ true$)\}]$ [M]

At the moment, I can't see anything wrong with (30).

Conclusion

Note that the semantics for *unless* and the one for *if* are now very similar. In fact, they only differ in the way they use the set of situations that are part of a fact that makes $[\![R]\!]^o$ true. While *unless* subtracts this set from the domain of quantification, *if* intersects it with the domain. In this respect then, *unless* is really just the negative counterpart of *if*, modulo the fact that their presuppositions get added in a positive way in both cases. The general interpretation schema for conditionals can now be given as in (31).

(31) **cond** $[\![R]\!]^o$, Q [C] [M]
$= Q[(C \cap [\![R]\!]^P) @ \{s \mid \exists s'(s' \geq s \,\&$ s' is a fact that makes $[\![R]\!]^o$ true$)\}]$ [M]

where @ stands for any set-theoretic operation.

[5]Again, this is not the place to compare the focus-based approach to the LF-approach. Also, we will have to ignore for the moment the criticisms of the situation-based approach put forward in Chierchia (1991).

Speculations

It is time to step back a little and reflect on what the focus-based analyses presented in this paper are doing. Note that for all conditional clause-types we posited the same mechanism. The domain of quantification C was restricted to those situation presupposed to be actual by the complement of the conditional complementizer. This process then looks perfectly regular. What kind of process is it?

Do we need to stipulate as in (31) that the quantifier domain C gets restricted to those situations compatible with the presuppositions of the conditional antecedent. Or can we say that this is just presupposition accommodation running its natural course? Conditionals on our view are operators on quantifier domains, their presuppositions get locally accommodated into their argument. I would hope that the account developed here will eventually help us to achieve a clearer picture of how presupposition projection and accommodation intervene in the semantics of natural language.

There is an interesting contrast between conditionals and other types of adverbial clauses. *Although*- and *because*-clauses are probably best treated as relating two complete proposition with the added ingredient of factivity. In any event, they presumably do not interfere with the internal semantics of the matrix clause. Therefore, we would not expect to find with such adverbials the intricate interactions that license donkey-binding of indefinites in conditionals. This prediction seems to be borne out as the sentences in (32) demonstrate.

(32) a. !!Although a farmer owns a donkey, he often beats it..
b. !!Because a farmer owns a donkey, he often beats it.

Neither sentence in (32) has the relevant donkey-reading which would be that "Many farmer-donkey pairs are such that the farmer beats the donkey although/because he owns it". Instead, if these sentences mean anything at all, it is the irrelevant interpretation that although/because farmers in general own donkeys, they beat them often. In other words, the adverbials cannot get at the internal structure of the quantified statement.[6]

[6]Also irrelevantly, when the adverbial is not in sentence-initial position but occurs sentence-finally, it can be interpreted as part of the nuclear scope of the quantification. But again, as the sentences in (i) show, the adverbial clause does not provide any restriction of the quantifier domain. Note also that this means that the adverbial has to contain pronouns and cannot contain indefinites.

(i) a. A farmer often beats a donkey although he owns it.
b. A farmer often beats a donkey because he owns it.

Roger Higgins (pc) pointed out that the somewhat obsolete example in (33) may have the relevant donkey-reading.

(33) †Though a farmer own a donkey, he beats it.

Interestingly, (33) shows a subjunctive verb form in the adverbial which might suggest that it is more intimately connected with the semantics of the matrix.

All of this leaves us with the following issues for further research: (i) The "semantic" approach developed here needs to be compared to more "syntactic" accounts. In particular, the relation between the use of focus in my system and the appeal to LF-scrambling by Diesing and Kratzer and the topic selection mechanism of Chierchia has to be clarified. (ii) Various general problems with the situation-based approach brought up by Chierchia have to be addressed. (iii) Cases with the E-type pronouns in the conditional clause and the indefinites in the matrix have to be treated. (iv) The connection between donkey-binding and mood interaction indicated by (33) should be pursued. Sequence of tense/mood and and also switch reference can be seen as other phenomena that need a tight link between matrix and adverbial clauses.

References

Berman, Steve: 1987, 'Situation-Based Semantics for Adverbs of Quantification', in Jim Blevins and Anne Vainikka (eds.), *University of Massachusetts Occasional Papers* **12**, GLSA, University of Massachusetts, Amherst.

Chierchia, Gennaro: 1991, 'Anaphora and Dynamic Binding', to appear in *Linguistics and Philosophy*.

Condoravdi, Cleo: 1992, 'Weakly and Strongly Novel Noun Phrases', Talk at WCCFL XI, UCLA.

Cooper, Robin: 1979, 'The Interpretation of Pronouns', in F. Heny and H. Schnelle (eds.), *Syntax and Semantics* **10**, 61-92.

Diesing, Molly: 1990, *The Syntactic Roots of Semantics Partition*, Ph.D. Dissertation, GLSA, University of Massachusetts at Amherst.

Evans, Gareth: 1980, 'Pronouns', *Linguistic Inquiry* **11**, 337-362.

von Fintel, Kai: 1991, 'Exceptive Conditionals: The Meaning of *Unless*', *NELS* 22.

Geis, Michael: 1973, '*If* and *Unless*', in Braj B. Kachru, Robert B. Lees, Yakov Malkiel, Angelina Petrangeli, and Sol Saporta (eds.) *Issues in Linguistics: Papers in Honor of Henry and Renée Kahane*, University of Illinois Press, Urbana, pp. 231-253.

Geis, Michael: 1985, 'The Syntax of Conditional Sentence', *Ohio State University Working Papers in Linguistics* **31**, 130-159.

Groenendijk, Jeroen and Martin Stokhof, 'Dynamic Predicate Logic', *Linguistics and Philosophy* **14**, 39-100.

Haiman, John: 1978, 'Conditionals are Topics', *Language* **54**, 564-589.

Heim, Irene: 1982, *The Semantics of Definite and Indefinite Noun Phrases*, Ph.D. Dissertation, GLSA, University of Massachusetts, Amherst.

Heim, Irene: 1990, 'E-Type Pronouns and Donkey Anaphora', *Linguistics and Philosophy* **13**, 137-178.

de Hoop, Helen: 1992, 'The Principle of Contrastiveness', Talk at WCCFL XI, UCLA.

Iatridou, Sabine: 1991, 'If *then* Then What?', *NELS 22*.

Kamp, Hans: 1981, 'A Theory of Truth and Semantic Representation', in Jeroen Groenendijk et.al. (eds.), *Truth, Interpretation and Information*, Foris, Dordrecht.

Kratzer, Angelika: 1989, 'An Investigation of the Lumps of Thought', *Linguistics and Philosophy* **12**, 607-653.

Kratzer, Angelika: 1990, 'How Specific is a Fact?', ms, University of Massachusetts, Amherst.

Kratzer, Angelika: 1991, 'Pseudoscope: Ambiguities in Opaque Contexts', Talk at ASL/LSA Conference on Logic and Linguistics, Santa Cruz.

Lewis, David: 1975, 'Adverbs of Quantification', in Edward L. Keenan (ed.), *Formal Semantics of Natural Language*, Cambridge University Press, pp. 3-15.

Lycan, William: 1991, '*Even* and *Even If*', *Linguistics and Philosophy* **14**, 115-150.

Rooth, Mats: 1985, *Association with Focus*, Ph.D. Dissertation, GLSA, University of Massachusetts at Amherst.

Rooth, Mats: 1989, 'Indefinites, Adverbs of Quantification, and Focus', ms.

Rooth, Mats: 1991, 'A Theory of Focus Interpretation or What is the Source of Association with Focus Ambiguities?', ms.

Stump, Greg: 1981, *The Formal Semantics and Pragmatics of Free Adjuncts and Absolutes in English*, Ph.D. Dissertation, Ohio State University.

Stump, Greg: 1985, *The Semantic Variability of Absolute Constructions*, Reidel, Dordrecht.

de Swart, Henriëtte: 1992, 'Genericity, Scope, and the Weak/Strong Distinction', Talk at WCCFL XI, UCLA.

Author's E-Mail Address: *Fintel@Linguist.Umass.Edu*

A Computational Approach to "Intake" Ordering in Syntactic Acquisition

ANDI WU
University of California, Los Angeles

In this paper I propose a computational approach to syntactic acquisition where the input strings are filtered so that only 'unambiguous' triggers are used for parameter setting. As a consequence of this filter, the 'intake' strings will be ordered in spite of the fact that the input strings are not.

1. Basic Assumptions

I will adopt the 'principles and parameters' approach to language acquisition where the learner's task is to set UG parameters upon the triggering of input data. The parameters to be considered in this paper are word order parameters. With the current X-bar theory (Chomsky 1986, Sportiche 1991), these parameters have taken on a new format. Since every category can have a head, a specifier and a complement, word order can now be represented as the relative positions of these three elements. In particular, the specifier and the complement can either precede or follow the head. Using 'L' for 'to the left of head' and 'R' for 'to the right of head', we can for instance represent the word order involved in the following tree as

(a) SPECIFIER(I,N,L), and

(b) COMPLEMENT(I,V,R).

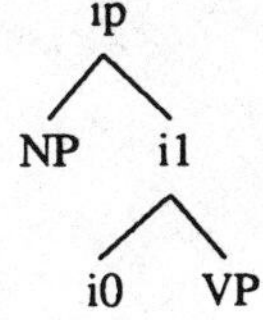

In these rules, the first argument is the category of the head, the second the category of the specifier or complement, and the third the direction of the specifier or complement. Thus (a) can be read as 'I(nfl) can have an NP specifier on its left' and (b) as 'I(nfl) can have a VP complement on its right'. I will assume that the values of the first two arguments are fixed as part of UG. For the two rules illustrated above, this will mean that it is universally possible for I(nfl) to have an NP specifier and a VP complement. The third argument is the DIRECTIONALITY PARAMETER whose value can be either L or R. The acquisition of word order then consists of setting the directionality parameter for the specifier and complement of each category. I will further assume the following.

(i) The directionality parameter is unset at the initial stage.[1]

(ii) A parameter cannot be reset once it is set (Clahsen 1991).

(iii) The directionality parameters for specifiers and complements are set independently for each different category, i.e., the way the parameters are set in one category has nothing to do with their settings in other categories.[2] An idea similar to this, though not specifically referring to word order parameters, is found in Wexler and Manzini (1987) where they proposed the INDEPENDENCE PRINCIPLE.

(iv) The child's input consists of categorized strings (i.e. strings labeled as IP, VP, PP, etc.) and the child knows the category of each content word in the string.[3]

In the model I am developing, parameter setting is accomplished in the parsing process. The parser used here is a HEAD-DRIVEN PARSER which is

[1]It has been suggested (e.g., Sano 1991) that there can be no default parameter values. While this view may be debatable for some parameters, it is certainly plausible for the word order parameters.

[2]As far as word order parameters are concerned, this idea may not sound right. As Greenberg has observed, the head-complement order in different categories tend to correlate with one another in a given language, with the result that some languages are predominantly head-initial and some others head-final. However, this is a tendency rather than a rule. Considering the fact that the orders are mixed in some languages, we have to assume the Independence Principle first and then try to find a way to build in the tendencies.

[3]It is assumed that function words (D, I, C) may not have been categorically labeled in the early stages.

designed to accept and analyze only those structures that conform to the constraints of X-Bar theory. In this sense, the parser can be regarded as a processing counterpart of UG. Upon exposure to language data, the child is supposed to use his/her present knowledge of the grammar to parse the input strings. If a string cannot be processed because of some unset parameter(s), he/she will try to set the parameter(s). In the case of word order, both L and R will be tried and the parameter will be set to the value which results in a successful parse. Take the string *in Boston* as an example. Given that both words are in the child's lexicon with *in* specified as a preposition and *Boston* as an NP, there are logically four possible rules to consider:

(1) SPECIFIER(N,P,?)[4]

(2) COMPLEMENT(N,P,?)

(3) SPECIFIER(P,N,?)

(4) COMPLEMENT(P,N,?)

Possibility (1) is ruled out by UG, since N never takes a PP specifier. Possibility (2) is out by the theta-criterion: the preposition in this case will not have a complement to assign its theta role to. Both (1) and (2) are also ruled out by Assumption (iv) above, since the child expects to parse a PP rather than an NP. Rule (3) is eliminated because of another UG constraint: a preposition does not assign its theta role to its specifier. What remains is (4) where we have to decide whether the direction should be L or R. Obviously, only the value R can make the parsing successful and so the following becomes a rule in the Child's grammar of English:

COMPLEMENT(P,N,R)

2. The Problem

The parameter setting model described above seems fairly easy to implement. However, difficulty can arise as soon as we take a slightly more complex input string, such as *Mary hit John.* By Assumption (iv) above, the child knows that this string is an IP and he/she also has the three words categorized in his/her lexicon. Suppose that no directionality parameter has been previously set. When the child tries to parse this string by setting some parameters, a serious problem emerges. As we can verify, the parsing of this

[4]The question mark here represents an unset parameter.

string can be successful with at least two sets of parameter values which are contradictory to each other:

Set 1: SPECIFIER(I,N,R) COMPLEMENT(V,N,L)

Set 2: SPECIFIER(I,N,L) COMPLEMENT(V,N,R)

Both settings are compatible with the input data, although we know that only Set 2 has the right values for English. If a child happens to choose Set 1, his/her grammar will contain an error unless the parameters are reset later on. Since resetting is not permitted in my model, the child will never be able to recover from his/her mistake. What we find here is a string which provides ambiguous information as to how the parameters should be set.

This problem may not show up if we assume that the child can somehow get the meaning of this sentence before he/she begins to parse it. In that case, he/she will know that *Mary* bears the agent role and *John* the patient role, and the values in Set 1 will not be considered. However, I prefer to assume as little semantic information as possible at this stage and try to solve the problem within syntax. This by no means implies that semantic information does not participate in the acquisition of word order. The preference for a syntactic solution is based on the following two considerations. First of all, it is unclear at this stage how much semantic information we should assume and how reliable the availability of such information is. So one strategy is to start with the null hypothesis that the acquisition can be successful with very limited semantic information and resort to meaning only if absolutely necessary. Even in that case the information should be made available piece by piece so that we may know exactly how much semantic assistance is actually required for the acquisition process to be successful. Furthermore, there is no need for the worry that, if there are both a semantic solution and a syntactic solution, one of the solutions will be redundant. Such redundancy may be necessary for the success in language acquisition which children invariably achieve. The existence of alternative strategies makes it possible for the learner to fall back on other means when one of the strategies fails.[5]

Having justified our approach, we will now try to find a syntactic solution. One thing we notice is that the error will not occur if the child has heard *hit*

[5]This is also true of other kinds of redundancy in natural languages. For instance, a language can use both word order and case marking to indicate grammatical relations. Such redundancy increases the success rate of linguistic communication and is not harmful at all.

John before he/she encounters *Mary hit John.* The string *hit John* is a VP and it is compatible with only one set of parameter values. It is parsable only if we set the directionality to R in the following rule:

COMPLEMENT(V,N,R)

Once this rule has been acquired, *Mary hit John* will not be ambiguous any more, as the values in Set 1 are no longer possible. The natural conclusion we will draw from this phenomenon is that, in order to prevent error in parameter setting, the input strings have to be ordered. Unfortunately, the input a child receives in the real world is typically unordered. So we have a paradox: the input is unordered but the child cannot acquire a language successfully unless the input is ordered.

3. The Logical Solution

To get out of this ordering paradox, we need to invoke the distinction between input and INTAKE originally made in Corder (1967) and further discussed in White (1980). This distinction is based on the hypothesis that children attend to the input data selectively and only a small subset of the input data is used for acquisition purposes. We can find similar ideas, without the term intake, in Braine (1971), Shipley et al. (1969), Waterson (1971), Newport et al. (1977), and Roeper (1978). Put in contemporary terms, this distinction simply refers to the notion that not everything in the input data is used for the purpose of parameter setting. We can thus define intake as follows:

Definition 1:

Intake is the part of input which serves as a trigger for parameter setting in language acquisition.

Given that the input data consists of a set of strings, the intake may differ from the input in two ways: (1) not every string in the input is in the intake, and (2) not every symbol in the input string has to be in the intake string. With this input/intake distinction, the paradox we have here about data ordering may be resolved. It is very likely that children have a way of filtering the data so that the strings which comprise the intake are ordered though the input strings are not. In our example, this means that children will somehow use *Mary smiled* as a trigger before they use *Mary hit John.*

The idea of input filtering has been discussed in the literature for a long time. Roeper (1978), for instance, suggests that the child is equipped with an input filter which excludes unknown material and admits material which fits in with the child's current hypotheses. However, no one has formalized this notion as an algorithm by which we can compute the input and extract the triggers. The main goal of this present paper is to propose such an algorithm.

We recall from the examples above that incorrect parameter values may be selected when 'ambiguous' input strings are used as triggers for parameter setting. The obvious solution to this problem is to ignore such sentences and use as triggers only those strings which are compatible with a unique set of parameter values. This idea is reminiscent of what Pinker suggested ten years ago: "The learner would be safe in positing new grammatical rules, ... , whenever the parser made a *single* prediction about what that analysis must be." (Pinker 1982) Pinker demonstrated that, in order to guarantee a unique analysis in each case, we need some 'scheduling principles' whereby different predictions are assigned different 'strengths' and only the strongest one is adopted as the actual analysis. In my model, however, this kind of scheduling or filtering is to be achieved in a logical way without the use of statistics. One way of doing it is to define triggers in a more formal way so that they can be recognized algorithmically. I propose the following definition which is based on the discussion in Stabler (1989).

> Definition 2:
>
> A string S is a trigger for parameter(s) P iff
>
> (1) S cannot be parsed with the current values of parameters,
>
> (2) P is not already set, and
>
> (3) there is exactly one way to set P which allows S to be parsed.

We can call this the NO AMBIGUOUS TRIGGER HYPOTHESIS. The definition will function as a filter on the input strings, with the result that (1) only a small subset of the strings children hear can be used as triggers, and (2) different strings may qualify as triggers at different time points in the acquisition process. We can see that no string is intrinsically a trigger or non-trigger, its status depending on the current values of parameters. As more and more parameters are set, the qualification for trigger-hood will change. The string *Mary hit John* cannot be a trigger at the initial stage, but it will become one as soon as the directionality parameter in one of the following two rules is set:

SPECIFIER(I,N,?)

COMPLEMENT(V,N,?)

As we can see, it is dynamic relationship between the current parameter values and the input strings which forces the triggers into a certain order.

The kind of filtering discussed here is similar in spirit to Sano's INDETERMINACY HYPOTHESIS' (Sano 1992):

> Only a certain set of data, namely, the triggering data, triggers the acquisition of grammar; given non-triggering data, a child does not make any decision as to his/her grammar.

Sano is working in a different area of language acquisition, namely, the acquisition of referentially dependent (RD) items, and the triggers he refers to there are used not for setting parameters, but for acquiring the features of lexical items. However, the idea behind it is basically the same.

3. The Computational Solution

So far we have solved a logical problem concerning parameter setting. The algorithm for computing triggers seems correct conceptually, but it is not clear whether it is computationally feasible as well. It turns out that the computation can be fairly efficient when the number of new parameter values to be considered in the parsing process is small. Suppose that only one more parameter needs to be set in order to make a given string parsable and this parameter has only two values as in the case of directionality parameters. To see if this string is a trigger, we only have to try two parses, one with each value, assuming no syntactic ambiguity relative to the child's grammar and the new parameter value.[6] However, if two or more parameters are involved, the number of parses to be explored can be very big. To make sure that one and only one set of values is compatible with the input string, we will have to try out all the value combinations of those parameters. If n is the number of new parameters involved, the number of possibilities to be considered can be as many as 2^n. This means that, if the first sentence a child ever hears is a long one whose parsing affects 4 parameters, he/she might attempt to parse the sentence in 16 different ways before he/she can decide whether to use this sentence as a trigger! Here we have another paradox: the test for triggerhood

[6] It is important to distinguish strings which are syntactically ambiguous and strings which are ambiguous for parameter setting. The former can be parsed in more than one way with the *same* set of parameter values.

is necessary but children cannot always be expected to be able to perform this test.

In order to avoid this paradox, we will need an algorithm which is computationally less expensive but has more or less the same filtering effect. As we have observed, the computation is simple when there is only one parameter to be set. Furthermore, we find that most of the triggers in the sense of Definition 2 turn out to affect one parameter only. Generally speaking, a string tends to provide ambiguous information for parameter setting if its parsing process affects two or more new parameters. A reasonable strategy to adopt then is to require that no string be used as a trigger if more than one parameter has to be set to parse it. This can be done by adding a new condition to Part (3) of Definition 2. The following is the new definition where the underlined part is the added condition.

Definition 3:

A string S is a trigger for a parameter P iff

(1) S cannot be parsed with the current values of parameters,

(2) P is not already set, and

(3) P is the only parameter that has to be set in the parsing process and there is exactly one way to set P which allows S to be parsed.

The new condition can be called the ONE PARAMETER AT A TIME HYPOTHESIS. In the case of directionality parameter, this new definition means that, without the complication of possible syntactic ambiguity, we will never have to construct more than two parses to find out if a string qualifies as a trigger. A string can be dismissed as a possible trigger as soon as a second unset parameter is encountered in the parsing process. This makes the computation much more efficient so that children are more likely to carry out the trigger test. As far as the logical consequences for parameter setting are concerned, Definition 3 is not much different from Definition 2. The triggers selected by Definition 3 form a subset of those selected by Definition 2. All the strings filtered out by Definition 2 will be filtered out by Definition 3 as well, though the reverse is not always true. Therefore, Definition 3 can be said to have improved the efficiency of Definition 2 while preserving the basic content of the latter.

4. The Ordering Effect

Both Definition 2 and Definition 3 will put the triggers in a certain order in the intake, but Definition 3 makes the ordering more computable. Given two strings $S1$ and $S2$, if the new parameters involved in the parsing of $S1$ is a proper subset of those involved in parsing $S2$, then $S1$ will necessarily qualify as a trigger before $S2$. In the head-driven parsing algorithm assumed here, the parser has to make a decision on tree attachment whenever a new maximal projection is produced. Each attachment decision has to consult at least one directionality parameter of a specifier rule or complement rule. Since each word in the string (not to mention empty heads) produces a maximal projection and each maximal projection has to be attached by consulting some parameter, the number of parameters involved in parsing a string is likely to increase as the string gets longer. This predicts that shorter strings will tend to be used as triggers before longer ones. In particular, it requires that children first pay attention to two-word strings which constitute the 'base cases'. In terms of primary linguistic data, it predicts that children's input will have to contain sentence fragments (NPs, VPs, PPs, etc.) as well as full sentences. These predictions are by and large consistent with empirical facts. Sentence fragments do seem available in children's input data. As shown in Newport et al. (1977), about 40% of maternal speech is composed of 'well-formed isolated phrases'.

However, the present account seems also to make some predictions that are not empirically confirmed. Among other things, it seems to predict (incorrectly) that a string like *The girl hit the boy*, which contains 5 words, will be ordered in the intake way after a string like *Mary hit John*, which contains only 3 words. But this can be accounted for on some independent grounds without changing our theory. In reality, children may not pay attention to every word in a string, as I have suggested earlier. In the model I am developing, a word will not be able to function as a head for projection unless it has been categorized (i.e. labeled as N,V,P,etc.). The head-driven parser will ignore any symbol in the string whose category label is yet unavailable. I further assume that functional categories (D,I,C) are not available in the early stages (Guilfoyle and Noonan 1988). Consequently, words like *the* will not participate in the parsing process and no parameter associated with them will have to be set. In this sense, *The girl hit the boy* is analyzed by children as *girl hit boy* which is no more complex than *Mary hit John.* What we are observing here is another kind of filtering which results in intake strings which contain fewer symbols than their input counterparts. I will not elaborate on this second filter in this paper.

5. Some Related Questions

5.1. Intake vs. Comprehension

In its traditional use, the term intake is often interpreted as the portion of input data which children actually comprehend. This interpretation, if applied to my model, will lead to the conclusion that children only understand the triggers. This is obviously false. For one thing, not every string comprehended is used as a trigger. Only one string is needed to set a parameter but, once the parameter is set, an infinite number of strings may be comprehended by referring to that parameter. Moreover, children may understand a sentence without using it as a trigger. In the case of those 'ambiguous' strings, children are very likely to understand something, since the strings CAN be parsed in some way. Finally, we cannot exclude the possibility that children have some other means of making sense of a sentence than by parsing it. Sentences comprehended in those other ways may be longer than the triggers. In short, I want to distinguish between the traditional sense of intake and my use of this word which is defined in terms of parameter setting only.

5.2. Intake vs. Output

It is a common observation that there is a big gap between children's input data and output utterances. Intake and output, however, may be more closely related. With the concept of intake in this paper, the relationship can be established in the following way. Let us assume that children have to use syntactic rules in their language production and they only use those 'active' rules where the parameters are already set. Then their output will be limited to those strings which can be generated by those 'active' rules. Formally, given a parameter P, no string whose generation refers to P can be produced until a trigger for P has been found. This correlation between intake and output may enable us to predict the relative ordering of children's output strings from the order of their intake strings. From the fact that the first group of triggers have to be two-word strings, for example, we can predict that children will utter two-word strings first. We can also predict that children's utterances will in general become longer over time. Other than that, however, we should not expect any one-to-one correspondence between intake ordering and output ordering. Nothing prevents children from uttering a three-word string when they are only using two-word triggers. Different two-word triggers can cause parameters in different rules to be set and the combination of those rules can generate a three-word string. For instance, *Mary smiled* and *hit John*, both two-word strings, may trigger the following two rules:

SPECIFIER(I,N,L)

COMPLEMENT(V,N,R)

The combination of these two rules, however, can generate *Mary hit John* which is a three-word string.

5.3. Other Parameters

So far I have limited my discussion to word order parameters. We may wonder if the theory proposed here applies to other parameters. There are two basic hypotheses in our theory, the 'no ambiguous trigger' hypothesis and the 'one parameter at a time' hypothesis. Let us see how these two hypotheses work for other parameters.

The 'no ambiguous trigger' hypothesis seems problematic for other parameters given the assumption that parameters are all unset at the initial stage. Take the binding domain for reflexives as an example. The English sentence *John hates himself* is ambiguous in the sense that it is compatible with any of the values of the binding domain parameter proposed in Wexler and Manzini (1987). Therefore this sentence cannot be used as a trigger. But there is no other sentence in English that is not ambiguous in this sense. As a result, no trigger will ever be found and the parameter will never be set. The same problem occurs with the null subject parameter and the bounding node parameter. However, the problem disappears if we allow for the existence of default values for those parameters. This suggests that there might be two different types of parameters, the preset ones which can be reset and the unset ones which has to be set once and only once. The difference corresponds to what Freidin and Quicoli have called the distinction between P-PARAMETERS and R-PARAMETERS (Freidin and Quicoli 1989). The binding domain parameter is an example of the former and word order parameter an example of the latter.

The 'one parameter at a time' hypothesis will also acquire some new interpretation when we start to consider other parameters. Since other parameters are all different in nature from one another, this hypothesis can be extended to mean that no two different types of parameters can be set at the same time. It is very hard to find out whether this is empirically true. But this assumption does us no harm unless we find one of the following situations:

1. The values of two parameters are mutually dependent and neither can be set without the other being set at the same time.

2. The values of two parameters are not mutually dependent but no string can refer to one of them without simultaneously referring to the other.

So far I have not been able to find such situations.

5.4. Modifiers

In my discussion of X-bar structures, I deliberately left out the modifiers which are adjoined to the main tree. Obviously, directionality parameters also have to be set in order for those adjuncts to be attached. However, the inclusion of modifiers in the discussion would not change the basic problem we tried to solve. Modifiers are similar to specifiers and complements in that each word has a maximal projection and each projection tree has to be attached. They will of course add to the complexity of the parsing process and increase the number of parses to be considered for a given string. While making a decision on tree attachment, we have to consider the possibility of an adjunct in addition to that of a specifier or complement. This will certainly increase the amount of computation involved in finding a trigger and make our logical solution even more impractical. But this is all the more reason why we have to adopt the computational solution expressed in Definition 3. With the 'one parameter only' restriction, the additional complexity associated with modifiers can be minimized.

Summary

In this paper I have proposed an algorithm for computing input strings and extracting from them the triggers for parameter setting. The original motivation for this algorithm is to avoid errors in parameter setting. It turns out, however, that the algorithm also makes some interesting predictions about intake ordering, output ordering and the linguistic environment of the children. There is reason to believe that this algorithm should be incorporated into a computational model of language acquisition.

References

Braine, M.D.S. 1971. On Two Types of Models of the Internalization of Grammars. *The Ontogenesis of Grammar*, ed. D. Slobin. New York: Academic Press.

Chomsky, Noam. 1986. *Barriers*. Cambridge, MA: The MIT Press.

Clahsen, Harald. 1991. Constraints on Parameter Setting: a Grammatical Analysis of Some Acquisition Stages in German Child Language. *Language Acquisition* 1(4):361–391.

Corder, S.P. 1967. The Significance of Learner's Errors. *I.R.A.L* 5:161–170.

Freidin, Robert and A.Carlos Quicoli. 1989. Zero-Stimulation for Parameter Setting. *Behavioral and Brain Sciences* 12:338–339.

Guilfoyle, E. and M. Noonan. 1988. Functional Categories and Language Acquisition. Text of paper presented to Boston University Conference on Language Acquisition.

Newport, E.L., H. Gleitman, and L.R. Gleitman. 1977. Mother, I'd Rather Do It Myself: Some Effects of and Non-Effects of Maternal Speech Style. *Talking to Children: Language Input and Acquisition*, eds. C.E. Snow and C.A. Ferguson. Cambridge, England: Cambridge University Press.

Pinker, Steven. 1982. A Theory of the Acquisition of Lexical Interpretive Grammars. *The Mental Representation of Grammatical Relations*, ed. Joan Bresnan. Cambridge, MA: The MIT Press.

Roeper, T. 1978. Linguistic Universals and Acquisition of Gerunds. *Papers in the Structure an Development of Child Language*, eds. H. Goodluck and L. Solan. University of Massachusetts Occasional Papers in Linguistics 4.

Sano, Tetsuya. 1991. A Note on Parameter Theory: Are There Default Values or Not? Manuscript at UCLA.

Sano, Tetsuya. 1992. The Acquisition of Referentially Dependent Items and Their Development. To appear in the present volumn.

Shipley, E.R., C.S. Smith, and L.R. Gleitman. 1969. A Study in the Acquisition of Language: Free Response to Commands. *Language* 45:322–342.

Sportiche, Dominique. 1991. Movement, Agreement, and Case. UCLA manuscript.

Stabler, Eadward P. 1989. What's a Trigger? *Behavioral and Brain Sciences* 12:358–360.

Waterson, N. 1971. Child Phonology: A Prosodic View. *Journal of Linguistics* 7:174–211.

Wexler, K and R. Manzini. 1987. Parameters and Learnability in Binding Theory. *Parameter Setting*, eds. T. Roeper and E. Williams Dordrecht: Reidel.

White, Lydia. 1980. *Grammatical Theory and Language Acquisition.* PhD thesis, McGill University. Reproduced by the Indiana University Linguistics Club.

A Degree-Based Semantics for Bare Positive Adjectives

JOOST ZWARTS
University of Utrecht

1. Introduction[1]

In most semantic theories, adjectives like *tall* or *red* are interpreted as sets of (tall or red) individuals. However, over the years several authors have argued for an alternative semantics of adjectives in terms of *degrees* (Seuren 1973, Cresswell 1976, Hellan 1981, Bierwisch 1989). In this degree-based semantics an adjective expresses a relation between an individual and a degree. The adjective *tall*, for example, is interpreted in terms of the relation 'x is tall to degree d'. The degrees of an adjective are ordered along a scale and comparative and superlative constructions are analyzed in terms of that ordering. That this leads to a simple and natural analysis of sentences with different adjectival constructions is illustrated in (1):[2]

(1) a. John is *this* tall
tall(john, *d*)

[1] I would like to thank Peter Coopmans and Henk Verkuyl for useful comments on an earlier version.

[2] These semantic representations are just given to illustrate the general tenets of the degree-based semantics. The proponents of this approach use different formulations and formalisms.

b. *How* tall is John?

$?d$ [**tall**(**john**, d)]

c. John is tall*er* than Mary

$\exists d\, \exists d'$ [**tall**(**john**, d) & **tall**(**mary**, d') & $d > d'$]

d. John is the tall*est*

$\exists d$ [**tall**(**john**, d) & $\forall d'$ [$\exists x$ [**tall**(x, d')] $\rightarrow d > d'$]]

e. John is *six foot* tall

$\exists d$ [**tall**(**john**, d) & $d =$ **6f**]

In (1a) the deictically specified degree of John's tallness is represented by a free variable over degrees *d*. In (1b) this degree-variable is bound by the question operator ?. In (1c) John's degree of tallness *d* is said to be higher on the scale than Mary's degree of tallness *d'*. In (1d) John's degree of tallness *d* exceeds all other degrees of tallness that anyone (from a contextually given set) has. In (1e) John's degree of tallness is identified with the tallness of six feet.

However, the degree-based approach loses much of its attractiveness when it is applied to *bare positive adjectives*, like the adjective *tall* in (2a).

(2) a. John is tall

b. $\exists d$ [**tall**(**john**, d)]

c. $\exists d$ [**tall**(**john**, d) & $d > d_A$]

(2a) does not just mean that John is tall to an arbitrary degree *d*, but that John's degree of tallness is on the 'higher part' of the scale of degrees of tallness. The semantic representation in (2b) is therefore not adequate: the existential quantifier $\exists d$ is not restricted and *d* can denote any degree on the scale. To accommodate this, a representation like (2c) is often proposed, in which John's degree of tallness is said to be higher than a contextually given degree d_A, which stands for the 'average' or 'normal' degree of tallness. This representation can be paraphrased as: 'John is taller than average' or 'John is taller than most people'. As the paraphrase makes clear, bare positive adjectives are then treated as a special kind of comparatives.[3]

[3] The average degree of tallness d_A is usually relativized to a *comparison class*, i.e. a class of objects (people, in this case) of which the average tallness can be determined. Different comparison classes (children-adults, mice-elephants) will have different average degrees. See Klein (1980) for a formal treatment of comparison classes. I will come back to the context-dependence of bare positive adjectives in section 5.

This paper argues against the analysis in (2c) and in favor of an analysis which is based on the idea that bare positive adjectives are the syntactic and semantic counterparts of *bare plurals*. This requires a model-theory for adjectives with degrees *and properties*, which also turns out to have interesting results for the interpretation of nominalized adjectives.

2. Some Problems for Average Degrees

If bare positive adjectives are analyzed as in (2c) they will have the same semantic structure as the comparative constructions in (3).

(3) a. John is too tall
    b. John is taller
    c. John is less tall

In each of the sentences in (3), John's degree of tallness is related to a contextually given degree d_C. They can be analyzed as in (4):

(4) a. $\exists d$ [**tall(john,** d) & $d > d_C$]
    b. $\exists d$ [**tall(john,** d) & $d > d_C$]
    c. $\exists d$ [**tall(john,** d) & $d < d_C$]

In these comparative constructions, measure phrases can be used to specify the distance between the degrees d and d_C:

(5) a. John is *one foot* too tall
    b. John is *one foot* taller
    c. John is *one foot* less tall

This can be represented schematically as in (6):

```
(6) d0-------------d-----dC-----d--------...
                   -1f     +1f
```

In this diagram, degrees are represented as positions on a scale, which starts with the zero-degree d_0. The measure phrase *one foot* can be interpreted as a unit **1f** which is added to or subtracted from d_C. This yields the semantic representations in (7):

(7) a. $\exists d$ [**tall(john,** d) & $d = d_C$ + **1f**]
   b. $\exists d$ [**tall(john,** d) & $d = d_C$ + **1f**]
   c. $\exists d$ [**tall(john,** d) & $d = d_C$ - **1f**]

Positive adjectives allow measure phrases too, but contrary to what we expect these cannot be treated as comparative adjectives.

(8) a. John is six foot tall
   b. $\exists d$ [**tall(john,** d) & $d = d_A$ + **6f**]
   c. $\exists d$ [**tall(john,** d) & $d = d_0$ + **6f**]

The measure phrase *six foot* in (8a) does not specify the distance between d and the average degree d_A, as in (8b), but with the zero-degree d_0, as represented in (8c).[4] This representation is equivalent to (1e), given that the normal zero-rule for addition ($x + 0 = y$ iff $x = y$) applies to addition of degrees. So, the first problem for the 'comparative' analysis of positive adjectives is that it yields the wrong predictions with respect to the interpretation of measure phrases.

The second problem is that analysis (2c) only seems to work for a certain class of adjectives. Adjectives can be classified in many different ways. A classification that is relevant for our purposes is given in (9).[5]

(9) Degree adjectives:
      Measure adjectives: *tall, short, old, young*
      Non-measure adjectives: *pretty, ugly, healthy, ill*
   Non-degree adjectives:
      dead, atomic, recursive

Adjectives are divided into *degree* adjectives, those that can be 'graded', and *non-degree* adjectives, those that can not be 'graded'. The degree adjectives can be further divided into *measure* adjectives and *non-measure* adjectives. Measure

[4] These two degrees are never identical, because $d_A > d_0$ in every context.

[5] See Klooster (1971) and Bierwisch (1989) for similar distinctions and Kamp (1975) for a more general classification of adjectives.

adjectives allow measure phrases (*six feet*, *ten years*), are associated with units of measurements and have clear zero-degrees. Non-measure adjectives do not allow measure phrases, are not associated with units of measurement and often do not have a zero-degree.

It turns out that the analysis in (2c) might work for measure adjectives, but it certainly does not work for non-measure adjectives.

(10) a. Ann is pretty
b. Bill is healthy
c. Carol is angry

(10b), for example, does not mean that Bill is healthier than average, or than most people. Neither does (10c) mean that Carol's degree of anger is above average. Moreover, it is unclear what the average degree of anger is.

There is another difference between measure and non-measure adjectives, concerning entailments from comparative to bare positive uses of adjectives. The analysis (2c) correctly predicts that such entailments are never possible for measure adjectives:

(11) a. Ann is taller than Betty
=/=> Ann is tall
b. Carol is too old for kindergarten
=/=> Carol is old
c. Dolly is younger than Eve
=/=> Carol is young

(11b), for example, shows that Carol's being too old for kindergarten does not imply that she is old, she may be five or six years old. The degrees of 'old' cover the whole scale of ages. In general, comparative and superlative uses of measure adjectives are *neutral*, i.e. they can denote any degree on the scale, even 'close' to d_0.

However, non-measure adjectives are different, as (11d)-(11f) show. The entailment from comparative to bare positive adjectives is usually possible.

(11) d. Ann is prettier than Betty
===> Ann is pretty

e. Carol is as healthy as Dolly
===> Carol and Dolly are healthy

f. Eve is lazier than Dolly
===> Eve and Dolly are lazy

In (11d), for example, Ann's being prettier than Betty entails that Ann is pretty. This shows that the comparative of a non-measure adjective quantifies over the same range of degrees as the bare positive. The strangeness of the sentences in (12) is also related to this:

(12) a. ? Ann is prettier than Betty although they are both ugly
b. ? Carol is as healthy as Dolly although they are both ill

If Ann's being prettier than Betty entails Ann's being pretty, a contradiction will arise when Ann is said to be ugly. The same is true for (12b).[6]

We have seen three problems for the view that bare positive adjectives should be analyzed in terms of a comparison with an average degree: (i) it incorrectly predicts that measure phrases in positive and comparative adjectives can be treated in the same way, (ii) the notion of an average degree leads to counterintuitive analyses of non-measure adjectives, and (iii) it does not account for the entailments of adjectives like *pretty*. I will not follow Klein's (1980) conclusion that these problems indicate that the whole degree-based approach is on the wrong track, but I will propose an analysis for bare positive adjectives that maintains the advantages of this approach.

3. Parallels between DP and DegP

My proposal is based on the idea that there are fundamental parallels between phrases of different categories, both syntactically and semantically. As for the syntactic parallelism, Abney (1987) argued that sentences, noun phrases and adjective phrases are all projections of a functional head with a lexical complement.

---

[6] Interestingly, the unacceptability seems to diminish when the order of the clauses is changed:

a. Although they are both ugly, Ann is prettier than Betty
b. Although they are both ill, Carol is healthier than Dolly

(13) a. [$_{IP}$ ... [$_{I'}$ INFL [$_{VP}$ ...]]]
b. [$_{DP}$ ... [$_{D'}$ DET [$_{NP}$ ...]]]
c. [$_{DegP}$ ... [$_{Deg'}$ DEG [$_{AP}$ ...]]]

In his view, adjective phrases are projections of the functional head DEG (for Degree), hence Degree Phrases. The DEG position can be occupied by different elements: *so*, *how*, *this*, *that*, *too*, *as*, *-er*, *-est*, *more*, *most*, *less*.[7] The specifier position of the DegP can be occupied by measure phrases and other specifying phrases, like *two miles*, *three times*, *much*, *far* and there can be modifiers in the DegP, like *very* and *fairly*.[8]

Abney also suggests that the syntactic parallelism in (13) corresponds with a semantic parallelism. The lexical projections VP, NP and AP can be interpreted as *predicates* over different sorts of elements: 'situations', 'objects', and 'attributes'. The functional heads INFL, DET and DEG are *operators* over these predicates.

I would like to suggest a more specific parallel between DP and DegP: that between bare positive adjectives and bare plurals. Syntactically, the functional head of both bare positive adjectives and bare plurals are empty:

(14) [$_{DegP}$ ... [$_{Deg}$ ∅] [$_{AP}$ tall]]
[$_{DP}$ ... [$_{D}$ ∅] [$_{NP}$ dogs]]

This means that there are no quantificational elements (like *too* and *-er* in DEG and *every* and *some* in DET); as a result bare plurals and bare positive adjectives have no inherent quantificational force.

Carlson (1978) gives a semantics of bare plurals which is based on the idea that there are two primitive model-theoretic entities: *kinds* and *stages*. Stages are spatiotemporal *realizations* of kinds (which is expressed by the relation R) and bare plurals are basically proper names for kinds (e.g., **Dog** in the generic sentences *I love dogs*) and in some contexts existential quantifiers over stages of a kind (e.g., $\exists s$ [R(s, **Dog**) & ...] in the non-generic use *I saw dogs*).[9]

---

[7] When the DEG is filled with the suffixes *-er* and *-est*, the adjective must be raised to DEG (an instance of head to head movement), resulting in comparative and superlative adjectives like *taller* and *tallest*.

[8] See Corver (1990) for more details about the DegP analysis.

[9] Actually, Carlson's proposal is more complicated than presented here. He makes a threefold distinction between *kinds*, *objects* and *stages*. Objects are atemporal instantiations of kinds and stages are spatiotemporal realizations of both kinds and objects. I do not want to make a

The semantics of bare positive adjectives can be given along more or less the same lines, if we assume the existence of two primitive model-theoretic entities: *properties* and *degrees*. Degrees are *realizations* of properties along a dimension of comparison, in the same way as stages are realizations of kinds in time and space. The property of being pretty, for example, can be manifested in different degrees of prettiness. The bare positive adjective *pretty* is basically a 'name' for a property, but in some contexts there is existential quantification over degrees of that property (e.g., $\exists d$ [R(d, **Pretty**) & ...]).

4. Degrees and Properties

In order to set up a model theory along these lines, we assume a non-empty set D of *degrees*, which is partitioned into a set of *scales*, where each scale is a pair (S_i,<) of a set S_i of degrees and an ordering < of S_i. That the scales partition the space of degrees D means that every degree is member of exactly one scale. Besides the set of scales there is also a non-empty set P of *properties*, more or less like primitive properties in certain property theories.

Properties and degrees are related by means of the realization relation R, which is restricted in a number of ways. First, if R is defined for a property p, then all realization of p are part of one scale. The degrees that realize the property of being pretty, for example, are all degrees on the prettiness-scale and not degrees of laziness or tallness. Second, for every property p, the set of degrees that realized p, is monotone increasing with respect to <. For example, if a degree d is a realization of the property of being pretty, then every higher degree of prettiness is also a realization of that property. Third, exactly one property will be associated with every scale.

There is a relation Attr between the set of individuals and the union of P and D, that attributes degrees and properties to individuals. This relation has the following characteristics. First, if Attr(x, d) and Attr(x, d') and d and d' are degrees on the same scale, then d=d'. This condition guarantees that an individual is not related to two different degrees of tallness, for example. Second, for every individual x and property p, Attr(x, p) iff $\exists$d [R(d, p) & Attr(x, d)]. This captures the following fact about properties and degrees: If we say that Rockefeller was rich and that Getty was rich, then we are attributing the *same property* to those

---

distinction between stages and objects and therefore use the term stage here for every realization of a kind.

individuals, although we know that both of them are related to possibly *different degrees* of wealth.

The structure of the resulting model is schematically given in the following diagram:

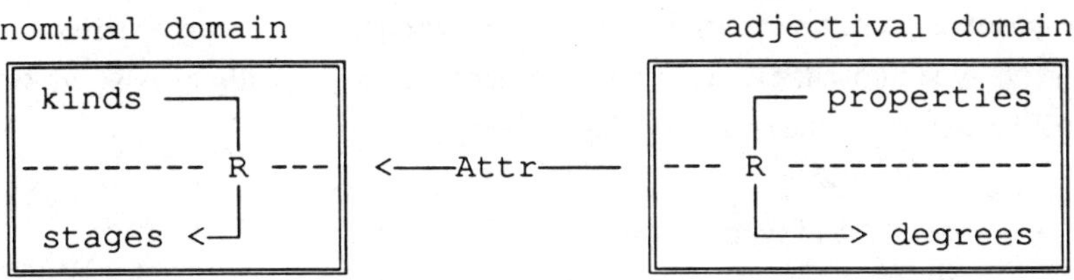

There are two sorts of entities in the universe of discourse: the right-hand box stands for the set of adjectival denotata, the left-hand box for the set of nominal denotata. These two sets are both 'stratified': kinds and properties are in some sense on a 'higher level' than stages and degrees, respectively. In both cases there is a realization relation R between the two levels. Finally, the attribution relation Attr attributes degrees and properties to stages and kinds.

On the basis of this model, the classification given in (9) can be explained model-theoretically. There is a fundamental difference between *dead* and *pretty* on the one hand and *tall* on the other: *dead* and *pretty* are basically names for properties, while *tall* denotes a complete scale of degrees, the set of all degrees of tallness, starting with the zero-degree of tallness. *Dead* and *pretty* are distinguished in the following way: the property of being pretty has degrees of prettiness, but there are no degrees of being dead. In other words: $\{d : R(d, p_{dead})\}$ is empty, but $\{d : R(d, p_{pretty})\}$ is not empty. A degree adjective (*pretty* and *tall*) can be characterized as an adjective that is directly or indirectly associated with a set of degrees.

For expository purposes, the formalism of type-theory will be used. To the set of basic types **e** and **t** of extensional type-theory, the types **p** for properties and **d** for degrees are added. We can now say that *dead* and *pretty* are of type **p** and that *tall* is of type **<d, t>**, as a lexical property. However, it is possible to *shift* the basic type of an adjective. There are two basic type-shift functions between degrees and properties, which can be defined in terms of the realization relation R:

(15) a. $\cup$: **p → <d, t>**, $\cup$p = {d : R(d, p)}

b. $\cap$: **<d, t> → p**, $\cap$S = p iff S is a scale and {d : R(d, p)} is a subset of S.

The first function, represented by the round cup, maps a property to the set of degrees that realize it. The second function, the round cap, maps a scale to the corresponding property. *Pretty* is basically of type **p**, but the cup-operator can change its type into **<d, t>**, i.e., a set of degrees. *Tall* is basically of type **<d, t>**, but can be mapped to the corresponding property:

(16) a. $\cup$**pretty** is of type **<d, t>**

$\cup$**pretty** = { d · R(d, **pretty**) }

b. $\cap$**tall** is of type **p**

$\cap$**tall** = the unique p such that { d : R(d, p) } is a subset of **tall**

The cup-operator is undefined for *dead* and other non-degree adjectives, because these do not have realizations.

The semantics of overt and empty DETs and DEGs can be characterized type-theoretically. Empty DETs and DEGs are not quantificational and have a vacuous semantics. The empty DEG of bare positive adjectives is of type **<p, p>**: it selects a property (type **p**) and maps it onto itself; similarly, the empty DET of bare plurals selects a kind and maps to onto itself. Overt DETs and DEGs on the other hand are quantificational. An overt DEG can be characterized type-theoretically in the same way as the overt DET of noun phrases: it maps a set of degrees to a generalized quantifier of degrees, i.e., it is of type **<<d, t>, <<d, t>, t>>**.

Given that empty DEGs are of type **<p, p>**, they can select adjectives like *dead* and *pretty* which are basically type **p**, but also the measure adjective *tall* when its type is shifted from its basic type **<d, t>** to type **p**. If we assume that the copula *be* is a direct lexical expression of the attribution function Attr, we arrive at the following semantic representations for bare positive adjectives in predicative position:[10]

---

[10] It would probably be more adequate to assume that Attr is the semantic counterpart of the syntactic predication relation between a subject and a DegP.

(17) a. The king is dead ⇒ Attr(**the-king**, **dead**)

b. Bella is pretty ⇒ Attr(**bella**, **pretty**)

c. Chris is tall ⇒ Attr(**chris**, $^\frown$**tall**)

Bare positive adjectives in predicative position denote properties, directly in (17a) and (17b) and after type-shifting in (17c). There is no existential quantification over degrees. However, given the nature of Attr, (17b) and (17c) allow the following entailments:

(17) b'. $\exists d$ [R(d, **pretty**) & Attr(**bella**, d)]

c'. $\exists d$ [R(d, $^\frown$**tall**) & Attr(**chris**, d)]

These semantic representations express that there are particular degrees of prettiness and tallness that are attributed to Bella and Chris, respectively, but these degrees are not specified in comparison to an average degree (as in (2c)) but as realizations of a property.

An overt DEG has to select an adjective that denotes a set of degrees. This can be either a measure adjective like *tall* that directly denotes a scale, but it can also be an adjective like *pretty* that is shifted from its basic type **p** to **<d, t>**. However, it cannot be *dead* because this adjective can never denote a set of types.

(18) a. *Jack is more dead than Jill

b. Bilbo is taller (than Frodo) ⇒
$\exists d$ [**tall**(d) & Attr(**bilbo**, d) & $d > d_{\text{Frodo}}$]

c. Bella is less pretty (than Berta) ⇒
$\exists d$ [$^\smile$**pretty**(d) & Attr(**bella**, d) & $d < d_{\text{Berta}}$]

The existential quantifier picks out one degree d from the set of degrees and compares this degree to the degree given by the extent clause. There is a crucial difference between **tall** and $^\smile$**pretty**. In (18b), the existential quantifier ranges over all degrees of the scale denoted by **tall**, without any restriction. In (18c) however, the existential quantifier ranges over the set $^\smile$**pretty** consisting of those degrees that are realizations of the property of being pretty, which is just a part of the prettiness-scale. The representation in (18c) entails the representation in (17b), which explains the entailment from *Bella is as pretty as Berta* to *Bella is pretty*.

5. The Context-Dependence of Degree Adjectives

It has often been discussed that the interpretation of bare positive measure adjectives depends on the context. This can most clearly be seen with adjectives that are used attributively:

(19) a. Tom is a tall boy

b. This is a tall building

(19a) does not entail (20a) or (20a') and (19b) does not entail (20b) or (20b').

(20) a. Tom is tall

a'. Tom is a tall person

b. This is tall

b'. This is a tall thing

The reason is that the set of individuals that count as tall depends on the context. This set is different in a context of boys, persons, buildings or things.

In our proposal this context-dependence has to be located in the realization relation R that relates the property of being tall to its degrees. This relation can be made context-dependent: $R_c(d, p)$ expresses that d is a degree of property p *in a context c*. Six foot, for example, may be tall in the context c_{boy} but not in the context $c_{building}$. This means that $\{d : R_c(d, {}^\frown\mathbf{tall})\}$, the set of degrees that realize the property of being tall, is in every context c a different subset of the scale **tall**.

Given this, we can represent the prenominal adjectives as in (21):

(21) a. tall boy $\Rightarrow \lambda x$ [$\mathbf{boy}(x)$ & $\mathrm{Attr}(x, {}^\frown\mathbf{tall})$]

b. tall building $\Rightarrow \lambda x$ [$\mathbf{building}(x)$ & $\mathrm{Attr}(x, {}^\frown\mathbf{tall})$]

In both cases the individual boys and buildings are attributed to the property $^\frown$**tall**. The representations in (21) entail those in (22):

(22) a. λx [$\exists d$ [$R_c(d, {}^\frown\mathbf{tall})$ & $\mathbf{boy}(x)$ & $\mathrm{Attr}(x, d)$]]

b. λx [$\exists d$ [$R_c(d, {}^\frown\mathbf{tall})$ & $\mathbf{building}(x)$ & $\mathrm{Attr}(x, d)$]]

The contextual index c of R makes it possible to restrict the existential quantifier in (22) to a contextually restricted set of degrees, which is different for boys and buildings.

6. Nominalized Adjectives

We have seen that degree adjectives can give rise to a 'degree-reading' and a 'property-reading', depending on the nature of the DEG selecting them. There is a context where adjectives are ambiguous between these two readings, namely when they are nominalized.

(23) a. Albert's intelligence
b. Bella's prettiness

The noun phrase *Albert's intelligence* can either denote his *property* of being intelligent, or his *degree* of intelligence. The same is true for the noun phrase *Bella's prettiness*. Given the distinction between degrees and properties, it is now straightforward to represent these two readings. In (24), the noun phrases of (23) are interpreted as iota-terms denoting a unique property p:

(24) a. $\iota p\ [\ p = {}^{\cap}\mathbf{intelligent}\ \&\ \mathrm{Attr}(\mathbf{albert}, p)\ ]$
b. $\iota p\ [\ p = \mathbf{pretty}\ \&\ \mathrm{Attr}(\mathbf{bella}, p)\ ]$

In (25), the iota-term denotes a unique degree of intelligence or prettiness:

(25) a. $\iota d\ [\ \mathbf{intelligent}(d)\ \&\ \mathrm{Attr}(\mathbf{albert}, d)\ ]$
b. $\iota d\ [\ {}^{\cup}\mathbf{pretty}(d)\ \&\ \mathrm{Attr}(\mathbf{bella}, d)\ ]$

Sometimes, one of the two readings can be forced by a specific linguistic context:

(26) a. Albert's intelligence made him famous
b. Albert's intelligence is greater than Bella's

In (26a), the favored reading for the subject is a property-reading, but in (26b) the degree-reading is necessary. Which reading is selected seems to depend on the nature of the predicate, but the non-linguistic context might also be important.

Conclusion

The problems that the degree-based approach approach has with bare positive adjectives can be solved when properties are added to it. This leads to a simple and explanatory treatment of different classes of adjectives, both in their predicative, attributive, and nominalized use. Moreover, it supports the idea that there are not only syntactic, but also semantic parallels between DPs and DegPs.

References

Abney, S. 1987. *The Noun Phrase in its Sentential Aspect.* Doctoral dissertation, MIT.

Bierwisch, M. 1989. The Semantics of Gradation. In M. Bierwisch & E. Lang, eds., *Dimensional Adjectives: Grammatical Structure and Conceptual Interpretation.* Berlin: Springer-Verlag. pp. 71-261.

Carlson, G. 1977. *Reference to Kinds in English.* Doctoral dissertation, University of Massachusetts, Amherst.

Corver, N. 1990. *The Syntax of Left Branch Extractions.* Doctoral dissertation, University of Tilburg.

Cresswell, M. 1976. The Semantics of Degree. In B. Partee, ed., *Montague Grammar.* New York: Academic Press. pp. 261-292.

Hellan, L. 1981. *Towards an Integrated Analysis of Comparatives.* Tübingen: Narr.

Kamp, H. 1975. Two Theories of Adjectives. In E. L. Keenan, ed., *Formal Semantics of Natural Language.* Cambridge: Cambridge University Press.

Klein, E. 1980. A Semantics for Positive and Comparative Adjectives. *Linguistics and Philosophy* 4, 1-45.

Klooster, W. 1971. *The Structure Underlying Measure Phrase Sentences.* Doctoral dissertation, University of Utrecht.

Seuren, P. 1973. The Comparative. In F. Kiefer & N. Ruwet, eds., *Generative Grammar in Europe.* Dordrecht: Reidel.

General Index

Language Index